Forensic Pathology

Second Edition

CRC SERIES IN
PRACTICAL ASPECTS OF CRIMINAL AND FORENSIC INVESTIGATIONS

VERNON J. GEBERTH, BBA, MPS, FBINA *Series Editor*

Forensic Pathology

Second Edition

Vincent J. DiMaio
Dominick DiMaio

CRC Press
Boca Raton London New York Washington, D.C.

Library of Congress Cataloging-in-Publication Data

Di Maio, Dominick J.
  Forensic pathology / Dominick J. Di Maio, Vincent J.M. Di Maio --2nd ed.
       p.   cm. (Practical aspects of criminal and forensic investigation)
  Includes bibliographical references and index.
  ISBN 0-8493-0072-X
  1. Forensic pathology. I. Di Maio, Vincent J.M., 1941- II. Title .III. CRC series in
  practical aspects of criminal and forensic investigations.
  [DNLM: 1. Forensic Medicine. 2. Pathology. W 700 D582f2001]
  RA1063.4 .D5 2001
  614′.1—dc21   2001025798

Visit the CRC Press Web site at www.crcpress.com

© 2001 by CRC Press LLC

No claim to original U.S. Government works
International Standard Book Number 0-8493-0072-X
Library of Congress Card Number 2001025798
Printed in the United States of America 1 2 3 4 5 6 7 8 9 0
Printed on acid-free paper

Dedication

This book is dedicated to our wives, Violet and Theresa, for their patience, understanding, encouragement, and support.

Foreword

The medicolegal investigation of death is the most crucial and significant function of the medical examiner within the criminal justice system. The medical examiner's office is primarily concerned with the investigation of violent, sudden, unexpected, and suspicious deaths.

Forensic pathology is the branch of medicine that applies the principles and knowledge of the medical sciences to the many legal issues within the field of law. The medical examiner is responsible for determining the cause and manner of death, identifying the deceased if unknown, determining the approximate time of death and injury, collecting evidence from the body that can be used to prove or disprove an individual's guilt or innocence and to confirm or deny the account of how the death occurred, documenting injuries or lack of them, deducing how the injuries occurred, documenting any natural disease present, determining or excluding other contributory or causative factors of death, issuing the death certificate, and documenting these events through an official autopsy report. This autopsy protocol is a complete medical record based on a thorough and conclusive review of all the facts and information.

Forensic pathology, the science of recognizing and interpreting diseases and injuries in the human body, is the basis of the medicolegal investigation. The medical examiner provides the expert testimony if the case goes to trial.

Forensic Pathology Second Edition, written by Dominick J. DiMaio, M.D. and Vincent J. DiMaio, M.D., provides the reader with more than 75 years of practical, hands-on experience in the essentials of forensic medicine. The material presented in this revised edition continues to be based on the personal experience of two forensic pathologists who are nationally renowned experts in their respective fields. Dominick J. DiMaio, M.D., a retired Chief Medical Examiner of New York City, is currently a forensic consultant. He served as the professorial lecturer in pathology for the State University of New York Health Science Center at Brooklyn.

Vincent J. DiMaio, M.D. is the Chief Medical Examiner for Bexar County in San Antonio, Texas. He serves as a professor for the Department of Pathology at the University of Texas Health Science Center in San Antonio.

The new and revised *Forensic Pathology Second Edition* begins with an overview of the medicolegal investigative systems and then delves into the substance and mechanics of forensic pathology. The authors present the essentials of forensic medicine in a concise, lucid, and comprehensive manner. They omit superfluous, confusing medical terminology and present medicolegal facts pertinent to the many and varied cases discussed, and have added new case histories and current information, bringing this remarkable text into the 21st century. *Forensic Pathology Second Edition* is geared toward medical practitioners, medical students, homicide detectives, medicolegal investigators, prosecuting and defense attorneys, and others interested in forensic pathology.

The first edition of *Forensic Pathology* addressed and corrected the insufficiencies that existed between criminal investigations textbooks and medicolegal investigations textbooks and established a recognized reference standard for medical examiners and homicide investigators. The second edition has been completely revised and expanded to include current statistical information. It has been updated and new photographs have been added, as well as two additional chapters that address the concerns of the medicolegal profession.

The new chapter dealing with "Deaths In Nursing Homes" addresses issues of improper health care resulting in drug overdoses, accidents not involving medication, homicide, and gross negligence. The revised information presents the dynamics involved in evaluating signs of neglect such as contractures, malnutrition, dehydration and the various stages of decubitus ulcers, which provide the practitioner with a frame of reference in a medicolegal determination. The chapter also addresses deaths caused by hospital-bed rails and medical restraints.

The new chapter on "Sudden Deaths During or Immediately after a Violent Struggle Unassociated with an Anatomical Cause of Death" is, without a doubt, an extremely important addition to this text. Deaths involving police or medical personnel who were attempting to restrain a violent or irrational individual are fraught with controversy. The medical examiner and investigator must be cognizant of the necessity for a complete and extensive medicolegal examination. The circumstances leading up to and surrounding the death should be obtained, and any medical records of the deceased should be reviewed. A complete autopsy with microscopic survey of all organs — especially the heart — as well as a complete toxicological screen should be performed. This chapter discusses the evaluation of excited delirium, catecholamine release, potassium and their effects on the heart. Drug actions, alcohol and acute psychotic episodes are covered, along with deaths ascribed to positional asphyxia. The authors present important information on the proper certification of death in these circumstances.

I have known Dominick J. DiMaio for more than 30 years. In fact, he was my mentor and instructor in forensic medicine when I was a young homicide detective in the New York City Police Department. When I retired as commanding officer of The Bronx Homicide, I became a homicide and forensic consultant.

I have continued my professional affiliation with Dr. DiMaio and we have been involved in many consultative investigations over the last 15 years. I have also known his son, Vincent J. DiMaio, M.D. for more than 21 years and have had the privileges of his professional affiliation in the sphere of medicolegal investigations and of editing his excellent edition in this series, *Gunshot Wounds: Practical Aspects of Firearms, Ballistics, and Forensic Techniques,* which is the recognized standard for the interpretation and evaluation of gunshot wounds.

According to the latter, the success of the medical examination and the homicide investigation is assured when a mutual cooperation exists between the forensic pathologist and the homicide investigator. Teamwork is essential. This teamwork is based upon a recognition and appreciation of each other's duties and responsibilities so that all parties can benefit from their contributions and expertise in the professional investigation of sudden death and homicide.

In my professional opinion as an expert in the sphere of practical homicide investigation, *Forensic Pathology Second Edition* is the must-have companion text to *Practical Homicide Investigation: Tactics, Procedures, and Forensic Techniques Third Edition.*

Forensic Pathology Second Edition provides an outstanding insight into the investigation of death and serves as a brilliant guide for any pathologist, investigator, or attorney who lacks the formal training of a board-certified forensic pathologist. This text provides practitioners with a foundation upon which they can build an excellent medicolegal investigation. The authors have provided graphic and descriptive photographs throughout the text that highlight for the reader exactly what to look for and how to handle specific situations. This revision carries this textbook well into the 21st century.

Forensic Pathology Second Edition by Dominick J. DiMaio, M.D. and Vincent J. DiMaio, M.D. continues to be the most comprehensive, definitive, and practical medicolegal textbook on forensic pathology today

Vernon J. Geberth, M.S., M.P.S.
Series Editor - CRC Press, LLC
Homicide and Forensic Consultant
Retired Homicide Commander
New York City Police Department

Acknowledgments

The authors thank Wanda Austin and Gloria Delgado for fending off individuals so that we would have time to think and write. We also thank Suzanna E. Dana, M.D., for reviewing the manuscript, and Vernon E. Geberth, the editor of this series, for giving us the opportunity to write this book. We must also, of course, acknowledge Cain, who initiated this field of endeavor.

From lightning and tempest; from earthquake, fire and flood; from plague, pestilence and famine; from battle and murder and from sudden death, Good Lord deliver us.

Litany

Table of Contents

4   Blunt Trauma Wounds

5 Blunt Trauma Injuries of the Trunk and Extremities

6 Trauma to the Skull and Brain: Craniocerebral Injuries

7   Wounds Caused by Pointed and Sharp-Edged Weapons

8   Asphyxia

9 Deaths Caused by Motor Vehicle Accidents

10 Airplane Crashes

11 Sudden Infant Death Syndrome

12   Neonaticide, Infanticide, and Child Homicide

13   Fire Deaths

21 Nursing Home Deaths

22 Sudden Death During or Immediately after a Violent Struggle

23 Interpretive Toxicology: Drug Abuse and Drug Deaths

Medicolegal Investigative Systems

1

Forensic pathology is a branch of medicine that applies the principles and knowledge of the medical sciences to problems in the field of law

The major duties of a medicolegal system in handling deaths falling under its jurisdiction are:

- To determine the cause and manner of death
- To identify the deceased if unknown
- To determine the time of death and injury
- To collect evidence from the body that can be used to prove or disprove an individual's guilt or innocence and to confirm or deny the account of how the death occurred.
- To document injuries or lack of them
- To deduce how the injuries occurred
- To document any natural disease present
- To determine or exclude other contributory or causative factors to the death
- To provide expert testimony if the case goes to trial

Deaths that come to the attention of the office of the medical examiner or the coroner generally fall into the following categories: violent deaths (accidents, suicides, and homicides), suspicious deaths, sudden and unexpected deaths, deaths without a physician in attendance, and deaths in an institution. There are variations to these categories, depending on the local jurisdiction.

Definition of Death

Because of advances in medical science, what was formerly not a problem has now become one—the definition of death. In simpler times, death was defined as the permanent cessation of cardiac and/or respiratory function. Today, instrumentation can keep a heart beating and an individual breathing

1

in spite of the fact that if this machinery were turned off, heart and respiratory activity would cease. This has brought about the concept of *brain death*. There is extensive literature on this subject, and the definition of brain death in adults and children is not necessarily the same.[1]

The declaration of an individual as brain dead, with all the requirements to be met, is mostly of academic interest to the medicolegal system in that a case is not reported until some clinician has pronounced the individual dead. The only time that difficulty might arise is in the harvesting of organs and the moving of brain dead individuals. Thus, in most jurisdictions, if harvesting of organs is intended and family permission has been obtained, and if the case is to be a medical examiner's or coroner's case, prior to removal of the organs, permission must also be obtained from the medical examiner or coroner. This is because, once the individual is "dead," he or she becomes a medicolegal case. Harvesting of organs at that time could then be interpreted as interfering with the duties of the medicolegal system and therefore could constitute a crime. Permission to harvest the organs after pronouncement of death is, for the most part, automatic in most medicolegal systems, because the importance of organ harvesting is recognized by medical examiner/coroner offices. If properly coordinated, the harvesting of organs can be performed without any interference to a subsequent medicolegal examination of the body, including homicides.

The only time the authors have had problems has been when it was decided to pronounce an individual dead, to maintain the person on life support systems, and to transport the body outside the jurisdiction of the medical examiner's office. Once the organs are harvested and the machines turned off, who then will perform the examination of the body? Because the body has been moved out of the legal jurisdiction where it was pronounced dead, does it have to be moved back to that jurisdiction or does the medicolegal agency in the area where the organs are harvested take jurisdiction? Does this medicolegal agency have the legal right, since the individual "died" in another jurisdiction? Fortunately, such problems can usually be settled beforehand with conferences involving the agency harvesting the organs and other medicolegal entities.

One other minor point should be mentioned. An individual may be pronounced dead, yet be maintained on a life support system for 2 to 3 days after pronouncement. This has sometimes resulted in confusion in the documentation of the date of death. This is more a problem of bureaucracy than science, however.

Delayed Deaths

Most people realize that violent deaths (accidents, suicides, and homicides) fall under the jurisdiction of a medicolegal system. What they often fail to realize is that this jurisdiction is retained even if there is a long delay between injury and death, as long as the death was a result of injuries. Thus, if an individual suffers a head injury resulting in irreversible coma, is put in a nursing home, and dies 2 or 3 years later of pneumonia, this is still a medical examiner's case because the medical condition was the result of trauma. In one case, an individual died of chronic renal failure within a few hours of admission to a hospital. The renal failure was due to chronic pyelonephritis, complicating paraplegia, which had in turn been caused by a gunshot wound to the spine 25 years prior. This case was not only still a medical examiner's case, but was a homicide, since the event that started the chain of events that resulted in the death was a gunshot wound. In this case, there were no legal problems, because the perpetrator had died 10 years prior to the victim.

Cause, Manner, and Mechanism of Death

Two of the most important functions of the medical examiner's or coroner's office are the determination of the cause and manner of death. Clinicians, lawyers, and the lay public often have difficulty understanding the difference between cause of death, mechanism of death, and manner of death. Simply put, the *cause of death* is any injury or disease that produces a physiological derangement in the body that results in the death of the individual. Thus, although differing widely, the following are causes of death: a gunshot wound to the head, a stab wound to the chest, adenocarcinoma of the lung, and coronary atherosclerosis.

The mechanism of death is the physiological derangement produced by the cause of death that results in death. Examples of mechanism of death would be hemorrhage, septicemia, and cardiac arrhythmia. One must realize that a particular mechanism of death can be produced by multiple causes of death and vice versa. Thus, if an individual dies of massive hemorrhage, it can be produced by a gunshot wound, a stab wound, a malignant tumor of the lung eroding into a blood vessel and so forth. The reverse of this is that a cause of death, for example, a gunshot wound of the abdomen, can result in many possible mechanisms of death, e.g. hemorrhage or peritonitis.

Medical examiners often have to review death certificates produced by clinicians. Not infrequently, the cause of death is listed as "cardiac arrest" or "cardiopulmonary arrest." Simply stated, this means that the heart stopped or the heart and lungs stopped. Experience tells us, however, that when any individual dies, the heart and lungs stop. These are not causes of death and, to a degree, are not even mechanisms of death. Yet, clinicians continue to list these diagnoses on the death certificate, and some government organizations accept them as causes of death.

The manner of death explains how the cause of death came about. Manners of death can generally be categorized as natural, homicide, suicide, accident, or undetermined. The authors also use the category "unclassified." Just as a mechanism of death can have many causes and a cause many mechanisms, a cause of death can have multiple manners. An individual can die of massive hemorrhage (the mechanism of death) due to a gunshot wound to the heart (the cause of death), with the manner of death being homicide (somebody shot the individual), suicide (they shot themselves), accident (the weapon fell and discharged), or undetermined (one is not sure what occurred).

The manner of death as determined by the forensic pathologist is an opinion based on the known facts concerning the circumstances leading up to and surrounding the death, in conjunction with the findings at autopsy and the laboratory tests. The autopsy findings may contradict or agree with the account of how the death occurred. Thus, if the story is that an individual shot himself and the autopsy reveals a gunshot wound to the back inflicted from a distance, obviously the account is incorrect. If, however, it is a contact gunshot wound of the temple, then the autopsy findings are consistent with the account. It must be realized that the manner of death can be changed if subsequent information that alters the circumstances surrounding the death is discovered. Thus, if we have an individual found with a contact gunshot wound to the temple, with no weapon present and no history of any suicidal threats, one might then conclude that this case is a homicide. If, subsequently, it turns out that the individual had embezzled half a million dollars from his company and was about to be indicted by the grand jury, and his body was found by his wife, who removed a gun and suicide note from the scene, the cause of death would be changed to suicide.

Just because a forensic pathologist makes a ruling as to the manner of death does not mean that it will be accepted by either families or other agencies. The author has ruled homicide in a number of cases that police agencies have written off as accidents. Sometimes, families will challenge a ruling and go to court to have the manner of death overturned. In most instances, the court will support the medical examiner. The medical examiner should not be upset if the court comes to a different ruling as to manner of death, because juries, especially in cases of suicide, are notoriously not impartial or objective. Thus, if a widow, challenging a medical examiner's ruling of suicide so that she can collect insurance, brings two or three young children to the trial, it would not be surprising if the jury should decide to rule the death an accident, no matter how much objective evidence had been presented to the contrary. Their reasoning is that the widow needs money and the insurance company has plenty of it.

Occasionally, there are cases in which the cause of death would ordinarily be considered natural, but the manner is homicide. Thus, we have the home-owner who surprises a burglar, engages him in a violent struggle, then collapses and dies of a heart attack. The mechanism of death is a cardiac arrhythmia and the cause of death is severe coronary atherosclerosis, but the manner of death is homicide, in that the arrhythmia was brought on or precipitated by the struggle. Some individuals will rule a case a homicide even if there is no physical struggle, just sufficient psychological stress to have precipitated the arrhythmia and death. This is very controversial.

In one case, what would ordinarily be considered a natural death based on cause of death was classified as a suicide. An elderly woman attempted to commit suicide by stabbing herself. She used a dull kitchen knife and could not break the skin. She then picked up a hammer and struck herself two or three times on the head, producing some minor contusions of the scalp. The stress of the attempted suicide precipitated a fatal cardiac arrhythmia due to severe coronary atherosclerosis. One of the authors ruled the cause of death to be coronary atherosclerosis and the manner suicide. Her family initially challenged this ruling. When the reasoning for the ruling was explained to them, much to the author's surprise, the family agreed that it was suicide. In another case, a young woman stood at the end of a pier, placed a gun to her chest, and pulled the trigger. The bullet struck her in the chest and she fell backward into the harbor. Her body was subsequently pulled out of the water by a police boat. At autopsy, she had a through-and-through gunshot wound of the left breast, with the bullet producing only soft tissue injury and not entering the chest cavity. The actual cause of death was drowning. The manner of death was ruled as suicide.

A manner of death is ruled undetermined when there is insufficient information about the circumstances surrounding the death to make a ruling, or, in some instances, when the cause of death is unknown. Thus, if one finds the skeletonized remains of a young adult male without evidence of trauma, one cannot say whether the manner of death was accident, homicide, or suicide, because the cause of death is not known. In other instances, there may be insufficient information concerning the circumstances surrounding the death to explain the manner of death. This situation often occurs in deaths due to drug overdoses. Thus, an individual dies as a result of an overdose of a central nervous system depressant drug. The individual has a long history of overmedicating, but, at the same time, has a history of attempted suicide. Is this a case of suicide or did the individual just take too much medication inadvertently, because that was his or her normal habit? Sometimes it is possible to differentiate on the basis of the metabolites of the drug present. Sometimes it is not.

An individual was found with a head injury, obviously due to a fall on the back of the head. There was suspicion, however, that the individual had been in a fight. Toxicological analysis revealed the deceased was intoxicated. Was there a fight and the individual was struck, fell backward, and hit his head, making the case a homicide? Or was there a fight in which the individual was not injured, walked away, and, while intoxicated, fell backward, striking his head, making the death an accident?

In some instances, based on the circumstances surrounding a death, a ruling as to the manner of death can be made without a cause of death. Thus, the decomposing body of a 32-year-old female was found in a ditch two miles from her burglarized house. She was clad in pajamas, barefoot (with the soles of her feet clean), and her hands were bound behind her back. An autopsy failed to reveal a cause of death. The cause of death was ruled undetermined; the manner homicide. The ruling as to manner was based on the circumstances surrounding the death and not the autopsy findings. In the autopsy report, it was suggested that she had either been strangled or smothered. The perpetrator was subsequently arrested and confessed to smothering her.

In addition to the usual classifications of manners of death, some forensic pathologists, ourselves included, use the term "unclassified." This refers to a death in which the cause and circumstances are known, but the death does not readily fall into any of the aforementioned categories. An example is the case of a woman who came into the hospital for an abortion. A hypertonic saline solution was injected; the woman went into labor and delivered a live 450-g infant. There were chemical burns of the skin due to the hypertonic saline solution. The child survived an hour and a half without mechanical assistance, then died. The death was obviously not a suicide, but was it a natural death, an accident, or a homicide? You can propose valid arguments for all three rulings. The manner of death was ruled unclassified. The authors also place in the unclassified category cases that some individuals call *medical misadventure*. Thus, a case of a perforated heart due to an intravascular catheter, and an air embolism complicating spinal fusion are classified as unclassified.

One must also understand that sometimes the classification of manner of death is based on tradition. Thus, if two people are "kidding around" with a gun and one individual points the gun at another and pulls the trigger, in some localities, this is classified as an accident, in others, as a homicide. An individual walking down the street is hit by an automobile; the driver stops. This is an accident. If the driver continues on his way, in a number of jurisdictions, this is classified as a homicide. If one drinks too much alcohol and dies of acute alcohol intoxication, this is an accident. If one drinks too much alcohol every day for 15 years and develops cirrhosis of the liver and chronic liver failure due to the alcohol, then the manner of death is classified as natural.

Sudden, Unexpected Natural Death

The largest category of deaths handled by most medical examiner's offices is natural deaths (Table 1.1). Most of these are sudden and unexpected deaths.

Table 1.1 Breakdown of Medical Examiner Cases as to Manner of Death: Bexar County Texas (1983 –1998)

Total	Naturals	Homicides	Suicides	Accidents	Other
31,502	14,718	4,893	3,440	7,693	758
(100%)	(46.7%)	(15.6%)	(10.9%)	(24.4%)	(2.4%)

These are individuals out functioning in the community, whose deaths are not expected, who suddenly collapse and die. Stress should be put on the sudden nature of these deaths, as many of these individuals may actually have a history of a serious disease.

The medical examiner's office will also see individuals who die as a result of a chronic or terminal disease, but who have elected to die at home. These individuals may be in a hospice or under hospice care. Some elderly individuals with chronic end-stage disease may have been cared for at home for years without seeing a physician. The absence of medical supervision means that these deaths become medical examiner's cases. In the case of hospice individuals, one of the authors (VJMD) has adopted a policy of *pre-registration* in his office. The hospice personnel send the office information on patients while they are still alive. This includes the name of the attending physician who has already agreed to sign the death certificate as well as the expected cause of death. When the individual eventually dies, the hospice just informs the office of the death; the time of death, and who made the pronouncement.

Sudden deaths can be instantaneous; sudden but not instantaneous, or cases where the individual is found dead. Most people, when talking about sudden death, envision *instantaneous deaths*. The best illustration of this is an individual walking along who suddenly collapses and is dead upon hitting the ground. The most common cause for this is a ventricular arrhythmia due to coronary artery disease. The individual will often show *impact abrasions* of the face, indicating that as he was going down, he was unconscious and was not even able to put his arm up in front of his face to prevent impacting the ground (Figure 1.1).

The sudden, but not instantaneous, death is illustrated by the individual who begins to complain of chest pain, difficulty in breathing, weakness, sweating, nausea, and vomiting, and then collapses. He is then transported to the hospital. On the way to the hospital, he goes into cardiac arrest and by the time he reaches the emergency room he is not resuscitatable. Another individual with the same initial symptoms may arrive conscious at the hospital only to experience his fatal cardiac arrhythmia 2 h after admission. Is this still a sudden death? This depends upon one's definition of sudden death. Many, if not most, medical examiners limit classification of sudden deaths as those occurring instantaneously or within 1 h of the onset of symptoms.

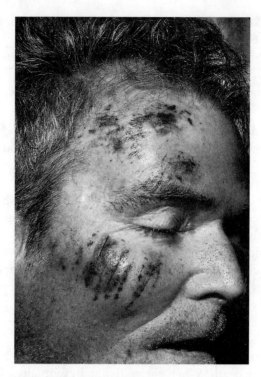

Figure 1.1 Impact abrasions of face indicating individual was unconscious or unable to protect his face from impact with ground. Such abrasions tend to overlie bony ridges.

If the individual complaining of chest pain and difficulty breathing survives long enough to get to the emergency room of a hospital, where an EKG shows an acute myocardial infarct and laboratory tests reveal elevated enzymes, then a diagnosis of myocardial infarct can be made and the case is not a medical examiner's case.

There is a third category of sudden unexpected deaths. These are the individuals in whom the death was unexpected, but was found dead in what may or may not have been an instantaneous manner. Sometimes, one can tell how rapid the death was by the how the individual was found. Someone found sprawled on the kitchen floor with impact-type abrasions of the face is most likely an instantaneous death. In the case of a person found dead in bed, death may have been sudden but not instantaneous. The great majority of sudden, unexpected natural deaths seen at a medical examiner's office are due to cardiovascular disease. Less common are deaths due to central nervous system lesions, pulmonary disease, and sepsis. The whole spectrum of natural disease associated with sudden death is discussed in Chapter 3.

The Coroner System

There are two general types of medicolegal investigative systems in the United States: **coroner systems** and **medical examiner** systems. As of 2000, 12 states had coroner systems; 19 states had state medical examiner systems; 3 states had county or regional medical examiner's offices but no coroner's offices; and 16 had a mixture of medical examiner and coroner systems.[2] Over the years, there has been a gradual decrease in the number of coroner systems, with replacement by medical examiner systems, though this seems to have slowed down recently. Coroner systems, however, still make up a significant proportion of the medicolegal coverage of the American population.

The coroner system, dating back to feudal England, is the older of the two medicolegal systems. The earliest reference appears in the Articles of Eyre (1194).[3] In the pure form of this system, an individual who is not a physician is elected the coroner. He then makes rulings as to the cause and manner of death in cases that fall under the coroner law. As a general rule, these cases constitute violent deaths, sudden and/or unexpected deaths, suspicious deaths, and cases in which a physician is not in attendance at the time of death. In making a ruling, the coroner is not required to consult a physician for advice, may or may not order an autopsy, and may or may not rule in agreement with autopsy findings if one is performed. The training the coroner receives for the position can range from absolutely none to a few hours or to 1–2 weeks. Based on this training — or lack of it — the coroner makes decisions as to cause and manner of death that may have significant criminal and civil consequences.

In some areas of the country, this system has been modified such that the coroner must be a physician, though not necessarily a pathologist. This gives a scientific veneer to the system. We now have physicians making decisions in a medical field usually having absolutely nothing to do with their areas of expertise. Thus, we have the obstetrician-coroner, the general practitioner-coroner, and so on. Occasionally, by chance, the coroner is a pathologist, though almost never a forensic pathologist.

Most people do not realize that exposure to forensic pathology in most general pathology training programs ranges from nonexistent to a few hours of instruction, or occasionally a short (2–4 weeks) rotation through a medicolegal system. Thus, certification as an anatomical (general) pathologist does not necessarily mean that an individual knows any forensic pathology. Physicians practicing outside their fields of specialty or with such minimal training as possessed by the physician-coroner would ordinarily be open to malpractice lawsuits and condemnation by the public, colleagues, and especially the legal community. No insurance company would provide malpractice coverage. The coroner-physician, however, works for a governmental organization that either does not care or know about qualifications for this work.

California often exemplifies the extremes of this country. Thus, in a number of counties in California, the coroner is also the sheriff. Thus, a deputy sheriff might kill a civilian and his boss, the sheriff, rules as to the cause and manner of death. Sheriffs also operate jails. The sheriff acting as the coroner thus makes rulings as to the cause of death of inmates dying in his jail. Obviously, to anyone but the California legislature, there is a conflict between having a single organization whose duties are to both enforce laws and make arrests and to conduct objective investigation of death in which rulings may impeach or conflict with the other half of the organization.

In many areas of the country, the coroner is also a funeral director. Here, again, there is at least the appearance of a conflict of interest. The coroner-funeral director makes a livelihood by conducting funerals, not by being a coroner. Some unscrupulous coroners are more interested in obtaining a family's permission to conduct the funeral than to make a ruling as to cause and manner of death. They may take great care not to make a ruling as to cause and manner of death that might offend a family and thus cost them business or potential votes in the next election.

The coroner system was developed at a time when the lay public knew as much about the science of medicine as the physicians practicing it. Times have changed. Medicine has become an extremely complicated, specialized, scientific field. Specialized knowledge is necessary not only to practice medicine in general, but to practice any of its numerous subspecialties. Thus, a dermatologist would not consider doing neurosurgery, nor would a neurosurgeon practice obstetrics/gynecology. The practice of forensic medicine has also become a specialty. Neither average hospital pathologists nor physicians who are not pathologists can adequately practice in this field no matter how well intentioned they are — and they are often very well intentioned.

Some non-forensic pathologists claim that any anatomical pathologist with a basic knowledge of pathology can handle 85% of medical examiner cases, with the remaining 15% needing a forensic pathologist in a fully equipped medicolegal facility. Therefore, only a small corps of experienced forensic pathologists is needed, to which the difficult 15% of cases can be referred.

Even accepting this somewhat dubious premise, the problem is how does one know ahead of time which of the cases are the 15% needing the forensic pathologist and the fully equipped medical examiner's office? Not even a forensic pathologist knows for sure in every case. One never knows when the simplest autopsy will turn out to be a complicated case with the most extreme repercussions. A witnessed "automobile accident" turned out, at autopsy, to be a capital homicide involving an armed robbery. A simple carbon monoxide suicide in a garage eventually ended up with a million-dollar lawsuit and involved the flying characteristics of light planes. A simple case of sudden death in infancy ended up as the final death in a decades-long chain of infanticide.

The Medical Examiner System

The medical examiner system was first introduced in the United States in 1877 in Massachusetts. The state was divided into a number of sectors, within each of which was designated a physician who functioned as a "medical examiner" to determine the cause and manner of death. Originally, medical examiners did not have the right to order autopsies. This was not corrected until the 1940s. Neither was a central laboratory for toxicological analysis available. It was only in the 1980s that a true State Medical Examiner System was established in Massachusetts.

The first true medical examiner system came into existence in 1918 in New York City.[4] A medicolegal system was established in which the individual designated as Chief Medical Examiner was to be a physician experienced in the field of pathology (forensic pathology did not become a subspecialty until 1959). The system described the type of cases that fell under the Medical Examiner Law; it stated that the medical examiner could perform autopsies in cases that he felt needed them, and it established a laboratory for his use. The cases that fell under the medical examiner system were violent deaths (accidents, suicides, homicides), suspicious deaths, sudden, unexpected deaths, and deaths occurring without the attendance of a physician. Most medical examiner systems in this country are variations of the original New York concept. Some of the newer systems specify that the chief medical examiner must be a forensic pathologist.

The creation of a medical examiner system does not necessarily mean that a community actually has a functioning or effective medical examiner system, nor does the fact that it once had one guarantee that it will continue to operate in an effective manner. Thus, by the mid 1980s, the New York City Medical Examiner System had been seriously damaged in its functioning by a change in the law that allowed families to prevent the performance of autopsies in cases in which the manner of death did not appear to be homicide; that is, the forensic pathologist had authority to perform an autopsy only in cases that were obviously homicide.

Unfortunately, it is not always possible to recognize a homicide until an autopsy is performed. In 10% of children beaten to death, there is no external evidence of trauma. In addition, without an autopsy, an accurate cause of death, the presence and extent of disease or injury, the incapacitation produced by them, and knowledge of whether there was any pain or suffering involved in an injury (an important question in civil cases) become sheer speculation.

Some legislatures have created medical examiner's offices and have not funded them adequately. In other instances, the offices are placed under state government agencies that should not be supervising the medical examiner's office. No medical examiner's office should function under a police agency. There is a direct conflict in values, goals, and philosophies. The police want to make an arrest and clear a case. The medical examiner's office wants to determine the cause and manner of death, independent of who did what. While these functions usually coincide, in some cases, they do not. One of the most controversial types of death is that of a civilian killed by police. By virtue of being a subdivision of a police agency, the impartiality of the medical examiner's office in such cases is open to serious question.

In some areas, the medical examiner's office functions under the public health department. This may or may not work out. Public health departments often have only a vague concept of the duties and functions of a medical examiner's office, which is a medicolegal agency rather than a pure medical agency. The contribution of the medical examiner's office to the public health is of a tenuous nature. Placing it under a department of public health tends to increase the bureaucracy between the office and the authority to which it is responsible. In addition, public health departments are often under funded and there is always the human tendency to dip into one section of a department for monies for another section. Just as police agencies should be separate from the district attorney's office, so, ideally, the medical examiner's office should be reportable to only the highest authority, for example, the mayor, county commissioners, or governor.

As a general rule, while some medical examiner's offices are handicapped by defective laws, underfunding, and political interference, they do a much better and more scientific job than a coroner. It is easier to convince ("coerce") a politician subject to election to change a ruling than a physician who can usually make more money in private practice doing the same work.

One argument for retention of the coroner system is that it is more economical than a medical examiner system. The coroner system, while cheaper in some jurisdictions in the short run because no experts or scientific investigations are used, becomes more expensive in the long run. Savings are lost when cases are invariably mishandled with resultant expensive and protracted litigation, both criminal and civil, retrials, the hiring of outside experts, and so on. More important than money, however, is that the coroner system often produces inferior and inaccurate results. Non-physicians cannot make medical decisions, no matter how many weeks of training they have. General pathologists can get through most cases, but the difficult case, the one that they often do not even recognize as difficult, can result in the imprisonment of innocent individuals and the release of the guilty. Just as we are guaranteed certain basic rights by our legal system, we should also have the right to a competent scientific medical investigation following a death, especially if there is the potential for civil or criminal litigation.

Some coroners argue that they can and do produce excellent work because they retain competent physicians and rely on them to make decisions. This is true. But, if coroners rely that much on their physicians, then what purposes do the coroners serve? They are just elected administrators subject to political influence who, if they desire, can ignore their experts. In addition, a conscientious, competent coroner may be defeated at the next election to be replaced by a venial incompetent.

A modern, well-organized medical examiner system is relatively cheap to operate, considering its benefits once the population serviced exceeds approximately 250,000. Cost to the community for a good system is approximately one quarter to one third the cost of a movie ticket per person per year. This money will fund a fully staffed medical examiner's office including an investigative staff and a toxicology laboratory. Some states or counties claim to be too big, with a population too scattered, for a state system. This can be handled by establishing either regional offices or a central state office to which bodies can be transported.

The main problem with establishing a quality medical examiner system is ignorance — ignorance not only by the general public, but, more importantly, by courts, judges, and attorneys. The courts permit untrained and sometimes incompetent individuals to routinely testify on the basis of a medical degree often coupled with vague forensic experience. While no judge would take his pregnant wife to a dermatologist for obstetrical care, he does permit an individual with no forensic training at all to testify in a case that may involve a sentence of lengthy imprisonment or even execution.

There is ignorance also on the part of politicians. They have very little idea of what a medical examiner's office does, do not visit the facilities, and show very little interest in the office — after all, the dead do not vote. The only time one hears from politicians is when there are lawsuits against the government because of incompetence in the medicolegal system. The public is often ignorant of the poor quality of the medicolegal system in their area because they assume what they see on television crime shows is also true in their own community.

The police are partly at fault because they do not realize the amount of help a quality medical examiner system can provide. In some instances, they do not like the data provided by a good medical examiner system. They prefer the charlatan who tells them what they want to hear to the expert who tells them unpalatable truths or that conclusions cannot be made. One of the characteristics of the unqualified expert in forensic pathology is an ability to interpret a case in exquisite detail. This "expert" sets the time of death, plus or minus a few minutes, accurately positions the deceased, and gives detailed analysis of the events surrounding the death and precise deductions about the assault. If the police have expressed prior opinions, it is not uncommon for the opinions of the "expert" to agree in almost complete detail with the police hypotheses. The experienced forensic pathologist tends to hedge, knows there can be more than one interpretation of a set of facts, and is more "wishy-washy" than the charlatan.

Because of the poor quality of forensic medicine in many parts of this country, there are individuals languishing in jail for homicides that were suicides and murderers walking the street after having committed a homicide that was interpreted as an accident or a natural death.

Operation of a Medical Examiner System

To perform its duties, a medical examiner system requires a number of basic essentials. First is an adequate law under which to operate. Under such a law, violent deaths (accidents, suicides, and homicides), suspicious deaths, sudden and unexpected deaths, deaths without a physician in attendance, and deaths in jails and penal institutions should fall under the medical examiner's jurisdiction. In many areas, there is also a broad "24-hour death" report law. That is, the death of any individual dying within 24 h of admission to a hospital must be reported to the medical examiner as a possible medical examiner case. This law is useful in picking up cases that might otherwise be missed.

After indicating the type of cases that fall under the medical examiner's jurisdiction, the law should then state that medical examiners have the right to perform an autopsy on any cases that they feel need one to accurately determine the cause and manner of death or to document injuries or disease processes. The law should also give medical examiners the right to subpoena records and individuals, if necessary, to help in making such determinations. The law should state that deaths are to be reported to medical examiners immediately after they occur or are discovered and that, at any crime scene, medical examiners have jurisdiction over the body. Overall jurisdiction of the scene, of course, lies with the police agency involved. The law should also provide medical examiners with a toxicology laboratory.

The right of the medical examiner to perform autopsies in any cases falling under the Medical Examiner's Law is especially important. This is because accurate determination of the cause and manner of death can be accomplished only by a complete autopsy. The absence of any external evidence of injury does not rule out massive internal injuries and the possibility that the case is a homicide. Thus, in the authors' experience, 10% of all children dying of blunt traumatic injuries show no evidence of injury externally. If one could not perform an autopsy in such cases, these homicides would be missed and death ascribed to natural causes. Obvious homicide cases are less of a problem than the more subtle ones that initially appear to be natural deaths or accidents.

It is also highly desirable that the medical examiner have some civil service protection. This is because medical examiners make unpopular decisions, decisions that politicians, police agencies, and sometimes the public may not want to hear. There is always the natural tendency of humanity to want to "kill" the bearer of bad news.

The second requirement for an adequate medical examiner system is qualified personnel. The chief medical examiner should be a **board certified forensic pathologist** with a number of years of experience. Under the chief medical examiner, there should be assistant medical examiners who are also board-certified forensic pathologists. If initially not certified, the individuals should be given a certain time limit (2–3 years) to obtain certification. To acquire and retain such qualified personnel, they must command competitive salaries.

What is a board certified forensic pathologist? A **board certified forensic pathologist is a physician** who has successfully completed a graduate medical education program in either anatomical or anatomical and clinical pathology approved by the Residency Review Committee and accredited by the Accreditation Council for Graduate Medical Education (ACGME) or The Royal College of Physicians and Surgeons of Canada; been endorsed by the training program director and successfully passed a written and practical examination designed and administered by the American Board of Pathology in this (these) field(s) of medicine, following which they have taken 1 full year of additional supervised training in forensic pathology in a program accredited for such training by the ACGME, and passed a written and practical examination designed and administered by the American Board of Pathology in this field.

Third, the medical examiner's office needs adequate staffing. Medical examiners alone do not constitute an office. There must be competent investigative, administrative, secretarial, and technical support staff.

Fourth, there must be an adequate facility. One cannot practice forensic medicine in the sub-basement of a county hospital or in the back of a funeral home. The facility must have sufficient space, an appropriate floor plan, electrical, plumbing, and cooling capabilities, and furnishings.

Fifth, there must be adequate instrumentation available for the scientific investigation of death. In some areas, x-ray equipment is considered a luxury, but it is basic equipment for an autopsy suite. There should be equipment in the toxicological laboratory capable of an accurate, precise analysis for the presence of drugs. The equipment should be of high quality and be in sufficient quantity to handle the caseload. Computerization of an office has now become mandatory.

Last, there must be consistent and adequate funding of the institution. Without this, a qualified staff is not possible, nor are adequate facilities or equipment.

How do medical examiners (forensic pathologists) approach a case? They approach it just like any other physician approaches a patient. In medical school, one is taught that, to make a correct diagnosis, one must take a history, perform a physical examination, and order relevant laboratory tests. Based on this, a diagnosis is made. The forensic pathologist performs all of these functions but with some variance. Thus, the history is not obtained from the patient, but from witnesses, relatives of the deceased, police agencies, treating physicians, and/or records (medical, nonmedical, police, governmental, etc.). It is an account of the events leading up to and surrounding the death.

In most major medical examiner systems in this country, reports of deaths do not come directly to medical examiners, but to lay investigators employed by the medical examiner's office, who are trained to screen the cases and make a determination as to whether a death is a medical examiner's case. If it is not, it is then released back to the reporting physician. If the case falls under the Medical Examiner's Law or if there is no physician to sign the death certificate, the case is accepted. Whether a case is accepted or not, a detailed report should be written up. In cases that are not accepted, the report should be subsequently reviewed by a medical examiner as soon as possible. If there is any disagreement with the conclusion of the investigator, the body will then be brought in from the funeral home to which it was sent. With well-trained, highly motivated investigators, this is an extremely rare occurrence.

The reason that physicians are not used to screen calls is both economical and logistic. In a community of a million people, one might get anywhere from 4000 to 6000 death calls a year. To have a physician personally screen each one of these calls — calling other physicians, double-checking records, talking to police agencies, and going to the scene of death — is uneconomical and a waste of professional time. *The U.S Department of Justice has published national guidelines for death investigation.*[5] In addition, there is now in existence the American Board of Medicolegal Death Investigators, which certifies death investigators based on a combination of experience and testing.[6]

If investigators accept the case as a medical examiner's case, they then must decide whether to go to the scene of the death. If the body has been moved from the scene to a hospital, the decision has already been made for them and the body can come directly in. If they decide to go to the scene, their job is to document all the findings at the scene regarding the body and to obtain a detailed history of the circumstances leading up to and surrounding the death. Investigators will document the scene with diagrams and photographs. In some communities, investigators videotape the scene. This material is then brought back to the office, where a detailed report is prepared for the medical examiner. At this time, the investigation report may be supplemented by telephone calls to other agencies and individuals. The lay investigator goes to hospitals to obtain medical records that may be of importance in making a determination of the cause of death. Based on the investigator's report, the medical examiner will then decide what to do with the case, whether to perform an autopsy, as well as what types of tests are to be performed.

In some jurisdictions, physicians routinely make all scene investigations or at least all violent death scenes. While this is satisfactory in small, low-volume offices, it is generally a waste of personnel, time, and money in large urban areas. In some areas of the country, a physician who visits a scene has the right to sign out the case without bringing it into the medical examiner's office. This practice should be condemned. There is no way to adequately examine a body at a scene as well as in a morgue. If a body is a medical examiner's case, it should come into the office, where, at the minimum, a complete external examination can be performed in an environment with adequate lighting, equipment, and support personnel. In addition, at the same time, body fluids can be obtained for toxicological analysis. If it is a medical examiner's case, it should come in. If it is not a medical examiner's case, then the medical examiner should refuse jurisdiction and let the patient's attending physician handle the case. When in doubt, however, bring the case in.

When the body comes in, the medical examiner then performs a physical examination and laboratory tests. The procedures may range from an external examination of the body to a complete autopsy. This will be determined by the information that has been provided to the medical examiner by the investigator, the type of case, the medical examiner's expertise, and local or regional differences. Performing autopsies on every case coming into a medical examiner's office is a waste of time and energy. The practice is common in areas where there are contract pathologists paid by the case. Thus, the more cases they autopsy, the more money they make.

For every case that comes into the office, at least blood, urine and vitreous should be obtained and retained. The blood should be obtained from the femoral or subclavian vessels. It should never be obtained from a blind thoracic puncture. It is the policy of one of the authors (VJMD) to perform a complete toxicological screen on the blood of most individuals younger than 70 years of age, whether they are autopsied or not. An exception would be a terminal cancer patient in the end stage of the disease. Routine drug screens on apparent natural deaths have, with regular monotony, revealed deaths from suicidal and accidental overdoses of drugs. Such extensive screening is not possible in most areas of the country because of limitations on the toxicology laboratory.

If an autopsy is performed, what specialized tests are done at the time of autopsy are determined by the type of case. Thus, a rape examination may be conducted in a suspected rape case, or hair obtained in a death with blunt-force injuries to the head.

For all cases coming to autopsy, it is recommended that, at the minimum, blood, vitreous, urine, and bile be obtained for toxicological analysis. Blood should be obtained from the femoral vessels. If this is not possible, other sites, in descending order of preference, are the subclavian vessels, the root of the aorta, the pulmonary artery, the superior vena cava and the heart. The blood should be collected with a clean needle and new syringe. Blood should never be obtained by incising a vessel or the heart and attempting to capture the fluid as it escapes. All body fluids should be placed in glass tubes or bottles, not plastic. If the body is decomposed, liver, kidney, and thigh muscle are retained. When suicidal overdose of oral medications is suspected, the stomach contents should be kept. Some laboratories retain portions of liver and kidney in all suspected drug overdose deaths — whether decomposed or not. With modern instrumentation and analytical methods, however, it is rarely necessary to analyze these materials.

The urine is generally of use only in screening for certain drugs. The detection of a drug in the urine indicates only that the individual has taken that drug at some time in the past, not that they were under its influence at time of death. It is the presence of the drug in the blood that is important. Because of this, toxicological procedures should be concentrated on the blood. Absence of a drug in the urine also does not necessarily indicate that it will not be found in the blood. Thus, an intravenous injection of heroin could cause death before any metabolites appear in the urine.

At the time of autopsy, tissue should be retained for possible microscopic examination, although this is not necessary in every case. Thus, in traumatic deaths, such as a shooting or motor vehicle accident, while a medical examiner may elect to do microscopic examination of the tissue, it is rarely necessary. Even if microscopic slides are not made, tissue should still be retained for this possibility. It is the opinion of the authors that toxicologic specimens and tissue removed for possible microscopic examination should be retained for 3–5 years. All microscopic slides and paraffin blocks should be retained indefinitely.

In homicide cases and cases where extensive civil litigation is expected, photographic documentation of the injuries is recommended.

NAME Accreditation

In 1997, the National Association of Medical Examiners (NAME) instituted a revised voluntary inspection and accreditation program for medicolegal offices. The new program is much more stringent than the prior program. The standards represent **minimum standards for an adequate medicolegal system**, emphasizing policies and procedures. Deficiencies are designated as Phase I or II. A single Phase II deficiency precludes accreditation. Evaluated are:

The facilities
Safety policies, procedures and equipment
Personnel
Notification, acceptance and release
Investigations
Body handling
Postmortem examinations
Identification
Evidence and specimen collection
Support services
Reports and records
Mass disaster plan
Quality assurance

One area addressed is medical examiner caseload. If a medical examiner performs more than 250 autopsies per year, this is considered a Phase I deficiency; if more than 400, a Phase II deficiency (there are plans to lower the 400 number to 350 and possibly 300).

Excessive caseload is a problem in many medicolegal offices. The recommended annual caseload for a forensic pathologist without administrative responsibilities is 250 autopsies. On a short-time basis, one can perform autopsies at an annual rate of 300, perhaps 325. By the time, caseload exceeds 350 autopsies, mistakes are being made and the quality of the autopsy is being sacrificed.

References

1. *Defining Death: A Report on the Medical, Legal and Ethical Issues in the Determination of Death.* President's Commission for the Study of Ethical Problems in Medicine and Biomedical and Behavioral Research. Washington D.C., U.S. Government Printing Office, 1981.

2. Hanzlick R and Combs D: Medical examiner and coroner systems: history and trends (special communication). *JAMA* 1998 279(11): 870-874.

3. Mant AK: The evaluation of the coroner's system and the present status in Great Britain. *Forensic Sci Gazette* 1971; 2(4):1-6.

4. The Office of the Medical Examiner of the City of New York: Report by the Committee on Public Health, New York Academy of Medicine. *Bull NY Acad Med* 1967. 43: 241-249.

5. National Medicolegal Review Panel: *Death Investigation: A Guide for the Scene Investigator.* National Institute of Justice, November 1999. (http://www.ncjrs.org/txtfiles/167568.txt)

6. American Board of Medicolegal Death Investigators: St. Louis, MO.

Time of Death

2

Determination of the time of death is important in both criminal and civil cases. In criminal cases, it can set the time of the murder, eliminate or suggest suspects, confirm or disprove an alibi. In civil cases, the time of death might determine who inherits property or whether an insurance policy was in force. Unfortunately, all methods now in use to determine the time of death are to a degree unreliable and inaccurate. They usually give vague or dubious answers. The longer the postmortem interval, i.e., the time between death and the attempt to determine time of death, the less precise the estimate of the interval. One obvious facet of time of death determination often not considered is that the time the fatal injury is incurred is not necessarily the time of death. One can incur massive fatal injuries, yet linger in an unconscious state for hours prior to death (Figure 2.1).

Many factors are or have been used in determining the time of death:

Livor mortis
Rigor mortis
Body temperature
Degree of decomposition
Chemical changes in vitreous
Flow-cytometry
Stomach contents
Insect activity
Scene markers (papers, letters, clothing, televisions, TV schedules, etc.)

Livor Mortis

Livor mortis (lividity, postmortem hypostasis) is a reddish purple coloration in dependent areas of the body due to accumulation of blood in the small vessels of the dependent areas secondary to gravity (Figure 2.2A). Postmortem lividity is occasionally misinterpreted as bruising by people unfamiliar with this phenomenon.

Dependent areas resting against a firm surface will appear pale in contrast to the surrounding livor mortis due to compression of the vessels in this area, which prevents the accumulation of blood. Thus, areas supporting the weight of the body, for example, the shoulder blades, buttocks,

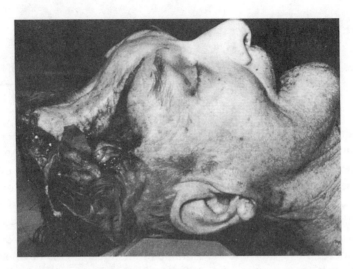

Figure 2.1 Contact wound of right temple with .357 Magnum. The deceased lived 1 hr and 34 min with no life support systems.

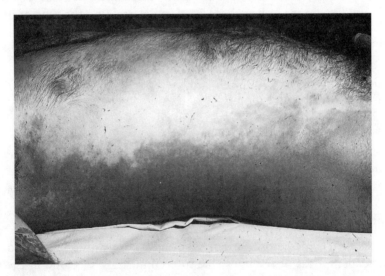

Figure 2.2 (A) Liver mortis in dependent areas of body (*continued*).

and calves in individuals lying on their backs, show no livor mortis, but appear as pale or blanched areas (Figure 2.2B, C). Tight clothing, for example, a brassiere, corset, or belt, which compresses soft tissues, collapsing the vessels, also produces pale areas.

Livor mortis usually, but not invariably, has a cherry-red to pinkish color in deaths due to carbon monoxide. This is due to carboxyhemoglobin. Identical coloration may be caused by exposure of a body to cold temperatures, and in deaths due to cyanide.Localized areas of bright red livor mortis are

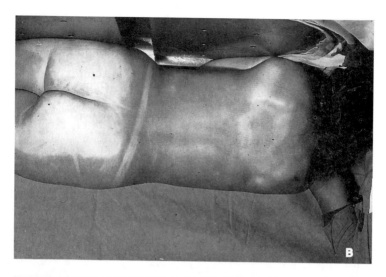

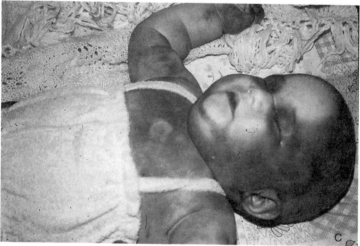

Figure 2.2 (*continued*) (B) Blanched areas of buttocks and shoulders due to compression of vessels by weight of body. (C) Infant with pale face from lying face down in crib.

also seen adjacent to chest tubes. In all three of the aforementioned entities, the coloration is caused by predominance of oxygenated hemoglobin.

Livor mortis is usually evident within 30 min to 2 h after death. In individuals dying a slow lingering death with terminal cardiac failure, livor mortis may actually appear antemortem. Livor mortis develops gradually, usually reaching its maximum coloration at 8–12 h. At about this time, it is said to become "fixed." Prior to becoming fixed, livor mortis will shift as the body is moved. Thus, if an individual dies lying on his back, livor mortis develops posteriorly, i.e., on the back. If one turns the body on its face, blood will drain to the anterior surface of the body, now the dependent aspect. Livor mortis becomes "fixed" when shifting or drainage of blood no longer occurs, or when blood leaks out of the vessels into the surrounding soft tissue due to hemolysis and breakdown of the vessels. Fixation can occur before 8–12 h if decomposition is accelerated, or at 24–36 h if delayed by cool temperatures. Thus, the statement that livor mortis becomes fixed at 8–12 h is really just a vague generalization. That livor mortis is not fixed can be demonstrated by applying pressure to a dependent discolored area and noting the subsequent blanching at the point of pressure.

Although livor mortis may be confused with bruising, bruising is rarely confused with livor mortis. Application of pressure to an area of bruising will not cause blanching. An incision into an area of contusion or bruising shows diffuse hemorrhage into the soft tissue. In contrast, an incision into an area of livor mortis reveals the blood to be confined to vessels, without blood in the soft tissue.

Livor mortis also occurs internally, with settling of the blood in the dependent aspects of an organ. This is most obvious in the lungs.

As the blood accumulates in the dependent areas, the pressure of the settling blood can rupture small vessels, with development of petechiae (minute hemorrhages or Tardieu spots) and purpura (patches of purplish discoloration) (Figure 2.3). This usually takes 18–24 h and often indicates that decomposition is fast approaching. This phenomenon is more common in asphyxial or slow deaths. Unfortunately, as time passes, it cannot always be determined with certainty whether the purpura produced are ante- or postmortem. Presence of petechiae and purpura only in dependent areas suggests a postmortem origin. In limbs hanging over the side of a bed or the legs and forearms of an individual who is hanging, Tardieu spots may develop even more rapidly, appearing as early as 2–4 h after death.

Livor mortis can cause difficulty in interpreting head injuries in decomposed bodies. In a body lying on its back, blood accumulates in the posterior or dependent half of the scalp due to gravity. In advanced decomposition, with lysis of red blood cells and breakdown of the vessels, there is seepage of blood into the soft tissue of the scalp. This gives the appearance of confluent bruising and cannot always be differentiated from true antemortem bruising. There will, of course, be no abrasion or laceration of the scalp, but all forensic pathologists have seen extensive scalp contusions without abrasions or lacerations. In decomposed bodies, blood collecting in the occipital areas of the brain due to gravity may escape through small vessels, producing very thin localized films of blood in the subarachnoid or subdural spaces coating the occipital lobes. The rest of the brain does not show subarachnoid or subdural hemorrhage. In drownings where the body floats head down, decomposition produces the picture of

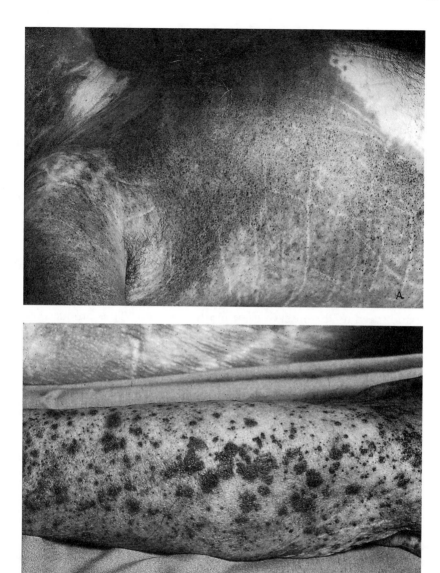

Figure 2.3 Tardieu spots. (A) Petechiae in area of livor mortis. (B) Petechiae and purpura in arm hanging over bed.

diffuse scalp hemorrhage. Rarely, postmortem leakage of blood into the soft tissue and muscle of the anterior aspect of the neck may also occur in drownings. This "bleeding" is minimal.

Livor mortis is not very important in determining the time of death. It is important, however, in determining whether the body has been moved.

Rigor Mortis

Rigor mortis, or stiffening of the body after death, is due to the disappearance of adenosine triphosphate (ATP) from muscle. ATP is the basic source of energy for muscle contraction. Muscle needs a continuous supply of ATP to contract because the amount present is sufficient to sustain muscle contraction for only a few seconds. The three metabolic systems responsible for maintaining a continuous supply of ATP in the muscle are the phosphagen system, the glycogen–lactic acid system, and the aerobic system. Under optimal conditions, the phosphagen system can provide maximal muscle power for 10–15 sec, the glycogen–lactic acid system for 30–40 sec, and the aerobic system for an unlimited period of time.[1] After exercise, these three systems need time to be replenished. After death, generation of ATP stops, though consumption continues. In the absence of ATP, actin and myosin filaments become permanently complexed and rigor mortis sets in. This complex remains until decomposition occurs.

Any violent muscular exertion prior to death will produce a decrease in ATP and speed up the onset of rigor mortis, since no ATP is produced after death. Some factors that cause a marked decrease in ATP prior to death are violent or heavy exercise, severe convulsions, and high body temperatures. All of these factors may cause rapid onset of rigor mortis, with onset appearing within minutes in some cases, and, in rare instances, instantaneously. The instantaneous appearance of rigor mortis is known as **cadaveric spasm.** In one instance, a man was chasing his wife with a straight razor when she turned and fired one shot, striking and killing him instantly. The deceased collapsed to his knees, holding the razor in his right hand in an upward position. At the scene, he was found dead, kneeling, with his right arm extended upward with the razor clasped in the hand. In cadaveric spasm, the object will be firmly clenched in the hand (Figure 2.4).

Rigor mortis disappears with decomposition. Cold or freezing will delay the onset of rigor mortis as well as prolong its presence. Rigor mortis can be "broken" by passive stretching of muscles. After rigor mortis is broken, it will not return. If only partial rigor mortis has set in prior to stretching, then the residual unbroken rigor mortis can still set in.

Rigor mortis usually appears 2–4 h after death, and fully develops in 6–12 h. This can vary greatly. In one case seen by the author, a young woman died following an overdose of aspirin. An EMS unit was summoned while she was in an agonal state. On arrival, she was still breathing and had a heart rate. Almost immediately, she suffered a cardiopulmonary arrest. Attempts at resuscitation were made and continued for approximately 15–20 min. Following this, she was pronounced dead. The body was then made ready to be transported to the medical examiner's office. At this time, it was realized that she was in full rigor mortis, only minutes

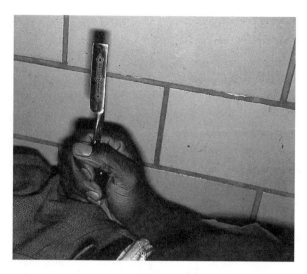

Figure 2.4 Cadaveric spasm in 43-year-old male with razor in right hand.

after being pronounced dead. Two hours later, at the morgue, she had a rectal temperature of 106°F.

Rigor mortis, when it develops, involves all the muscles at the same time and at the same rate. However, it becomes most evident in the smaller muscles. Thus, rigor mortis is said to appear first in the smaller muscles, such as the jaw, and then to gradually spread to large muscle groups. The classical presentation of rigor mortis in its order of appearance is jaw, upper extremities, and lower extremities. It passes off in the order in which it appeared. Rigor mortis is lost due to decomposition. In temperate climates, rigor mortis disappears in 36 h, but may be present up to 6 days. In hot climates, such as in Texas, a body can be in a moderately advanced to advanced state of decomposition in 24 h, in which case, there will be no rigor mortis present.

In a case seen by one of the authors (VJMD), the decomposing body of a 14-year-old boy was pulled from a cold lake. He had drowned 17 days prior. The body was in an early to moderate state of decomposition externally: a swollen face, discolored skin with slippage and marbling. The internal organs were in an early state of decomposition — not as decomposed as one might expect with the external changes. The most unusual aspect of the case was that the body was still in full rigor mortis. One can only speculate that the immersion in the cold water was the reason the rigor mortis persisted.

Rigor mortis may be delayed or be very weak in emaciated individuals. Its onset may also be very rapid in infants. Poisons, such as strychnine, that produce convulsions can accelerate the development of rigor mortis. Any disease or environmental factor that raises body temperature accelerates the development of rigor mortis. Thus, hyperthermia, loss of body regulatory

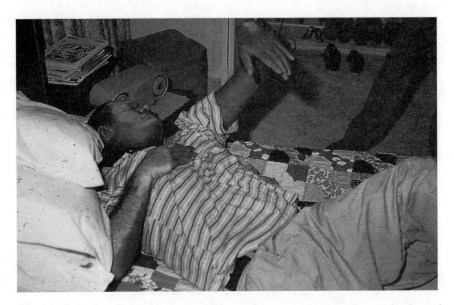

Figure 2.5 Body originally found face down, but now turned onto back. Left arm in air. Blanching of right side of face, back of right hand and forearm, and back of left wrist.

temperature due to cerebral hemorrhage, and infection may accelerate the development of rigor mortis.

In drowning deaths, rigor mortis may develop fully within only 2 to 3 h. This is apparently due to exhaustion of ATP through violent struggling while drowning. Individuals who are being chased prior to their deaths may show more rapid development of rigor mortis in their legs than in the rest of their musculature. This, again, is due to exhaustion of ATP by the muscles of the legs caused by running. Like livor mortis, rigor mortis can indicate whether a body has been moved (Figure 2.5).

Body Temperature

Some physicians attempt to determine how long an individual has been dead by the temperature of the body. Such determinations make two assumptions that may not be true: first, that the body temperature at death was normal, and second, that body cooling follows a progressive repetitive pattern such that one can project what the prior body temperature was and what it will be.

Determination of the time of death by body temperature usually involves using a formula. A number of formulas have been devised, some of which are quite complicated. Two of the formulas that are the easiest to use are:

(1) Time since death = 37°C – Rectal temperature (C) + 3

$$(2) \text{ Time since death} = \frac{98.6°\text{F} - \text{Rectal Temperature (F)}}{1.5}$$

The problem with all formulas using body temperature to determine time of death is that they are based on the assumption that the body temperature at time of death is "normal." What is normal? "Normal" body temperature is an average. Some people have higher and some have lower body temperatures. Traditionally, the normal mean oral temperature has been said to be 98.6°F (37.0°C). These figures are based on testing done during the 19th century. More recent work indicates that mean oral temperature, for healthy adults age 40 or younger, is really 98.2°F (36.8°C) with 99.9°F (37.7°C) the upper limit of the normal temperature range.[2] Body temperature also varies with time of day, with the nadir at 6 a.m. and the zenith at 4–6 p.m. Women showed slightly higher normal temperatures.

A second problem: Even if we know what the deceased's normal temperature is, was the temperature normal at the time of death? Strenuous exercise can raise rectal temperatures up to 104°F. Infection obviously causes a rise in body temperature. Intracerebral hemorrhages or injury to the brain can cause dysfunction of the thermoregulatory system of the brain stem, which causes increased body temperatures. Exposure to cold can cause hypothermia, i.e., low body temperatures.

In other words, body temperature varies from the site where it was taken (oral or rectal, brain or liver), from individual to individual, by time of day, by the activity of the individual, and by the health of the individual. To make matters even worse, Hutchins, in comparing recent premortem rectal temperatures with postmortem rectal temperatures, observed elevation of rectal body temperature in the early postmortem period and feels that this is probably the rule.[3] Utilizing linear regression analysis of the pre- and postmortem rectal temperature difference as a function of time, he concluded that, on the average, postmortem rectal temperature took about 4 h to return to premortem levels after death. He hypothesized that continuing metabolic activity of body tissues and of bacteria in the bowel was the cause of this effect.

Another factor to be considered is that death may not occur immediately following an assault. Patients could be injured and lie in a coma for several hours. They might develop pneumonia, increasing the body temperature, or die slowly in coma, becoming hypothermic. Thus, even if one knew exactly when an individual died, the time might not correspond to the time of the assault.

If the forensic pathologist decides to take rectal temperatures, the rectum must always be examined prior to insertion of the thermometer. In cases of possible sexual assault, swabs should be taken prior to insertion of the thermometer.

In addition to the aforementioned problems with "normal" body temperatures, we have the problem that body cooling does not necessarily follow a uniform, repetitive pattern such that one can project what the body temperature was. In a dead body, heat is lost by conduction (absorption of heat by objects in contact with the body), radiation (loss in the form of infrared heat rays), and convection (movement of air). Thus, we can see that loss of body heat is passive. If the temperature of the environment surrounding the body is greater than 98.6°F, the body will get warmer; if the same, the body will remain at 98.6°F; and, if colder, the body will cool. There is, unfortunately, no control over environmental temperature.

At a scene, there may be air conditioning or heating. A body lying in sunlight will retain heat longer than in shade. But the sun moves, changing the conditions of exposure to sunlight, and thus, heat. A wet body conducts heat more rapidly. Is the body lying on stone, which is excellent for conduction, or on a bed, which acts as an insulator? Is the individual fat or thin? Clothed or nude? Clothing and fat act as insulators that tend to retain heat. Children and infants cool rapidly because they have a large surface area relative to mass. The opposite occurs with obese individuals, i.e., they have a small surface area relative to their mass. Cachectic (emaciated) individuals, of course, cool faster than obese individuals.

To recapitulate, the problems with using postmortem body temperatures to make a determination of the time of death are that one does not know what the temperature of the body was at the actual time of death and one does not know at what rate it has cooled.

Decomposition

Decomposition involves two processes: autolysis and putrefaction. Autolysis is the breakdown of cells and organs through an aseptic chemical process caused by intracellular enzymes. Since it is a chemical process, it is accelerated by heat, slowed by cold, and stopped by freezing or the inactivation of enzymes by heat. Organs rich in enzymes will undergo autolysis faster than organs with lesser amounts of enzyme. Thus, the pancreas autolyzes before the heart.

The second form of decomposition, which to most individuals is synonymous with decomposition, is putrefaction. *This is due to bacteria and fermentation.* After death, the bacterial flora of the gastrointestinal tract spread throughout the body, producing putrefaction. This is accelerated in septic individuals because bacteria have already spread throughout the body prior to death.

When we talk about decomposition, we usually mean putrefaction. The onset of putrefaction depends on two main factors: the environment and the body. In hot climates, the more important of these two factors is environment.

Most authorities would give the following sequence of events in decomposition of bodies. First there is greenish discoloration of the lower quadrants of the abdomen, the right more than the left, usually in the first 24–36 h. This is followed by greenish discoloration of the head, neck, and shoulders; swelling of the face due to bacterial gas formation; and "marbling." Marbling is produced by hemolysis of blood in vessels with reaction of hemoglobin and hydrogen sulfide and development of greenish black coloration along the vessels (Figure 2.6). The body soon undergoes generalized bloating (60–72 h) followed by vesicle formation, skin slippage, and hair slippage. By this time, the body is a pale green to green-black color.

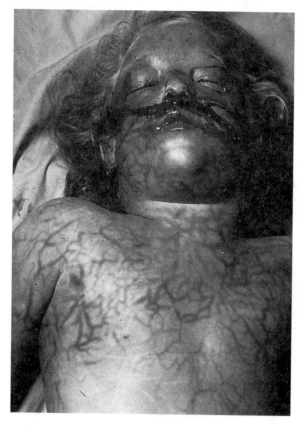

Figure 2.6 Marbling.

Bloating of the body is often noted first in the face, where the features are swollen, the eyes bulge, and the tongue protrudes between the teeth and lips. The face has a pale greenish color, changing to greenish black, then to black (Figure 2.7A). Decomposition fluid (**purge fluid**) will drain from the

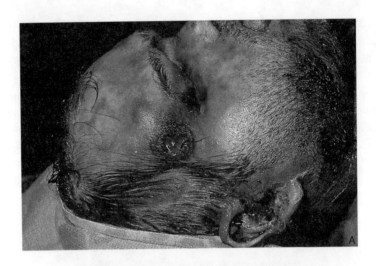

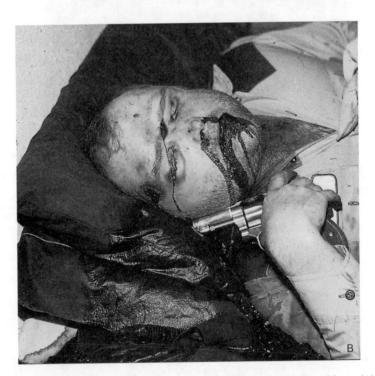

Figure 2.7 (A) Decomposition with discoloration and early marbling. (B) Same individual 12 hours prior. Body was immediately refrigerated after discovery, yet decomposition continued.

mouth and nose (Figure 2.8). This is often misinterpreted by the inexperienced as blood, and head trauma is suspected. Decomposition fluid will accumulate in body cavities and should not be confused with hemothorax

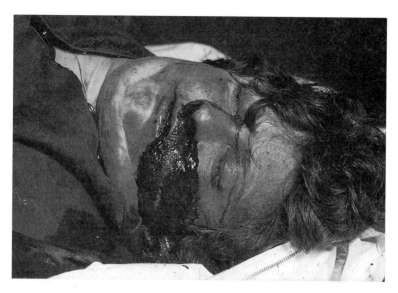

Figure 2.8 Early decomposition with bloody purge fluid flowing from nostrils.

in the case of the pleural cavities. Usually, the fluid accumulating in each pleural cavity is less than 200 mL.

As decomposition continues, hemolyzed blood leaks out into the tissue. Especially in the scalp, this cannot readily be differentiated from antemortem bruising. Thus, in the dependent areas of the head in decomposed bodies, one must be very cautious in interpreting blood in the tissue as a contusion.

This description of the gradual decomposition of a body assumes a temperate environmental climate. With high temperature, this process can be accelerated. Thus, in Texas, a body left in a car during the summer will take less than 24 h to go from a fresh state to a swollen, greenish-black body with marbling, vesicle formation, skin slippage, and purge fluid.

Cold weather slows down and may even stop decomposition. A frozen body will not undergo decomposition until it defrosts. Extreme examples of this are mammoths frozen in Siberia for thousands of years.

Decomposition is hastened by obesity, heavy clothing, and sepsis, all of which keep the body warm. Decomposition is delayed by tight clothing or by the body's lying on a metallic or stone surface that will rapidly cool it by conduction. In the case of generalized sepsis, the authors have seen bodies undergo accelerated decomposition in spite of the fact that they were immediately refrigerated. A septic body dead 6–12 h may have the appearance of one dead 5–6 days even if refrigerated.

Even in the non-septic body, if decomposition has set in, immediate refrigeration of the body may not necessarily stop decomposition completely (Figure 2.7A, B). Thus, the authors have seen a number of bodies in which there was early decomposition with opaque eyes, a reddish tinge to the skin of the face, and bloody purge fluid in the mouth and nostrils when the body was initially viewed at the scene. When the body came to autopsy 6–12 h later, after having been refrigerated the whole time, the face was bloated and greenish black.

As decomposition progresses, hair slips off the head and skin from the hands. Thus, one finds "gloves" of skin. Hair may be taken by birds in the area and used to build nests. As the body decomposes and swells, one often gets the impression of a very heavy individual. When the body is actually weighed, however, the weight will be found to be significantly less than estimated on gross examination of the body. As decomposition proceeds, the weight of the organs decreases.

In hot, dry climates, the body can dehydrate rapidly and may go into **mummification** rather than decomposition. While the skin will have a brown to black leathery appearance, the internal organs will continue to deteriorate, often reduced to a blackish-brown putty-like consistency.

Bodies are embalmed to delay decomposition. The success of embalming is variable and depends on the quality of the embalming, the climate, and the nature of the ground where the body is buried. Rarely will a body be perfectly preserved for years. One of the authors disinterred the body of an elderly white female buried for 6 years that was in perfect condition and could have been "viewed" at a funeral. There was no odor, no observable changes to the outside of the body, and no fungus present. Microscopic sections from the embalmed organs were perfectly preserved. The body of another female buried the same length of time, but in ground where water leaked into the coffin, was completely skeletonized. The authors have seen bodies buried for a year perfectly preserved, except for some drying of the fingertips and patches of fungus, while other bodies buried 2–3 weeks are in an advanced state of decomposition.

The time necessary for skeletonization of a body is also variable. In areas where the body is exposed to the elements and scavengers, it can proceed quite rapidly, occurring in 9–10 days. In rare instances, it may be even faster than this. The uterus and prostate are two of the last organs to decompose.

Occasionally, a decomposing body will undergo transformation to adipocere (Figure 2.9). Adipocere is a firm, greyish-white to brown wax-like material composed of oleic, palmitic, and stearic acids. It is produced by conversion of neutral fats during putrefaction to the aforementioned acids. It is most prominent in subcutaneous tissue, but can occur wherever fat is present. Adipocere is really a variation of putrefaction. It is seen most

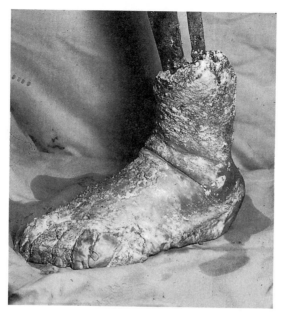

Figure 2.9 Adipocere.

commonly in bodies immersed in water or in damp, warm environments. In adipocere, fat undergoes hydrolysis to free fatty acids by virtue of endogenous lipases and bacterial enzymes. Bacterial enzymes, principally from *Clostridium perfringens,* convert these free fatty acids to hydroxy fatty acids.[4] Adipocere is said to take several months to develop, though development can be as short as several weeks. It is relatively resistant to both bacteriologic and chemical degradation.

A brief mention should be made of maceration of infants in intrauterine deaths. This is not truly putrefaction, but rather an aseptic autolytic process. It is described in a separate section.

Eye changes postmortem are difficult to interpret. Changes depends on whether the eyes are open or closed and on the environment. *Tache noire* is seen, but often not observed. It is an artifact of drying consisting of a brown to black band of discolored sclera where the eyes are partly open and exposed to the air (Figure 2.10). In closed eyes, by 24 h, there is usually a white scummy deposit on the cornea, which, in turn, is cloudy.

Chemical Changes in Body Fluids

Quantitation of vitreous potassium has been put forward as a reliable method of determining the time of death. It is known that, as time since death increases, so does the concentration of potassium. Sturner and Gantner developed a formula for estimating the time of death based on a uniform

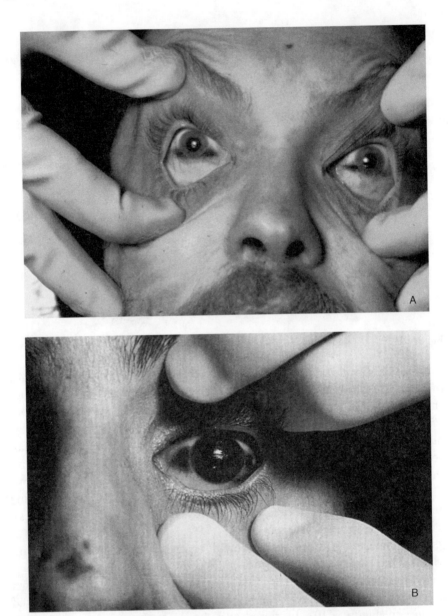

Figure 2.10 *Tache noire.* (A and B) Postmortem drying of sclera of eyes.

increase in vitreous potassium.[5] However, this formula has since been proven incorrect. Graphs published in the same article are also of little help due to their wide margin of error. Coe estimates that, when using potassium levels to determine time of death, in the first 24 h after death, the potential variability is ±10 h; the first 48 h ±20 h, and the first 72 h ±30 h (John Coe, personal communication). The wide variation is because increases in potassium concentration in the vitreous are controlled by the rate of decomposition. Anything that accelerates decomposition, e.g., high temperature, will increase potassium rise.

Flow-Cytometry

Flow-cytometry is being investigated as a tool in determining how long an individual has been dead and, thus, the time of death. This procedure is still experimental, and whether it is completely reliable or how practical, is still to be determined. Present analyses involve use of splenic tissue. In flow-cytometry, one correlates the degree of DNA degradation in tissue from the deceased with tissue from other individuals whose time of death is known i.e., controls.[6]

Gastric Emptying and Digestion

One way of attempting to determine the time of death is by establishing the time interval between eating and death and then finding the time the deceased last ate. A perusal of standard forensic textbooks gives a number of estimations of how long it takes to digest a meal. Spitz and Fisher state that a small meal (a sandwich) is digested in 1 h and a large meal takes 3–5 h.[7] Adelson says gastric emptying depends on the size and content of the meal, with a light meal taking 1/2–2 h to digest, a medium size meal 3–4 h, and a heavy meal 4–6 h.[8]

For stomach contents to be of value in making an estimate of the time of death, a knowledge of gastric emptying is necessary. The introduction in 1966 of radioisotopic methods measuring gastric emptying has led to more accurate measurement of gastric emptying than the old barium contrast meal and tube recovery technique. Thus, it is now possible to simultaneously measure gastric emptying of both liquid and solid components of normal meals without an invasive technique. Such studies have shown that there are no significant differences in solid food emptying rates between young and aged men, though a delay in liquid emptying has been observed in aged men.[9]

Dual radionuclide methods employing noninvasive simultaneous monitoring of liquid and solid meal gastric emptying have been used to determine the influence of weight and caloric content of a meal on gastric emptying. These methods have revealed that, if water is ingested with a solid meal, the water is emptied rapidly and separately and is not influenced by either the weight or total calories of the accompanying solid meal. The rate of emptying is exponential and identical to that of non-nutrient liquid meals ingested without solid portions. In contrast, the emptying pattern of calorie-containing liquids is slower and more linear, which indicates a more constant rate of emptying. Thus, in a study by Brophy et al., the mean liquid half-emptying time for 150 g of orange juice was 24 ± 8 min (range 12–37 min).[10]

If the caloric content of a meal is kept stable but the weight is increased, the result is an increase in the rate of emptying; that is, the emptying rate (expressed as grams of solid food emptying from the stomach per minute) increases directly with meal weight. This is felt to be due to activation of gastric wall stretch or volume receptors stimulating peristalsis of the antrum by the increased meal weight and volume. In contrast, if the meal weight is held constant and the caloric content is increased, there is a progressively slower rate of emptying.[11,12]

Most studies done on gastric emptying utilize an artificially structured meal, unlike what the ordinary person would eat. This meal is designed to give a certain weight and/or number of calories. The favorite of many of the experimenters seems to be beef stew, though one used lettuce. In contrast is a study by Moore et al.,[11] where the subjects were given a self-selected meal that included meats, seafoods, vegetables, soups, salads, pastries, desserts, and a variety of beverages. The subjects were allowed to eat as much as they wanted and to stop when they felt full. The meals were consumed in 30 min. The total amount of food ingested ranged from 1024 to 2408 g with a mean of 1692 g. The weight of the solid food consumed ranged from 693 to 1279 g with an average of 865.5 g. The gastric half-emptying time ($T\frac{1}{2}$) for these meals ranged from a low of 60 to a maximum of 338 min with an average half-emptying time of 277 ± 44 min. There was great variability in meals of approximately the same weight. Thus, a 1474-g meal in one individual had a half-emptying time of 195 min, a 1549-g meal 126 min in another, a 1562-g meal 60 min in a third, a 1260-g meal 143 min, and a 1923-g meal 124 min. This study also revealed that, in several subjects, there was a long lag time following ingestion of the meal during which no emptying occurred. As expected, the liquids emptied significantly more rapidly than the solid food. For the liquids, the mean half-emptying time was 178 ± 22 min, compared with 277 ± 44 min for solids.

As part of these experiments, the same individuals were given 900- and 300-g meals. It was observed that the larger meals were associated with a longer emptying time

The half emptying time of 277 ± 44 min for an ordinary meal is much longer than most of the studies in the literature.[11] Most studies, however, usually involved smaller meals that were artificial in composition. Studies show that the longer emptying times are associated with larger meals and that gastric emptying appears to be more closely correlated with the total number of calories in the meal than with meal weight.[11,12]

Brophy et al. investigated differences in emptying rates in healthy subjects fed the same meal on separate days.[10] Both solid and liquid times were studied. The meal administered consisted of 150 g of beef stew and 150 g of orange juice, with both elements isotopically labeled. As a result of these experiments, it was concluded that meal emptying time is a variable phenomenon in healthy subjects with significant differences from day to day in the same and in different individuals. Thus, for liquids, the half-emptying time was an average of 24.88 ± 8.66 min. In one individual, however, over 4 d, the half-emptying time for 150 g of orange juice was 30, 12, 28, and 12 min. The range of half-emptying times for the whole group was from 12 to 38 min. For solid food, the half-emptying time was 58.58 ± 17.68 min. The overall range was from 29 to 92 min. Thus, this study demonstrates that the gastric emptying of either liquids or solids is subject to relatively wide differences in the same and different individuals even if the same meal is ingested. If, in addition to this, we added differences in the weight, caloric content, and composition of the meal, we would see even greater differences in half-emptying time.

Insect Activity

Another factor that may be of use in determining the time of death is insect activity. Just as in life, after death the tissues of humans are still attractive to a variety of insects. Different insects are attracted at different stages of decomposition of the body. These insects follow a set pattern of development in or on the body. Identification of the type of insects present and their stage of development, in conjunction with knowledge of the rate of their development, can be used to determine approximately how long a body has been dead. In addition, this identification might indicate that the body has been moved from one area to another.

In their development from egg to adult stage, insects undergo either complete or incomplete metamorphosis. In incomplete metamorphosis, small versions of the adult hatch from the egg. These subsequently mature into the full adult form. In complete metamorphosis, the insect hatches from the egg as a larva. The larva is markedly different in appearance from the adult, e.g., the maggot that develops into a fly. After a series of molts, the larva enters a resting stage, the pupa. From the pupa emerges the fully formed adult insect.

The insects that are attracted to a dead body fall into three categories: the necrophagous species, which feed on the body itself; the predators and parasites, which feed on the necrophagous insects; and the omnivorous species, which feed on both the body and on the other insects. The necrophagous species are the most important in determining the time of death. Depending upon the time of day and the species of insect, insects may settle on the body and begin to feed immediately after death. As the body decomposes, successive waves of insects settle on the body. Varying factors, such as the rate of decomposition, burial, immersion in water, mummification, and geography, determine how soon and how many types and waves of insects will attack the body. The temperature and humidity of the environment are the major factors controlling the laying of eggs and the rate of development of the necrophagous insects. Extremes of temperature may impair, prevent, or cause cessation of insect development. Obviously, temperature and humidity are tied into the season of the year, which also controls what insects are available. Temporary storing of the body in an area where there is no access for insects will prevent the laying of eggs on the body and thus impair determination of the time of death. In addition, moving the body from one area to another may interfere with the cycle of insect development and introduce new species.

Flies are the most common form of insect associated with decomposing bodies. They tend to lay their eggs in orifices of the body and in open wounds. This latter attribute may result in either destruction or alteration of the appearance of a wound. Eggs are generally deposited immediately after death in the daytime. Blowflies do not normally lay eggs at night. If the body has not been moved and only eggs are present on the body, one can assume that the duration of death has been about 1–2 d. This is quite variable, however, depending on the temperature and humidity, as well as the species of fly. After hatching, the maggots grow progressively larger until they reach the pupa stage. This can take anywhere from 6–10 d under ordinary conditions. The adults emerge in 12–18 d. All of these figures, however, are quite variable and greatly dependent on the species involved and the temperature of the environment. Because of this, it is the authors' opinion that any attempt to determine time of death using entomological evidence from bodies should be done only with the aid of an entomologist. For more detailed information concerning methods and techniques used and the different species of insects, the authors recommend *A Manual of Forensic Entomology* by Kenneth G.V. Smith.[13]

Scene Markers

This last method of attempting to determine when an individual died, though unscientific, is often more accurate than determinations made by scientific means. This is especially true in badly decomposed bodies. Scene markers include:

- Uncollected mail or newspapers.
- Whether the lights are on or off.
- A TV schedule opened to a time and date.
- How the individual is dressed.
- Any food that is out or dirty dishes in the sink.
- Sales receipts or dated slips of paper in the deceased's pockets.
- When the neighbors last saw the individual or observed a change in his habits. Thus, if he typically went for a walk every evening and

suddenly is no longer seen, then one might conclude that death occurred on or about the day he failed to take his walk.

References

1. Guyton AC and Hall JE. *Textbook of Medical Physiology.* 10th ed. WB Saunders Co. Phil. 2000.

2. Mackowiak PA, Wasserman SS, and Levine MM. A critical appraisal of 98.6 degrees F, the upper limit of the normal body temperature and other legacies of Carl Reinhold. *JAMA* 1992. 268(12):1578-80.

3. Hutchins GM: Body temperature is elevated in the early postmortem period. *Hum Pathol* 1985;16:560-561.

4. Cotton GE, Aufderheide AC, and Goldschmidt VG: Preservation of human tissue immersed for five years in fresh water of known temperature. *J Forensic Sci* 1987;32:1125-1130.

5. Sturner WO, Gantner GE: The postmortem interval: A study of potassium in the vitreous humor. *Am J Clin Pathol* 1964;42:134-144.

6. Di Nunno N, Costantinides F, and Melato M. Determination of the time of death in a homicide-suicide case using flow-cytometry. *Am J Forensic Med Path* 1999 20(3):228-231.

7. Spitz WV and Fisher RS, (Eds): *Medicolegal Investigation of Death,* ed 2. Springfield, IL, Charles C Thomas, 1980.

8. Adelson L: *The Pathology of Homicide.* Springfield, 111, Charles C Thomas, 1974.

9. Moore JG, Tweedy C, Christian PE, et al.: Effect of age on gastric emptying of liquid-solid meals in man. *Digestive Dis Sci* 1983;28:340.

10. Brophy CM, Moore JG, Christian PE, et al: Variability of gastric emptying measurements in man employing standardized radiolabeled meals. *Digestive Dis Sci* 1986;31:799-806.

11. Moore JG, Christian PE, Brown JA, et al: Influence of meal weight and caloric content on gastric emptying of meals in man. *Digestive Dis Sci* 1984;29:513-519.

12. Moore JG, Christian PE, and Coleman RE: Gastric emptying of varying meal weight and composition in man. *Digestive Dis Sci* 1981;26:16-22.

13. Smith KGV: *A Manual of Forensic Entomology.* London, British Museum (Natural History); Ithaca, NY, Cornell University Press, 1986.

Deaths Due to Natural Disease

3

Ring around the rosy
Pocket full of posies
Ashes, ashes
All fall down

Most natural deaths seen in a medical examiner's office are sudden and unexpected. The definition as to what constitutes sudden death is variable. It is based on the amount of time between the onset of symptoms and death. Depending on one's definition, the maximum time interval varies anywhere from 1–24 h. Most witnessed deaths handled by the medical examiner are what are called instantaneous deaths. Literally, the individual falls down dead. In such cases, everyone agrees that these are sudden deaths. In other cases, the individuals usually die within 1 h of the onset of symptoms.

Cardiovascular Disease

Cardiovascular disease is the most common cause of death in the United States. Sudden cardiac death causes between 300,000 and 400,000 deaths a year. It is the leading cause of death in men between 20 and 65 years of age. Zipes and Wellens estimate that up to 80% of individuals dying suddenly of cardiac disease die of coronary artery disease.[1] Of 853 individuals, 18 years of age or older, coming to autopsy in San Antonio, Texas, 591 (69.3%) died of cardiovascular disease; 76.3% (451) of the 591 of coronary artery disease. Cardiomyopathy accounted for a significant but smaller number (13%), with occasional deaths from valvular heart disease, myocarditis, and other less common forms of cardiovascular disease.

There is a circadian variation in the incidence of sudden death, with a peak incidence in the early morning. Willich et al. reported the peak incidence of sudden cardiac death as between 7 and 9 a.m. (after discounting individuals found dead during this time), which was 70% higher than the average rate during the rest of the day.[2] They suggest that one possible explanation for this is increased activity of the sympathetic nervous system, known to occur in the morning, which may predispose to cardiac arrhythmias.

Coronary Atherosclerosis

The most common cause of death from cardiovascular disease is coronary atherosclerosis. Approximately half the individuals with coronary artery disease die suddenly. Sudden death is, in fact, the initial symptom in approximately 25% of individuals dying of coronary atherosclerosis. In the authors' experience, coronary artery disease accounts for 76.3% of adults' dying suddenly and unexpectedly of cardiovascular disease who come to autopsy. The frequency will change to some degree depending on the population handled by a particular office and the criteria used for selection of cases for autopsy.

In contrast to the number of individuals who die in the hospital of coronary artery disease, in a medical examiner's office, acute coronary thrombosis and acute myocardial infarcts are the exception rather than the rule. In a study of 500 consecutive autopsies of individuals aged 20–99 years who died suddenly and unexpectedly of coronary artery disease, only 67 (13.4%) showed acute thromboses, grossly.[3] The left coronary artery and its branches showed a slightly higher incidence of thrombosis compared with the right. The low incidence of thrombosis in individuals' dying suddenly is in agreement with other authorities. In contrast, studies of hospitalized patients show a high rate of thrombosis — 87.3% by DeWood et al.[4] Gross myocardial scarring representing previous areas of old infarction has been reported as being present in 34.8% of individuals dying suddenly, with 8.4% demonstrating evidence of acute myocardial infarction, grossly.

What is present in all deaths due to coronary atherosclerosis is severe atherosclerosis of the coronary vessels. Significant obstruction of the coronary artery lumen usually requires 75% narrowing of the lumen (Figure 3.1). In individuals with hypertensive cardiovascular disease, one often does not see the classical eccentric narrowing due to plaque formation of pure coronary atherosclerosis, but rather concentric thickening of the walls by atherosclerotic deposits. In individuals older than 60 years of age, the coronary arteries may present yet another picture. While the lumina are patent, the vessels are rigid calcified tubes because of calcium deposits in the walls of the vessels.

In some individuals, while the epicardial coronary arteries appear non-occluded, microscopic examination of the myocardium reveals severe, occlusive dysplasia of the intramural coronary arteries.[5] The dysplasia is characterized by severe medial thickening, with smooth muscle disorganization and marked luminal narrowing. Burke and Virmani describe four sudden deaths due to this entity in young (12–31 years) individuals. [5]

In most individuals who die suddenly and unexpectedly of atherosclerosis of the coronary arteries, at least two vessels are involved. Occasionally, an

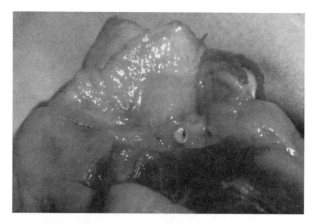

Figure 3.1 Left anterior descending coronary artery of 21-year-old male with 75% narrowing of lumen due to atherosclerosis.

individual will die with single vessel disease with a single strategically located atherosclerotic plaque. This plaque, which produces at least 75% narrowing of the lumen, is usually found in the proximal portion of the left anterior descending coronary artery (the "widow-maker") almost immediately after its origin. This is an extremely critical point in this vessel, in that the left coronary artery begins supplying significant myocardial tissue shortly after its origin. In contrast, the right coronary artery does not supply any significant amount of myocardial tissue until it gives off the posterior descending vessel. In a study of 451 deaths due to CAD, in 54 of the cases (11.9%) significant disease was confined to one vessel. The vessel was the left anterior descending coronary in 40 cases; the circumflex in 4 and the right coronary in 10.

Bridging

Sudden death has been described in a condition called **bridging**.[6,7] In this entity, the left anterior descending coronary artery (very rarely the right coronary), instead of lying in the epicardial fat of the heart, dips down into the myocardium (Figure 3.2). Coronary angiography has demonstrated bridging in from 0.5 to 1.6% of individuals.[7] In adults with hypertrophic cardiomyopathy, bridging occurs in 30–50% of individuals.[7] In bridging, there is compression of the vessel during systole with either partial or complete occlusion of the lumen. Generally, this is a benign phenomenon, because nearly all coronary blood flow to the left ventricle occurs during diastole. With tachycardia, however, there is a shortening of diastolic perfusion. This may allow the systoli compression to become significant. This would explain the observation that sudden death in bridging is seen more often in association with exercise. Septal fibrosis from repeated systolic compression may occur. Death from bridging is rare.

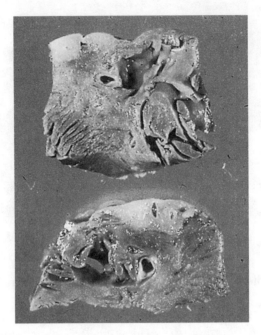

Figure 3.2 "Bridging" of left anterior descending coronary artery.

Dissecting Coronary Aneurysm

A dissecting aneurysm of the coronary artery may be either secondary to extension of an aortic root dissection or primary and limited to the coronary artery. Primary dissecting aneurysms may be either spontaneous or due to trauma (e.g., chest trauma, coronary angiography). Spontaneous coronary artery dissection is a rare condition, usually presenting as sudden death.[8–10] It consists of an intramural hematoma of the media of the vessel wall, which flattens and occludes the lumen, reducing blood flow (Figure 3.3). Communication with the lumen may occur. There may be a diffuse adventitial inflammatory reaction consisting mainly of eosinophils present. This is felt to be reactive and not related to causation. Most (80%) spontaneous dissecting aneurysms occur in females, particularly in the peripartum period. Three quarters of the cases involve the left anterior descending coronary artery. In men, dissection of the right coronary artery appears to be more frequent.[10] Changes of cystic medial necrosis may be present.

Coronary Artery Spasm

In some individuals, angina coupled with symptoms consistent with development of an acute myocardial infarction occurs immediately prior to sudden collapse and death. At autopsy, however, there is no infarct and the coronary arteries are found to be patent, without significant atherosclerosis

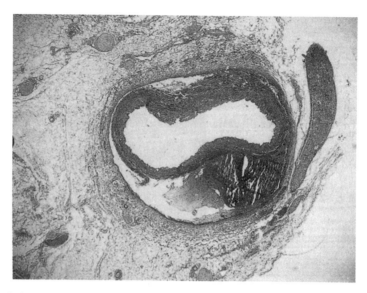

Figure 3.3 Postpartum dissecting aneurysm of left anterior descending coronary artery.

or congenital anomalies. Death is believed to be due to transitory coronary artery spasm. The phenomenon of coronary artery spasm without anatomical narrowing of the coronary arteries in association with angina has been demonstrated angiographically and has actually been witnessed during operative procedures.[11–13] Myocardial infarction secondary to coronary artery spasm induced by use of cocaine is a well recognized phenomena.

Mechanism of Sudden Death

The mechanism of sudden death in most individuals with coronary artery disease is the sudden onset of ventricular tachycardia, which either is sustained or, in most cases, progresses to ventricular fibrillation (approximately 80%). This has been demonstrated in individuals wearing portable cardiac monitors who collapsed and died with the terminal event's being recorded. Asystole or a bradyarrhythmia accounts for the remaining 20% of cases of sudden cardiac death.[14,15]

The death rate following out-of-hospital cardiac arrests is dependent on the type of arrhythmia that caused the arrest, prompt initiation of cardiopulmonary resuscitation (CPR), and how soon after arrest defibrillation is instituted. The public's perception of the success of CPR is based to a great degree on information communicated to them by the media — especially television. An unrealistic impression is routinely conveyed. In a television study of CPR, 75% of "patients" survived the immediate arrest, with apparently 67% surviving to discharge.[16] Virtually none had neurological *sequelae*.

The arrest was due to trauma in the majority of cases, with the patients typically young.

In actuality, short-term success of CPR (the return of the patient's blood pressure and pulse for 1 h) is, at most, 40%, with survival until discharge from the hospital varying from 2–30 % for cardiac arrests outside the hospital.[15–16] While 83% of the patients on television were nonelderly, in reality, the elderly are the most common group. On TV, 28% of the underlying diseases were primary cardiac, in reality, 75–95% are cardiac in origin. For the elderly, long-term survival after cardiac arrest outside the hospital is 5% or less. In arrests due to trauma, the long-term survival rate varies from 0–30%.[16]

Schneider reviewed 19,955 patients in 98 studies who had CPR after in-hospital cardiac arrest.[17] Resuscitations were successful in 15% of cases. The rate of CPR success did not change over time. The nature of the cardiac rhythm affected CPR success rates with 20% success with ventricular fibrillation or tachycardia; 7% with electromechanical dissociation; 6% with asystole; and other, 10%. A small number of patients (2%) with successful resuscitation had central nervous system impairment.

Sudden Death: Exercise and Climate

Sudden death in association with coronary artery disease can occur at any time of the day, during any activity. The individual might be sleeping or participating in strenuous activity. Severe climatic conditions such as heat and cold may stress the heart, predisposing to anginal attacks and sudden deaths.[18] However, there is no doubt that strenuous activity predisposes a person to sudden cardiac death.[19–21] In individuals over the age of 35, coronary atherosclerosis is the most common cause of death in exercise-related deaths.[19] In younger individuals, the most frequent causes are hypertrophic cardiomyopathy and congenital anomalies of the coronary arteries.[22] The most common coronary anomaly is anomalous origin of the left coronary artery from the right sinus of Valsalva.[22]

Hypertensive Cardiovascular Disease

Sudden death in individuals with hypertension is usually associated with, and probably in most instances due to, accompanying coronary atherosclerosis. The atherosclerosis present can be either the usual form, with eccentric plaque-like deposits of atheromatous material, or a concentric form with uniform thickening of the coronary arteries. In the latter case, while the lumen may be technically patent, the severe concentric narrowing of the vessels accomplishes the same hemodynamic effect as the eccentric plaques, that is, a reduction in blood flow to the myocardium.

In some individuals with a history of hypertension who die suddenly and unexpectedly, the autopsy will reveal only an enlarged heart with marked left ventricular hypertrophy and minimal or absent coronary atherosclerosis.[23] The mechanism of death in these cases is a cardiac arrhythmia, most likely ventricular fibrillation. It has been known clinically for some time that patients with left ventricular hypertrophy have significantly more ventricular premature contractions than normal individuals or individuals with hypertension without left ventricular hypertrophy.[24–26] This clinical observation is in agreement with the observations of forensic pathologists that a small but significant number of individuals who die suddenly and unexpectedly with a clinical history of hypertension have only left ventricular hypertrophy, without severe atherosclerotic involvement of their coronary arteries or the small vessels of the myocardium. In contrast to individuals with hypertension coming to autopsy in hospitals, most individuals dying suddenly and unexpectedly of a cardiac arrhythmia with a clinical history of hypertension do not show the gross changes of hypertension in their kidneys, that is, the fine granularity of the cortical surfaces, though, microscopically, there is evidence of arteriosclerosis.

In regard to the left ventricular hypertrophy in individuals with hypertension, electrocardiographic studies have shown increases in left ventricular mass in young individuals 12–20 years of age, before arterial pressure reached levels considered abnormal in adults.[27] This is in agreement with the observation of the authors that some individuals in their late teens and early twenties in populations that are particularly susceptible to hypertension (e.g., blacks) have shown left ventricular hypertrophy consistent with hypertension without any clinical history of hypertension but with a family history of hypertension.

Cardiomyopathy

The cardiomyopathies constitute a diverse group of diseases of both known and unknown etiology characterized by myocardial dysfunction, that is, diseases that are not the result of arteriosclerotic, hypertensive, congenital, or valvular disease.[28] Cardiomyopathies can be grouped into three general categories: **dilated** or **congestive**, **hypertrophic**, and **restrictive-obliterative**. The last category is usually rarely encountered by the forensic pathologist, since it deals with entities such as amyloidosis, hemochromatosis, sarcoidosis, glycogen storage disease, and hypereosinophilic syndrome, conditions not usually associated with sudden death and mostly of an infiltrative nature to the myocardium. The exception is sarcoidosis, which, while uncommon, is occasionally encountered. It must, of course, be realized that within the three categories of cardiomyopathy, there can be some overlap.

The largest category of cardiomyopathies is the congestive or **dilated cardiomyopathies**. This condition is characterized by enlargement, sometimes massive, of the heart, with dilatation of all four chambers (Figure 3.4A). *Probably the most common cause of dilated cardiomyopathy in America is chronic alcohol abuse.* The myocardial damage in this case can be due to the direct toxic effect of the alcohol, the nutritional effects of chronic alcoholism, or the toxic effects of an additive to the alcohol (e.g., cobalt). Other causes of dilated cardiomyopathy are peripartum cardiomyopathy and chronic myocarditis. There is also an idiopathic form of dilated cardiomyopathy in which the cause is unknown.

Patients with peripartum cardiomyopathy present with heart failure during the last month of pregnancy or during the first 5 months postpartum.[29] In approximately half the patients, the enlarged heart returns to normal within 6–12 months. Occasionally, sudden death occurs. There is some thought that this entity is a form of myocarditis secondary to an infectious, autoimmune or idiopathic process.

In dilated cardiomyopathy, the heart is markedly enlarged, with flabby myocardium and dilatation of all chambers. Mural thrombi are common. Microscopically, there is degeneration and/or hypertrophy of muscle fibers, focal or diffuse myocardial fibrosis, scattered mononuclear cell infiltrates, and, occasionally, fatty infiltrates.

Congestive cardiomyopathy has also been associated with certain toxic substances such as cobalt and adriamycin. The secondary cardiomyopathy due to toxic substances may be caused by the direct cardiac toxic action of the drug, an atypical reaction to it, or excessive doses of some of these substances, such as adriamycin. In all forms of congestive cardiomyopathy, sudden deaths occur and are recognized by both forensic pathologists and clinicians. Arrhythmias are, in fact, clinically associated with this condition.

The most interesting of the three cardiomyopathies is **hypertrophic cardiomyopathy**. It has also been known as idiopathic hypertrophic subaortic stenosis and hypertrophic obstructive cardiomyopathy. Hypertrophic cardiomyopathy is principally a familial cardiac disorder, with an autosomal dominant pattern of inheritance, said to be present in approximately 0.2% of the population.[30] In this condition, there is massive myocardial hypertrophy without ventricular dilatation, in the absence of any cardiac or systemic disease that could produce these changes. The heart usually shows a disproportionate asymmetrical hypertrophy of the interventricular septum compared with the free wall of the left ventricle (Figure 3.4B). In some cases, however, the left ventricular hypertrophy is symmetrical, with thickening of both the septum and free wall. Ninety-five percent of the cases of hypertrophic cardiomyopathy show disarray in the ventricular myocardial fibers, with fibers running in all

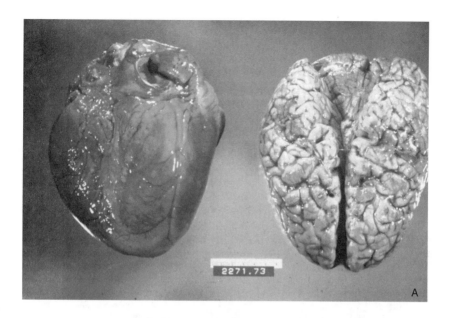

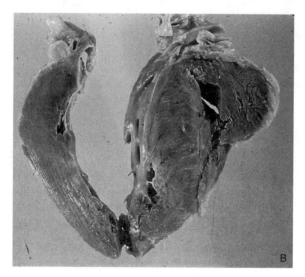

Figure 3.4 (A) Congestive cardiomyopathy. Heart weight 1050 g. Note size of heart in relationship to adult brain of normal size. (B) Hypertrophic cardiomegaly with asymmetrical hypertrophy of interventricular septum.

directions in an apparent haphazard pattern and with the myocardial cells hypertrophied and bizarre. These bizarrely shaped and haphazardly arranged myocardial cells are typically seen in the septum. They are less common in the free wall. The haphazardly arranged bizarre cells are not specific for hypertrophic cardiomyopathy, but have been noted in a number of other conditions usually associated with left ventricular strain. The disarray, however, is not nearly so marked or extensive. Ventricular and supraventricular arrythmias are common in individuals with this condition.

Echocardiographic evidence of hypertrophic cardiomyopathy is usually present in one or more closely related family members. In adolescents and young adults, hypertrophic cardiomyopathy may be the most common cause of sudden cardiac death.

Valvular Disease

Sudden death due to valvular disease usually involves either mitral valve prolapse (floppy mitral valve; myxomatous degeneration of the mitral valve) or aortic stenosis. Rarely, sudden death will be due to an acute bacterial valvulitis (Figure 3.5). The valve involved is usually the tricuspid valve and the individual an intravenous drug abuser.

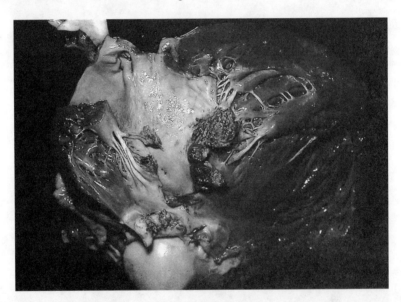

Figure 3.5 Acute bacterial endocarditis involving mitral and aortic valves in 32-year-old drug addict.

Until recently, it was estimated that 5–15% of the population had mitral valve prolapse. A study by Freed et al. of 1646 men and 1845 women, representing an unselected, community-based sample of ambulatory patients, and using current two-dimensional echocardiographic criteria, revealed an overall incidence of 2.4%.[31] The mitral valve prolapse syndrome refers to a condition characterized by nonspecific symptoms (dyspnea, fatigue, dizziness, palpitation, anxiety, atypical chest pain), electrocardiographic abnormalities, and arrhythmias.[31–33] The characteristic auscultation findings are midsystolic clicks and late systolic murmurs. The arrhythmias are widely varied, with premature ventricular complexes being the most prevalent. The anatomical findings are voluminous, thickened, redundant valve leaflets showing myxomatous transformation of the valve substance, in the absence of any inflammatory change, and dilatation of the mitral annulus (Figure 3.6). The posterior leaflet of the mitral valve is allegedly involved more than the anterior, though this has not been the authors' impression.

Clinically, there is protrusion of the mitral leaflets into the left atrium during systole. Complications of mitral valve prolapse are sudden death due to ventricular fibrillation, infective endocarditis, transient ischemic attacks and partial strokes secondary to clot or platelet aggregations originating from the prolapsed valve, ruptured chordae tendinae, and progression to mitral insufficiency.[31–32]

Deaths due to mitral valve prolapse are uncommon. Diagnosis of this entity as a cause of death is made by exclusion. One would have to do a complete autopsy, including a thorough toxicological screen, to exclude other possible causes of death before making the diagnosis. In the cases the authors have seen, the myxomatous degeneration of the valves has been extremely marked and has involved both leaflets of the mitral valve. The victims have generally been female, with the youngest 12 years of age and the rest in their late teens, twenties, and early thirties. Some have had a previous history of arrhythmias. One 18-year-old girl, who had been on propranolol for her arrhythmias, had her medication stopped approximately a month before collapsing and dying in front of a number of witnesses.

After mitral valve prolapse, the next most common cause of sudden death due to valvular disease is aortic stenosis (Figure 3.7). Mitral stenosis, once a common finding in the medical examiner's office, has almost disappeared due to the marked decline in rheumatic fever and the surgical treatment for mitral stenosis. Aortic stenosis may have four etiological causes: congenital malformation of the valve, rheumatic inflammation with fusion of the cusps, secondary calcification of congenital bicuspid valves, and primary degenerative calcification of normal aortic valves.[34]Congenital aortic stenosis, which excludes the bicuspic aortic valve, refers to conditions present at the time of birth. Congenital stenotic valves will develop secondary calcification as the individual gets older. This condition is rarely seen in the medical examiner's office because diagnosis has usually been made and treatment administered.

Rheumatic aortic stenosis is becoming uncommon for the same reason that mitral stenosis is uncommon — the relative absence of rheumatic fever in the population. In rheumatic aortic stenosis, there is fusion of the cusps due to the inflammatory process. Calcification develops in patients as they grow older, generally over the age of 40.

In both secondary calcification of the bicuspid valves and primary degenerative calcification of the normal aortic valve, it is the calcium deposit that is the principal cause of the stenosis. With the bicuspid aortic valves, calcification begins in the 6th, 7th, and 8th decades of life, developing at the free

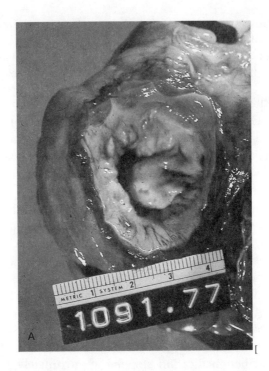

Figure 3.6 Floppy mitral valve. (A) Viewed from atrium. (B) Opened up with lower two thirds of left ventricle amputated.

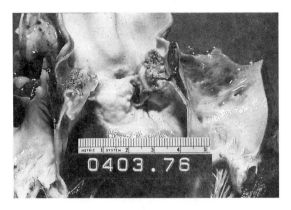

Figure 3.7 Aortic stenosis.

edges of the cusps and progressing toward the base. In primary degenerative calcification of normal aortic valves, the calcification progresses from the base toward the edges and usually involves individuals in the 8th and 9th decade of life.

At the present time, the most common cause of aortic stenosis is calcification of bicuspid valves. It should be noted that bicuspid aortic valves, the precursor of calcific aortic stenosis, are present in approximately 0.4% of the population.

The aspect of aortic stenosis of most interest to the forensic pathologist is the propensity for sudden death. The mechanism of death is presumably acute myocardial insufficiency secondary to obstruction of the left ventricular outflow. The most disturbing case that the authors have seen with calcific aortic stenosis was that of a commercial airplane pilot in his late forties who collapsed and died while jogging. This condition apparently was not detected in any of his physical examinations.

Coronary Artery Anomalies

Sudden death in adults and children may be associated with congenital anomalies of the coronary arteries. There are many variations.[35,36] There may be a single right coronary ostium, with the left coronary artery arising from the proximal portion of the right coronary artery; the left main coronary artery arising from the right sinus of Valsalva with passage of the artery between the aorta and pulmonary artery; the right coronary artery arising from the left sinus of Valsalva; coronary artery hypoplasia, etc.

Myocarditis

The clinical manifestations of acute myocarditis may range from none to acute fulminating congestive heart failure to sudden death.[28] The cases of interest to the forensic pathologist are those involving individuals who are asymptomatic or have had only minor complaints and then suddenly collapse and die.

Myocarditis can be caused by infectious agents (bacterial, rickettsial, viral, protozoal, fungal), connective tissue diseases (e.g., rheumatic fever, rheumatoid arthritis), physical agents (chemical poisons, or drugs) or can be idiopathic. With infectious myocarditis, injury to the myocardium may be directly due to invasion by the organism or by toxin produced by the organism. Microscopically, there are patchy or diffuse areas of necrosis with interstitial inflammation. The inflammation may be focal and minor or extensive and severe. Degeneration and necrosis of muscle fibers is usually present. The infiltrate may vary from mostly neutrophils to lymphocytes, plasma cells, and esosinophils. Grossly, the appearance of the heart may be normal or pale and flabby with dilated chambers.

Most cases of infectious myocarditis are probably viral in origin. Initially, there is infiltration by neutrophils and lymphocytes accompanied by necrosis of muscle fibers. Subsequently, lymphocytes and macrophages predominate. There may or may not be subsequent interstitial fibrosis on healing. If fibrosis develops, it may be either minor or extensive and may or may not be associated with subsequent arrhythmias. In a case seen by one of the authors, a 17-year-old boy at age 13 had a documented episode of viral myocarditis. Following that, he developed arrhythmias with occasional episodes of ventricular extrasystoles and tachycardia. He was told never to engage in any strenuous activities. At age 17, while participating in a basketball game, he collapsed and died. For the 4 years following his episode of myocarditis, he had been followed by a cardiologist, who had documented his numerous episodes of arrhythmias. It was the expectation of the cardiologist that the heart would show extensive interstitial scarring. At autopsy, the heart appeared grossly normal. Multiple microscopic sections of the heart taken from all areas, including the conduction system, were completely unremarkable. This shows that a viral inflammation of the heart can cause injury to the conduction system of the heart that cannot be detected or evaluated microscopically. This condition is probably the cause of some instances of sudden death in which the autopsy findings are completely negative.

In occasional cases of fatal myocarditis, the myocarditis is not widespread, but consists of a single strategically located lesion. Thus, the case of a 32-year-old housewife found dead on the kitchen floor, whose autopsy and toxicological examination were completely negative. Microscopic sections of the heart showed a single focus of acute myocarditis in the conduction system. Death in this case was due to the unfortunate location of a relatively small lesion. This points out the importance of taking multiple sections of the heart, especially through the conduction system, in any complete examination of the heart for heart disease. It should be realized that a single small collection of mononuclear cells in the myocardium does not necessarily indicate that the individual is suffering from myocarditis. This is a "normal" finding in many hearts if one takes sufficient microscopic sections. In cases where myocardial disease is suspected, the authors recommend taking a minimum of six microscopic sections of myocardium for proper evaluation of the myocardium. At least one of these should involve the conduction system.

Aortic Dissection

Aortic dissection occurs when blood dissects between the middle and outer two thirds of the aortic media, creating a blood filled channel within the aortic wall.[37] The process usually arises in the ascending aorta and is manifested by an intimal tear, a necessary component of a dissecting aortic aneurysm. The tears have sharp edges and run transversely or longitudinally rather than obliquely. A combined longitudinal and transverse tear produces T- or cross-shaped tears. The tear tends to arise in relatively normal appearing areas of the aorta. In some case, the tears are seen to be preceded and arise in areas of intramural hematoma. The dissection then proceeds peripherally down the aorta. It usually breaks out again into the lumen of the aorta. It might, however, rupture into the pericardial sac. The predisposing factors are hypertension, heredity and inflammation. In Marfan's syndrome, there is both dilatation and dissection of the aorta.[38] Marfan's syndrome affects fibrillin, a glycoprotein that sees to the adhesion and alignment of the sheets of collagen in the aorta. Fragmentation of the elastic fibers results in weakening of the wall and dissection. Focal areas of cystic medial necrosis may be seen.

The term aortic dissection is often used to describe rupture of the aorta due to simple dilatation rather than true dissection. Genetic abnormalities of the collagen, such as those found in osteogenesis imperfecta and Ehlers-Danlos, lead to dilatation of the aorta. This, in turn, can result in rupture at the site of the aneurysm.

Familial degeneration of the aortic media in the absence of any of the well-characterized diseases of the connective tissue can occur. These cases show cystic medial necrosis. Most individuals with dissection, however, have none of the aforementioned conditions. What they do have is hypertension. Hypertension is the most important risk factor in developing aortic dissection.

Weight lifting and use of cocaine have been associated with aortic dissection.[38,39] In regard to cocaine, the individuals tend to be men, long-term cocaine users, and have a history of hypertension or idiopathic cystic medial necrosis.[39] The dissection occurred shortly after recent use of cocaine. The weight lifters may have had predisposing cystic medial necrosis.

Sudden Death on a Physiological Basis

Up to this point in the discussion of sudden cardiac death, lesions of the heart that are visible either grossly or microscopically have been described. Sudden cardiac death on a physiological basis without a visible etiology can also occur. Thus, sudden death can be, though rarely, one of the *sequelae* of Wolff -Parkinson-White syndrome.[1,40] Sudden cardiac death is also seen in conjunction with the Q-T interval syndrome.[1] There are two forms of this syndrome: the congenital hereditary form and the acquired form. The Jervell and Lange-Nielsen syndrome and the Romano-Ward syndrome are the two hereditary forms. The acquired form is secondary to drugs, electrolyte abnormalities, toxic substances, hypothermia, anorexia nervosa, and diet programs involving liquid protein diets. In the acquired form of the Q-T interval syndrome, removing the inciting factor abolishes the syndrome. The mechanism of death in both anorexia nervosa and dieting with liquid protein diets is the same — development of a prolonged Q-T interval with subsequent ventricular arrhythmias.[41,42]

Deaths Due to Intracranial Lesions

Sudden deaths due to lesions of the brain are considerably less common than those due to cardiac disease. The most common causes encountered by the medical examiner are epilepsy, nontraumatic subarachnoid hemorrhage, intracerebral hemorrhage, meningitis, and tumors. Occasional rare lesions such as cysticercosis are also encountered.

Epilepsy

Probably the most common cause of sudden death due to an intracranial lesion is epilepsy. Epileptic deaths constitute approximately 3–4% of all natural deaths coming to autopsy in a medical examiner's office. The estimated incidence of sudden unexplained death among epileptics is 2–17%.[43] Very few of these individuals die in status epilepticus.

Typically, individuals dying suddenly and unexpectedly of epilepsy are young and show either subtherapeutic levels or absence of epileptic medications on toxicological analysis. Usually, but not always, such deaths are unwitnessed, with the victims often found dead in bed in the morning. If a death is witnessed, there may be no seizures or only one seizure with collapse.[43,44] In individuals found dead in bed, there is usually no evidence of seizures, either in the environment (sheets and blankets undisturbed, no loss of urine) or on the body (bite marks of the tongue are absent in 75% of the cases). That individuals are commonly found dead in bed is probably because sleep predisposes to epileptic attacks and, in fact, is used as a provocative diagnostic technique. Sleep has also been found to affect cardiac vulnerability to arrhythmia in that sudden death secondary to arrhythmias often occurs in the morning, immediately before or at the time of awakening.

Diagnosis of death due to epilepsy is, for the most part, a diagnosis of exclusion. At autopsy, there are no pathonomonic findings. In approximately 25% of the cases, a bite mark of the tongue might indicate a seizure, but seizures as a terminal event can occur in other entities. To make a diagnosis of death due to epilepsy, the examiner must have a clinical diagnosis of epilepsy in the past or a well-documented history of seizures, a scene not inconsistent with such a finding, and a complete autopsy, including removal of the tongue, with no findings, grossly, microscopically, or toxicologically, to explain death.

Most epileptic deaths are natural. If, however, the epilepsy was due to trauma, documented, and uncontestable, then the manner would more properly be classified as accident. Some epileptics die of accidental means precipitated by an epileptic attack; for example, an individual may have an epileptic attack while in water and drown (Figure 3.8). No matter what the manner of death, it is very common for epileptics dying suddenly to have

Figure 3.8 A 27-year-old epileptic drowned in the bathtub.

subtherapeutic levels or absence of anticonvulsive medication. Careful examination of the brain in most instances does not reveal a lesion that could have caused the epilepsy. The actual incidence of finding such lesions varies considerably, depending on the authority, but, to a degree, is influenced by the type of population being handled. The only thing that one can say is that, in the vast majority of the cases, no lesion to explain the seizure disorder will be found at autopsy. If lesions are found, they may be foci of sclerosis, arteriovenous malformations, or adhesions between cortex and dura. Again, it must be realized that the finding of such lesions is uncommon. One finding, sclerosis of Ammon's horn, is most probably a secondary phenomenon related to cerebral edema during epileptic attacks, with compression of the vessels supplying blood to this region (branches of the posterior cerebral artery) against the edge of the tentorium by a herniating hippocampal gyrus.

Because the diagnosis of death due to epilepsy is on an exclusionary basis, the actual incidence of such deaths is probably underestimated. Thus, if an individual dying of a seizure disorder happens to have significant coronary atherosclerosis, the cause of death would probably be ascribed to the coronary artery disease rather than the epilepsy.

The mechanism of death in epilepsy is most probably due to a cardiac arrhythmia precipitated by an autonomic discharge.[43–45] Alterations in cardiac activity and respiration have been documented in individuals dying during an epileptic attack. It is not known, however, why a seizure, apparently no different from those that the patient had previously had in the past, should prove fatal at this particular time. The autonomic nervous system, especially the sympathetic portion, is important in the regulation of cardiac and vascular physiology. Cortical loci exert a more specific autonomic control of cardiovascular changes than do the lower levels of the brain. Cortical stimulation can produce changes in heart rate, blood pressure, and cardiac extrasystoles. Stimulation of portions of the hypothalamus can also produce cardiovascular changes, for example, cardiac arrhythmias, because the hypothalamus exerts considerable control over the autonomic function. Production of extrasystoles by stimulation of the hypothalamus is due to the stimulation of the sympathetic pathways to the heart or stimulation of pathways controlling secretion of epinephrine.

The sympathetic nervous system can lower the vulnerable threshold of even electrically stable myocardium, thereby facilitating the onset of ventricular fibrillation, if the activity of the sympathetic nervous system is increased by neural or neurohumoral action. Increased sympathetic nervous activity can predispose to ventricular fibrillation by the direct action of neuroepinephrine on neuroeffector sites in the myocardium. The aforementioned findings indicate that sudden death during epileptic seizures is most likely due to a lethal cardiac arrhythmia induced or propagated by the disorganized neural discharges of a seizure.

Nontraumatic Subarachnoid Hemorrhage

The second most common cause of sudden unexpected death due to natural disease of the brain is nontraumatic subarachnoid hemorrhage. Early in this century, spontaneous subarachnoid hemorrhage was considered a disease entity in itself. With the advancement of medical knowledge, it was realized that it was a syndrome with multiple causes. Berry aneurysms are the most common cause of subarachnoid hemorrhage, followed by intracerebral hemorrhages and, to a lesser degree, rupture of arteriovenous malformations. Arteriovenous malformations probably account for only a few percent of nontraumatic subarachnoid hemorrhages. They tend to cluster in the early decades of life, though they can be found at any age. Uncommon causes of nontraumatic subarachnoid hemorrhage would be blood dyscrasias; endocarditis with embolic phenomenon; overuse of anticoagulants; tumors, both primary and metastatic; and sickle cell hemoglobinopathy.

Berry Aneurysms

In the medical examiner's office, rupture of a **berry aneurysm** is the most common cause of nontraumatic subarachnoid hemorrhage. Berry aneurysms per se are not uncommon — unruptured aneurysms have been reported in 4.9% of all routine autopsies when searched for.[46] While Berry aneurysms are rare in children, they increase in frequency with age. They are located, for the most part, at the point of bifurcation and branching of the cerebral arteries, with approximately 90% found in the anterior cerebral, middle cerebral and internal carotid arteries. Berry aneurysms are thought to be the result of developmental weakness of the vessel walls. This abnormality generally consists of a defect in the formation of the media at the branching point. The intimal elastic lamina and the muscularis terminate at the neck of the aneurysm, with the wall of the sac made up of thickened hyalinized intima and the adventitia. Persistence of incomplete involuted embryonic arteries with residual medial weakness is the explanation proposed for aneurysms away from the point of bifurcation.

Hypertension and cigarette smoking are predisposing factors. Atherosclerosis may also play a secondary role, leading to focal destruction and weakening of the vessels walls. Multiplicity of aneurysms is quite common, multiple aneurysms being reported in anywhere from 12 to 31.4% of cases.[47]

Berry aneurysms almost invariably rupture at the apex. *When rupture occurs, there is generally hemorrhage into the subarachnoid space.* Hemorrhage may also occur into the substance of the brain. The patient usually complains of an excruciating headache and loses consciousness almost immediately. *Death is due to generalized vasospasm triggered by the subarachnoid hemorrhage, with resultant ischemic injury to the brain.* Minor leakage from the aneurysm may precede rupture. In such cases, the patient often complains of headache for days or weeks prior to rupture.

Most of the statistical data on ruptured intracranial aneurysms are based on hospital cases, that is, those individuals who survive a rupture long enough to be admitted to a hospital. There are, however, two studies in the literature that include large numbers of individuals who died prior to or on arrival at a hospital.[47,48] These studies more accurately represent the cases seen in the medical examiner system. In both reports, 60% of the patients died immediately after rupture. Of those who survived the initial insult, more than half died less than 24 h after admission to a hospital.

In Freytag's study, the ages of the individuals ranged from 14 to 77, with a mean age of 46 years.[47] Eighty-four percent of the aneurysms were located in the anterior portion of circle of Willis and 16% in the posterior portion; 27% were present in the middle cerebral artery, 25% in the internal carotid artery, 24% in the anterior communicating artery, and 10% in the basilar artery. Patients with aneurysms of the posterior circle of Willis or the internal carotid artery showed a greater tendency (69–79%) to die at the time of rupture than those in other areas (49–53%). Of the 24 aneurysms in the basilar artery, 20 were present at the branching point of the posterior cerebral arteries. Evidence of previous bleeding from the aneurysms was present in 13% of the cases.

In ruptured berry aneurysms, massive subarachnoid hemorrhage was present in 96% of the cases, subdural hemorrhage in 22%, and intracerebral hemorrhage in 43%. Subarachnoid hemorrhage was the only lesion in 49% of the cases, with intracerebral hemorrhage and subdural hemorrhage alone in 1% of each of the cases. Intracerebral hemorrhage was present in 24% of those who died immediately, but in 71% of those who survived some time, thus indicating a better chance of survival if the aneurysm had ruptured into the brain tissue. Hemorrhage into the ventricular system occurred in 17% of the cases with intracerebral hemorrhage. Such hemorrhage into the ventricular system may be as rapidly fatal as bleeding into the subarachnoid space. Twenty-two percent of the cases showed hemorrhage in the subdural space. Only 5% of the cases, however, were space-occupying (over 50 mL).

In deaths due to subarachnoid hemorrhage from a ruptured berry aneurysm, the largest quantity of blood is on the ventral surface of the brain, with lesser amounts laterally and dorsally (Figure 3.9A). Large pools of blood on the ventral surface of the brain often make it difficult to locate the aneurysm if the brain is not examined when fresh. The arachnoid membrane should be removed with forceps and the ventral surface of the brain flushed with

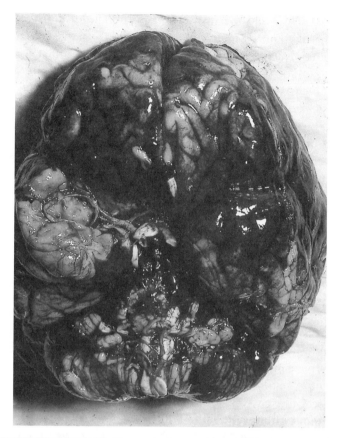

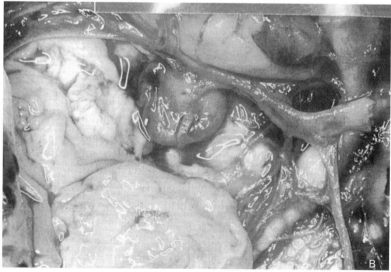

Figure 3.9 (A) Massive subarachnoid hemorrhage from ruptured aneurysm of right middle cerebral artery. (B) Berry aneurysm

running water. This will allow inspection of the circle of Willis for aneurysms (Figure 3.9B). In approximately 10% of all cases in which subarachnoid hemorrhage is present and in which the presentation is that of a ruptured berry aneurysm, no aneurysm can be found. If we exclude all other causes of the subarachnoid hemorrhage, then, in all probability, the cause is a rupture of a small aneurysm that has been completely obliterated by the blowout of the vessel.

A small percentage of the cases of nontraumatic subarachnoid hemorrhage are due to bleeding from an **arteriovenous (AV) malformation**. These are complex tangles of abnormal arteries and veins linked by one or more fistulas.[49] They lack a capillary bed and the small arteries have a deficient muscularis. They range from small to large; cortical to deep. Most of these lesions are visible on the surface of the brain, appearing as a wedge of arteries and veins extending into the subcortical white matter. Deep arteriovenous malformations may lie in the white matter, basal ganglia, thalamus or brainstem. The majority of arteriovenous malformations of the brain involve the central parietal cortex.

Most arterio-venous malformations derive part of their blood supply from at least one branch of the middle cerebral artery. There may be severe bleeding from these lesions into the subarachnoid space or into the substance of the brain, presenting as a massive intracerebral hemorrhage. It is estimated that 0.1% of the population have AV malformations with 12% of these symptomatic.[49] Sturge-Weber syndrome is characterized by multiple arteriovenous malformations of the cerebral hemispheres associated with vascular nevi of the face and/or neck and epilepsy. The most common clinical presentations are intracranial hemorrhage (30–82%); seizures (16–53%); headache and focal neurological deficits.[49] Two percent of all strokes are due to AVs. The death rate from hemorrhage is 10–15%.

A rare cause of subarachnoid hemorrhage is **sickle cell disease**. At autopsy, there is diffuse subarachnoid hemorrhage distributed evenly over the convexities of the cerebral hemispheres, as well as on the ventral surfaces of the brain. The marked concentration of subarachnoid hemorrhage on the ventral surface of the brain seen in rupture of a berry aneurysm is not present. The brain must be carefully examined to rule out the presence of arteriovenous malformations or berry aneurysms.

Whatever the cause of the nontraumatic subarachnoid hemorrhage, as soon as blood enters the subarachnoid space, it causes a mild inflammatory reaction in the meninges.[509] Fibrosis subsequently develops in many cases. Following hemorrhages into the subarachnoid space, a meningeal reaction is generally not seen for at least 2 h, when there are small accumulations of polymorphonuclear cells around pial blood vessels. By 4–16 h, a more intensive polymorphonuclear reaction is seen. Lymphocytes begin to accumulate around the pial vessels. After 16–32 h there are large numbers of polymorphonuclear cells and lymphocytes. Reaction of the mesothelial cells lining the subarachnoid space and arachnoid trabeculae appears 24 h after the subarachnoid hemorrhage. Breakdown of the erythrocytes can be seen as early as 16–32 h after subarachnoid hemorrhage. By the third day, the polymorphonuclear reaction has reached its peak. Because of a rapid increase in lymphocytes and macrophages, however, it accounts for only half of the cells present. Hemosiderin granules can be seen inside macrophages. By 7 days, no more polymorphonuclear reaction is present. At this time, lymphocytic infiltration is most prominent, with macrophages and hemosiderin. Some intact red blood cells are still present. Fibrosis of the pia matter develops in about 10 days. Since slight fibrosis of the pial and arachnoid membranes may be present as a "normal" aspect of these membranes, especially with advancing age, interpretation of minimal fibrosis is difficult.

Intracerebral Hemorrhage

Intracerebral hemorrhage is characterized clinically by an abrupt onset and rapid evolution. Intracerebral hemorrhages are more common in males and show a higher incidence in blacks than in whites, probably due to the greater incidence of hypertension. Blacks dying of intracerebral hemorrhages are generally younger than their white counterparts.

Intracerebral hemorrhages are uncommon in the younger age groups. The hemorrhage usually occurs in individuals who are up and active rather than asleep. Hypertension is virtually always present. There is usually only one episode of hemorrhage at the time of the attack. Recurrence of bleeding is not usually encountered. The patient usually develops symptoms over a period of 2 h to hours. The primary sites for intracerebral hemorrhages are the putamen and adjacent internal capsule, the thalamus, the cerebellar hemispheres, the pons, and the white matter (Figure 3.10).

In hemorrhage in the putamen, the speech becomes slurred and the muscles of the face, arms, and legs gradually weaken. In thalamic hemorrhage, hemiparesis occurs secondary to pressure on the adjacent internal capsule. The sensory deficit is greater than the motor weakness. Cerebellar hemorrhage usually takes a period of several hours to develop. Loss of consciousness is uncommon. Repeated vomiting, occipital headache, vertigo, and inability to walk or stand are symptoms. Occasionally, the individual is thought to be intoxicated. In pontine hemorrhage, consciousness is lost almost immediately.

As in the case of ruptured berry aneurysms, most of the literature about intracerebral hemorrhage is clinically oriented and concerns hospital cases. The paper by Freytag is probably most relevant to a medical examiner's office, because 80% of the cases were autopsies carried out in a medical examiner's

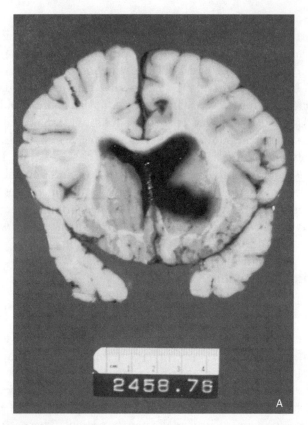

Figure 3.10 Primary intracerebral hemorrhages involving (A) basal ganglia with rupture into ventricular system (*continued*).

office.[51] Of the 393 cases studied, 40% of the hypertensive intracerebral hemorrhages originated in the striate body area, 16% in the pons, 15% in the thalamus, 12% in the cerebellum, and 10% in the cerebral white matter. Neither the cerebral nor cerebellar hemorrhages showed predilection for any side. Three percent of the cases showed multiple areas of origin for the hematomas, with five being the greatest number of multiple sites. There was no direct correlation between the severity of atherosclerosis of the basilar vessels and the development of intracerebral hemorrhage.

The age of the individuals ranged from 30 to 88 years of age, with an average of 55.5 years. Freytag pointed out that more than 50% of the hematomas occur between 40 and 60 years of age. Eleven percent of the patients, however, were in their thirties. Survival time was relatively short. Thus, 35% of the individuals were found dead or were dead on arrival at a hospital, 75% were either dead on arrival at a hospital or died within the first 24 h. Only 10% lived longer than 3 days. When hemorrhage occurred in the pons, 95% of the patients died within 24 h. Seventy-five percent of the hematomas

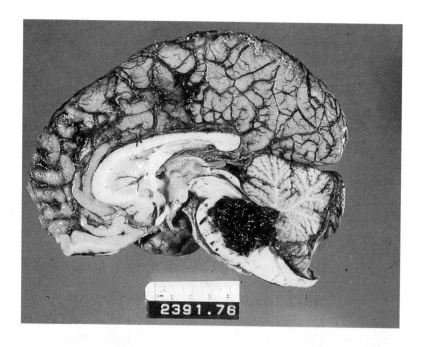

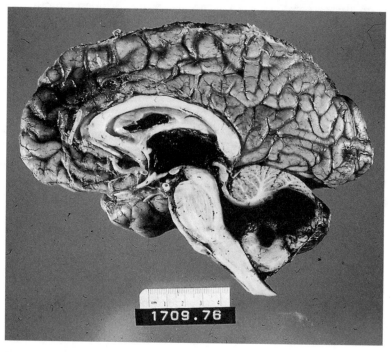

Figure 3.10 *(continued)* Primary intracerebral hemorrhages involving (B) pons, and (C) cerebellum.

ruptured through the ventricular walls into the ventricles. Hemorrhages at sites close to the ventricles penetrated into the ventricles more often than those in remote areas. Thus, 97% of the thalamic hemorrhages ruptured into the ventricles, compared with only 40% of the cerebral white matter hematomas. In 6% of the cases, the intracerebral hematomas penetrated through the cortex and subarachnoid membrane into the subdural space. This was most common with the cerebellar hemorrhages. Only 15% of the intracerebral hemorrhages penetrated through the cortex, producing subarachnoid hemorrhage. More than half (54%) of the patients developed secondary brain stem hemorrhages and edema.

In intracerebral hemorrhage, the brain is asymmetrically swollen, with the swollen hemisphere containing the hemorrhage. Subarachnoid hemorrhage may or may not be present on the base of the brain. On sectioning, the brain tissue adjacent to the hemorrhage is swollen and edematous. No brain tissue is present in the hematoma. Microscopic sections of adjacent brain tissue usually show severely sclerotic hyalinized arteries and arterioles. Occasionally, aneurysmally dilated arterioles and small arteries may be found. Death is generally due to compression and distortion of the midbrain, or hemorrhage into the ventricles. While deaths due to ruptured berry aneurysms or intracerebral hemorrhage are generally considered natural, in certain circumstances, they might be classified as homicide. Thus, if an individual ruptures an aneurysm during a fight in which physical violence is involved, the case should be classified as homicidal in manner. But, whether there are any criminal actions involved is something for the courts to decide, not the medical examiner.

Primary Brain Tumors

Sudden, unexpected death may, on rare occasion, be due to an undiagnosed primary brain tumor. In a study of 10,995 consecutive medicolegal autopsies in Dallas, Texas, DiMaio et al. found 19 sudden, unexpected deaths due to primary intracranial neoplasms, an incidence of 0.17%.[51] In another study of 17,404 autopsies performed at the Brooklyn Office of the Medical Examiner, DiMaio and DiMaio found an incidence of 0.16% of sudden, unexpected deaths due to primary intracranial neo-plasm.[53]

In the 19 deaths due to primary intracranial neoplasm reported by DiMaio et al., nine (47.4%) were in the astrocytoma-glioblastoma category.[52] The remainder included four cases of oligodendroglioma and one case each of medulloblastoma, microglioma, meningioma, teratoma, colloid cyst, and pituitary chromophobadenoma (Figure 3.11). Six deaths occurred following abrupt loss of consciousness or the individuals were found dead. Five of these had no known preceding symptoms. Thirteen individuals had symptoms of increased intracranial pressure, epilepsy, and psychiatric manifestations. Comparison of

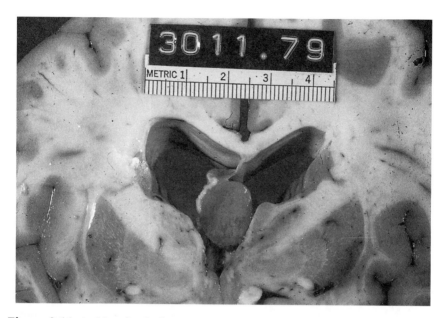

Figure 3.11 Sudden death due to unsuspected colloid cyst of third ventricle.

the duration and the type of symptoms exhibited by these patients and those of a hospital patient population in which death was caused by a previously diagnosed primary intracranial neoplasm revealed that there was a shorter duration of acute symptomatology in the sudden, unexpected death cases seen by the medical examiner. The symptoms also tended to be nonlocalizing and there was a lack of progression or change of symptoms in those patients in whom epilepsy was a primary manifestation of their underlying disease. There was also a lower incidence of focal neurological deficits as presenting symptoms.

Meningitis

Meningitis is an occasional cause of sudden unexpected death.[54] Until the late 1980s, most of the victims were children between the ages of 3 months and 3 years, with the organism involved being *Hemophilus influenza*. Mass inoculation of children with *Hemophilus* vaccine has resulted in the virtual disappearance of such cases. At present, acute bacterial meningitis is a disease of adults. It is seen in association with infections of the ears and sinuses; alcoholism; splenectomy, pneumonia, and septicemia. The most common organisms now encountered are *Streptococcus pneumoniae* (40–60%); *Neisseria meningitis* (15–25%); *Listeria monocytogene* (10–15%) and *Haemophilus influenzae* (5–10%).[54] In neonates, the coliform bacilli and group B streptococci predominant.

Most cases of meningitis develop secondary to septicemia. *S. pneumoniae* may develop secondary to pneumococcal pneumonia. This organism is also

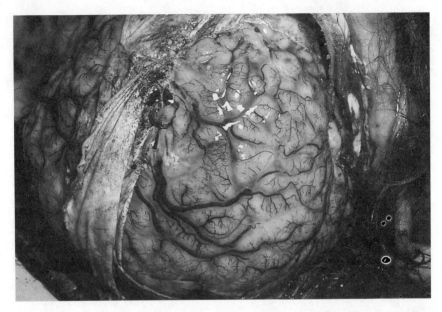

Figure 3.12 A 29-year-old female with pneumococcal meningitis. Purulent exudate in subarachnoid space.

the most common organism associated with head trauma in which the dura is disrupted. Hemophilus, pneumococcal, and meningococcal meningitis all may develop by direct extension from middle ear infections.

At autopsy, the brain is markedly swollen. The meninges appear cloudy on the ventral surface of the brain and, to a lesser degree, laterally due to purulent exudate (Figure 3.12). The exudate may be so slight as not to be seen grossly, or severe with copious quantities. In all cases of meningitis, the middle ears should be opened and examined to make sure that this is not the source of the meningitis.

Among bacteria that cause meningitis is *Neisseria meningitidis*.[55] The posterior nasopharynx is the natural reservoir for this organism, with 2–15% of healthy individuals carrying the organism in non-epidemic times. Meningococcal is now second only to pneumococcus in causing meningitis and is more common than *Hemophilus influenza* in both children and adults. The fatality rate is approximately 3%. Infection may present as a pure purulent meningitis, meningococcemia (septicemia), or as both.

Meningococcemia may present as a mild febrile illness, a fulminant disease (Waterhouse-Friderichsen Syndrome) or a chronic illness. The patient may have chills, high fever, dizziness, nausea, headaches, or weakness. Petechiae appear on the body in 75% of cases. They may coalesce, forming purpura and intracutaneous lesions. In 10% of the cases, there is a rapidly progressive course with toxemia, shock, and collapse. The individual may die less than 10 h after onset of symptoms. Occasionally, a person who is walking around will suddenly collapse, die, and, at autopsy, be found to have meningococcemia. In such a case, one can only speculate that the symptoms were not severe enough to inconvenience the person. At autopsy, there will be cyanosis; a blotchy erythematous rash, petechiae and purpura of the skin, and conjunctivae and acute bilateral hemorrhagic adrenal necrosis, but no meningitis (Figure 3.13). Cultures of the blood and spinal fluid for meningococcus are generally negative after refrigeration of the body due to the fragile nature of the organisms and/or antemortem administration of antibiotics. In such cases, diagnosis can be made from blood by detection of specific meningococcal capsular polysaccharides using immunoelectrophoresis, latex agglutination or polymerase chain reaction.[56] These, in the presence of the aforementioned autopsy findings, make the diagnosis of meningococcemia.

The same clinical and autopsy presentation that occurs in meningococcemia may occur from pneumococcal septicemia. The latter condition is commonly associated with absence of the spleen, either through surgery or congenital aberration. The pneumococcus organisms can usually be cultured from the blood even after refrigeration of the body.

Viral encephalitis is rarely seen in the medical examiner's office due to its protracted course, which leads to a clinical diagnosis. The brain will show severe edema with perivascular cellular infiltrates and infiltration of the meninges. The cells are predominantly lymphocytes and polymorphonuclear cells. Acellular plaques of necrosis may be seen throughout the brain.

Reyes Syndrome

Reyes syndrome is an entity of unknown etiology affecting children, in which an upper respiratory tract infection, chicken pox, and, rarely, gastroenteritis are followed by vomiting, convulsion, coma, hypoglycemia, elevated blood ammonia, and abnormal serum transaminase values. Individuals dying of the entity show fatty metamorphosis of the liver, with multiple small fatty cytoplasmic vesicles in the hepatocytes, myocardial fibers, and tubular cells of the kidneys. These are extremely fine vesicles compared with the coarse deposit seen in alcoholic fatty metamorphosis of the liver. Reyes syndrome can be confused with inborn errors of metabolism with which it may share many of the same clinical characteristics. The only way to be absolutely sure of the diagnosis is to demonstrate specific mitochondrial changes in liver tissue.

An increased incidence of this syndrome was noted in children who had taken aspirin for flu-like illnesses or chicken pox. Because of this, the use of aspirin in the treatment of children was discontinued in the 1980s. This has led to the virtual disappearance of the entity. Thus, from 1980 to 1997, 1207 cases of Reyes Syndrome were reported with a peak incidence of 555 cases in 1980.[57] Since 1994, no more than two cases per year have been reported.

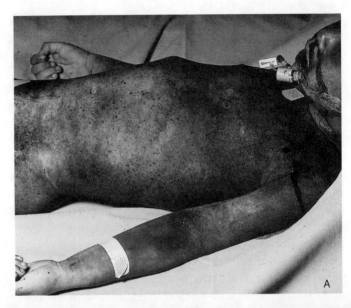

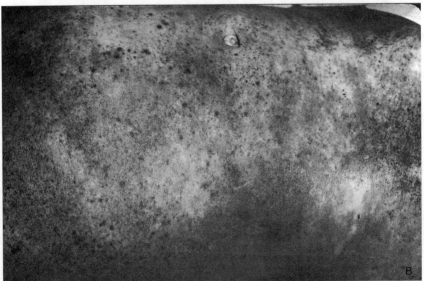

Figure 3.13 Meningococcemia. (A and B) Blotchy erythematous rash with petechiae and purpura (*continued*).

Hydrocephalus

Sudden and unexpected death is also seen in association with hydrocephalus. Here, the patient will usually have a long history of hydrocephalus, often with a shunt procedure performed in the past. The patient appears to be asymptomatic, then suddenly dies. At autopsy, one will find chronic

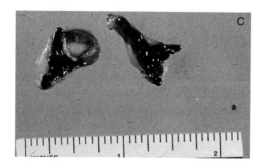

Figure 3.13 *(continued)* Meningococcemia. (C) Bilateral acute hemorrhagic necrosis of adrenals.

hydrocephalus, generally without any acute process. Such deaths are apparently a manifestation of the "final straw that broke the camel's back." These individuals were apparently borderline stabilized as to intracranial pressure, when some minor physiological change sufficient to raise the intracranial pressure caused death.

Psychiatric Patients

Sudden death is occasionally seen in psychiatric patients, usually chronic schizophrenics on phenothiazine, in whom there are therapeutic or high, but not lethal, levels of this drug. Such deaths are believed to be due to one or more of the following: cardiac arrhythmias induced by this drug, which does have a recognized potential to produce arrhythmias; hyperthermia; hypotension with development of tachycardia and cardiovascular collapse; respiratory dyskinesias; laryngeal-pharyngeal dystonias; neuroleptic malignant syndrome; and seizures.[58] Ascribing a death to the use of phenothiazines can be decided on only after obtaining a medical history, an account of the circumstances leading up to and surrounding the death, a scene investigation, a complete autopsy, and a thorough toxicological analysis. This is to prevent deaths from other causes being incorrectly attributed to phenothiazines.

Another subpopulation of schizophrenics whose deaths are not related to phenothiazine medication even though many have been prescribed this drug in the past, die suddenly and unexpectedly. At autopsy, these individuals show no anatomical cause of death. A complete toxicological analysis using the most refined techniques will reveal no drugs in toxic levels and, in most cases, absence of any drugs at all. In some cases, histories have shown that the individuals have been off their medications for several months prior to death. These deaths are sudden and unexpected and in some instances have been witnessed.

Respiratory System

Sudden death due to diseases of the respiratory system makes up only a small proportion of all sudden deaths. This has not always been the case. Thus, in the textbook by Gonzales et al., published in 1937, diseases of the respiratory tract accounted for 23% of unexpected deaths.[59] Gonzales et al. grouped respiratory deaths into four large categories: asphyxia, hemorrhage from air passages, pneumothorax, and infections of the lung.

Nowadays, sudden, unexpected deaths from lung diseases are relatively uncommon. The group that Gonzales et al. referred to as "asphyxia" included asthma and pulmonary embolism. Deaths due to these entities are still seen. Diphtheric or luetic inflammation of the larynx are not seen anymore. Also included in this category were deaths allegedly due to inhalation of vomitus. It is now realized that vomitus in the tracheobronchial tree is almost invariably an agonal event.[60] It is only when the airway is completely occluded by foreign material in an individual who has severe neurological impairment that one should attribute death to massive aspiration.

Epiglottitis

While conditions like luetic or diphtheric laryngitis are no longer seen, occasional cases of acute epiglottitis will be seen in the medical examiner's office. Most people think of this as a disease of young children. Increasingly, however, it has become a disease of adults.[61,62] With acute epiglottitis, there is always the potential for sudden fatal airway obstruction, which can occur extremely rapidly. The individual may have very minor symptoms such as a sore throat, difficulty swallowing, and hoarse speech. From there, the patient can rapidly develop airway obstruction, even while talking to a physician. Acute epiglottitis is often a medical emergency, requiring immediate tracheostomy or insertion of an endotracheal tube if the individual begins to develop acute airway obstruction.

H. influenzae has traditionally been the most common cause of this condition in both children and adults. In the last decade, there have been significant changes in the epidemiology of epiglottitis, with its now occurring almost exclusively in adults, and with a lower incidence of *H. influenzae* infection.[61,62] Since the introduction of *H. influenzae* vaccination in Sweden in 1992–1993, there has been a >90% reduction in the incidence of acute epiglottitis in the youngest age group.[62]

Other causes for obstruction of the larynx by natural disease are extremely rare. Occasionally, large numbers of polyps combined with sudden edema due to temporary obstruction by the polyps may cause death. One case the authors saw involved an individual with an undiagnosed squamous cell carcinoma of the larynx that virtually occluded the airway. The individual had had symptoms, but refused to see a physician, when suddenly he developed edema, which completely closed off the airway, and died.

Pulmonary Thromboemboli

Gonzales et al. list asthma and pulmonary embolus as causes of asphyxia.[59] These two conditions are not fatal as often as they formerly were, but still represent a significant number of deaths due to respiratory disease. Death from massive pulmonary thromboembolus is due to impaction of dislodged thrombi in the pulmonary artery or its main tributaries (Figure 3.14). Thrombosis has been classically described as being caused by three factors: stasis, injury to a vein, and hypercoagulability. Most pulmonary thromboemboli originate in the deep veins of the lower extremities. Occasionally, they will arise in the pelvic veins, especially in pregnant women. In one case, the source of the embolus was a pelvic vein in a woman who had a serocystadenoma the size of a basketball pressing on the vein. Any trauma to the lower extremities or pelvis may injure a vein and cause the formation of thrombi, which can be subsequently dislodged.

Stasis is a cause for the formation of thrombi, with the classic example the individual confined to bed. Thrombi can develop in individuals who are in bed following a traumatic injury that does not involve a vein of the lower extremity or pelvis. Thus, an individual might be in bed for a head injury, develop thrombosis of the veins of the lower extremities, and throw

Figure 3.14 Bilateral massive pulmonary thromboemboli

a massive pulmonary thromboembolus. Here, even though the mechanism of death is natural, i.e., a pulmonary thromboembolus, the manner of death would be accident because the individual was confined to the bed due to trauma. If the individual had been assaulted, then the case would be classified as homicide.

Death from massive pulmonary thromboembolus is caused by a combination of mechanical obstruction of the blood flow by the embolus plus vasoconstriction that further reduces the lumen of the pulmonary arteries. Symptoms of massive pulmonary thrombolus are syncopy, chest pain, and dyspnea. Approximately one third of the people dying of massive thromboemboli die within an hour. In all deaths due to massive thromboemboli, the source of the emboli should be sought. The veins of the pelvis and legs must be examined. Incisions should be made bilaterally into the popliteal fossae and calves.

There has recently been speculation that hereditary thrombotic disease, manifested by the presence of factor V Leiden and factor II/20210A alleles coupled with acquired factors, accounts for a large number of fatal cases of pulmonary thromboemboli. A number of studies, however, have shown that the incidence of factor V Leiden and factor II/20210A allele in patients with fatal pulmonary thromboemboli is not greater than the incidence of these factors in the general population.[63,64]

Asthma

Asthma, which affects 3% of the population, is also a cause of sudden and unexpected death in the medical examiner's population.[65] Deaths from it, while uncommon, do occur, with death rates of from 1.1 to 7% reported. Since 1960, there has been an increase in the incidence of deaths from asthma, either because of increased prevalence of the disease or an increase in severity. Deaths in blacks are twice that of whites. Sudden, unexpected death can occur in asthmatics without long-term deterioration or a prolonged attack. The frequency of death from asthma is increased at night or in the early morning, possibly due to a pronounced diurnal variation in airflow limitation. Up to one fourth of deaths from asthma occur within 30 min of onset of the attack.

In acute asthmatic attacks, there is a reduced airflow rate, air trapping, and a ventilation-perfusion imbalance that leads to decreased oxygenation of the blood, elevated carbon dioxide, increased pulmonary vascular resistance, a right ventricular systolic overload, and an increase in the effort needed to breathe. The reduction in airflow is due to a combination of smooth muscle contraction, tenacious mucoid secretions in the bronchi, and an inflammatory infiltrate in the walls of the bronchi. These may develop either gradually or in a very short order. If airflow obstruction is not relieved, there will be steady progression to elevated carbon dioxide, metabolic acidosis, exhaustion, and death.

At autopsy, the lungs usually appear overexpanded, completely, occupying their respective chest cavity. This hyperexpanded state may not be present if extensive cardiopulmonary resuscitation has been carried out. In addition to the hyperexpansion of the lungs, a sticky tenacious white mucus deposit will fill the bronchi. Microscopic sections of the lung show a chronic inflammatory infiltrate with numerous eosinophils around the bronchi. The basement membrane of the bronchi is thickened and has a wavy appearance.

A large increase in deaths in the 1960s in Great Britain was originally attributed to abuse of aerosol bronchodilators. It is now generally accepted that such use is not a cause of death from asthma. Rather, the excessive use of bronchodilators is a reflection of the need for more effective therapy for these individuals. The increasingly accepted view is that many deaths from asthma are due to inadequate or delayed treatment.

In the workplace, two types of asthma are encountered: work-aggravated and occupational.[66] The former is preexisting asthma that is aggravated by irritants in the workplace. *Occupational asthma is caused by exposure to irritants in the workplace.* Occupational asthma without a latency period follows exposure to high concentrations of irritant gases, fumes, or chemicals on one or several occasions. The most common examples of such agents are chlorine and ammonia. Occupational asthma with a latency period is the most common type and is caused by exposure to irritants over a period of time that can vary from a few weeks to several years. The majority of individuals developing occupational asthma with latency do not recover.

Pneumonia

The medical examiner will see numerous individuals with bronchopneumonia. In most cases, this is a secondary complication of another disease process that has brought the case into the office. Thus, individuals hospitalized for several days or weeks following head trauma from an accident quite commonly will develop bronchopneumonia. Sudden deaths due to primary pneumonia are uncommon. When they do occur, one sees either a lobar pneumonia or a confluent bronchopneumonia involving at least one lobe. Such deaths usually involve alcoholism. Occasionally, one will see cases of bilateral acute fulminating tuberculous pneumonitis. In these cases, the deceased is usually an alcoholic or has an impaired immune system. Occasionally, one will see a young child with a vague history of some respiratory symptoms over a couple of days, interpreted as being nothing but a cold by the parents. These children are often found to have patchy bronchopneumonia involving all lobes or bronchiolitis.

Hemoptysis

A fourth type of sudden, unexpected death due to pulmonary disease is
massive hemoptysis (Figure 3.15). There are generally two causes, depending on the population served. First is a tumor eroding into a pulmonary
vessel with subsequent massive hemoptysis and exsanguination. In a population with a large number of alcoholics or individuals with impaired
immune systems, however, one will see fatal hemoptysis caused by cavern-
ous tuberculosis.

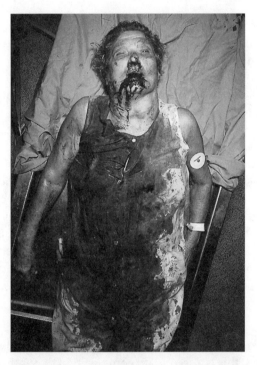

Figure 3.15 An 80-year-old female who exsanguinated from massive hemoptysis due to tuberculosis and bronchiectasis.

Spontaneous Pneumothorax of Newborns

One other pulmonary cause of sudden death should be mentioned. This is
spontaneous pneumothorax of the newborn.[67,68] This entity is relatively
uncommon, occurring in 1–2% of live births, and is usually benign, with
virtually all term infants having resolution without *sequelae*, often without
the condition's being diagnosed. It should be suspected in any apparently
healthy newborn who dies suddenly and unexpectedly in a hospital nursery.
An X-ray prior to autopsy will make the diagnosis (Figure 3.16).

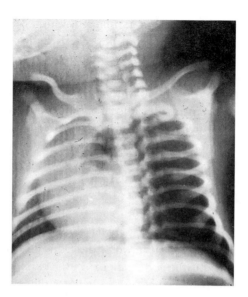

Figure 3.16 Pneumothorax of newborn with left tension pneumothorax and displacement of heart and left lung into right chest cavity.

Urogenital and Gastrointestinal Tracts

Diseases of the urogenital and digestive organs caused 13% of the sudden and unexpected deaths in 1937.[59] Nowadays, such cases are uncommon, with possibly the most common entity a massive hematemesis due to esophageal varices complicating cirrhosis of the liver. Occasionally, one will see a death following a duodenal ulcer eroding into a major blood vessel with massive GI hemorrhage. There are occasional deaths caused by peritonitis from a perforated duodenal ulcer or an acute peritonitis. These latter deaths are more common in alcoholics and psychotic patients on heavy doses of antipsychotic medications that could mask the symptoms of these conditions and the patients' awareness of their illness.

Spleen

A spleen massively enlarged due to undiagnosed leukemia may rupture, causing exsanguination. Absence of the spleen, either surgically or congenitally, is associated with pneumococcal septicemia and bilateral adrenal hemorrhages. Presentation of this syndrome may be the same as that due to acute fulminant meningococcemia.

Pancreas

Sudden death from diseases of the pancreas generally involve two entities, acute fulminating pancreatitis and diabetes mellitus. Deaths from acute pancreatitis in which the patient is mobile and walking around are uncommon. As in instances of unsuspected peritonitis, they are associated with alcoholism and individuals on high doses of antipsychotic medications, which can mask or obscure symptoms.

Sudden, unexpected death due to the acute onset of diabetes mellitus is relatively rare.[69] The classic symptoms of diabetes are polydipsia, polyuria, polyphagia, and loss of weight. In some instances however, diabetic coma may be the initial symptom. If the individual dies without medical attention or if the cause of the coma is not diagnosed before death, these cases become medical examiner cases.

Diabetes is a metabolic disorder characterized by hyperglycemia and a failure to a greater or lesser extent to secrete insulin. Approximately one third of all diabetics are juvenile onset diabetics. In this condition, the lack of insulin may be complete. This type of diabetes is differentiated from the mature onset diabetes by the tendency of the juvenile diabetic to develop ketoacidosis. Most individuals with juvenile onset diabetes present with the classical symptoms of diabetes previously mentioned. Approximately one third, however, initially present in acidosis or diabetic coma. In a number of instances, the onset of diabetes seems to be triggered by an infective illness. In diabetic ketoacidosis, blood glucose levels are seldom under 300 mg/dL or over 1000 mg/dL, with an average blood level reported as 736 mg/dL.

The biochemical derangement in diabetic ketoacidosis may be extremely severe with increased metabolism of fatty acids, resulting in the formation of ketone bodies and acidosis. There is loss of large quantities of electrolytes and water. The hyperglycemia produces osmotic diuresis with hypertonic dehydration. Free acetone is elevated in the blood in cases of coma. Levels of free acetone in normal individuals are generally less than 0.17 mg/dL. In diabetic coma, levels have been reported as ranging from 14.5 to 74.95 mg/dL.[70]

There is an aketotic form of diabetic coma that differs in several respects from the classical form of ketoacidosis. The patients tend to be older and blood glucose levels in this condition are extremely high, with an average level of 1949 mg/dL. Dehydration is intense, with serum sodium and potassium usually normal or high. Free acetone is only mildly elevated (up to 5.81 mg/dL) if at all.[70]

Sudden, unexpected death due to the acute onset of diabetes is a problem to the forensic pathologist in that postmortem blood glucose levels are generally of no value because of the great fluctuation in the level of glucose after death. Elevated blood acetone levels, while suggestive of diabetes, are not diagnostic, because they may be the result of another condition, such as malnutrition. In addition, in the aketotic form of diabetic coma, elevated levels of ketones may not be present. Glucose in the urine is also not diagnostic, because it can occur in many conditions. The presence of glycogen in the cells of the proximal convoluted tubules of the kidney (Armanni-Ebstein lesion) is said to be diagnostic of uncontrolled diabetes. Unfortunately, this lesion is often absent.

The most reliable indicator of diabetes mellitus in the postmortem state is elevated glucose in the vitreous humor. Vitreous humor provides an easily obtainable fluid for the postmortem diagnosis of diabetic coma. *An elevated vitreous glucose level is an accurate reflection of an elevated antemortem blood glucose level.* Fortunately, marked agonal rises in blood glucose level, a not uncommon occurrence, do not manifest themselves as rises in the vitreous glucose. Thus, in studying 102 nondiabetics in whom perimortem peripheral blood glucose concentrations exceeding 500 mg/dL resulted from a terminal rise in blood sugar from a variety of causes, Coe found the vitreous glucose in all of these cases was below 100 mg/dL.[71] Even if intravenous glucose infusions are administered for hours prior to death, the vitreous glucose level in normal subjects is generally less than 200 mg/dL. Thus, glucose levels significantly above 200 mg/dL are diagnostic of diabetes mellitus even if intravenous glucose infusions are being administered. Of course, as the time between the death and autopsy increases, there will be a fall in the glucose level of the vitreous. This decrease, however, is relatively gradual in the diabetic because of the markedly elevated levels of glucose present, and significantly elevated levels of glucose will remain for prolonged periods of time.[72]

Liver

Sudden death in association with liver disease is uncommon. Rarely, individuals will die of massive hepatic necrosis caused by fulminating hepatitis. One should always worry in such cases that the hepatitis is of a toxic nature such as that caused by an overdose of acetaminophen. In children, Reye's syndrome can cause relatively rapid death, but the condition is usually diagnosed prior to death.

Another cause of massive hepatic necrosis is ingestion of poisonous mushrooms. *Amanita phalloides* is one of the most commonly encountered poisonous mushrooms in the United States. It is the most dangerous, accounting for almost all fatalities. It is found in many regions of the U.S., including California, the Pacific Northwest, and the Northeast. It contains cyclopeptide toxins,[73] which are potent hepatotoxins with no taste or smell that are not destroyed by cooking. Ingestion of even one mushroom can cause death. Following ingestion, there are no symptoms for several hours. Then, the victims develop nausea, vomiting, severe abdominal cramps, and watery diarrhea. They then seem to be getting better, when they develop hepatic and renal failure, become jaundiced, and develop a coagulopathy and impaired neurologic status. The signs of fulminant hepatic necrosis may not appear for a day or two. The mortality rate for *Amanita phalloides* poisoning is 20–30%.

In alcoholics with cirrhosis of the liver, there is a relatively obscure entity characterized by massive non-traumatic intra-abdominal hemorrhage. Di Maio reported three cases[74] in which no source for the bleeding was found. Of the three, one who was briefly hospitalized showed evidence of a disseminated intravascular coagulopathy. It was the author's opinion that this was the most likely cause of the intra-abdominal hemorrhage in the two other cases and could be attributed to the cirrhosis of the liver. Two of these deaths were obviously sudden and unexpected, with one 44-year-old woman observed to become rigid and collapse while seated in a chair at home. She was found to have 2750 mL of non-clotted blood in her abdominal cavity and advanced micro-nodular cirrhosis. A second individual was a 38-year-old man who collapsed while walking from a convenience store to a parked truck. Again, there was no evidence of trauma, and 4800 mL of non-clotted blood was found in the abdominal cavity. The liver showed micro-nodular cirrhosis of an advanced degree. The third individual, who was hospitalized for 21 h, had between 2500 and 3000 mL of non-clotted blood in his abdominal cavity.

Occasionally, chronic alcoholics die suddenly and unexpectedly, without any anatomical or toxicological cause of death. At autopsy, the only finding is an enlarged liver with severe fatty metamorphosis. The toxicological screen usually shows absence of alcohol. This entity was first described by Le Count and Singer in 1926.[75] By tradition, these deaths have been signed out as "fatty metamorphosis of the liver."

Alcohol, in both moderate and heavy doses, has a direct toxic effect on hepatic triglyceride metabolism, with resultant accumulation of triglycerides and phospholipids in the liver cells.[76] Large and small vacuoles of fat are present in the hepatocytes and Kupffer cells. While the most common cause of the accumulation of fat in the liver is chronic abuse of alcohol, this condition can also be seen in obesity, diabetes, and viral infections as well as due to toxic compounds of phosphorous and chlorinated hydrocarbons.

While the death is certified as due to fatty metamorphosis, no one seriously believes that it is the actual cause of death. Rather, it is a marker of chronic abuse of alcohol. The present thought is that such deaths are due to cardiovascular etiologies.[76] Alcoholics have a tendency to develop arrhythmias. Recent study has also demonstrated an increased QT interval and elevated plasma norepinephrine.[77,78] It is thought that the effects of chronic alcoholism on the heart are fatal arrhythmia and death.

Adrenals

The adrenal is rarely a primary cause of sudden death. Bilateral adrenal cortical hemorrhages are seen in sepsis (the Waterhouse-Friderichsen syndrome), classically with meningococcemia, though other organisms can produce the same picture. There have been rare sudden deaths in association with a pheochromocytoma of the adrenal gland.[79] Minor trauma and surgery are common precipitants. This tumor secretes epinephrine, norepinephrine, or both. Sudden death on a cardiac basis from release of these chemicals can occur.

Miscellaneous

Sudden, unexpected death could be caused by rupture of a tubal pregnancy. The woman may have only vague symptoms of abdominal pain, often ascribed to gastroenteritis. Rupture of the tubal pregnancy can result in massive hemoperitoneum with 2–3 L of blood present (Figure 3.17). Other causes of sudden, unexpected death due to natural disease seen by the authors include idiopathic pulmonary hemosiderosis, central pontine myelinosis, cysticercosis, a stasis ulcer of the ankle with erosion into a vessel, an aneurysm of the femoral artery with erosion through the vessel wall and skin with massive exsanguination (Figure 3.18), and undiagnosed malignant tumors.

Tumor and Trauma

There is no medical proof that a single traumatic event can give rise to a malignant tumor.[80] However, a causal relation between head trauma, such as a fracture of the skull, and the subsequent development of a meningioma

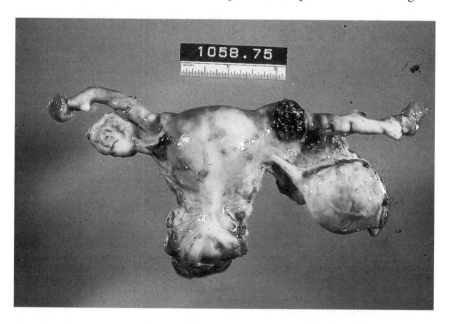

Figure 3.17 Rupture of tubal pregnancy with massive hemoperitoneum in 28-year-old female. Incidental finding: teratoma of ipsilateral ovary.

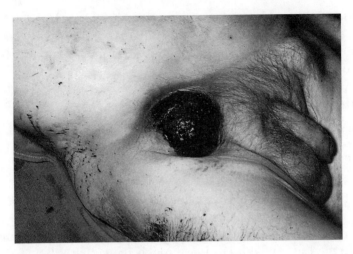

Figure 3.18 Aneurysm of right femoral artery with erosion through skin, perforation, and exsanguination in a 75-year-old male. Second uneroded aneurysm visible in left inguinal region.

has been suggested, with Schiffer et al. reporting three such cases.[81] Trauma has also been linked to the metastatic spread of a preexisting malignant tumor. Multiple episodes of trauma in conjunction with other factors may cause cancer, for example, chronic irritation of the skin and squamous cell carcinoma. If, under the category of trauma, one includes radiation (including ultraviolet light), carcinogenic chemicals, and chronic exposure to heavy metals, there is no doubt that, with repeated exposure, an individual can develop a malignant tumor.[80]

References

1. Zipes DP and Wellens HJJ. Sudden cardiac death. *Circulation* 1998; 8(21):2334-2351.

2. Willich SN, Levy D, Rocco MB, et al.: Circadian variation in the incidence of sudden cardiac death in the Framingham heart study population. *Am Cardiol* 1987; 60:801-806.

3. Di Maio V.J.M. and Di Maio DJM, Incidence of coronary thrombosis in sudden death due to coronary artery disease *Am J Med & Path* 1993; 14(4):273-5.

4. De Wood MA, Spores J, Notske R et al. Prevalence of total coronary occlusion during the early hours of transmural myocardial infarction. *NEJM* 1980 303:897-902.

5. Burke AP and Virmani R. Intramural coronary dysplasia of the ventricular septem and sudden death. *Hum Path* 1998; 29(10):1124-7.

6. Morales AR, Romanelli R, Boucek R, The mural left anterior descending coronary artery, strenuous exercise and sudden death. *Circulation* 1980;62(2):230-237.

7. Cutler D and Wallace J M, Myocardial bridging in a young patient with sudden death *Clin. Cardiol* 1997; 20:581-583.

8. DiMaio VJM, DiMaio DJ, Postpartum dissecting coronary aneurysm. *NY State J Med* 1971; 71:767-769.

9. Smith JC, Dissecting aneurysms of coronary arteries. *Arch Pathol* 1975;99:117-121.

10. Basso C, Morgagni GL, and Thiene G., Spontaneous coronary artery dissection: a neglected cause of acute myocardial ischaemia and sudden death *Heart* 1996; 75:451-454.

11. DeMaria AN, Lee G, Amsterdam EA, et al., The anginal syndrome with normal coronary arteries. *JAMA* 1980; 244:826-828.

12. Manzar KJ, Padder FA, Conrad AR, Freeman I, and Jonas EA. Acute myocardial infarction with normal coronary artery: a case report and review of the literature. *Am J Med Sci.* 1997; 314(5):342-345.

13. Yasue H and Kugiyama K. Coronary spasm: clinical features and pathogenesis. [Review] *Intern Med.* 1997; 36(11):760-5.

14. Bigger JT and Coromilas J, Identification of patients at risk for arrhythmic death: Role of Holter ECG recording, in Josephson ME (Ed): *Sudden Cardiac Death Cardiovascular Clinics 1513.* Philadelphia, FA Davis Co, 1985; pp 131-143.

15. Weaver W, et al., Use of the automatic external defibrillation in the management of out-of-hospital cardiac arrest. *NEJM* 1988; 319:661- 665.

16. Diem SJ, Lantos JD, and Tulsky JA, Cardiopulmonary resuscitation on television – Miracles and misinformation *NEJM* 1996; 334(24) 1578-1582.

17. Schneider AP II, Nelson DJ, Brown DD, In-hospital cardiopulmonary resuscitation: a 30-year review *J Am Board Fam Prac.* 1993; 6(2):91-101.

18. Kavanagh T, A cold weather "jogging mask" for angina patients. *Can Med Assoc J* 1970;103:1290-1291.

19. Coplan NL, Gleim GW, Nicholas JA, Exercise and sudden cardiac death. *Am J Heart* 1988; 1 15:207-212.

20. Mittleman MA, Maclure M, Tofler GH et al., Triggering of acute myocardial infarction by heavy physical exertion *NEJM* 1993; 329:1677-1683.

21. Willich SN, Lewis M, and Lowel H et al., Physical exertion as a trigger of acute myocardial infarction. *NEJM* 1993; 329:1684-1690.

22. Maron BJ, Cardiovascular risks to young persons on the athletic field. *Ann Intern Med.* 1998; 129(5): 379-386.

23. Kragel AH and Roberts WC, Sudden death and cardiomegaly unassociated with coronary, valvular congenital or specific myocardial disease. *Am J Cardiol* 1988; 61:659-660.

24. Messerli FH, Ventura HO, Elizardi DJ, et al., Hypertension and sudden death. *Am J Med* 1984; 77:18-22.

25. Haider AW, Larson MG, Benjamin EJ, and Levy D, Increased left ventricular mass and hypertrophy associated with increased risk for sudden death. *JACC* 1998; 32(5):1454-9.

26. Frolich ED, Left ventricular hypertrophy and sudden death (Editorial Comment) *JACC* 1998; 32(5):1460-2.

27. Wagner BM, Left ventricular hypertrophy and sudden death. *Hum Pathol* 1986; 17: 1.

28. Wynne J and Braunwald E, The cardiomyopathies and myocarditis: toxic chemical and physical damage to the heart, in Braunwald E (Ed): *Heart Disease* 4th ed. WB Saunders, Philadelphia 1992.

29. Brown CS and Bertolet B, Peripartum cardiomyopathy: a comprehensive review. *Am J Obst Gynec* 1998; 178(2):4091414.

30. Maron BJ, Hypertrophic cardiomyopathy. *Lancet* 1997; 350 (9071):127-133.

31. Freed LA, Levy D, Levine RA, et al., Prevalence and clinical outcome of mitral valve prolapse *NEJM* 1999; 341(1):1-7.

32. Kligfield P, Levy D, Devereux RB, et al., Arrhythmias and sudden death in mitral valve prolapse. *Am Heart J* 1987; 1 13:1298-1307.

33. Scala-Bamett DM, Donoghue ER: Sudden death in mitral valve prolapse. *J Forensic Sci* 1988;33:84-91.

34. Selzer A, Changing aspects of the natural history of valvular aortic stenosis. *NEJM*1987; 317:91-98.

35. Perloff JK, Congenital heart disease in the adult, in Braunwald E (Ed): *Heart Disease* 4th ed. WB Saunders, Philadelphia 1992.

36. Sharbough AH and White RS, Single coronary artery. *JAMA* 1974; 230:243.

37. Davies MJ, Treasure T, and Richardson PD, The pathogenesis of spontaneous arterial dissection. *Heart* 1996; 75:434-435.

38. Fikar CR and Koch S. Etiologic factors of acute aortic dissection in children and young adults. *Clin Ped* 39(2): 71-80.

39. Rashid J, Eisenberg MJ, and Topol EJ, Cocaine-induced aortic dissection. *Am Heart J*. 1996; 132(6):1301-1304.

40. Dreifus LS, Haiat R, Watanobey, et al., Ventricular fibrillation, a possible mechanism of sudden death in patients with Wolff-Parkinson-White syndrome. *Circulation* 1971; 43:520-527.

41. Insner JM, Roberts WC, Heymsfield SB, et al., Anorexia nervosa and sudden death. *Ann Intern Med* 1985; 102:49-52.

42. Insner JM, Sours HE, Paris AL, et al., Sudden unexpected death in dieters using the liquid-protein modified-fast diet. *Circulation* 1979; 60:14011412.

43. Ficker DM, Sudden unexplained death and injury in epilepsy. *Epilepsia* 2000; 41 Suppl 2:S7-12.

44. Hirsch CS, Martin DL, Unexpected death in young epileptics. *Neurology* 1971; 21:682-690.

45. Jay GW, Leestma JE, Sudden death in epilepsy. *Acta Neurol Scand* 1981; 63(suppl 82):1-66.

46. Chasson JL, Hindman WM, Berry aneurysms of the circle of Willis. *Neurology* 1958; 8:41-44.

47. Freytag E, Fatal rupture of intracranial aneurysms. *Arch Pathol* 1966; 81:418-424.

48. Dinning TAR, Falconer MA, Sudden or unexpected natural death due to ruptured intracranial aneurysms: Survey of 250 forensic cases. *Lancet* 1953; 2:799-801.

49. The Arteriovenous Malformation Study Group, Current Concepts: Arteriovenopus malformations of the brain in adults. *NEJM* 1999; 340(23):1812-1818.

50. Hammes EM, Reaction of meninges to blood. *Arch Neurol Psychiat* 1944; 52:505-514.

51. Freytag E: Fatal hypertensive intracerebral haematomas. *J Neurol Neurosurg Psychiat* 1968; 31:616-620.

52. DiMaio S, DiMaio VJM, Kirkpatrick J, Sudden death due to primary intracranial neoplasm. *Am J Forensic Med Pathol 1980*; 1: 29-46.

53. DiMaio TM, DiMaio DJ, Sudden deaths due to colloid cysts of third cerebral ventricle. *NY State J Med* 1974; 74:1832-1834.

54. Hirschmann JV, Bacterial infections of the central nervous system 1999. In Dale DC and Federman (Eds) *Scientific American Medicine. Sci Amer.* NY 53A.

55. Samore MH and Karchmer AW, Infections due to Neisseria. In Dale DC and Federman (Eds) *Scientific Amer. Medicine. Sci Amer.* NY.

56. Challener RC, Morrissey AM, and Jacobs MR, Postmortem diagnosis of meningococcemia by detection of capsular polysaccharides. *J Forensic Sci* 1988; 33:336-346.

57. Belay ED, Bresee JS, Holman RC, et al., Reyes Syndrome in the United States from 1981 through 1997. *NEJM* 1999; 340(18): 1377-1382.

58. Laposata EA, Hale P Jr, Poklis A, Evaluation of sudden death in psychiatric patients with special reference to phenothiazine therapy: Forensic pathology. *J Forensic Sci* 1988; 33:432-440.

59. Gonzales TA, Vance M, Helpern M: *Legal Medicine and Toxicology.* New York, Appleton-Century, 1937.

60. Knight BH, The significance of the postmortem discovery of gastric contents in the air passages. *Forensic Sci* 1975; 6:229-234.

61. Mayo-Smith MF, Spinale JW, Donskey CJ, Yukawa M, Li RH, Schiffman FJ, Acute epiglottitis: An 18-year experience in Rhode Island. *Chest* 1995; 108:1640-7.

62. Garpenholt O, Hugosson S, Fredlund H, et al., in Sweden before and after introduction of vaccination against *Haemophilus influenzae* type b. *Ped Infect Dis J* 1999; 18(6):490-3.

63. Slovacek KJ. Harris AF. Greene JF Jr, et al., Fatal pulmonary embolism: a study of genetic and acquired factors. *Molec Diag* 2000; 5(1):53-8.

64. Kohlmeier RE, Cho CG, Bux RC, et al., Prothrombin gene mutation uncommon in pulmonary embolism. *SMJ* 2000; 93(11):1073-1077.

65. Benatar SR, Fatal asthma. *NEJM* 1986; 314:423-439.

66. Chan-Yeung M. Malo JL, Occupational asthma. *NEJM*,1995; 333(2):107-12.

67. Norton LE. DiMaio VJ. Zumwalt RE, Spontaneous pneumothorax in the newborn: a report of two fatalities. *J Forens Sci.* , 1978 Jul; 23(3):508-10.

68. Mayo P, Saha SP, Spontaneous pneumothorax in the newborn. *Am Surg.* 1983 Apr; 49(4):192-5.

69. DiMaio VJM, Stumer WQ, Coe J, Sudden and unexpected deaths after the acute onset of diabetes mellitus. *J Forensic Sci* 1977; 22:147-151.

70. Sulway JJ, Trotter W, Trotter MD, et al., Acetone in uncontrolled diabetes. *Postgrad Med J* 1971; June Suppl, pp 382-387.

71. Coe JI, Peripheral blood glucose and cardiopulmonary resuscitation. *Forensic Sci Gazette* 1975; 6(4):1-2.

72. Coe JI, Postmortem chemistries on human vitreous humor. *Am J Clin Pathol* 1969; 51:741-750.

73. Pomerance HH, Barness EG, Kohli-Kumar M, et al., A 15-year-old boy with fulminant hepatic failure. *J Pediat* 2000 Jul; 137(1):114-8.

74. DiMaio VJM, Sudden unexpected deaths due to massive non-traumatic intra-abdominal hemorrhage in association with cirrhosis of the liver. *Am J Forensic Med Pathol* 1987; 8:266-268.

75. Le Count ER and Singer HA, Fat replacement of the glycogen in the liver as a cause of death. *Arch Path.* 1926; 1:84-89.

76. Chejfec G, Fat replacement of the glycogen in the liver as a cause of death. *Arch. Pathol. Lab Med* 2001; 125:21-24.

77. Bernardi M, Calandra S, Colantoni A, et al., Q-T interval prolongation in cirrhosis: prevalence, relationship with severity, and etiology of the disease and possible pathogenetic factors. *Hepatology* 1998; 27(1):28-34.

78. Day CP, James OFW, Butler TJ, et al., Q-T prolongation and sudden cardiac death in patients with alcoholic liver disease. *Lancet* 1993; 341:1423-1428.

79. Primhak RA, Spicer RD, Variend S, Sudden death after minor abdominal trauma:An unusual presentation of phaeochromocytoma. *Br Med J* 1986; 292:95-96.

80. Monkman GR, Orwoll G, Ivins JC, Trauma and oncogenesis. *Mayo Clinic Proc* 1974; 49:157-163.

81. Schiffer L, Avidan D, Rapp A; Post-traumatic meningioma. *Neurosurgery* 1985; 17: 84-87.

Blunt Trauma Wounds

4

The severity, extent, and appearance of blunt trauma injuries depend on:

- The amount of force delivered to the body
- The time over which the force is delivered
- The region struck
- The extent of body surface over which the force is delivered
- The nature of the weapon

If a weapon deforms or breaks on impact, less energy is delivered to the body to produce injury, because some of the energy is used to deform or break it. Thus, the resultant injury is less severe than one would have if the weapon did not deform or break. Similarly, if the body moves with the blow, this increases the period of time over which the energy is delivered and decreases the severity of the injury.

For any given amount of force, the greater the area over which it is delivered, the less severe the wound. The size of the area affected by a blow depends on the nature of the weapon and the region of the body. For a weapon with a flat surface, such as a board, there is diffusion of the energy and a less severe injury than that caused by a narrow object, for example, a steel rod delivered with the same amount of energy. If an object projects from the surface of the weapon, then all of the force will be delivered to the end of the projection and a much more severe wound will be produced. If a blow is delivered to a rounded portion of the body, such as the top of the head, the wound will be much more severe than if the same force is delivered to a flat portion of the body, such as the back, where there will be a greater area of contact and more dispersion of force.

Blunt force injuries fall into four categories:

1. Abrasions
2. Contusions
3. Lacerations
4. Fractures of the skeletal system

It should be realized that a wound might display more than one type of injury. Thus, one may have a laceration with abraded margins lying in the center of an area of contusion.

Abrasions

An abrasion is an injury to the skin in which there is removal of the superficial epithelial layer of the skin (the epidermis) by friction against a rough surface, or destruction of the superficial layers by compression. Antemortem abrasions have a reddish-brown appearance (Figure 4.1) and heal without scarring. Abrasions produced after death are yellow and translucent with a parchment-like appearance. They are important to the forensic pathologist in that they indicate where a blunt instrument or a blunt force has interacted with the body. They may be the only external evidence of trauma to the body. Abrasions are not always present in areas of blunt force injury.

There are three types of abrasions:

1. Scrape or brush abrasions
2. Impact abrasions
3. Patterned abrasions

In **scrape (brush) abrasions**, the blunt object scrapes off the superficial layers of the skin, leaving a denuded surface. At times, these abrasions may be fairly deep, extending down to the dermis. In such instances, there may be leakage of fluids from vessels with deposit of a serosanguineous fluid on the surface of the abrasion. This dries, forming the familiar reddish brown scab. One of the most common types of scrape abrasions is the linear abrasion known as the scratch. Extensive scrape-like abrasions (graze or sliding abrasions) are seen in pedestrians who slide across the pavement (Figure 4.1A) after being hit by a motor vehicle. Particles of gravel, dirt, or glass may be embedded in such wounds. An incision made into these areas usually fails to reveal underlying soft tissue hemorrhage (Figure 4.1B). Similar scrape abrasions may be produced when a victim's body is dragged over a rough surface. Nooses or ligatures can also produce scrape abrasions.

It is quite common to read in textbooks of the heaping up of epidermis at the distal end of a scrape abrasion, enabling one to determine the direction of movement of the blunt object or the body across a rough surface. The phenomenon is more theoretical than real and usually does not occur to a significant degree.

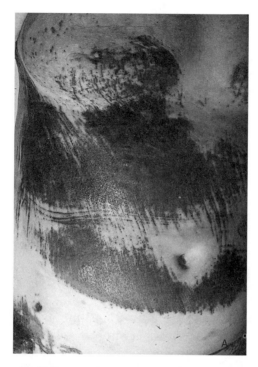

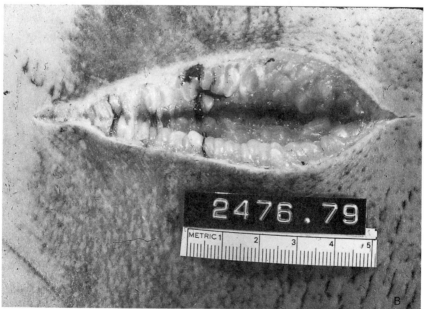

Figure 4.1 (A) Scrape-like abrasion from sliding across pavement. (B) Incision shows injury confined to epidermis.

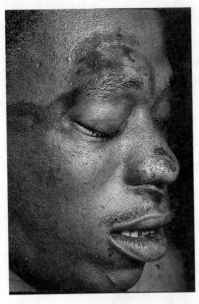

Figure 4.2 Impact abrasions of right side of face.

In **impact abrasions**, the blunt force is directed perpendicular to the skin, crushing it. Such abrasions tend to be focal and are commonly seen overlying bony prominences where a thin layer of skin covers bone. Impact abrasions over the supraorbital ridge (eyebrow), zygomatic arch (cheek-bone), and the side of the nose are commonly seen in individuals who are unconscious when they collapse, and strike their heads on the ground (Figure 4.2).

A **patterned abrasion** is a variation of an impact abrasion. Here, the imprint of either the offending object, such as a pipe, or intermediary material, such as clothing, is imprinted or stamped on the skin by the crushing effect of the blunt object (Figure 4.3).

Postmortem insect bites and diaper rash are occasionally misinterpreted as abrasions by the inexperienced physician (Figure 4.4A-B). Another artifact that can be confused with an abrasion is drying of the skin of the scrotum and, less commonly, of the vulva (Figure 4.4C). The skin in these areas seems to be very susceptible to drying, especially if exposed to the open air. It has a reddish brown or yellow coloration and may be interpreted as an abrasion.

Dating of Abrasions

Unlike attempts at dating of contusions in which histological examination of the injuries has not been helpful, histological examination of abrasions in an attempt to determine their age is possible to a degree. Robertson and Hodge probably provide the most authoritative and logical method of approach.[1]

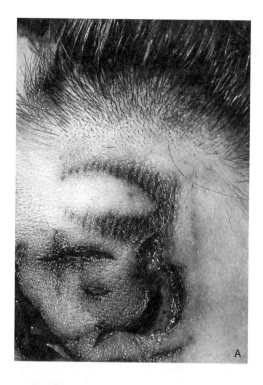

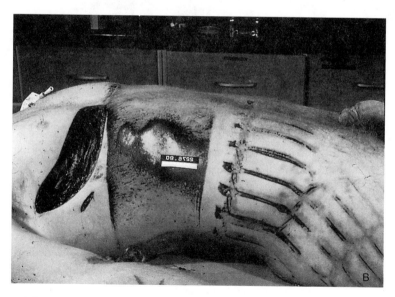

Figure 4.3 Patterned abrasions. (A) Thread marks of pipe (lacerations below abrasion). (B) Grill marks in individual who jumped off eight-story building, landing on metal grill.

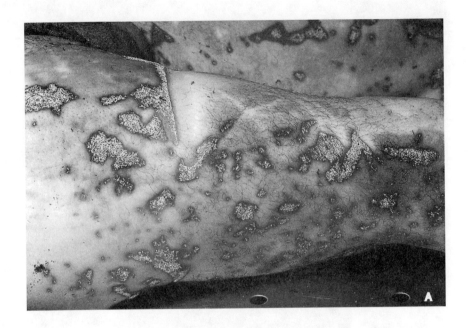

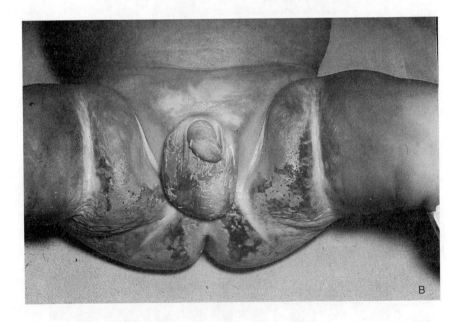

Figure 4.4. A. Postmortem ant bites simulating abrasions. B. Diaper rash (*continued*).

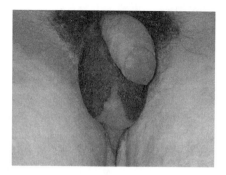

Figure 4.4. (*continued*) C. Drying of scrotum.

They describe four stages in the healing of abrasions:

1. Scab formation
2. Epithelial regeneration
3. Subepithelial granulation and epithelial hyperplasia
4. Regression of epithelium and granulation tissue

The first stage is **scab formation**. Serum, red cells, and fibrin are deposited on the abrasion. These are not used for aging, but do indicate survival following the injury. The infiltration of polymorphonuclear cells in a perivascular formation signifies that the injury is 4–6 h old. The earliest time for such a cellular reaction is 2 h, but it is usually not clearly visible until 4–6 h. By 8 h, the bed of the scab is marked by a zone of infiltrating polymorphonuclear cells underlying the area of epithelial injury. At 12 h, there are three layers: a surface zone of fibrin and red cells (or crushed epithelium in the case of impact abrasions), a deeper zone of infiltrating polymorphonuclear cells, and a layer of damaged abnormally staining collagen. For the next 12 to 18 h, the last zone is progressively infiltrated by polymorphonuclear cells.

The second stage is **epithelial regeneration**. Regeneration of the epithelial cells arises in surviving hair follicles and at the edges of the abrasion. Epithelial growth may appear as early as 30 h in superficial scrape-like abrasions and is clearly visible by 72 h in most abrasions.

The third stage is **subepidermal granulation**. This becomes prominent during days 5 to 8. It occurs only after epithelial covering of an abrasion. Perivascular infiltration and chronic inflammatory cells are now prominent. The overlying epithelium becomes progressively hyperplastic, with formation of keratin. This stage is most prominent during days 9 to 12 after injury.

The last stage is **regression**. It begins at about 12 days. During this phase, the epithelium is remodeled and becomes thinner and even atrophic. Collagen fibers, which began to appear in the late subepidermal granulation phase, are now prominent. There is a definite basement membrane and the vascularity of the dermis decreases.

Contusions

A **contusion** or **bruise** is an area of hemorrhage into soft tissue due to rupture of blood vessels caused by blunt trauma (Figure 4.5). Contusions may be present not only in skin, but also in internal organs, such as the lung, heart, brain, and muscle. A large focal collection of blood in an area of contusion is referred to as a hematoma. A contusion can be differentiated from an area of livor mortis in that, in a contusion, blood has escaped into soft tissue and cannot be wiped or squeezed out, as in an area of livor mortis. The extent and severity of a contusion depends not only upon the amount of force applied, but also on the structure and vascularity of the tissue that is contused. Thus, contusions are more readily incurred in areas with thin, lax skin and in fatty areas.

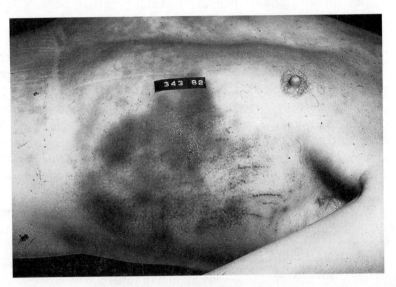

Figure 4.5 Non-patterned contusion. Perpetrator jumped on deceased's chest, rupturing left lung and lacerating liver.

Contusions might reflect the configuration of the object used to produce the contusion; that is, they might be patterned (Figure 4.6). When an individual is struck with a flat object, such as a board, it is quite common to find parallel linear contusions corresponding to the edges of the board, with normal-appearing tissue in between. A contusion at a site does not necessarily indicate the point of trauma, since soft tissue bleeding will follow the path of least resistance. Deep bruises may not be visible externally and may be

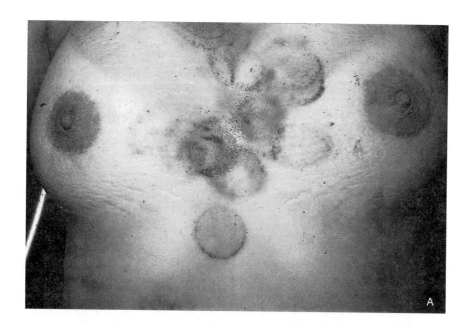

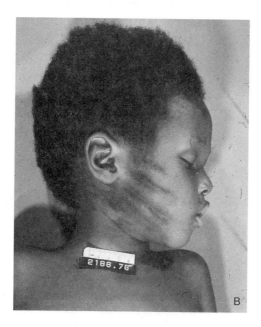

Figure 4.6 Patterned contusions caused by (A) end of flashlight (B) imprint of left hand (*continued*).

discovered only on incising the soft tissue. In other instances, deep bruises may not become visible externally until hours after death. Scalp bruises are frequently not visible externally unless there is swelling (Figure 12.4). Bruises can also be difficult to detect in dark-skinned individuals.

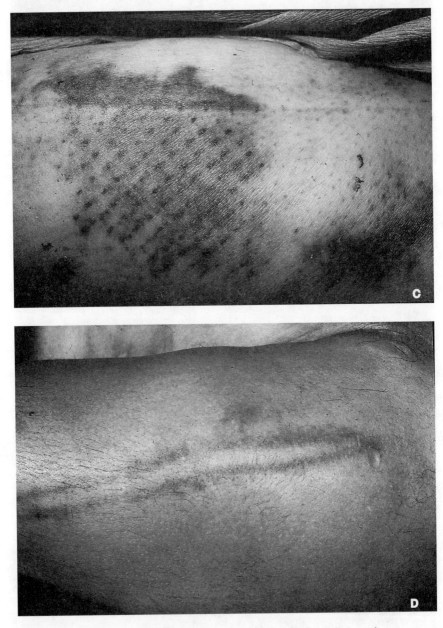

Figure 4.6 (*continued*) Patterned contusions (C) clothing (D) pool cue.

Contusions, like abrasions, indicate that blunt force has been applied to a particular area. Absence of a bruise, just as absence of an abrasion, does not indicate that there was no blunt force to that area. This is especially true of the anterior abdominal wall, where there may be massive internal injury in the absence of external evidence of trauma. Another point to remember is that a contusion might be much larger than the object that produced it.

As a rule, bruises are not fatal. However, multiple contusions with extensive soft tissue hemorrhage may produce shock and death from massive blood loss. This is seen occasionally in battered children.

The size and severity of a contusion is not always indicative of the amount of force applied, though, obviously, the greater the force, the greater the contusion. Certain factors influence the size of a contusion: age, sex, the condition and health of the victim, and the site and type of tissues struck. Children and the elderly bruise more easily because of loose delicate skin in the former and loss of subcutaneous supportive tissue in the latter. Senile purpura (ecchymoses) on the forearms of the elderly may be mistaken for bruises. Women, especially if obese, seem to bruise more easily. Well-conditioned, muscular individuals are more resistant to bruising. Soft, lax, vascular tissue, such as in the eyelid, is more susceptible to bruising than areas such as the palm. Alcoholics with cirrhosis, individuals with bleeding diatheses, and individuals taking aspirin bleed more easily. A single therapeutic dose of aspirin irreversibly inhibits platelet function for the 7-d life of the platelets with resultant inhibition of hemostasis and a prolonged bleeding time.[2]

Dating of Contusions

The forensic pathologist is often asked the age of a bruise, as such information could be of potential importance in a case. Methods used to age a bruise are (1) histology and (2) color changes. The first method can be disposed of very rapidly. Consistent microscopic dating of contusions has been found to be impossible.[3]

The method most commonly employed in dating contusions is based on the changes in color a contusion undergoes as it heals. The depth of a contusion and skin pigmentation may affect the appearance and detection of the colors. Yellow coloration is visible sooner in superficial bruises than in deep bruises; dark pigmentation may conceal a bruise. The depth and location of the bruise can influence its time of appearance, with superficial bruising and bruises of the eyelids (with their loose soft tissue) appearing immediately, and deep bruising not appearing for days.

As a bruise ages, it undergoes an evolution in its color due to the degradation of the hemoglobin. The time and order of the changes is how one ages a bruise. Problems arise, however, in individuals' disagreeing on color terminology and the chronology of the development of colors, and that bruises are not consistent in appearance, color or evolution.

There is no standard terminology in use to describe the color of a bruise. The same bruise might be described as violet, reddish purple, bluish purple, purple, or blue. Most bruises appear initially as red, dark blue, purple, violet or black. As the hemoglobin in the bruise is broken down, the color gradually changes to violet, green, dark yellow, and pale yellow before disappearing. These changes can occur over a matter of days to weeks. Unfortunately, the rate of change is quite variable, not only between persons, but in the same person and from bruise to bruise. Not uncommonly, the color change goes directly from violet to yellow with no green coloration. In the same individual, one can have two bruises that were incurred at the same time, and one will go from blue to violet to yellow and disappear while the other is still violet. A brown coloration to a contusion is said to indicate that it is not recent. The authors, however, have seen numerous pale brown contusions of the anterior chest overlying the sternum produced by perimortem cardiopulmonary resuscitation, and have seen contusions develop a pale yellow color in 2 to 3 d. Langlois and Gresham concluded that all one could say about a bruise with yellow coloration is that it is more than 18 hours old.[4] They also concluded that absence of a yellow color does not mean that the bruise is less than 18 hours old. Color changes should be considered only as general guidelines in interpreting how old a bruise is. The best thing to do is to just state that the bruise appears either recent or old.

Postmortem Bruising

One of the most commonly heard statements in regard to contusions is that they indicate that the injury was incurred prior to death, because one cannot form a contusion after death. This is not absolutely correct. Contusions can be produced postmortem if a severe blow is delivered to a body within a few hours of death.[3] The blow can rupture capillaries, forcing blood into the soft tissue and producing a postmortem contusion identical in appearance to an antemortem contusion. Postmortem contusions rarely occur and are most commonly seen in skin and soft tissue overlying bone or bony prominences such as in the head. Microscopic examination of a contusion to determine whether it is antemortem or postmortem is usually of no help, because, in most cases, the antemortem injuries are incurred immediately prior to death and there is insufficient time for tissue reaction.

The Eyes and Eyelids

Surgical removal of corneas or the globes of the eyes shortly after death can result in hemorrhage into the eyelids indistinguishable from antemortem traumas (Figure 4.7A). Removal of vitreous shortly after death can result in scleral hemorrhage at the puncture site (Figure 4.7B).

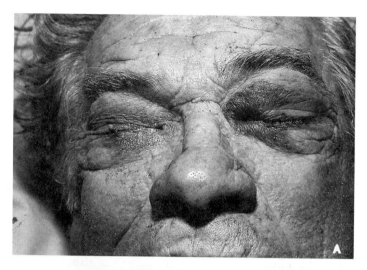

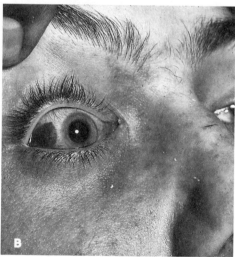

Figure 4.7 (A) Hemorrhage into eyelids following removal of corneae. (B) Scleral hemorrhage following removal of vitreous.

Confluent hemorrhage in eyelids can occur after death in cases of head trauma with fracture of the orbital plates. One can prove this by taking the body of an individual with skull fractures, but without hemorrhage in the eyelids, and placing it face down for a number of hours. Blood will drain from the cranial cavity through the orbital plate fractures into the eyelids.

Decomposed Bodies

In decomposed bodies, especially in the scalp, hemolysis of erythrocytes produces a diffuse discoloration of the soft tissue, which makes attempts to distinguish between an antemortem contusion and an area of livor mortis impossible. In areas of livor mortis, blood vessels break down with leakage of erythrocytes into the soft tissue. Erythrocytes still in the vessels and those that diffuse into soft tissue hemolyze. Erythrocytes in soft tissue from bruising will also hemolyze, giving identical appearances to these lesions.

Lacerations

A laceration is a tear in tissue caused by either a shearing or a crushing force (Figure 4.8). Just as with contusions, one can have lacerations of internal organs as well as the skin. Lacerations of the skin tend to be irregular with abraded contused margins. They are caused by blows from blunt objects, falls, or impact from vehicles. The appearance of the laceration may not accurately reflect the instrument that produced it. Thus, a steel rod might produce not only a linear laceration of the scalp, but also a Y-shaped one. As a general rule, however, long, thin objects, such as pipes and pool cues, tend to produce linear lacerations, while objects with flat surfaces tend to produce irregular, ragged, or Y-shaped lacerations. Just as with contusions, determining the age of lacerations is difficult.

Lacerations occur most commonly over bony prominences, such as in the head, where the skin is fixed and can more easily be stretched and torn. Since different components of soft tissue have different strengths, there is usually incomplete separation of the stronger elements, such as blood vessels and nerves, so that when one looks into the depth of the laceration, one sees "bridges" of tissue running from side to side (Figure 4.9). The presence of bridging proves decisively that one is not dealing with an incised wound. The depths of the laceration should be explored for the presence of foreign material that could have been deposited there by the weapon or surface that caused the laceration.

If the blow or impact that causes a laceration is delivered at an angle, rather than perpendicular to the surface of the body, one will find undermining of the tissue on one side, which indicates the direction that the blow was delivered (Figure 4.10). The other side of the laceration, the side from which the blow was coming, will be abraded and beveled.

While most lacerations have irregular, abraded, even contused margins, if an individual is struck with a heavy object having a relatively sharp edge along the impacting surface, the wound produced may greatly resemble an incised wound (Figure 4.11). Careful examination of the wound, however, will usually reveal at least some abrasion of the margin, plus bridging in the depths of the wound. Occasionally, a very dull knife may produce an incised wound with abraded margins. Again, careful observation of the edges and base of the wound with a dissecting microscope usually makes differentiation

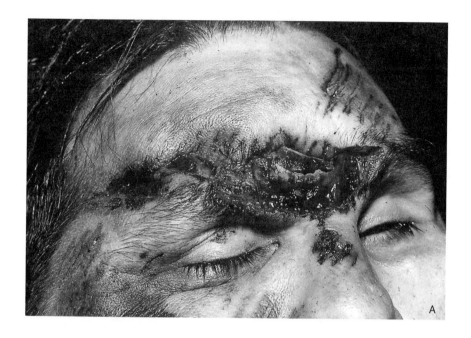

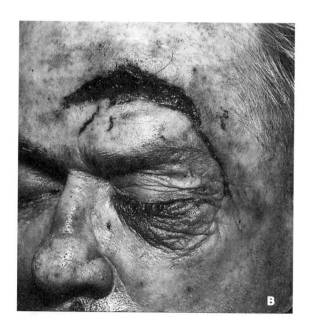

Figure 4.8 (A) and (B) Lacerations.

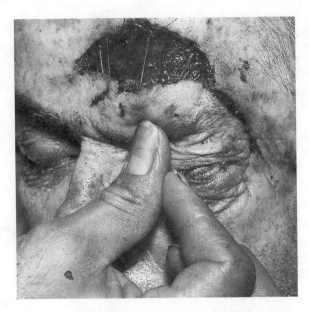

Figure 4.9 Laceration with bridging.

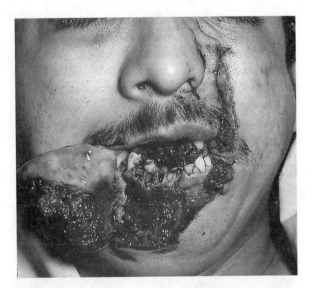

Figure 4.10 Laceration with avulsion of skin. Blow delivered from deceased's left to right.

between an incised wound and a laceration relatively easy. In some instances, however, differentiation is not possible. Differentiation of a laceration from an incised wound of the head in a decomposed body is often not possible.

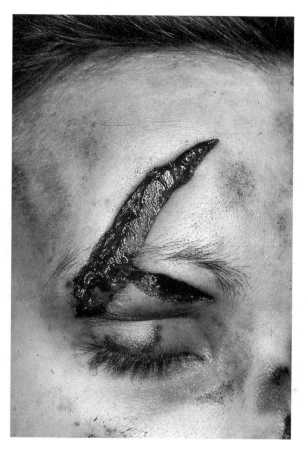

Figure 4.11 Laceration with sharp, almost incised margins.

An avulsion or avulsive injury to the outside of a body is a form of laceration where the force impacting the body does so at an oblique or tangential angle to the skin, ripping skin and soft tissue off the underlying fascia or bone. Thus, tires passing over an extremity may avulse soft tissue off the bone. In a case of extreme avulsion, an extremity or even the head can be torn off the body. Internally, organs can be avulsed or torn off in part or in toto from their attachments.

A variation of an avulsive laceration is one produced by shearing forces, where the skin shows no signs of injury but the underlying soft tissue has been avulsed from the underlying fascia or connective tissue, creating a pocket that may be filled with a large quantity of blood. This injury is occasionally encountered on the backs of the thighs of pedestrians struck by motor vehicles. As the hood of the car impacts the back of the thigh and lifts up the pedestrian, it imparts a shearing force to this region, avulsing the skin and subcutaneous tissue off the fascia and creating pockets where blood can accumulate.

Defense Wounds Due to Blunt Force

Just as one can have defense wounds from a knife attack, one can have defense wounds from an attack with a blunt object. There are generally abrasions and contusions on the back of the hands, wrists, forearms, and arms (Figure 4.12). Lacerations are less common and may contain embedded fragments of the weapon in the wounds. Even less common are fractures. When these occur, they generally involve the forearm, and are incurred in attempts to ward off a blunt object.

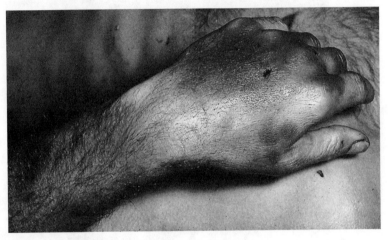

Figure 4.12 Abrasions and contusions of back of hand representing defense-type wounds.

Determination of Whether a Wound is Ante- or Postmortem

At present, determination of whether a wound is either ante- or postmortem is made by gross or microscopic examination of the wound. The presence of bleeding into the tissue is presumed evidence that the deceased was alive, or, at least, the heart was beating at the time the injury was incurred. The problem with this principle is that, on occasion, trauma to a recently dead body can cause bleeding into soft tissue. This is seen most commonly with withdrawal of vitreous. The needle is inserted through the sclera and the vitreous aspirated. Within minutes, hemorrhage develops around the needle-stick site (Figure 4.7B). This phenomenon may cause confusion to a forensic pathologist who is unaware of it. Much rarer is the postmortem contusion of the scalp previously mentioned in this chapter.

Another method of determining if an injury is antemortem is microscopic examination of the injury in search of an inflammatory reaction. The problem with this technique is that some tissues do not show an inflammatory reaction unless the victim has survived for at least several hours after the injury.

Techniques to identify antemortem injuries involving use of histochemistry, enzymology and biochemistry have been developed.[5] None of these techniques are used on a routine basis, if at all, in the United States. Analysis of enzyme activity in antemortem wounds has demonstrated a zone of decreased enzyme activity at the center of the wound, with increased enzyme activity at the periphery. The increased enzyme activity occurs over a specific time interval, with the interval different for different enzymes. Enzyme activity can be detected up to 5 d after death. The enzyme activity can be used to demonstrate that a wound was antemortem as well as to date it. In addition to enzymes, other markers such as DNA, C 3 factor, vasoactive amines and catecholamines have also been used. Thus, histamine and serotonin are both increased in antemortem wounds.

Fractures of the Face

Fractures of the mandible, maxilla, zygoma and zygomatic arch are produced predominantly by assaults and motor vehicle accidents. All can be fractured by a single blow. Maxillary fractures can be placed in five categories (Figure 4.13):

1. Dentoalveolar
2. LeFort I
3. LeFort II
4. LeFort III
5. Sagittal

In **dentoalveolar fractures**, direct force applied anteriorly or laterally causes separation of a fragment of the mandible. This fragment generally contains a number of teeth. **The LeFort I fracture** is a transverse fracture of the maxilla, above the apices of the teeth, through the nasal septum and maxillary sinuses, the palatine bone and the sphenoid bone. The **LeFort II** (the "pyramidal") fracture has the same path posteriorly. As it proceeds anteriorly, however, it curves upward near the zygomatic-maxillary suture, through the inferior orbit rim onto the orbital floor, through the medial orbital wall and across the nasal bones and septum. The **LeFort III** is a high transverse fracture of the maxilla that goes through the nasofrontal suture, through the medial orbital wall and fronto-zygomatic suture, across the arch and through the sphenoid. **Sagittal fractures** run in a sagittal plane through the maxilla.

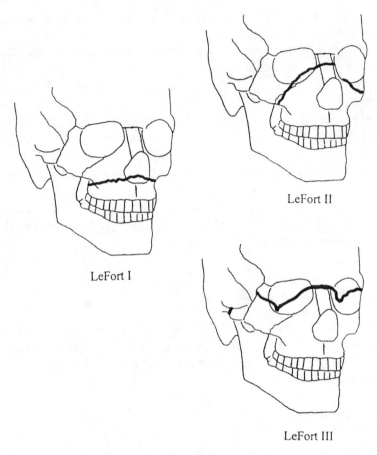

LeFort II

LeFort I

LeFort III

Figure 4.13 Fractures of the face: LeFort I, LeFort II, LeFort III.

Fractures of the the Extremities

Fractures of the bones of the extremities can be produced by either the **direct** or **indirect** application of force to the bone.[6]

Fractures from Direct Application of Force

When a blunt object impacts a long bone, it tends to bend the bone, producing disruption or cracking of the bone on the side opposite the impact i.e., the convex or tension side of the bone. With significant impact, however, there is crushing on the side of the bone to which the force is applied (the concave side), prior to the bone's cracking. In comminuted fractures, the bone is broken into more than two pieces.

Fractures caused by direct application of force to a bone site can be divided into penetrating, focal or crush fractures, depending on the amount of force applied to the bone and the size of the area to which it is applied. **Penetrating fractures** are caused by a large force acting on a small area. Because, for all practical purposes, this category is synonymous with gunshot wounds, penetrating fractures will not be discussed in this book.

In **focal fractures**, a small force is applied to a small area and the resultant fracture is usually transverse. Overlying soft tissue injury is relatively minor, for example, an abrasion, contusion, or small laceration. In areas where two bones are adjacent to each other, such as in the forearm or calf region, typically only one bone is fractured. Focal fractures, produced by weapons such as a bat or pipe, are seen in forearms when an individual has tried to ward off blows from such instruments (Figure 4.14A).

In **crush fractures**, a large force is applied over a large area, with resultant extensive soft tissue injuries and, often, comminuted fractures of the bone. In the forearm and lower legs, there is usually fracture of both bones at the same level. Most crush fractures of the extremities involve the legs, with motor vehicle-pedestrian accidents the most common etiology. The fractures produced are called **bumper fractures** (Figure 9.18).

In severe impact injuries of the legs, a number of possible fracture patterns can be produced (transverse; oblique; spiral; segmental; comminuted; longitudinal split; tension wedge; compression wedge).[7] The two most common patterns are tension wedge and oblique (Figure 4.14B). Tension wedge

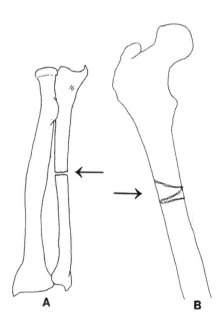

Figure 4.14 Direct fractures. (A) Focal (B) Crushing. Arrow indicates direction of force.

fractures can be used as an indicator of the direction of impact. In tension wedge fractures, the fractures begin opposite to the point of impact and radiate back through the bone at a 90° angle, giving rise to a wedge of bone whose point is directed in the direction of the force and whose base is at the point of impact. What appears to be an oblique fracture on X-ray may turn out to be a tensile wedge fracture on dissection. On occasion, one will see compressive wedge-type fractures. These are extremely rare and may be confused with the common tension wedge fracture.

Fractures Caused by Indirect Application of Force

Indirect fractures are produced by a force acting at a distance from the fracture site. In this regard, it should be noted that bone is weaker to tension (stretching) than compression. Indirect fractures can be classified into six types (Figure 4.15):

1. Traction
2. Angulation
3. Rotational
4. Vertical compression
5. Angulation and compression
6. Angulation, rotation, and compression fractures

In **traction fractures**, the bone is pulled apart by traction. An example would be violent contraction of the quadriceps muscle with resultant transverse fracture of the patella. In **angulation fractures**, the bone is bent until it snaps. The concave surface is compressed and the convex surface is put under traction. This usually results in a transverse fracture.

In **rotational fractures**, the bone is twisted and a spiral fracture is produced. *Spiral fractures* occur only when the bone is subjected to torsional force. In the femur, most spiral fractures occur in the proximal third. The proximal and distant ends of a spiral fracture are connected by what Porta et al. call a "hinge."[8] The hinge distinguishes it from an oblique fracture. To determine in which direction a bone was twisted, ascertain the direction the spiral runs from the end twisted. This indicates the direction of torque.

Vertical compression fractures produce an oblique fracture of the body of long bones, with the hard shaft of the long bone driven into the cancellous end. In femurs, a T- or Y-shaped fracture is typically seen at the distal end of the femur. Such fractures may occur following impaction of the end of the femur into the instrument panel in motor vehicle crashes.

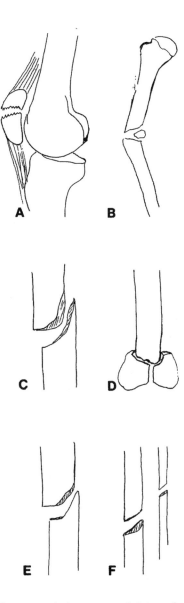

Figure 4.15 Indirect fractures. (A) Traction. (B) Angulation. (C) Rotational. (D) Vertical compression. (E) Angulation and compression. (F) Angulation, rotation, and compression.

In **angulation** and **compression fractures**, the fracture line is curved, with an oblique component due to compression, and a transverse component due to angulation. The last category is **angulation, rotation,** and **compression fractures**. The angulation plus rotation produces an oblique fracture, with the compression increasing the tendency toward fracture.

Pelvic Fractures

Fractures of the pelvis deserve special mention because of two unusual aspects. First, an immense amount of force is required to disrupt the pelvic ring. Second, because the pelvis is a ring, disruption of any portion of it is usually associated with disruption of another portion of the ring. Pelvic disruption or fractures are classified by the direction of the force.[9,10] There are four categories:

1. Anterior-posterior compression
2. Lateral compression
3. Shear
4. Complex fractures

In fractures due to antero-posterior compression, there is a direct blow to either the pubic symphysis or the posterior iliac spines, or violent external rotational forces applied to the femurs. Anteriorly, there is separation of the pubic symphysis. Posteriorly, there is bilateral separation of the sacroiliac joints anteriorly, with the posterior iliac ligaments generally intact.

In lateral compression, the force is applied either to the iliac crest directly or to the greater trochanter by the femoral head's being propelled into the acetabulum. Anteriorly, the pubic rami on the side of impact are usually fractured. However, there may be contralateral fracture of the pubic rami or, less commonly, fracture of all four pubic rami or even disruption of the pubic symphysis. Posteriorly, there is ipsilateral impaction of the sacroiliac joints with the posterior ligaments generally intact. If the femoral head produces lateral compression by being propelled into the acetabulum, there are usually ipsilateral fractures of the pelvic rami, disruption of the sacroiliac joints with impaction, and fractures of the acetabulum.

Shearing injuries of the pelvis are due to extremely severe force. There is application of a shearing force to one or both of the sacroiliac joints. The force is perpendicular to the trabecular pattern of the posterior pelvic complex, which results in disruption of both the anterior and superior sacroiliac ligaments with gross disruption of the joints. With massive forces, the hemipelvis can be avulsed from the body. Anteriorly, there may be disruption of the pubic symphysis, two pubic rami, or all four pubic rami.

In complex fractures, multiple forces from different angles have been exerted at the pelvis and one cannot simply classify the injuries as being due to the three aforementioned modes.

Healing of Fractures

Healing of fractures depends on the ages of individuals and their nutritional status. After adulthood, age does not play an important role. Fractures of cancellous bone unite faster than those of cortical bone. In children, a callus is visible radiologically within 2 weeks of the fracture. The bone is consolidated in 4–6 weeks, though it usually takes 2–3 months to heal solidly. In adults, consolidation takes approximately 3 months, though in the case of the femur, it could take 4–5 months. These are only very general time periods.

In healing, fractures of the bone undergo a number of stages that end in repair of the bone. Initially, there is hemorrhage at the point of fracture secondary to rupture of vessels, with production of a fusiform hematoma surrounding and joining the ends of the bone. The periosteum is torn from the outer surface of the bone; the endosteum from the marrow. Fibrin is deposited in the hematoma. This is followed in 24 to 48 hours by an inflammatory response with edema, continuing deposit of fibrin and the accumulation of large numbers of polymorphonuclear cells. As time passes, increasing numbers of machrophages appear.

The next stage begins 48 hours after injury and is characterized by the appearance of fibroblast and mesenchymal cells with gradual development of granulation tissue. Necrosis of the bone adjacent to the fracture becomes evident, with empty lacunar spaces due to death of osteocytes. The line of demarcation between dead bone, with its empty lacunae, and live bone is evident. There is marked proliferation of the cells of the deep layer of the periosteum and, to a lesser degree, of the cells of the endosteum.

As the days pass, the periostial proliferation results in formation of a collar around what is becoming the callus. At the same time the periosteal cells are proliferating, capillaries begin to grow out into the hematoma. Osteoblasts begin to appear and form new trabeculae. Approximately a week after injury, granulation tissue, fibroblasts, osteoblasts, chondroblasts and small islets of cartilage in the fibrous stroma appear. Osteoblasts produce a matrix of collagen and polysaccharide, which becomes impregnated with calcium to produce immature "woven" bone. The callus reaches its maximum size in 2–3 weeks. The next stage appears in 3–4 weeks and is marked by a hard bony callus, with the bone forming from periostial and endochondrial ossification. In the last stage, there is remodeling of the new bone from a woven appearance to mature bone.

References

1. Robertson I and Hodge PR, Histopathology of healing abrasions. *Forensic Sci* 1972;1:17-25.

2. Medical Letter, Jan.8, 1993. Vol 35 (Issue 887) p 1.

3. Robertson I, Antemortem and postmortem bruises of the skin: Their differentiation. *J. Forensic Med* 1957; 4:2-10.

4. Langlois NEI and Gresham GA, The aging of bruises: a review and study of the color changes with time. *Forensic Sci. Int* 1991 50:227-238.

5. Hernandez-Cueto C, Girela E, and Sweet DJ, Advances in the diagnosis of wound vitality: a review. *Am J. Forensic Med. Path.* 2000. 21(1):21-31.

6. Harkness JW, Ramsey WC, and Ahmadi B, Principles of fractures and dislocations, in Rockwood CA, Green DP (Eds): *Fractures in Adults,* Vol 1. Philadelphia, JP Lippincott, 1984.

7. Kress TA, Porta DJ, Snider JN, et al., Fracture pattern of human cadaver long bones. Presented 1995 International IRCOBI Conference on the Biomechanics of Impact. Sept 13-15, 1995. Brunnen Switzerland.

8. Porta DJ, Kress TA, Fuller PM, et al., Spiral fractures — definition and determination of torsional direction from radiographs. Presented at the Annual Meeting of the American Academy of Forensic Science, Nashville, February 19-24, 1996.

9. Pennal GF, Tile M, Waddell JP, et al, Pelvic disruption. *Clin Orthoped Related Res* 1980; 151:12-21.

10. Tile M, *Fractures of the Pelvis and Acetabulum.* Baltimore: Williams & Wilkins, 1984.

Blunt Trauma Injuries of the Trunk and Extremities

5

Blunt Force Injuries of the Chest

The thorax, or chest, is a bony-cartilaginous cage containing and protecting the heart, the lungs, and their major blood vessels. The posterior surface (the back) is formed by the 12 thoracic vertebrae and posterior aspect of the ribs. The sides are formed by the ribs, separated from each other by the intercostal spaces, 11 in number, which are occupied by the intercostal muscles. The sternum and the ribs make up the front. The diaphragm forms the floor of the chest cavities and separates the thoracic from the abdominal cavities.

The heart lies between the two lungs in the middle of the chest, enclosed within a sac, the pericardium; each lung is enclosed by a serous membrane, the pleura. The heart is placed obliquely in the chest behind the body of the sternum and adjoining parts of the ribs. It projects farther into the left chest cavity than the right, such that about one third of it is situated to the right and two thirds to the left of the midline.

Nonpenetrating blunt force injuries of the chest organs can occur with or without external evidence of injury to the chest wall. In some cases, the absence of external injury is attributed to the clothing worn by the victims. Children and young adults, whose chests are pliable and elastic, may sustain severe injuries to the intrathoracic viscera without fractures of the sternum and ribs, whereas in older people, fractures of the ribs and sternum are frequent.

Injury to the Ribs

There are four general types of rib fractures:

1. **Pathologic (spontaneous) rib fractures.** These occur in primary bone disease and tumors of bone.
2. **Iatrogenic (therapeutic) rib fractures.** During cardiopulmonary resuscitation (CPR), the patient may sustain multiple rib or sternal fractures,

mediastinal hemorrhage, and pneumothorax. In the elderly, and in chronically debilitated or malnourished individuals, the ribs are fragile and easily broken when minimal pressure or violence is applied to the chest. These fractures usually involve the first six ribs, tend to be more left sided than right, and are either anterolateral or anterior.

3. **Rib Fractures caused by direct localized violence.** Depending on where the force is applied, one or more of the underlying ribs might be fractured. If severe localized direct force is applied to the chest, the fractured ribs can contuse the underlying lung parenchyma or the sharp, pointed fragments of rib can be driven into the pleural cavity, lacerating the pleura, lung, or heart, resulting in pneumothorax or hemopneumothorax. Fractures of the first three ribs are frequently associated with severe injuries to the tracheobronchial airway and great vessels of the upper anterior chest, whereas fractures of ribs 10 through 12 can be associated with injuries to the diaphragm, liver, and spleen.

4. **Rib fractures caused by indirect violence.** In indirect violence, severe anteroposterior (front-to-back) compression of the chest, such as would be caused by a fall from a height or a car rolling over the chest, may fracture the ribs, most often on their curved lateral portions. If the compressing force is from behind toward the front, the ribs tend to be fractured near the spine; if from the sides of the chest, the ribs fracture near the spine and the sternum. The sharp, pointed fragments of the fractured ribs can lacerate the underlying pleura, lungs, and heart.

The complications of fractured ribs are:

- Flail chest
- Lacerations of the intercostal blood vessels with hemothorax
- Laceration of the lung with pneumothorax
- Laceration of the lung with hemopneumothorax
- Impaling wounds of the heart
- Pleurisy, empyema, and pneumonia

The Sternum

Injuries of the sternum can be either iatrogenic, e.g., during CPR, or the result of direct violence. Fractures are usually transverse and occur most frequently in the body of the sternum. They are caused by a violent impact on the anterior chest, e.g., impacting a steering wheel, someone's jumping on a chest, or from severe anteroposterior compression of the chest, such as might be caused by a car's running over the victim. Fractures secondary to CPR usually occur at the level of the third or fourth interspace.

The Heart

Blunt trauma to the thorax can produce a spectrum of life-threatening or fatal cardiac injuries ranging from commotio cordis to cardiac contusion to rupture of the heart.

Commotio Cordis

Sudden death from cardiac arrest following a sudden, blunt, non-penetrating impact to the chest in an individual with a normal heart and unassociated with structural injury to the heart, occurs, though rarely. It is most often reported in association with sports activities and young athletes.[1,2] The usual description of the event is of an individual struck in the chest by a baseball, a karate kick, etc., who then collapses virtually instantaneously or after a brief delay. The blow does not appear to be of sufficient magnitude to cause cardiac arrest. Evidence of impact is not present in a substantial number of cases (approximately half). Impact points appear to be mainly over the left ventricle. These deaths are believed to be caused by a primary ventricular dysrhythmia induced by an abrupt, blunt, pre-cordial blow incurred at an electrically vulnerable phase of ventricular excitability, e.g., the upstroke or peak of the T wave. CPR, even if performed immediately or in a timely period, appears to be ineffectual. This event has been reproduced in experiments where baseballs were propelled at high speed at animals' chests.[3]

Structural Injuries of the Heart

Any massive crushing force applied to the anterior chest can cause bursting lacerations of the pericardium. These lacerations are almost invariably associated with injury to the heart or major blood vessels. The heart, protected in front by the sternum and ribs, is suspended in the pericardial sac by the aorta, pulmonary artery, and vena cava. The front or anterior surface of the heart is formed chiefly by the right ventricle and, to a lesser extent, the left ventricle. Traumatic injuries of the heart are caused by severe direct violence to the anterior chest. The nature of the injuries depends on the severity of the localized violence, whether the impact is inflicted while the heart is filled with blood, and whether the force applied is sufficient to compress or crush the heart between the sternum and vertebral column. Injuries to the heart are usually associated with injury to other structures of the chest. Blunt chest trauma is frequently caused by automobile accidents. The driver sustains this trauma when the chest forcibly strikes the steering wheel, the front-seat passenger when the chest strikes the dashboard. Air bags, and a lap belt combined with a good shoulder belt or harness can prevent or minimize this injury.

A localized force applied directly to the chest might be sufficient to cause a contusion of the anterior wall of either ventricle or the interventricular septum. Hemorrhage can occur in the conduction system with resultant arrhythmias.[4] Grossly, recent contusions appear as dark red, hemorrhagic areas. They must not be confused with an acute myocardial infarct. If the localized impact drives the heart against the vertebral column, a contusion of the posterior wall of either ventricle or the interventricular septum could result. A posterior cardiac contusion must not be confused with postmortem lividity, a change frequently found on the posterior ventricular surfaces of the heart. Microscopic study of the antemortem contusion will reveal localized interstitial hemorrhage and injured myocardial fibers. With cellular injury, there are EKG changes and release of cellular enzymes (e.g., troponin). Primary trauma to the heart must, but cannot always, be differentiated from iatrogenic injury due to CPR, open cardiac massage, or intracardiac injections, especially if resuscitation is prolonged. The contused myocardium usually heals without any *sequelae* or residual injury. Rarely, it may undergo necrosis with rupture into the pericardial sac several days after the injury. It may also heal with fibrotic replacement of the contused myocardium and, rarely, form an aneurysm. Killen et al. reported a case of a posttraumatic pseudo-aneurysm of the left ventricle.[5] They collected 12 more cases from a review of the literature. Complications were arrhythmia, cardiac failure, and embolism.

Lacerations of the heart occur primarily when a very severe crushing force is applied to the anterior chest. They can involve one or more areas of the heart, that is, atria, interatrial septum, ventricles, interventricular septum, papillary muscles, chordae tendinae, or cardiac valves. Cardiac lacerations infrequently occur as isolated injuries (Figure 5.1). Most often, they occur with other severe chest injuries. Rapid cardiac failure occurs whenever a cardiac valve, chordae tendinae, or papillary muscle is lacerated. Bolooki et al., while reporting two cases of ventricular septal defects produced by penetrating chest injuries, noted that defects caused by blunt trauma have been reported more frequently in the literature than defects from penetrating trauma.[6]

In 1971, Simson described the chin-sternum-heart syndrome.[7] This syndrome is known to occur in parachutists wearing protective helmets when there is incomplete deployment or partial failure of a parachute. The pattern of cardiac injury, multiple atrial, endocardial and myocardial lacerations, is associated with sternal compression by the chin with laceration of the chin. One of the authors (DJD) has encountered a similar syndrome in individuals who have fallen down stairs, sustaining severe flexion injury to the neck. There is injury to the chin, compression or fracture of the sternum, cardiac injury, and cervical spine fracture with injury to the spinal cord. In some cases of blunt trauma to the chest, the ribs are fractured, with the fractured ends puncturing the heart.

If the pericardial sac is not torn, a laceration of the heart will result in rapid death due to cardiac tamponade. As little as 150 mL of blood can cause death. The resultant increase in the intrapericardial pressure due to cardiac tamponade interferes with the entry of blood into the right heart and produces

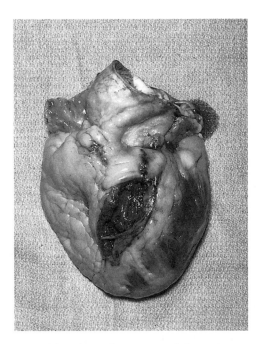

Figure 5.1 A 62-year-old male with rupture of the right ventricle of the heart at the interventricular septum due to impact of chest on steering wheel. No external injuries present.

mechanical interference with the contractility of the ventricular myocardium. If the pericardial sac is lacerated, bleeding will occur into the pleural cavities.

On rare occasions, blunt force trauma to the anterior chest causes direct injury to a coronary artery, almost invariably the left anterior descending branch. Atherosclerotic vessels are more susceptible to trauma. Injury to coronary arteries can produce coronary occlusion from an intraluminal thrombus, hemorrhage into an atherosclerotic plaque, intimal laceration or a traumatic dissecting aneurysm.[8,9] Because of its medicolegal implication, the diagnosis of traumatic coronary thrombosis must be made with caution. Objective evidence supportive of this diagnosis is:

- Injury to the chest wall and/or heart (fracture of the sternum and/or ribs overlying the thrombosed coronary artery, and/or injury to the myocardium adjacent to the thrombosed coronary artery)
- An incomplete tear of the wall of the thrombosed coronary artery, especially if survival is greater than 8–12 h and a myocardial infarction is present
- Finding the age of the infarct, when observed microscopically, to be consistent with the time interval between alleged coronary artery injury and death

In addition, serial electrocardiograph studies and cardiac enzyme determinations consistent with the time interval from trauma to testing support the hypothesis of injury to a coronary artery. It must not be forgotten, however, that posttraumatic coronary artery thrombosis may occur not as a primary complication of trauma but secondary to shock and intravascular stasis of blood, factors that are conducive to thrombus formation in victims with coronary atherosclerosis.

The Aorta

The heart is suspended in the pericardial sac by the aorta, pulmonary artery, and superior vena cava. Any force that violently compresses the anterior chest and forces the heart downward may exert sufficient traction on the aorta to tear it transversely. The superior vena cava and the pulmonary artery are rarely torn. Aortic lacerations are most often seen in automobile accidents, less commonly in falls. In automobile accidents, aortic lacerations occur in both head-on and side-impact crashes.

Virtually all lacerations of the thoracic aorta involve the descending portion, immediately distal to the origin of the left subclavian artery (Figure 5.2). The arch of the aorta is anchored by the great vessels arising from the aortic arch, that is, the right innominate, left common carotid, and subclavian arteries, and the ligamentum arteriosum (which connects the left pulmonary artery to the arch of the aorta). Partial or complete lacerations of the descending aorta occur at almost precisely the same location — just distal to the origin of the left subclavian artery, at the junction of the aortic arch and the descending aorta (figure 5.2–5.3).

The precise mechanism of this injury is not known. The relatively constant location of aortic lacerations, the relative fixation of the descending aorta just below the aortic isthmus, the relative fixation of the aortic arch by the vessels, and the constant association of the aortic laceration with deceleration injuries, such as automobile collisions, suggest that the abrupt deceleration of the body and resulting forceful compression of the anterior chest and underlying mediastinal structures cause the heart and great vessels to be jerked away from the posterior chest wall to which the thoracic aorta is attached. This traction on the ligament ductus arteriosus and descending aorta at its point of fixation is sufficient to lacerate the aorta immediately below the origin of the left subclavian artery.

Rarely, a periaortic hematoma due to an aortic laceration may evolve into a false aneurysm. The blood at the periphery of the hematoma, which is contained by the periaortic and mediastinal soft tissue undergoes organization until a restraining fibrous connective tissue wall is formed — the false aneurysm. This outer wall becomes adherent to the surrounding mediastinal structures, e.g., the tracheobronchial tree and esophagus, incorporating them

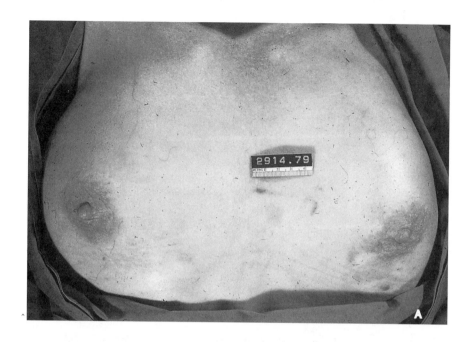

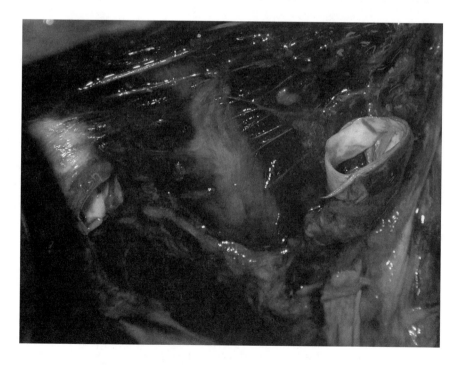

Figure 5.2 (A and B) Operator of motor vehicle with minor contusion of chest and complete transection of aorta.

Figure 5.3 Small laceration of aorta, distal to origin of left subclavian artery.

into the wall. Ultimately, the lining of the aneurysmal sac becomes continuous with the endothelium lining the aortic lumen. Because the false aneurysmal wall is composed of fibrous tissue without elastic tissue, continued aneurysmal enlargement is inevitable.

Bursting rupture of the ascending portion and arch of the aorta occur when a violent force compresses the heart and intrapericardial portion of the ascending aorta, producing a sudden rise in intracardiac and intraluminal pressure that results in a transverse tear of the aorta immediately above the cusps of the aortic valve (**Figure** 5.4).[10,11] This usually involves only a portion of the aorta's circumference. Death rapidly ensues from severe hemorrhage. These injuries are associated with fractures of the upper ribs and sternum.

While transmural rupture of the aorta due to trauma is common, traumatic dissection of the aorta is relatively rare.[12] Even rarer is a traumatic dissecting aneurysm of the ascending and arch of the aorta.[13,14] With regard to traumatic dissecting aortic aneurysms, Papadopoulos et al. reported the case of a 50-year-old hypertensive male who had sustained a steering wheel injury 4 years prior to admission to the hospital for sudden onset of pain in the lower back and left lower extremity.[15] The pain subsided rapidly, but the patient developed severe intermittent claudication. A translumbar aortogram revealed a dilated aorta with complete occlusion of the left common iliac artery. At surgery, a huge dissecting aneurysm of the descending thoracic aorta was found, with the intimal tear starting just distal to the left subclavian

Figure 5.4 Motor vehicle accident with compression of chest and laceration of ascending aorta.

artery. The true lumen of the distal thoracic aorta was very narrow. A review of the literature up to October 1975 by these authors revealed 138 cases of chronic traumatic aneurysmal lesions of the thoracic aorta.[15]

Traumatic rupture of the ascending aorta must not be confused with spontaneous ruptures associated with cystic medial necrosis, which frequently occur in this area. Grossly, the lesions might resemble each other. However, absence of injuries and the microscopic characteristics of cystic medial necrosis will differentiate the nontraumatic from the traumatic rupture. In cases of suspected traumatic laceration of the aorta, all natural diseases that might cause spontaneous rupture or aneurysmal formation, e.g., atherosclerosis, syphilis, or cystic medical necrosis, must be sought. It must be realized, however, that even if these conditions do exist, rupture could still be due to trauma.

Heggtveit et al. reported two cases of innominate artery aneurysms occurring after blunt trauma following a motor vehicle accident.[16] In such a case, the victim sustains injury to the chest just to the right of the sternum. This impact may produce nonpenetrating injury to the innominate artery and development of an aneurysm.

Traumatic rupture of the abdominal aorta, either partial or complete, is relatively uncommon, if not rare. Most but not all are caused by automobile accidents.[17] Rupture is commonly associated with fracture-dislocation of the underlying vertebrae.

Diaphragm

Traumatic rupture of the diaphragm is most often caused by severe blunt trauma to the lower anterior chest. It is frequently associated with fractures of the ribs and thoracoabdominal injuries. Violent compressive force applied to the lower anterior chest will cause overstretching and twisting of the diaphragmatic leaf, which ultimately ruptures. Forcible upward displacement of the abdominal viscera against the undersurface of the diaphragm may also create sufficient pressure to rupture the diaphragm. The severe crushing force applied to the lower chest-upper abdomen may produce a large hemidiaphragmatic defect with ragged hemorrhagic edges. The defect is usually large enough for protrusion of the abdominal viscera into the thoracic cavity. Traumatic rupture of the diaphragm is more common on the left. This is allegedly thanks to the protection afforded the right diaphragmatic leaf by the liver.

Rupture of the left hemidiaphragmatic leaf permits the stomach, intestine, omentum, or spleen to herniate into the left pleural cavity. The left lung is compressed and the heart displaced to the right. Herniation occurs because of the difference between the positive pressure cavity of the abdomen and the negative pressure cavity of the thorax. The presence of the liver on the right side acts as a plug if an opening is made. Rarely, a part of the liver can pass through and become tightly constricted at the margin of the rent like a strangulated hernia.

Lungs

Pneumothorax may be due to natural disease, medical procedures, or trauma. Spontaneous pneumothorax may occur following rupture of an emphysematous bulla. Iatrogenic pneumothorax can be caused by external cardiac massage, percutaneously inserted subclavian catheters and continuous ventilatory support.[18,19] Thus, in 168 cases of pneumothorax, 54 occurred during or immediately following closed chest cardiac massage (49 on the left side and 5 on the right).[18] There were associated ipsilateral anterolateral rib fractures in 43 of these patients. Of the 54 patients, 45 had also received intracardiac medication administered percutaneous through the left side of the chest. Whether this contributed to the pneumothorax was unknown. In 51 patients, pneumothorax occurred following percutaneous insertion of a catheter in the subclavian vein. In addition, 61 patients developed pneumothorax during continuous ventilatory support, and two patients during tracheo-stomy. In 1982, Newman et al. noted the increased frequency of catheter complications involving the subclavian and internal jugular veins secondary to total parenteral nutrition.[19]

Traumatic rupture of the intrathoracic trachea and bronchus is usually the result of severe compressive injury of the chest. The most frequent site of rupture of the tracheobronchial tree is within 2.5 cm of the carina, especially in the main bronchi. Cases of combined injury to the trachea and bronchus occur infrequently. Approximately 30% of the victims have anterior fractures of the second and third ribs. Winter and Baum[20] reviewed the various mechanisms that have been suggested as being responsible for these injuries:

- Compression of a main bronchus against the vertebral column
- Direct compression by the sternum against a closed glottis
- Sudden rise in intraluminal pressure during forced expiration against a closed glottis with explosive effect
- Shearing forces that cut across the hilar areas
- Deceleration of the pendulous lungs moving forward against the relatively more fixed trachea and proximal bronchi

Most likely, there are several causative mechanisms with any one or a combination of these mechanisms producing bronchial or tracheal injury.

In children, adolescents, and young adults, severe trauma to the chest may cause the flexible thoracic cage to be markedly compressed without fracturing the sternum, ribs, and costal cartilages. A normal lung, because of its elastic structures, is capable of withstanding gradual compression without injury. However, a sudden forcible blow to the chest could be sufficient to cause a contusion of the lung secondary to an inward bending of the rib(s). In children, it is not unusual to see a distinct subpleural hemorrhage corresponding to the width of the impacting rib. A localized blow to the chest compresses air within the alveoli that normally escapes via the air passages. If the air is trapped within the alveoli because the air passages are obstructed, the intra-alveolar air pressure will increase until it exceeds the limits of alveolar elasticity, at which time the alveoli rupture, resulting in intra-alveolar hemorrhage.

Osborn refers to contusions of the posterior surface of the lungs as *contrecoup* contusions.[21] He found them to be in an almost constant position corresponding to the angle of the ribs. He further stated that the thorax is typically compressed from the front and sides, the posterior parts near the spine being relatively fixed; hence, the typical contrecoup lesion is posterior. If the alveoli under the site of impact fail to absorb the force of the striking rib, the anterior alveoli transmit the force to the posterior alveoli, causing the contusion of the posterior surface of the lung. Resolution of a pure pulmonary contusion is rapid and complete without residual scarring. Generally, improvement occurs within 48 h and clearing is complete a few days later.

Multiple unilateral or bilateral rib fractures give rise to the "flail" chest with consequent paradoxical respiration. In such instances, inspiratory effort resulting from diaphragmatic descent is associated with inward motion of the injured thoracic wall, with little or no ensuing ventilatory exchange. The increased work of breathing creates only increased negative intrapleural pressure changes, which in turn cause more paradoxical motion of the chest wall. This, combined with reduced pulmonary ventilatory efficiency caused by trauma to lung parenchyma, leads quickly to hypoxia.

If a person is run over by an automobile or crushed beneath an overturned car or falling debris, the resulting injuries to the lung may consist of bursting ruptures. These occur most often when the glottis is closed and a severe compressive force is applied to the chest. The compressed intra-alveolar and intrabronchial air is trapped because it is unable to escape via the normal air passages, which are occluded. The intrabronchial and intra-alveolar air pressure will progressively increase, causing marked dilatation of the alveoli, which ultimately rupture, resulting in intrapulmonary hemorrhage and possibly a pneumothorax. In adults, the crushing force applied to the anterior chest will fracture the ribs, costal cartilages, and sternum, whereas the same force applied to the posterior chest will drive the fractured ribs and vertebrae into the chest cavities. In children, adolescents and young adults, the flexible and elastic rib cage will resist fracturing.

A grinding force will produce multiple fractures of the ribs, costal cartilages, and sternum, with mangling of the lungs. Intrapulmonary tears (lacerations) occur when the crushing force drives the chest inward, compressing the intrathoracic organs and exerting downward traction on the lung tissue. The intrapulmonary tears may be small and multiple, or single and large beneath an intact pleura.

Usually, a simple fracture of the rib will neither contuse nor lacerate the underlying lung. However, if the impact to the chest is forceful enough to cause inward displacement of the fractured ends of the ribs, they may puncture and lacerate the underlying pleura and lung. During postmortem examination, the inwardly driven broken ends of the fractured ribs may not be evident because they may have rebounded, giving the appearance of a simple fracture.

Complications of Lung Injuries

Hemothorax may result from lacerations of the lungs. Bleeding into the pleural cavity is not significant if the laceration is small because of the

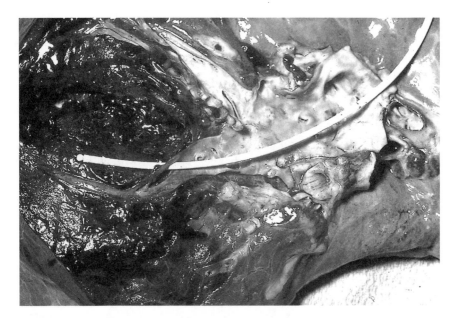

Figure 5.5   Perforation of pulmonary artery by Swan-Ganz catheter with massive dissecting hemorrhage into pulmonary parenchyma and rupture into chest cavity.

contractility of the elastic lungs and compression of the laceration by the expanding hemothorax. Massive intrapleural bleeding occurs, however, if the laceration is large and involves large blood vessels. Hemothorax might be augmented by bleeding from lacerations of the mediastinal tissues, diaphragm, and internal mammary or intercostal arteries following fractures of the sternum and/or ribs. Blunt chest trauma can overstretch and lacerate old pleural adhesions, producing intrapleural bleeding. The amount of bleeding is dependent on the degree of vascularization of the pleural adhesions. During therapeutic or diagnostic thoracentesis, the needle may puncture and lacerate the intercostal artery, causing bleeding into the pleural cavity. Perforation of a pulmonary artery by a Swan-Ganz catheter may occur with a resultant hemothorax (Figure 5.5).

Lacerated wounds of the lung can also result in leakage of air into the pleural cavity, producing a pneumothorax. When the pneumothorax is associated with intrapleural bleeding, it is called a pneumohemothorax. A tension pneumothorax can develop when the laceration penetrates deep into the lung and severs a large bronchus. With each inspiration, air entering the bronchus escapes into the pleural cavity. On expiration, the lacerated edges of the bronchus act as a valve to prevent the air from passing out of the pleural cavity through the bronchus. With each inspiration, the volume and pressure of the trapped air increases until the air pressure is high enough to collapse the lung and displace the mediastinum and heart to the opposite side. At autopsy, the pleural cavity contains a collapsed lung with air under pressure, a concave depressed diaphragm, and displacement of the heart and mediastinum to the opposite side. When a lacerated wound of the lung involves a pulmonary vein and adjacent bronchus, air exiting the bronchus may enter the pulmonary vein and be conveyed to the left atrium and ventricle, with resultant cardiac and cerebral air embolus.

If the blood in a pleural cavity is not removed, it will gradually break down, undergoing a series of color changes, red to brown, with the ultimate formation of a chocolate brown pigment deposit and turbid brown fluid. Intrapleural blood may be diluted by serous effusion. The lacerated lung, hemothorax, and diluting serous fluid are vulnerable to bacterial injection with production of pneumonia, lung abscesses, pleurisy, and empyema.

A diagnostic needle biopsy of the pleura or lung or a diagnostic or therapeutic thoracentesis may terminate in sudden death during insertion of the needle into the pleural cavity with no anatomical cause of death at autopsy. The exact mechanism of death is unknown.

Blunt Force Injuries of the Abdominal Viscera

The abdominal organs are vulnerable to a variety of injuries from blunt trauma because the lax and compressible abdominal walls, composed of skin, fascia, and muscle, readily transmit the force applied to the abdominal viscera. If the victim anticipates the blow and tightens the abdominal muscles, this will disperse the force of impact and thereby reduce the probability of internal injuries. Thus, the boxer who has conditioned his abdominal muscles and is prepared to receive such blows will sustain no injury to his abdominal organs.

The type of injury an abdominal organ will sustain depends on the organ involved. The soft, compact, vascular liver and spleen may be lacerated or crushed; a distended hollow organ, such as the stomach or intestines, will burst due to the rapid increase in intraluminal pressure produced by the force of impact. The severity of trauma is relative to the size of the blunt object, the force of impact, the organ traumatized and its condition at the time of impact. It cannot be overemphasized that absence of external injury (contusions or abrasions) to the abdominal walls does not exclude injury, even massive injury, to one or more of the internal abdominal organs (Figure 5.6). The lack of external injuries is attributable to the lax and compressible abdominal walls and protection afforded by clothing. If a traumatized victim complains of abdominal pains, but lacks visible signs of injury to the abdomen, the emergency room physician or surgeon may fail to clinically detect

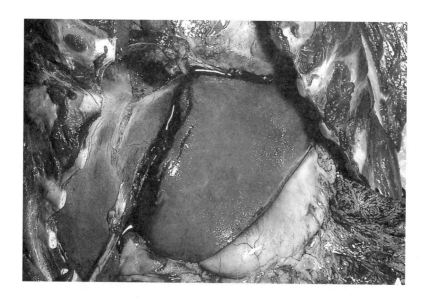

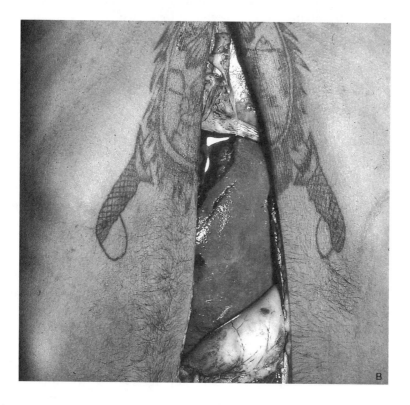

Figure 5.6 (A) Complete transection of liver (B) without any evidence of external trauma to anterior abdominal wall.

the early signs of intra-abdominal injury, and thus delay a lifesaving operation. This is especially true of intoxicated victims and individuals on high doses of tranquilizer whose condition renders them insensible to pain and obscures the signs of peritoneal irritation.

A 21-year-old male, involved in a motor vehicle accident, was admitted to a local hospital with pain in the left abdominal region. Vital signs were normal; physical examination was essentially negative, except for severe tenderness in the periumbilical area. The patient's abdomen was flat and soft. Bowel sounds were normal. X-ray studies of the abdomen, in the flat and upright position, revealed no evidence of abnormality. The intestinal gas pattern was normal. The hepatic, splenic, renal, and psoas outlines were unremarkable. There was no evidence of free abdominal air or fluid. Approximately 28 h later, he was DOA at another hospital. At autopsy, 2000 mL of purulent material was found in the peritoneal cavity. Fifty centimeters from the duodenum, there was a 2 x 2-cm laceration of the proximal jejunum, with communication with the peritoneal cavity. The mesentery showed a 3 x 5-cm contusion and recent thrombi of the superior mesenteric veins.

Trauma to the abdomen may be generalized, involving the abdomen as a whole, as exemplified by an individual run over by a vehicle, or localized, such as would occur if an individual was kicked in the abdomen. Most homicides resulting from blunt force involve localized injuries to the abdomen. Possibly only through a thorough investigation of the circumstances surrounding the victim's death will one be able to determine whether the blunt force injury was of a homicidal or accidental nature.

Since many individuals receive cardiopulmonary resuscitation nowadays, it is extremely important to differentiate iatrogenic injuries of the abdominal organs from those due primarily to trauma. Thus, with vigorous, slightly misplaced cardiopulmonary resuscitation, the authors have seen lacerations of the liver where it overlies the vertebral column. Several hundred milliliters of blood were present in the abdominal cavity in some cases, even though these injuries were, in a sense, postmortem.

In 1983, Ducatman et al. described three cases of fatal rectus sheath hematoma.[22] This entity is characterized by apparent spontaneous nontraumatic hemorrhage into the rectus sheath, usually occurring after anticoagulant therapy. It may be either an immediate or contributory cause of death.

Liver

The liver lies in the upper right quadrant of the abdominal cavity. It is partly protected by the lower ribs and the xiphoid process of the sternum. It is the largest of the solid abdominal organs and is the one most frequently injured by blunt trauma to the abdomen. Severe localized blunt trauma applied to the right upper quadrant will often lacerate only the liver, whereas generalized blunt trauma tends to injure not only the liver, but the other abdominal organs, though with less frequency. Fractures of the adjacent ribs may or may not be present, depending on the age of the individual and the calcification of the ribs.

The liver is susceptible to trauma because of its large size, its anatomic position in the upper abdomen, its inability to give with trauma, and the solid nature of its tissue. A preexisting liver disease, such as fatty metamorphosis or hepatitis, may make the liver more friable and thus easier to injure. In addition, fatty metamorphosis is often associated with impairment of the coagulability of blood. Injuries of the liver can be classified as **transcapsular lacerations**, in which both capsule and parenchyma are torn, and **subcapsular lacerations**, in which the capsule is still intact and the injury is either beneath an intact capsule or intraparenchymal. The right lobe is injured five times as frequently as the left, with the lesions occurring more commonly on the convex surface. Any severe localized force applied directly to the front of the liver will drive the liver in a posterior direction, crushing it against the posterior vertebral column, and producing a transcapsular laceration at the junction between the right and left lobes, immediately beneath the site of external impact (Figure 5.6). A variation of this is the contrecoup laceration of the liver where the laceration occurs on the posterior surface of the right lobe, at the point where it rests against the vertebral column. The same localized force that can produce transcapsular lacerations, if violent enough and directed to the front of the liver, may compress the liver, not only in a backward direction, but also in a lateral direction, causing an internal (subcapsular) laceration of the parenchyma.

Blunt trauma applied directly to the front of the liver may strip the capsule from its parenchymal attachment at the point of impact, resulting in the development of a subcapsular hematoma. Either the hematoma will undergo complete organization and be replaced by a thick fibrous connective tissue capsule, or continuous subcapsular bleeding may create sufficient pressure to rupture with a resultant fatal intraperitoneal hemorrhage. Rupture of the subcapsular hematoma may occur days after the time of impact.

If the force impacting the front of the liver is directed upward, it may lacerate the inferior (under) surface of the liver, whereas, if the force is directed downward and backward, there is deformation of the dome of the liver with lacerations of the superior surface. Multiple superficial capsular lacerations of the diaphragmatic or superior surface of the right lobe of the liver are common in motor vehicle accidents.

If the force is directed straight at the liver, along its anterior margin, there can be lacerations of both the concave and convex surfaces. With severe crushing force applied over the front of the liver, such as might occur in a severe automobile accident or a brutal kick to the abdomen, there could be complete amputation of the left lobe of the liver when it is crushed between the anterior abdominal wall and the vertebral column.

In addition to injuries to the parenchyma of the liver itself, there may also be injuries to the portal vein, hepatic artery, and inferior vena cava. Isolated injury to these vessels themselves are extremely rare, since any force sufficient to injure them would also produce extensive injuries to the liver.

Mays, in an experimental study, attempted to determine the amount of energy necessary to produce injuries to the liver.[23] He found that, in the energy range of 27–34 ft lb, there were tears and lacerations of the capsule, but intrahepatic damage to the vascular and biliary trees was absent. If the energy was increased to 106–134 ft lb, there was crevicing of the liver externally, but only an occasional disruption of a small bile duct or hepatic artery. There was no disruption of the major vascular or biliary trees. Increasing the energy to 285–360 ft lb caused extensive pulpefaction of the liver, bursting injuries, and severe disruption of the tributaries of the hepatic artery, portal vein, and bile ducts, though the major divisions themselves remained intact.

As previously noted, not all injuries to the liver are of a primary traumatic basis. Thus, one can have injuries caused by cardiopulmonary resuscitation, liver biopsy, angiographic vascular studies, and introduction of chemotherapeutic agents via the hepatic arteries. The authors have seen cases in which needle biopsies were performed only to have the patient exsanguinate a number of hours later due to massive intra-abdominal hemorrhage from the biopsy site. Intraperitoneal hemorrhage may also be due to rupture of a hepatic tumor.

Isolated traumatic rupture of the gallbladder due to blunt trauma is uncommon. Bursting rupture of the gallbladder, if present, is usually associated with massive injury to the liver. Isolated rupture of the gallbladder is said to be more common in children and young adults, possibly because their chests are more easily compressed. Leakage of bile into the abdominal cavity would cause chemical peritonitis.

Pancreas

The pancreas is located retroperitoneally, closely applied to the posterior abdominal wall. It is composed of a head, neck, body, and tail, with the head lodged in the curve of the duodenum. The neck and body are in proximity to the portal vein, inferior vena cava, and aorta, overlying the body of the second lumbar vertebra. The tail crosses the upper pole of the left kidney, terminating in the gastric surface of the spleen, in contact with the left flexure of the colon. Blunt force injuries to the pancreas are not common because of its posterior location and considerable distance from the anterior abdominal wall. If a severe localized force were applied to the epigastric region of the abdomen and injury to the pancreas incurred, it would generally be at the point where the pancreas overlies the second lumbar vertebra. Contusions, lacerations, and transections can occur at this point. With lacerations of the pancreas, there is associated injury to the pancreatic ducts, with loss of pancreatic secretions into the abdominal cavity and chemical peritonitis.

Trauma to the pancreas can result in residual pseudocysts, either peripancreatic or intrapancreatic. In the peripancreatic cyst, blood and pancreatic secretions accumulate around the pancreas, beneath the intact peritoneum, forming a peripancreatic hematoma. Resolution leads to the formation of a cyst filled with clear fluid. The cyst wall is devoid of epithelial lining, but does contain hemosiderin-laden macrophages and hemosiderin deposits in the fibrous connective tissue wall. In an intrapancreatic cyst, there is intrapancreatic bleeding, resulting in the formation of hematoma. With resolution, there is a cyst whose wall, again, is devoid of epithelial lining but contains hemosiderin. In contrast, neoplastic or congenital cysts have a distinct epithelial lining. Most pseudocysts of the pancreas are not caused by trauma, but rather are a result of pancreatitis.

Spleen

The spleen lies in the left upper quadrant of the abdomen, extending to the epigastric region and lying between the fundus of the stomach and the diaphragm. It is not as frequently injured as the liver because of its well-protected position in the left upper quadrant of the abdomen. Spontaneous rupture of the spleen, unassociated with any significant trauma, is associated with any condition that produces splenomegaly and an increased fragility of the parenchyma. The most common of such conditions are infectious mononucleosis, malaria, and leukemia. While this rupture is said to be spontaneous, it may actually be due to a trivial, perhaps unrecalled, traumatic episode that would have absolutely no significance in a normal individual.

Iatrogenic splenic rupture during cardiopulmonary resuscitation is extremely uncommon. If it does occur, it is probable that the spleen was not normal to begin with, but enlarged.

Severe trauma to the left upper quadrant of the abdomen can produce lacerations or bursting ruptures of the spleen. The extent of injury depends on the severity of the force and whether it is localized or generalized. Injuries can range from a small superficial capsular laceration up to virtual disintegration of the spleen. In some instances, the force delivered to the spleen is sufficient to lacerate the splenic parenchyma, but not to injure the capsule. If internal bleeding continues, a subcapsular hematoma could form. This may stop enlarging after a time and resolve, resulting in an area of scarring. If the bleeding continues, there will be a progressive increase in subcapsular pressure with rupture of the capsule and resultant intraperitoneal hemorrhage. The rupture of the capsule may occur hours or even days after the trauma. It might be due just to the buildup in pressure or be precipitated by another incident of trauma, even if it is minor. Microscopic sections will show that one is dealing with a delayed rupture of a subcapsular hematoma. During the period of development of the subcapsular hematoma and prior to its rupture, the patient may be either asymptomatic or complain of vague abdominal pain.

Gastrointestinal Tract

Traumatic injuries of the esophagus secondary to blunt trauma are rare and of little interest to the forensic pathologist, because they rarely result in death. Probably of most interest is **agonal** or **postmortem esophagogastromalacia** (autodigestion of the lower esophagus and stomach). This phenomenon is occasionally seen in debilitated patients or individuals who die after a prolonged coma. While the lower esophagus may be involved, it is the stomach that is principally involved. The tissue has a grayish-white to black appearance and is extremely friable. Microscopically, there is absence of any inflammation. This phenomenon occurs either immediately prior to death or, more probably, immediately after death and is of no clinical significance.

Repeated violent vomiting can produce lacerations of the esophagus, even perforations, at its lower end, where it meets the stomach. These lacerations are usually single in number, longitudinal, and on the lateral or posterior wall. They can range from superficial, involving only the mucosa, to complete lacerations of the wall with perforation. Lacerations of the esophagus in this area are most frequently seen in alcoholics, following prolonged bouts of violent and excessive vomiting (Mallory-Weiss Syndrome). Normally, in vomiting, the pyloric sphincter contracts and the lower and upper esophageal sphincters relax prior to contracture of the gastric musculature. It is postulated that, during violent spasmodic vomiting, if the upper esophageal sphincter fails to relax, the powerful contractions of the gastric musculature, aided by abdominal wall contractions, will propel the gastric contents into the esophagus. There is sufficient violence to cause a rapid rise in intraesophageal pressure, with rupture of the esophagus at its weakest point, the posterior lateral wall. This could result in mediastinal emphysema, bilateral hydrothorax, hydropneumothorax, or massive hemorrhage, which is the terminal event in the Mallory-Weiss syndrome.

Rupture of the hollow abdominal viscera, for example, the stomach or bowel, is relatively uncommon because of the mobility of the individual segments, which enables them to be easily displaced by the full impact of a blow. When rupture does occur, death is usually due to peritonitis that resulted from the spillage of intestinal contents into the peritoneal cavity. The stomach lies in the left upper quadrant of the abdomen, extending to the epigastric and umbilical region. The greater part of the stomach, the fundus and body, is protected by the ribs. Injuries to the stomach are virtually all caused by localized blunt force applied to the epigastric or left upper quadrant, for example, a kick or a blow with the fist. This crushes the stomach between the anterior abdominal wall and the posterior vertebral column. Depending on the severity of the injury, there might be a contusion or actual perforation of the wall of the stomach. While injury to the stomach may be a solitary traumatic lesion, more often it occurs in association with other major abdominal trauma. The stomach may perforate immediately or the contusion may progress to a point of necrosis with subsequent perforation due to the digestive action of the gastric acids.

In most cases of rupture of the stomach, the stomach is distended with food or drink.[24] The more distended, the more vulnerable the stomach is to blunt force injury. An impact to the anterior abdominal wall compresses the stomach between the abdominal wall and the vertebral column, creating a sudden increase in intragastric pressure that is distributed uniformly over the entire stomach. If the pyloric sphincter and cardiac orifice are relaxed, the compressing force displaces the stomach contents into the duodenum and esophagus and the stomach is partially protected from the injury. If, however, the stomach contents are not evacuated, the rapid increase in intra-gastric pressure will overcome the resistance of the gastric wall, with resultant rupture. Rupture can occur in any portion of the stomach, but the anterior wall seems to be most often involved. There is usually a circular defect with ragged ecchymotic edges. In addition to the aforementioned causes of perforation, the stomach can also be perforated during endoscopic examination or biopsy, or by a feeding tube.

There are three possible mechanisms for rupture of the bowel: compression between the anterior abdominal wall and the vertebral column or pelvis; deceleration at points of fixation (usually the Ligament of Treitz or the ileocecal junction) or a local area of increased intra-luminal pressure.

Immediately distal to the stomach is the duodenum. It is situated in the umbilical region. Beginning at the pylorus, it is divided into four regions: the superior, descending, horizontal, and ascending portions.

The first three portions encircle the head of the pancreas. The ascending fourth portion overlies the vertebral column from the fourth to the second lumbar vertebrae where it becomes the jejunum. The ascending portion of the duodenum and the duodenojejunal flexure are fixed by the ligament of Treitz. Severe blunt force trauma to the abdomen may injure the duodenum, with the most common site of injury in the vicinity of the ligament of Treitz.

The fixed distal portion of the duodenum is compressed between the anterior abdominal wall and the lumbar vertebrae. Injury may range from a contusion to perforation to transection. The contusion may subsequently evolve into a perforation if it is severe enough to devitalize the wall by hemorrhage. In such a case, the duodenal perforation might occur hours or days after the injury was sustained. If the duodenum is distended at the time of impact, there could be a bursting rupture at the duodenojejunal flexure. The points of rupture are usually small and ovoid, with ragged ecchymotic edges.

The jejunal portion of the small bowel principally occupies the umbilical and left iliac region, while the ileum chiefly occupies the umbilical, hypogastric, right iliac, and pelvic regions. The terminal portion of the ileum usually lies in the pelvis in the right iliac region, where it opens into the cecum. The jejunum and ileum are attached to the posterior abdominal wall by a fold of peritoneum, the mesentery, which allows free movement of the jejunum and ileum. Blood vessels and nerves run through the mesentery. There is an increased incidence of injury to the jejunum and ileum in comparison with the stomach and duodenum, with the jejunum injured more often than the ileum.[25]

In most instances of severe abdominal impact, the small intestine is crushed between the anterior abdominal wall and the vertebral column or pelvis. The resultant lesion, a contusion, perforation, or transection, depends on the severity of the blunt force and the area over which it is applied. A severe contusion can progress to a delayed perforation several hours or days after injury. Transection of the jejunum usually occurs just distal to the ligament of Treitz, where the jejunum is firmly attached to the posterior abdominal wall. In transection of the small bowel, there is usually associated injury to the mesentery. Spontaneous rupture of the small bowel may occur due to infarctions secondary to incarceration, strangulation, various ulcerative diseases of the mucosa, and thrombosis of the mesenteric vasculature.

With severe blunt trauma to the abdomen and injury to internal organs, the mesentery of the small intestine is often contused or torn. There can be either single or multiple lacerations. The mesentery appears to be torn most often by a tangential blow to the abdomen that exerts traction on the membrane. Death could occur solely from injury to the mesentery if there is laceration of one of the large blood vessels coursing through the mesentery.

The large intestine differs from the small intestine in its larger caliber, more fixed position and less vulnerability to trauma. The midportion or transverse colon is the most open to trauma because of its relation to the vertebral column and its exposed position in the mid abdominal cavity. A severe impact to the anterior abdominal wall may crush the midportion of the transverse colon between the anterior abdominal wall and the lumbar vertebrae. The resulting traumatic lesion depends on the severity of the blunt force and might range from a contusion to a laceration to transection. Rupture of the colon may also occur following insertion of foreign objects, hands, or animals for sexual stimulation.[26] Iatrogenic rupture of the colon can occur during sigmoidoscopy, proctoscopy, or a high colonic enema. Occasionally, a barium enema will result in perforation of the colon.

Kidneys

The kidneys are situated in the posterior part of the abdomen on either side of the vertebral column behind the peritoneum. The right kidney is usually slightly lower than the left. The posterior surface and upper portion of the right kidney rest on the 12th rib; the left kidney usually rests on the 11th and 12th ribs. The anterior surface of the right kidney is in contact with the right adrenal gland, liver, and the right colic flexure. The anterior surface of the left kidney is in contact with the left adrenal gland, stomach, spleen, jejunum, colon, and, medially, the pancreas.

Spontaneous rupture of the normal kidney does not occur. Blunt force injuries to the kidney are uncommon. They are usually seen following motor vehicle accidents or falls from great heights when there is massive blunt force trauma to the abdominal cavity. Blunt force applied to the flank may crush the kidney between the abdominal wall and the lumbar vertebrae. The most common injury to a kidney is a contusion. Aside from contusions, the majority of injuries to the kidney are small transverse lacerations beneath an intact capsule with minimal hemorrhage. Injuries producing massive lacerations of the kidneys up to fragmentation are uncommon and are associated with massive injury to the other abdominal organs.

Urinary Bladder

In adults, the empty urinary bladder is placed entirely within the pelvis, behind the pubic symphysis. When distended, the bladder may extend into the abdominal cavity. In children, the anterior surface of the bladder is in contact with the lower two-thirds of the abdominal wall between the symphysis pubis and the umbilicus. Beginning at puberty, it slowly begins to descend to its final position in the pelvis. Iatrogenic rupture of the urinary bladder may occur during instrumentation for diagnostic or therapeutic purposes. More commonly, severe blunt trauma to the pelvis and lower abdomen causes rupture. The degree and type of injury that occurs usually depends on the volume of urine in the bladder.

There are two types of rupture: **extraperitoneal** and **intraperitoneal**. Extraperitoneal occurs when the bladder is empty or contains only a small amount of urine. In extraperitoneal rupture, the bladder lies within the pelvis and is protected by the strong bony pelvis. Here lacerations of the urinary bladder are associated with fractures of the pelvis. Only rarely will extraperitoneal rupture occur without pelvic fractures. This is when blunt force is applied to the lower abdominal wall in a downward direction.

Intraperitoneal rupture of the urinary bladder occurs when the bladder · is markedly distended by urine. At this time, a kick, a blow, or any blunt force to the lower abdominal wall can compress the posterior wall of the bladder against the sacrum, raising the pressure within the bladder lumen and rupturing it, with urine entering the abdominal cavity.

Internal Genitalia

Injuries of the nonpregnant uterus are extremely rare. When they do occur, they are usually associated with extensive fractures of the pelvis. Blunt trauma injuries to the pregnant uterus and/or fetus are usually caused by automobile accidents, with falls and assaults accounting for a significantly smaller number of cases.[27,28] Placental separation is the leading cause of fetal death. Separation occurs at the moment of trauma but may not become evident for a few hours. This is probably due to a small separation at the edge of the placenta, with development of a retroplacental hematoma that takes a while to grow and kill the fetus. In the absence of any direct trauma, the cause for the separation is severe distortion of the uterus that can occur with violent motion. Following the death of the fetus, labor usually begins within 48 h, though it may be delayed up to a few weeks. During this time, the mother may develop a disseminated intravascular coagulopathy. With fractures of the pelvis, there may be not only placental separation but direct fetal injury, for example, fracture of the fetal skull and/or internal injuries to the fetus.

Blunt Force Injuries of the Extremities

These injuries may be limited to the skin and subcutaneous tissues or extend to muscles, blood vessels, nerves, bones, and joints. Injuries to bone are described in Chapter 4.

Avulsive wounds of the lower extremities are most frequently seen in automobile–pedestrian accidents. If an automobile wheel passes over the lower extremities, it can exert tangential pressure on the skin and subcutaneous tissues, separating them from the underlying muscles. The pocket created is soon filled with blood and liquefied fat. In other instances, the skin and subcutaneous tissue are also torn, forming a large flap of skin (Figure 5.7). A blood-filled pocket may also be produced in the back and/or lateral (outer) aspect of the thigh in pedestrians impacted by the front of the hood. The tangential force of the hood impacting the thigh strips the skin and subcutaneous tissue from the muscle, creating a blood-filled pocket (Figure 5.8).

Complications of Blunt Force Injuries to the Lower Extremities

Shock — caused by severe crushing, soft tissue injuries, and/or compound fracture.

Hemorrhage — occurs from traumatic amputation, compound fracture with severing of a large vessel, multiple lacerations, or severe avulsive wounds

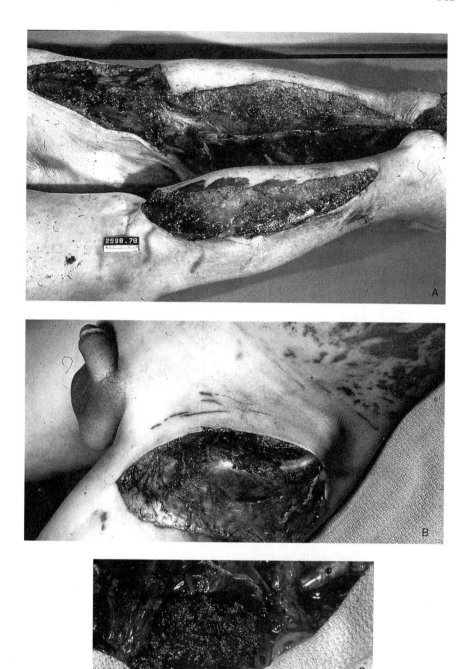

Figure 5.7 (A) Bilateral avulsion injuries of lower extremities caused by truck wheel passing over legs. (B) Avulsive injury of left thigh with (C) transection of femoral artery.

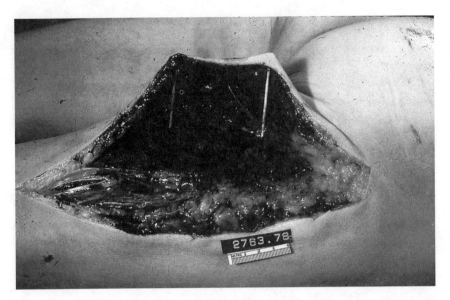

Figure 5.8 Blood-filled cavity (incised) in back of thigh caused by impact with front of automobile hood, with skin and subcutaneous tissue avulsed from muscle.

of the skin and subcutaneous and underlying tissues, with tearing of numerous small vessels.

Venous thrombosis with fatal pulmonary embolism — Veins may be injured directly by fracture of the lower extremity, with resultant thrombosis. Thrombosis may also be secondary to venous stasis following prolonged immobilization of the lower extremity when the patient is confined to bed with a fractured extremity. There may be crushing injuries rather than fractures of the lower extremity with either direct injury to the veins or stasis bv compressing hemorrhage and edema resulting from the leg injury.

Fat embolism — Fat embolism follows mechanical trauma that mobilizes the fat from an injured fat deposit in the body. This happens rapidly, usually within a few seconds after injury. A few heartbeats are sufficient to bring fat to the lungs and even to the systemic circulation. For this reason, fat may be found even when death seems to be instantaneous —although, with sudden death, the amount of fat is usually small. The amount of fat in those surviving injury is proportional to the degree of injury and to the time of survival up to 24 h. Older persons are prone to have more massive fat embolization. Microscopic sections of the lungs show massive amounts of intravascular fat droplets, as well as free fat in the alveoli. Outside the lungs, fat emboli are more frequently seen in the kidney than in the brain. Microscopic sections of the brain show petechiae (small hemorrhages) throughout, with fat droplets within the capillaries.

Infection — Compound fractures are frequently contaminated with bacteria carried into the wound and lodged in the devitalized traumatized tissues. Depending on the virulence of the bacteria and immediateness and extent of surgical attention and cleansing of the wound, the infection may be limited to the skin or soft tissue or extend to the bone (osteomyelitis). A combination of aerobic and anaerobic organisms may cause gangrene of the lower extremity, a terminal hemolytic anemia, hemoglobinuric nephrosis, uremia, and septicemia. Wounds contaminated with soil are occasionally infected with tetanus.

Crush syndrome: crushing injuries of the extremities — In this entity, there is traumatic or ischemic muscle necrosis in persons pinned by beams and falling debris. This causes myoglobin release with resultant acute tubular necrosis.

Effects of injury on preexisting natural disease — There may be delirium tremens in alcoholics, uremia in patients with chronic renal disease, cardiac decompensation in patients with heart disease, cerebral damage during shock, etc.

Injury to upper extremities occurs in association with motor vehicle accidents, falls, and assaults. In the case of homicide, the upper extremities should be closely scrutinized for defensive and offensive injuries. The fingernails, fingers, hands, and forearms should be carefully examined for abrasions, contusions, and lacerations. Broken or avulsed fingernails in a rape victim may indicate that the victim tried to protect herself. Fractured fingers and forearms are sustained by victims when they attempt to ward off a blunt instrument. Contusions, abrasions, and superficial lacerations over the knuckles may corroborate a perpetrator's contention of self-defense. Absence of injuries to the hand, however, does not exclude the possibility that blows were struck with the fists. Injuries to the back of the arms may indicate the victim was attempting to ward off blows.

References

1. Maron BJ, Poliac LC, Kaplan JA, and Mueller FO, Blunt impact to the chest leading to sudden death from cardiac arrest during sports activities. *NEJM* (1995) 333:337-42.

2. Viano DC, Andrzejak DV, Polley TZ, and King AI, Mechanism of fatal chest injury in baseball impact: development of an experimental model. *Clin J Sport Med* (1992) 2:166-71.

3. Link MS, Wang PJ, Natesa GP, Bharati S. et al., An experimental model of sudden death due to low-energy chest-wall impact (commotio cordis). *NEJM* 1998 338:1805-1811.

4. Bharati S and Levi M, The pathology of sudden death, in Josephson ME (Ed): *Sudden Cardiac Death (Cardiovascular Clinics) 15/3*. Philadelphia, FA Davis Co, 1985, pp 1-27.

5. Killen DA, et al., Posttraumatic aneurysm of left ventricle. *Circulation* 1969; 39:101-108.

6. Bolooki H, Karlson KE, Garzon AA, et al., Ventricular septal defects produced by penetrating chest injuries. *NY State J Med* 1969; 69:24712474

7. Simson LR Jr, Chin-sternum-heart syndrome: Cardiac injury associated with parachute mishaps. *Aerospace Med* 1971; 42:1214-1218.

8. Suzuki I, Sato M, Hoshi N, and Manjo H, Coronary arterial laceration after blunt chest trauma. *NEJM* 2000; 343(10):742-3.

9. Cherng WJ, Bullard MJ, Chang HJ et al., Diagnosis of coronary artery dissection following blunt chest trauma by transesophageal echocardiography. *J Trauma* 1995; 39:772-74.

10. Arajarvi E, Santavirta S and Tolonen J, Aortic ruptures in seat belt wearers. *J. Thorac Cardiovasc Surg.* 1989; 98:355-61.

11. Symbas PJ, Horsley WS and Symbas PN, Rupture of the ascending aorta caused by blunt trauma (Review). *Ann Thorac Surg* 1998; 66(1):113-7.

12. Rogers F, Osler TM and Shackford SR, Aortic dissection after trauma: Case report and review of the literature. *J. Trauma* 1996; 41(5):906-908.

13. Ono M, Yagyu K, Furuse A, Kotsuka Y and Kubota H, A case of Stanford Type A acute aortic dissection caused by blunt chest trauma. *J Trauma* 1998; 44(3):543-544.

14. Gammie JS, Katz WE, Swanson ER and Peitzman AB, Acute aortic dissection after blunt chest trauma. *J Trauma* 1996; 40(1): 126-7

15. Papadopoulos CD, Potter RT, Manoli AN, et al., Chronic traumatic dissecting aortic aneurysms. *NY State J Med* 1975; 75:2181-2184.

16. Heggtveit HL, Campbell JS, and Hooper GD, Innominate arterial aneurysms occurring after blunt trauma. *Am J Clin Pathol* 1964; 42:69-74.

17. Harkin DW, Kirk G, and Clements WDB, Abdominal aortic rupture in a child after blunt trauma on a soccer field. *Injury*, 1999; 30:303-304.

18. Steier M, Ching N, Bonfils-Roberts E, et al., Iatrogenic causes of pneumothorax: Increasing incidence with advances in medical care. *NY State J Med* 1973; 73:1296-1298.

19. Newman LL, San Filippo JA, Halata MS, et al., Pneumothorax and hydrothorax following placement of central catheter. *NY State J Med* 1982; 82:341-343.

20. Winter B and Baum R, Complete traumatic rupture of the bronchus with minimal trauma. *JAMA* 1968; 206:370-372.

21. Osborn GR, Findings in 252 fatal accidents. *Lancet* September 4, 1943; pp 277-284.

22. Ducatman BS, Ludwig J, and Hurt RD, Fatal rectus sheath hematoma. *JAMA* 1983; 249:924-925.

23. Mays ET, Bursting injuries of the liver. *Arch Surg 1966; 93:92-106.*

24. Semel L and Frittelli G, Gastric rupture from blunt abdominal trauma. *NY State J Med* 1981; 81:938-939.

25. Vance BM, Subcutaneous injuries of the abdominal viscera. *Arch Surg 1928;* 16:631-679

26. Reay DT, Sexual abuse and death of an elderly lady by "fisting," *Am J Forensic Med Path.* 1983; 4:347-349.

27. Rothenberger D, Quattlebaum FW, Perry JF, et al., Blunt maternal trauma: A review of 103 cases. *J Trauma* 1978; 18:173-179.

28. Crosby WM, Traumatic injuries during pregnancy. *Clin Obstet Gynecol* 1983; 26:902-912.

Trauma to the Skull and Brain: Craniocerebral Injuries

6

Injuries to the head can be grouped into two broad categories based on the mechanism by which the injury is produced: **Impact injuries** and **acceleration or deceleration injuries.**

Impact injuries are caused when an object strikes or is struck by the head. These injuries consist of the local effects of contact between the head and the object. Typically, these injuries are:

- Soft tissue injuries: lacerations, abrasions, and contusions of the scalp
- Fracture of the skull
- Contusions of the brain
- Epidural hematomas
- Intracerebral hemorrhages

Acceleration or deceleration injuries are due to sudden movement of the head the instant after injury, with resultant production of intracranial pressure gradients and the subjecting of the brain to both shearing and tensile forces. Two types of injuries are typically produced: (1) **Subdural hematomas** and (2) **diffuse axonal injury.**

Subdural hematomas are secondary to tearing of the subdural bridging veins; diffuse axonal injury is secondary to injury to the axons.[1] While acceleration or deceleration injuries are associated with impact, theoretically, impact is not necessary for the production of these injuries, just sudden angular rotation of the head. In situations encountered by forensic pathologists, however, acceleration or deceleration injuries of the brain involve impact.

Impact Injuries

Soft Tissue Injuries

When the head is either struck by an object or strikes the ground, the initial injuries are incurred by the scalp — lacerations, contusions, or

147

abrasions. Lacerations can produce profuse bleeding due to the great vascularity of the scalp. Only under the most unusual circumstances would this be life threatening.

Fractures of the Skull

The second type of injury that can be incurred is to the skull. In general, whenever a head is either struck with or strikes an object having a broad flat surface area, the skull at the point of impact flattens out to conform to the shape of the surface against which it impacts. As the skull is flattened and bent inward, adjacent, but more distant areas, are bent outward by a wave of deformation consisting of the central area of inbending and the peripheral outbending (Figure 6.1)[2,3] This outbending can occur at a considerable distance from the point of impact. Where the skull curves sharply, the extent of inbending and outbending is not so great as in less-curved areas. If a fracture of the skull occurs, the fracture does not begin at the point of impact, but at the point of outbending. Linear fractures begin on the external surface of the skull by the forces produced by the outbending of the bone. After inbending, the skull attempts to return to its normal configuration. As the inbent portion of the skull does so, the fracture line extends from its originating site toward the area of impact, as well as in the opposite direction. The fracture line may or may not reach the point of impact and could actually continue through it.

In any fall or blow to the head, the degree of deformation of the skull, the generation of a fracture and the extent of any fracture produced is dependent on a number of factors:

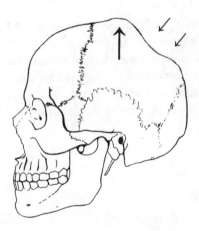

Figure 6.1 Indenting of skull at point of impact with outward bending at periphery.

- The amount of hair
- The thickness of the scalp
- The configuration and thickness of the skull
- The elasticity of the bone at the point of impact
- The shape, weight, and consistency of the object impacting or impacted by the head
- The velocity at which either the blow was delivered or the head strikes the object

The amount of energy required for production of a single linear fracture from a low-velocity blow or fall depends on whether the head strikes a hard unyielding surface or a relatively soft yielding surface. With a yielding surface, a large proportion of the impacting energy is transferred to the surface by way of the deformation of the surface, thus decreasing the amount of energy available to cause head injury. In the case of a hard unyielding surface, e.g., a steel plate, in which there is essentially no energy transferred to the impacted surface, it takes approximately 33.3–75 ft lb of energy to produce a single linear fracture.[3,4] This energy is absorbed in 0.0012 s. The first 0.0006 s is used in deforming and compressing the scalp and the residual 0.0006 s is used in deforming the bone.[3] The amount of energy necessary to produce multiple linear fractures or stellate fractures is almost identical to that needed to produce a single linear fracture, with only a slight increase required.[3] In fact, the same amount of force necessary to produce a single linear fracture could produce a stellate fracture in another area of the skull. That skull fractures commonly occur when individuals fall on the back of the head becomes obvious when one realizes that a free-fall of 6 ft for a head weighing 10 lb gives an available energy of 60 ft lb, well within the range necessary to produce a linear fracture of the skull if it impacts an unyielding surface. The velocity of the head at the time of impact is approximately 20 ft/s or 13.5 mph.[3]

If a head strikes or is struck by a deformable object, not all the energy possessed by either the object or head will be available for deformation of the skull. At impact, the object will tend to indent and deform so as to wrap itself around the head. Thus, the energy delivered is no longer in a localized focus but is dispersed over a considerable area, reducing the possibility of a skull fracture. Linear or comminuted fractures of the skull produced by impaction of a head and a relatively soft and flexible object, such as the instrument panel of a motor vehicle, require kinetic energy levels at impact of between 268 and 581 ft lbs.[4] Impact velocities are from 43 ft/s (29 mph) to 65 ft/s (45 mph). In one test, a human head impacting at 577 ft lb of energy did not fracture.[4] The fractures produced with a head impacting an unyielding surface (in which 33.3 to 75 ft lb of energy is needed to fracture the skull) are essentially identical to fractures produced with heads impacting a yielding surface and requiring 268 to 581 ft lb to fracture.[4] Thus, the magnitude of energy necessary to produce a skull fracture is approximately 33.3 to 75 ft lb, with other energy being utilized to deform and dent objects it impacts.

One point that has been stressed by numerous authors and should be repeated is that there is no absolute correlation between the severity of brain injury and the production of a linear skull fracture. Skull fractures can occur without any significant or detectable brain injury or any impairment of consciousness. Conversely, death may result from extensive brain injury without a skull fracture.

Simple linear fractures are typically seen in low-velocity impacts with a large area of contact between the head and impacting object. A fall to the pavement is the best example. With increased velocity and, thus, greater force, one may have a series of complete or incomplete **circular fractures** encircling the impact point (Figure 6.2). These fractures result from failure of the external surface of the bone at the edge of the inbent area, due to extreme inbending at the time of impact.[2] If the velocity and energy of impact are increased even more, one gets **stellate fractures**, where there is depression of the bone at the point of impact. The severe inbending about the impact site produces fractures on the inner surface that radiate out from the site of the blow.[2] Fractures resulting from the outbending of the bone at a distance from the point of impact, and arising in the outer surface of the skull, extend toward the point of impact and join with the fractures radiating outward from the point of impact. Circular fractures may occur at the junction of the inbending bone on its external surface (Figure 6.2). The concentric or circular fracture lines may be incomplete in that they stop at a linear fracture, indicating that the linear fracture preceded the concentric fracture. The opposite may also occur with the linear fractures stopping at the concentric fracture lines, which indicates that the latter preceded the former.

A **depressed skull fracture** occurs when the skull is struck with an object having a relatively large amount of kinetic energy but a small surface area, or when an object with a large amount of kinetic energy impacts only a small area of the skull. The scalp does not significantly affect the nature of the injuries to the skull. Large deformations occurring at a distance from the point of impact are no longer present.[2,3] At the point of impact, there is a depressed fracture, possibly with fragmentation. The fractures are due to failure of the inner surface of the skull secondary to the inbending. An example of this type of fracture is the circular depressed fracture of a hammer blow (Figure 6.3). Here there are no linear fractures radiating to or from the circular depression in the skull. If there is insufficient energy to produce fractures of both the outer and inner tables of the skull, there will be a

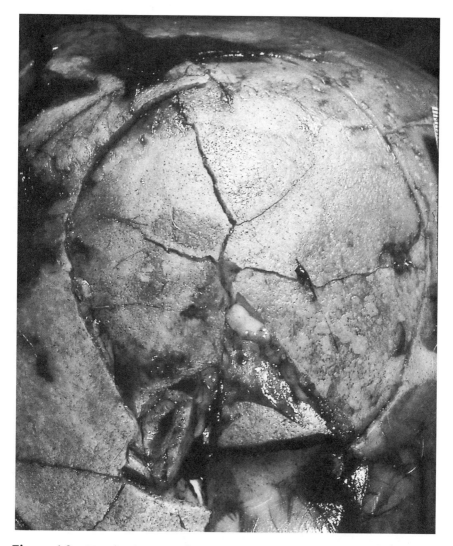

Figure 6.2 Circular fracture of cranial vault from fall onto top of head.

depressed fracture in the outer table, with the inner table intact. The fracture of the outer table is almost always larger than the fracture of the inner table. Most depressed fractures are compound in that there is an associated laceration of the scalp. Epilepsy is a complication in a small percentage of depressed fractures.

Blows in different areas of the head can have different effects. A blow to the top of the head tends to produce a cranial vault fracture that might or might not extend into the temporal region or base of the skull. A blow in the occipital region generally produces a linear fracture of the posterior fossa; a blow to the temporo-parietal region fractures through the temporal bone

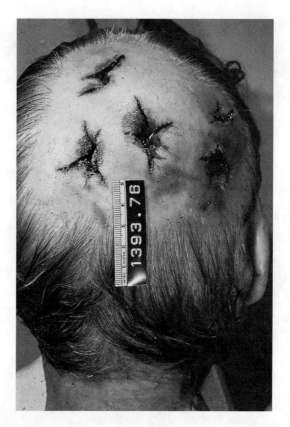

Figure 6.3 Blows to head with hammer, with (A) stellate lacerations of scalp. (*continued*).

to the base of the skull; and a mid frontal blow produces fractures running to the orbits and sometimes into the maxilla.[3]

Basilar skull fractures are quite common in forensic medicine. The base of the skull, by virtue of its construction and irregular shape, is weak. Almost any diffuse impact to the vertex of the skull will produce basilar fractures. Basal skull fractures can occur from blows anywhere along the circumference of the skull below the cranial vault. They can run anterior-posteriorly, posterior-anteriorly, side to side and any combination of these three. Basal skull fractures may be missed on X-rays of the skull. With a basal fracture, intracranial passage of a nasogastric tube or nasophrayngeal airway can occur.[5]

Hinge fractures are transverse fractures of the base of the skull that completely bisect the base of the skull, creating a "hinge." The authors divide them into three categories (Figure 6.4(A)). Type I run in the coronal plane, extending from the lateral end of one petrous ridge, through the sella turcica, to the lateral end of the contralateral petrous ridge. Type II run from front to the contralateral back, passing through the sella turcica. Type III run from side to side in the

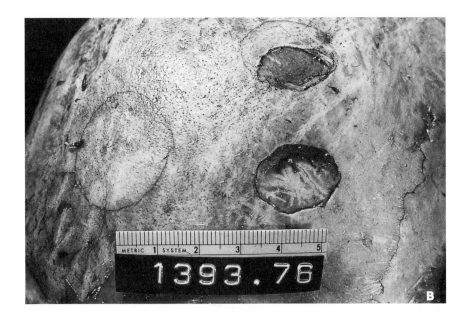

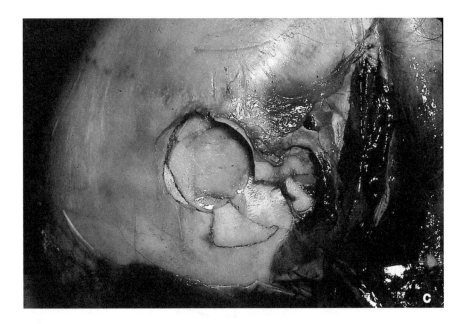

Figure 6.3 *(continued)* Blows to head with hammer, with (B and C) depressed circular skull fractures.

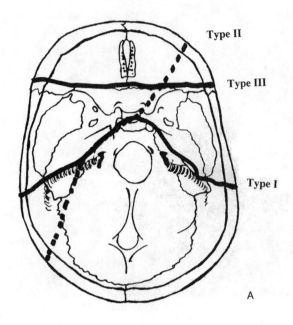

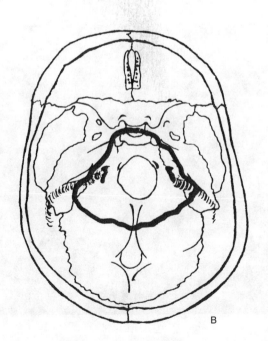

Figure 6.4 (A) Hinge fractures: Types I, II and III; (B) ring fracture.

coronal plane but do not pass through the sella turcica. *Type I hinge fractures are the most common form of transverse fractures of the base of the skull.* They have traditionally been ascribed to impacts on the side of the head and, less commonly, to impacts on the tip of the chin. In the latter instance, one would expect a laceration of the tip of the chin, though not necessarily fracture of the mandible.

Ring fractures are circular fractures of the base of the skull that surround the foramen magnum. Typically, they run from the sella turcica partly down the petrous ridges, before turning posteriorly, and then medially, joining in the posterior fossa, enclosing the foramen magnum (Figure 6.4(B)) They may be due to impacts on the top of the head that drive the skull downward onto the vertebral column, falls on the buttocks that drive the spine into the base of the skull, and impacts to the tip of the chin. In ring fractures from impacts on the tip of the chin, almost invariably there is a laceration of the chin. Even though the force of impact is transmitted through the mandible to the base of the skull, in most instances, fractures of the mandible are not present. Experiments have revealed that more force is needed to fracture the mandible than to produce a basal fracture.[6]

Humphry et al. reviewed 86 cases of basal skull fracture.[7] They found no correlation between the site of impact and generation of a hinge or ring fracture. *Hinge and ring fractures of the base of the skull can be produced by impacts anywhere on the circumference of the head.*

In skulls in which the sutures are not completely fused, suture lines represent areas of weakness and fractures may travel along them (**diastatic fractures**). Rarely, in infants and young children, diastatic fractures can be produced by severe cerebral edema. Thus, the authors had a case of an 18-month-old male admitted to a burn unit with burns over most of his body. He was never conscious and died a week after admission. At autopsy, there was separation of the coronal, sagittal, and lambdoidal sutures due to the edema (Figure 6.5).

Contre-coup fractures of the anterior cranial fossae are isolated fractures of the anterior cranial fossae associated with contre-coup injuries of the brain, with the impact point on the opposite side of the skull. In a study of 171 deaths from cranio-cerebral trauma due to falls, Hein and Schulz found that contre-coup fractures of the anterior cranial fossae occurred in 12% of the cases.[8] All cases had fractures at the impact site, which was the occipital region. If one considered only falls where there was occipital impact, then 24% of the cases had contre-coup fractures.

Contusions of the Brain

Impact injuries can produce contusions and lacerations of the brain. Contusions are the most frequently encountered traumatic lesion of the brain. Contusions involve the crests of the gyri, but can extend into the white matter as wedge-

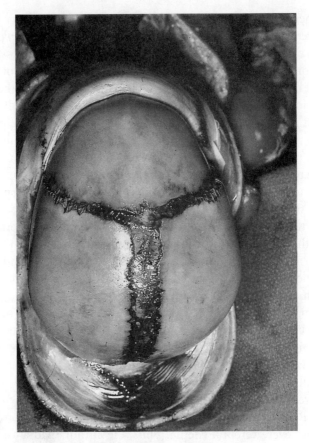

Figure 6.5 An 18-month-old child with separation of sutures due to severe cerebral edema.

shaped lesions.[9] Contusions are more severe when associated with skull fractures and are less severe in brains with diffuse axonal injury.[1] Cortical contusions consist of areas of hemorrhage and necrosis that originate at the moment of impact. Occasionally, hemorrhage may be present without necrosis or necrosis with little or no hemorrhage.[9] The contusion hemorrhages are located at or near the crest of a gyrus. They are usually multiple in number, streak-like, and densely arranged (Figure 6.6) though occasionally solitary. If the hemorrhage is close to the surface of the cortex, there may be overlying focal subarachnoid hemorrhage. If death is not immediate, the bleeding will continue. The amount of bleeding depends on the type (small artery, capillary, vein) and caliber of the vessel injured as well as if there is any adjacent necrosis. If necrosis is present, the contusions develop a wedge-shaped appearance with the base of the wedge at the crest and the point toward the white matter. If there is profuse bleeding, the areas of hemorrhage may expand into the white matter or subarachnoid space, essentially forming an area of intracerebral hemorrhage.

Figure 6.6 Streak-like linear contusions of cerebral cortex.

Contusion necrosis, just as contusion hemorrhage, tends to be in the cortex, at the crest of the gyri, sparing the cortex of the sulci.[9] The area of necrosis is wedge shaped, with the base of the wedge at the cortical crest. The area of necrosis is usually delineated by accompanying hemorrhage, though the exact extent of the necrosis may not become clear for 10–12 h. If the necrosis is purely ischemic, without hemorrhage, the lesion becomes visible grossly 10–12 h after the injury as an area of swollen gelantinous parenchyma.[9,10] Microscopically, it becomes visible at 3–5 h. Over time, contusions are reabsorbed with resultant golden-brown areas of gliosis.

Contusions are most often found in the frontal and temporal lobes of the brain. Less commonly, contusions are present on the lateral and ventral surfaces of the cerebral hemispheres. Contusions are not usually seen in infants. Rather, one sees lacerations involving the white matter, most commonly in the frontal and temporal lobes.[9,11] *Contusions may be absent in severe open fractures of the skull, with massive lacerations or even evisceration of the brain.* Thus, in jumps and falls from great heights, massive lacerations of the brain are often unaccompanied by contusions.

There are six types of contusions.[9]

1. **Coup contusions.** These occur at the site of impact and are due to the inbending bone snapping back (rebounding), inflicting tensile force injuries to the brain.[12] Coup contusions are less common than the second type of contusion.

2. **Contrecoup contusions** occur in the brain at locations directly opposite to the point of impact (Figure 6.7).They are tensile force

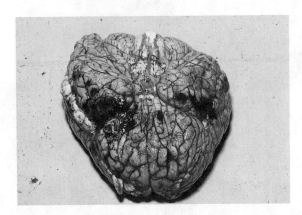

Figure 6.7 Contrecoup contusions of temporal poles due to fall on back of head.

injuries due to the brain rebounding backward from the skull following impact.[12] They are seen most commonly in the frontal poles,
orbital gyri and temporal lobes. Contrecoup contusions are classically associated with falls. As their name indicates (*contre* being
French for opposite), they develop opposite to the point of impact.
Thus, an individual falling on the left side of the back of his head
will have contrecoup contusions of the right frontal and temporal
lobes. A fall onto the top of the head would result in contusions of
the ventral surface of the cerebral hemispheres. Contrecoup contusions are virtually never seen in the occipital lobes, in spite of the
frequent occurrence of individuals' falling on their faces. While usually, one has only contrecoup injuries following a fall, and no coup
injuries, on occasion, an individual might have both coup and contrecoup contusions (Figure 6.8). When this occurs, the contrecoup
contusions will always be much more extensive and severe than the
coup contusions.

With blows to the head, if contusions are produced, they should be
only coup contusions. Occasionally, however, the coup contusions are
accompanied by contrecoup contusions. In these instances, the contrecoup contusions will be less extensive and less severe than the coup
contusions. The usual teaching is that, with blows to the head, if there
are no coup contusions, there are no contrecoup contusions. This may
not be completely correct. The authors have seen rare cases in which
individuals have been struck on the head and there were small contrecoup contusions, but no coup contusions. There is always the possibility in these cases that, after such individuals were struck, they
collapsed, striking their heads and incurring a contrecoup contusion
from the fall.

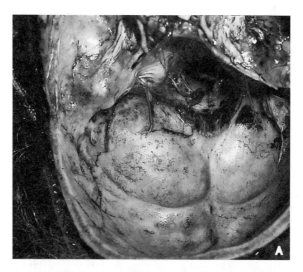

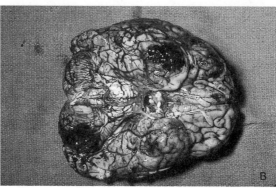

Figure 6.8 (A) Fracture of skull in left posterior fossa with, (B) coup contusions of left cerebellar hemisphere and contrecoup contusions of right temporal pole. Eight-day survival.

3. **Fracture contusions** are associated with fractures of the skull. They do not necessarily bear any relation to the point of impact, as the fracture line can be some distance from this point.

4. **Intermediary coup contusions** are hemorrhagic contusions in the deep structures of the brain, for example, the white matter, basal ganglia, corpus callosum, brain stem, and along the line of impact — that is, between the location of the coup and contrecoup points. They are said to be seen only in falls.[9] Intermediary contusions should not be mistaken for gliding contusions.

5. **Gliding contusions** are focal hemorrhages located in the cortex and underlying white matter of the dorsal surfaces of the cerebral hemispheres, principally in the frontal region. They are seen in falls and

motor vehicle accidents.[9,13] They are independent of the site and direction of impact and are often found in association with diffuse axonal injury.[13]

6. **Herniation contusions** are caused by impaction of the medial portion of the temporal lobes against the edge of the tentorium, or the cerebellar tonsils against the foramen magnum. These are also independent of the site and direction of impact.

The most important fact to remember about contusions is the relation of coup and contrecoup contusions to falls and blows. A fall on the head will produce contrecoup contusions opposite the point of impact and no or very minor coup contusions at the point of impact. A blow to the head results in coup contusions and no or minor contrecoup contusions.

Intracerebral hematomas are discrete collections of blood within the cerebral parenchyma that are not in contact with the surface of the brain.[14] They are principally located in the white matter of the fronto-temporal lobes and are caused by impact. They are said to differ from hemorrhagic intermediary coup contusions in that they are well demarcated, homogeneous collections of blood, in contrast to contusions that are blood and contused cerebral parenchyma. In the authors' opinion, this distinction is artifactual, and may just reflect a longer survival time by the intracerebral hematomas with continued bleeding. One of the most interesting aspects of intracerebral hematomas is that they can appear hours to days after the injury.[15–17] There have been numerous cases where a computerized tomography (CT) scan on admission has shown no intracerebral hematomas, but subsequent CT scans, taken several hours to several days after admission, revealed some. In some instances, their development has been followed by successive CT scans. Primary intracerebral hemorrhages involving the basal ganglia are found in approximately 10% of fatal head injuries. They are caused by deceleration/acceleration forces and are commonly found in association with diffuse axonal injury and gliding contusions.[14] In 90% of the cases, the cause of the injury was either a motor vehicle accident or a fall. In the study by Adams et al. 43 of 63 patients had small (less than 20 mm) hematomas.[13]

Lacerating, Penetrating, and Perforating Wounds of the Brain

Lacerating and penetrating wounds of the brain are most commonly due to fractures of the skull. Injuries to the brain by fragments of bone may occur in the presence of an intact scalp. Lacerations of the corpus callosum or septum pellucidum may occur due to blunt trauma to the head without any fractures of the skull (Figure 6.9). This latter phenomenon appears to be more common in younger individuals, who have more elastic bone. Lacerations of the brain may show little and even no bleeding around them. This

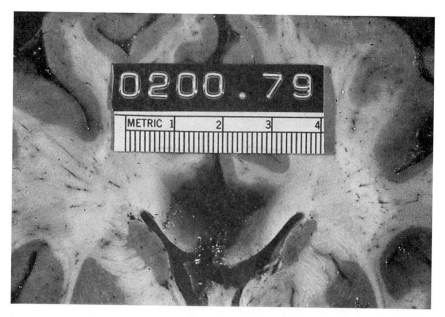

Figure 6.9 A 33-year-old male with transaction of corpus callosum. Impact top of head. No skull fracture.

is apparently due to vasospasm of arteries, which can maintain a bloodless field for as long as one hour.[9]

With severe hyperextension of the head, such as occurs in motor vehicle accidents when individuals are thrown forward, their faces impacting the windshield or visor region, and their bodies continuing forward, there may be injury to the brain stem. This injury can range from tears and hemorrhages in the pyramids at the junction of the medulla oblongata and pons to avulsion of the brain stem at the pontomedullary junction (Figure 6.10).[18] These injuries are commonly associated with fractures of the base of the skull and fractures of the upper cervical vertebrae. Subarachnoid hemorrhage is usually present over the brain stem.

In contrast to adults, impact trauma in infants (5 months or younger) does not produce cortical contusions, but rather, grossly visible lacerations in the cerebral white matter and microscopic lacerations of the outermost layer of the cortex, which run parallel to the surface of the brain.[11] The lacerations of the cerebral white matter occasionally extend through the cortex or wall of the ventricles or both. They are most often present in the orbital and temporal lobes and in the first and second frontal convolutions. Minimal bleeding is present in the lacerations and sometimes in the adjacent white matter. The earliest cellular reaction is seen at 36 h and is obvious by 72 h. Unlike contusions in the adult brain, the location and distribution of the white matter lacerations cannot be used to indicate whether the injuries were from a fall or a blow.

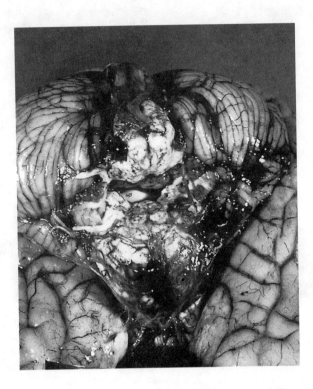

Figure 6.10 Complete avulsion of brain stem at pontomedullary junction.

Epidural Hemorrhages

The dura is a gray membrane of connective tissue firmly adherent to the inner surface of the skull. Arteries run along the inner surface of the dura at its point of attachment with the skull. The potential space between the skull and dura is the epidural space, with an actual space, the subdural space, between the dura and brain. The brain, in turn, is enclosed in two thin, transparent membranes: the inner pia and the outer arachnoid. The subarachnoid space is between the arachnoid and pial membranes. It and the subdural space contain fluid. The fluid in the subarachnoid space is cerebrospinal fluid, produced by the choroid plexus that reaches the subarachnoid space through the foramen of Magendi of the fourth ventricle.

Epidural hematomas are primary impact injuries. They are relatively infrequent and are seen most commonly in falls and traffic accidents. They are infrequent in the elderly and the very young (less than 2 years of age) due to strong adherence of the dura to the skull in both these age groups.

Epidural hematomas are caused by trauma to the skull and the meningeal vessels (principally the arteries) at the point of impact. At impact, the skull is bent inward, with stripping of the dura and laceration of meningeal vessels. A fracture is virtually always present at this point (90–95% of the time) in association with the epidural hematoma.

The area of avulsion from the dura is extended by arterial bleeding that strips the dura from the bone, permitting accumulation of blood. The inability of the venous system to generate sufficient pressure to strip dura from bone accounts for the infrequency of epidural hematomas following venous injury. Epidural hematomas unassociated with fractures are uncommon. These usually occur in children who have very elastic bones, such that the dura can be avulsed from the bone without fracture. In most such cases, bleeding is minor.[9,19]

Epidural hematomas usually have a thick, disk-shaped appearance (Figure 6.11(B,C)). They are virtually always unilateral. Most epidural hematomas result from fractures of the squamous-temporal bone, with laceration of the middle meningeal artery (Figure 6.11(A)). Thus, most epidural hematomas are in the temporal region. Less commonly, there are lacerations of the anterior and posterior meningeal arteries with frontotemporal and parieto-occipital hematomas, respectively. Epidural hematomas caused by venous bleeding are the result of injury to the diploic veins, middle meningeal veins, and dural sinuses.

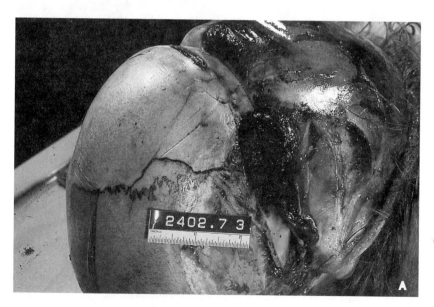

Figure 6.11   (A) Fracture of squamous temporal bone with laceration of middle meningeal artery *(continued)*.

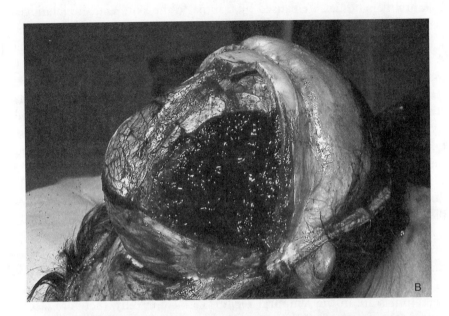

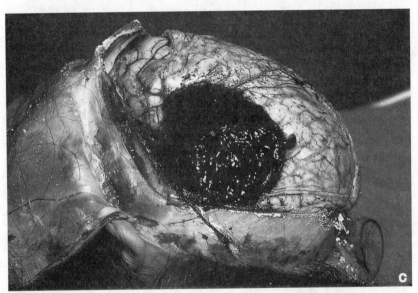

Figure 6.11 *(continued)* ((B and C) epidural hematomas.

Symptoms from an epidural hematoma usually occur 4–8 h after injury. There is a lucid interval prior to the development of severe symptoms in approximately one third of patients. Occasionally, an individual will develop an epidural hematoma so rapidly that death will occur in as little as 30 min.[9] Death is caused by displacement of the brain with compression of the brain stem. With large fractures, there may be decompression of the epidural hematoma and survival.

Chronic epidural hematomas are rare.[20] They produce their signs and symptoms over a lengthy period of time. These lesions might lie quiescent for many days and then suddenly bring about death. It is hypothesized that chronic epidurals are more commonly associated with tears of venous rather than arterial structures. However, in some cases, tears in meningeal arteries have been demonstrated. Frequently, however, no point of bleeding is found. Symptoms are usually present from the time of the trauma, though they may be very minor in nature, such as headache or nausea. Drowsiness may or may not be present. Chronic epidural hematomas may or may not be associated with fractures of the skull. They are seen most commonly in older children and young adults. This is thought to be due to the ease with which the dura can be stripped from the skull in such individuals. Generally, an epidural hematoma is considered chronic when more than 48–72 h passes from injury to identification. In some individuals, the interval has been as long as 18 days.

Acceleration/Deceleration Injuries

Acceleration or deceleration injuries are due to sudden movement of the head the instant after injury, with resultant production of intracranial pressure gradients and the subjecting of the brain to both shearing and tensile forces. Two types of injuries are typically produced: **subdural hematomas** and **diffuse axonal injury.** Subdural hematomas are secondary to tearing of the subdural bridging veins; diffuse axonal injury is secondary to injury to the axons.[1] While acceleration or deceleration injuries are associated with impact, theoretically, impact is not necessary for the production of these injuries, just sudden angular rotation of the head. In situations encountered by forensic pathologists, acceleration or deceleration injuries of the brain involve impact.

An impacting force to the head can produce linear acceleration, rotational (angular) acceleration, or a combination of both. In **linear acceleration,** the force passes through the center of the head, accelerating the head in a straight line. In **rotational** or **angular acceleration** the force does not pass through the center of the head and thus the head will rotate about its center. Impacts to the front and back of the head tend to produce linear acceleration while those to the side produce a combination of linear and angular. A combination of linear and angular acceleration of the head in the coronal plane e.g., side impact is more injurious to the brain than similar acceleration in the sagittal plane (frontal impact) as angular acceleration sets up shear strains in the brain.[21–23]

Subdural Hematomas

The subdural hematoma is the most common lethal injury associated with head trauma (Figure 6.12). The high mortality associated with subdural hematomas is due in part to associated brain damage.[14] Since a large number of subdural hematomas are caused by falls, it is not uncommon to find contrecoup contusions in association with subdural hematomas. Unlike epidural hematomas, subdural hematomas are often not associated with a fracture of the skull and can occur in the absence of cerebral contusions or any other visible brain injury. Subdural hematomas are more common in the elderly and alcoholics.

Clinically, approximately 72% of all subdural hematomas are due to falls and homicidal assaults, with motor vehicle accidents accounting for only 24%.[1] This is in contrast to diffuse axonal injury, where approxi-

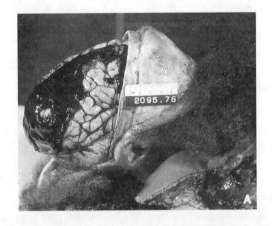

Figure 6.12 (A and B) Subdural hematoma.

mately 89% of cases are due to motor vehicle accidents and only 10% to falls and assaults.

Subdural hematomas can be acute, subacute, or chronic. Acute subdural hematomas manifest themselves clinically within 72 h of injury; subacute between 3 days and 2–3 weeks, and chronic more than 3 weeks after injury. Subdural hematomas are caused by the stretching and tearing of the parasagittal bridging veins that drain the surface of the cerebral hemispheres into the dural venous sinuses. These injuries occur after the head impacts a hard surface and the brain is accelerated. This rapid acceleration causes the tearing of the bridging veins. The more rapid the acceleration or deceleration, and the shorter the time of acceleration or deceleration, the more likely one will have a subdural hematoma rather than diffuse axonal injury.[1,14,24] The reason that subdural hematomas are less common in motor vehicle accidents, in contrast to diffuse axonal injury, is that in a motor vehicle accident, the head typically strikes a yielding or energy-absorbing surface, thus extending the time interval in which the acceleration or deceleration occurs. This reduces the probability of a subdural hematoma's occurring, because it requires a large acceleration or deceleration over a short time. It does, however, predispose the brain to diffuse axonal injury.

Part of the lethality associated with subdural hematomas is because of injury to the cerebral parenchyma by the same acceleration/deceleration force that produces the acute subdural hematoma.[14] This acceleration or deceleration force may also induce brain injury of the diffuse axonal injury type. The severity of this injury would vary from totally recoverable to such that, regardless of the subdural hematoma, death would occur.

There is no consistent relation between the presence or location of skull fractures and the presence of subdural hematomas. A fracture might be either on the same or contralateral side to the hematoma or may not even be present (which is more common in elderly individuals). Subdural hematomas may be on the same or contralateral side as the point of impact or bilateral.[9] Subdural hematomas can occur without apparent head injury or with very minor injury in the elderly and in individuals on anticoagulants or who have bleeding dyscrasias. Occasionally, a cerebral aneurysm or intracerebral hemorrhage will rupture into the subdural space, producing a subdural hematoma.

In subdural hematomas, the onset of symptoms is usually rapid. In elderly individuals, however, symptoms may develop over days. There may be a relapse of symptoms secondary to recurrent hemorrhage. In an adult, a rapidly developing (acute) subdural hematoma becomes life threatening when it reaches approximately 50 mL in size. With slow bleeding, a considerably larger subdural hematoma can be tolerated without symptoms or serious side effects. In infants, a smaller volume is life threatening. Renewed bleeding into an old subdural hematoma can occur. It can be either "spontaneous" or the result of new trauma to the head. It originates from the sinusoidal vessels in the outer neo-membrane formed during the organization of the initial hematoma. Rapid development of a subdural hematoma with mass displacement of the brain with or without generalized cerebral edema may result in compression of the brain stem and development of secondary (Duret's) hemorrhage. These may develop in as little as 30 min after trauma (R. Lindenberg, personal communication).

In subdural hematomas, the blood presses on both the crests and depths of the gyri so that the cerebral convolutions retain their normal contours. The hematoma, however, causes displacement of the cerebral hemispheres with flattening of the convolutions of the opposite hemisphere as they are pressed against the dura and bone. If rebleeding occurs within the sac formed by an organized subdural hematoma, the convolutions on the side of bleeding will become flattened as the fibrous membrane presses on the crests of the gyri.

If a person does not immediately die from a subdural hematoma, the hematoma will gradually become encapsulated by cells from the dura. The arachnoid does not participate in this encapsulation. Therefore, the capsule is attached to the dura and not the arachnoid. When formed, this sac of blood will press on the underlying gyri, flattening them, deforming the surface of the brain immediately underneath this sac. There is, however, no shifting of the hemisphere toward the other side, which is seen in the acute non-organized subdural hematoma.

Organization of a subdural hematoma follows a protracted course.[9] The subdural space has only a limited absorptive capacity, thus, a subdural hematoma is removed by a process of organization initiated by the dura. For the first few days immediately following a subdural bleed, the clot is not adherent to the dura. At about 4–5 days, the clot begins to become adherent at multiple sites.

About 24 h after formation of the subdural hematoma, a layer of fibrin is deposited on the dura beneath the subdural hematoma. Fibroblastic activity starts at the junction with the dura by 36 h with a layer of fibroblasts 2–5 cells thick present after 4–5 days.[9] Invasion of the subdural hematoma by capillaries and fibroblasts is evident by 5–10 days. Hemosiderin-laden macrophages are obvious. Erythrocytes begin to lake. By 8 days, a membrane 12–14 cells thick is present on the dura. The neocapillaries in the membrane are the source for rebleeding into the subdural hematoma. The arachnoid surface of the subdural hematoma is initially coated only by fibrin. The membrane enclosing the arachnoid surface of the hematoma begins to form in about 14 days, at which time the dural membrane is one third to one half the thickness of the dura. By 3–4 weeks after injury, the hematoma is covered by a membrane of fibrous tissue that grows inward from the edges of the clot. By 4–5 weeks, the arachnoid membrane has half the thickness of the dura, with the dural surface equal in thickness to the dura. The clot is completely liquefied and hemosiderin-laden macrophages are present in the membranes. At 1–3 months, the membrane is hyalinized on both its inner and outer aspects, with large capillaries invading the clot. This goes on to eventual complete resorption, with only a residual gold-colored membrane adherent to the dura.

Some individuals do not develop significant symptoms of a subdural hematoma for weeks to months after head injury. The resultant hematoma is a **chronic subdural hematoma**. In this entity, instead of the initial acute subdural hematoma's becoming organized and then smaller as it is reabsorbed, it begins to enlarge. This continues until the chronic subdural hematoma produces sufficient symptomology.

The victims of chronic subdural hematomas tend to be either infants younger than 6 months of age or the elderly.[14,25] Both have cranial cavities that can accommodate the slow accumulation of large quantities of blood. In the case of infants, this is due to incomplete fusion of bony plates; in the elderly, increased intracranial space due to brain atrophy. In infants, chronic subdural hematomas may result in enlargement of the head. Adults with chronic subdurals often tend to be alcoholics. Because of the prolonged time between trauma and symptoms, in a significant percentage of individuals with chronic subdural hematomas, no history of trauma can be elicited. Chronic subdural hematomas are rarely seen in medicolegal offices.

The etiology of chronic subdural hematomas is generally thought to be rebleeding from thin-walled sinusoidal blood vessels in the neo-membrane of a resolving acute subdural hematoma. Lee et al., however, feel that most chronic subdurals originate as subdural hygromas.[26]

A **subdural hygroma** is an accumulation of spinal fluid in the subdural space.[14,26] Trauma to the brain causes effusion of spinal fluid through the arachnoid, with development of a hygroma. A small amount of bleeding may also be present, giving the fluid a xanthochromic color. Hygromas can also develop secondary to meningitis. If the hygroma, instead of being reabsorbed, continues to grow, it can produce the same space-occupying effects as a subdural hematoma.

Diffuse Axonal Injury

Immediate prolonged coma unaccompanied by an intracranial mass lesion occurs in almost half of patients with severe head injuries. The etiology of this coma and the cause of death in fatal cases is diffuse axonal injury (DAI). Diffuse axonal injury results from the effects of head motion on the brain. It is caused by sudden acceleration or deceleration of the head. While, theoretically, impaction of the head against a hard object is not necessary, in reality, brain injury in humans requires contact, not just acceleration or deceleration. For all practical purposes, it is the impact that starts the acceleration or deceleration injury to the brain.

Diffuse axonal injury is a continuum, varying from mild brain injury and dysfunction to severe irreversible dysfunction and injury, and even death. The severity of injury is determined by the amount of acceleration or deceleration of the brain, the time span over which it occurs, and the direction of movement.[21,22] Experiments have shown that only motion in the coronal plane causes severe injuries. Sagittal head movement produces diffuse axonal injury of mild, or at most, moderate type.

At low levels of acceleration or deceleration, there is no anatomical disruption of the axons, only physiological dysfunction. This may lead to either complete recovery of an axon or its degeneration. As the physical force increases, there will be a progressive increase in the extent of irreversible physiological injury to axons (thus making it more likely that they will subsequently undergo degeneration) plus an increase in the amount of immediate structural disruption of axons (transaction) with immediate cessation of all activities.

Concussion is defined by Kelly et al. as "a trauma-induced alteration in mental status that may or may not involve loss of consciousness."[27] In **mild concussion**, there is confusion and disorientation, but no loss of consciousness. Retrograde amnesia may or may not develop. If it does, it develops 5 or 10 min after the trauma and, while it might subsequently decrease, there will always be some residue.[23] In **cerebral concussion**, there is immediate loss of consciousness, which usually returns within minutes but can persist for hours (< 6 h) as confusion and retrograde, or posttraumatic, amnesia. What is clinically called concussion is thought to be a manifestation of diffuse brain injury, with no or insignificant irreparable physical injury to the brain. Blumberg et al. reported on autopsy findings of five individuals who died from other causes after incurring cerebral concussion.[28] Using immunostaining with B-amyloid precursor protein (B-APP), they found multifocal axon injury.

In the **second-impact syndrome**, individuals incur a minor head injury, followed by a second head injury before the symptoms of the first have disappeared.[29] These individuals appear dazed, may complete the activity they were performing at the time of second impact, but then collapse into coma. This entity is seen virtually exclusively in sports. Mortality is approximately 50%.

The term **diffuse axonal injury** (DAI) is used clinically to characterize a condition of diffuse injury of the axons of the brain associated with immediate unconsciousness and coma longer than 6 h of duration.[23] In mild DAI, there is coma of 6–24 h; in moderate DAI, coma of more than 24 h without prominent clinical signs of brain stem dysfunction; and, in severe DAI, coma of more than 24 h with brain stem signs. Severe DAI usually results in severe disability or death. Axonal injury of a greater or lesser degree is the pathological lesion common to all three forms of DAI.

With mild DAI, the injury is predominantly physiological. Some axons, however, may show immediate physical disruption with cessation of functions. In other axons, the physiological disruption will eventually lead to degeneration. As the acceleration or deceleration force increases, the proportion in each category changes, until, with severe DAI, the predominant injury is shearing of axons and immediate cessation of functioning. In severe DAI, there is mechanical disruption of the axons in the white matter of the cerebral hemispheres, the corpus callosum, and upper brain stem. Focal hemorrhages are usually grossly visible in the corpus callosum and dorsolateral quadrant of the rostral brainstem. Occasionally, laceration or even transection of the corpus callosum can occur. Gliding contusions of the gray matter of the cerebral hemispheres and hippocampi may be present.

The histologic hallmark of DAI is axonal swelling or "retraction balls" (see below).[30–33] Evidence of axonal injury is not visible for approximately 12 to 24 hours using hematoxylin and eosin stains and 15–18 h with silver stains. If one employs immunohistochemical techniques, injury may be visible in 6 h using ubiquitin and 3 h or less with B-APP. Injury to axons has been detected as early as 1.5 h with B-APP. These axonal changes by B-APP are not specific for DAI, however. Similar changes have been seen in non-traumatic cases with cerebral hypoxia.[31–33] As time passes, the extent and degree of axonal injury increase.

In DAI, the axons first appear dilated, like sausage links; then club shaped, and finally (in 18–24 h) as round balls known as "retraction balls." Retraction balls represent axons that are transected. They are seen in the cerebral white matter, corpus callosum, and upper brain stem. The number of retraction balls increases during the first week after injury. This is because, while the initial trauma causes transection of some axons with formation of retraction balls, other axons are irreversibly injured but continue functioning for a while prior to cessation of function and degeneration. Two to three weeks after injury, the number of axon retraction balls begins to decrease and clusters of microglial cells, the most prominent lesion, appear. This will be followed by astrocytosis and demyelinization.[23]

In diffuse axonal injury, experiments have revealed that it is not only the magnitude of acceleration that produces the injury, but the time over which the acceleration occurs. Severe angular accelerations over a short time period result in subdural hematomas; acceleration over a long time period, diffuse axonal injury.[7,14,24] This agrees with the observation that diffuse axonal injury is more common in vehicular accidents, where the time of impact may be prolonged due to absorbing materials, but rare in falls, where there is no absorption of impact. When diffuse axonal injury has been documented following falls, these have been falls from a considerable height.[34] It is extremely unlikely for diffuse axonal injury to occur from a fall from a person's own height.

Death Due to Cerebral Concussion

The authors have seen a number of deaths following blunt trauma to the head in which no, or at least insignificant, anatomical injury to the brain could be documented. They fall into two categories. The first is illustrated by the case of an 8-year-old boy riding in the back seat of a motor vehicle that was involved in a head-on collision with another vehicle. The boy was propelled over the back seat, striking the top of his head against the windshield. He was dead at the scene within minutes of the accident. At autopsy, there was no evidence of any injury to the scalp, skull, brain, or neck (anterior and posterior dissection). A complete autopsy and toxicological screen were negative.

A second, similar case involved a 20-year-old man who fell 20 ft to the ground from a ladder. Death was immediate. At autopsy, there was a small laceration of the scalp in the temporal region without fracture of the skull or gross evidence of injury to the brain. A number of small perivascular hemorrhages were identified in the brain stem. There was no other evidence of injury. The neck was examined anteriorly and posteriorly. Death in this and the previous case was presumably due to diffuse axonal injury.

The second category of deaths involves individuals who, while acutely intoxicated with alcohol, are severely beaten about the head, usually with fists and feet (Figure 6.13). The individuals collapse and are subsequently found to be dead. At autopsy, the face shows extensive soft tissue injury. There is no intracranial hemorrhage (subdural, subarachnoid or intracranial). There are no skull fractures, though fractures of the nose may be present. Anterior and posterior dissection of the neck is unremarkable. The airway is patent. The blood alcohol is high, but not in the lethal level, i.e., above 0.15 %, but less than 0.400%. Analysis of vitreous humor indicates that, even if there had been prolonged survival, the blood alcohol level was never in the lethal range.

Milovanovic and Di Maio reported five such deaths.[35] In all cases, there was extensive soft tissue injury to the face and head; no intracranial bleeding; no injury to the neck; no airway obstruction and no skull fractures. Three of the five individuals did, however, have nasal fractures. All five were intoxicated, with blood alcohol levels from 0.22 to 0.33 g/dl. Three of the five died within minutes of the assault; two were found dead.

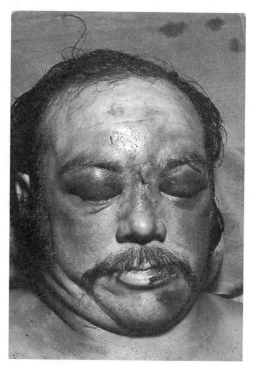

Figure 6.13 A 35-year-old male severely beaten about face with fists. Blood alcohol 280 g/dL. No visible injury to brain.

The cause of death in this category of cases is posttraumatic apnea due to a combination of concussion and acute alcohol intoxication.[35–36] Concussion, alone or in combination with alcohol, can produce posttraumatic apnea. With concussion alone, however, posttraumatic apnea is rare, brief, relatively mild and not life-threatening. Concussion in combination with alcohol produces apnea that can cause death. This was demonstrated by Zinc and Feustel in animal experiments.[36] They concluded that alcohol augments the effects of concussive brain injury with resultant posttraumatic apnea.

Subarachnoid Hemorrhage

Subarachnoid hemorrhage is the most common *sequela* of trauma to the head. Subarachnoid hemorrhage can be focal or diffuse, minor or severe. In very rapid deaths, subarachnoid hemorrhage tends to be multifocal. In most cases, it is of a diffuse nature, overlying the cerebral hemispheres, with minimal pooling on the ventral surface of the brain. Large collections of blood in the subarachnoid space of the base of the brain are more common in natural diseases than trauma, e.g., a ruptured berry aneurysm.

Traumatic subarachnoid hemorrhage over the base of the brain can be caused by lacerations of the internal carotid, vertebral, or basilar arteries. These injuries can be almost immediately fatal. Hyperextension can cause bleeding because of lacerations of the basal or vertebral arteries. Blows to the face might produce lacerations of the internal carotid artery or a vessel of the circle of Willis. Blows to the neck can cause lacerations of a vertebral artery with dissection of blood superiorly into the subarachnoid space.

In some instances, subarachnoid hemorrhage may be the only visible sign of trauma to the brain. Such was the case of an individual struck repeatedly about the head with the barrel of a rifle, with resultant multiple lacerations of the scalp, but no fractures of the skull. The brain showed massive subarachnoid hemorrhage, but no contusions or lacerations. That subarachnoid hemorrhage in itself can cause death is illustrated by deaths following rupture of a berry aneurysm or laceration of a vertebral artery. While most subarachnoid hemorrhage is of venous origin, occasional cases are caused by lacerations of the vertebral artery or one of the basilar arteries of the brain.

It is possible to have massive injury to the brain with minor focal subarachnoid hemorrhage, especially if death is rapid. This is seen most commonly in cases with massive mutilating injuries of the head, such as when an individual jumps several stories to the ground. There are massive, gaping, compound fractures of the skull, with partial or even complete avulsion of the brain. The brain may show spotty subarachnoid hemorrhage and no contusions. Absence of contusions in such cases is common. In one case, an individual had his head caved in with a baseball bat in front of a number of witnesses. The brain showed virtually no subarachnoid hemorrhage and no contusions, though there were extensive lacerations. Absence of hemorrhage following lacerations to the brain has been reported as much as 1 h after injury, and is presumably due to prolonged spasm of vessels.[9] Subarachnoid hemorrhage may cause subsequent development of communicative hydrocephalus because of a lack of reabsorption of cerebrospinal fluid relative to production. This is due to subarachnoid hemorrhage causing scarring of the arachnoid villi, such that it impedes their ability to reabsorb cerebrospinal fluid.

Subarachnoid hemorrhage can be produced postmortem secondary to decomposition, with lysis of blood cells, loss of vascular integrity, and leakage of blood into the subarachnoid space. In addition, minimal subarachnoid hemorrhage may be produced during the process of removing the brain. In this case, in the process of removing the skull cap, cerebral veins and the arachnoid are torn, with subsequent diffusion of blood into the subarachnoid space in the posterior aspect (dependent portion) of the cerebral hemispheres and cerebellum. While this hemorrhage is usually very minor, if the brain is not removed from the cranial cavity immediately but rather left to sit for a while, a considerable quantity of subarachnoid hemorrhage may accumulate.

Vertebral Artery Injury (Laceration)

Blunt trauma to the neck can cause severe injury to the vertebral arteries. The upper third of the cervical region is the area where the vertebral artery is most susceptible to trauma. Two types of trauma can result. In the most common form, there is a traumatically induced dissection in the vessel wall, along a length of vertebral artery, with rupture into the subarachnoid space at the base of the brain (Figure 6.14). The second type of injury also involves dissection but, instead of rupture of the vessel wall, there is thrombosis of the lumen with infarction of brain tissue. Opeskin and Burke reported on 25 cases of vertebral artery trauma.[37] In 19 cases, there was rupture with subarachnoid hemorrhage, while in four, there was thrombosis with ischemia. The remaining two cases had rupture, but death was too rapid for subarachnoid hemorrhage.

The most common causes of vertebral artery trauma are blows to the neck, motor vehicle accidents, falls, and cervical spine manipulation. In most of Opeskin and Burke's cases, considerable force was involved.[37] Chiropractic manipulation with resultant vertebral artery injury was the cause for two of their deaths. Injury of the vertebral artery should be suspected when an individual collapses and dies almost immediately after receiving a blow to

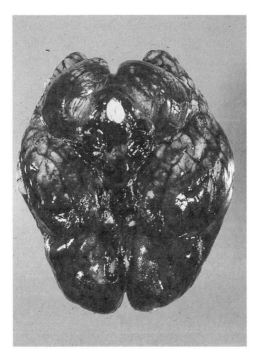

Figuren 6.14 Massive subarachnoid hemorrhage secondary to laceration of vertebral artery.

the neck. In cases caused by rupture of the artery, an autopsy reveals subarachnoid hemorrhage primarily concentrated on the ventral surface of the brain and around the brain stem.

In rupture of the artery due to blunt trauma, Opeskin and Burke noted bruising and abrasions below and behind the ear in 50% of 18 cases.[36] Fractures of the cervical spines were present in 10 of 25 cases. Demonstration of the vertebral artery injury is easiest by injection of radio-opaque dye into the vertebral arteries with radiological demonstration of the injury. Only after such demonstration should there be dissection of the neck, because dissection is extremely difficult and, if not done correctly, may produce artifactual defects in the vessels.

Of 19 individuals with rupture and subarachnoid hemorrhage in the study of Opeskin and Burke, 14 died immediately and five in 10 h to 3 days.[37] Four of the five delayed deaths were unconscious from the time of trauma. In the fifth case, rupture occurred 2–3 days after neck manipulation. Of the four individuals who died secondary to vertebral artery thrombosis, symptoms did not appear for 1 d to 4 weeks, with survival time of 3 days to 7 weeks.

Traumatic Injury of the Carotid Artery

This entity is probably more common than realized.[38,39] It occurs mostly in motor vehicle accidents, where it is often missed because of other injuries to the head. The injury can be in the neck or in the cranial cavity. In the neck, it may be found in association with hyperextension injury or spinal fracture. Intracranial injury is commonly associated with a fracture of the skull. Neurological symptoms may be delayed. Thus, of 29% of patients seen by Cogbill et al., significant neurological deficits developed more than 12 h after a normal admission neurological examination.[39] The injury to the carotid arterial wall might be caused by:

- An intimal laceration with development of a thrombus
- An intimal laceration with subsequent dissection into the media in the presence of an intact adventitia, with development of a true aneurysm
- Rupture of the wall of the artery

One of the authors reviewed a case of a thrombosis of the internal carotid artery just distal to the bifurcation of the common carotid artery. The injury was incurred in a low-speed motor vehicle collision and was due to deployment of an airbag.

Traumatic Dissection of Intracranial Arteries

Dissection of intracranial arteries due to trauma is relatively uncommon.[40] If it does occur, however, it can cause cerebral infarction. It is caused by subintimal dissection of the intracranial anterior circulation arteries. Unlike other areas of the body where dissection is in the media, here it occurs subintimal, with resultant occlusion of the lumen by mechanical effects and the production of infarction.

Traumatic Brain Swelling and Edema

Following significant head injury, whether clinically mild or severe, swelling of the brain can occur. Brain swelling may be focal, adjacent to an area of brain injury; or diffuse, involving one or both cerebral hemispheres. Brain swelling is due to an increase in intravascular cerebral blood volume secondary to vasodilatation (congestive brain swelling), or an absolute increase in the water content of the brain tissue, or a combination of the two. An increase in tissue water content, or cerebral edema, is often incorrectly considered synonymous with brain swelling. If continued long enough, brain swelling caused by an increase in the intravascular cerebral blood volume progresses to cerebral edema, presumably due to increased vascular permeability. The magnitude of the brain swelling does not necessarily correspond to the severity of the injury. Massive cerebral (congestive) swelling can occur within 20 minutes following head trauma.[41]

Swelling of one cerebral hemisphere is seen most commonly with an ipsilateral subdural hematoma. The secondary swelling may, in fact, cause a more serious mass effect than the hematoma. The rapid onset of the swelling suggests that the etiology is congestive.

With severe brain injury, diffuse brain swelling of a severe degree may occur immediately without the individual regaining consciousness. Brain swelling, however, might not occur immediately after an injury, but rather develop minutes to hours later. Delayed brain swelling of a significant degree is rare. It is usually diffuse and more often associated with the less severe forms of brain injury. Typically, the patient receives a concussion, regains consciousness, only to become stuporous and lapse into coma minutes to hours later. Until recently, it was felt that children were more susceptible than adults to developing diffuse swelling, even after minor trauma.[42,43] Recent studies have challenged this contention. Lang et al. found that, while diffuse swelling might occur more readily in children it is more benign.[44] Thus, in their study, 75% of children with diffuse swelling had a benign course, while two thirds of adults had a poor outcome The researchers believed that a number of the previous studies had problems in that they were not able to adequately study changes in the brain in children because the studies were performed without CT scans.

If brain swelling develops to a severe degree and continues over a sufficient time, there can be herniation of the brain or secondary brain stem hemorrhage. A rapidly expanding intracranial mass or severe brain swelling

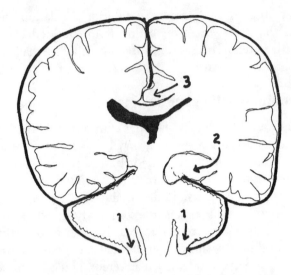

Figure 6.15 (1) tonsillar, (2) transtentorial, and (3) subfalcial herniation of brain.

can produce tonsillar, transtentorial, or subfalcial herniation of the brain, with resultant necrosis, secondary infarction, and Duret hemorrhages (Figure 6.15). Herniation may be either symmetrical, due to brain swelling, or asymmetrical, due to a mass in one side of the brain or subdural space, e.g., a subdural hematoma or intracerebral hemorrhage. In the case of diffuse brain swelling, there is usually symmetrical herniation of the cerebellar tonsils without brain stem hemorrhage. The brain stem and cerebellar tonsils are forced into the foramen magnum, with resultant dysfunction or even infarction of the brain stem. The individual becomes unconscious and develops respiratory difficulty that proceeds to arrest and death. Severe herniation of the cerebellar tonsils can result in infarction. In some individuals with prolonged survival, the authors have seen the upper spinal cord encased in necrotic cerebellar tissues shed into the cerebrospinal fluid. In dealing with an asymmetrical herniation caused by a subdural hematoma, in addition to ipsilateral cerebellar tonsil herniation, one often has a secondary brain stem hemorrhage (a Duret hemorrhage) involving the midbrain and pons.

Transtentorial or uncal herniation is due to a rapidly expanding supratentorial mass lesion. It may be either unilateral or bilateral, though unilateral herniation is more common because rapidly expanding lesions are usually unilateral. A rapidly expanding mass in a cerebral hemisphere means that ipsilateral uncal herniation can be expected. If severe enough, there will be displacement of the brain stem against the contralateral tentorial edge with injury to the brain stem and production of Kernohan's notch.

The third type of herniation is subfalcial or transfalcial herniation. This occurs when there is a rapidly expanding mass in one cerebral hemisphere or at least in the subdural space on one side. This causes herniation of the cerebral hemisphere across the midline below the edge of the falx. The herniating tissue is most often the cingulate or supracingulate gyrus.

As previously noted, herniation with compression of the brain stem can result in Duret hemorrhages. These are secondary herniation hemorrhages of the midbrain and pons. They might range from small streaks to massive confluent hemorrhage. They are in the midline and are most commonly associated with asymmetrical herniation of the brain stem. Duret hemorrhages may develop in only 30 min.

Boxing Injuries

Professional boxers and, to a lesser extent, amateur boxers can suffer both acute and chronic injuries in the sport. In 1928, Martland described the "punch drunk syndrome" in boxers.[45] This syndrome, in its final form, is characterized by slurred speech, ataxia, impaired memory, dementia, a broad-based gait, and a Parkinsonian-like facial appearance.[45,46] These brain injuries result from the cumulative effect of multiple subconcussive blows. The brain injury is apparently irreversible and, in some cases, progresses even after the fighter stops boxing. Corsellis et al. described a unique neuropathological pattern of injuries in such boxers.[47] It is characterized by:

- A fenestrated cavum septi pellucidi
- Scarring of the cerebellum and cerebral hemispheres, with marked loss of Purkinje cells and loss of neurons with subsequent gliosis in the cerebral hemispheres and with resultant reduction in brain weight and enlargement of the lateral and third ventricles
- Degeneration and loss of the pigmented cells of the substantia nigra
- Neurofibrillary tangles throughout the cerebral cortex and brain stem, most commonly in the medial temporal gray matter and the laterally placed temporal, insular, and frontal cortex

In fights, most punches to the head result in rotational acceleration. Thus, not unexpectedly, most ring fatalities are due to subdural hematomas. These, as well as DAI, are due to rotational or angular acceleration. Although less common, blows to the head can produce linear acceleration of the brain with resultant focal ischemic lesions, especially in the cerebellum.[48] These develop a few days after trauma. Straight blows to the face can also produce hyperextension of the neck, with resultant damage to the axons in medullopontine angle and the reticular substance of the brain, as well as retinal detachment. Blows to the neck can cause injury to the carotid arteries, with development of dissecting aneurysms or thrombosis.[48] Also, if the boxer is knocked out, he can strike his head as he collapses to the mat, incurring contrecoup contusions.

Occipito-Cervical Injuries

The cervical vertebrae are divided into the upper, C1–C2, and the lower, C3–C7, vertebrae. The occiput, C1 and C2, form a functional unit bound together by ligamentous bands. There is no intervertebral disc between the occiput and C1, and C1 and C2. The vertebral arteries pass through the foramina of the transverse processes from C-1 to C-6 and are, thus, subject to injury from lateral fractures.

Atlanto-occipital (occipitocervical) dislocation due to craniocervical ligamentous separation is an extremely severe injury commonly associated with death. Dislocation may be anterior, posterior, vertical and lateral. This injury is commonly seen in pedestrians struck by motor vehicles and in the occupants of motor vehicles involved in crashes. In a study of 100 consecutive deaths from motor vehicle accidents, 24 had cervical spinal injuries, with 8 having atlanto-occipital dislocation.[49] The other injuries involved the first cervical vertebra in three cases; the second in nine cases; the third to the seventh in four cases.

Of the eight individuals with atlanto-occipital dislocation, only three had osseous injury (two involved a condyle, one a fracture of C1). Adams studied 12 cases of atlanto-occipital dislocation occurring secondary to traffic accidents.[50] Five had osseous injuries (two of the occipital condyles; three of C1). Nine of the twelve cases had pontomedullary brainstem lacerations, four had midbrain lacerations.

The Atlas (C1) is a ring-like structure between the occipital condyles and the axis (C2). Isolated fractures are usually not associated with neurological injury. Fractures can be classified based on the location and stability of the fractures. Anterior arch injuries are usually due to hyperextension and may vary in severity from minimally displaced to comminuted to unstable; lateral mass fractures are due to lateral loading; posterior arch fractures are caused by hyperextension together with axial loading; burst fractures by axial loading.[52]

Fractures of the axis (C2) involve the dens, the neural arch or the body of the vertebra. Neurological injury from fractures of the dens is rare. If there is injury, it can vary from minor to fatal. Odontoid fractures are the most frequent spinal fracture in children below 8 years of age and adults above 70 years. They may be caused by falls on the head. Excluding the dens, the most common fracture is that of the neural arch between the superior and inferior articular processes, the "hangman's fracture." The most common mechanism is axial loading with extension or flexion. It is seen commonly in motor vehicle accidents and falls.

Less dramatic, and more difficult to detect than atlanto-occipital dislocations, are atlantoaxial (C1–C2) dislocations. Adams studied 14 traffic fatalities with C1–C2 dislocation.[51] Thirteen had sprains of the atlantoaxial facet joints; one a healed C1 fracture. Six of the 13 — two children and four older individuals — had odontoid fractures. In sharp contrast to atlanto-occipital dislocations, there was only one pontomedullary laceration and two lacerations of the brainstem.

Most fractures of the lower cervical vertebrae can be divided into five types (Figure 6.16).[52] They vary in severity from mild to severe. Only the severe forms of each type will be considered, as these are the injuries of interest to the forensic pathologist.

Flexion-distraction: a flexion injury characterized by disruption of the posterior ligaments with anterior displacement of a vertebra.

Flexion-compression: a more severe version of the flexion-distraction injury. There is disruption of the posterior ligaments with anterior and inferior displacement of a vertebra with compression and fracturing of the adjacent vertebra.

Extension-distraction: extension injuries that are the opposite of flexion-distraction injuries. There are no fractures of the vertebrae, but rather anterior disruption at the discs as they are pulled apart with posterior displacement of vertebrae.

Extension-compression: a more severe form of extension-distraction with fracture of the posterior elements of the vertebral bodies and increased anterior separation at the disc space.

Vertical compression: involves compression and fracturing of a vertebra.

Lacerations of the Brainstem

Violent hyperextension of the head and neck can cause laceration at the junction of the pons and medulla.[18,53] These laceration may be either partial or complete, and are usually associated with fractures of the cervical spine, hinge fractures, or ring fractures.[50,53] Occasionally, the injury will not be associated with either cervical or cranial fractures. The only evidence of injury to the brain, aside from the laceration, is generally subarachnoid hemorrhage around the brainstem. While death is almost always immediate, partial laceration is sometimes associated with survival of a few hours. While generally ascribed only to hyperextension, some individuals feel that these injuries can be a form of diffuse axonal injury due to angular acceleration of the head.[53]

Traumatic Intracranial Aneurysms

Traumatic intracranial aneurysms[54,55] are relatively uncommon, with approximately 100 reported in the literature. Most occur in association with fractures of the base of the skull and involve the extracranial portion of the internal carotid artery. When the aneurysms occur intracranially, they most

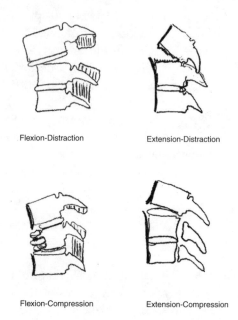

Flexion-Distraction   Extension-Distraction

Flexion-Compression   Extension-Compression

Figure 6.16 Fractures of lower cervical vertebrae

commonly involve the anterior aspect of the circle of Willis. Traumatic aneurysms might be either true or false aneurysms. Those involving the cerebral
arteries are true aneurysms, as they are formed due to the lack of an external
elastic lamina in the cerebral vessels.

Cerebral Palsy

Deaths complicating cerebral palsy (CP)[56] are occasionally seen in a medicolegal system. Pneumonia or seizures are the typical presenting causes of
death. Usually, the only reason the death becomes a medical examiner's case
is that it occurred at home. Cerebral palsy is not a single disease, but rather
a group of diseases producing non-progressive motor impairment due to
lesions or anomalies that arose in the early stages of brain development.
Twenty-five percent of afflicted individuals are unable to walk; 30% are
mentally retarded and 33% have epilepsy. Despite dramatic changes in obstetrical and perinatal care, there has been no decline in CP's prevalence among
full term births. In fact, it has increased overall because of the increase in
survival of premature infants. The lower the birth weight and the earlier the
gestational age, the higher the risk of cerebral palsy. Current medical opinion
is that, for the vast majority of children with CP, the injuries are not caused
by birth trauma or hypoxic insult at birth, but rather by intrauterine insult.

References

1. Graham DI and Gennarelli TA, Pathology of brain damage after injury. In Cooper PR and Golfinos JG(Eds), *Head Injury*, 4th ed McGraw-Hill, NY 2000.

2. Gurdjian ES, Webster JE, and Lissner HR, The mechanism of skull fractures. *Radiology* 1950:54:313-338.

3. Lissner HR and Evans FG, Engineering aspects of fractures. *Clin Orthoped* 1958; 8:310-322.

4. Evans FG, Lissner HR, and Lebow M, The relation of energy, velocity and acceleration to skull deformation and fracture. *Surg Gynecol Obstet* 1958; 107:593-601.

5. Castiglione AG et al., Intracranial insertion of a nasogastric tube in a case of homicidal head trauma, *Am J Forens Med Path.* 1998; 19(4): 329-334.

6. Hopper RH, McElhaney JH, and Myers BS, Mandibular and basilar skull tolerance. Experiments carried out under the auspices of Duke University.

7. Humphrey J, Di Maio VJM, Bux R et al., Basal skull fractures in relationship to head impact site (in preparation).

8. Hein PM and Schulz E, Contrecoup fractures of the anterior cranial fossae as a consequence of blunt force caused by a fall. *Acta Neurochir* (Wien) 1990; 105:24-29.

9. Lindenberg R, Trauma of meninges and brain, in Minckler J (Ed), *Pathology of the Nervous System,* Vol 2. McGraw-Hill, 1971.

10. Lindenberg R and Freytag E, Morphology of cortical contusions. *Arch Pathol* 1957; 63:23-42.

11. Linderberg R and Freytag E, Morphology of brain lesions from blunt trauma in early infancy. *Arch Pathol* 1969; 87:298-305.

12. Gennarelli TA, Mechanisms of cerebral injury. Presented at the 34th Annual Meeting of the National Association of Medical Examiners. Indianapolis, September 14-19 2000.

13. Adams JH et al., Deep intracerebral (basal ganglia) haematomas in fatal non-missile head injury in man. *J Neurol Neurosurg & Psych*; 49(9):1039-43, 1986.

14. Cooper PR, Posttraumatic intracranial mass lesions. In Cooper PR and Golfinos JG (Eds): *Head Injury*, 4th ed McGraw-Hill, NY 2000.

15. Ninchoji T et al., Traumatic intracerebral haematomas of delayed onset. *Acta Neurochirugica* 1984; 71:69-90.

16. Young HA et al., Delayed traumatic intracerebral haematoma: Report of 15 cases operatively treated. *Neurosurgery* 1984; 14:22-25.

17. Gentleman D, Nath F, MacPhersen P, Diagnosis and management of delayed traumatic intracerebral hematoma. *Br. J. Neurosurg* 1989; 3:367-372

18. Linderberg R and Freytag E, Brainstem lesions characteristic of traumatic hyperextension of the head. *Arch Pathol* 1970; 90:509-515.

19. Mealey J Jr, Acute extradural hematomas without demonstrable skull fractures. J *Neurosurg 1960;* 1 7:27-34.

20. Iwakuma T and Brunngraber CV, Chronic extradural hematomas: A study of 21 cases. *J Neurosurg* 1973; 38:488-493.

21. Gennarelli TA et al., Diffuse axonal injury and traumatic coma in the primate. *Ann Neurol* 1982; 12:564-574.

22. Adams IH, Graham DI and Gennarelli TA, Head injury in man and experimental animals: neuropathology. *Acta Neurochirugica Suppl* 1983; 32:15-30.

23. Le Roux PD, Choudhri H, and Andrews BT, Cerebral concussion and diffuse brain injury. In Cooper PR and Golfinos TA.(Eds): *Head Injury,* 4th ed McGraw-Hill, NY 2000, Chap 7.

24. Gennarelli TA and Thibault LE, Biomechanics of acute subdural hematoma. *J Trauma* 1982 22(8): 680-686

25. Weiner HL and Weinberg JS, Head injury in the pediatric age group In Cooper PR and Golfinos TA (Eds): *Head Injury,* 4th ed McGraw-Hill, NY 2000.

26. Lee KS et al., Origin of chronic subdural haematoma and relation to traumatic subdural lesions (Review). *Brain Injury;* 1998 12(11):901-910.

27. Kelley JP et al., Concussion in sports: Guidelines for the prevention of catastrophic outcome. *JAMA* 1991; 226: 2867-69

28. Blumberg PC et al., Staining of amyloid precursor protein to study axonal damage in mild head injury. *Lancet* 1994; 344:1055-56.

29. Cantu RC, Second-impact syndrome. *Clin Sport Med* 1998 17:37-60.

30. Gultekin SH and Smith TW, Diffuse axonal injury in craniocerebral trauma. *Arch Path. Lab Med.* 1994; 118:168-171.

31. Geddes JF, What's new in the diagnosis of head injury? *J Clin Path* 1997; 50(4): 271-274.

32. Oehmichen M et al., Axonal injury — a diagnostic tool in forensic neuropathology? (Review). *Forensic Sci. Inter.* 1998; 95(1):67-83.

33. Oehmichen M et al., Pontine axonal injury after brain trauma and nontraumatic hypoxic-ischemic brain damage. *Int. J. Legal Med.* 1999; 112:261-267.

34. Adams JH et al., Diffuse axonal injury in head injuries caused by a fall. *Lancet,* December 22/29, 1984; pp 1420-1422.

35. Milovanovic A. and Di Maio VJM, Death due to concussion and alcohol. *Am J Forens Med Path.* 1999; 20(1):6-9.

36. Zink BJ and Feustel PJ, Effects of ethanol on respiratory function in traumatic brain injury. *J Neurosurg* 1995; 82:822-8.

37. Opeskin K. Burke MP, Vertebral artery trauma. *Am J Forens Med Path..* 19(3):206-17, 1998.

38. Martin RF et al., Blunt trauma to the carotid arteries. *J. Vasc Surg.* 1991; 14(6): 789-93.

39. Cogbill TH et al., The spectrum of blunt injury to the carotid artery: a multicenter prospective. *J Trauma* 1994; 37(3):473-479.

40. Rutherfoord GS, Dada MA and Nel J.P., Cerebral infarction and intracranial dissection in closed head injuries. *Am J Forens Med Path*1996; 17 (1): 53-57.

41. Kobrine AI et al., Demonstration of massive traumatic brain swelling within 20 minutes after injury. Case report. *J Neurosurg* 1977; 46(2):256-8.

42. Bruce DA et al., Diffuse cerebral swelling in children: The syndrome of "malignant brain edema" *J Neurosurg* 1981; 54:170-178.

43. Snoek IW et al., Delayed deterioration following mild head injury in children. *Brain* 1984;107:15-36.

44. Lang DA et al., Diffuse brain swelling after injury: more often malignant in adults than children. *J Neurosurg* 1994; 80: 675-680.

45. Martland HS, Punch drunk. *JAMA* 1928; 91:1003-1007.

46. Morrison RG, Medical and public health aspects of boxing. *JAMA* 1986: 255:2475-2480.

47. Corsellis J, Burton CJ, and Freeman-Browne D, The aftermath of boxing. *Psychol Med* 1973; 3:270-303.

48. Lampert PW and Hardman JM, Morphological changes in brains of boxers. *JAMA* 1984; 251: 2676-2679.

49. Bucholz RW et al., Occult cervical spine injuries in fatal traffic accidents. *J Trauma* 1979; 19(10): 768-771.

50. Adams VI, Neck injuries, I occipitoatlantal dislocations — a pathologic study of 12 traffic fatalities *J Forens Sci* 1992; 37(2):556-564.

51. Adams VI, Neck injuries, II atlantoaxial dislocations: a pathologic study of 14 traffic fatalities *J Forens Sci* 1992; 37(2):565-573.

52. Chapman JR and Anderson PA, Chapter 60: Cervical Spine Trauma P1245-1295. In Frymoyer JW. (Ed) *The Adult Spine: Principles and Practice.* 2nd ed. Lippincott-Raven 1997.

53. Ezzat W, Lee CA, and Nyssen J, Pontomedullary rent: A specific type of primary brainstem traumatic injury: *Am J Forens Med Path*1995;16 (4) 336-339.

54. Opeskin K., Traumatic pericallosal artery aneurysms. *Am J Forens Med Path* 1995; 16 (1): 11-16.

55. Soria ED, Paroski MW, and Schamann ME, "Traumatic aneurysms of cerebral vessels: A case study and review of the literature. *Angiology* 1988 39:690-15.

56. Kuban KCK and Leviton A, Cerebral Palsy (Medical Progress). *NEJM.* 1994; 330(3): 188-195.

Wounds Caused by Pointed and Sharp-Edged Weapons

7

One, two! One, two! And through and through
The vorpal blade went snicker-snack!
  —Lewis Carroll, Jabberwocky

Wounds caused by pointed and sharp-edged weapons can be divided into four categories:

1. Stab wounds
2. Incised wounds (cuts)
3. Chop wounds
4. Therapeutic/diagnostic wounds

Stab Wounds

Stab wounds are produced by pointed instruments. Most are homicidal. In stab wounds, the depth of the wound track in the body exceeds its length in the skin. The edges of the wound in the skin are typically sharp, without abrasion or contusion (Figure 7.1). In describing stab wounds, one should never use the term laceration. A laceration is a tear in the skin caused by blunt force.

The most commonly used weapon to produce a stab wound is a knife, which, by virtue of its cutting edge, can also produce incised wounds. The typical weapon is a flat-bladed, single-edged kitchen, pocket, or folding knife with a 4- to 5-in. blade. Other devices, such as ice picks, scissors, screwdrivers, broken glass, forks, pens, and pencils, have been used to inflict stab wounds.

The force needed for a knife to perforate the skin depends on the configuration and sharpness of the tip of the knife. The sharper, more needle-like the tip, the more readily it will perforate the skin.[1] Once the tip has perforated the skin, the rest of the blade will slide into the body with ease. As long as it does not contact bone, a knife can readily pass through organs with very little force. Thus, even if a knife blade is driven its complete length into the body, this does not necessarily mean that the stab wound was inflicted with great force.

Figure 7.1 Stab wound by single-edged knife. Top squared off, lower end V-shaped.

Depth of Stab Wounds

In stab wounds, the length of the wound in the skin can be equal, less or greater than the width of the knife. It may be greater if, as the knife perforates the skin, the cutting edge of the blade is drawn against the skin, slicing through it, enlarging the wound. The elasticity or laxness of the skin can also change the dimensions of the wound in the skin, increasing or decreasing it by a millimeter or two beyond the actual dimensions of the knife.

The depth of the stab wound can be equal to, less than, or greater than the length of the knife blade. If the knife is not inserted all the way, the wound track is less than the length of the blade. Or, the knife may be plunged deeply into the body with such force as to indent the abdominal or chest wall, so that the length of the knife track exceeds the length of the knife blade. If there are numerous stab wounds in the body, one can usually get an approximation of the length and the width of the knife blade by examining them all.

The depth a stab wound needs to achieve to produce a life threatening or fatal wound depends on the area of the body stabbed. Minimum skin-to-organ distances for various organs have been determined by Connor et al. using computer tomography (CT).[2] There was no significant difference between the minimum skin to organ distances for males (44 cases) and females (27 cases). Table 7.1 gives the minimum, maximum and mean skin to organ distances for various organs. These distances may overstate the distance a knife needs to penetrate to reach an organ in that in real life situations the skin and subcutaneous tissue may be compressed by the force of the thrust.

Table 7.1 Distance from Skin to Organs (mm)

	Pleura	Pericardium	Liver	Spleen	Kidney	Thoracic aorta	Abdominal aorta	Femoral artery
Minimum	10	15	9	12	19	31	65	13
Maximum	48	45	36	39	79	93	102	25
Mean	22	31	19	23	37	64	87	18
Standard Deviation	7.9	7.1	6.3	7.0	13	15.1	10.3	3.9

Appearance of Stab Wounds in Skin

The size and shape of a stab wound in the skin depends on the nature of the blade and knife, the direction of the thrust, the movement of the blade in the wound, the movement of the individual stabbed, and the state of relaxation or tension of the skin. The sharpness of a weapon will determine the appearance of the margins of the wound: sharp and regular; abraded and bruised, or jagged and contused. With a blunt cutting edge, the edges of the wound may be abraded. If an individual is stabbed such that the flat surface of the knife blade is at an oblique angle to the skin, the stab wound will have a beveled margin on one side with undermining on the other, indicating the direction from which the knife entered.

The parts of a single-edge knife (Figure 7.2) are:

- Grip
- Guard
- Ricasso
- Back
- Spine
- Edge
- Point

The appearance of a stab wound can be influenced by how deep the knife is thrust in and what portion of the shaft penetrates or contacts the skin. If

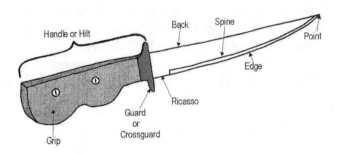

Figure 7.2 Parts of single-edge knife.

the knife is thrust with great force into the body up to the guard, then the imprint of the guard could be on the skin. If the knife is thrust in up to the ricasso, the wound can be squared at both ends.

The shape of a stab wound in the skin is determined not only by the shape of the blade, but by the properties of the skin. If a stab wound is inflicted when the skin is stretched, the resulting long, thin wound will assume a shorter, broader appearance when the skin relaxes. Langer's lines can also influence the appearance of a wound. Langer's lines are a pattern of elastic fibers in the dermis of the skin, which is approximately the same from individual to individual. Plastic surgeons take advantage of this pattern of fibers to conceal scars. If one is stabbed across these lines, that is, perpendicular to the fibers, the fibers will pull apart the edges of the wound, creating a gaping wound (Figure 7.3). Stab wounds parallel to Langer's lines produce narrow slit-like wounds. Between the two extremes are oblique wounds. Here, depending on the pattern of the fibers, the wounds may be asymmetrical or semicircular. If the edges of a gaping wound are drawn together, the size of the restored wound approximates the maximum possible width of the knife blade.

If a double-edged weapon is used to stab an individual, the wound produced will show bilateral pointed ends. If a single-edged weapon is used, theoretically, one end of the stab wound is pointed and the other is squared off or blunted (Figure 7.1). However, stab wounds with double-edged weapons are uncommon in the U.S. Virtually all stab wounds seen are made with single-edged weapons. When actual wounds are examined, it becomes obvious that a number of stab wounds caused by single-edged weapons have bilateral pointed ends like those made with double-edged weapons. There are two explanations for this. First, as the tip of the knife perforates the skin,

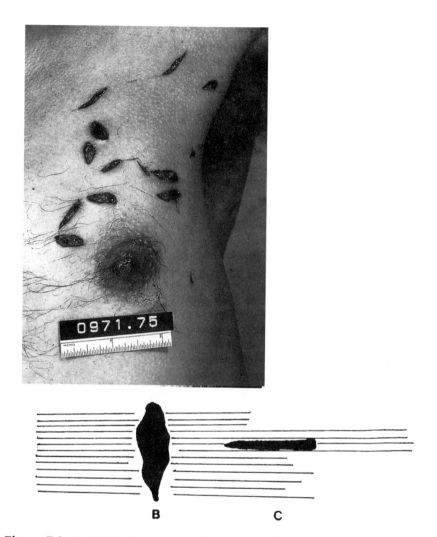

Figure 7.3 (A) Multiple stab wounds with same knife. Varied shapes to wounds due to Langer's lines. Effect of Langer's lines on stab wound perpendicular to (B) and parallel to (C) lines.

it is pulled down, with the cutting edge slicing through the skin and the squared-off back of the knife not imparting its configuration to the skin because it does not contact it. Second, many single-edged knives have a cutting edge on the back of the knife at the tip. Thus, the initial plunge into the skin will produce a double-pointed wound. Then, as the rest of the knife goes through the skin, if it is pulled down slightly, the back or squared off portion of the knife will never contact the skin.

Thus, while in theory one can look at a stab wound and say the weapon was single- or double-edged, in reality, it is not always possible through examination of a single wound. If an individual is stabbed multiple times with a single-edged knife, examination of the wounds will eventually disclose the typical single-edged configuration.

As a knife is withdrawn from the body, it may be twisted or the person stabbed may move. In such a case, the knife might produce a Y- or L-shaped wound (Figure 7.4). There will be a primary stab wound with an extension caused by the knife's edge cutting a secondary path as it exits. A variation of this can be seen when the knife is only slightly rotated or the individual moves only slightly, such that one end (the cutting end) of the stab wound will have an inverted V-shaped notch or "fork" in it (Figure 7.5)Thus, in this situation with a single-edged knife, one end of the stab wound will be squared or blunted and the other will be forked.

This picture of a fork at one end of a stab wound caused by the cutting edge of the knife can be simulated by tears in the skin at the squared-off end of the stab wound produced by the back of the blade (the ricasso) lacerating the skin as the blade is plunged in. These tears can usually be differentiated from the fork cuts in that they are not as sharp and clean and are often confined to the superficial layers of the skin (Figure 7.6).

The most common reason for a large, irregular knife wound is movement of the victim as the weapon is withdrawn. Prosecutors, however, often contend that this is due to the perpetrator's twisting the knife in the body after stabbing the individual.

If a knife is plunged into the body with such great force that the full length of the blade enters, a patterned abrasion around the stab wound can be caused by the guard (Figure 7.7), which is a metal piece between the blade and handle originally designed to keep the user's hand on the handle. Use of the term "hilt" is technically incorrect, because that term refers to swords. A mark from a guard will be symmetrical if the knife is plunged straight in. (Figure 7.7A) If the knife is plunged in a downward angle, then the guard mark will be prominent above the stab wound; if the knife is plunged upward, the guard mark will be below the stab wound. In oblique stab wounds, a knife plunged in from the right will have a guard mark on the right (Figure 7.7 (B, D)).

In some stab wounds, examination of the wound will reveal both ends to have a squared-off or blunt appearance. This is caused by the knife's being plunged in the full length up to the guard. In most weapons, between the true edge of the knife and the guard, there is a short, unsharpened section of blade called the ricasso. This generally has a squared-off configuration that is identical on both the back and the cutting edge of the knife. Thus, if the knife goes in all the way, one end of the stab wound will be squared off by the back of the knife, and the other by the ricasso.

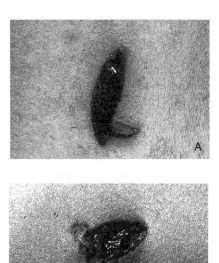

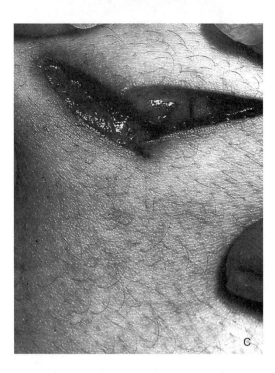

Figure 7.4 (A, B and C) Irregular configuration of stab wounds caused by knife's being twisted or movement of victim as blade is withdrawn.

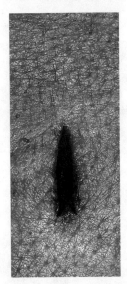

Figure 5.5 (A) Stab wounds from a single-edge knife with small forks at the cutting-edge end caused by the knife's being withdrawn. (B) Double-edged stab wound with fork at one end.

Stab Wounds from Weapons Other than Knives

When an individual is stabbed with an implement other than a knife, the stab wound may have a characteristic appearance because of the unusual nature of the weapon. Because ice picks are no longer common household objects, ice pick wounds are rarely seen nowadays. Ice picks produce small, round, or slit-like wounds that can be easily missed or confused with wounds caused by .22-caliber bullets or shotgun pellets (Figure 7.8). A single ice pick wound might be missed on a cursory examination of a body, especially if there is little or no external bleeding (Figure 7.18).

If a victim is stabbed with a barbecue fork, there will be clusters of two or three wounds, depending on the number of prongs on the fork (Figure 7.9A). Each of the stab wounds will be equally spaced, as are the prongs of the fork. Perforation of the skin with a kitchen fork is generally not possible. The authors have seen only one death due to a stab wound with a kitchen

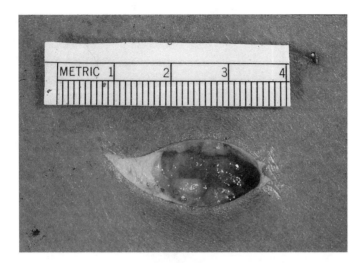

Figure 7.6 Tearing at squared-off margin of stab wound from single-edged knife produced by back of blade's lacerating skin.

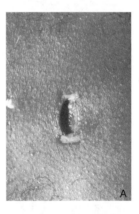

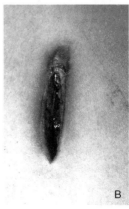

Figure 7.7 Patterned abrasions around stab wounds due to single-edged knife with guard. (A) Symmetrical marking at superior and inferior margins. (B) Knife plunged in a downward angle with guard mark at squared off margin *(continued).*

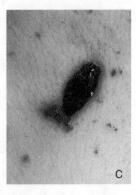

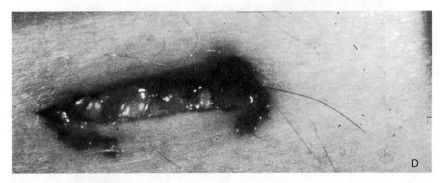

Figure 7.7 *(Continued)* Patterned abrasions around stab wounds due to single-edged knife with guard. (C) Knife plunged upward with guard mark on inferior margin of stab wound. (D) Oblique stab wound with guard mark on inferior margin.

fork (through the chest wall into a lung), though they have seen numerous attempts. What one sees is a pattern of three or four (depending on the number of prongs) abrasions or superficial penetrating wounds of the skin caused by the prongs of the fork (Figures 7.9 B,C).

The authors have seen fatal stab wounds inflicted with pens, pencils, broken pool cues, etc. In one case, an individual was stabbed on the left side of the neck with a ballpoint pen. The pen perforated skin, muscle, and ligaments; penetrating into the spinal column at the atlanto-occipital junction, and perforating the spinal cord (Figure 7.10).

The appearance of stab wounds made with scissors depends on whether the scissors were open or closed at the time of stabbing (Figure 7.11). If closed, the tip of the scissors splits rather than cuts the skin, producing a linear stab wound with abraded margins. If the screw holding the two blades is not flush but protrudes, it can produce an angular laceration in the mid portion of one of the skin margins. If the two blades are separated, two stab wounds will be produced with each stab.

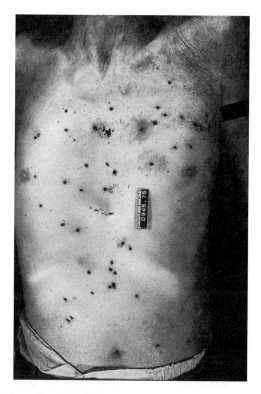

Figure 7.8 Elderly individual with multiple ice pick wounds of chest originally believed to be shotgun pellet wounds.

Figure 7.9 (A) Stab wound with barbeque fork *(continued)*.

Stab wounds with screwdrivers may show very characteristic configuration if the weapon is a Phillips screwdriver. In such instances, the X-shaped point of the blade will cause a circular wound with four equally spaced cuts and an abraded margin (Figure 7.12 A, B). A standard-blade screwdriver will produce a slit-like stab wound with squared ends and abraded margins

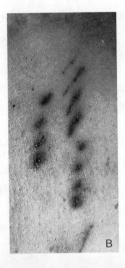

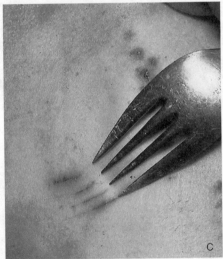

Figure 7.9 *(continued)* (B and C) Superficial stab wounds caused by kitchen fork.

(Figure 7.12 C). Thus, one cannot be absolutely sure whether a wound has been produced by a screwdriver or by a knife with a narrow, dull blade, plunged in up to the guard.

Stab wounds inflicted with a broken bottle tend to occur as clusters of wounds of different sizes, shapes, and depths (Figure 7.13 A, B). The stab wounds are sharp edged but ragged and there are differences in the depth of penetration for the individual wounds. Most fatal stab wounds with broken bottles are homicides, occasionally suicides, and, rarely, accidents (Figure 7.13 C). In one case, an individual died when he fell on a broken bottle. The broken end penetrated into the right side of the neck, severing a major vessel.

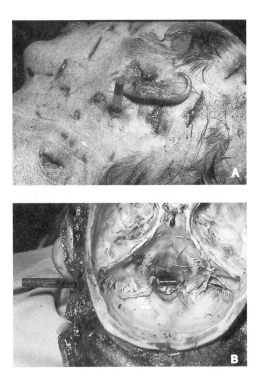

Figure 7.10 Stab wound of neck from ballpoint pen with perforation of spinal cord at atlanto-occipital junction.

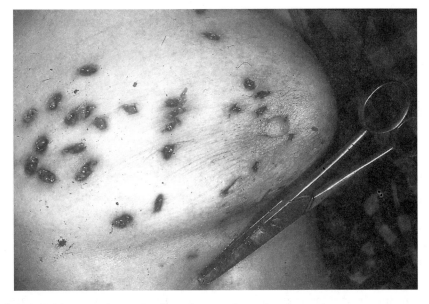

Figure 7.11 Suicide. Multiple stab wounds with scissors.

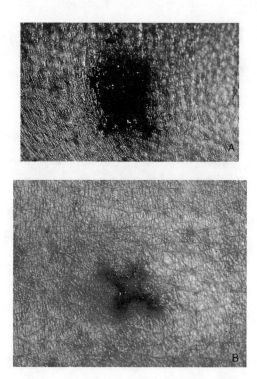

Figure 7.12 (A and B) Stab wounds with Phillips screwdriver.

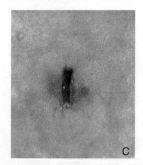

Figure 7.12 (C)   Stab wounds from
traditional screwdriver

Stab wounds caused by swords and lances are virtually unheard of in the U.S. The authors have encountered only one, a sword wound. Occasionally, one sees deaths caused by arrows or crossbow bolts. These are, in a way, stab wounds. The appearance of the wound depends on the arrowhead. Target arrows have pointed conical ends. They produce circular entrance wounds in the skin similar in appearance to bullet wounds. Hunting arrows have from two to five knife-like edges (four or five are the most common). The wounds produced are cross-like or X-shaped with the four-edged arrowhead. The margins of the wound appear incised, without abrasions.

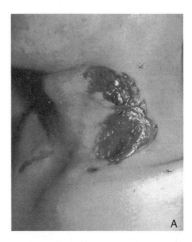

Figure 7.13 (A and B) Stab wounds from broken bottle.

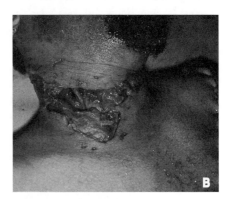

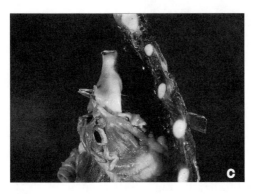

Figure 7.13 (C) Sliver of glass perforating stemum and aorta. Deceased fell through glass door.

Identifying the Weapon

The pathologist is often asked to give an opinion as to the characteristics of a knife used in a killing. Was the knife single- or double-edged? What was the length of the knife blade? The width? Was the blade serrated? Was more than one knife used?

One should be extremely cautious in giving answers to these questions. In most cases, on examining a wound, the most information that can be deduced is the maximum width of the blade, an approximation of the length of the blade, and whether it is single-edged. If the stab wound passes at an oblique or perpendicular angle to Langer's lines, one must reorient the wound edges to see the true appearance of the blade.

One can never definitely link a knife to a wound unless the tip of the knife has imbedded itself in the body and broken off (Figure 7.14). If the knife is recovered, this tip can be matched to the knife by tool mark comparison. A physical match in such a case is as valid as a ballistics match of a bullet.

In most instances, the most that one can do when presented with a knife and asked if it was the weapon that produced a specific wound is state that it could have been. To be sure that a knife blade was serrated from the appearance of the wound is rare (Figure 7.15).

All knives thought to have injured or killed an individual should be examined for the presence of blood or tissue. Any blood or tissue present can be typed by DNA techniques so as to link the weapon to the victim. It is possible for a knife or similar weapon to not show microscopic blood staining after it has been used to stab an individual. In stab wounds of solid organs, bleeding occurs only after the knife is withdrawn because pressure of the knife *in situ* prevents bleeding. During withdrawal of the knife, the muscular and elastic tissue of the solid organs stabbed or the elastic tissue of the skin may contract about the knife and wipe off the blood present on the blade of the knife. During its withdrawal from the body, the knife may also be wiped clean by the clothing. If a knife appears to be free of blood, the handles should be removed to see if any blood is there. With folding knives, the recess for the blade should also be tested for blood. Even though the blade or recess may appear to be free of blood or tissue, analysis of wipings of the blade might still yield sufficient tissue to perform at least limited DNA analysis and typing. This may be sufficient to link a weapon to a victim.

On rare occasions, a knife is found embedded in the body. To remove it, the thumb and index finger should grasp the sides of the handle immediately adjacent to the skin. This will enable the examiner to avoid touching that portion of the knife handle that was in contact with the assailant's hand, where fingerprints may have been left.

Rarely, the weapon is found firmly clenched in the deceased's hand (Figure 2.4). Cadaveric spasm, an intense muscular contraction of the hand, which occurs at the moment of death, provides unequivocal proof that the person had the weapon in his hand prior to death.

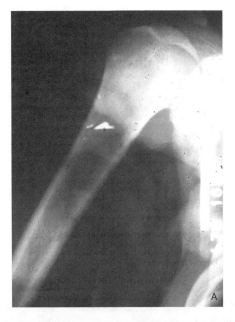

Figure 7.14 (A) Broken knife blade embedded in humerus. (B) Match made with murder weapon.

Usually, following a suicidal stabbing, the weapon is found immediately adjacent to or a short distance from the body. Absence of blood on the hand is inconsistent with a suicidal cutting of the throat, but may occur with suicidal stab wounds of the chest or abdomen. The absence of a weapon at the scene of a death suggests a homicide because an assailant usually does not leave the weapon at the scene of death. Rarely, a suicide victim survives

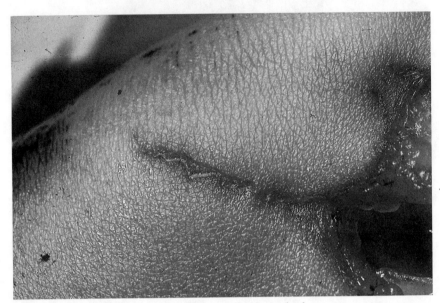

Figure 7.15   Stab wound from blade with serrated edge.

long enough to clean the weapon and replace it in its usual storage area or hide it. It is also possible for a perpetrator to leave the weapon near the body to suggest a suicide.

Manner of Death

Most deaths due to stab wounds are homicides. In such killings, multiple wounds are usually widely scattered over the body. Most of the wounds often fail to penetrate deeply and, thus, are not life threatening. Most life-threatening wounds involve the chest and abdomen. Death is usually fairly rapid and due to exsanguination.

Suicide by stabbing is uncommon. When individuals decide to stab themselves, they will often unbutton or pull aside their clothing to expose the area that they intend to stab. Most suicidal stab wounds involve the mid and left chest and are multiple in number, with many wounds showing minimal penetration or just barely breaking the skin (Figure 7.16(A)). The latter are "hesitation" stab wounds. Suicidal stab wounds vary in size and depth with usually only one or two "final" stab wounds going through the chest wall, into an internal organ. Occasionally, a knife will be plunged into the body without any evidence of hesitancy (Figure 7.16 (B)). In some instances, the knife is left *in situ*. In one case the authors are aware of, an individual stabbed himself with two knives and left them embedded in his abdomen.

Once connected with the traditions of Japanese Samurai warriors, *seppuku* (commonly called *hara-kiri*) is an unusual form of suicide involving an

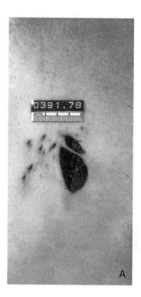

Figure 7.16 (A)　Multiple suicidal stab wounds of chest with only one penetrating into chest cavity. (B) Single stab wound to the left chest with knife embedded in chest

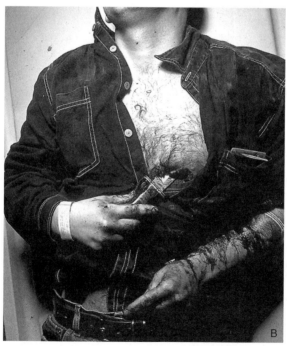

abdominal stab wound. A single large wound is inflicted in the abdomen. The sudden evisceration of the internal organs results in an immediate decrease of intra-abdominal pressure and cardiac return, which results in sudden cardiac collapse. The proper method for performing seppuku involves plunging a short sword into the left side of the abdomen, drawing the blade across to the right side of the abdomen and then turning it upward, producing an L-shaped cut.

Impaling injuries are very uncommon. When they do occur, they are usually caused by falls and traffic accidents. Rarely, one encounters deliberate sexually motivated impalement, usually involving the anus and genital area. Occasionally, individuals fall on an object that they are carrying, e.g., a pencil. More commonly, individuals fall or jump from a structure onto a pointed object such as a fence.[3] Falling pipes and metal rods have also impaled individuals. In traffic accidents, a vehicle might crash into an obstacle, e.g., a fence, which, in part or in whole, is driven into the car (usually the windshield), impaling the driver or a passenger (Figure 7.17). Shifting cargo, e.g., metal pipes, in the back of a vehicle can slide forward and impale the driver or passenger if the vehicle abruptly stops. Rare cases have been reported involving wood splinters in a tornado.

Stab Wounds by Anatomical Location

Most fatal stab wounds are located in the left chest region. Among a number of explanations is that most people are right handed and, when facing a victim, will tend to stab the left chest. In addition, if the intention is to kill someone, one would stab in the left chest where the heart is thought to be.

Most fatal stab wounds of the chest involve injury to the heart or aorta. Deaths due solely to a stab wound of the lung are less common. Fatal stab wounds of the right chest usually involve injury to the right ventricle, aorta, or right atrium. Stab wounds of the left chest usually injure the right ventricle when parasternal, and the left ventricle as the stab wounds become more lateral and inferior.[4] While hemopericardium is common, death caused solely by cardiac tamponade is not. In cardiac tamponade, once a victim acutely accumulates more than 150 mL of blood in the pericardial sac, death can occur at any time. Rather than this scenario, however, most deaths are due to a combination of hemothorax, external blood loss, and hemopericardium.

Stab wounds of the heart with severing of the left anterior descending coronary artery are rapidly fatal. In stab wounds, damage to the atria or great vessels leading to and from the heart are more serious than those of the ventricles because the ventricular muscle can contract, thus slowing or terminating bleeding. Stab wounds of the heart are typically inflicted over the front of the chest, occasionally the sides, and least commonly the back. The majority of the stab wounds of the left chest also perforate the lungs. Some individuals survive stab wounds of the heart.

Stab wounds of the lungs, like those of the heart, typically occur from wounds over the front of the chest, less commonly the sides, and only occasionally the back. Most such wounds are associated with wounds of the heart.

Death from stab wounds of the lungs alone are usually due to exsanguination with massive hemothorax. Pneumothorax may also occur.

Stab wounds of the lower chest can produce injuries to not only the heart and lungs, but also to the abdominal viscera. Fatal stab wounds of the abdomen usually involve injury to the liver or a major blood vessel, e.g., the aorta, vena cava, iliac, or mesenteric vessels. Occasionally, in wounds of the abdomen, death is not immediate. Rather, the victim develops peritonitis because of a wound of the bowel. The forensic pathologist, by virtue of his work, sees a biased sampling of cases — only those individuals who die of their injuries. Thus, in regard to all stab wounds of the abdomen, only two thirds enter the abdominal cavity and less than half of these inflict significant injury to the viscera.[5]

Less common are stab wounds of the head and neck. Stab wounds of the neck can produce rapid death by exsanguination; air embolism or asphyxia due to massive soft tissue hemorrhage with compression of the trachea and vessels in the neck. Delayed deaths might be due to cellulitis, or arterial thrombosis with cerebral emboli and infarction. In cases in which there are stab wounds of the head and neck, X-rays of the chest are suggested to rule out air embolus. Occasionally, in a stab wound of the neck, the knife will sever not only a major blood vessel, but also the trachea, with resultant massive hemorrhaging into the pulmonary tree.

Stab wounds of the brain are uncommon. Most occur through the eye or the temporal region because of the thinness of the bone in these areas. Often, single stab wounds of the brain are not immediately fatal, and the victim may walk or run away from the assailant. In some instances, victims may not realize that they have been stabbed.[6,7] Rarely, stab wounds of the brain are not discovered until years after the assault. Sometimes, the knife blade might still be present. Victims of stab wounds of the brain have, on occasion, been hospitalized and the knife's entry into the brain not discovered because the wound was concealed by hair; in the fold of the eye or under the eyelid.[6] Death in such cases was due to either continuing intracranial bleeding or infection. At autopsy, the skull defect produced by the weapon will match the width and thickness of the knife blade or screwdriver or the diameter of an ice pick. Bleeding from a stab wound of the brain may be subdural, subarachnoid, intracerebral, or a combination of all three.

Stab wounds of the spine are uncommon. Like stab wounds of the head, the knife blade may break off and be found in the spine. Injury to the cord will produce either complete or partial paralysis below the level of injury. Delayed presentation is rare, but occurred as long as 30 years after the stabbing in one case.[8]

While most lethal stab wounds involve the trunk, head, or neck, occasionally one will have a lethal stab wound of an extremity. Most commonly,

Figure 7.17 Impaling injury from a pipe.

the vessel involved is the femoral artery. In virtually all these cases, the individuals stabbed are intoxicated and do not realize the lethality of their injury. Instead, they keep walking around bleeding copiously before they collapse and die.

Most stab wounds of the upper extremities are sustained by victims as they try to defend or protect themselves from assailants. Defense wounds of the lower extremities occur but are uncommon.

In rare instances, the weapon used to inflict a stab wound, e.g. an ice pick, may produce an inconspicuous external wound, with minimal or no external bleeding (Figure 7.18). This stab wound can be overlooked in examination of the body at the scene, where conditions for ideal examination are lacking.

Probing of stab wounds is usually of very little benefit, in that the probe, with very little force, will produce multiple erroneous wound tracks. Thus, probing is not recommended.

Incised-Stab Wounds

An incised-stab wound is a stab wound that is converted to an incised (slashing) wound. The wound starts out as a stab wound with the knife plunged into the body. The knife, instead of being immediately withdrawn, is pulled toward the assailant, slicing through the tissue, extending the length of the

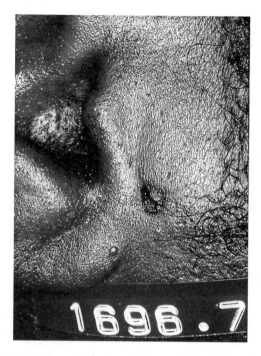

Figure 7.18 Inconspicuous single ice pick wound in front of ear. Ice pick perforated vertebral artery.

wound in the skin such that the wound is now longer than deep. This is accomplished in one continuous flowing movement. In Figure 7.19, the deceased was stabbed on the right side of the neck with the tip of the knife penetrating into the third cervical vertebra. The knife was then pulled anteriorly, toward the assailant, slicing through skin, muscle and the jugular veins.

Usually, one cannot tell the direction the knife was drawn through the tissue from examination of the wound alone. The only way a differentiation can be made is if there is a nick or forked configuration to one end of the wound. If present, this indicates that the blade was drawn toward this end.

Physical Activity Following a Fatal Stab Wound

The question of whether an individual is capable of physical activity, i.e., able to walk or run away from the assailant after receiving a fatal stab wound, depends on the organ(s) injured, the extent of the injury, the amount of blood lost, and the rapidity with which the blood is lost. With profuse bleeding, physical activity is limited or lost rapidly; with slow bleeding, the victim is capable of walking away from the assailant. Not infrequently, a trail of blood will mark the path of escape. A stab wound that will disable one victim will not necessarily affect the physical activity

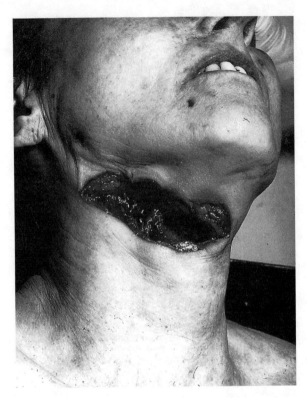

Figure 7.19 Incised-stab wound of right side of neck. The assailant was facing the deceased at the time the wound was inflicted.

of another. The authors have seen prolonged survival (several hours) following stab wounds of major vessels.

Karger et al. evaluated 12 cases of suicide from sharp pointed weapons in order to estimate the potential for physical activity following injury.[9] In all cases, the suicidal action and the subsequent behavior were witnessed. Seven of the victims had stab wounds of the heart. These latter deaths fell into three categories, based on time of survival and physical activity: immediate incapacitation (one case); short-term survival (two cases) and long-term survival (four cases). The short-term group collapsed in approximately 10 seconds; the long-term 2–10 minutes.

The individual who collapsed immediately had a 15 mm wound of the heart and a 450 ml tamponade. In the short-term group, both individuals collapsed in 10 seconds; both had tamponade, one 250 ml with the other not specified. The stab wounds of the heart were 14 and 20 mm long, compared with 7–10 mm for the long-term group. In two of the long-term group, cardiac tamponade of 300 and 400 ml were found. No mention of tamponade is made in the other two cases. The individual with the 400 ml tamponade lived the longest — 10 min. An eighth case involved a stab wound of the heart with a cannula. This individual survived 2 h and was found to have a 600 ml tamponade.

In the eight cases with stab or puncture wounds of the heart, the right ventricle was punctured three times; the left five. All injuries to the heart perforated only the anterior wall. The case with the longest time of physical activity (2 h) and three of the four individuals in the long-term physical activity group had wounds of the left ventricle, while both cases in the short-term group had wounds of the right ventricle. In another case, an individual stabbed himself in the right chest, injuring his lung and liver. He survived 2 h and was found to have a 2200 right hemothorax and a 700 ml hemoperitoneum.

Force Necessary to Inflict Fatal Stab Wounds

It is impossible to exactly quantitate the force exerted by an assailant in inflicting a fatal stab wound. After comparing and correlating the relation of each of the following four variables with those of the fatal stab wound, it is possible, however, to state in comparative terms the force required to inflict the fatal stab wound:

1. *The condition of the knife*: a sharp point; a dull point; a sharp or dull cutting edge; a thin or thick blade; double-edged or single-edged cutting blade. A sharp, pointed, double-edged, thin knife requires less force or effort to penetrate tissues or organs than a single-edged, blunt, pointed, dull blade.
2. *The resistance offered by the different tissues or organs penetrated*. Penetration of skin, cartilage, and bone, which are tough structures, requires greater force than that required for penetration of soft tissue, such as fat. Therefore, the tissue or organs penetrated by the knife will indicate the amount of force exerted by the assailant.
3. The depth and length of the stab wound. A 2-in blade causing a 4-in-deep stab wound must be inflicted with great force.
4. The amount of clothing and its composition will also determine the amount of force to be exerted. For example, leather belts, thick leather jackets, fur coats, and so on will require a greater force for penetration than scant, soft clothing.

In regard to the above item # 2, O'Callaghan et al. measured the force necessary for a knife to penetrate different tissues.[10] They inflicted a series of stab wounds to a depth of 10 cm in cadaveric tissue and amputated specimens. They determined that the mean force to penetrate skin, subcutaneous fat and muscle was 11.1 lb (49.5 N) with a range of 7.9 to 12.4 lb; for subcutaneous fat and muscle 7.8 lb (35 N); for muscle 8.4 lb (37.5 N) and for fat 0.5 lb (2 N).

Postmortem Bleeding

Drainage from a postmortem incised or stab wound is usually minimal due to the small quantity of blood present in the severed blood vessel. However, should a large blood vessel be severed after death and the vessel be located in a dependent area of the body, the quantity of blood lost could be considerable. The dependent position enables the network of blood vessels communicating with the severed vessel to drain or "bleed" through the severed vascular wall. In postmortem experiments, one of the authors severed large blood vessels in the chest and abdominal cavities to determine the quantity of blood that could be lost in each body cavity; 300–500 mL of blood leaked out into the cavities. This quantity of blood is small in comparison with the usual amount of blood that accumulates during antemortem wounding.

When a victim is stabbed multiple times and bleeds heavily, the last stab wound inflicted may appear bloodless. In such cases, the medical examiner may experience difficulty in deciding whether this stab wound was inflicted before, during, or soon after death.

During movement or transportation of a body, blood may escape from the wounds and stain the clothing. Thus, blood stains on the clothing at the time of autopsy may have occurred during movement and transportation of the victim's body. Blood stains or blood-stain patterns initially present on the clothing may be enlarged, increased in number, or obliterated by the flow of postmortem blood during transportation.

Incised Wounds

Incised wounds or cuts are produced by sharp-edged weapons or instruments. A knife is the classical example of a weapon used to inflict an incised wound, though, in fact, any instrument with a sharp edge can do so e.g., a piece of glass, metal, or paper. The sharp edge of the instrument is pressed into and drawn along the surface of the skin, producing a wound whose length is greater than its depth.

In incised wounds, the length and depth of the wound will not provide information as to the weapon. A 3-in-long incised wound could have been produced by a 6-in blade, a 2-in blade, a razor, or even a piece of glass. Incised wounds should not be confused with lacerations. Incised wounds have clean-cut straight edges free of abrasion or contusion (Figure 7.20). There is no bridging in the depth of the wound. Lacerations, which are tears in the skin caused by blunt force, generally have ragged, abraded margins with bridging

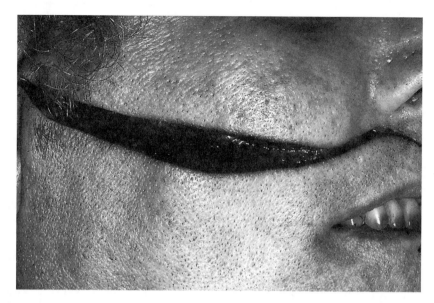

Figure 7.20 Incised wound of face caused by razor. Note sharp, clean margins.

of the base. One must realize, however, that a dull, irregular-edged, or nicked cutting edge can produce an incised wound with irregular, contused, or abraded margins because the wound is caused more by the pressure applied by the weapon than by the cutting edge. No bridging in the depth of the wound will occur, however.

Wounds of the scalp produced by heavy, usually metallic, objects with sharp edges can produce lacerations with sharp, non-abraded margins that can be confused with incised wounds. Careful examination of the base of the wound usually produces evidence of bridging, thus indicating a laceration. In some instances, however, just by examining a wound alone, it will not be possible to determine if it is an incised wound or a laceration. Other wounds on the body will often suggest the etiology of the ambiguous wound.

Incised wounds often begin very superficially, deepen, and then become superficial again. If the blade is held at an oblique angle to the skin, the wound will present a beveled or undermined edge. If the angle is extreme, a skin flap will be produced. On occasion, a single slash with a sharp, edged weapon might produce more than one incised wound. These are **wrinkle wounds**, which occur when the skin is not flat, but "wrinkled," that is, in folds. Here, the cutting edge skips from crest to crest of the skin, leaving a string of cuts, all of which have resulted from a single slash (Figure 7.21). Usually, these lie in a straight line and it is fairly simple to deduce what has occurred. If the skin is thrown into irregular folds, an irregular zigzag wound may be produced by a single swipe of the blade. In such a case, the blade rolls up the skin before cutting through it.

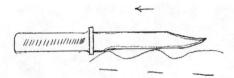

Figure 7.21 Incised "wrinkle" wound caused by knife drawn across skin from crest to crest.

The edges of an incised wound tend to separate or gap. The extent to which the wound gaps and the shape it subsequently assumes depend on whether it is parallel, transverse, or oblique to the direction of the elastic fibers in the skin (Langer's lines). Thus, an incised wound parallel to the contractile fibers will gap less than one made at a right angle or obliquely across the fibers because the fibers will pull the skin apart and evert the edges.

Incised wounds are usually not fatal. Most are seen in emergency rooms, where they are treated with a few sutures and the victims released. Incised wounds are most frequently inflicted on the exposed portions of the body: the head, neck, and arms. If the victim survives, the wounds usually heal by primary intention, leaving a thin, linear scar. Fatal incised wounds generally involve the arms and neck and are usually suicidal. Homicidal incised wounds almost always involve the neck.

Suicidal incised wounds are generally inflicted on those parts of the body most accessible to the victim. The victim may expose the portion of the body to be incised. For example, he may open his collar before cutting his throat, or pull up his shirt before cutting his chest or abdomen.

In self-inflicted incised wounds, one will often find **hesitation marks** (Figure 7.22). These are superficial incised wounds adjacent to, a continuation of, or overlying the fatal incised wound. They are very superficial and often do not go through the skin. One has the impression that the deceased attempted to cut the skin, but either because of pain or hesitancy, did not initially cut deep, but rather made multiple, very superficial cuts, almost like paper cuts, until finally, he built up enough courage to actually cut through the skin. Very superficial incised wounds identical to hesitation marks occasionally can be seen in homicidal incised wounds of the neck. This could be caused by either struggling of the individual prior to the infliction of the fatal wound or perhaps the perpetrator's initial hesitancy to cut the victim's throat.

Fatal incised wounds of the arms are almost always suicidal. As a means of attempting suicide, cutting one's wrists is a poor method. Most people have a vague knowledge of anatomy and do not know where to sever a major vessel. In addition, they usually do not cut deep enough. Some individuals cut their forearms vertically, rather than horizontally, due to an ignorance of

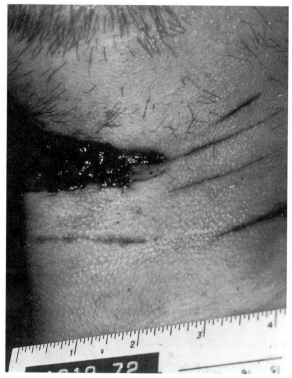

Figure 7.22 Incised wounds of neck with hesitation marks.

anatomy (Figure 7.23 A). One individual who did so had this fact explained to him by his physician. When the patient cut his wrist again later in the week, he cut the radial artery correctly and bled to death.

In self-inflicted incised wounds of the extremities, right-handed individuals usually cut the left wrist or forearm; left-handed individuals, the right wrist or forearm. These incised wounds are typically found on the flexor surface and radial aspect of the forearm (Figure 7.24 (A and B)). Thus, the presence of linear scars on the flexor surface in these areas suggests that an individual has attempted suicide in the past.

Defense wounds are wounds of the extremities incurred when an individual attempts to ward off a pointed or sharp-edged weapon. They are most commonly found on the palms of the hands, due to attempts to grasp or ward off the knife; the back (extensor surface) of the forearms and upper arms and on the ulnar aspect of the forearms (Figures 7.24 (C and D); 7.25). Rarely, defense wounds will be found on the feet or legs. In such a case, the

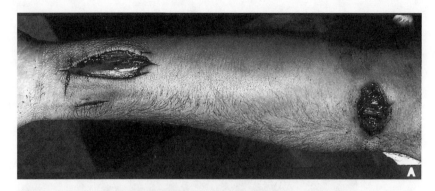

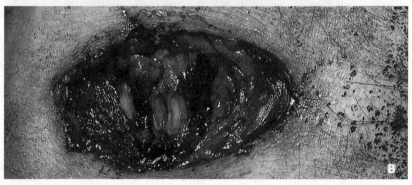

Figure 7.23 (A) Three self-inflicted incised wounds of flexor surface of left forearm, the two in the wrist, vertical in orientation. (B) Detail of wound of antecubital fossa showing partial severing of artery and vein.

individual might have kicked out at the knife to try to ward it off, or he might have curled up and tried to cover his vital areas with the legs.

In self-inflicted incised wounds using double-edged razor blades, the blade will often cut the fingers of the hand holding it. If individuals are using a knife and there is a lot of blood, there is a possibility that their hands could slip from the handle onto the blade, incurring an injury. In both instances, the wounds produced simulate defense wounds.

Incised Wounds of the Neck

Incised wounds of the neck can be accidental, homicidal, or suicidal. Accidental wounds are extremely rare, usually seen only when an individual goes through a sheet of glass or is struck in the neck by a flying fragment of glass or some other sharp-edged projectile. Thus, in one case, a 13-year-old male was struck by flying glass when a bottle containing dry ice exploded. The fragment of glass severed his left jugular vein, causing exsanguination.

Homicidal incised wounds of the neck present two different pictures, depending on whether they are produced from the back or the front. Most

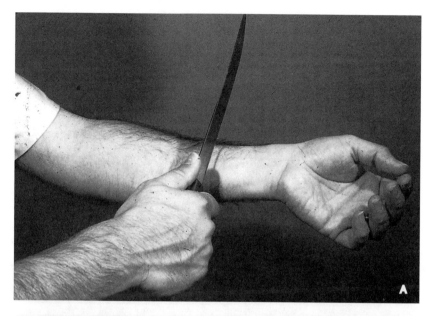

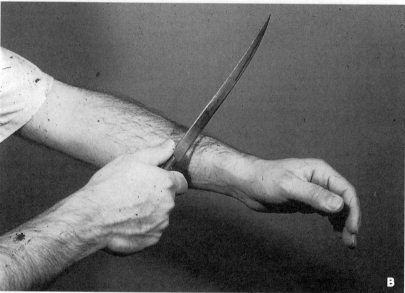

Figure 7.24 Demonstration of (A) self-inflicted incised wound of flexor surface of wrist (B) self-inflicted incised wound of radial aspect of forearm *(continued)*.

commonly, a person's throat is cut from behind. The head is pulled back, exposing the neck, and the knife is then drawn across it. Often, the victim is face down on the floor or ground at the time the wound is inflicted. The perpetrator usually starts the incision high up on the side of the neck

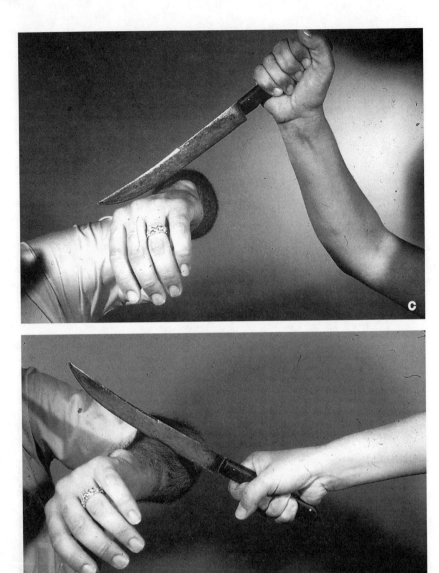

Figure 7.24 *(Continued)* Demonstration of (C) defense wound of back of forearm, (D) defense wound of ulnar aspect of forearm.

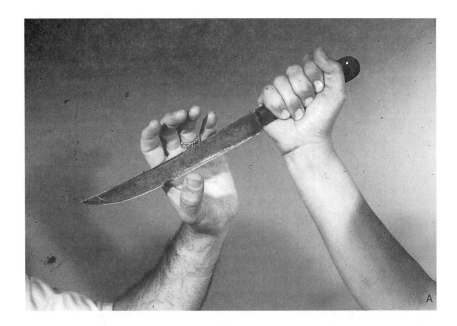

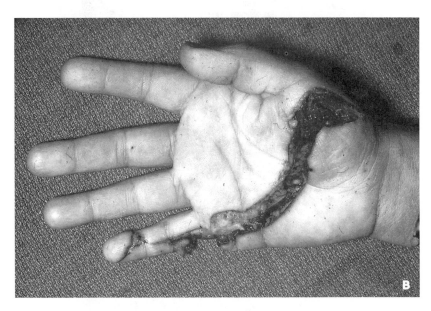

Figure 7.25 (A and B) Defense wound of palm of hand incurred in attempt to grasp knife.

opposite to the hand he is using. The knife is drawn across the neck, from left to right by a right-handed assailant and from right to left by a left-handed individual. The wound inflicted is first shallow, then deeper and then shallow again, terminating on the opposite side of the neck. The wound generally starts below the ear; runs downward and medially at an angle, then straight across the midline of the neck, and then upward, ending on the opposite side of the neck, lower than its point of initiation (Figure 7.26).

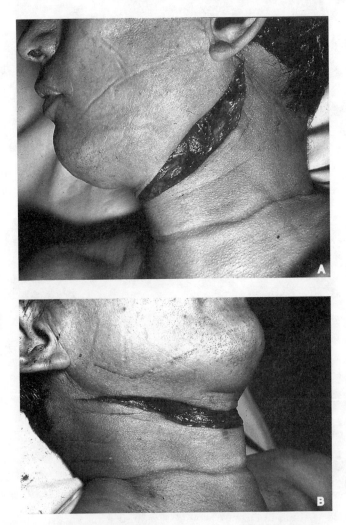

Figure 7.26 Homicidal incised wound of neck inflicted from back beginning below left ear (A) running downward and medially across the midline of the neck and upward on the opposite side of the neck, ending lower than its point of initiation (B).

Homicidal incised wounds of the neck inflicted from the front tend to be short and angled (Figure 7.27). A right-handed individual typically inflicts incised wounds on the left side of the victim's neck, with the slashes running downward and medially at an oblique angle. If the wounds are inflicted on the right side, they tend to be fewer in number. Wounds across the front of the neck tend to be horizontal and short, extending a short distance to the right or left of the midline. Horizontally incised wounds inflicted from the front of the neck are the least common. The characteristics of the wounds produced by a frontal attack are obvious with an understanding of the etiology. Instead of the neck's being cut with one long, continuous motion, these wounds are inflicted by "swipes" or slashes made while facing the individual.

In self-inflicted wounds of the neck, the same general pattern holds as for a homicidal assault from the rear. The wound usually begins higher on the neck on the side opposite to where it terminates. Suicidal incised wounds of the neck are usually, but not always, accompanied by hesitation marks (Figure 7.28). In rare instances, a fatal self-inflicted incised wound of the neck may be accompanied by cadaveric spasm (instantaneous rigor mortis) with the knife or razor found firmly clenched in the victim's hand — unequivocal proof of suicide. In some suicides, the weapon might not be present at the scene. Another person may have altered the scene, or, if the initial wound was not immediately incapacitating, the suicide victim was allowed time to conceal the weapon prior to death.

Incised wounds of the neck may be extremely deep and extend completely to the vertebral column. This is most common in homicidal wounds inflicted from the rear.

Death from incised wounds of the neck may be due not only to exsanguination, but to massive air embolus. An X-ray of the chest for the detection of air in the venous system and heart is recommended. Subsequently, the heart should be examined for air emboli. The length of time it takes to die following an incised wound of the neck depends on whether the venous or arterial systems are severed and whether there is air embolism.

Miscellaneous

Pieces of glass have been used to cut wrists and throats and to slash people. They have been used in both homicides and suicides. Occasionally, an accidental death will be caused by glass. The authors have seen a number of cases in which an intoxicated individual knocked out a pane of glass with a hand or fist. In the process, as the arm went through the glass, or when it was pulled back, a jagged projection of glass cut the arm, inflicting a deep wound and severing a major vessel, with resultant exsanguination (Figure 7.29).

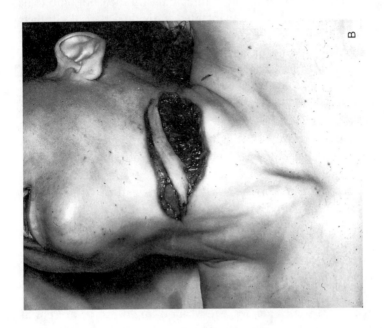

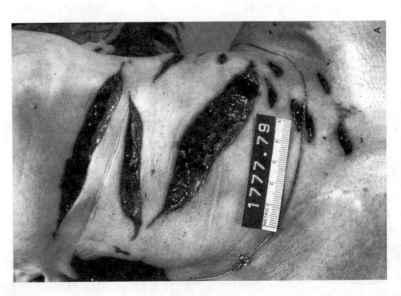

Figure 7.27 (A, B) Homicidal incised wounds of the neck inflicted from the front. Note short slashing nature of wounds.

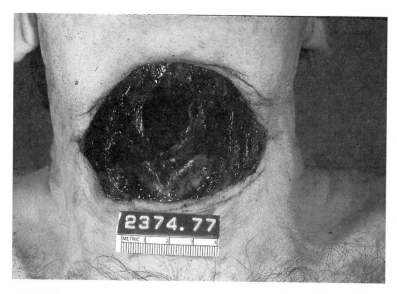

Figure 7.28 Self-inflicted incised wound of neck with hesitation marks.

Psychotic individuals may use edged weapons to mutilate either themselves or others. Mutilation usually involves the genitalia, ears, or nose. Non-psychotic individuals may mutilate as a warning, in revenge, or to collect souvenirs (usually ears). Husbands occasionally mutilate the genitalia of cheating wives. Sexual mutilation of prostitutes occurs, though rarely.

In bodies in which there is prolonged immersion in water, the water can leach out the blood in both stab and incised wounds, giving an almost postmortem appearance to these wounds, suggesting that they were inflicted after death rather than before (Figure 7.30).

In both incised and stab wounds, one should always examine the clothing to see if there are defects corresponding to the wounds. This is to rule out an individual's being stabbed or cut and then the body dressed.

Chop Wounds

Chop wounds are produced by heavy instruments with a cutting edge, e.g., axes, machetes, and meat cleavers. The presence of an incised wound of the skin, with an underlying comminuted fracture or deep groove in the bone, indicates that one is dealing with a chopping weapon (Figure 7.31). When the perpetrator pulls out a weapon that has embedded itself in the bone, he might give it a sharp twist, fracturing or breaking off the adjacent bone. In tangential wounds of the skull, chopping instruments may cut off disks of bone.

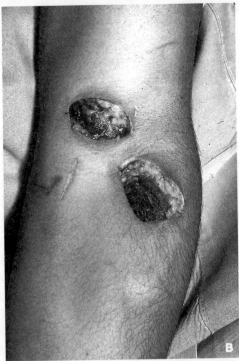

Figure 7.29 (A, B) While intoxicated, the deceased attempted to break a window and enter. He incurred wounds of the left arm, with severing of major vessels and exsanguination.

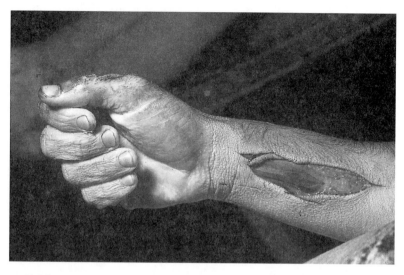

Figure 7.30 Antemortem incised wound of right forearm with blood leached out following prolonged immersion in water.

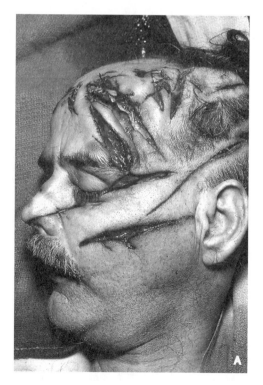

Figure 7.31 (A) Chopping wounds of head from machete. Note incised-like nature of wounds with cutting of underlying bone *(continued)*.

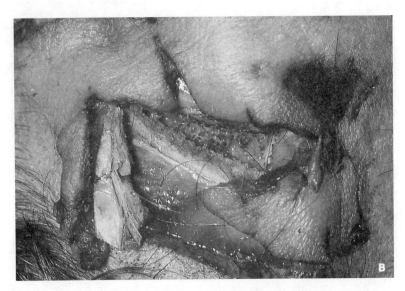

Figure 7.31 (*continued*) (B) Chopping wounds of head from machete. Note incised-like nature of wounds with cutting of underlying bone

While most chop wounds appear incised, when there is a combination of cutting and crushing, they can have both incised and lacerated characteristics.

Chopping weapons cutting through bone can impart characteristic striations on the bone unique to each type of weapon. Humphrey and Hutchinson evaluated hacking trauma on bones produced by cleavers, machetes and axes.[11] Hacking blows produce wounds in bone characterized by at least one smooth, flat side with, in the case of angled impacts, fracturing of the other side. Cleavers produce clean, narrow wounds without fractures at the entry site; machetes wider, less-clean wounds with small fragments of bone at the entry site and fractures in the bed of the cut. Axes make crushing, fragmenting wounds with fractures. Microscopic examination of these wounds by Tucker et al. found that cleavers produce thin, fine striations that are sharp and distinct.[12] Striations produced by machetes were more pronounced but coarse and less distinct. Axe wounds showed no striations on the bone. The authors thought that microspcopic analysis of hacking wounds of bone could distingish different classes of weapons. They also saw a potential to identify specific weapons. Boat or airplane propellers can produce chop-like wounds of the body. On occasion, a body will be pulled from the water with multiple chop wounds (Figure 7.32). The question then arises as to whether these are ante- or postmortem. If, on examination of the site of injury, there is hemorrhage in the soft tissue, one can be fairly sure that this is an antemortem injury. Absence of bleeding into a chop wound does not prove that the injury was postmortem, because prolonged immersion in water might result in the

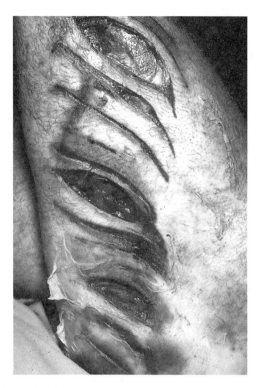

Figure 7.32 Body pulled from water; wounds caused by boat propeller.

leaching out of the blood from the wound, giving the appearance of a postmortem injury.

Therapeutic or Diagnostic Wounds

These are wounds produced by medical personnel during the treatment of a patient. Common examples are thoracotomy incisions; surgical stab wounds of the chest or abdomen for insertion of tubes and drains; laparotomy incisions; incisions for peritoneal lavage; cutdowns of the wrists, antecubital fossae, and ankles; and tracheostomy incisions.

Some of these surgical wounds may be mistaken for primary traumatic injury; e.g., a surgical stab wound of the chest for a drain could be interpreted as a homicidal stab wound. In other instances, the traumatic wounds are obliterated by the surgical procedure; e.g., a stab wound of the left chest might be incorporated into a thoracotomy incision. Occasionally, a homicidal stab wound is converted to a therapeutic use, e.g., a surgical drain might be placed into the chest cavity through a stab wound of the chest. If the individual dies and the drain tube is left in the stab wound, the wound could be misinterpreted at autopsy.

To avoid misinterpretation of therapeutic wounds, therapeutic tubing should never be removed prior to sending a body to the medical examiner; the chart should be reviewed prior to autopsy and, if any questions arise, the treating physicians should be consulted.

References

1. Knight B, The dynamics of stab wounds. *Forens Sci* 1975; 6:249-255.
2. Connor SEJ, Bleetman A, and Duddy MJ, Safety standards from stab-resistant body armour: a computer tomographic assessment of organ to skin distances. *Injury* 1998; 29(4):297.299.
3. Missliwetz, J, Fatal impalement injuries after falls at construction sites. *Am J Forens Med Path* 1995; 16 1):81-3.
4. Wilson RF and Bassett JS, Penetrating wounds of the pericardium or its contents. *JAMA* 1966; 195:513-518.
5. Moore EE and Marx JA, Penetrating abdominal wounds: Rationale for exploratory laparotomy. *JAMA* 1985; 253:2705-2708.
6. DiMaio VJM and DiMaio DJ, An unsuspected stab wound of the brain. *Military Med* 1972; 137:434-435.
7. Deb S et al., Stab wounds to the head with intracranial penetration *J. Trauma* 2000. 48(6):1159-1162.
8. Kulkani AV et al., Delayed presentation of spinal stab wounds: case report and review of the literature. *J. Emerg. Med* 2000; 18(2):209-213.
9. Karger B, Niemeyer J, and Brinkmann B, Physical activity following fatal injury from sharp pointed weapons. *Int. J. Legal. Med* 1999; 112:188-191.
10. O'Callaghan PT et al., Dynamics of stab wounds: force required for penetration of various cadaveric human tissues. *Forens Sci. Int* 1999; 104:173-178.
11. Humphrey, JH and Hutchinson, DL, Characteristics of hacking trauma. *J Forens Sci* 2001; 46 92 0 228-233.
12. Tucker BK et al., Characteristics of microscopic hacking trauma on bone. *J Forens Sci* 2001; 46(2) 234-240.

Asphyxia

8

Asphyxial deaths are caused by the failure of cells to receive or utilize oxygen. The deprivation of oxygen can be partial (hypoxia) or total (anoxia). The classical signs of asphyxia are visceral congestion, petechiae, cyanosis, and fluidity of blood. These are nonspecific, however, and can occur in deaths from other causes. Visceral congestion is due to obstructed venous return and capillovenous congestion. The latter is a result of the susceptibility of these vessels to hypoxia, with resultant dilatation of the vessels and stasis of blood.

Petechiae are pinpoint hemorrhages produced by rupture of small vessels, predominantly small venules. Rupture appears to be mechanical in etiology and is caused by sudden over distention and rupture of the vessels following abrupt increases in intravascular pressure.[1,2] These are most common in the visceral pleura and epicardium. In asphyxial deaths from strangulation, petechiae are classically seen in the conjunctivae and sclerae. Petechiae, as nonspecific markers,[1,2] may be seen in the conjunctivae and sclerae in association with many different conditions, not all fatal, and not just in asphyxial deaths. They are routinely seen in the reflected scalp in all types of death and are of no diagnostic significance in this area. Petechiae of the epiglottis are also of no significance. Gordon and Mansfield documented development of epicardial petechiae after death.[2]

Petechiae can develop after death in dependent areas of the body e.g., an arm hanging over the side of a bed. Here, gravity causes increased intravascular congestion and pressure with resultant mechanical rupture of small vessels. If the petechiae become larger or confluent, they are called ecchymoses.

Cyanosis is, of course, nonspecific and caused by an increase in the amount of reduced hemoglobin. It does not become observable until at least 5 g of reduced hemoglobin is present. Postmortem fluidity of blood is not characteristic of asphyxia or any cause of death, but rather the result of a high rate of fibrinolysis that occurs in rapid deaths, possibly by high agonal levels of catecholamines.[3]

Asphyxial deaths can be loosely grouped into three categories:

1. Suffocation
2. Strangulation
3. Chemical asphyxia

These deaths might be accidental, suicidal or homicidal in manner. Compared with other causes of homicide, homicides via asphyxia are relatively uncommon in the U.S. They predominantly involve strangulation — manual and ligature strangulation. In the last ten years, murders ascribed to strangulation have averaged 286 a year, with a range of 366 to 211. There seems to have been a gradual decrease in the number of such cases over the years. Murders caused by "asphyxiation" (no further description but excluding strangulation) have averaged 107 a year, with this number being fairly constant over the ten-year period.[4]

Suffocation

In deaths from suffocation, there is failure of oxygen to reach the blood. There are six general forms of suffocation:

1. Entrapment/environmental suffocation
2. Smothering
3. Choking
4. Mechanical asphyxia
5. Mechanical asphyxia combined with smothering
6. Suffocating gases

Entrapment / Environmental Suffocation

In suffocation by entrapment or environmental hazard, asphyxia is caused by inadequate oxygen in the environment. These deaths are almost exclusively accidental in nature. In **entrapment**, individuals find themselves trapped in an air-tight or relatively air-tight enclosure. Initially, there is sufficient oxygen to breathe. However, as respiration continues, they exhaust the oxygen and asphyxiate. The best example of this is a child trapped in a discarded refrigerator. Fortunately, this specific form of death by entrapment is becoming rare, as modern refrigerators do not have a latch system of locking and can be pushed open from the interior. Suicide and homicide by entrapment are rare, but do occur.

In **environmental suffocation**, an individual inadvertently enters an area where there is gross deficiency of oxygen. This deficiency is not due to displacement of the oxygen by suffocating gases, which will be discussed in another section, but rather that the oxygen has been depleted by some mechanism. Thus, the authors reported two deaths caused by lack of oxygen in an underground chamber.[5] The normal percentage by volume of oxygen in the atmosphere is 20.946%. In this particular case, the percentage by volume was 9.6%. This lethal atmosphere was caused by fungus-like organisms and low forms of plant life present on the vault walls and in the sediment on the floor. The metabolic processes of the fungi and plant life resulted in depletion of oxygen by these organisms, with production of carbon dioxide. Thus, carbon dioxide, which is normally 0.033% in air, in this case, was 7.0%. The increased quantity of carbon dioxide, however, was insufficient in itself to have caused death by displacement of oxygen. It was the absolute lack of oxygen that caused death. At oxygen concentrations of 10 to 15%, there is impairment in judgment and coordination. Loss of consciousness occurs at 8 to 10%; death at 8% and less. At oxygen concentrations of 4 to 6%, there is loss of consciousness in 40 sec and death within a few min.

In deaths due to **entrapment** or **environmental suffocation**, the cause of death cannot be determined by autopsy alone, because there are no specific findings. *All that one finds is nonspecific acute visceral congestion.* It is only by an analysis of the circumstances leading up to and surrounding death, and the exclusion of other causes, that one can make a determination as to the cause of death.

Smothering

Asphyxia by smothering is caused by the mechanical obstruction or occlusion of the external airways, i.e., the nose and mouth. Deaths such as these are usually either homicide or suicide, very rarely accident (Figure 8.1).

The most common form of suicidal smothering is the placing of a plastic bag over an individual's head (Figure 8.1 A). If it is heavy plastic, it may be secured at the neck. More commonly, suicides employ the thin, filmy plastic bag used by dry cleaners. Here, there is often no necessity to secure the bag at the neck, because it clings to the face, occluding the airways. These filmy plastic bags also account for the rare accidental deaths by smothering when these bags are used to cover a mattress or pillow in a crib of a young child. The child becomes enmeshed in the bag and smothers. In all the deaths that the authors have seen in which plastic bags have been placed over the head, there have been no specific autopsy findings. Petechiae of the face, sclerae, and conjunctivae were virtually always absent. Petechiae of the epicardium or pleural surfaces of the lung were sometimes present, but these are so nonspecific that the authors do not give any weight to them. If an individual commits suicide by use of a plastic bag and the bag is removed prior to notification of the authorities, a medical examiner cannot determine the cause of death by the autopsy.

There are occasional allegations of infants smothering in their cribs because of heavy blankets or bedding placed over them. The authors feel that these cases are examples of sudden infant death syndrome (SIDS) and that it is just coincidental that they are found covered by bed clothes. One can pile a number of blankets on an infant without causing any respiratory difficulty.

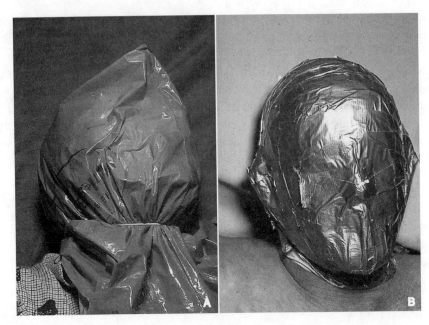

Figure 8.1 (A) Suicide of elderly female who secured plastic bag over head with tie around neck. (B) Accidental smothering in mentally retarded, 43-year-old male who wrapped face in duct tape. Deceased had performed this act before.

Occasionally, an alcoholic is found face down on a pillow, dead. Circumferential oral and nasal pallor is noted and death is attributed to smothering. This pallor, however, can be caused post mortem by passive pressure of the dependent head on the pillow. Thus, the diagnosis cannot be made on this "evidence." The authors have grave reservations about this diagnosis. An individual would have to be in an alcoholic coma to smother this way. Alcoholic coma, however, puts them in grave danger of death anyway and this is more likely the cause of death, rather than the alleged suffocation.

Accidental smotherings can occur with defective cribs. Here, an infant is trapped either between a too-small mattress and the frame of the crib, or between a defective crib and mattress, with the face wedged against the mattress (Figure 8.2). The child is unable to move and smothers.

Gags obstructing the nose and mouth can cause death by smothering. Such deaths, though unintentional, are still homicides if the victims die during the commission of a crime. Typically, a gag is placed around the face obstructing the mouth and nose (Figure 8.3). Victims are usually elderly individuals who are either unable to struggle sufficiently to move the gag or who are unusually susceptible to the anoxia by virtue of natural disease. Mucus and fluids may accumulate in the nasal cavities and airways, contributing to asphyxia. In the elderly, there may be congestion of the face with

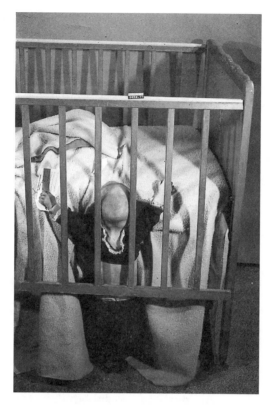

Figure 8.2 A 9-month-old child who slipped between frame and mattress of defective crib. Face wedged against mattress.

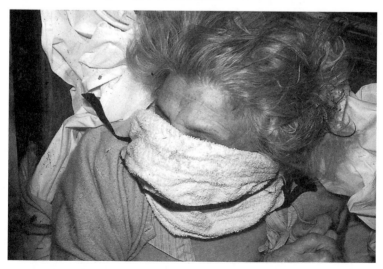

Figure 8.3 A 75-year-old woman, victim of robbery. Asphxyiated from towel secured over mouth and nose.

scattered fine petechiae of the sclerae, conjunctivae, and skin of the face. This has not been the case in young individuals in whom petechiae are usually absent. It is the discovery of the gag obstructing the airways that makes the diagnosis, not alleged signs of asphyxia.

In homicide by smothering, the implements used are usually pillows, bedding, and the hands. Infants may be placed in plastic bags. The victims tend to be very young, very old, debilitated, or incapacitated by restraints, disease or drugs. It is extremely difficult to smother adults in full control of their faculties.

When a pillow is used, it is placed over the face and pushed down. This causes obstruction of the nose and mouth, asphyxia, and death. There are usually no marks on the face. The face is not congested and there are no petechiae of the sclerae or conjunctivae (Figure 8.4). Abrasion injuries of the face will occur only if the victim puts up a vigorous resistance. In a review of 15 smothering deaths involving children below the age of 2 years, of the 13 who could be evaluated for the presence of petechiae, only one had findings. This child had a single petechia of the conjunctiva and a single area of scleral hemorrhage. Because of the circumstances of this case, there was the possibility that the child might also have been choked. Pushing the face into the bedding will accomplish the same end as using a pillow.

Smothering can also be accomplished using the hands. The nose is pinched off with one hand, while the other hand is used to push the jaw closed. In small children, one hand can accomplish both these tasks. In infants and adults unable to put up any effective resistance, an autopsy will fail to disclose any injury due to this process. In adults, even those who can muster only a minimal struggle, there may be abrasions on the nose or chin from the fingernails, and contusions of the lips from pressure of the palm (Figure 8.5).

The sequence of physiological events in smothering is:

- Bradycardia (decrease in heart rate)
- Decrease in respiration to agonal gasps with eventual cessation of respiration
- Slowing and finally flattening of the electroencephalogram (EEG)

The heart will continue to beat even after flattening of the EEG. In infants, bradycardia has been observed to start 30 sec after the initiation of smothering, and flattening of the EEG at 90 sec.[6] If, after cessation of respiration, the pillow or hand is removed from the face, respiration will not usually restart spontaneously. The individual must be resuscitated. Violent struggles with increased utilization of oxygen can speed up this sequence of events, just as natural disease could make the individual more susceptible to the effects of hypoxia.

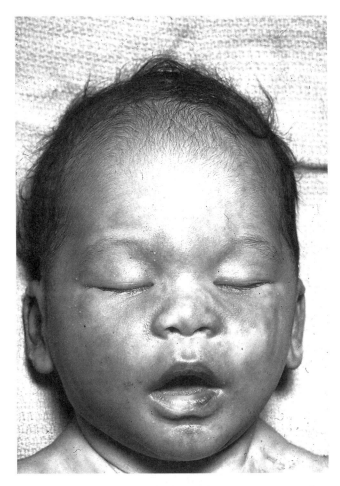

Figure 8.4 A 2-month-old infant smothered by parent. No petechiae of sclerae, conjunctivae, or face.

Choking

In choking, asphyxia is caused by obstruction within the air passages. The manner of death can be natural, homicide, or accident. Natural deaths are seen in individuals with acute fulminating epiglottitis, where there is obstruction of the airway by the inflamed epiglottis and adjacent soft tissue. Such individuals represent medical emergencies and can die literally in front of a physician. The individual develops a sore throat, hoarseness, respiratory difficulty, inability to speak and then suddenly collapses as the airway is completely obstructed. Inhalation of steam can cause a similar picture, with a markedly edematous, beefy-red mucosa in the larynx with obstruction (Figure 8.6).

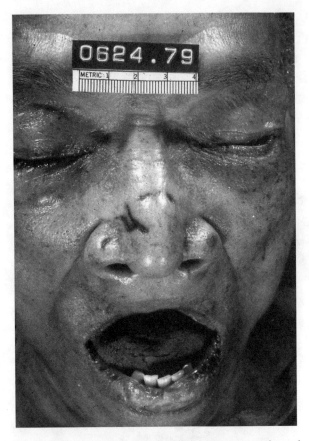

Figure 8.5 Elderly female smothered with hand. Fingernail marks on nose.

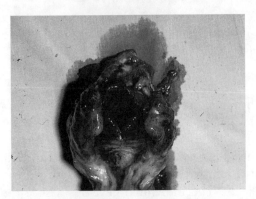

Figure 8.6 Massive laryngeal edema caused by inhalation of steam.

Homicidal deaths by choking are relatively uncommon. In infants, one occasionally sees a newborn murdered by stuffing toilet paper into its mouth. Figure 8.7A illustrates the case of an infant killed by her father by ramming

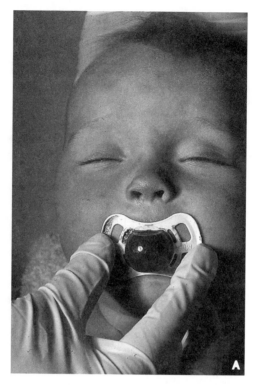

Figure 8.7 (A) Pacifier rammed into mouth by father *(continued)*.

a pacifier into her mouth. In adults, individuals sometimes die during a robbery or burglary when a cloth or sock is rammed into the mouth to silence the individual. This is often done in conjunction with gagging (Figure 8.7B). This method of gagging individuals is shown quite frequently on television without any harmful consequences, but, unfortunately, in real life, the cloth can work its way backward, completely obstructing the posterior pharynx and causing the individual to asphyxiate.

Most choking deaths are accidental in manner. In 1997, there were approximately 3300 deaths ascribed to unintentional inhalation of food or other objects, resulting in obstruction of the respiratory passages.[7] In children, choking usually involves aspiration of a small object into the larynx with occlusion of the airway, e.g., a small rubber ball or a balloon (Figure 8.8). Deaths have occurred in classrooms, where children have choked on the top of ballpoint pens they were biting on.

In adults, choking virtually always involves food (Figure 8.9). Here, it is commonly associated with acute alcohol intoxication, bad-fitting dentures, neurological injury, or senility. The piece of food will wedge in the larnygopharynx and larynx, completely obstructing the airway. Such deaths have

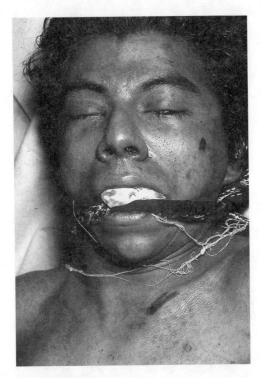

Figure 8.7 *(continued)* (B) Choked on gag that was secured by a bandana.

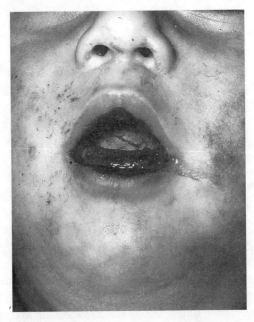

Figure 8.8 A 2-year-old choked to death on a wine cork.

Figure 8.9 A 39-year-old male choked on a ham sandwich.

acquired the name of "cafe coronary." The individual is eating, suddenly stops talking, stands up, and collapses. Cardiopulmonary resuscitation is begun in the belief that the individual has suffered a heart attack. In fact, he has choked on food and his airway is completely occluded. Thus, cardiopulmonary resuscitation is ineffective. If the individuals giving mouth-to-mouth resuscitation are observant, they will see that the chest is not rising when they blow into the airway, which indicates obstruction.

Coughing during a collapse suspected of being caused by choking rules out this diagnosis as one must have an open airway to cough. Coughing involves the inspiration of 2 to 2.5 liters of air, followed by closing off of the epiglottis and the vocal cords, contraction of the abdominal muscles to force up the diaphragm, while, at the same time, the expiratory muscles contract. The epiglottis and vocal cords open up and the air is then expelled out of the lungs, under pressure, usually carrying with it any foreign material present in the bronchi and trachea.[8] The expelled air can reach velocities of 75 to 100 miles per hour.

Occasionally, choking deaths occur when an individual falls into finely ground material, such as cornmeal or sawdust. There is involuntary inhalation and the airway is completely occluded by this material.

The finding of small amounts of food material in the airway at autopsy does not indicate that the individual choked to death. Approximately 20–25% of all individuals aspirate food agonally, independent of the cause of death.[9] One can attribute a death to aspiration only if the airway from the larynx down is completely occluded by food. Death caused by massive aspiration of food is rarely seen in a medical examiner's office. It is most common in comatose patients who have impaired functioning of the central nervous system.

The diagnosis of choking death is made at autopsy when the airway is found occluded. If the individual had an occluded airway and the object or food was removed during resuscitation, the only way to make the diagnosis would be by history. There are no specific autopsy findings indicative of choking except for occlusion of the airway.

Some medical personnel will ascribe a death to choking even though the airway was never completely occluded. They suggest that laryngospasm is the cause of death. There is, however, no objective evidence that this can occur. If laryngospasm did occur, one would expect relaxation of the larynx as the victim became agonal. This, in turn, would lead to opening up of the airway and recovery. Others hypothesize that a fatal "vagal reaction" or "reflex cardiac death," mediated through the parasympathetic nervous system, occurred through hypersensitivity of the larynx to aspirated food. Again, there is just no objective proof that this entity exists.

Mechanical Asphyxia

In mechanical asphyxia, pressure on the outside of the body prevents respiration. Mechanical asphyxia is almost always accidental in manner. It can be subdivided into three types:

1. Traumatic asphyxia (a term often used interchangeably with mechanical asphyxia)
2. Positional asphyxia
3. Riot-crush or "human pile" deaths

Traumatic Asphyxia

Traumatic asphyxia occurs when a heavy weight presses down on an individual's chest or upper abdomen, making respiration impossible. One common form of traumatic asphyxia is individuals under a car, repairing it, when the jack slips and the vehicle falls on top of them (Figure 8.10). At autopsy, there is congestion of the head, neck, and upper trunk with numerous petechiae in these areas, the sclerae, the conjunctivae and the periorbital skin. Retinal hemorrhages may also be present. Internally, there is often no evidence of trauma in spite of the heavy weight on the chest. Individuals who survive an episode of traumatic asphyxia usually make an uneventful recovery, though occasionally there is some permanent visual impairment due to retinal hemorrhage. One individual who survived described a severe crushing pain and suffusion of his face followed by immediate unconsciousness.[10] Rarely, traumatic asphyxia is homicidal. Thus, in one instance, an individual was knocked to the ground and a refrigerator and stereo were piled on top of him. An occasionally encountered form of accidental traumatic asphyxia involves individuals buried in cave-ins with their heads above the ground.

The most unusual case of traumatic asphyxia seen by the authors was that of a 5-month-old infant killed by a python. The snake wrapped itself around the baby, tightening its coils whenever the child exhaled. At autopsy, the only marks on the child were teeth marks on the face where the snake had tried to swallow the child whole (his head was too big for the snake's mouth) (Figure 8.11). There were no petechiae, hemorrhage, or bruising.

Positional asphyxia

Positional asphyxia is virtually always an accident and is associated with alcohol or drug intoxication. In this entity, individuals become trapped in restricted spaces, where, because of the position of their bodies, they cannot move out of that area or position. This results in restriction of their ability to breathe, followed by death (Figure 8.12). There is usually marked congestion, cyanosis, and petechiae. Positional asphyxia might occur if individuals fall down a well and are wedged between the walls. Every time they exhale, they slip farther and farther down the well, preventing inhalation.

Riot-crush

Riot-crush, as the name implies, occurs in riots, when the chest is compressed by stampeding people piling on top of each other. Respiratory movements are, thus, prohibited by this human pile.

Traumatic Asphyxia Combined with Smothering

Traumatic asphyxia combined with smothering is a combination of both these entities. It can be accidental or homicidal. An accidental form is **overlay**, where an infant is placed in bed for the night with either an adult or a larger child. Subsequently, the infant is found dead. During the night, the other individual rolled onto the infant, killing it by a combination of

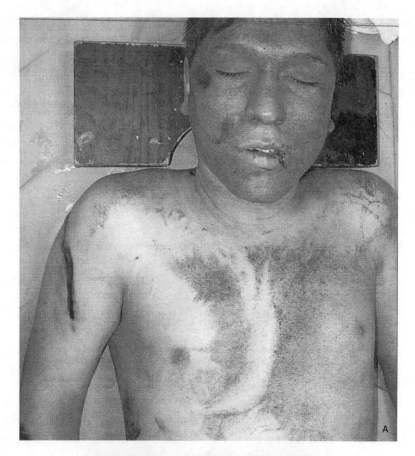

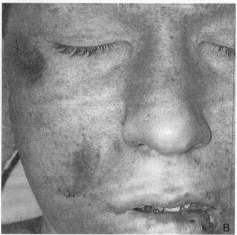

Figure 8.10 Traumatic asphyxia. (A) Deceased pinned under overturned vehicle. (B) Marked congestion of face with petechiae.

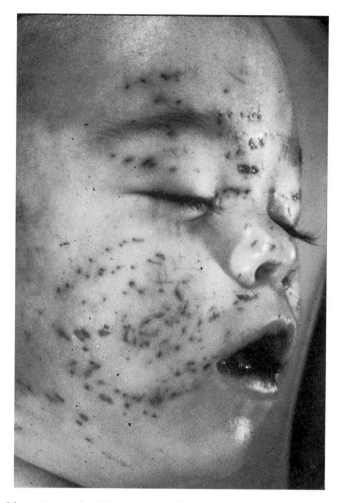

Figure 8.11 A 5-month-old infant killed by python. No petechiae, hemorrhage, or bruising of body. Puncture marks on face have a semicircular configuration and are caused by the needle-like teeth of the python.

smothering and traumatic asphyxia. If the circumstances surrounding the child's death are not known, such a case is often ascribed to SIDS. In fact, an autopsy cannot differentiate between the two. Other deaths in this category are individuals buried in cave-ins, grain, or sand, etc. The physical findings at autopsy are generally nil. Rarely, a few fine petechiae of the facial skin, but not of the sclerae or conjunctivae, will be found.

Burking is a combination of suffocation and traumatic asphyxia developed (or at least perfected) by the "resurrectionists" Burke and Hare in the early 19th century.[11] These men made their living by digging up bodies from graveyards and supplying them to medical schools for dissection. They

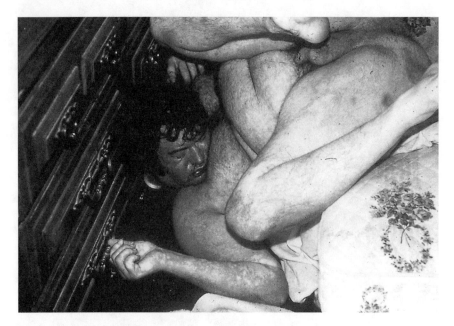

Figure 8.12 Positional asphyxia in acutely intoxicated individual.

decided, however, to eliminate the chore of digging up bodies and go straight to the source. Victims, usually intoxicated, were brought to the ground, whereupon Burke knelt or sat on their chests, expelling the air and interfering with inspiratory efforts. He then put one hand over the victim's nose and mouth and used the other hand to press the lower jaw towards the upper. Visible injuries were virtually nonexistent. The two now had a fresh body for the schools.

Suffocating Gases

Deaths from suffocating gases are caused, not by the toxic nature of the gases, but rather by displacement of oxygen from the atmosphere. Carbon dioxide and methane are the two most commonly encountered suffocating gases. Both are essentially nontoxic and odorless. Both are found in sewers and mines. Methane is the principal constituent (94–96%) of natural gas that is used for cooking. It is odorless; the smell we detect from natural gas is an added ingredient to make leaks detectable. Reduction of atmospheric oxygen to less than 25% of normal (5–6% by volume of oxygen) by displacement of oxygen by inert gases, such as carbon dioxide and methane, produces unconsciousness in seconds and death in a matter of minutes. Determination of the cause of death in such cases is by knowledge of the circumstances surrounding the death. There are no specific findings at autopsy. Toxicological analysis of the blood is of no help in the case of carbon dioxide, because it is a normal constituent of blood. Methane can be detected in the blood. Since the gas is not toxic, however, all that its identification would indicate is that the individual was exposed to an atmosphere containing methane, not that death was due to it.

Strangulation

Strangulation is a form of asphyxia characterized by closure of the blood vessels and air passages of the neck as a result of external pressure on the neck. There are three forms of strangulation:

1. Hanging
2. Ligature strangulation
3. Manual strangulation

Virtually all hangings are suicide and all ligature and manual strangulations homicide. In total numbers per year, murder by strangulation is uncommon. In the last ten years, murders ascribed to strangulation have averaged 286 a year, with a range of 366 to 211.[4] The numbers may be slightly higher in that some deaths ascribed simply to asphyxiation were strangulation. The increase would be minor, as the total number of homicides ascribed to just asphyxiation in that same time period averaged 107 a year.

In all three forms of strangulation, the cause of death is cerebral hypoxia secondary to compression and, thereby, occlusion of the vessels supplying blood to the brain. The arteries supplying blood to the brain are:

- The internal carotids
- The vertebrals
- The small spinal arteries
- Anastomatic connections of branches of the external carotid and subclavian arteries

The venous drainage is chiefly by way of the jugular veins and the cervicalis profunda veins.

The carotid arteries, by virtue of their location, are easily compressed by direct pressure to the front of the neck. In contrast, the vertebral arteries are resistant to direct pressure, but can be occluded by severe lateral flexion or rotation of the neck.[12] Such a condition can occur in hanging. The amount of pressure necessary to occlude the carotid arteries is approximately 11 lb; for the vertebral arteries it is 66 lb.[13] Pressure on the neck in the area of the carotid arteries causes unconsciousness in an average of 10 sec.[14] If pressure is immediately released, consciousness is regained in 10–12 sec. Electrocardiographic (EKG) changes are minimal. Respiratory movements are inhibited in the inspiratory phase. Electroencephalograms (EEG) show an increased amplitude of their waves, similar to the picture seen during an epileptic seizure. The pattern returns to normal in approximately 20 sec.[15]

Rossen et al. conducted an extensive study involving occlusion of not only the carotid arteries but the vertebral arteries and the anastomatic connections of branches of the external carotids and subclavian arteries.[16] This was accomplished using an inflatable pressure cuff placed on the lower third of the neck that produced 600 mm of mercury within one-eighth of a second of inflation. Only the small spinal arteries were not occluded. The subjects were 126 normal male volunteers between the ages of 17 and 31 years. Repeated tests were conducted on 85 of the subjects. Acute occlusion of the arterial circulation resulted in blurring of vision, constriction of visual fields, loss of consciousness and hypoxic convulsions. The pressure cuff was released upon loss of consciousness with complete recovery within 1 or 2 min after the procedure and no subsequent *sequelae*. The convulsions occurred after loss of consciousness, were mild, generalized tonic and clonic, and rarely continued more than 6–8 seconds. The EEG showed large, slow waves correlated with loss of consciouness. The EKG changes were minimal. Half the subjects loss consciousness in 6 to 6.5 sec. The overall range was approximately 5 to 11 sec.

Rossen et al. then studied the effects of prolonged occlusion of cerebral circulation on 11 individuals.[16] Complete occlusion of the cerebral blood flow was not achieved in every case, as in the other experiment. Cervical pressure was maintained for as long as 100 sec in some tests. The subjects regained consciousness in 30–40 sec and were able to walk from the room in 2 min. Convulsions, cyanosis, involuntary urination and defecation in some patients, bradycardia, and dilatation of the pupils followed loss of consciouness. The convulsions were relatively mild, continuing during the whole period of unconsciousness in some individuals, lasting 30–40 sec in others. Initially, after loss of consciouness, the heart rate was stable. Subsequently, bradycardia developed, with the heart rate dropping as much as 50%. Respiration continued throughout the test, increasing in rate.

Venous drainage of the head is by the jugular and vertebral venous systems. The vertebral venous system consists of an external plexus of veins in the deep muscles of the neck adjacent to the vertebral column and an internal vertebral plexus within the spinal canal. This internal vertebral plexus, though limited in its blood transport capacity, cannot be affected by pressure on the neck. In contrast, the amount of pressure necessary to occlude the jugular veins is 4.4 lb.[12]

Hemorrhage over the back of the larynx and in soft tissue overlying the cervical spine should be interpreted as traumatic in etiology only with great care. In the majority of cases, it is not due to trauma to the neck, but rather is an artifact produced by over-distention and rupture of the venous sinuses, forming the pharyngolaryngeal plexus.[12] Such hemorrhage can and does occur in deaths from natural causes and might be either peri- or early post-mortem in origin.

In virtually all fatal cases of ligature and manual strangulation, there are petechiae of the conjunctivae. The presence of petechiae does not indicate that death was due to strangulation, because they can be seen in a number of other conditions, including natural disease.[17] Petechiae may develop in victims of attempted strangulation who do not incur any life-threatening degree of asphyxia. Thus, in a study of 79 surviving victims of attempted strangulation (both ligature and manual), who showed stigmata of strangulation, conjunctival petechiae were observed in 14 victims, only eight of whom became unconscious, and with only four experiencing sphincter incontinence.[18] This suggests that petechiae are not necessarily an indication of life-threatening asphyxia, but rather the effect of local venous congestion.

Hanging

In hanging, asphyxia is secondary to compression or constriction of the neck structures by a noose or other constricting band tightened by the weight of the body. There may be either complete or incomplete suspension of the body (Figure 8.13). Incomplete suspension, with the toes or feet (less commonly the knees or buttocks) touching the ground, is extremely common. Virtually all hangings are suicidal. Accidental hangings are uncommon and homicidal hangings very rare. Death is caused by compression of the blood vessels of the neck such that an insufficient amount of oxygenated blood reaches the brain. Obstruction of the airway can also occur, either through compression of the trachea or, when the noose is above the larynx, elevation and posterior displacement of the tongue and floor of the mouth. Blockage or compression of the air passages is not necessary to cause death in hanging. A number of individuals have hanged themselves with the noose above the larynx and a permanent tracheostomy opening below. Fracture of the neck plays virtually no role in non-judicial hangings. It is rare and, in our experience, is usually seen only in individuals with advanced degenerative disease of the cervical spine, such as osteoarthritis, in combination with complete suspension of the body, a sudden drop, and, frequently, obesity.

The amount of pressure necessary to compress the jugular veins is 4.4 lb; the carotid arteries, 11 lb; and the vertebral arteries, 66 lb. Compression of the trachea requires 33 lb of pressure.[13] Because of the small amount of pressure necessary to compress the carotid arteries, one can hang oneself

Figure 8.13 (A) Hanging with complete suspension *(continued)*.

sitting, kneeling, or lying down. The weight of the head (10–12 lb) against a noose is sufficient to occlude the carotid arteries and cause death. The authors have seen cases where individuals have hanged themselves from a bedpost while lying in bed next to a sleeping spouse. Hangings in kneeling and sitting positions are common.

Virtually all hangings are suicidal. Depending on the area of the country and the sex of the victim, hanging is either the second or third most popular method of suicide. Rarely, couples hang themselves together, some with the same rope. In hangings, a simple slipknot type of noose is typically used. The noose is constructed from anything that is handy. Most common are ropes, electrical cords, and belts. In jails and prisons, convicts typically tear sheets into strips as well as using T-shirts, undershorts, trousers, or even socks. Occasionally, to prevent a change of mind, the victim ties his hands together. The authors have seen a number of cases where the victims have actually handcuffed their hands behind themselves. (Figure 8.13B)

Figure 8.13 *(continued)* (B and C)
Hanging with (B) hands cuffed behind
back (C) incomplete suspension..

The most common point of suspension is the side of the neck, followed
by the back and the front. At the time of suspension, the noose typically slips
above the larynx, catching under the chin (Figure 8.14). Present on the neck
will be a furrow. This furrow generally does not completely encircle the neck,
but rather slants upward toward the knot, fading out at the point of suspension — the knot (Figure 8.15). If the knot is under the chin, its site might
be indicated by an abrasion or indentation beneath the chin. The clarity and
configuration of the furrow depend on the material used. A rope will give a
deep, well-demarcated, distinct furrow, often with a mirror-image impression
of the twist of the rope on the skin (Figure 8.16A). This furrow initially has
a pale yellow parchment appearance, with a congested rim. With time, the
furrow dries out and becomes dark brown. If the ligature is a soft material,
the groove might be poorly defined, pale, and devoid of bruises and abrasions
(Figure 8.16B). In some cases, the lower margin of the groove is pale, with
the upper margin red, caused by postmortem congestion of vessels. A towel
can give poorly defined superficial areas of abrasion.

In the majority of suicidal hangings, the noose consists of a single loop.
Less commonly, there are two loops. This results in two furrows that may be

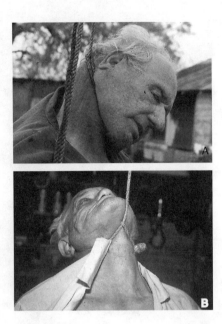

Figure 8.14 Hanging with point of suspension on (A) side of neck and (B) front of neck.

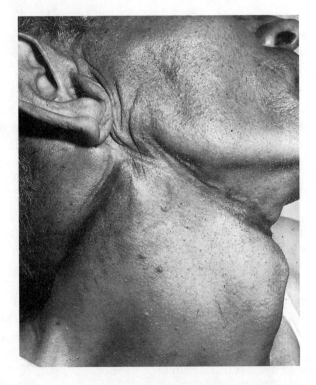

Figure 8.15 Furrow from noose slanting upward toward point of suspension.

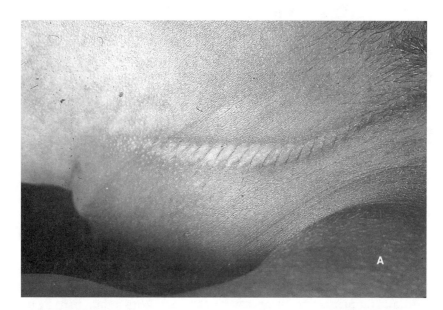

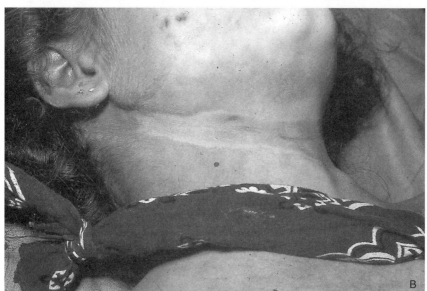

Figure 8.16 (A) Noose mark with pale yellow base and congested rim. (B) Broad pale furrow due to soft noose.

parallel, overlap at points, or follow two completely different paths, e.g., one oblique and the other horizontal. The two loops might pinch the skin between them, producing a hemorrhagic strip of skin (Figure 8.17). If the noose is a belt, there are usually two parallel ligature marks on the neck where the upper and lower edges of the belt dig into the skin (Figure 8.18).

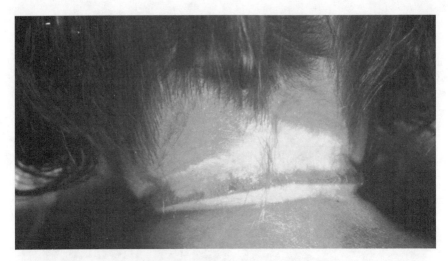

Figure 8.17 Suicide with double loops pinching skin.

If a soft noose, such as a towel, is used and the body is cut down shortly after death, no marks may be present on the neck. With a thin, hard ligature, the groove will be narrow, deep, and distinct. The longer the body remains suspended, the more prominent the mark. The furrow will be shallow and broad with a wide ligature such as a strip of cloth. The ligature mark is deepest opposite the point of suspension. Rarely, scratch marks will be seen above and below the ligature mark, where the victim tried to undo the noose.

In most hangings, the face is pale and the tongue is protruding and "black" from drying (Figure 8.19). Exceptions to this usually involve partially suspended individuals, where the noose is tightened only by the weight of the head or the torso. In these instances, while the carotid arteries and venous

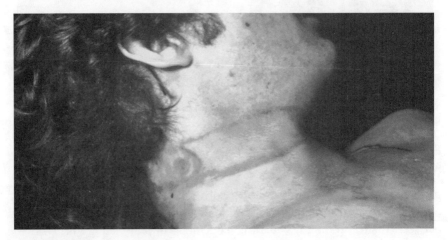

Figure 8.18 Suicide with belt.

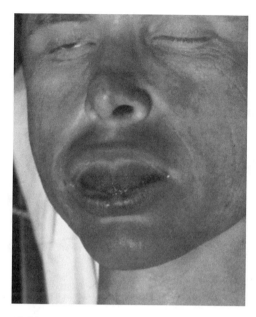

Figure 8.19 Suicidal hanging with protrusion of tongue and drying.

drainage are completely occluded, the vertebral arteries continue to supply blood to the head, producing congestion of the face and petechiae. In hangings, blood will pool in the dependent areas of the body, usually the forearms, hands, and lower legs, secondary to gravity. With time, punctate hemorrhages and Tardieu spots, caused by hydrostatic rupture of vessels, will be seen (Figure 8.20).

Prior to removal of the noose from the neck, its nature and composition, width, mode of application, location, and type of knot should be described in detail. After removal, the ligature mark on the neck should also be minutely described. One should describe the direction of the furrow (obliquely upward, horizontal, etc.), whether it is continuous or interrupted, its color, its dimensions (depth and width), whether there is a distinct imprint to the ligature pattern, the areas of the neck involved, and its relation to local landmarks.

Usually, except for ligature marks, there are no other external marks (injuries) on the body. If some are present, the medical examiner must decide whether they are self-induced, occurred during the convulsive phase preceding death, were produced when the body was cut down or during attempted resuscitation, occurred when a swinging body contacted other objects, or were produced by a second party, making the case a homicide.

On examination of the internal structures of the neck, in more than half of the cases, there are no injuries. Of 83 consecutive hangings examined prospectively, only ten (12%) had fractures. Nine showed fractures of the thyroid

Figure 8.20 Tardieu spots.

cartilage, specifically the superior horns; none fracture of the hyoid, and one a fracture of the cervical spine (VJM DiMaio, personal communication). This last case involved an obese woman with arthritic changes of the cervical vertebrae who stepped off a ladder, dropping a short distance before being fully suspended. Of the nine cases with fracture of the superior horns of the thyroid cartilage, seven were unilateral and two bilateral. Four of the unilateral fractures were contralateral to the point of suspension, two ipsilateral, and one unknown. Seventeen (20.5%) of the 83 cases, excluding those with fractures, showed hemorrhage in the strap muscles of the neck. Petechiae of the conjunctivae or sclerae were present in 21 of the 83 cases (25.3%) including four with fractures and six with hemorrhage in the neck. Absence of petechiae in most hangings is because there is complete obstruction of the arterial system, so there is no pooling of blood in the head, no increased pressure, and, therefore, no petechiae. A dried rivulet of saliva often runs from a corner of the mouth and down the chest. Blood-tinged fluid may be present in the nostrils.

The low incidence of fractures of the neck organs observed by one of the authors (VJMD) was also observed by Feigin.[19] In a retrospective study of 307 suicidal and accidental hangings, fractures of the neck organs were present in only 9.5% (29) of cases. In three cases, there were fractures of the cervical spine, C1–2, C3–4 and C6–7 (one in association with a fracture of the thyroid cartilage), 14 cases with fractures confined to the thyroid cartilage, nine fractures of the hyoid and three fractures of the hyoid and thyroid cartilage. No individual had more than two fractures of the neck organs.

Fractures were not associated with height of suspension, sex, or the width of the ligature. The likelihood of fractures did increase with age.

The best way to examine the interior of the neck in strangulation deaths, whether manual or caused by hanging or ligature, is to remove the viscera from the chest and abdominal cavities and then remove the brain. After there has been drainage through the cranial and chest cavities, the neck can be dissected in a relatively blood-free field. Fractures of the thyroid cartilage, the cricoid cartilage or the hyoid bone can only be considered antemortem if there is blood at the fracture site. In the authors' opinion, blood detectable only microscopically at a fracture site is insufficient to prove that the fracture was antemortem.

Homicidal hanging is very rare. It is virtually impossible for one of two healthy adults, equally matched physically, to hang the other unless the victim was beaten unconscious or rendered helpless by alcohol or drugs. In the first instance, one would suspect homicide by virtue of the injuries on the victim. In the second scenario, or if the victim was rapidly subdued by two or more stronger assailants, there might be no marks on the body except the noose mark or possible contusions of the arms, inflicted while being forcibly restrained by the assailants. If there is also a marked disproportion in strength between the assailant and victim, for example, an adult and a child or a large man and a small woman, it would also be possible to hang an individual without marks of violence. A person might also be ligature strangled and then strung up. But in this instance, the neck markings would not have the classic inverted-V configuration of a hanging. The authors, however, have seen suicidal hangings involving incomplete suspension where the noose mark overlaid the larynx and was horizontal, not sweeping upward to the point of suspension in an inverted-V configuration. To rule out any violence that might not be visible and to make sure the individual was not drugged, in all alleged suicidal hangings, a complete toxicologic screen should be performed and, in most instances, a complete autopsy.

Accidental hangings usually involve children who are playing at hanging or get entangled in a rope, or adults engaging in the practice of sexual (erotic) asphyxia (see Sexual Asphyxia). Rarely, infants will accidentally hang themselves from a pacifier suspended around their neck on a cord or get entangled in a toy or mobile placed above their cribs.[20] Accidental hangings of infants and toddlers have also been reported with venetian-blind cords and drawstrings on clothing.[21,22]

In all deaths from hanging, the police agency involved should notify the medical examiner's office immediately. If the victim is obviously dead, the body should not be cut down, so that proper photographic documentation and investigation of the scene can be made. The noose should never be cut from the body, but left intact for transport with the body to the morgue.

When the medical examiner removes the noose from the neck, the knot should not be untied. The noose should either be slipped off the head or cut opposite to the knot and the cut ends secured together with tape.

Research has been performed on the hanging of dead bodies. Between 1817 and 1855, Casper performed 23 experiments to determine the effect of hanging on a dead body.[23] He concluded that the noose marks seen on the neck in hanging during life could be produced by a ligature applied to a neck within 2 h or if not later after death. Thus, noose marks on the neck do not necessarily mean that an individual was alive when he was hanged.

In **judicial hangings**, death is caused by fracture-dislocation of the upper cervical vertebrae with transaction of the cord. The knot is placed under the left ear or, less commonly, under the chin. A trapdoor is sprung and the prisoner falls a specific distance determined by his weight. If he falls an insufficient distance, he strangles rather than breaking his neck; if he falls too far, he is decapitated. In properly performed judicial hangings, the victim abruptly stops at the end of his fall when his head is jerked suddenly and violently backward, fracturing his spine. Ideally, one then has the classical hangman's fracture — fracture through the pedicles of C2 with the posterior arch remaining fixed to C3. C1, the odontoid process and the anterior arch of C2 remain in articulation with the base of the skull. This injury pattern is caused by hyperextension and distraction and results in injury of the cord at C2–3. This classic fracture does not always occur in hangings. Thus, in an anthropologic study of six judicial hangings by Spence et al., there were fractures of the hyoid, the styloid processes, and occipital bones as well as the cervical body of C2 and the transverse processes of C1–3 and C5.[24]

In a report by Hartshorne and Reay on two recent hangings, they found bilateral vertebral artery lacerations with associated basilar subarachnoid hemorrhage; fractures of the hyoid and thyroid cartilage and hemorrhage into the cervical muscle.[25] In one of the cases, there was also a fracture or separation at C2 and C3 with complete transection of the cord, bilateral carotid intimal tears and a subdural hematoma. In this latter case, the fall was 5.5 feet, with the knot slipping to the subaural area. In the other case, the fall was 7 feet, with the knot secured in the subauricular area.

In judicial hangings, consciousness is lost immediately, though the heart may continue to beat for 8–20 min and there may be muscular contractions of the facial muscles, twitching and convulsions of the limbs and trunk, and violent respiratory movements of the chest. In non-judicial hangings, where the mechanism of death is strangulation, if there is complete suspension with occlusion of both the carotid and vertebral arteries, based on the experiments of Rossen et al., the victim should lose consciousness in 5–11 sec, with half losing consciousness in 6 to 6.5 sec. If the suspension results only in occlusion of the carotid arteries, unconsciousness may not occur for 10–15 seconds.

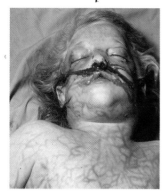

Color Figure 2.6
Marbling.

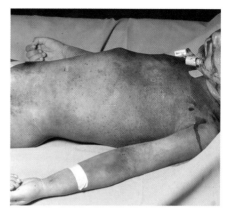

Color Figure 3.13
Meningococcemia. Blotchy
erythematous rash with petechiae
and purpura.

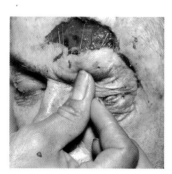

Color Figure 4.9
Laceration with bridging.

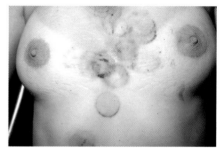

Color Figure 4.6
Patterned contusions caused
by the end of a flashlight.

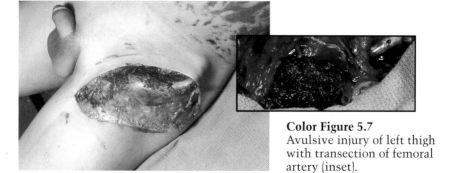

Color Figure 5.7
Avulsive injury of left thigh
with transection of femoral
artery (inset).

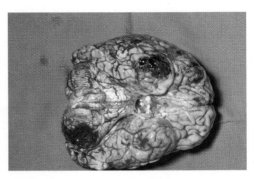

Color Figure 6.8
Fracture of skull in left posterior fossa with coup contusions of left cerebellar hemisphere and contrecoup contusions of right temporal pole. Eight-day survival.

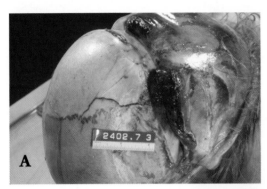

Color Figure 6.11
(A) Fracture of squamous temporal bone with laceration of middle meningeal artery and (B and C) epidural hematomas.

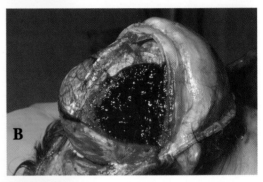

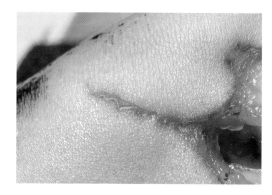

Color Figure 7.15
Stab wound from blade with serrated edge.

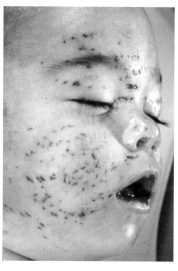

Color Figure 8.11
A 5-month-old infant killed by python. No petechiae, hemorrhage, or bruising of body. Puncture marks on face have a semicircular configuration and are caused by the needle-like teeth of the python.

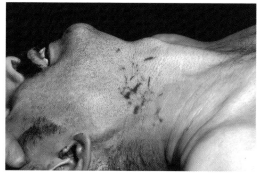

Color Figure 8.24
Manual strangulation with fingernail marks and scratches on sides of neck.

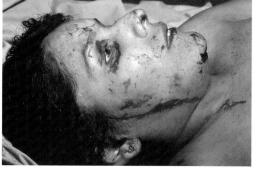

Color Figure 9.11
Acid burns of face from ruptured battery.

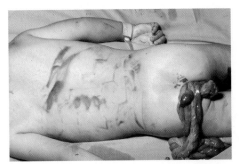

Color Figure 9.19
A 3-year-old child run over by a truck, with tire marks on the back.

Color Figure 13.6
Postmortem epidural thermal hematoma.

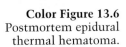

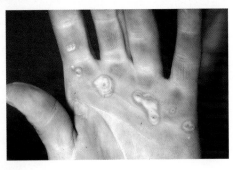

Color Figure 13.7
Postmortem burn with erythematous rim.

Color Figure 16.1
Electrical burns of hands representing points of entry.

Color Figure 19.2
Air bubbles in epicardial veins of heart in death caused by air embolism.

Ligature Strangulation

In ligature strangulation, the pressure on the neck is applied by a constricting band that is tightened by a force other than the body weight. Virtually all cases of ligature strangulation are homicides. In the authors' experience, ligature strangulation is the most common method of homicidal asphyxia, though the incidence of manual strangulation follows fairly closely. In a study of 133 homicides caused by asphyxia, ligature strangulation accounted for 48 of the deaths; manual strangulation for 41.[26] In ligature strangulation, females predominate as victims, though not as much as in the case of manual strangulation. Of the 48 victims of ligature strangulation, 27 were females and 21 males. In the authors' experience, the most common motive for ligature strangulation of females is rape. Suicides and accidents are rare. The mechanism of death is the same as in hanging — occlusion of the vessels supplying blood and thus oxygen to the brain. With constant compression of the carotid arteries, consciousness is lost in 10–15 sec.

In contrast to hanging deaths, the face and neck above the ligature mark appear markedly congested, with confluent scleral hemorrhage and petechiae of the conjunctivae. Fine petechiae might also be present on the skin of the face, especially in the periorbital regions. In the authors' experience, petechiae are present in 86% of the cases of ligature strangulation.[26] The presence of a congested face, petechiae, and scleral hemorrhage in ligature strangulation occurs because, unlike in hanging, there is no complete occlusion of the vasculature. Blood continues to go into the head from the vertebral arteries. It cannot escape, however, because of the compressed venous system. This results in increased intravascular pressure, congestion, and rupture of the vessels.

Ligatures used range from electrical cords, neckties, ropes, and telephone cords to sheets and hose. The appearance of a ligature mark on the neck is subject to considerable variation, depending on the nature of the ligature, the amount of the resistance offered by the victim, and the amount of force used by the assailant. The ligature mark might be faint, barely visible, or absent in young children or incapacitated adults, especially if the ligature is soft, e.g., a towel, and removed immediately after death (Figure 8.21). If a thin tough ligature is used, there will be a very prominent deep mark encircling the neck. Initially, it has a yellow parchment-like appearance that turns dark brown.

In ligature strangulation, in contrast to hangings, the ligature mark usually encircles the neck in a horizontal plane often overlying the larynx or upper trachea (Figure 8.22). When a wire or cord is used, it often completely encircles the neck. There might be a break in the furrow, however, usually in the back of the neck, where a hand has grasped the ligature and tightened it at this point. Aside from the ligature mark, abrasions and contusions of the skin of the neck are usually not present. They can occur, however, if the

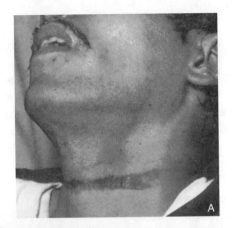

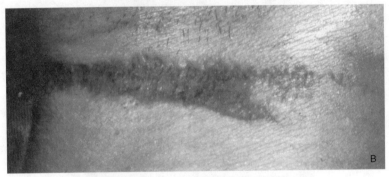

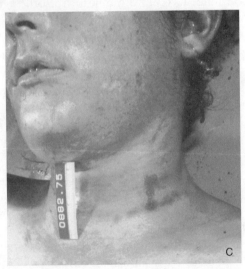

Figure 8.21 (A, B, C (A) Ligature strangulation with cloth band. Ligature marks on anterior and lateral aspects of neck. (B) Close-up showing vertically oriented pattern of cloth. (C) Poorly defined ligature marks on a young girl strangled with T-shirt *(continued)*.

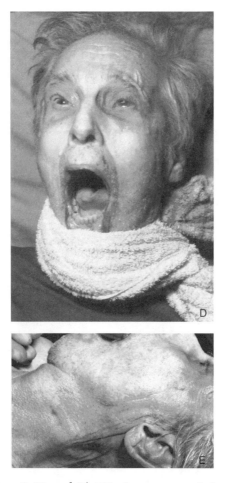

Figure 8.21 *(continued)* (D and E) Elderly man strangled with towel.

assailant places his hands beneath and around the ligature and twists it, tightening it around the neck, or if the victim claws at his neck in an attempt to remove the ligature or relieve the pressure. If there is more than one loop of the ligature around the neck, there could be bruising of the skin if the ligature pinches the skin between two loops. Edema fluid may be present in the nostrils.

Injury to the internal structures of the neck is the exception rather than the rule. In a study of 48 ligature strangulation deaths, fractures of the hyoid or thyroid cartilage were present in only six cases (12.5% of the total cases) — five of the males (23.8%) and one (3.7%) of the females.[26] Altogether, there were 12 fractures in the six cases, seven of the hyoid and five of the thyroid cartilage. Four of the victims had fractures of both the thyroid and

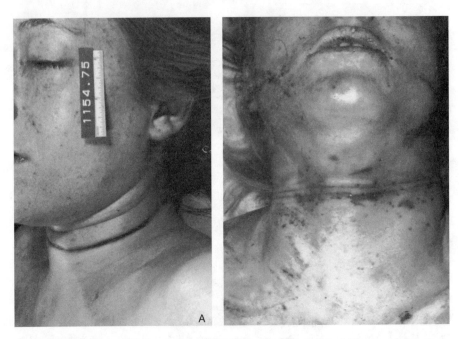

Figure 8.22 Victim strangled with (A) telephone cord and (B) boot lace. Face congested with numerous petechiae. Horizontally oriented ligature mark overlying larynx, encircling neck.

hyoid; two, only the hyoid. The fractures of the thyroid cartilage all involved the superior horns.

Suicide using a ligature is rare. In such cases, the victim usually ties a ligature tightly around the neck (Figure 8.23A). Because some individuals remain conscious for 10–15 sec after complete occlusion of the cartoid arteries, they have sufficient time to tie at least one, if not more, knots. Instead of tying a knot, some individuals tightly wrap a ligature several times around the neck, securing it in place by the overlapping loops. Other individuals use a tourniquet method: a ligature is loosely wrapped around the neck, knotted, and then tightened by a stick inserted beneath the ligature and twisted multiple times. Clothing or the individual's own weight on the stick holds it in place, maintaining the "tourniquet." In one case, an individual used a plastic lock-tie to strangle himself (Figure 8.23B).

Accidental ligature strangulation is rare. It is seen when a tie, scarf, shirt, or other article of clothing gets entangled in a moving machine. Isadora Duncan, the dancer, died of accidental strangulation when a scarf she was wearing became entangled in an automobile wheel.[27] Other deaths have involved motorcycles, snowmobiles, ski lifts and massage devices.[27]

Despite decomposition, ligature marks tend to be well preserved and recognizable. The marks resist decomposition presumably because the

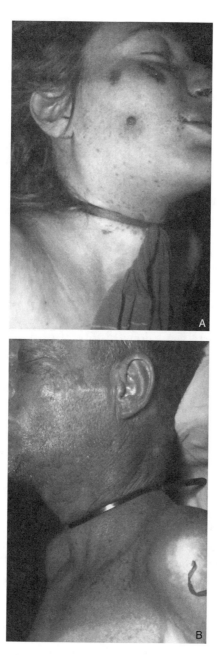

Figure 8.23 (A) Suicidal ligature strangulation using stocking. Six previous attempts at suicide. (B) Suicidal strangulation using plastic lock-tie.

ligature has compressed the underlying blood vessels, restricting access to the area by the putrefying bacteria. In infants, the elderly, and decomposing bodies, there can be pseudo-ligature marks that suggest strangulation. In infants, pale crease marks between overlapping folds (rolls) of neck skin can be mistaken for ligature marks. This can be further complicated in newborns by the presence of petechiae, which can be normally present in newborns delivered vaginally because of compression of the chest.

A similar picture of pseudo-ligature marks can be seen in the elderly — pale crease marks caused by overlapping rolls of skin, petechiae of the sclerae and conjunctivae (caused by cardiac failure) — with the addition of retropharyngeal hemorrhage. Petechiae are often seen in acute cardiac failure, not uncommonly the cause or mechanism of death in elderly individuals. The case that comes to mind is that of an elderly woman found dead in bed with a pillow propping up her head, such that her chin was against her chest. There was a long history of cardiac disease. When the body was examined at the medical examiner's office, there was a horizontal mark across the front of her neck that simulated a ligature. The face above the mark was congested and there were fine petechiae of the sclerae, conjunctivae, and periorbital skin, as well as retropharyngeal hemorrhage. At the time the body was initially autopsied, a full account of the circumstances and scene surrounding the death was unknown. For example, it was not known that the head had been propped up, that there was a long history of cardiac failure, and that the woman died in a room with no windows and with a single entrance that was blocked by a bed in which her bedridden husband slept. Death was, in fact, caused by her long-standing coronary artery disease. The "ligature mark" was just an artifact — a crease caused by the positioning of the head. Pseudo-ligature marks can also be seen in decomposing bodies with tight collars or other clothing around the neck. The body, as it decomposes, swells around the tight-fitting garment, which produces a deep furrow that simulates a ligature mark.

In victims of homicidal ligature strangulation, hair is often found clutched in the hands. This should be recovered and retained. A control sample of the victim's hair should be obtained for comparison, because the hair found in the hands almost invariably turns out to be that of the victim. Fingernail scrapings or cuttings (the latter are preferred) should be taken to look for tissue of the perpetrator under the nails. Unfortunately, unlike in fiction, such scrapings or cuttings have traditionally been of little help, with foreign tissue rarely identified. With the new STR and mitochondrial DNA techniques, this should change, with a greater success in detecting tissue of an assailant on fingernail cuttings.

Manual Strangulation

Manual strangulation is produced by pressure of the hand, forearm, or other limb against the neck, compressing the internal structures of the neck. The mechanism of death is occlusion of the blood vessels supplying blood to the brain i.e., the carotid arteries. Occlusion of the airway probably plays a minor role, if any, in causing death. Virtually, all cases of manual strangulation are homicide. In the authors' experience, it is the second most common method of homicidal asphyxia. In a study by DiMaio of 41 deaths caused by manual strangulation, females predominated, with the ratio of females to males 1.9 to 1 (27 to 14).[26] Of the 27 females manually strangled, the motive was rape in 14 cases and domestic violence in 10.

One cannot commit suicide by manual strangulation because, as soon as consciousness is lost, pressure is released and consciousness regained. A choke hold can result in manual strangulation if it is maintained long enough.

Occasionally, it is claimed that the death of a healthy individual ascribed to manual strangulation is unintentional and caused by a vasovagal reaction (reflex cardiac death) brought on by touching, grasping, or striking the neck. This is an interesting theory, but unproven by objective evidence. The mechanism of death in such a case would be an arrhythmia produced by stimulation of the carotid sinuses. The carotid sinus is a focal area of enlargement of the common carotid artery where it bifurcates into the external and internal carotid arteries. Compression or stimulation of the carotid sinuses causes an increase in blood pressure in these sinuses with resultant slowing of the heart rate (bradycardia), dilatation of blood vessels (vasodilation), and a fall in blood pressure. Pressure on the common carotid artery below the sinuses reduces the blood pressure within the sinus by reducing the amount of blood flowing into it. This mimics hypotension or decreased blood supply from hemorrhage or shock, causing the heart to beat faster (tachycardia), the blood vessels to constrict (vasoconstriction), and a rise in blood pressure. This explains the fact that, while in most cases of manual strangulation there is bradycardia, vasodilation, and fall in blood pressure, in some cases, if the hands are lower down on the neck, there might instead be tachycardia, vasoconstriction, and a rise in blood pressure.

In normal individuals, pressure on the carotid sinus causes minimal effects with a decrease in heart rate of less than six beats per minute and only a slight reduction in blood pressure (less than 10 mm Hg).[28] Some individuals, however, show extreme hypersensitivity to stimulation of the carotid sinuses. In such individuals, there is slowing of the heart and cardiac arrhythmias ranging from ventricular arrhythmias to cardiac stand-still and hypotension. There are cases reported in which turning of the neck in varying positions or a high or tight collar has produced dizziness and fainting.[28,29] Some articles refer to cases of stimulation of the carotid sinus that have allegedly produced bradycardia, progressing to cardiac arrest and death.[29] Review of the original case reports almost invariably indicates that these individuals were elderly suffering from some severe cardiovascular disease that in itself was capable of causing sudden death.

In manual strangulation, the face usually appears congested and cyanotic, with petechiae of the conjunctivae and sclerae. Di Maio found petechiae present in the conjuctivae or the sclerae in 89% of his cases.[26] Fine petechiae might also be present on the skin of the face. The petechiae are most noticeable on the bulbar conjunctivae and conjunctival sac, the skin of the upper and lower eyelids, the bridge of the nose, the brows, and the cheeks. Conjunctival hemorrhages will be larger if the victim struggles and the assailant responds with increased pressure about the neck. The petechiae are caused by rupture of venules and capillaries secondary to increased intravascular pressure as a result of the obstructed venous return (the internal jugular veins) in conjunction with incomplete arterial obstruction, which permits the vertetbral arteries to continue supplying blood to the brain. The characteristic signs of asphyxia — cyanosis, and multiple petechiae — are most striking above the site of manual compression of the neck. Petechiae are not pathognomonic of asphyxial deaths, however. They are also seen in other diseases, for example, acute heart failure. In severe vomiting or coughing, occasional petechiae might be seen. If the body remains in the prone position for a prolonged length of time, such that it is approaching decomposition, postmortem petechiae can form in the distribution of the livor mortis. These petechiae may be present on the skin, conjunctivae and sclerae. On occasion, in cases of manual strangulation, pulmonary edema is present, with foamy edema fluid visible in the nostrils.

In most cases of manual strangulation, the assailant uses more force than is necessary to subdue and kill his victim. Hence, marks of violence are frequently present on the skin of the neck. Typically, there are abrasions, contusions, and fingernail marks on the skin (Figures 8.24, 8.25). Rarely, no marks are present. Dissection of the throat usually reveals hemorrhage, often extensive, into the musculature. Depending on the age of the victim and the amount of force used, there might be fractures of the hyoid bone or thyroid cartilage. As age increases, so does calcification of these structures and the tendency to have fractures. Thus, these fractures are less common in individuals in their teens and late twenties than in individuals over 30 years of age. One must be careful not to mistake the cartilagenous separations between the greater horns of the hyoid and its body and the superior horns of the thyroid cartilage and thyroid plates for fractures. Hemorrhage must always be present at an alleged fracture site before it can be called an antemortem fracture.

The incidence of fractures in manual strangulation is high if a careful dissection of the neck is conducted. In the 41 cases of manual strangulation studied by DiMaio, the incidence of fractures was 68.1% (28 cases) — 100% of the males (14 of 14 cases) and 52% (14 of 27 cases) of the females.[26] Harm and Rajs reported an incidence of 70% of their 20 cases; Simpson and Knight 92% of 25 cases.[18,30] In DiMaio's cases, of the 14 females with fractures, all

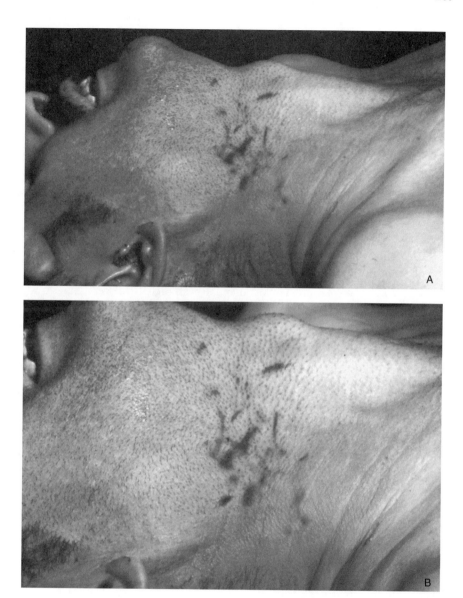

Figure 8.24 (A and B) Manual strangulation with fingernail marks and scratches on sides of neck.

had fractures of the hyoid, either alone (5 cases) or in combination with the thyroid cartilage (4); in combination with the cricoid (3) or in conjunction with both the thyroid and cricoid (2). Of the 14 males, 10 had fractures of the hyoid, either alone (4 cases) or in combination with other structures (6); two had fractures limited to the thyroid cartilage; two to the cricoid cartilage. There were 60 individual fractures in Di Maio's 28 cases. Unilateral fractures

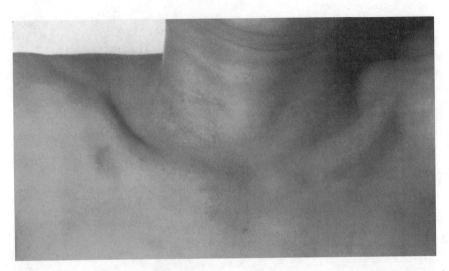

Figure 8.25 A 38-year-old female manually strangled. Bilateral fractures of superior horns of thyroid cartilage and fracture of cricoid cartilage. No external evidence of manual strangulation. Horizontal mark on neck is a surgical scar.

of the hyoid predominated over bilateral fractures 3 to 1. With unilateral fractures of the hyoid, fractures of the left side dominated 11 to 7. All the fractures of the thyroid cartilage involved the superior horns rather than the body of the thyroid. The latter fractures tend to be vertical and are usually caused by a blow to the thyroid cartilage.

Because of its location high up in the neck, the hyoid bone is relatively safe from injury by direct blows unless the neck is arched. In direct blows to the neck, fractures of the hyoid are generally seen only in association with a fracture of the mandible. The U shape of the hyoid does make it susceptible to fracture by compression. Thus, fractures of the hyoid are, as a rule, seen only in strangulation. Whether the fractured ends of the hyoid bone are driven inward or outward is immaterial.

The larynx, lying in front of the fourth through sixth cervical vertebrae, is protected in the midline only by skin and two layers of fascia. It is therefore susceptible to direct neck trauma, i.e., blows to the neck. Thus, fractures of the body of the thyroid cartilage can be seen in blows to the neck. Lateral compression of the larynx, as might be expected in manual strangulation, causes fractures of the cornu (horns) of the thyroid. Fractures of the cricoid cartilage occur most frequently when the cartilage is compressed in an antero-posterior direction against the vertebral column. These fractures, which are usually vertical, might occur in the midline or laterally.

In manual strangulation, there is usually trauma to both the external and internal aspects of the neck. Because of the way the neck is usually grasped, the tips of the four fingers with their associated fingernails dig into the neck.

Depending on the length, sharpness, and regularity of the nails, they can produce linear or semilinear abrasions, scratches, and scrapes (Figure 8.24). The tips of the fingers can produce contusions or erythematous marks. Pressure as applied by the thumb tends not to be at the tip, but on the pad. Therefore, nail marks are less common from the thumb, though a contusion may be present.

Various methods of manual strangulation are used. The simplest involves using one hand and attacking the victim from the front. In this method of attack, one sees small contusions and erythematous marks in association with nail marks on one side of the front of the neck caused by the fingers. An erythematous mark or contusion and, less commonly, a nail mark caused by the thumb, might be present on the opposite side of the neck. If the right hand is used, this thumb mark is on the right side of the neck. If two hands are used and the victim is attacked from the front, there are usually erythematous marks and contusions or nail marks on both sides of the front of the neck, usually posterior to the sternocleidomastoid muscles. A variation of a two-handed attack to the front of the neck involves using pressure applied by two thumbs on the central aspect of the neck. Here, the assailant presses both thumbs directly against or along the sides of the larynx and trachea. This results in erythematous markings or contusions of the anterior aspect of the neck. The area of hemorrhage can be either in a bilateral parasagittal plane or confluent across the midline. Fingernail marks, contusions, and erythematous marks caused by the fingers will be on the lateral aspects of the neck.

If either one or two hands are used and the victim is attacked from the back, erythematous marks or contusions from the fingertips, as well as nail marks, are generally found on the front of the neck between the larynx and sternocleidomastoid. With one hand, the marks would be on only one side of the neck; with two hands, on both sides. Bruises from the thumbs will be present on the back of the neck.

A less common method of strangulation is an assault from the front using the palm of the hand to apply pressure to the neck without using the fingertips. The authors have seen this in a number of instances, all of which involved adults who were unconscious through acute alcohol intoxication, or young children. There was no evidence of trauma externally that could be related to either the fingertips or fingernails. In all but one instance, there was congestion of the face and petechiae of the conjunctivae and sclerae, as well as periorbital petechiae of the skin. No hemorrhage was noted internally and there was no injury to the internal structures of the neck.

Nail marks can be classified into three types using the classification of Harm and Rajs: impression marks, claw marks, and scratch marks. Impression marks are "regularly curved, comma-like, exclamation mark-like, dash-like, or oval, triangular, rectangular epidermal injuries measuring 10–15 mm in length and up to a few millimeters in breadth." [18] They are produced when the fingertip digs into the skin at a right angle to it with the fingernails penetrating through the epidermis to the dermis. In the case of curved imprints, the concave surface does not necessarily correspond to the concave surface of the nail, but might just as easily be a mirror image.

Claw marks are U-shaped injuries of both the epidermis and dermis, varying in length from 3–4 mm to a few cm. In claw marks, the fingernails dig into the skin at a tangential angle, cutting the epidermis and dermis tangentially and undermining it. Scratch marks are parallel linear abrasions or erythematous bands in the epidermis up to 1.0 cm wide, produced when the fingernails dig into the epidermis at a vertical angle and then are drawn across the skin, producing an elongated injury.

While, in most manual strangulations, there is evidence of both external and internal injury to the neck, in some cases, there is no injury, either externally or internally. One of the authors (VDM), over a period of 3 months, saw three women who had been manually strangled. The first showed absolutely no evidence, either externally or internally; the second showed congestion of the face with fine petechiae of the conjunctivae and skin of the face, but no evidence of injury to the neck, either externally or internally; and the third victim had abrasions and scratches of the skin with extensive hemorrhage into the muscles of the neck. All three women were killed by the same individual. All three had blood alcohols above 0.300 g/dL. The *modus operandi* of the perpetrator was to meet a woman in a bar, buy her liquor until she was extremely intoxicated, and then go off with her and have sexual intercourse. He would then strangle her. At the time of strangulation, the women were unconscious through acute alcohol intoxication, so a very minimal amount of pressure was necessary. He would place his hand over their necks and push downward, compressing the vessels of the neck. In the last case, the individual regained consciousness and struggled, with the resultant injuries. The perpetrator admitted having killed a number of other women the same way over the past years in a number of states.

In manual strangulation, the victims are usually female. When they are male, they are often highly intoxicated. It is suggested that, in all manual strangulations, a complete toxicological screen be performed.

Sphincter incontinence is thought to be quite characteristic in strangulation. Harm and Rajs addressed this question in a study of 37 dead and 79 surviving victims of strangulation.[18] Of the 37 dead victims, 60% (22) had an empty urinary bladder, compared with 14% of 54 control autopsies whose causes of death were other than violence. Of the 79 surviving victims of asphyxia, 5% (4) had sphincter incontinence. Thus, sphincter incontinence, while more common in strangulation, is not an absolute finding.

In cases of strangulation, the presence of fractures of the larynx or hyoid indicate only that pressure or force has been applied to the neck. These fractures by themselves do not cause death. They are just markers of neck trauma. The authors have seen cases where someone has attempted to strangle an individual, causing fractures of the thyroid cartilage or hyoid, only to give up and stab or beat the victim to death.

One must be sure that the fractures are antemortem, because it is not uncommon to fracture the larynx at the time of autopsy. The distinguishing characteristic of an antemortem fracture is hemorrhage at the fracture site. This hemorrhage should be grossly visible. Hemorrhage demonstrable only microscopically can be a postmortem artifact. In handling suspected strangulation cases, one must be very careful about the interpretation of retro-esophageal and paravertebral cervical hemorrhage. Bleeding over the front and sides of the larynx is virtually always diagnostic of trauma e.g., strangulation, a blow, or an intravenous line. This is not the case for retro-esophageal and paravertebral cervical hemorrhage. These are almost always an artifact and are often seen in natural deaths, especially in elderly individuals dying slowly, i.e., hypoxic deaths.[2,31] The presence of petechiae of the mucosa of the epiglottis or larynx is not diagnostic of strangulation or any specific form of asphyxia.

Injuries of the Pharynx and Larynx Produced by Resuscitative Intubation

Resuscitative injuries of the pharynx and larynx secondary to intubation can mimic injuries caused by strangulation and neck holds. In a study of 50 individuals who had endotracheal intubation prior to reaching an emergency room, in an unsuccessful attempt at resuscitation, 37 (74%) had injuries of the airway following the intubation.[32] Injuries to the mouth consisted of focal contusions, lacerations, and focal abrasions of the lips and buccal mucosa. Injuries of the posterior oropharynx and laryngopharynx were contusions of the base of the tongue, contusions of the epiglottis, petechiae of the epiglottis, contusions of the piriform recesses, and laceration of the epiglottis (one case). Injuries to the larynx (32 cases) included contusions and petechiae of the mucosa as well as seven cases in which there were hemorrhages in the superficial and deep muscles of the larynx. As noted previously, petechiae of the epiglottis, larynx and trachea are of no diagnostic significance. In regard to hemorrhage in the neck musculature, Raven et al. do not give the exact location of these hemorrhages and their extent.[32] Externally, the individuals had cutaneous neck abrasions in two cases; facial petechiae in three and conjunctival petechiae in ten. The occurrence of the petechiae was ascribed to chest compression during resuscitation.

Injuries to Perpetrators of Strangulation

The paper by Harm and Rajs is unusual in that, not only does it consider the characteristics and patterns of injuries in victims of both manual and ligature strangulation, but also documents injuries in the assailant.[18] The authors studied 37 fatal cases of strangulation — 20 manual, 12 ligature, and five both manual and ligature. In 32 instances, the perpetrators were known. Twenty were examined for injuries. Of these, 13 (65%) showed a total of 98 injuries. Interestingly, the presence or absence of defense injuries on the victims did not correlate with the presence of injuries on the perpetrator. Thus, of the victims killed by the 13 assailants who showed evidence of injury, six showed defensive injuries of the hands and arms, while seven showed no injuries and thus no indication of a struggle even though the injuries on the assailant indicated that they did struggle.

Nail marks (impressions, claw marks, and scratches) constituted 82% of the injuries incurred by the 13 assailants. The other 18% of injuries were nonspecific in nature. Eleven (85%) of the assailants had from two to 26 nail marks. Seventy percent of these nail marks on ten of the 11 assailants were on the backs of the hands and forearms and were predominantly impressions. Most of the nail marks were concentrated on the back of the index finger and thumb. The face and right shoulder were secondary sites of injury.

When the distribution of the injuries in the stranglers was compared with those received by rapists who did not strangle their victims, it was found that the most common lesions in rapists were parallel scratches on the trunk caused by nails. Nail marks (mostly scratches and claw marks) were more often on the face and neck in rapists and nonspecific injuries were more common than in stranglers (47 to 18%).

Chemical Asphyxiants

In chemical asphyxia, inhalation of a gaseous compound prevents utilization of oxygen at the cellular level. The most common chemical asphyxiant encountered by a medical examiner is carbon monoxide. Carbon monoxide poisoning is discussed in Chapter 14.

Hydrogen cyanide and its salts, potassium and sodium cyanide, are potent, rapidly acting poisons. Cyanide produces cellular hypoxia by combining with the ferric iron atom of intracellular cytochrome oxidase. There is no cumulative effect from ingestion or inhalation of cyanide. One either dies or survives. Cyanide salts are used in photography, engraving, electroplating, and chemical laboratories. Most deaths caused by ingestion of cyanide are suicide and involve individuals who work in laboratories in which cyanide is used. It is a favorite method of suicide for chemists. Cyanide salts are harmless until they come into contact with acid, at which time there is production of hydrogen cyanide gas. Inhalation of this gas in a small room, in very high concentrations, such as a gas chamber, can produce almost immediate collapse and death. This, however, is the exception. In most instances, it takes minutes to die following inhalation of cyanide gases. Even in the Nazi death chambers, where pure cyanide gas in large quantities was pumped into a closed chamber, it took minutes to cause death. Ingestion of cyanide salts can produce rapid death if the salts contact gastric acid and the stomach is empty. With a full stomach, there might be a delay of several minutes to an hour before death occurs. According to Baselt[33] and J. Garriott (personal communication), the minimum adult lethal dose is approximately 200 mg for either sodium or potassium cyanide.

At the autopsy of an individual who ingests a cyanide salt, the mouth and stomach give off the distinct smell of bitter almonds. Unfortunately, the ability to smell cyanide is governed by a genetic trait and a significant percentage of the population cannot smell it. The gastric mucosa and blood will have a bright red color. Livor mortis is often bright pink. This coloration is caused by cyanide's inhibition of the cytochrome oxidase system, which prevents utilization of circulating oxyhemoglobin. It is oxyhemoglobin that gives the bright pink color to the blood, not cyanohemoglobin, which is not formed in any significant quantity in life. If a strong solution of potassium or sodium cyanide was ingested, there may be some alkaline burns of the gastric mucosa. If there was some vomiting of this material, these burns might be seen in the skin adjacent to the mouth. If hydrogen cyanide is inhaled, the only changes at autopsy are a bright pink color to the blood and livor mortis.

Analysis of the blood for the presence of cyanide should be conducted as soon as possible, because it decomposes with time. Conversely, in normal blood, cyanide is formed over time. Cyanide is detoxified by the liver into thiocyanate. Normal thiocyanate concentrations in the blood range from 1 to 4 mg/L in nonsmokers and from 3 to 12 mg/L in smokers. Blood cyanide levels in healthy subjects range from 0.016 to 0.041 mg/L. Toxic levels of cyanide range from 0.1 to 2.2 mg/L, with fatal levels generally greater than 1.1. mg/L (J. Garriott, personal communication). Individuals in industries exposed to cyanide on a chronic basis may have a mean level of 0.232 mg/L for smokers and 0.183 mg/L for nonsmokers. One worker, a smoker, had a level of 2.2 mg/L, which would ordinarily be considered a lethal level.[34]

Hydrogen sulfide (H_2S) is produced by fermentation of organic matter. It is found in sewers, sewage plants, and cess pools, as well as in the oil and chemical industries. Hydrogen sulfide, in conjunction with CO_2 and methane formed in sewers, is known as sewer gas. Deaths caused by H_2S are, almost without exception, accidental in manner. Just like cyanide, there is no cumulative effect to the inhalation of H_2S. In low doses, hydrogen sulfide is easily detected by its pungent, rotten-egg odor. In higher concentrations (150 parts per million), it can produce paralysis of the olfactory nerves.

In low concentrations, H_2S is a severe local irritant. In concentrations of 1000–2000 ppm (0.1–0.2%), there can be rapid, almost immediate death. At autopsy, the deceased appears cyanotic with dark-colored blood. This is caused by the reduction of oxyhemoglobin and the formation of methemoglobin. Sulfhemoglobin is not formed during acute exposure to H_2S. Normally, a small quantity of sulfhemoglobin exists in the blood. It is also formed postmortem secondary to decomposition. Fatal levels of sulfide in the blood range from 0.9 to 3.8 mg/L (J. Garriott, personal communication).

Sexual Asphyxia (Autoerotic Asphyxia, Autoerotic Deaths)

These are asphyxial deaths, principally caused by hanging, in which transitory anoxia is intentionally induced to enhance sexual arousement produced by masturbation.[35] Such deaths are rare, with the victim virtually always a male. Only a few cases involving females have been reported.[36] The victim is typically found in a private area, nude or partially nude; sometimes wearing female clothing. There may be erotic literature, sexual paraphernalia or a mirror opposite the individual so that he can observe his actions.

Typically, the deceased is found hanging by the neck, with a towel or some article of clothing interposed between the noose and the skin to prevent rope burns or marks on the neck (Figure 8.26). This pattern of behavior is repetitive and there may be evidence that the individual has performed this act numerous times over many years. While the individual is typically found

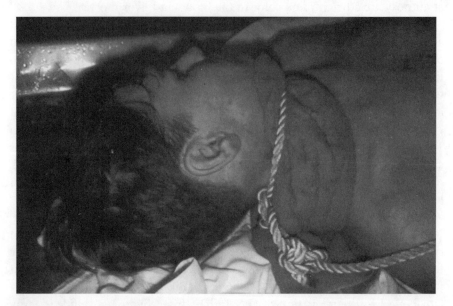

Figure 8.26 A 21-year-old male. Sexual asphyxia. Placed towel between noose and skin.

with a simple noose around the neck, there may be elaborate binding with multiple turns of the rope around the body, or the hands bound either in front of or behind the body. Analysis of the binding will reveal that the individual was capable of binding himself. He is not completely suspended; his feet are on the ground. Thus, he can relieve the pressure of the noose just by standing a little straighter. In some instances, rather than a noose, a ligature or some other device capable of applying pressure to the neck is used. There is always some self-rescue device so that the individual can relieve pressure before losing consciousness. Unfortunately, because of equipment failure, a flaw in design or construction of the device, or loss of control by the individual, accidental deaths occur.

Crucifixion

One unusual, historical, form of asphyxia was crucifixion.[37] The victim was typically nailed to a cross with nails driven through the wrists into the crossbar and through the feet into the upright post. Death was caused by shock, both hypovolemic and secondary to the pain of nailing, plus dehydration and asphyxia. The weight of the body on the outstretched arms would interfere with exhalation by maintaining the intercostal muscles in an inhalation state. Exhalation would then become primarily diaphragmatic. Over a prolonged time, this would lead to impaired respiration and asphyxia.

Death Caused by Upside-Down Suspension

If an individual is suspended upside down for a long enough period of time death can result. The mechanisms of death might be either acute cardiac or respiratory failure or a combination of both. The length of time it takes for death to occur depends on the health of the individual. It could range from a few hours to a day, perhaps somewhat longer.

Deaths from Choke or Carotid Holds

Neck holds are used by law enforcement agencies to subdue violent individuals. Rarely, one will encounter a death alleged to have occurred due to application of either a choke hold or a carotid sleeper hold.[38–41] These terms are often used interchangeably, but, in fact, refer to two different holds whose purpose is to produce transient cerebral ischemia and unconsciousness. Neither involves use of a mechanical implement. Rather, the arm and forearm are used to compress the neck, producing cerebral ischemia and unconsciousness. Occasionally, a baton, large metal flashlight, or some other device, will be used to compress the neck. The authors have seen a number of deaths involving use of such instruments. In such cases, there is usually extensive hemorrhage in the neck and fractures of the hyoid or larynx.

With **choke (bar arm) holds**, the forearm is placed straight across the front of the neck. The free hand grips the wrist, pulling it back, collapsing the airway and displacing the tongue rearward, which occludes the hypopharynx. Incapacitation is caused by collapse of the airway and the carotid arteries with resultant decrease in the supply of oxygen to the brain. Compression of the carotid arteries is the prime mechanism for loss of consciousness. If too much force is used, there could be fracture of the larynx or hyoid. In two cases reported by Reay and Eisele and in a case seen by the authors, there were unilateral fractures of the greater cornu of the thyroid cartilage.[38] Both of Reay and Eisele's cases had fractures on the left side of the neck, the right forearm was across the neck and the left hand was used to pull it backward. Thus, pressure was eccentrically transferred to the neck, predominantly to the left side. In the case seen by the authors, the left forearm was across the neck and the fractures were on the right side of the neck. The authors' case also had a fracture of the hyoid bone on the same side. Following loss of consciousness, the chokehold is released and the victim should regain consciousness within 30 sec. There should be no permanent *sequelae*. Obviously, if the choke hold is maintained for too long, death will ensue, and one now has a case of manual strangulation.

In the **carotid sleeper hold**, symmetrical force is applied by the forearm and upper arm to the front of the neck such that there is compression of only the carotid arteries and jugular veins and not the trachea. The arm is placed about the neck with the antecubital fossa or crook of the arm centered at the midline of the neck. The free hand grips the wrist of the other arm and pulls it backward, creating a pincher effect. This produces transient cerebral ischemia. The carotid sleeper hold impedes blood flow in the carotid arteries by pressure exerted on both sides of the neck by the pincher effect of the arm and forearm. If properly applied, the compression of the carotid arteries will cause loss of consciousness in approximately 10–15 sec. On relaxation of the hold, cerebral blood flow will be restored and consciousness will return in approximately 10–20 sec, without any serious side effects. Experiments by Reay and Holloway demonstrated that, during application of the carotid sleeper hold, blood flow is decreased an average of 85% to the head.[39] The range in five subjects was 82 to 96%. The time to minimum blood flow averaged 6 sec (range 3.2 to 7.2 sec).

In theory, the carotid sleeper hold will cause rapid unconsciousness without injury to the individual. Unfortunately, in violently struggling individuals, a carotid sleeper hold can easily and unintentionally be converted into a choke hold, as the individual twists and turns to break the hold.

Maintenance of the pressure in a carotid sleeper hold, after loss of consciousness, becomes manual strangulation and, if continued long enough, will cause death. One would not expect trauma to the structures of the neck in such an instance. The compression of the carotid arteries, with resultant decreased cerebral blood flow, can theoretically precipitate a stroke in an individual with atherosclerotic disease of the carotid or cerebral vasculature. The pressure can cause dislodgment of atherosclerotic material with a stroke caused by an embolus. Blood flow to the brain is from both the carotid and the vertebral arteries. If the vertebral arteries have impaired blood flow due to atherosclerosis, then occlusion of the carotid arteries can threaten an already compromised circulation, resulting in thrombosis or stroke.

Both choke and carotid sleeper holds are safe if properly used, though the latter is the safer of the two. In weighing how much force is acceptable in a situation, one must realize that any action involving force always has the potential of producing severe injury and death.

References

1. Ely SF and Hirsch CS, Asphyxial deaths and petechiae: a review. *J Forens Sci* 2000; 45(6):1274-1277.

2. Gordon I and Mansfield RA, Subpleural, subpericardial and subendocardial hemorrhages. *J Forens Med* 1955; 2:31-50.

3. Gilg T et al., Investigations on postmortem coagulation and fibrinolytic reactions in blood. *Beitr Gericht Med* 1986; 44:399-405.

4. U.S. Department of Justice, Federal Bureau of Investigation, *Crime in the United States: 1999.* Superintendent of Documents, Washington D.C., 2000.

5. DiMaio DJ and DiMaio VJM, Two deaths caused by a lack of oxygen in a water vault. *J Forens Sci* 1974; 19:398.40 1.

6. Rossen CL et al., Two siblings and recurrent cardiorespiratory arrest: Munchausen syndrome by proxy or child abuse? *Pediatrics* 1983; 71:715-720.

7. National Safety Council, *Accident Facts:1998* Itasca, Ill.

8. Guyton AC and Hall JE, *Textbook of Medical Physiology* 10th ed. W.B. Saunders, Philadelphia 2000.

9. Knight BH, The significance of the postmortem discovery of gastric contents in the air passages. *J Forens Sci* 1975; 6:229-234.

10. Feldman EA, Traumatic asphyxia: Report of three cases. *J Trauma* 1969; 9:345-353.

11. Roughead W, *Burke and Hare,* ed 3. Edinburgh, Cited in Polson C, Gee DJ, Knight B: *The Essentials of Forensic Medicine,* New York, Pergamon Press, 1985.

12. Camps FE and Hunt AC, Pressure on the neck. *J Forens Med* 1959; 6:116-135.

13. Brouardel P, Cited in Polson CJ, Gee DJ, Knight B, *The Essentials of Forensic Medicine.* New York, Pergamon Press, 1985.

14. Ikai M et al., Physiological studies on choking in judo, in *Bulletin of the Association for the Scientific Studies on Judo, Part 1, Studies in General*, 1958; pp 1-12.

15. Suzuki E, Medical studies on choking in judo, with special reference to electroencephalographic investigation, in *Bulletin of the Association for the Scientific Studies on Judo*, 1958; pp 23-48.

16. Rossen R; Kabat H., and Anderson JP, Acute arrest of cerebral circulation in man. *Arch Neurology and Psych* 1943; 50:510-528.

17. Rao Vj and Weti CV, The forensic significance of conjunctival petechiae. *Am J Forens Med Pathol* 1988; 9:32-34.

18. Harm T and Rajs J, Types of injuries and interrelated conditions of victims and assailants in attempted and homicide strangulations. *Forens Sci Int* 1981; 18:101-123.

19. Feigin G. Frequency of neck organ fractures in hanging. *Am J Forensic Med. Path* 1999; 20(2):128-130.

20. DiMaio VJM, Accidental hangings due to pacifiers. *JAMA* 1973; 226:790.

21. Rauchschwalbe R and Mann NC, Pediatric window-cord strangulations in the United States, 1981-1995. *JAMA.* 1997; 277:1696-1698.

22. Petruk J et al., Fatal asphyxiations in children involving drawstrings on clothing. *Can. Med. Assoc. J.* 1996; 155(10):1417-1419.

23. Casper JL, *Handbook of the Practice of Forensic Medicine*, vol 2, ed 3, GW Balfour (trans). London, New Syndenham Society, 1982, pp 169-182.

24. Spence MW et al.,. Craniocervical injuries in judicial hangings: an anthropologic analysis of six cases. *Am J Forens Med Pathol* 1999; 20 (4):309-322.

25. Hartshorne NJ, Reay DT, Judicial Hanging (letter), *Am J Forens Med Pathol* 1995; 16 (1):87.

26. DiMaio VJM, Homicidal Asphyxia, *Am J Forens Med Pathol*, 2000; 21(1):1-4.

27. Habal M, Meguid MM, and Murray JE, The long scarf syndrome — A potentially fatal and preventable hazard. *JAMA* 1972; 221:1269,1270.

28. Weiss S, Baker JP, The carotid sinus reflex in health and disease. *Medicine* 1933; 12:297-354.

29. Thomas JE, Hyperactive carotid sinus reflex and carotid sinus syncope. *Mayo Clin Proc* 1969; 44:127-139.

30. Simpson K and Knight B, *Forensic Medicine*, ed 9. Baltimore, Edward Arnold, 1985.

31. Paparo GP and Siegel H, On the significance of posterior crico-arytenoid muscle hemorrhage. *Forens Sci* 1976; 7:61-65.

32. Raven KP, Reay DT, and Harruff RC, Artifactual injuries of the larynx produced by resuscitative intubation. *Am J Forens Med Pathol*, 1999; 20(1):31-36.

33. Baselt RC, Disposition of Toxic Drugs and Chemicals in Man, 5th ed, Chemical Toxicology Institute, Foster City, 2000.

34. Chandra H et al, Chronic cyanide exposure — A biochemical and industrial hygiene study. *J Anal Toxicol* 1980; 4:161-165.

35. Uva JL, Review: autoerotic asphyxiation in the United States, *J Forens Sci*, 1995; 40(4):574-581.

36. Byard RW, Hucker SJ, and Hazelwood RR, Fatal and near-fatal autoerotic asphyxial episodes in women. *Am J Forens Med Pathol*, 1993; 14(1):70-73.

37. Edwards WD, Gabel WJ, and Hosmer FE, On the physical death of Jesus Christ. *JAMA* 1986; 255:1455-1463.

38. Reay DT and Eisele JW, Death from law enforcement neck holds. *Am J Forens Med Pathol*, 1982; 3:253-258.

39. Reay DT and Holloway GA, Changes in carotid blood flow produced by neck compression. *Am J Forens Med Pathol*, 1982; 3:199-202.

40. Koiwai EK, Deaths allegedly caused by use of "choke holds" (ShimeWazal). J *Forens Sci* 1987; 32:419-432.

41. Kornblum RN, Medical analysis of police choke holds and general neck trauma: I, II. *Trauma*, February 1986; 27(51:7-60; June 1986;28(l):13-64.

Deaths Caused by Motor Vehicle Accidents

9

In motor vehicle deaths, autopsies are performed to:

- Determine the cause of death
- Confirm that death was caused by injuries suffered in the accident
- Determine the extent of these injuries
- Detect any disease or factor, e.g., drugs, that could have precipitated or contributed to the accident or death
- Detect any criminal activity associated with the death
- Document all findings for subsequent use in either criminal or civil actions
- Establish positive identification of the body, especially if it is burnt or severely mutilated

The injuries in motor vehicle crashes are the result of:

- Impaction of the individual on some portion of the interior of the car
- Violation of the integrity of the passenger compartment by intrusion of part of the car or of another object, e.g., another vehicle or a lamppost, into the passenger compartment
- Ejection from the motor vehicle, either in part or entire
- Fire

Causes of Motor Vehicle Accidents

The most common cause of a fatal motor vehicle accident in the U.S. is impairment of the driver by alcohol, drugs, or a combination of both. As a general rule, approximately half of all motor vehicle operators killed in crashes are under the influence of alcohol. If one considers only drivers who cause the accidents, it would be safe to say that 65–75% are to some degree under the influence of alcohol or drugs.[1] These drugs are not necessarily drugs of abuse, but can be prescription medications. In addition, at least 15.9% of drivers, in some areas, are under the influence of marijuana at the time of the crash, though what the significance of specific levels of the active ingredients of marijuana means is not known at the present time, just that the active ingredients of marijuana are detectable in the blood.[1]

The second most common cause of fatal motor vehicle accidents is human error — speed, reckless driving, and falling asleep at the wheel. Excess speed, in most instances, plays only a marginal factor as a cause of an accident. It is, in fact, usually associated with alcohol intoxication, which would be the primary cause of the accident. With present day motor vehicles, crashes at 55 versus 75 mph are not significantly different in their fatal outcome.

The third most common cause is environmental hazards, such as bad weather, slick or icy roads, poorly marked roads, and poorly constructed roads. After this, come a host of miscellaneous causes such as defective vehicles and natural disease. An example of the latter would be the individual who suffers a fatal heart attack at the wheel.

Natural Disease as a Cause of Motor Vehicle Accidents

Accidents caused by natural disease are rare and do not represent a serious danger to the public. Sudden natural deaths at the wheel generally result in the death of only the driver, with the cause of death usually the natural disease. The driver is often able to stop the vehicle. When a collision does occur, usually only minor injuries result. Buttner et al.[2] reviewed 147 cases of sudden death in association with operation of a motor vehicle in which 134 of the individuals were male and 13 female. The main cause of death was ischemic heart disease — 113 cases (76.9%). Aortic aneurysm accounted for six cases, cerebrovascular disease for eight and epilepsy for two. In the cases resulting from cerebrovascular disease, six were caused by rupture of an aneurysm and two by intracerebral hemorrhage.

Not all the 147 individuals were driving at the time of death — 43 were found dead in the driver's seat of a parked vehicle, and 28 individuals were driving and able to stop the vehicle before they died. In one case, the deceased was driving and a passenger stopped the vehicle. Eight died while driving but were not involved in a collision, 55 died while driving by colliding with either another vehicle (26 cases) or with an object. In two cases, a pedestrian was injured, five cases caused minor injury to a passenger not necessitating hospital admission, and in three cases, a passenger incurred severe injuries. In only one case did the collision result in the death of others (two people in a shop).

Categories of Motor Vehicle Accidents

Motor vehicle accidents can be divided into four categories, depending on how the accident occurred:

1. Front impact crashes
2. Side impact crashes
3. Rollovers
4. Rear impact crashes

The probability of a fatality depends to a degree on the size and type of vehicle involved in a crash. Small vehicles, by virtue of their size, are less able to absorb crash energy. Thus, severe injury and fatalities are more common with such vehicles. Utility vehicles and pickups are generally heavier than are automobiles, therefore, the occupants of the former vehicles are more likely to survive crashes with cars. Pickups and sports utility vehicles, however, are more likely than cars to be involved in fatal single-vehicle crashes. In sports utilities, this is caused by their tendency to rollover.

Deaths are slightly more common in multiple vehicle crashes than single vehicle crashes. In fatal single vehicle crashes involving a car, the frequency of the type of crash causing death, in descending order, is: frontal impact; side impact, rollover and rear impact.[3] For utility vehicles and pickups, it is rollovers, frontal impacts, side impacts and rear impacts. In fatal multi-vehicle crashes involving a car, the frequency of type of crash in descending order is: frontal and side impacts (approximately equal), followed by rear impacts and then rollovers. For pickups and utility vehicles, it is frontal impact; side impact; rear impact and finally rollover.

Front Impact Crashes

Front impact crashes are the type of crash that most people think of when talking about motor vehicle accidents. Textbooks tend to concentrate on this type of accident, because it is easy to explain and understand. When two vehicles crash head-on, or a vehicle crashes into a fixed object, unless the driver and passengers are restrained, they will continue their forward movement, even though the car has stopped. If unrestrained, the driver's knees will impact the instrument panel; the chest the steering wheel; and the head the windshield, sun visor region above the windshield, or the frame (generally in this order). The same pattern of injuries would be true for unrestrained passengers, except they would impact the dashboard rather than the steering wheel. If the front impact is off-center, the driver or passenger might impact the A pillar with their head.

If the driver is restrained by belts, but without an airbag, the knees still impact the instrument panel but the head flexes forward, with the chin impacting either the sternum or, in severe collisions, the steering wheel. Unrestrained individuals in the back seat will hit the back of the front seat, the passengers in the front seat come up against the windshield or the sun visor area.

Objects protruding from the instrument panel, such as levers or knobs, can produce patterned abrasions on the victims.

If the drivers and passengers have restraint devices and if the passenger compartment retains its integrity, then the occupants of the vehicle should survive without any significant injury. The intrusion of part of the vehicle or another object into the passenger compartment may be transitory, with the portion of car or the object springing back. Thus, it might not at first be obvious that there has been violation of the integrity of the passenger compartment.

If the head of the driver or front seat passenger impacts the windshield, there will be abrasions and superficial cuts of the forehead, nose, and face, with the injuries having a vertical orientation (Figure 9.1)Thin slivers of windshield glass might be embedded in the wounds or be found loose on the clothing. The glass cuts, *per se*, are not serious, thanks to the construction of the windshield. Windshields are designed to prevent serious cuts and people going through them. The latter phenomenon, however, can still occur if the windshield pops out of the frame. Present-day windshields consist of thin outer and inner layers of glass with a thick core of plastic. Impaction of the head against the windshield with great force can cause the glass to shatter, but the plastic will only bulge.

Blunt force impact on the windshield, while not causing serious incised wounds, can, with enough force, produce fairly severe soft tissue injuries. There can be partial avulsion of the skin with the avulsed skin anchored superiorly (Figure 9.2). These wounds, because of their location, often bleed very heavily, appearing very dramatic and life threatening. This has caused emergency room physicians to concentrate all their attention on these seemingly severe, but actually non-life-threatening head injuries, and to neglect chest and abdominal injuries that eventually caused death (Figure 9.3). In addition to the external injuries, impaction of the head with the frame of the car above the windshield can cause basilar skull fractures, closed head injury, and fractures of the neck. Basilar fractures tend to run along the length of the petrous ridges passing through the sella turcica ("hinge fractures"). Less common are ring fractures and multiple fracture lines of the base of the skull.

In neck injuries, the most common fatal injuries are upper cervical fractures or dislocation at the atlanto-occipital junction (Figure 9.4). This

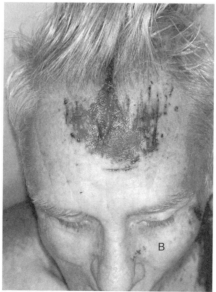

Figure 9.1 (A and B) Abrasions and superficial cuts of the forehead caused by impacting the windshield.

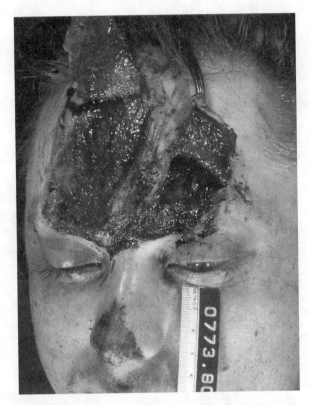

Figure 9.2 Avulsion of skin caused by impact with windshield.

can result in either complete transection or crushing of the cord. In other instances, the cord is violently pulled down, with partial or complete avulsion of the brain stem, ventrally, at the ponto-medullary junction.

The chest of the driver can impact the steering wheel; the chest of the passenger, the dashboard. Evidence of injury from such an impact varies from imprinted abrasions/contusions of the wheel or instrument panel to complete absence of any evidence of external injuries (Figure 9.5). The following internal injuries are fairly typical, depending on the amount of force and the age of the victim:

- Transverse fracture of the sternum (usually at the third intercostal space)
- Bilateral rib fractures
- Impaling injuries of the lung caused by fractured ribs
- Contusions, internal lacerations, and rupture of the pulmonary parenchyma
- Rupture of the heart
- Transection of the aorta
- Lacerations of the liver and spleen

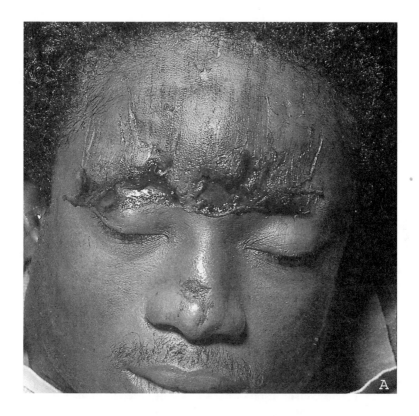

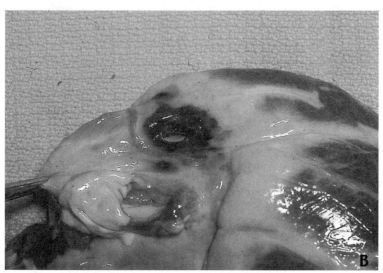

Figure 9.3 (A) A 24-year-old male with severe laceration of forehead caused by impact with windshield. Treated for non-existent brain injuries. (B) Cause of death: a 1-cm laceration of right atrium with hemopericardium (250 ml).

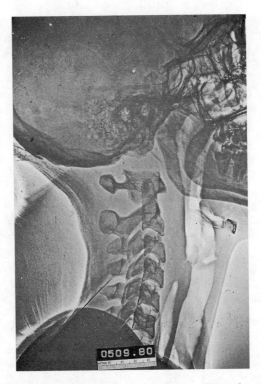

Figure 9.4 Fracture-dislocation of neck at atlanto-occipital joint.

Because of the elastic nature of the sternum or ribs in young individuals, there can be extensive thoracic injuries without fracture. Serious chest injuries from impaction against the steering wheel became less frequent with the introduction of energy-absorbing compressible steering wheel columns in the late 1960s. At the time, this was estimated to have reduced overall driver fatalities in frontal crashes 12%, with serious injury (including fatalities) reduced by 38%.[4]

One of the most common fatal thoracic injuries is transsection of the aorta (Figures 5.2 and 5.3). Typically, this occurs immediately distal to the origin of the left subclavian artery. Occasionally, one will see at autopsy individuals who have survived motor vehicle accidents in the past and died for other reasons. On opening the aorta, faint, horizontally oriented, linear scars on the intimal surface of the aorta distal to the left subclavian artery can be seen. These represent incomplete lacerations of the intima that subsequently healed. While the etiology of thoracic aortic lacerations has classically been ascribed to rapid deceleration, more recent work suggests that it is caused by chest compression.[5]

Injury to the heart is less common than aortic injuries. The most common injuries are myocardial contusion, laceration of the pericardial

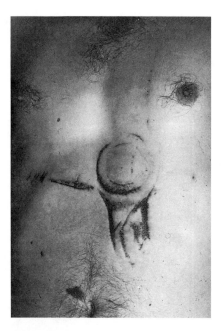

Figure 9.5 Imprint of steering wheel on chest.

sac, rupture of the right atrium, rupture of the right ventricle anteriorly at the interventricular septum, rupture of the left atrium, and laceration of the interatrial septum (Figure 9.6). Occasionally, individuals die from intraparenchymal pulmonary hemorrhage caused by massive pulmonary contusions.

In addition to the chest injuries, there can be lacerations of the liver and spleen. The injuries of the liver range from superficial capsular lacerations to bursting rupture. With massive blunt trauma, there might be rupture of the left hemi-diaphragm. With both splenic and hepatic injuries, the extent of the injuries may not be appreciated initially, when there may only be production of subcapsular hematomas. The individual will be examined and thought to have only minor injuries. A peritoneal tap will reveal no blood. The patient will die hours, if not days, later when the subcapsular hepatic or splenic hematoma ruptures. The authors have seen deaths in individuals where the physicians were so concentrated on other injuries that they ignored the possibility of abdominal injuries. In one case, the patient was given an initial peritoneal tap with no blood found. Although the patient subsequently complained of abdominal pain and had a drop in hematocrit, the physicians were so concerned with the other injuries that they lost their patient to the liver injury.

Occasionally, there will be a motor vehicle accident in which the driver impacts the steering wheel and in which no anatomical cause of death

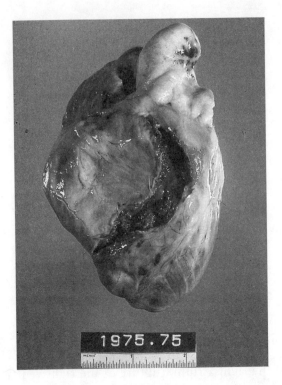

1975.75

Figure 9.6 Rupture of heart caused by chest's impacting steering wheel.

presents after a complete autopsy and toxicological screen. There may be soft tissue trauma to the chest and a fractured sternum or ribs, but insufficient injuries to explain death. Such deaths are caused by fatal cardiac arrhythmia secondary to a cardiac contusion. Examination of the heart might fail to reveal any evidence of impact because of the suddenness of the death. Some individuals do not develop cardiac arrhythmias until hospitalized. In these individuals, the presence of a cardiac contusion is confirmed by enzymatic tests and EKGs. The patients usually recover, though occasionally, they will die from an arrhythmia. Rarely, the authors have seen traumatic dissecting aneurysms of the left anterior descending coronary artery caused by blunt trauma to the chest.

Before death can be ascribed to cardiac contusion, positional or traumatic asphyxia must first be ruled out. A careful dissection of the neck, both anteriorly and posteriorly, in the upper cervical region must also be performed. The authors have seen a number of deaths caused by posterior fracture or dislocation of the upper cervical region, while no hemorrhage was seen anteriorly or in the subarachnoid space of the brain stem. This injury would have been missed if the posterior aspect of the cervical spine had not been explored. These injuries are caused by hyperflexion of the head.

In any automobile death in which no cause of death is found at autopsy, the back of the neck should be explored.

In elderly individuals, death can occur with injuries that a younger person might survive. Thus, rib fractures, minor cardiac contusions, pulmonary contusions, and some minor intrathoracic or intraabdominal injury that younger people will survive might cause death in an elderly individual with an unstable cardiac status.

If the knees impact the dashboard, there may be fractures of the patella or the distal femur, as the patella is driven as a wedge between the malleoli. There also can be dislocation at the hip joint or a fracture of the femur at its neck. In one case the authors saw, a woman in her early fifties was a passenger in the front seat of a car. She impacted her knees against the dashboard in a minor crash. She was seen in the emergency room of a prestigious trauma center where she complained of leg pains and had obvious bruising of the knees. The knees were X-rayed, but no fractures were seen. The woman said that she could not walk, so she was given crutches and sent home. A day and a half later, she was found dead in bed. At autopsy, a fracture of the neck of the right femur was found, with massive bleeding into the musculature and soft tissue of the thigh. Death was caused by exsanguination. The doctors in the emergency room, while dutifully X-raying the knees, had not examined the rest of the femur and had completely missed the fracture that produced death.

If the integrity of the passenger compartment is violated by the engine's being driven backward, the injuries produced can be the massive crushing injuries previously noted, plus injuries of the pelvis. Occasionally, the compartment may be violated, the injuries produced minor, yet death occurs. Death in these cases is usually caused by traumatic asphyxia with compression of the chest by the intruding portion of the car so that respiration is impossible.

In unrestrained individuals, the usual sequence and pattern of injuries is knee–femur–hip–chest–head. In restrained (belted) individuals, the nature of the injuries is dependent on the severity (force) of the crash. Knee contact usually still occurs. In moderate-speed collisions (30 mph and above), the forward movement of the head is such that it might impact the steering wheel. In all collisions, the individual is propelled toward the point of impact. This is true in angled front impact collisions. Thus, in an impact to the left front of the vehicle, the head of the driver moves front-left and might impact the A pillar while the passenger might impact the rearview mirror.[6]

If the driver and passenger are restrained by seat (lap and shoulder) belts and there is no intrusion into the passenger compartment, the probability of survival is great. In addition to preventing, or at least minimizing, occupant-to-interior impacts, seat belts virtually eliminate the risk of ejection, even in rollover crashes. Use of seat belts reduces the risk of fatalities to front-seat occupants by 45%.[7]

Seat belts and airbags, while effective in decreasing the incidence of death and injury, can, themselves, produce injuries, even death. Lap belts can produce tears of the mesentery and omentum and occasionally laceration of the bowel. Shoulder belt use may be reflected by a linear abrasion running downward and medially on the left side of the neck of the driver or the right side of the neck of the front passenger (Figure 9.7A). A poorly defined area of abrasion and contusion indicating the distribution of the belt might be seen on the skin of the lower abdomen (Figure 9.7B).

In addition to the aforementioned injuries, one also sees dicing injuries, which are superficial cuts of the skin caused by the fragments of glass produced when the side and back windows of a car shatter (Figure 9.8). Glass used in these windows is tempered glass, which is designed to shatter into little glass cubes on violent impact. This is to prevent the individuals in the car from incurring serious cuts from slivers of glass. The marks produced by these little cubes of glass tend to be linear, right angled, and very superficial. They are not life threatening. Drivers typically have them on the left side of the face and forehead and the left arm; passengers on the right side of the face and forehead and right arm.

In head-on crashes, the floorboards can be driven upward and inward, twisting the foot on the ankle and causing a fracture. In other instances, if the seat goes forward, the foot can be trapped beneath the seat, breaking the ankle.

Side Impact Crashes

The second type of collision is the side impact. In fatal crashes involving passenger cars, it is second in frequency to front impacts. These crashes usually occur at intersections when a car is struck broadside by another vehicle going through the intersection at right angles to the first. In such cases, dicing injuries can be found on either one or both sides of a driver, depending on whether the side glass is propelled into the driver; the driver into the glass, or both. Side impact crashes can also occur when a car skids sideways, striking a fixed object such as a tree or pole with its side.

In car-to-car collisions, where the impact is to the driver's side, force is applied from the shoulder level downward. The head can flex laterally through the side window, striking the impacting vehicle. It might also impact the A or B pillars. If the impacting vehicle is a truck, the force is delivered from roof to floor level, and the intruding vehicle can make direct contact with the head. A seatbelt or frontal airbag in this situation yields virtually no benefit. External injuries — abrasions, lacerations, dicing injuries, and fractures — will tend to be on the left side of the body, and the

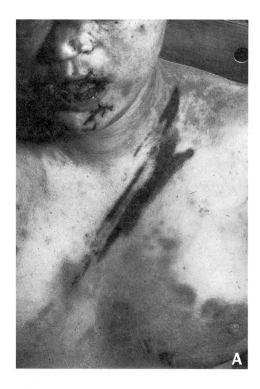

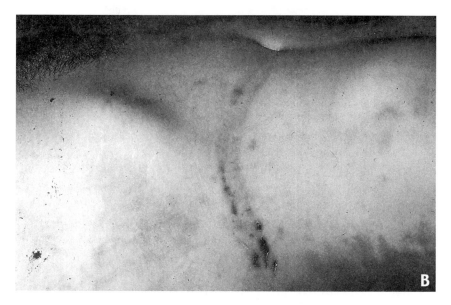

Figure 9.7 Abrasions caused by (A) shoulder belt and (B) lap belt in 26-year-old female driver dying of craniocerebral injuries. Manner of death: suicide.

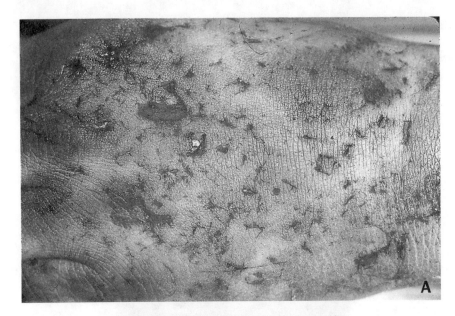

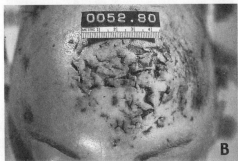

Figure 9.8 Dicing injuries of back of left hand (A) and forehead (B).

left arm and leg may be fractured. Internally, fractures of the ribs tend to be predominantly on the left side. While textbooks always discuss transections of the aorta from head-on collisions, these injuries can result from a side impact as well. In addition, there might be rupture of the heart, with the same type of injuries as those in head-on collisions. Lacerations of the liver and, to a lesser degree, the spleen, can be present, as well as lacerations of the left kidney. Basilar fractures and fractures of the neck might occur. The overall impression with such cases, however, is that the injuries to the left side of the body are more severe than the right. In the case of passengers in this vehicle, the injuries will tend to be to the left side. Unrestrained front seat passengers might be cushioned by the driver, reducing the severity of the injuries to some degree. Use of a seatbelt by the passenger can reduce the severity of or even eliminate injuries by preventing the passenger from making contact with the driver, the impacting vehicle, or structures in the passenger compartment.

If the impact is from the right (i.e., the passenger's) side, the injuries will tend to be more severe on the right side of the body. Transection of the aorta may occur, though it is less common than from front or left-side impacts. Lacerations of the heart, liver, and spleen; fractures of the neck; and basal fractures can also occur.

As noted, seat belts tend to keep people in place rather than having them hurled from one side of the vehicle to the other. They are less effective in preventing injuries in side impacts than in head-on crashes, because the sides of motor vehicles are constructed of thin sheet metal.

When a side impact occurs, fatalities usually occur in the car impacted rather than the car impacting, because the engine protects the impacting driver and passengers. In side impact collisions with fixed objects, that is, when a car slides sideways into a fixed object, the driver or a passenger if not restrained may partially pop out the window, impact the fixed object, and then pop back into the vehicle.

Rollovers

Rollover crashes are generally less lethal than head-on and side impact collisions, provided the individual is not ejected or the vehicle rolls into an unyielding object such as a tree. Anything that prevents ejection of an occupant increases the probability of survival. Because of better design, present-day car doors usually do not open in rollovers. Instead, the unrestrained individual is ejected out the window. Thus, use of a seat belt is very beneficial in such accidents. If one is not wearing a seat belt, one may be thrown about the passenger compartment like a rag doll and not infrequently ejected from the vehicle. Ejection may be complete with the car rolling over the ejected individual, or just the head and upper trunk may protrude to be rolled over by the vehicle. The body may then pop back into the car. It is not uncommon in rollover accidents to see a blood-stained depression in the roof of the car adjacent to a window (Figure 9.9). The head of one of the individuals in the vehicle has protruded through the window as the car rolled over, with the head causing the depression as it was crushed. Paint from the roof is sometimes left on the head of the victim in such instances.

The injury patterns in rollover accidents in which an individual is not restrained are much more variable because the individual is thrown about, impacting surfaces willy-nilly. There is no specific injury pattern. If the individual is ejected and the car rolls over his trunk but not his head, there may be no external evidence of trauma (Figure 9.10). Subsequent autopsy, however, can reveal massive ruptures of the lungs, heart, liver, spleen, and mesentery.

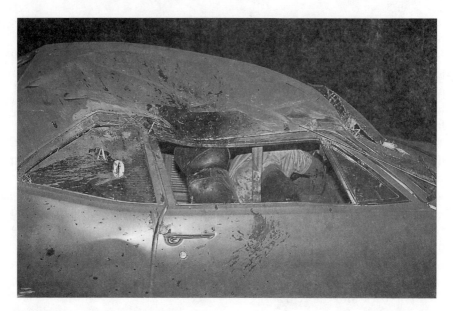

Figure 9.9 Blood-stained depression in roof of car adjacent to window where head popped out and was rolled over.

Rollovers account for approximately 18.8% of all fatal motor vehicle accidents.[3] In passenger cars, crash direction is most commonly from the front, with rollovers accounting for 15.1% of fatal accidents. In contrast, rollovers account for 36% of fatal crashes involving utility vehicles; 24.5% for pickups; 20.3% for vans and 13.8% for large trucks. [3]

Most single-vehicle rollover accidents involve a vehicle's running off the roadway, followed by an abrupt attempt to steer it back onto the road. The attempted correction causes the vehicle to skid sideways. As it does, it begins to tip over toward the leading side. If there is sufficient lateral momentum, the tires will plow into the surface and the vehicle will roll over. If the momentum is insufficient, the vehicle will fall back onto its wheels. The point at which the vehicle begins to roll over is approximately where the tire marks stop. The propensity of the vehicle to tip is determined not only by the side momentum but also by the height of the vehicle's center of gravity (thus, the increased tendency of utility vehicles to roll over) as well as the nature of the ground surface. A vehicle is more likely to roll over on dirt than pavement.

As a vehicle begins to roll, it becomes airborne. With a low center of gravity, such as in automobiles, the rolling vehicle tends to land on the edge of the roof opposite to the side of the car that is leading the rollover. In vehicles with a high center of gravity, such as utility vehicles, the impact point is more likely to be the leading edge of the vehicle roof. After impact, the vehicle continues to roll, often coming to rest back on its wheels. When a

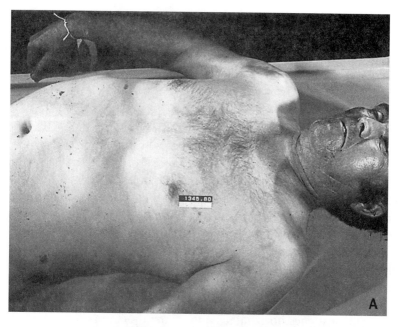

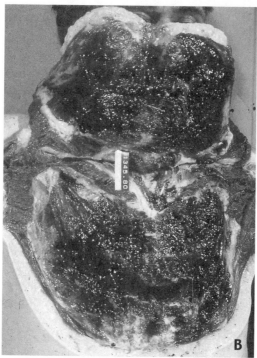

Figure 9.10 Tractor rolled over deceased with (A) no external evidence of injury but (B) massive internal injuries with fractures of ribs and sternum and rupture of internal organs.

vehicle does roll over, it usually doesn't do it more than once. By studying the scene and the vehicle, an accident reconstructionist can estimate the speed of the vehicle at the time of rollover, the number of rolls, the impact points on the vehicle, and the direction of the roll.

Rear Impact Crashes

Rear impact crashes are the least common form of fatal accident. This is because the occupants of the front seat of the impacted car are protected by the trunk and rear passenger portion of the vehicle. These usually decelerate the impacting vehicle sufficiently to protect individuals in the front seat. People in the impacting automobile are protected by their car's engine. Rear impact crashes account for many civil suits involving whiplash syndrome. Although relatively uncommon, one of the potential dangers with the rear impact crash is rupture of the gas tank, with ignition of the fuel. Rupture of the tank is, of course, proportional to the speed of impact. In the authors' experience, most fatal automobile fires begin under the hood of the car and are not related to rear impact.

In rear impact collisions, there may be seatback failure such that the back of the front seat goes horizontal. At the same time, the occupant of the seat can go backward, impacting the rear seat or the roof, or even be ejected out the rear window. This can result in serious, if not fatal, head and/or neck injuries. This can occur even if the individual is wearing a seatbelt. In one case seen by the authors, the seat partially failed after a rear impact, creating a ramp, with the driver propelled backward and upward. His head impacted the roof of the car with such force as to embed hair in the cloth lining. The impact fractured his neck, producing quadriplegia.

Conclusions

In the aforementioned discussion of injury patterns associated with different types of crashes, we have neatly divided all crashes into four categories: front impact, side impact, rollover, and rear impact. This is, of course, an artificial distribution. There can be a combination of the types. Thus, there might be a front impact where the car is deflected, rolls over, and slams sideways into a tree.

One minor, infrequent, but interesting injury should be mentioned here. Occasionally, an individual is brought into the morgue with a gray- to pale-green-colored face and a leathery texture to the skin (Figure 9.11). This is caused if the car battery ruptures and sprays the victim's face with acid.

Seat Belts and Air Bags

There are three forms of automobile belt-type restraints: lap belts; shoulder (diagonal) belts and three-point belts (lap plus shoulder belt). Lap belts were

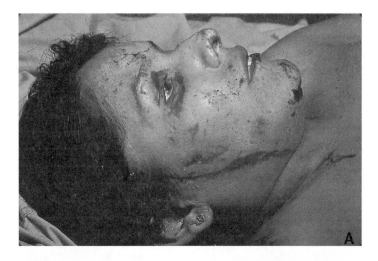

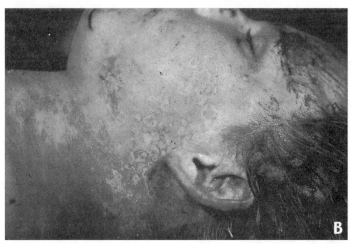

Figure 9.11 (A and B) Acid burns of face from ruptured battery.

the first form of restraint offered, becoming standard in automobiles in 1964. They are still found in older vehicles and in the back seats of some newer vehicles. All new vehicles use the three-point belt. As of December 1997, it was estimated that 69% of motor vehicle occupants use safety belts.[7]

Lap belts are effective in reducing mortality and morbidity, predominantly by preventing ejection of the driver and passengers at the time of a crash. In frontal collisions, they prevent impact of the head of the driver or passenger with the windshield frame and reduce injuries that would be caused by impacting the steering wheel and dashboard. On frontal impact, the head and chest will jackknife over the belt such that the driver's head can impact the steering wheel and the front passenger's head the dashboard. Both can incur serious and fatal injuries. Lap belts also prevent rear passengers from impacting or being propelled over the front seats.

While successful in reducing mortality and injury, on occasion, a lap belt can also cause injury. If the belt is worn too high (above the pelvis), the body can violently jackknife, producing compression fractures of the lumbar vertebrae; transverse fractures of the vertebral bodies; as well as fractures of the pedicles, transverse processes and lamina of the lumbar vertebrae.[8–11] The vertebral injuries are caused by severe flexion combined with shearing forces. Soft tissue injuries produced by lap belts consist of contusions and lacerations of the duodenum, jejunum and ileum and lacerations of the spleen and pancreas. In intestinal injuries, the lacerations are on the anti-mesenteric side of the bowel. While all of the aforementioned injuries occur from wearing the lap belt too high, such injury can still take place if it is worn properly through a phenomenon called "submarining," where, at impact, the pelvis sinks down into the seat and slides under the belt. Most abdominal and spinal injuries, however, are caused by wearing the lap belt too high.

Injuries to the small intestine, colon and lumbar spine, in the plane of the lap belt, are referred collectively to as the "seat belt syndrome." Contusions and abrasions on the abdominal wall, in association with this syndrome, and caused by the belt, are called the "seat belt sign."[11]

Use of the shoulder restraint without the lap belt can produce fractures of the cervical, thoracic and lumbar spine; fractures of the ribs and sternum and injuries of the larynx, liver, spleen and kidney.[10] With combined use of lap and shoulder belts(three-point restraints), the benefits of the lap belt are augment by the benefits of the shoulder belt. Impaction with the steering wheel and dashboard are prevented. However, the three-point restraint still can produce injuries such as rib fractures (single more likely than multiple), fractures of the clavicles, and sternum and cervical spine fractures.[9,10]

While lap–shoulder belts can produce injuries, such hazards are outweighed when one realizes that they reduce fatalities for drivers of passenger cars by 45%.[7] The part played by seat belts in saving lives is further evidenced in their ability to prevent individuals from being ejected from vehicles — 75% of occupants ejected from passenger cars are killed.[12] Only 1% of occupants who are restrained are ejected compared with 22% of unrestrained occupants.

Air Bags

Air bags were introduced to reduce serious injuries and deaths in automobile crashes, especially in those individuals not using seat and lap belts. *They are intended to provide protection only in frontal crashes and to be used in conjunction with seat belts.* Compared with lap–shoulder belts, air bags are significantly less effective. Thus, airbags alone have an estimated effectiveness of 14% in reduction of fatalities in drivers in crashes of all types compared with 45% for lap–shoulder belts used alone. The estimated reduction in fatalities when used together is 50%.[7]

To perform their function, air bags should fill as much of the space as possible between the driver and the steering wheel or the passenger and the dashboard. In addition, the air bag must deploy as rapidly as possible. As with any life-saving device or drug, there is the potential for adverse side effects. Thus, air bags can produce injury, and, on rare occasion, death.

There is a wide variance in the design of air bags including:

- Collision speed that triggers deployment
- Speed of deployment
- Distance of extension
- Physical characteristics of the airbag, etc.

Deployment of airbags occurs when crash sensors detect an impact equivalent to hitting a solid barrier at 10–15 mph.[7] There is some thought that the threshold for deployment is too low, and that there is no risk of severe injury or fatalities to drivers until impact speed is approximately 30 kph (18 mph). Some suggest that 18 mph should be used for the threshold for deployment, at least for belted individuals.[13]

Some vehicles have a higher threshold than the 10–15 mph while others have dual thresholds. An example of dual threshold deployment is found in Mercedes automobiles, and has been so for driver airbags since 1988 and passenger air bags since 1989.[13] The threshold for deployment is 12 mph if the passenger is unbelted and 18 mph if belted.

Inflation of the air bag is usually by a pyrotechnic device with production of gas. The velocity of deployment ranges from 100 to 200-plus mph, with older air bags deploying faster than newer. Deployment time is at least 30 milliseconds. Airbags can be tethered or untethered. In the former, tethers control the excursion of the bag toward the occupant as well as the shape. The distance that the air bag can travel from wheel to driver can range from 12 to 20 inches, with the untethered bags traveling farther. Newer air bags will be less powerful and able to modify the amount of inflation depending on the size of the driver or passenger. Side-impact airbags are smaller than front-impact bags and must inflate faster.

Just like seat belts, air bags can cause injuries, but, unlike seat belts, the injuries can be immediately lethal. Deaths are usually associated with women of small stature and children below the age of 13 years, especially when the children are unrestrained or out of position. Rear-facing infant or child restraints should never be used in front seats, as they place the child's head and body very close to the air bag housing. Infants in the front seat, in rear-facing infant seats, have predominantly craniocerebral injuries. Drivers seated too close to the steering wheel (less than 10 inches) can be seriously injured or killed by deploying air bags. Short drivers are injured more frequently because they must sit closer to the steering wheel to reach the gas and brake pedals.

In some vehicles, e.g., Mercedes, there are "pre-tensioners" that are activated by the same sensor system that activates the air bag. Pre-tensioners pull the slack out of the shoulder strap before the airbag deploys, pulling wearers back in the seat before they begin to move forward, reducing the subsequent force of impact between the air bag and the person. This reduces the likelihood of air bag injury.

Fatal injuries ascribed to airbag deployment include cervical spine dislocations or fractures, basal skull fractures, and injuries to thoracic and abdominal viscera. The injured person may show characteristic abrasions of the anterior neck and under surface of the jaw (Figure 9.12). Abrasions of the chest might also be present. In one relatively minor accident reviewed by the authors, there was blunt trauma to the right internal carotid artery, just

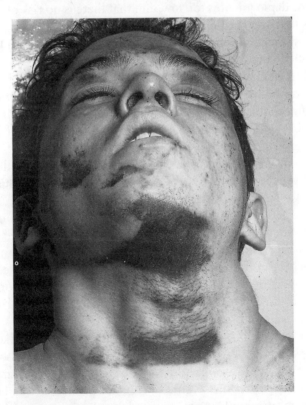

Figure 9.12 Abrasions on undersurface of chin and on neck caused by deploying airbag. Cause of death was fracture of cervical spine.

distal to the bifurcation of the common carotid artery. At the scene, the driver appeared somewhat disoriented. She was seen at a hospital and sent home, only to be re-admitted 12 hours later, with a history of convulsions. She was alert, oriented, and could speak but had left-sided hemiparesis. An angiograph showed complete occlusion of the right internal carotid artery caused by thrombosis. She gradually deteriorated over the next few days, dying of widespread infarction of her right cerebral hemisphere. The traumatic injury of the internal carotid artery was demonstrated at autopsy.

By November 2000, the National Highway Traffic Safety Association (NHTSA) had documented 169 deaths ascribed to airbags since 1990.[14] One hundred involved children 12 years of age or younger. Ninety-eight were killed by passenger bags; two by driver's air bags. Of the 98 children fatally injured by deployment of passenger air bags:

- 69 were unrestrained or improperly restrained
- 18 were in rear-facing child safety seats
- 5 were in forward-facing child safety seats
- 6 were wearing lap and shoulder belts

Of the 69 adults, 63 were drivers and six were passengers. Only 18 of the drivers were belted, and 23 of the drivers and three of the passengers were 62 inches or less in height.

Motor Vehicle Fires

Fires secondary to a motor vehicle crash are uncommon. When they do occur, and involve fatalities or severe injuries, they almost invariably result in a major lawsuit against the automobile manufacturer. Because of this, in any motor vehicle accident where there is a fire and a burned body is removed from the vehicle, a complete and thorough autopsy should be performed. This should involve examination of the neck, both anteriorly and posteriorly, especially if there are no evident traumatic injuries to explain death. Blood carbon monoxide analysis should be performed. If no blood can be obtained, use spleen, marrow, liver or muscle in that order.

Fire occurs in approximately 2.9% of fatal motor vehicle crashes — 5.7% of large truck crashes; 2.9% of light truck and 2.5% of passenger car.[3] In absolute numbers, for example in 1998, fatal fires occurred in 738 crashes involving passenger cars; 565 light trucks and 279 large trucks.

A number of experiments have been conducted involving burning vehicles. No propellants were used in these experiments. In one case, a fire was started in the passenger compartment of an automobile.[15] The four windows were left open and a 10 km/h wind blew steadily through the windows from the driver's to the passenger's side. Maximum temperatures in the compartment ranged from 867 to 1133°C. The maximum carbon monoxide level was 15,100 ppm; the carbon dioxide level 122,000 ppm. Oxygen concentration dipped down to 8.5%.

In a similar experiment, the same type of car was burned, again with the fire started in the passenger compartment, but with the windows closed.[16] After a period of smoldering and heavy smoke formation, the fire erupted with a flash-over. It burned for less than 1 min before it went out, presumably because of lack of oxygen. The temperature rise away from the immediate vicinity of the fire was minimum (maximum of 30°C). At the time of flash-over, the temperature rose to 29°C on the floor, 266°C at the driver's head level and 603°C at the headliner. After the flash-over, the temperatures dropped to below 50°C. Prior to the flashover, the CO was from 110–260 ppm; the CO_2 levels 700–1000 ppm. Subsequently, CO rose to 24,800 ppm; CO_2 59,000 with O_2 falling to 8%.

Motorcycle Accidents

There is a classic line that goes, "Buy your son a motorcycle for his last birthday." This, in a way, summarizes motorcycle accidents. The motorcycle, by its design, is intrinsically dangerous. An accident that might result in minor injuries with an automobile can result in death with a motorcycle. Approximately 6% of all traffic fatalities involve motorcycles.[12] In accidents involving automobiles, the most dangerous thing that can happen to an individual is to be ejected from the vehicle. Motorcycles involved in accidents always eject their operators or passengers. Individuals dying in motorcycle accidents typically die of either head or neck injuries, with the former more common. There are usually extensive skull fractures, predominantly basal. The injuries occur from impacting the ground or another object, e.g., a curb or a lamppost. If the individuals are not wearing protective clothing, and even when they are, there can be extensive confluent scrape-like abrasions as they slide across the pavement. An incision into this area typically reveals no underlying subcutaneous hemorrhage, because these injuries are very superficial and limited to the skin (Figure 4.1). Passengers falling off the backs of moving motorcycles typically have lacerations of the back of the head, fractures of the posterior fossa, contrecoup contusions of the frontal lobes of the brain, and abrasions of the back and elbows. If the person tumbles forward, there will be abrasions of the face. While motorcycle helmets reduce the incidence of head trauma in low-speed accidents, at moderate and high speeds their sole function is to prevent brain matter from being spread over the highway.

The most common causes of motorcycle accidents are alcohol or drugs, environmental factors (oil slicks, bumps or potholes in the road,), reckless driving, and failure of drivers of cars to see the motorcycle. The most common cause of a motorcycle fatality is running off the road. Approximately 28% of motorcycle operators involved in fatal crashes have a blood alcohol level of 0.10 g/dl or greater.[12]

The authors have seen a number of motorcycle operators beheaded or having arms avulsed due to cables or wires stretched across roads or used as supports to poles or towers (Figure 9.13). Injury occurs when the operator does not see the cable or wire. Examination of the amputated heads and extremities shows the edges of the wounds to be sharp, almost as if they had been produced with a knife. If one found such a head and body without knowing the individual had been on a motorcycle and beheaded by a wire, one would think that the head had been cut off with a sharp, edged instrument, so sharp are the edges of the wound.

Occasionally, a motorcycle rider, seeing a car stop abruptly in front of him and knowing he will not be able to stop in time, will drop his motorcycle on its side and skid toward the vehicle in an attempt to prevent impacting it. The authors have seen a number of cases in which this was effective in

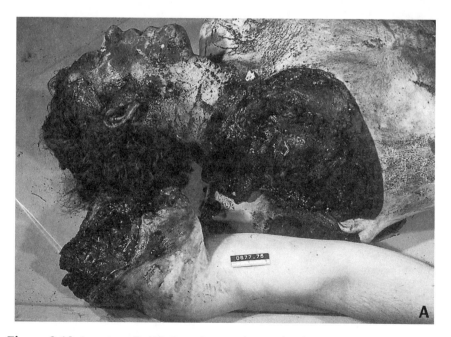

Figure 9.13 *(continued)* (A) Complete avulsion of right arm by guy wire. Note sharp margins.

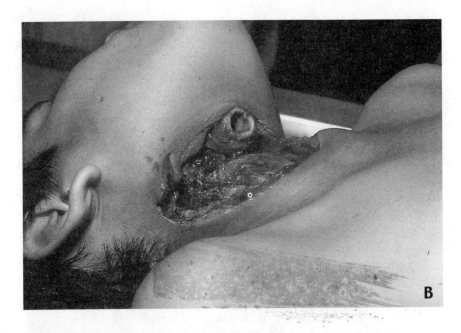

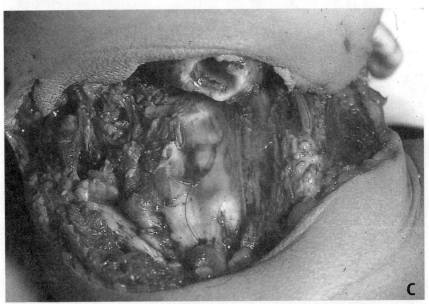

Figure 9.13 *(continued)* (B) Incomplete beheading due to wire. (C) Sharp margins to wound, almost as if neck had been cut with a knife.

preventing any serious damage to the motorcyclist. Unfortunately, in one case, the operator skidded beneath the car, hooking his chin on the bumper and dislocating his neck at the atlanto-occipital juction.

As mentioned previously, operators of automobiles often do not see motorcyclists, either because of their low profile, or because auto drivers are not attuned to looking for motorcycles. Automobiles will turn in front of a motorcycle and the motorcycles will crash into the car. Automobiles going through an intersection will crash into a motorcycle, failing to see it. Most experienced motorcyclists assume that individuals driving cars do not see them.

The aforementioned discussion of motorcycles also applies to a degree to off-the-road, all-terrain vehicles (ATVs). These are now all four-wheeled vehicles. Three-wheeled vehicles are no longer sold in the U.S. because they are believed to be unsafe. Fatal injuries tend to involve the head and neck, with occasionally the ATV's turning over and landing on top of the operator. The operators who are killed often are young children, too young to legally operate motor vehicles or motorcycles.

Mention at this time can also be made of snowmobiles. One of the more common causes of death with these vehicles is drowning. This occurs when a driver attempts to cross a frozen lake and does not realize that the ice is not thick enough to support the vehicle.

Suicide by Motor Vehicles

A small number of single motor vehicle accidents are suicides. Typically, drivers crash their cars head-on into a fixed object such as a concrete bridge, an embankment, or a utility pole. The individual turns off the road and drives a significant distance, straight into the object, without using the brakes. It is usually obvious from a study of the tire tracks that such individuals had sufficient time to turn back onto the road or avoid the obstacle if they had accidentally gone off the road. In addition, if the death was witnessed, no brake lights would have been observed. There are probably other such suicides that go undetected. The cause of the "accident" in such cases is attributed to drinking or falling asleep at the wheel.

Usually, individuals committing suicide with a motor vehicle will have a history of prior suicide attempts or treatment by a psychiatrist. In one instance, the victim was a mother who had just killed her daughter. In all suspected cases, one should examine the soles of the shoes of the driver to see if there has been transfer of the pedal pattern to the shoe sole. If the pattern is that of the gas pedal, then one knows that, at the time of impact, the individual was still accelerating. This is confirmatory evidence of a suicide.

Determination of Who Was Driving

Occasionally, accidents occur in which there are two or more occupants in a vehicle and it is not clear who the driver was. In some cases, all the people may be dead, or a survivor, although he might have been the driver, to avoid legal liability might claim that a deceased individual was driving. In such instances, examination of the body, car, and clothing can be decisive in determining who actually was the driver. The pattern of injuries, for example, dicing or an imprint of a steering wheel, might identify the driver. In other instances, examination of the car might show fibers in the broken steering wheel or in the sun visor that correspond to the clothing of one of the individuals. Examination of the soles of shoes for a pedal pattern from an accelerator or brake might be of aid. There might be deposits of blood on the steering wheel, visor or windshield that can be typed by DNA to identify the driver.

In one case, a 20-year-old girl was suspected of driving a motor vehicle involved in a fatal collision. Her blood alcohol showed that she was intoxicated at the time of the accident. She claimed that the other individual in the car, who had been killed, was the driver. Her shoes and the pedals of the car were examined. There could be no transfer of the pedal pattern to the soles of her shoes because they were covered by fine parallel grooves that would not take an impression from the pedals. Examination of the pedals, however, revealed the pattern of the sole of the shoes (Figure 9.14). This indicated that she had been the driver of the motor vehicle.

Motor Vehicle–Train Accidents

Collisions between trains and motor vehicles are virtually all of the side impact-type, with the train impacting the side of a vehicle that is either trying to beat the train through the intersection, or is stalled on the tracks. Less commonly, a speeding vehicle impacts the side of a train. The nature of the injuries varies from typical side- and front-impact automobile injuries to the more common nonspecific pattern of massive mutilating injuries. Since many of these cases evolve into civil suits, a complete autopsy and analysis for alcohol and drugs is mandatory. Many of the drivers are, in fact, under the influence of alcohol.

Toxicology in Motor Vehicle Accidents

In all fatal motor vehicle accidents, a complete toxicologic screen for alcohol and drugs, and in certain circumstances carbon monoxide, should be performed on both drivers and passengers. Tests for alcohol alone are not sufficient. Drugs tested for should include alcohol; carbon monoxide; acid, basic, and neutral drugs. Marijuana testing is optional. In select cases, analysis for opiates is indicated.

In 1999, 38% of traffic fatalities were alcohol related compared with 49% in 1989.[12] The intoxication (blood alcohol of 0.10 g/dL or greater) rates for

Figure 9.14 Brake pedal with imprint of sole of shoe.

drivers in fatal crashes were: 17% passenger cars, 20% light trucks, 28% motorcycles, and 1% for large trucks.

At least 10–15% of drivers involved in automobile accidents will be under the influence of other drugs, either illicit or prescribed.[1] Whether a drug is a cause of an accident, either wholly or in part, can be decided only by individual analysis of a case. Drug testing on passengers is recommended for two reasons — first, a "passenger" occasionally turns out to have been the driver; second, the presence of a drug or alcohol in a passenger often reflects the toxicologic status of the driver.

Often victims of motor vehicle accidents do not die immediately and are transported to a hospital. Here, intravenous fluids are started and massive blood transfusions begun. Prior to instituting a transfusion, blood is virtually always drawn for type and cross matching. Unused blood for this purpose is retained in the blood bank for at least 7 d. Thus, it is usually possible to obtain original, pre-transfusion blood for toxicologic analysis within 1 week of admission to a hospital.

If, in spite of the transfusions and medical attention, the victim dies within a few hours of admission, toxicologic screens should still be performed on blood and vitreous fluid removed at autopsy. In spite of massive transfusions, we have been able to document elevated or intoxicating levels of alcohol in the blood in many people. This is because alcohol, being water soluble, distributes itself throughout the body of a drinker. When he is then transfused, the alcohol diffuses back into the blood from water in the tissue in an attempt to equalize the concentrations. Vitreous is valuable in that it reflects alcohol and drug levels 1–2 h prior to death and is essentially unaffected by the transfusions.

Carbon monoxide levels should be performed in most motor vehicle deaths, since occasionally death might be caused by, or the accident precipitated by, acute carbon monoxide poisoning. The source of the carbon monoxide is usually a defective exhaust system in the vehicle.[17]

Pedestrian Deaths

When a pedestrian is struck by a motor vehicle, the pattern and severity of the injuries, as well as their etiologic mechanisms, depend, for the most part, on four factors:

1. The speed of the vehicle
2. Its physical characteristics
3. Whether it was braking
4. Whether the victim was a child or an adult

Relationship between Speed at Impact and Injuries

The speed of the vehicle is probably the most important factor in the causation of severe injuries. Between 20 and 40 km/h, the nature of the injuries produced changes, becoming severe. This is not to say, however, that severe, even fatal, injuries cannot occur at lower speeds.[18]

Karger et al. studied 47 pedestrian–passenger car fatalities in regard to impact velocity and injury.[18] They found that four types of injury appeared to be correlated with impact velocity:

1. Fracture of the spine
2. Rupture of the thoracic aorta
3. Inguinal skin rupture
4. Dismemberment

With regard to fractures of the spine, they found that: almost half involved the cervical spine, first appeared at an impact velocity of 27.5 km/h, were common above 45 km/h, and were present in all cases with impact velocity above 67.5 km/h.

Ruptures of the thoracic aorta first appeared at 63 km/h, were always present above 85 km/h, and were associated with corresponding fractures of the thoracic spine.

Ruptures of the inguinal skin first occurred at 66 km/h and were always present at 95 km/h and above.

Dismemberment first occurred at 98 km/h. In regard to this last observation, Zivot and Di Maio reviewed 85 fatal motor vehicle–pedestrian deaths, and, in five cases, found amputation of a limb, and in two, transection of the torso. In all seven instances, the vehicles were going a minimum of 55 mph (88.5 Km/h).[19]

Child Pedestrians

In children struck by non-braking or late-braking motor vehicles, impact with the front of the vehicle is above the body's center of gravity. The victim is impacted, slammed down, and run over. If the vehicle is braking hard prior to the impact, the front of the vehicle dips below the child's center of gravity and the child may be thrown forward.

Adult Pedestrians

If an adult is struck by a truck with a high front, the situation is the same as with a child. With non-braking or late-braking, the impact to the adult is above the center of gravity and the individual is slammed down and run over. If the truck is braking hard prior to impact, the individual is thrown forward.

If adults are struck by an automobile or light truck, rather than a truck with a high front, a different pattern of injuries occurs because victims are impacted below the center of gravity. With non-braking or late-braking automobiles at very high speed, the pedestrian is picked up and thrown over the top of the car. Examination of the automobile reveals either scuff marks or dents on the bumper, as well as denting of the front of the hood in most instances. There may be dents on the roof or trunk of the car, when the individual is hurled over it. The authors have seen this pattern in individuals struck at high speeds, i.e., the high 60s and 70s mph range. In these cases, there is often mangling of the body with partial or complete amputation of a limb by the massive blunt trauma (Figure 9.15). The skin in the groin area may show traumatic striae (stretch marks) if it has been violently stretched by impact at the buttocks (Figure 9.16). Striae might also be present on the neck because of violent bending with subsequent massive fracture of the cervical vertebrae.

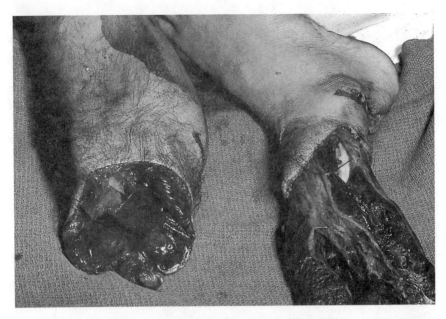

Figure 9.15 Traumatic amputation of lower extremities by motor vehicle moving at high rate of speed. Note the sharp edges of amputated limbs.

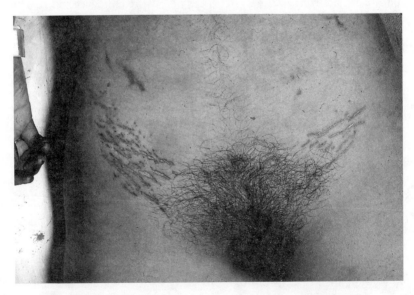

Figure 9.16 Striae in inguinal regions caused by overstretching of skin. Deceased pedestrian was struck in buttocks by speeding motor vehicle.

If the motor vehicle is traveling at a moderate speed at the time of impact, the pedestrian will be picked up, land on the hood, and slide backward, then impacting the windshield and sliding off. The automobile will then present

Figure 9.17 Typical pattern of damage to motor vehicle that has impacted a pedestrian. Dented hood and impact site on windshield.

the classic picture of a pedestrian impact: scuffing or dents on the bumper, indentation of the front and top of the hood, and an impact site on the windshield (Figure 9.17). Fragments of glass from the windshield may be found in the hair of the victim, because often it is the head that hits the windshield. In addition, hair might be found in the windshield. The authors have also seen the weave pattern of clothing imprinted on the hood. In some instances, threads have been caught by the deformed hood, which could be linked to clothing. As the body impacts the front of the hood and indents its top, paint smears can be imparted to the clothing. All of the aforementioned trace evidence can be used to link a victim and car in cases of hit and run.

If the pedestrian is struck by the extreme lateral or outer portions of the front of the vehicle, i.e., the headlight area, the individual will be picked up onto the fender and will roll off. Damage to the car will generally be confined to the headlight area and the fender, with no damage to the top of the hood or the windshield.

If an automobile traveling at either high or moderate speed brakes hard prior to impact with an adult, there are two possibilities, in both of which the pedestrian is struck below the center of mass by a rapidly decelerating vehicle. In the first possibility, the pedestrian is thrown forward. In the second, the individual is struck by the vehicle, picked up, lands on the hood, and is then propelled forward, again coming to rest in front of the rapidly decelerating vehicle. In the latter case, there will be damage to the front and top of the hood.

The first portion of a motor vehicle to impact a pedestrian is the bumper. If the automobile is not braking, in most present-day vehicles the impact point in a male of average height would be the knee region or just below it. Obviously, with shorter individuals, it will be higher. Most drivers, however, are able to brake prior to hitting a pedestrian. Because of this, the bumper impacts the mid or lower aspect of the tibia and fibula, that is, the calf region. Depending on the speed of the vehicle and the strength of the bones, there might be fractures of either or both the tibia and fibula, with the fractures either closed or open. These are called "bumper fractures" (Figure 9.18). Not uncommonly, bumper fractures are at different levels

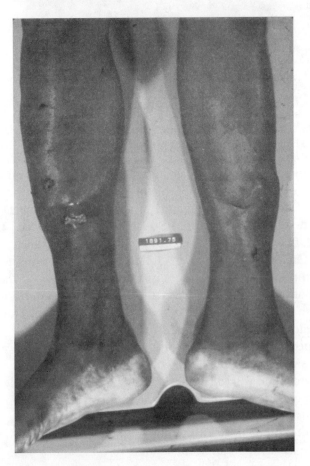

Figure 9.18 "Bumper" fractures of lower legs.

on the two legs. This suggests that the individual was either walking or running at the time of impact, with the higher-placed injury indicating the leg that was in contact with the ground and supporting the body weight. If the individual was oriented sideways to the impacting vehicle, the "bumper fractures" might be confined to one leg. In some instances, there are no fractures, just abrasions of the skin and hemorrhage into the calves. In other cases, there might be no visible injuries and it is not until an incision is made in the calf that one sees internal hemorrhage. Occasionally, no injury is present. The long-bones fractures produced by impaction with the bumper are usually of two types — first, a wedge-shaped fracture with the apex of the wedge pointing in the direction of the force, and, second, an oblique fracture.[20]

On impact, the pedestrian is picked up with the head and trunk impacting the hood and windshield. Often, the body pivots on impact such that the buttocks and upper thigh region strike the front of the hood. The tangential force directed by the hood to the buttock and thigh may cause stripping of the skin and subcutaneous tissue from the muscles, creating a pocket in the upper thigh–buttock region. There can be extensive bleeding into these pockets, with collection of 1–2 L of blood. These pockets are often not visible externally. They can be readily palpated and then exposed with an incision (see Figure 5.8).

As the individual is picked up and thrown by the vehicle, he can literally be stripped of his clothing. The authors have seen cases in which bodies have been found on a highway dressed only in a shirt and undershorts. At first, it was thought that the individuals were intoxicated and were walking around half dressed. Subsequent examination at the scene revealed their trousers, often turned inside out, with paint smears on the outer surface. In other words, these individuals were struck by the motor vehicle and, as they were thrown through the air, the trousers and shoes were stripped from the body. Horizontal linear marks on the ankles may represent the edges of shoes that were torn off the feet.

If an individual is run over by a wheel, there are often tire tread marks on one surface of the body with scrape-like abrasions on the opposite side, i.e., the pavement side (Figure 9.19). The abrasions are caused by the body's scraping along the ground as the spinning tire pushes it backward. Tire tread marks are not invariably present, but if they are, may be on the clothing as well as, or instead of, the skin (Figure 9.20). If the wheel passes over a limb, the spinning movement of the tire may avulse skin and subcutaneous tissue from the fascia and muscle (Figure 9.21).

In hit-and-run deaths, photographs of the tread marks with a ruler in the field should be taken for subsequent comparison with a tire. In passing over a victim, grease or dirt from the undersurface of the car can be deposited

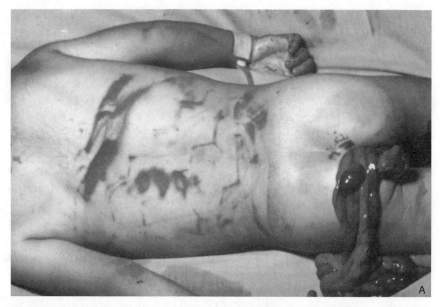

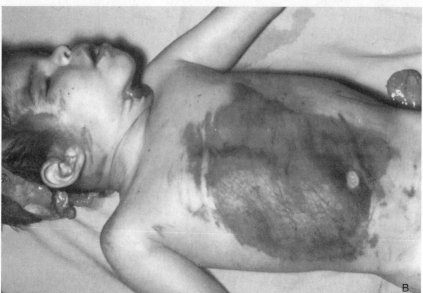

Figure 9.19 A 3-year-old child run over by a truck with (A) tire marks on the back and (B) scrape abrasions on chest, which was in contact with pavement.

on the body or clothing. Head hair, samples of grease from the body, and the clothing should be retained. When a suspect vehicle is found, the under-surface should be examined for blood, hair, and clothing fibers. Any material recovered can then be compared with material removed from the body.

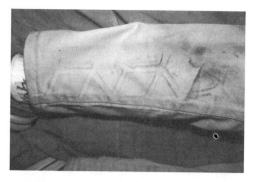

Figure 9.20 Tire tread marks on clothing in a hit-and-run death.

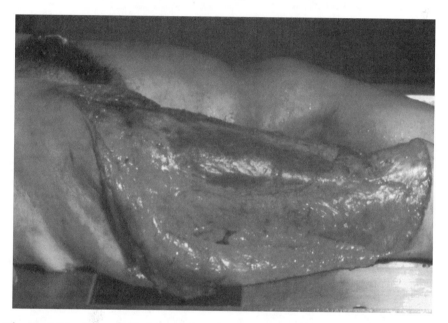

Figure 9.21 Skin avulsed from thigh by wheel running over leg.

In pedestrian accidents, the most common causes of death are head injuries and fracture-dislocations of the cervical spine, predominantly at the atlanto-occipital joint. In many pedestrian accidents, injuries to the chest and abdomen are minimal or absent. The determining factor as to amount of injury appears to be the velocity of the vehicle and whether the individual was thrown into a fixed object. There are usually abrasions and lacerations of the face where the head has impacted the ground after the body is thrown. Extensive scrape-like abrasions may be present on the body where it has skidded across the pavement. If the individual was fully dressed in heavy material, there might be virtually no injuries on the outside of the body, except for some minor abrasions of the face and head.

Just as thoracic aorta lacerations occur in drivers and passengers, so can they also occur in pedestrians struck by a vehicle. Brundage et al. reported a 12.7% incidence of traumatic rupture of the thoracic aorta in a review of 220 pedestrian fatalities.[21] The predominant site of laceration was immediately distal to the origin of the left subclavian artery (15 of 28 cases, or 53.6%). Four (14.3%) were in the ascending aorta or arch of the aorta. In half the individuals with aortic injury, there was associated thoracic spinal injury.

Occasionally, an individual will be found on a road or a parking lot with crushing injuries of the body, tire tread marks on one surface, and brush abrasions on the opposite side (Figure 9.22). No evidence of an impact with the front of a motor vehicle will be seen. Toxicology virtually always will show acute alcohol intoxication. These are individuals who have gone to sleep or passed out on a road or in a parking lot, only to be subsequently run over by a vehicle whose driver did not see them.

Sensing Diagnostic Modules: "Black Boxes"

In motor vehicle accidents resulting in death or serious injury, there are often civil suits. In such cases, there is often controversy as to the speed of the vehicle at the time of the accident, the force of impact, whether the driver was braking or taking evasive action, whether seat belts were being used, and whether the airbag properly deployed. Were the injuries incurred consistent with the account of the accident, the use of seat belts, and the result of a deploying air

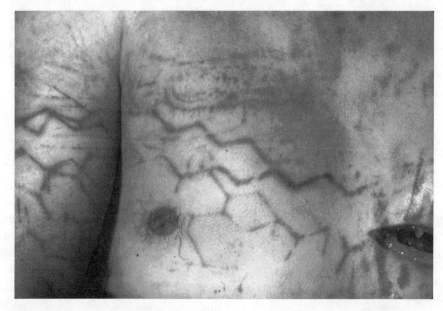

Figure 9.22 Tire tread marks across arm and chest in a 42-year-old male who, while asleep in a parking lot, was run over by a truck.

bag? The forensic pathologist might be asked to answer those questions pertaining to injuries. Unfortunately, in regard to seat belt use, more often than not, a lap or chest belt does not leave identifiable markings on the body.

Virtually all of the aforementioned questions regarding the vehicle, the actions of the driver, use of seat belts and deployment of air bags will no longer be speculative. Motor vehicles are now being equipped with Sensing Diagnostic Modules ("black boxes"). Some manufacturers have been equipping their cars with these devices for years (e.g., Mercedes). These devices are continually monitoring a number of the vehicle functions (speed, throttle position, engine RPM, brake use, impact velocity, seat belt use, airbag deployment, etc.). On impact, the device stores all the recorded data collected over the past 5 sec or so. This can then be played back to determine the events immediately preceding and at the time of crash.

References

1. Garriott JC, DiMaio VJM, and Rodriguez RG, Detection of cannabinoids in homicide victims and motor vehicle fatalities. *J Forens Sci* 1986; 31:12741282.

2. Buttner A, Heimpel M, and Eisenmenger W, Sudden natural death 'at the wheel':retrospective study over a 15-year time period (1982-1996) *Forens Sci Intern*, 1999; 103:101-112

3. National Highway Traffic Safety Administration, Traffic Safety Facts 1998; Washington D.C.

4. Kahane CJ, An Evaluation of Federal Motor Vehicle Safety Standards for Passenger Car Steering Assemblies, DOT HS 805 705. Washington D.C., National Highway Traffic Safety Administration, January 1981.

5. Crass JR, et al., A proposed new mechanism of traumatic aortic rupture: the osseous pinch. *Radiology* 1990; 176:645-649.

6. MacKay M, Mechanisms of injury and biomechanics: Vehicle design and crash performance. *World J Surg* 1992; 16:420-427.

7. National Highway Traffic Safety Administration. Fourth report to Congress: Effectiveness of occupant protection systems and their use. May 1999; Washington, D.C.

8. Williams N and Ratliff, Gastrointestinal disruption and vertebral fracture associated with the use of seat belts. *Ann Royal Coll Surgeons* 1993; 75:129.132.

9. Hendey GW and Votey SR Injuries in restrained motor vehicle accident victims. *Ann Emerg Med* 1994; 24:77-84.

10. Sims JK, et al., Automobile accident occupant injuries. *JACEP* 1976; 5:796-808

11. Chandler CF, Lane JS, and Waxman KS, Seatbelt sign following blunt trauma is associated with increased incidence of abdominal injury. *Am Surgeon.* 1997; 63:885-888.

12. National Highway Traffic Safety Administration, Traffic Safety Facts 1999 – Overview. Washington, D.C.

13. Kallina, Ingo (head of design and safety at Mercedes Benz), Testimony at NTSB Air Bag Public Forum, March 1997.

14. National Highway Traffic Safety Administration. Special Crash Investigation Report (November 2000).

15. Abu-Isa, IA, Fleck LL and Jacques CHM, Research Report PO -399, AN 87: Vehicle combustion experiments II. Electrical ignition of interior with windows opened. GMC Research Labs. March 1979.

16. Abu-Isa, IA, Fleck LL and Jacques CHM, Research Report PO -363, AN 67: Vehicle combustion experiments I. Electrical ignition of interior with windows closed. GMC Research Labs. October 1977.

17. Baker SP, Fisher RS, Masemore WC, et al., Fatal unintentional carbon monoxide poisoning in motor vehicles, *Am J Pub Hlth,* November 1972; pp 1463-1467

18. Karger B, Teige K, Buhren W and DuChesne A, Relationship between impact velocities and injuries in fatal pedestrian–car collisions. *Int. J. Legal Med.* 2000; 113:84-88.)

19. Zivot U and Di Maio VJM, Motor vehicle–pedestrian accidents in adults: relationship between impact speed, injuries and distance thrown. *Am J Forens Med Path* 1993; 14(3):185-186.

20. Kress TA, et al., Fracture patterns of human cadaver long bones. Presented at 1995 International IRCOBI Conference on the Biomechanics of Impact. September 13-15, 1995- Brunnen, Switzerland.

21. Brundage SI, et al., The Epidemiology of thoracic aortic injuries in pedestrians. *J Trauma* 1998; 45 (6):1010-1014.

Airplane Crashes 10

Air crashes may involve hot-air balloons, gliders, motorized gliders, hang gliders, helicopters, light aircraft, commercial aircraft, or military aircraft. The role of the forensic pathologist in an air crash depends on the nature of the craft, the number of passengers or crew and the circumstances of the crash.

Crashes Involving Light Planes

In light-plane crashes, the forensic pathologist usually deals with only a few bodies, which are generally in much better condition than those from the crash of a commercial aircraft. If there is more than one individual involved, the forensic pathologist may have to determine who was the pilot by the pattern of injuries. Patterned abrasions and contusions from restraint belts, the console or controls might indicate who was the pilot. Recovery of tissue from these surfaces with subsequent DNA typing might also identify the pilot.

Differentiation of a pilot from a passenger is said to be possible by the finding of "control surface injuries." These are alleged to occur when the forces generated by the impact of the crash are transmitted to the pilot's arms and legs through the aircraft controls. Control surface injuries of the arms consist of lacerations of the palms, fractures of the carpal and metacarpal bones, and fractures of the distal radius and ulna. In the legs, there are fractures of the tarsal and metatarsals and of the distal tibia and fibula. In a review of 100 aircraft fatalities, however, Campman and Bexfield found a high incidence of these injuries in the passengers as well.[1] They concluded that the presence of these injuries lacked sufficient sensitivity and specificity to indicate that the individual who incurred them was the pilot in control of the aircraft.

As in all air crashes, the pathologist must identify charred and dismembered bodies, document injuries, and determine whether natural disease, drugs or violence played a role. Because of the smaller number of bodies, identification is usually easy. Most identifications are based on fingerprints and dental records, occasionally on comparison of ante- and postmortem X-rays and, though rarely, the use of DNA.

319

Crashes of Commercial Aircraft

In crashes involving commercial planes, the main role of the forensic pathologist is to identify the bodies. Initially, identification should be attempted using fingerprinting, dental identification and comparison of ante- and postmortem X-rays. If these methods are unsatisfactory, one can use DNA typing. DNA identification procedures can be used not only for whole bodies but also for body fragments. As a last resort, it might be necessary to utilize nonscientific methods of identification, such as documents on the bodies, jewelry, exclusion (for example, knowing that there is only one child on board), or use of nonspecific characteristics such as tattoos and scars. The forensic pathologist should always have a team of dentists on call for any major airplane crash. Both forensic and non-forensic dentists are usually willing to volunteer to make up the team. All medicolegal offices should have disaster plans in place to be used if a major air crash occurs.

In addition to identifying the passengers' remains, the forensic pathologist will autopsy the flight crew in attempting to determine whether natural disease or drugs might have contributed to the accident, although, because of the size of the flight crew and the sophisticated instrumentation of commercial planes, this is highly unlikely. The forensic pathologist will search for trauma unrelated to the crash that might explain why the crash occurred. Thus, one will look for gunshot wounds and evidence of an explosion. Bodies may be X-rayed to look for bomb fragments. Autopsies on passengers will usually be selective and intended to shed light on how the plane crashed, whether gases produced by fire played a part in the deaths, and whether there is evidence of explosive injuries.

Causes of Crashes

Whether in light or commercial plane crashes, the pilot (flight crew in commercial planes) should have a complete toxicological screen for the presence of alcohol; acid, basic, and neutral drugs; alkaline drugs; narcotics; carbon monoxide and, possibly, marijuana. Generally, one is looking for drugs, not in toxic levels, but in therapeutic levels that could impair reflexes and thinking to a degree sufficient to contribute to or cause the accident. Because of this, very sensitive and specific methods of analysis must be utilized in the toxicological screen. Only rarely will natural disease or drugs play a role in airplane crashes. When they do, virtually all instances involve light planes. For the most part, airplane crashes are due to pilot error, mechanical defects, weather, or a combination of these factors. In light planes, there is often use of poor judgment, such as flying in inappropriate weather.

Crash Scene

The majority of airplane accidents occur as planes are taking off and landing. Rutherford, in reviewing 473 civilian air crashes throughout the world, found that 34.9% occurred as the planes took off; 36.9% as they descended and landed; 26.4% in mid-flight and 1.8% while parked. The number of fatalities per crash was relatively few. Thus, in 50.7% of the crashes, there were fewer than five fatalities, and in 72.7%, fewer than 20.[2]

The most important initial act at a crash site is to secure the scene, document it, and preserve any evidence for the team of investigators that will come. Body parts should not be indiscriminately moved, but should be left in place and documented as to where they were recovered in relation to other body parts and whatever is left of the plane. Unfortunately, in commercial crashes, one is often dealing with parts, rather than with bodies. Also, unfortunately, airplane crashes bring out souvenir hunters and looters.

The actual handling of body identification and processing of the bodies will vary from area to area. One may set up a temporary morgue adjacent to the crash site with refrigerated trucks and a tent-like arrangement. Identification can then be made directly at the scene. In other instances, the bodies may be transported to a morgue. Again, use of a refrigerated truck is usually necessary because of the large number of bodies involved and the convenience of using such a device. There also may be a combination of identification at the scene and at the morgue. If there is suspicion of bomb involvement, x-rays of bodies should be taken and external examination for explosive residue conducted.

The forensic pathologist should be realistic and realize that in a major commercial airplane disaster, he plays a relatively minor role. Other investigators, including accident reconstruction specialists, human factor specialists, meteorologists, bio-mechanical experts, power plant engineers, metallurgists, and aero-dynamicists, play a greater role than the forensic pathologist. This is because the primary goal in airplane accidents is to determine why the accident occurred. These experts have three major areas of concern: the pilot (or flight crew), the aircraft, and the environment (weather, mountain ranges, other planes, etc.).

Crash Patterns

There are six basic patterns of airplane crashes:[3]

1. The hole in the ground
2. The spin impact
3. The spiraling impact
4. The small angle of impact

5. In-flight disintegration
6. The wire strike

The hole-in-the-ground pattern is caused by a high-speed dive into the ground at a nose-down attitude of between 45 and 90°. The heavier components of the airplane, such as the engines, will be found at or buried in the bottom of the crater. In such accidents, the pilot was obviously not in control of the aircraft.

In the spin impact, the plane dives into the ground, usually at a nose-down attitude, while spinning. Because of the relatively low speed associated with spins, the crater produced is shallower than the hole-in-the-ground pattern. The wings will have scarred the ground outside the impact crater. The inside wing of the spinning aircraft is usually the first to strike the ground, with the outside wing creating a ground scar directly opposite the scar produced by the inside wing. The scars on the ground will indicate the direction of rotation. While most airplane crashes impacting in spin-type accidents do nose down, occasionally some will impact flat.

When a plane hits the ground while spiraling, the spiral impact pattern is created. Here, the inside wing strikes the ground first and then the outside wing. Unlike the pattern from the spin impact, however, wreckage is spread over a relatively large, fan-shaped area. The wings may be torn from the aircraft but come to rest some distance from the fuselage. The engines usually separate from their mounts when mounted on the wing and remain near the initial point of impact.

Small-angle-of-impact accidents may be either high- or low-speed. The low-speed, small-angle-of-impact accident is usually the result of a forced landing. Here, the aircraft damage is substantially less than that of a high-speed impact and individuals may survive. In the high-speed, small-angle-of-impact, there are long, fan-shaped debris patterns, with the aircraft breaking into many pieces, the heavier parts traveling the farthest forward in the pattern of debris. As the plane begins to impact, the first mark seen could be from the wheels if the landing gear is down, or the propellers, if the plane is a propeller aircraft. In wooded areas, the wings can be damaged by tree tops long before contacting the ground. High-speed, small-angle-of-impact accidents are essentially caused by a controlled flight into the ground because of flying too low.

In in-flight disintegration, major parts of the aircraft are scattered over a wide area without an apparent logical pattern. This type of pattern-less scattering is seen in in-flight explosions, major structural failure and midair collisions. Mid-flight accidents account for 26.4% of all accidents.[2] If only one aircraft is involved, the case should be treated as an in-flight bombing. The bodies should be X-rayed for bomb fragments or fragments of the plane propelled into the body by an explosion. Burns caused by proximity to a detonating bomb should be sought. Clothing should be saved for analysis for explosive residue. Swabs of the skin should also be taken for such purposes.

Wire strikes usually involve low-level flights by helicopters and crop dusters. They occur when the low-flying vehicle strikes a wire.

In-Flight Fire

In-flight fires are indicated by elevated carbon monoxide levels in the passengers or crew, as well as the presence of soot downstream from the area of fire damage in the aircraft. Beads of molten aluminum will also be blown downwind along the fuselage from the area of fire damage. In post-crash fires, there is a widespread pattern of soot and fire damage without any specific distribution of soot and melted aluminum. Carbon monoxide levels are negative in the passengers.

Helicopter Crashes

These might involve a crash into a stationary object (e.g., a tower or an electrical line), as well as a mid-air explosion, a mid-air crash into another aircraft, sudden loss of power or impact into the ground. The only unusual aspect of these crashes, compared with those involving fixed-wing aircraft, is that, if a helicopter loses power or is somehow incapacitated in flight (e.g, a mid-air crash), the helicopter might drop straight down. The resultant injuries might be more similar to those from falls rather than traditional aircraft crashes

Hot-Air Balloons

Hot-air ballooning is popular in some areas of the U.S. Fatalities are uncommon. Cowl et al. reviewed 495 hot-air-balloon crashes that involved 1533 individuals, occurring over a 32-year period.[4] There were 92 fatalities and 384 serious injuries. Most crashes occurred while approaching a landing zone (20.6%) or during landing (46%). Collision with a power line accounted for 27.7% of the crashes and 44.6% of the fatalities. Contact with a power line can cause the basket to overturn, or the basket cables to be severed by the wires, or electrocution. The cause of the crashes was predominantly pilot error or incapacitation (85.1%). Equipment failure was responsible for 7.3%.

Lightning Strikes

Lightning-related aircraft accidents are very uncommon. Thus, Cherington and Mathys were able to identify only 40 such incidents from 1963–1989.[5]

These resulted in 290 fatalities. Thirty of the accidents involved private planes and 10 commercial aircraft. Lightning can cause an accident by (1) entering the fuel compartment and igniting the fuel, (2) temporarily blinding the pilot by the bright flash, or (3) disrupting the electrical system. Because of upgrading of the fuel, electrical and automatic control systems, Cherington and Mathys felt that accidents caused by lightning should become even less common. With the use of composite materials in airplane construction, another problem has arisen. These materials are not conductive. Thus, if they are stuck by lightning, the lightning could burn a hole through the material. Manufactures are developing methods to conduct electricity from lightning strike points.

References

1. Campman SC and Bexfield KD, The sensitivity and specificity of control surface injuries in aircraft accident fatalities. Presented at the 34th annual meeting of NAME. Indianapolis, Sept. 16, 2000.

2. Rutherford WH, An analysis of civil air crash statistics 1977-1986 for the purposes of planning disaster exercises. (1988) Injury 19:384-388.

3. Horton NL, cited by Schiff B: After the fall. *AOPA Pilot* 1988; 31:67-70.

4. Cowl CT, et al., Factors associated with fatalities from hot-air-balloon crashes. *JAMA.* 1998; 79(13):1011-1014.

5. Cherington M and Mathys K, Deaths and injuries as a result of lightning strikes to aircraft. *Aviation, Space Environ Med*, 1995; 66(7): 687-689.

Sudden Infant Death Syndrome

11

Sudden infant death syndrome (SIDS), or crib death, is characterized by the sudden, unexpected death of an apparently healthy infant who is less than 1 year of age, in which an examination of the scene of death, a review of the clinical history and a complete postmortem examination fail to reveal a cause of death. SIDS accounts for approximately 3–4000 deaths per year in the U.S. The national incidence has been dropping over the last decade. In 1992, the incidence of SIDS was 1.2 per 1000 live births. By 1996, it had declined to 0.74 per 1000 (a drop of 38%) and appeared to still be dropping.[1]

This syndrome is presumably composed of a heterogeneous group of disease processes and is not due to a single entity. **SIDS is a diagnosis of exclusion**. These facts are often misunderstood by both the public and the medical profession. In addition to a natural etiology, some of the deaths that are certified as SIDS are undoubtedly accidents due to overlay, while others are homicides, usually caused by smothering. This does not detract from the fact, however, that the vast majority of these cases are of a natural etiology.

In the past, SIDS deaths have been ascribed at various times to status thymolymphaticus, interstitial pneumonitis, or suffocation. The former condition was manifested by an "enlarged" thymus, in fact, a normal finding in infants. Interstitial pneumonitis was just as nonexistent and essentially referred to the normal hypercellular appearance of the alveolar septae of an infant. In the 1930s and early 1940s, crib deaths were often thought to be caused by suffocation from blankets, bedclothing, or mattresses. Thus, Abramson, in a paper in 1944, reported 139 deaths from suffocation during a 5-year period in New York City alone, a number greater than the total number of deaths from measles, scarlet fever, and diphtheria.[2] Gafafer claimed suffocation accounted for more than one third of all accidental deaths in infants under 1 year old.[3] Wooley, in a paper in 1945, was critical of this concept.[4] He thought that complete autopsy examinations should be performed in any unexplained death of an infant and, when no cause of death was determined, the medical profession should admit that it is ignorant of the cause of death rather than alleging that the child had smothered in its bedclothes. Wooley pointed out that he had analyzed the atmosphere breathed by infants covered in various manners by different types of bedding. Under ordinary bedding, there was no discomfort to the child. He also attempted to induce anoxia by having the subject sleep with the nose and mouth closely pressed to pillows and mattresses. Even the smallest child, however, was capable of rolling aside to obtain a patent airway. Wooley thus concluded that the importance of suffocation as an explanation of sudden death in infancy could not be substantiated.

Incidence of SIDS

Over the last decade, the incidence of SIDS has been dropping such that, while in 1992 the incidence was 1.2 per 1000 live births, by 1996, it had dropped to 0.74 per 1000 and appeared to still be dropping.[1] This drop seems to correspond with a change in positioning of infants that has occurred since then. In 1992, the American Academy of Pediatrics Task Force on Infant Positioning and SIDS recommended that healthy newborn infants, born at term, be placed on either their sides or backs to sleep as this seemed to reduce the incidence of SIDS.[5] In 1996, the recommendation was changed slightly so as to recommend that infants be placed on their backs. This modification was made so as to prevent infants placed on their sides rolling onto their stomachs.

Presentation of Cases

As stated previously, there are approximately 3000–4000 deaths per year in the U.S. from SIDS. Most occur between 2 and 4 months of age, with a rapid decline after this age. In a 1-year study by the authors of 187 SIDS deaths in New York City, 92% occurred in children 6 months or younger and 74% in children 1–4 months of age. No death should be ascribed to SIDS beyond the age of 12 months. In fact, 10 months is probably a much more accurate cutoff age. The authors, as a general rule, do not blame SIDS for deaths below the age of 1 month, especially those occurring in the first week or two of life. While these may also be of unknown etiology, they are most probably not the result of the same conditions that cause death after a month of age. Most probably, these are disorders associated with neonatal development and adaptation to a new world.

Premature infants seem to be at a greater risk for SIDS. However, the vast majority of SIDS deaths involve full-term infants. As in most disease entities, males outnumber females. Race does not appear to be a factor, but the socioeconomic status of the family does. SIDS deaths appear to vary with the environmental temperature. As the temperature decreases, there tends to be more SIDS deaths. This could, in part, be because overlay cases are being confused with SIDS deaths, or to a "cold" (more common in cold weather), that triggers a mechanism causing death.

SIDS deaths occur almost invariably while the child is asleep. Most children are found dead in their cribs in the morning when their parents go to feed them. The peak incidence for crib deaths appears to be between midnight and breakfast. SIDS deaths, however, occur throughout the day and not only in cribs and beds, but in baby carriages, the backs of autos, and even while the child is being carried by a parent. The child always appears to be asleep at the time of death, however.

Non-Hereditary Nature of SIDS

SIDS deaths appear to occur in families at random. There is no evidence of a genetic etiology. Siblings of SIDS victims have the same risk as the general population. There is a small number of reports of more than one SIDS death in a family and of SIDS deaths in twins.[6,7] Some of these cases can probably be attributed to pure random chance; some to undetected environmental hazards. The majority, however, probably represent infanticide. It is the general policy of the authors to ascribe the first death in a family presenting as SIDS to SIDS. The second death by the same mother is labeled undetermined, and a more intensive investigation of the circumstances surrounding the death is conducted. The police are usually asked to interview the family, though in a discreet fashion. A third death with the same mother is thought by the authors to be homicide until proven otherwise. Infanticide by smothering and repetitive episodes of apnea and cyanosis caused by smothering, presenting as near-miss SIDS cases, are discussed elsewhere in the book. It is the authors' opinion that, while a second SIDS death with one mother is improbable, it is remotely possible and she should be given the benefit of the doubt under most, but not all, circumstances. A third case, in our opinion, is not possible and is a case of homicide. The second case is labeled "undetermined" rather than SIDS to flag the case, that is, to make it stand out for future reference.

In multiple-SIDS homicide cases that go to trial, the defense is sometimes made that the children were suffering from some rare nondiagnosed hereditary disease that causes sudden death. Allusions are made to mitochondrial disorders, fatty acid oxidation disorders etc.[8,9] Of course, the specific disease is never positively identified and diseases alluded to do not present the way the cases did or can readily be differentiated. When autopsying the third case, one might consider saving frozen samples of skin, muscle, liver, kidney, lung, brain and heart as well as performing the most recent battery of tests for hereditary disease.

Diagnosis of SIDS

Because SIDS is a diagnosis of exclusion, the diagnosis cannot be made unless a complete autopsy has been conducted, and no physician should sign a death certificate as SIDS without one. If physicians work in jurisdictions where families can prevent an autopsy on a suspected SIDS case, they should label the cause and manner of death "undetermined," not SIDS, and not "natural."

The autopsy should include, not only a gross examination of the organs, but microscopy and toxicology. The authors have seen cases of apparent SIDS in which a routine toxicology screen revealed death to have been caused by a drug. Part of the toxicological screen should consist of an electrolyte examination performed on the vitreous. This might reveal electrolyte abnormalities or dehydration.

The diagnosis of SIDS is made when an investigation of the circumstances surrounding a death plus the autopsy fail to reveal a cause of death or any substantial disease process. Externally, the body of the child appears unremarkable. There may be some blood-tinged edema fluid in the nostrils or mouth. Not uncommonly, feces is present in the diaper. Internally, pulmonary congestion with edema is often present. Petechiae of the thymus, epicardium, and pleural surfaces of the lungs are common. These, like the edema and congestion, are nonspecific and might be absent in obvious cases of SIDS and present in non-SIDS cases. The petechiae are caused by nonspecific agonal anoxia. The rest of the autopsy will be negative. There have been reports of hypertrophy and hyperplasia of the muscular media of small pulmonary arteries, right ventricular hypertrophy, and brain stem gliosis.[10] These findings, however, have either been refuted or are highly suspect.

In some autopsies, small accumulations of chronic inflammatory cells might be seen in the larynx and trachea, with a few scattered deposits around bronchi or in the alveoli. In such cases, there is always a possibility that one is dealing with death due to bronchiolitis. This is a judgment call by pathologists based on experience. They will have to decide whether the amount of inflammation around the bronchi or in the alveoli is sufficient to explain death.

Etiology of SIDS

The etiology of SIDS is presumably multifocal and includes not only natural causes, but accidents and, rarely, homicides. New theories as to etiology seem to arise every few years, then disappear only to be resurrected in future years. Theories have included prolonged QT interval; immunopathogenesis; unstable homeostatic control, etc. Two hypotheses should be mentioned, however. First is that SIDS deaths can be produced by DPT (diphtheria-pertussis-tetanus) inoculations. A study by the National Institute of Child Health and

Human Development shows that of 716 cases of SIDS, 40% had received DPT vaccine.[11] In a control group matched by age, race, and birth weight, 53% of the children had been immunized. Thus, no link has been found between DPT inoculation and SIDS.

The second theory is that of hereditary idiopathic apnea. In 1972, Steinschneider described five infants suffering from multiple cyanotic and apneic episodes of unknown etiology during sleep.[12] Two of these children, siblings, subsequently died. Steinschneider hypothesized that prolonged sleep apnea was a cause of SIDS. There then arose an extensive literature on this subject. Brought into prominence were "near-miss" SIDS cases. These were characterized by infants who were successfully resuscitated after being brought into the emergency room with episodes of apnea and cyanosis. In some children, there was repeated admission for this entity. In most, however, nothing subsequently developed. It must be realized that the initial observation of the apnea and cyanosis was often at home by nonmedical observers and the validity of their observations is open to question. In other instances, there is absolutely no doubt that these near-miss episodes represented multiple episodes of assault on the child by smothering, thus constituting what some call Munchausen Syndrome by Proxy.[13–15] In 1995, the deaths described in Steinschneider's paper were found to be homicide by smothering.[16]

After many years of study, there is still absolutely no proof that apneic spells commonly seen in premature infants and SIDS are related.[17,18] Southall et al. studied the breathing patterns of 6914 full-term and 2337 premature infants over 24-h periods prior to hospital discharge in an attempt to see if they could detect SIDS cases.[19] Sudden death occurred in 29 of the infants studied. None of these had had prolonged apneic episodes while studied. None of the infants who had had prolonged apnea during the test period died.

Because SIDS was thought by some authorities to be the result of apnea secondary to immature development of the brain stem, and to be hereditary, the use of apnea monitors came into fashion. There is no proof that they have prevented any deaths from SIDS. Since the underlying rationale for their use (the apnea theory of Steinschneider) has been discredited, there is no valid reason for their use.[12,16]

Investigation of the Death

In any SIDS death, just as in any death investigated by the medical examiner's office, there are three components to the investigation: the scene investigation, the autopsy, and the laboratory studies. If the body has not been moved, investigators should go to the scene and document it. The parents or caretakers of the child should be questioned as to the circumstances leading up to and surrounding the death: the last time the child was seen alive, the last time it was fed, and when it was put to bed. It should be determined in what position the child was found, face down or face up. Was the infant's head covered by a blanket or wedged between the mattress and slats? If the body has been moved prior to the investigation, the individuals who moved the body should be questioned to obtain this information.

Questioning of the parents should be done with a sensitive, sympathetic, and compassionate approach. The parents of a dead infant are subjected to severe psychological trauma with, not infrequently, feelings of guilt that they did something to cause the death. Many individuals are unaware of what a SIDS or crib death is. Attempts should be made to ease the grief and prevent a guilt-ridden reaction. Investigators, in addition to investigating the scene, should do their best to convince the parents that they are in no way at fault or to blame for the infant's death and that there was no way they could have prevented it. If, subsequently, the case turns out not to be SIDS-related, or there is something that the parents could have done to prevent the death, no harm has been done by this approach.

Occasionally, postmortem lividity is mistaken by medical or police personnel for bruising. They then become suspicious that the parents killed the child. Blood-tinged froth from the mouth and nose is sometimes mistaken for blood and trauma is suspected. Diaper rash is also on occasion mistaken for trauma.

At the scene, investigators should approach the parents in a sensitive, nonaccusatory manner and should interview, not interrogate. The parents should be permitted to tell their story without interruption. They should be allowed as much time as they need to describe the circumstances surrounding their infant's death. Most frequently, the bulk of the information needed will be ascertained by simply listening to the distressed parents. If some circumstances preceding or surrounding the infant's death need clarification, the examiners' questions should be neither inflammatory nor accusatory. Otherwise, they will reinforce the guilt feelings frequently present in the parents and cause them to become resentful and uncooperative.

The following information should be obtained by the investigator:

- Age, date of birth, birth weight if known, race, and sex.
- Who was the last person to see the infant alive (date and time)?
- Who discovered the dead infant (date and time)?
- What was the place of death (the child's crib or bed, the parent's bed, or elsewhere)?
- What was the position of the infant when found dead?
- Was the infant's original position changed (why and by whom)?
- If resuscitation was attempted, give the method and the name of the person who attempted the resuscitation.
- Had the infant been sick lately? Have a cold or sniffles? Any other minor illnesses?

- Was a physician consulted? Who?
- What treatment had been prescribed?
- Was the child on any medication? What type?
- When was the child last seen by a physician? Why and by whom?
- Was the infant exposed to any illnesses recently?
- Had there been any illnesses in the family recently?
- Was the child breast-fed or bottle-fed? When was the time of the last feeding? What was fed?
- Had there been a difference in the appearance or behavior of the child within the last few days?
- Have there been any other SIDS deaths in the family?
- If someone other than the parent was caring for the child, have any other children died in his or her custody?

Communication with the Parents

Following the investigation, medical investigators, if seeing nothing suspicious, should indicate to the parents that the most likely cause of death was SIDS. They should then explain to them what SIDS is. Important facts to be conveyed to them are:

- SIDS can neither be predicted nor prevented — even by a physician.
- For the present, the exact mechanism of death is unknown.
- SIDS is not contagious.
- SIDS is not hereditary.
- SIDS occurs very quickly, without suffering, distress, or warning, and is assumed to occur while the infant is asleep.
- SIDS occurs most frequently during the first 6 months of life and virtually never beyond 10 months.
- The child usually appears healthy prior to death.
- SIDS is not caused by smothering or choking following aspiration of regurgitated or vomited food.

The parents should also be told that in approximately 15% of the cases that appear to be SIDS, a different cause of death will be determined at autopsy. Therefore, they should check with the agency to determine what the final diagnosis is. It should be pointed out that a complete autopsy will not only confirm or disprove the diagnosis of SIDS, but also determine whether the child died from a contagious or inheritable disease.

All examiners are well aware that a number of cases of what appears to be SIDS turn out to be homicide. In some cases, it is a "gentle" homicide, a smothering. In others, even though no injuries appear on the external surface of the body, the autopsy will reveal extensive internal injuries. Since the parents are most commonly the individuals who inflict such injuries, there is nothing to be gained by discussing the possibilities of trauma prior to an autopsy with the parents. If the parents are guilty, they know about it. If the child has not died of trauma, then there is no reason to subject them to additional emotional stress because of a hypothetical possibility.

After the body has been removed from the scene, the parents not uncommonly examine the crib. They may find some blood-tinged fluid or vomitus present. One should explain that the fluid does not mean there was any trauma and that vomiting is a common agonal action in death and that the child did not choke to death.

Following a ruling as to the cause of death, it is not uncommon for the parents to contact the medical examiner again to discuss the case. Usually, the discussion is focused around guilt feelings that the family has about the child. They will say that the child had a slight cold and that if they had taken him to the doctor, the death would not have occurred. They should be reassured that there is no evidence that the child died of any disease related to the cold and that sniffles and cold symptoms are quite common in this age group and, therefore, taking the child to a physician would not have prevented the death. The family may say that if they had just looked in on the child more often, they might have prevented death. Again, it should be explained that this would not have helped. The family will often ask if the child suffered. One should reassure them this did not occur.

Sometimes, the family will ask about the possibility of the child's suffocating in a blanket or a comforter or bedding, or the face turned down into the pillow. Often, well-meaning family friends will suggest that this is a possibility. One should point out that virtually all medical authorities feel that a healthy infant cannot smother in its bedclothes, under a blanket, or with its face down in a pillow. The parents should be referred to organizations such as the National Foundation for SIDS for additional information or help with the emotional problems arising from the death of the child.

References

1. Willinger M, et al., Factors associated with the transition to nonprone sleep positions of infants in the United States: The national infant sleep position study. *JAMA* 1998; 280(4):329-335.

2. Abramson H, Accidental mechanical suffocation in infants. *J Pediatrics* 1944; 25:404-413.

3. Gafafer WM, Time changes in mortality from accidental mechanical suffocation among infants under one year in different geographical regions of the United States, 1925-32; Studies on fatal accidents of children. *Pub Health Rep* 1936; 51:1641-1646.

4. Wooley PV, Mechanical suffocation during infancy. *J Pediatr* 1945; 26:572-575.

5. American Academy of Pediatrics Task Force on Infant Positioning and SIDS, Positioning and SIDS, *Pediatrics* 1992; 89:1120-1126.

6. Oren J, Kelly DH, and Shannon DC, Familial occurrence of sudden infant death syndrome and apnea of infancy. *Pediatrics* 1987; 80:355-358.

7. Ramos V, Hernandez AF and Villanueva E, Simultaneous death of twins: an environmental hazard or SIDS, *Amer. J. Forensic Med. Path* 1997; 18(1):75-78.

8. Bowles RG, et al., Retrospective biochemical screenings of fatty acid oxygenation in postmortem livers of 418 cases of sudden death in the first year of life. *J Peds* 1998; 132(6): 924-933.

9. Wang SS, Fernhoff PM, and Khoury MJ, Is the G985A allelic variant of medium-chain acyl-CoA dehydrogenase a risk factor for sudden infant death syndrome? A pooled analysis. *Pediatrics* 2000; 105(5):1175-6.

10. Valdes-Dapena M, Sudden Infant Death Syndrome Morphology. Update for *Forensic Pathology*, 1985.

11. Wyngaarden JB, SIDS not linked to DPT shots. *JAMA*, July 1986; 256.

12. Steinschneider A, Prolonged apnea and the sudden infant death syndrome: Clinical and laboratory observations. *Pediatrics* 1972; 50:646-654.

13. Berger D, Child abuse simulating "near miss" sudden infant death syndrome. *J Pediatr* 1979; 95:554-556.

14. Minford AMB, Child abuse presenting as apparent "near miss" sudden infant death syndrome. *Br Med 1*1981; 282:521.

15. Rosen CL, et al.,Two siblings with recurrent cardiorespiratory arrest: Munchausen syndrome by proxy or child abuse. *Pediatrics* 1983;71:715-720.

16. Firstman R and Talan J, *The Death of Innocents*, New York Bantam Books, 1997.

17. Milner AD, Apnea monitors and sudden infant death. *Arch Dis Childhood* 1985; 60:76-80.

18. Avery ME and Frantz ID, To breathe or not to breathe: What have we learned about apneic spells and sudden infant death? (editorial retrospective). *NEJM* 1983; 309:107-108.

19. Southall DP, et al., Identification of infants destined to die unexpectedly during infancy: Evaluation of predictive importance of prolonged apnoea and disorders of cardiac rhythm or conduction. *Br Med J* 1983; 286:1092-1096.

Neonaticide, Infanticide, and Child Homicide

12

"Speak roughly to your little boy,
And beat him when he sneezes."
—Louis Carroll, Alice's Adventures in Wonderland

The number of children murdered each year in the United States is relatively small in relation to the total number of murders. This fact has been obscured by the media, which report thousands of children being murdered each year. This dramatic pronouncement is obtained by considering any individual below the age of 21 years as a child. Data for 1999 as to number of murders by age is:[1]

Table 12.1 Data for 1999 Showing Breakdown of Child Murders by Age

AGES	TOTAL MURDERS
Infants (under 1yr)	205
1 to 4 yrs	280
5 to 8 yrs	95
9 to 12 yrs	79

Most child murders occur in the first two years of life, with most of these in the first year. The deliberate killing of a child in the first year of life by either act or omission is infanticide. Most such cases represent filicide, the killing of a child by its parent. In 1999, in the United States, approximately 205 children less than 1 year of age were reported murdered. The most commonly cited weapons used were "personal weapons" — hands, feet fists etc, — 105 cases. Other weapons or manners were strangulation and asphyxia, 29 cases; blunt objects, ten; firearms, four cases: and knives and cutting instruments, six cases; other or not stated, 51.

Neonaticide

This can be defined as the deliberate killing of a child within 24 h of its birth. The perpetrator is usually the mother. She delivers the child and kills it. Occasionally, she is assisted by a relative or a friend, but usually neonaticide is an act committed by a single individual with no witnesses. Most of the perpetrators are young and unmarried. Some claim not to have realized they were pregnant until they went into labor. Their goal is either to conceal the fact that they gave birth to a child or to dispose of an unwanted child.

Finding dead infants in sewers, trash dumps, and public bathrooms is fairly common in large metropolitan areas. These infants are either victims of neonaticide or are stillborn. The mother is usually the individual who abandoned the child. If apprehended, her defense is usually that the child was stillborn; she panicked and disposed of the body. Thus, in cases of suspected neonaticide, the first fact to establish is whether the child was alive at the time of birth. This is often one of the most difficult things to do. The presence of milk or any food material in the stomach would indicate that the child was alive. Unfortunately, in cases of neonaticide, the killing usually occurs immediately after birth and one does not find milk or food material in the stomach.

The standard test to determine if a child has breathed has traditionally been the hydrostatic test. This consists of determining whether the lungs float in water. If they sink, the child is presumed to have been stillborn, and if they float, the child is presumed to have been born alive. There are problems with this test. If putrefaction has taken place, then, even in the stillborn, the lungs might float. Second, some children who are delivered alive take only a few breaths and do not aerate their lungs enough to float. Because of this, physicians have resorted to microscopic examination of the lungs. If the alveoli were collapsed, then it was presumed that the children had not breathed. If they were completely and uniformly distended (presumably by air), then the child obviously had breathed. Unfortunately, microscopic examination is even more inaccurate than the hydrostatic test. If there has been attempted resuscitation, there may be distention of the air passages and alveoli by air and it will not be possible to determine whether the child was alive or stillborn. One of the authors had a case of a child dead 10 h intrauterine who, on microscopic examination of the lungs, showed uniform distention of all alveoli, which is consistent with a child who has breathed for several hours. The lungs did not float, however.

At the present time, the authors place most reliance on the hydrostatic test. We determine if both lungs float *in toto* and then we attempt to float sections of the lungs. If all float, then in our opinion, the child breathed and was, therefore, alive. This, of course, assumes that there has been no attempt at resuscitation and that there is no decomposition. Other findings used to determine whether a child was alive include petechiae of the lungs or heart and air in the stomach on radiological examination. Neither of these criteria is valid. Petechiae are nonspecific and can occur from intrauterine stress, and gas in the stomach can be due to labored respiratory efforts as the infant is in transit through the birth canal.

Once it has been established that a child was born alive, then one has to determine how it was killed. The simplest, most convenient, and probably the most common method of killing infants of this age is by suffocation. This can be accomplished by the direct application of a hand over the face, by obstructing the nose and mouth with an object such as a pillow, or by placing the child in a plastic bag. Less common methods are strangulation, stuffing the mouth with rags or toilet paper, drowning the child in a toilet, throwing the child off a building, and abandonment, with death caused by exposure or lack of care.

Deaths following abandonment may be unintentional in that the mother places the child in an area where she expects it to be found, but for some reason it is not, or environmental conditions (such as temperature) change radically. Given moderate temperatures, newborns can survive 7–10 days without food or water. This was illustrated in the Mexico City earthquake of September 1985 where 44 newborns were buried beneath tons of debris when a hospital collapsed.[2]

The more violent methods of homicide used on older children are rarely used in neonates. People generally do not bash heads against the wall or stomp neonates. Unfortunately, suffocation of a neonate usually leaves no physical signs. Thus, the pathologist can make this diagnosis only if the mother leaves the baby in a plastic bag, leaves toilet tissue in the mouth, or confesses. If none of these occur, then one can only speculate as to the cause of death.

If the body of a newborn is placed in a warm dry atmosphere, it will frequently undergo mummification. This may be aided by the relatively bacteria-free condition of a newborn. Mummified infants are occasionally found in trunks in attics and beneath floorboards of old houses.

Infanticide and Child Murder

Once past the first few days of life, the methods used to commit homicide change radically. In addition, the mother is joined by the husband, boyfriend, or babysitter as possible perpetrators. Most child homicides occur in the first two years of life, the majority in the first year, with a steep decline after the second year. In 1999, 280 children between the ages of 1 and 4 years were murdered in the U.S. The most commonly used weapons were hands, feet, and fists, 123 cases; firearms, 39 cases; blunt objects, 33; asphyxia and stran-gulation, 16 and knives, 10 cases; other or not stated, 59.

The murders of young children can be placed in a number of categories. There is the classical battered child, with its variant the neglected or starved child; the "impulse" or "angry" homicide, with its variant the "punished" child (often a scalded child); and the "gentle" homicide, smothering, with its variant the lethal form of Munchausen's Syndrome by Proxy. There is also a miscellaneous category for deaths that do not fit into any of these categories.

Contrary to what one would conclude from reading the clinical medical literature and the popular press, deaths of children do not usually involve the classical battered baby syndrome, but rather are more likely "impulse" or "angry" homicides. In the authors' experience, most child homicides fall in this category.

In a series of 184 homicides of children ages 5 years or younger who died of blunt force injuries, in 10% of the cases, the children showed absolutely no external evidence of injury. In others, external injuries were relatively mild and tended to be about the head and neck. Of the 184 children, 42.4% were 12 months of age or less, 78.3% were 24 months or less. Craniocerebral injuries accounted for 64.1 %, 23.4% were abdominal injuries, 4.4% were head and abdominal injuries, and 2.2% were head, abdominal, and chest injuries (Table 12.2). If one correlates age with the cause of death:

- In children 12 months of age or less, isolated head injuries accounted for 85.8% of deaths, compared with 2.6% each for chest and abdominal injuries alone and 2.6% for head, abdominal, and chest injuries.
- In contrast, children 13 to 24 months of age had isolated fatal head injuries in 53% of deaths and abdominal injuries alone in 34.9%.

Thus, as the age of the child increases, abdominal injuries become more common as a cause of death.

In children dying of head injuries, the most common findings are subarachnoid or subdural hematoma with or without a skull fracture. The authors reviewed a series of deaths of young children in which there was epidural, subdural, or subarachnoid hemorrhage or a combination of these. The five cases of epidural hematoma all showed fractures. In four children with only subarachnoid hemorrhage, one showed no fractures. In 39 children dying with subdural hematoma, (in four cases bilateral), 17 (43.6%) did not show skull fractures. The four cases with bilateral subdural hematomas had skull fractures. Fractures of the skull seem to be more commonly associated with bilateral subdural hematoma and subarachnoid hemorrhage than single-sided subdural hematomas.

In the children dying of abdominal injuries, 43% showed no external evidence of injury to the abdominal wall, though virtually all showed external evidence of trauma. Of these children, 80% died as a result of lacerations of

Table 12.2   Blunt Force Homicides in Children 5 Years of Age or Less*

Age (mos)	Head	Chest	Abdomen	Head/ abd.	Chest/ abd.	Head, chest, abd.	Other	Total
0–12	67 (85.8)	2 (2.6)	2 (2.6)	3 (3.8)	0	2 (2.6)	2(2.6)	78 (42.4)
13–24	35 (53)	1 (1.5)	23(34.9)	3 (4.5)	1 (1.5)	1 (1.5)	2(3)	66 (35.9)
25–36	9(36)	0	12 (48)	1 (4)	2 (8)	0	1 (4)	25 (13.6)
37–48	7 (53.8)	0	4(30.8)	1 (7.7)	0	1 (7.7)	0	13 (7.1)
49–60	0	0	2(100)	0	0	0	0	2(1)
Total	118(64.1)	3(1.6)	43(23.4)	8(4.4)	3(1.6)	4(2.2)	5 (2.7)	184(100)

*Numbers in parentheses are percentages.

the liver with or without associated lacerations of the mesentery, bowel, spleen, and pancreas. The other 20% showed lacerations of the mesentery, duodenum, pancreas, and spleen.

In children dying of blunt force injuries, there are usually multiple contusions and abrasions of the body, recent and healing, most commonly about the head. Lacerations, burns, and patterned injuries caused by belts, coat hangers, and sticks might also be present. Parallel rows of linear contusions with intervening pale skin suggest a belt or stick; loop-shaped marks suggest a coat hanger or electric cord (Figure 12.1). Contusions may be very difficult to see, especially in dark-skinned children. Therefore, it is suggested that long cuts be made down the back, buttocks, and extremities to look for soft tissue hemorrhage (Figure 12.2). The interior of the mouth should always be examined for lacerations and contusions of the frenulum, gums, and lips, as well as for dislodged teeth that might have been caused by blows to the mouth (Figure 12.3).

At a trial, defense attorneys might attempt to ascribe injuries to the face, lips, and gums to attempted resuscitation. While some minor injuries of the lips can occur with resuscitation, multiple abrasions and contusions of the face do not. One of the authors (DJD) examined the bodies of 123 children who had cardiopulmonary resuscitation. None showed the multiple abrasions and contusions about the face and neck that are seen in children beaten about the face.

Battered Baby Syndrome

The battered baby syndrome refers to a condition characterized by repeated intentional acts of trauma to a young child inflicted at the slightest or most trivial provocation. Deprivation of food and water is a variant of this trauma. Classically, the child presents to a physician or an emergency room with an acute injury accompanied by evidence of both old and recent bruises, fractures, and other injuries. There might be skull or extremity fractures, ruptured viscera, subdural hematomas, or burns. There is often a delay in

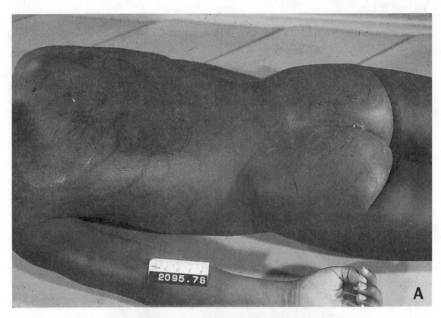

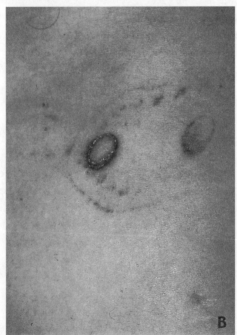

Figure 12.1 (A) Loop-shaped contusions caused by coat hanger. (B) Imprint of belt.

bringing the child to the hospital, with an explanation by the parents that they did not realize that the child was so ill. There is usually a significant

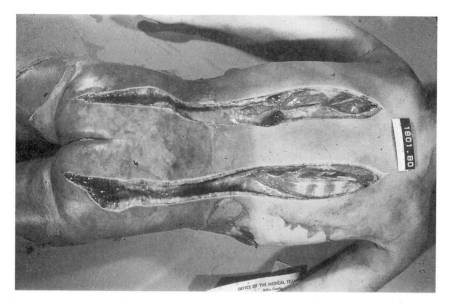

Figure 12.2 Long incisions made down back in search of soft tissue hemorrhage.

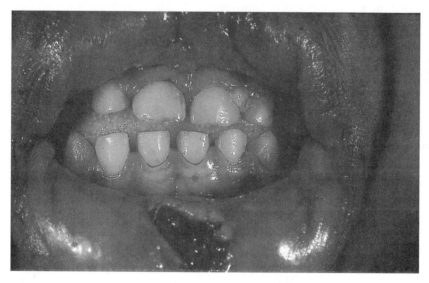

Figure 12.3 Laceration of mucosa of lip caused by blow to mouth.

discrepancy between the history given by the parents and the clinical findings. The explanation as to how the recent trauma occurred is vague, inconsistent, or contradictory with the injuries. Multiple bruises are ascribed to the fact that the child "bruises easily" or is "always falling down." Head injuries are said to have occurred when the child fell from the arms of the parent, fell out of a high chair, or rolled off a table or bed. In the case of burns, children are alleged to have put their hands in boiling water, pulled a pot of hot water on themselves, climbed into a tub and turned on the hot water (or it may be alleged that a sibling turned on the hot water). If a child is starved and dehydrated, he is described as a "fussy eater" who seems to "spit everything up." There is often severe diaper rash, which is said to be because the child has "very tender skin" and seems to be "allergic to everything."

Prior to 1962, the battered baby syndrome was unrecognized. In 1946, John Caffey, a Pittsburgh radiologist, wrote an article entitled "Multiple Fractures in the Long Bones of Infants Suffering from Chronic Subdural Hematoma."[3] Dr Caffey described in detail the history of six infants aged 2 weeks to 12 months with chronic subdural hematomas and a total among them of 23 fractures of the long bones. In retrospect, these are classic textbook examples of repeated assaults on infants. Caffey, however, failed to recognize the true nature of the cases; he did not comprehend the etiology of this trauma, even after he had systematically eliminated all possible disease processes.

In 1953, Silverman determined that, in children presenting this way, a history of trauma could be obtained, even if the initial history was negative, provided the family was carefully interviewed.[4] The history he obtained from the parents is the usual one given by individuals who batter children: the baby fell from the arms; the parent fell down the stairs with the baby; the baby's arms and legs got caught in the crib slabs; the parent grabbed the child to save it from a collapsing bassinet; the parent was throwing the child in the air, playing a game, and missed; and so forth. Silverman did not realize the inadequacy and incompatibility of the history to the injury and felt that there was possibly an individual factor that predisposed some children to injury more than others.

It was left to Kempe et al. in 1962 in their article "The Battered Child Syndrome" to give widespread recognition to this syndrome.[5] The authors detailed the etiology of the trauma in infants and charged physicians with the duty to see that repetition of such injuries did not occur. Since then, there has been a tremendous amount of literature on child abuse, such that it has become almost a trendy social issue in certain circles. Thus, one sees bumper stickers stating "It Shouldn't Hurt To Be A Child." The popularity of this entity in certain sociological circles has led to an under diagnosis of other forms of child abuse and murder. This is because everyone is looking for the classic battered baby syndrome, which is often not the presentation of a murdered child.

At autopsy, the battered baby will present with multiple bruises of various ages over the body, especially about the head and chest. Most children, when they incur bruises accidentally, as in falls while playing, receive them on the lower legs or the forearms. Battered children tend to have injuries to the head. There may be patterned bruises of the extremities caused by the child's being gripped firmly with the fingers or patterned bruises of the trunk caused by the child's being hit with a belt or coat hanger (Figure 12.1). In some instances, however, the bruises are not visible in spite of beatings. Thus, in cases of deaths following suspected child abuse, long incisions should be made down the back, buttocks, and extremities to reveal underlying soft tissue hemorrhage. (Figure 12.2) One must be careful not to confuse the Mongolian spot, an area of hyperpigmented skin in the lumbosacral region in some young children, with a bruise. Rarely, death will be due solely to exsanguination from massive bleeding into the soft tissue, caused by a beating.

Blows to the face may cause tears of the frenulum and dislodge teeth. There may be cuts on the inner surface of the lips in older children from the lips being driven against the teeth. There might be cigarette burns on the body. On occasion, the child might have been disciplined by having its hand plunged into hot water or held against a hot surface. Hot fluids might have been thrown onto the child. There may be trickle-like burns where the water has run down the body. X-rays might reveal fractures.

Most battered children die as a result of head trauma. There are subdural and subarachnoid hemorrhages with or without fractures of the skull. It is not at all uncommon to find brain injury without skull fractures. Occasionally, a fracture might lead to secondary meningitis. There may be evidence of old subdural hematomas, as well as recent ones. Fractures of the skull and injury to the brain may be present with no or only insignificant injury to the skin and soft tissue of the head. The absence of external trauma to the head does not rule out trauma (Figures 12.4, 12.5). In fact, neither does the absence of internal scalp hemorrhage. A head might impact a flat, yielding surface with enough force to incur brain injuries but without incurring contusions of the scalp, either externally or internally.

Severe head injuries are often associated with retinal hemorrhage. If the child survives, retinal scarring may result. Retinal hemorrhage can occur naturally from birth trauma, but in these instances, scarring does not occur.[6] While retinal hemorrhage is more common in homicides, it can occur in severe accidental head injuries. Retinal hemorrhages are also seen in bleeding disorders, sepsis, vasculopathies, increased intracranial hemorrhage and, rarely, when there is abrupt and severe compression of the chest.[7,8] Examples of the last entity are cardiopulmonary resuscitation and the effects of a shoulder harness in a car crash.[8]

After head injuries, the next most common cause of death in battered children is injuries to the abdomen. The child is either punched or kicked in the abdomen. There may be no external evidence of injury at all to the

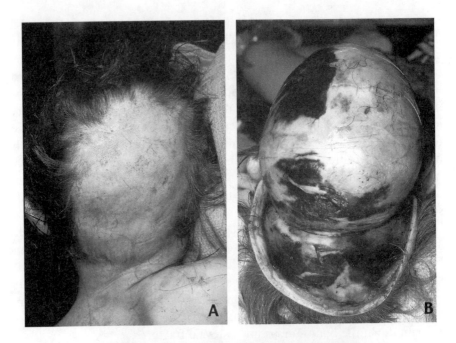

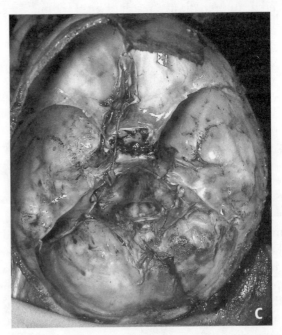

Figure 12.4 A 2-year-old child admitted to hospital in an unconscious state. (A) No external evidence of trauma, even after shaving scalp. (B) Retraction of scalp reveals massive scalp hemorrhage (C) with subdural bleed and 15.5-cm fracture of posterior fossa.

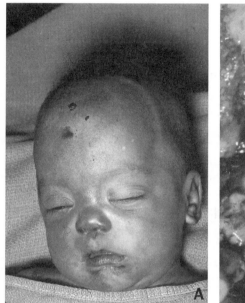
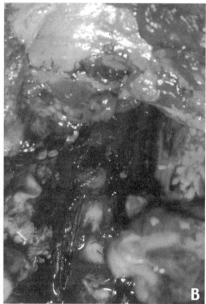

Figure 12.5 A 32-month-old child brought to Medical Examiner's Office with diagnosis of SIDS. Externally, (A) three healing scabs of forehead and excoriation of chin. At autopsy, (B) fracture of neck at C6–7. Parent admitted slamming child's head against bed, face down.

abdominal wall, yet, within the abdominal cavity, there may be lacerations of the liver, rupture of the spleen, tears in the mesentery, rupture of the bowel and a massive hemoperitoneum. A severe blow to the abdomen might cause transection of the liver at the point where it overlies the vertebral column. In the authors' experience, the most common organs lacerated, in order of frequency, are the liver, mesentery and bowel. In cases of isolated bowel injury, death may be due to peritonitis.

Some attorneys have used as a defense that the abdominal injuries were caused by cardiopulmonary resuscitation. Price et al. reviewed 324 child fatalities caused by natural disease who were resuscitated.[9] None had abdominal injuries. Distribution by age was: below the age of one year, 75.93%; between the ages of 1 and 4 years, 19.75% and between 5 and 10 years 4.32%. CPR was by medical personnel in 70.06% of cases; a relative in 18.21%; a friend in 5.25% and others in 6.48%.

Bush et al. reviewed 211 child fatalities in children less than 12 years of age who died of nontraumatic causes, who had cardiopulmonary resuscitation.[10] Fifteen children had at least one injury; seven of which were considered medically significant. There were no injuries to the abdominal organs. Only three children had potentially life-threatening injuries: a pneumothorax; an epicardial hematoma, and pulmonary interstitial hemorrhage associated with hemoperitoneum.

The neglected or starved child is a variant of the battered baby syndrome. Here, the child is fed insufficiently or sporadically and left to lie in its own feces and urine. The child presents with sunken, wizened features, a sunken abdomen, prominent ribs, wrinkled, loose skin with loss of turgor, and an overall emaciated appearance (Figure 20.1). There is usually severe, ulcerating diaper rash.

There are three possible explanations for a child presenting this way: criminal neglect, parental ignorance of the care and feeding of an infant, or a congenital disease e.g., malformation of the gastrointestinal tract, a malabsorption syndrome. Malnutrition can be the result of the mother's ignorance of proper feeding and care of the child if she is young, poor, uneducated, or retarded. The child, in this instance, is often only marginally nourished. If it develops severe diarrhea, in a matter of several hours its underlying malnutrition can be so exacerbated as to cause the child to present in a serious condition.

Most starved and neglected children are hospitalized at least once before they die. If their condition is not due to congenital disease, they rapidly gain weight in the hospital and are discharged in a healthy, well-nourished state. If such children are subsequently found dead in a starved condition, one then can conclude that this was a purposeful action and the case is a homicide. In cases where there are no prior admissions, one must first exclude any possible natural disease causing malnourishment.

The "Impulse" or "Angry" Homicide

The majority of cases of infanticide or child murder fall into this category. These children are the victims of a sudden violent act brought on by a slight or trivial provocation. The perpetrator is often a husband or boyfriend or, less often, the mother. Children crying or dirtying their diapers give rise to a sudden venting of suppressed anger and frustration by the perpetrator. Typically, the child is picked up and thrown or slammed against an object, floor, or wall. Aside from the fatal injuries, the child may be relatively well cared for and well nourished. Some might show a few minor old injuries but not the severe multiple injuries of different ages shown by children of the battered baby syndrome. Death is usually caused by head trauma. Less commonly, there are severe abdominal injuries following a blow or kick to the abdomen. The severe nature of the internal injuries may not be visible externally. Occasionally, cases presenting as SIDS have turned out to be impulse homicides with massive non-visible (at least externally) head or abdominal trauma. Explanations for the trauma usually are "He fell out of my arms"; "I was throwing him up in the air and catching him when I missed"; "He fell from his high chair"; "He rolled off the bed"; and so on.

Some individuals use immersion of a child in hot water as a disciplinary measure. Thus, an individual might plunge a child's hand or foot into boiling water to "teach" him not to perform a certain act. The forensic pathologist, however, more commonly sees the child who has been lowered into water up to his waist. Children who incur intentionally induced scalding burns are initially seen in the emergency rooms of hospitals, usually with a story that the child had been accidentally burned. Often, there will be a delay between the time of the injury and the child's being brought to the emergency room. Adults will usually ascribe this to their not having realized the severity of the injury. Yet, one will be presented with a child with second- or third-degree burns over half of the body with injuries so severe as to be obvious to even a layperson. The story of how the burns are incurred usually follows one of a few scenarios. The individual may say that they were bathing the child and did not realize the water was so hot until the child began to scream. Yet, these same adults show no evidence of any burns to their hands. With older children, they state that the child climbed into the bathtub and turned on the hot water and inexplicably was unable to get out. A variation of this is that the child was placed in the bathtub and a sibling turned on the hot water. A careful analysis of these stories shows they do not make sense, nor does the pattern of burns match the history.

In most cases of child abuse caused by scalding, adults intend to punish the child for some infraction such as dirtying a diaper. Typically, they will run water into a sink or bathtub, grasp the child underneath or by the arms and lower them into the water. What they fail to realize is that the water heater in many houses and apartments is set at around 140 °F. At this temperature, full-thickness burns can be inflicted in a matter of several seconds following immersion.[11] As the temperature of the water decreases, the time needed to inflict full-thickness burns increases.

On lowering a child into the water, the child's feet contact the water first. This causes an involuntary withdrawal of the feet such that there is flexion at the knees and hips. Thus, the child is immersed in a squatting position. In most instances, the water is not very deep, somewhere between 6 and 12 in. Because of the position of the child as it is placed in the water, there will be a very characteristic distribution of burns (Figure 12.6). The skin in the popliteal fossae and in the knee region is spared because the child flexes its legs such that the knees project above the water and the flexed thigh and calf protect the skin of the popliteal fossa. If the thigh is brought back hard against the abdomen, which is often the case, there may also be sparing of the inguinal regions. If the child is wearing a diaper and immersion is not very long, there may be some sparing of the inguinal region by the diaper.

Table 12.3 shows the correlation between water temperature and time necessary to cause epidermal damage and full-thickness burns. It is based on

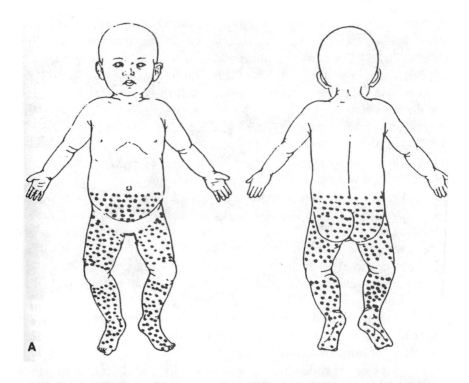

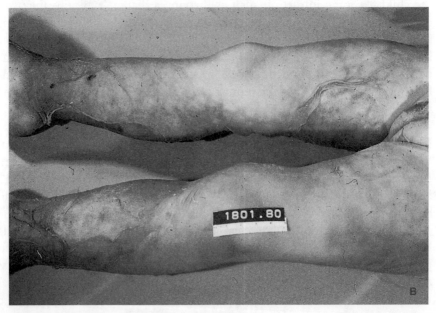

Figure 12.6 (A) Illustration of usual distribution of scalding burns with sparing of knees, popliteal fossae, and inguinal regions. (B) Sparing of knees *(continued)*.

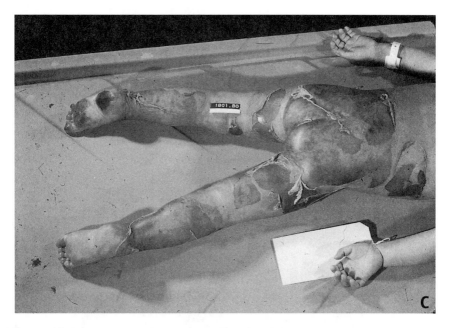

Figure 12.6 *(continued)* (C) Sparing of popliteal fossa.

Table 12.3   Water Temperature in Relation to Scalding Burns Time

Temperature (°F)	Threshold for epidermal injury	Full-thickness burns
120	290 s*	600 s
125	50 s	120 s
130	15 s	30 s
140	2.6 s	~7 s
150	<1 s	2.3 s

* s = seconds

human experimentation.[11] Because the individuals involved were adults, it is probable that the times are actually shorter for young children since they have thinner, more delicate skin.

"Gentle" Homicides and the Lethal Variant of Munchausen's Syndrome by Proxy

Probably the most commonly missed method of homicide in infants and young children is smothering. Based on the authors' experiences, smothering is, after impulse homicides, the second most common type of homicide in infants. In infants, smothering is very easily accomplished. One closes off the child's nose with two fingers, at the same time pushing up on the lower jaw with the palm to occlude the airway. Other methods have involved placing a pillow or towel over the child's face and pressing down; pushing the face down into bed clothing, or just covering the nose and mouth with one's hand. These descriptions are based on either confessions or witnessed homicides. In a few cases, attempted homicides have been videotaped.

The true number of smotherings in infants is not known and can never be known until there is some scientific test to determine whether an individual has been smothered. The amount of force necessary to produce smothering is so minor in this age group that there is virtually never evidence of trauma. Autopsy findings are essentially unremarkable, the same as those found in SIDS deaths (Figure 12.7). Undoubtedly, a small percentage of SIDS deaths are due to smothering. This has been estimated as high as 10%. It has been the authors' opinion, that this percentage was too high and smotherings disguised as SIDS probably accounted for only a few percent of alleged SIDS cases. If the campaign to reduce SIDS deaths by placing infants on their backs

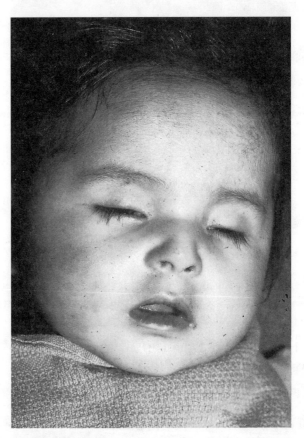

Figure 12.7 A 2-month-old child brought to Medical Examiner's office as a SIDS death. At autopsy, no injury and no petechiae. Mother subsequently admitted smothering child with towel.

is truly successful in reducing SIDS deaths, then the percentage of SIDS-attributed deaths that are really caused by smothering will increase and approach, if not exceed, the previously cited 10%.

The amount of time necessary to smother an infant, such that their electroencephalogram is flat and there is no spontaneous respiration, has been documented at 70–90s.[12,13] Deaths caused by smothering tend to be missed in large urban communities with high crime rates, where both the medical examiner's office and police agencies are overworked and cannot afford to expend the time on detailed investigations of all cases.

While most homicidal suffocation of infants is sporadic, a small number of individuals, virtually all of whom are mothers, practice a lethal form of Munchausen's syndrome by proxy, a form of child abuse in which children are brought to physicians and hospitals for induced signs and symptoms of illnesses in conjunction with a fictitious history.[14] The child is usually subjected to multiple hospital admissions and extensive medical evaluations, treatments and procedures for these nonexistent medical conditions. Thus, a child might be brought into the hospital with hypoglycemia because the mother is administering insulin or there may be blood in the urine because the mother pricks her own finger and adds blood to the child's urine.

With the more common forms of Munchausen's, the diagnosis is usually made after a number of admissions because the symptoms and signs usually do not make sense clinically and appear bizarre. Male and female children are affected equally and, in virtually every instance, the perpetrator is the mother. The father is usually supportive of the mother, is unaware of what she is doing, and usually stands by her after she is accused. Initially, multiple and varied tentative diagnoses are considered. The mother and child seem to be extremely close and it is difficult for the physician or social worker to realize what the mother is doing.

Forensic pathologists are familiar with a much more lethal version of this entity in which the individual, again virtually always the mother, repeatedly smothers the child into unconsciousness. Children are then either resuscitated by the parent or brought to an emergency room in a semi-moribund state, with a history of apnea, cyanosis, and losing consciousness. This continues to recur until the children are admitted to the hospital. After admission, the children are worked up extensively, with no abnormal findings. Usually, these children never have these episodes of apnea and cyanosis while in the hospital. If they do, a careful history reveals that the parents who have witnessed these attacks outside the hospital are alone with the children in the hospital room at the time the attack occurs. After discharge from the hospital, the "attacks" continue until either the diagnosis is made or the children killed.

The more lethal variant of Munchausen's syndrome by proxy was long unrecognized by pediatricians, though it was described in the forensic pathology literature, without resort to this terminology, by Di Maio and Bernstein in 1974.[15] Rosen et al. were the first to describe two siblings with recurrent cardiorespiratory arrest caused by smothering by the mother, in which the act was documented on videotape.[12] The first child was a 5-month-old girl admitted for cardiorespiratory arrest. Her 4-year-old brother had had a similar medical history. The mother gave a history of almost daily episodes of apnea, cyanosis, bradycardia, and loss of consciousness since 1 week of age. The attacks were very common, with the longest period between attacks only 72 h. These attacks occurred whether the child was asleep or awake. The child had been extensively worked up by computerized tomography, ECG, and EEG and had been given multiple anticonvulsive medications. She had had multiple apneic episodes in the hospital and was found apneic, cyanotic, bradycardic, and unresponsive. Ventilation with oxygen and closed chest massage always resuscitated the child. On this admission, however, the physicians became suspicious and, using video equipment, were able to document the mother smothering the child by placing the palm of her right hand over the baby's face. She kept the hand in position for 90 s. The heart rate began to fall 30 s after the obstruction of the airway. The EEG slowed and flattened at 90 s.

As awareness of this syndrome spread among pediatrians, and because of the availability of video cameras, other cases have been discovered and documented. Thus, Southall et al. reported two cases of apneic episodes induced by smothering that were documented by video cameras.[13] In one instance, the mother placed a T-shirt over the nose and mouth of a 22-month-old child and forced his head onto the mattress. In the second child, 6 months of age, the mother also placed a garment over the face of the child and forced its head onto the mattress. In a prior episode, which was not videotaped, but during which monitoring was being conducted, the child was found unconscious and cyanotic apparently after 2 min of smothering.

The videotapes showed that both the children struggled violently until they lost consciousness. Thus, the term "gentle" homicide is a misnomer. It took at least 70 s before electroencephalographic changes, probably associated with loss of consciousness, occurred. No marks were seen on the lips or nose. Southall et al. describe a series of physiological changes observed by their recording during the smothering.[13] Initially, there was the sudden onset of large body movements, apparently the child's violent struggling against the smothering. At 1 min, there was the appearance of a series of deep breaths occurring at a relatively slow rate with a prolonged expiratory phase, in other words, a "gasping" respiratory pattern. About this time, the electroencephalogram showed large slow waves progressing to an isoelectric baseline indicative of cerebral hypoxemia.

The authors have encountered a number of fatal cases of Munchausen's syndrome by proxy, such as the previously mentioned case described by Di Maio and Bernstein, where a woman was convicted of smothering her adopted child after repeated episodes of admission to the hospital for cyanosis and apnea.[15] She was also linked to six other deaths. Other cases encountered by the authors have involved anywhere from one to three deaths. In one instance, a mother was indicted by the grand jury for smothering two children, though she was never tried for either death, because the district attorney refused to try the case. He was advised by a pediatrician that the two deaths were examples of hereditary SIDS and was quoted the work of Steinschneider (see next section). One of the authors was also consulted in a case occurring in Houston, in which a child, who was repeatedly admitted for cyanotic episodes with essentially negative workups, subsequently died and was felt to represent a variant of SIDS. When a second sibling presented with the same history of multiple episodes of cyanosis, a video camera recorded the mother smothering the child (M. Munier, personal communication). The mother subsequently confessed to having smothered the first child as well.

Probably the most bizarre case of Munchausen's syndrome by proxy one of the authors (VJMD) has encountered involved a nurse in a pediatric intensive care unit. She was suspected of administering heparin, potassium chloride, and succinylcholine (alone and in various combinations) to infants and young children to precipitate a medical crisis (massive bleeding, cardiac and pulmonary arrest) so that she could resuscitate them and be viewed as a heroine. Unfortunately, she was not always able to resuscitate them. She was convicted of killing one child with succinylcholine and injuring another with heparin. Attorneys involved in the case suspected her of causing the deaths of from 15 to 30 other children.

Deaths from the lethal form of Munchausen's Syndrome by Proxy may be diagnosed as cases of near-miss SIDS (an entity which may not exist). Thus, Berger presented two cases of child abuse by suffocation presenting as near-miss SIDS.[16] Fortunately, both children survived. The perpetrator was the mother in both instances. She apparently put her hand over her child's nose and mouth. Minford also reported child abuse presenting as apparent near-miss SIDS.[17] Again, the child did not die. The mother admitted holding his nose, causing the child to become cyanotic and apneic.

The existence of cases of near-miss SIDS is debatable. Whether such cases actually represent potential cases of SIDS aborted due to the intervention of another or whether they are a misinterpretation of a normal apneic episode of an infant by an inexperienced observer is not clear. The importance of near-miss SIDS is that Munchausen's syndrome by proxy can be confused with it or some obscure apneic disorder. The presentation of the lethal variant of Munchausen's cases, however, is usually the same. Repeated apneic episodes in the presence of one individual (usually a parent), with the child's becoming cyanotic and limp; resuscitation, and repeated presentation in an emergency room or hospital with numerous admissions to a hospital, at which time the child has no problems unless left alone with the parent. Unfortunately, if suspicion is not aroused, there is a possibility that this will lead to the death of the child.

SIDS and the Munchausen Syndrome by Proxy

Over the years, a number of causes have been proposed for SIDS. One suggestion was that the episodes of prolonged apnea seen in premature infants are a *form frustre* of SIDS. This concept was proposed by Steinschneider in an article in *Pediatrics* in 1972.[18] He studied five infants, three of whom were referred to him at about 1 month of age because of cyanotic episodes of undetermined etiology. Two subsequently died of what was called the sudden infant death syndrome; three survived. One of the two was a 29-day-old female seen because of recurrent cyanotic episodes. The first occurred at the 8th to 9th days of life; the second 5 days later. She was admitted to the hospital at the time and discharged at the age of 25 days without a diagnosis. She was then re-admitted following another severe cyanotic episode. This pattern of admission, discharge and readmission occurred until her death at home at 79 days of age. During her workup by Steinschneider, the child allegedly suffered multiple episodes of apparent prolonged apnea.

The second child, a male, was studied from age 5 days to 33 days. The morning following discharge, he had an alleged episode of prolonged apnea and cyanosis. A similar alleged episode occurred 15 to 20 min later. The child was hospitalized for 34 days and then discharged. He was re-admitted the following day for a period of 6 days because of apparent aspiration during feeding. He was discharged and, on the morning following, had an apneic episode, became cyanotic, and died.

The two deaths reported by Steinschneider that form the basis for the contention that apneic episodes are associated with SIDS cases involved a brother and sister. In addition to these two deaths, mention is made in the article that three other children in the family had also died. The first male developed recurrent cyanotic spells and died suddenly at 102 days of age; the second, a female, turned blue and died at 48 days of age. Neither of the two children was autopsied. The third cried out and died suddenly at 28 months of age. An autopsy was negative, except for the fact that the adrenal glands were "considered to be of small size."

The Steinschneider article became one of the most quoted articles in the field of SIDS.[18] It led to the introduction of apnea monitors to "prevent" SIDS. In addition, the article indicated that there was hereditary basis for SIDS. Following its publication, a number of articles appeared in the medical literature describing multiple cases of SIDS in families, thus appearing to confirm that SIDS was indeed hereditary.

Forensic pathologists were immediately skeptical about the article, strongly suspecting serial homicide. In the first edition of this book, the authors stated that the deaths in the article were homicide and that Steinschneider's article was describing a lethal variant of Munchausen's syndrome by proxy. In March 1994, the mother of the two dead children in Steinschneider's article confessed to smothering all five children because she couldn't stand their crying. She was subsequently tried and convicted of homicide.[19]

Miscellaneous Causes of Child Deaths

The last category of homicides in children is a very broad one, encompassing a multitude of different causes including poisoning, stabbing, clubbing, drowning, and shooting. Generally, the perpetrators fall into one of a number of types. There is the psychotic assailant, often a parent, who will shoot, stab, or club the child for some delusional reason. These assailants usually make no attempt to conceal their actions. They might say that the child was possessed by the devil or is the devil. Such deaths present very little problem to either the medical examiner or the police agency, because the perpetrators are quite willing to describe in detail what they have done and the cause of death is quite obvious.

The second type of perpetrator is the sane individual who commits murder for reasons that might or might not be apparent. Such an individual might use obvious violence (e.g., stabbing), but claim that the assailant was another individual, or that the child was kidnapped. They might attempt to make a death appear to be an accident. Thus, the perpetrator will relate that a child accidentally drowned in the bathtub or fell into a river. The deaths may be more subtle, especially if poison is used. Poisoning is very easy in children, because they are dependent on adults for feeding. The perpetrators are generally not psychotic, but just wish to dispose of a child for some reason or other. Because of this, it is a very good idea to perform complete toxicological analysis on young children in which no anatomical cause of death is apparent. This is especially true of SIDS cases. The authors have had a number of apparent SIDS deaths in which toxicological analysis revealed the deaths to be caused by drug overdose. In one 2-year span, one homicide was obvious, one was an accident blamed on the mother's misinterpreting the dispensation of medication, and a third undetermined as to manner, but most probably a homicide. In a fourth case, where a child died of asphyxia when cotton was wedged down its throat, there was also a toxic level of propyl alcohol in the blood.

Occasionally, infants and young children are killed by their siblings. They may beat them or even smother them. Sibling jealousy might be a motive.

Radiological Evidence of Child Abuse

The radiological features of skeletal injury can play a significant role in the diagnosis of child abuse. Radiological evidence of skeletal trauma occurs in about a third of abused children, with most such injuries occurring in the first 2 years of life.[20] The location, nature, and multifocal aspect of the skeletal injuries have to be considered. Thus, epiphyseal-metaphyseal fractures of the long bones of the arms and legs and rib fractures exclusive of the newborn period are considered specific for child abuse. Multiple repetitive fractures of other areas are only suggestive of child abuse, but are not specific.

The majority of battered children are young — a third less than 1 year old and half less than 2.[21] In nonfatal cases exhibiting skeletal trauma, the most frequent sites of injury are the extremities (77%), the skull (34%), and the rib cage (19%). [20] In the extremities, epiphyseal-metaphyseal injuries are considered by many to be diagnostic of child abuse.[20–22] This is because the forces necessary to produce these fractures do not generally occur in accidental trauma at this age. In this entity, there is partial or complete separation or fracture of the epiphysis, the physis, and a thin layer of metaphyseal bone due to violent traction or torsion of the limb. Microscopically, there is a transmetaphyseal disruption (microfractures) in the subepiphyseal area.[22] The typical epiphyseal-metaphyseal fractures associated with abuse are said to be fracture-separation of one or both corners of the metaphysis ("corner fracture"), fracture-separation of an arc of the metaphysis (the "bucket-handle" fracture), and complete separation with displacement of the metaphyseal fragment.

In infants and children, the periostium can be sheared off the bone by twisting and pulling. This results in subperiosteal bleeding, with accumulation of blood between the periosteum and the cortex of the bone. New bone formation takes place in the hematoma, with bone formation along the shaft of the bone. On X-ray, the subperiosteal calcification appears as a thin line paralleling the bone.[23] In some instances, the subperiosteal bone formation can be very extensive (Figure 12.8).

Diaphyseal injuries are four times as frequent as epiphyseal-metaphyseal fractures.[20,21] The type of fractures produced may be either spiral or transverse. **Spiral fractures** are caused by twisting of an extremity. Especially in the non-walking child, they are highly suggestive of abuse. Spiral fractures, however, can occur accidentally from a fall and are not diagnostic of child abuse. **Transverse fractures** are produced by either a direct blow to the bone or a bending of the bone. Again, these can be of an accidental

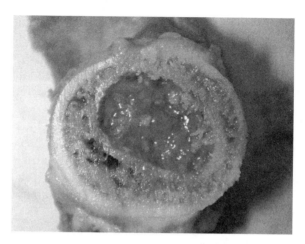

Figure 12.8 Healing fracture of femur with extensive ring of subperiosteal bone.

nature. Transverse fractures caused by blows are much more common than spiral fractures in child abuse cases.

Head trauma is, in fact, the most frequent cause of death and morbidity in abused children. Accidental trauma rarely causes intracranial injury in infants. Most (95%) of serious or life-threatening head injuries in young children and infants can be blamed on abuse; accidental trauma, such as motor vehicle accidents; falls from great heights; other less common, extremely traumatic situations account for the other cases.[24] An infant's falling from a bed, couch, or high chair at most suffers a mild concussion. Trying to explain an intracranial injury with such a situation is not viable. This conclusion is consistent with a study by Helfer et al. of 85 children who fell from a crib, bed, or examination table while in the hospital.[25] The height of the falls was approximately 36 in. (90 cm). The 85 falls resulted in 57 cases in which there was no apparent injury, 20 children in which there was a bump or contusion, 17 cases in which there was a small cut, scratch, or bloody nose, and one instance in which there was a fracture of the skull. (The total number of findings add up to more than 85 because there was more than one finding in some cases.) In the child with the fractured skull, there was neither serious or apparent *sequelae*. There was, in fact, no sign of soft tissue injury over the site of the fracture.

A common type of injury seen in child abuse are rib fractures.[20,21] Rib fractures outside the neonatal period in a young child without an obvious history of trauma of an accidental nature, such as an automobile accident, and free of intrinsic bone disease are virtually specific for child abuse.[20,21,26,27] They are caused by sudden, violent compression of the chest. In battered children, they are often multiple in number, bilateral, and most frequently posterior adjacent to the costo-vertebral junction. Most occur in children younger than 2 years of age. On X-ray, there might be evidence of healing fractures of different ages. Posterior rib fractures in child abuse cases are believed to be due to squeezing or direct trauma to the ribs. Lateral fractures of the ribs would be due to violent anterior-posterior compression of the chest.

Occasionally, attempts have been made to explain rib fractures in young children as being caused by resuscitation. Feldman and Brewer studied 50 patients, ages newborn to 97 months (mean age 27 months) who received cardiopulmonary resuscitation.[26] Only one of these showed evidence of a rib fracture and this child was subsequently shown to have suffered child abuse. Betz and Liebhardt reviewed 94 cases of non-traumatic death in children ages several days to 7 years who had cardiopulmonary resuscitation.[27] In two of the cases, there were rib fractures. The first was a 2-month-old with a diagnosis of SIDS. The child had bilateral, midclavicular fractures of ribs 2–5. The second child was 5 years old and had fractures of ribs 2–6 on the right in the midclavicular line. Both children had been resuscitated by physicians. Children resuscitated by non-medical personnel had no fractures. Betz and Liebhardt point out that the fractures they observed were anterior, while most fractures from abuse are posterior. This is in agreement with the observations of Bush et al., who reviewed 211 non-traumatic fatalities of children below 12 years of age who received cardiopulmonary resuscitation.[10] In only one case were there rib fractures. This was a 3-month-old infant, dying of SIDS, who had bilateral fractures of the eighth and ninth ribs at the sterno-chondral junction. Thus, in children, especially infants, fractures from resuscitation are extremely rare and, when present, are anterior in location, at the sterno-chondral junction and midclavicular line.

Fractures of the clavicle are relatively uncommon in child abuse cases. Most occur in the midportion and are similar in location to those resulting from accidental trauma. Fractures of the distal ends of the clavicle are less common and are caused by sudden traction on the extremity.[21] These are more suggestive of child abuse.

The Shaken Baby Syndrome

"If any one of them can explain it," said Alice ... " I'll give him sixpence. I don't believe ... there's an atom of meaning in it." Lewis Carroll, *Alice's Adventures in Wonderland*

The concept of the shaken baby syndrome (SBS) was introduced by Caffey in 1972 to describe a clinical pathological entity in infants characterized by retinal, subdural, or subarachnoid hemorrhages caused by violent shaking.[28] The injuries produced were allegedly caused by the resultant whiplash action of the child's relatively heavy head in association with weak neck muscles; an immature, partially membranous skull; a relatively large subarachnoid space; and a soft, immature brain. In other words, these injuries were not caused by direct-impact injuries to the head, but rather by indirect acceleration–deceleration traction stresses caused by the head's whipping back and forth. Since then, this diagnosis has gained a considerable following among clinicians. Interestingly, many of the cases described in Caffey's original paper would not be classified as examples of SBS nowadays, as no brain injury was involved. Caffey's paper also suffered from a number of problems in regard to his case material, e.g., the source of 15 of the 27 cases was *Newsweek* magazine. Other theories expressed in his paper are extremely dubious, e.g., over-vigorous "burping" might be fatal; breath-holding spells, body-rocking and head-rolling could be damaging to the brain.[28]

In most of the original reports on SBS, the diagnosis was made on a clinical basis. If death occurred, autopsies were not always performed and scant mention was made of the findings. Following the initial description, as more cases of this syndrome were diagnosed and studied, injuries to the scalp and skull (contusions and fractures), explainable only by impact trauma, began to be detected in alleged cases. Thus, Duhaime et al. reported on 48 infants and young children diagnosed as SBS.[29] Thirteen of these children died. Seven showed no evidence of blunt trauma to the head clinically (i.e., scalp contusions, subgaleal or subperiosteal hemorrhage, or a skull fracture). At autopsy, however, all 13 children had evidence of blunt head trauma: eight had soft tissue contusions and five had contusions and skull fractures. Of the seven deaths in which blunt trauma to the head was missed clinically, four presented with the classical symptoms of retinal hemorrhage, subdural hematoma, and subarachnoid hemorrhage. The other three, while having subdural hematoma and subarachnoid hemorrhage, did not have retinal hemorrhage.

Because of the unchallengeable detection of impact trauma in cases alleged to be due to SBS, some authors modified the terminology to the "shaken impact syndrome."[30] In this "revised" version of the syndrome, the child is shaken, presumably causing retinal hemorrhages and intracranial bleeding, and then the head is impacted against a hard surface, causing contusions and fractures and presumably additional intracranial hemorrhage. No way of differentiating pre-impact intracranial trauma from post-impact is given. To many observers, the "shaken impact syndrome" appears to be an attempt to explain away inconvenient observations that call into question the existence of the shaken baby syndrome itself.

In formulating the SBS, Caffey took a number of diverse observations, intracranial bleeding (subarachnoid or subdural), retinal hemorrhage and no evidence of head impact and constructed a unifying hypothesis that is the SBS.[28] A hypothesis, however, is not necessarily a truth. One is obligated to either prove or refute a hypothesis. The way to accomplish this is by experimentation and repeated objective observations to exclude other possible explanations.

Establishment of the validity of a hypothesis by observation is dependent on the quality of the observations and the observer. Observations might be handicapped by limitations of the senses or equipment employed. The quality of the observer is determined by training and experience but might be modified by prejudice and emotions. These latter qualities might cause individuals to either consciously or unconsciously distort the evidence to fit a preconceived theory. The individual charged with injury to a child cannot be considered an objective unbiased observer. Most people charged with injuring or killing a child would rather confess to or be charged with shaking a baby than slamming its head against an object or throwing it across a room like a football. Obviously, it is easier to claim as a defense ignorance of the consequences of shaking, rather than the other actions.

To prove the concept of SBS by observation, one must have objective evidence that excludes other etiologies. The original observations, in which head impact was "excluded," were almost all clinical and did not involve autopsies. By virtue of this, the quality of the observations is open to serious question. Cases where the child does not die and the absence of signs of impact are based on external and radiological examinations cannot be used to substantiate the existence of this entity, as there can be extensive impact injury, such as skull fractures, without either external or radiologic evidence of trauma. Absence of external or radiological evidence of injury, in cases where massive trauma is demonstrated at autopsy, is routinely seen by all experienced forensic pathologists. When alleged cases of SBS began coming to autopsy, evidence of impact (contusions, fractures) was observed.[29] If there is a skull fracture, a subgaleal hematoma or scalp hemorrhage, one cannot logically or in good conscience make the diagnosis of SBS because there is already a proven etiology for all the findings — an impact. One cannot blithely propose two causes for injuries in a case where one will be sufficient just because this fits a preexisting theory or prejudice. One also cannot use these cases, as the proponents of the shaken impact syndrome do, to prove the existence of SBS since one already has a plausible and accepted explanation for the injuries — an impact of the head.

An attempt to validate SBS experimentally with a biomechanical study was made by Duhaime et al.[29] They subjected models of 1-month-old infants, implanted with an accelerometer, to repetitive violent shaking by adult males and females. After each shaking episode, the occipital area of the model was impacted against either a metal bar or padded surface. The results of 69 shaking tests were then compared with 60 impacts. The mean peak tangential acceleration was 9.29 g for the 69 shaking episodes and 428.18 g for the 60 impacts. Mean time interval was 106.6 msec and 20.9 msec, respectively. Thus, acceleration due to impact exceeded acceleration due to shaking by a factor of nearly 50 times. As expected, impact against a padded surface was associated with significantly smaller acceleration (mean 380.6 g) and a longer time pause (mean 24.22 ms) than against a metal bar (489.5g and 17.13 ms).

Both the magnitude of angular acceleration and the time interval of the acceleration are important biomechanical factors influencing the nature of the injuries. Large angular accelerations over short time intervals tend to result in subdural hematomas, while longer intervals are associated with diffuse axonal injury. Based on work by Thibault and Gennarelli on subhuman primates, the angular acceleration and velocity associated with shaking is below the injury range for concussion, subdural hematoma or diffuse axonal injury, while the results from the impacts are within the range.[29, 31] Thus, attempts to verify SBS experimentally indicate that the injuries cannot be caused by shaking.

What about the rare case of traumatic intracranial bleeding in a child where there is no evidence of impact on the scalp or skull? Absence of trauma does not preclude impact. The authors have seen numerous cases of witnessed impact involving both adults and children who subsequently died of head trauma in which there was no evidence of impact in the scalp or skull at autopsy. This observation is in agreement with the opinions of Bernard Knight, who, in his book *Forensic Pathology*, in discussing acute subdural hematomas, states "... blunt impacts may leave no sign in the scalp, externally or internally, and no skull fracture."[33] As to the concept of shaken baby syndrome, Knight states: "Although shaking presumably may cause subdural hematoma (SDH), it is likely that it is a relatively uncommon cause, compared with impact. This situation may well have arisen because a blunt impact upon the head of an infant, if spread over a wide area following contact with a flat surface, can leave no external scalp mark, no subscalp bleeding and no fracture of the skull — yet the transmitted forces can still be sufficient to cause high strain — shearing stresses within the cranial cavity leading to subdural bleeding."

Some practitioners contend that retinal hemorrhages are pathognomonic of the shaken baby syndrome and make the diagnosis of this entity based on their presence alone. The problems with this assertion are twofold. First, the underlying premise (the existence of the shaken baby syndrome) is unproven. Second, retinal hemorrhage occurs with other etiologies: accidental trauma (especially subdural hematoma); resuscitation (rarely); papilledema; in 14.2 percent of vaginally delivered newborns (resolves by 1 month of age); 0.8% of caesarean deliveries; sudden compression of the thorax; subarachnoid hemorrhage of non-traumatic origin; sepsis and coagulopathy.[6-8, 32] The mechanism(s) causing retinal hemorrhages are unknown. Suggested are increased retinal venous pressure, extravasation of subarachnoid blood, and traction of retinal vessels at the vitreo-retinal interface due to angular deceleration.[32]

Another aspect of the shaken baby theory that appears to be ignored by proponents of this entity are the lack of neck and cervical spinal cord injuries. If the head is whipping back and forth with such velocity as to tear cerebral blood vessels and cause retinal hemorrhage, why are there no fractures of the cervical spinal column? When challenged in regard to this, the reason is said to be the suppleness (bendability) of the spine in small children. This explanation, however, does not explain the lack of spinal cord injuries. The cord should be crushed by the "supple" vertebrae shifting back and forth — or, if not crushed, at least torn or severely stretched. There should be evidence of spinal cord injury. Such injury is not described in these cases.

Some advocates of SBS contend that the presence of epidural hemorrhage in the cervical spinal area confirms the diagnosis of shaking. Harris and Adelson studied 19 infants dying of natural disease or SIDS.[34] They found epidural hemorrhage of varying degrees in 18 cases. They concluded that the presence of epidural hemorrhage in the cervical cord area was not related to trauma, not damaging to the cord, and probably due to hemodynamic forces. Case, in a study of this phenomenon in 50 children below the age of 3 years, some of whom had been allegedly shaken, found no relationship between shaking and epidural hemorrhages.[7]

The authors have grave reservations as to the existence of SBS. This was expressed in the first edition of this book. Since then, we have had no reason to change this opinion but rather to solidify it. There is just no conclusive evidence that this entity exists. The authors feel that head injury ascribed to shaking is due to impact of the head

Unintentional Causes of Intracranial Hemorrhage

While most children presenting in the first few years of life with intracranial bleeding and retinal hemorrhage are victims of child abuse, this is not absolute. Children do have accidents. Most such accidents, however, are clear-cut and involve significant violence e.g., a motor vehicle accident, or a fall from a great height.

In rare instances, natural disease can present a picture resembling child abuse. One rare example is rupture of a cerebral aneurysm.[35] Another is late-form hemorrhagic disease of the newborn,[36] which is caused by vitamin K deficiency. Typically presenting 4–6 weeks after birth, it is manifested by intracranial bleeding (subdural, subarachnoid, intracerebral) as well as bleeding in the skin, gastrointestinal tract and urogenital tract. Rutty et al. described the case of a 9-week-old boy brought to the hospital unconscious, with a right subdural hematoma and bilateral retinal hemorrhage. With such a presentation, the first thought is child abuse. In this case, because the child lived long enough to get to the hospital and survived 24 hours, hematological tests could be performed. They revealed prolonged prothrombin and partial thromboplastin times with a normal thrombin time and fibrinogen levels. Additional tests performed after death, but on antemortem blood, revealed elevated levels of "protein-induced vitamin K absence" (PIVKA). Severe vitamin K deficiency results in production of this nonfunctioning protein. This and other tests confirmed the diagnosis of late-form hemorrhagic disease of the newborn. If the child had died at home or had been dead on arrival at the hospital, the diagnosis of a natural disease would not have been made and the case thought to be child abuse. As no impact points to the head would have been found, many individuals would have described the death as a classic case of SBS.

References

1. Federal Bureau of Investigation, Crime in the United States 1999. Washington, D.C.

2. *Time,* October 7, 1985;126(14):38.

3. Caffey J, Multiple fractures in the long bones of infants suffering from chronic subdural hematoma. *Am J Roentgenol Radiat Ther* 1946; 56:163173.

4. Silverman F, The roentgen manifestations of unrecognized skeletal trauma in infants. *Am J Roentgenol Radiat Ther* 1953; 69:413-426.

5. Kempe C, et al., The battered child syndrome. *JAMA* 1962; 181:17-24.

6. Sezen F: Retinal hemorrhage in newborn infants. *Br Ophthalmol* 1970; 55:248-253.

7. Case MES, Neuropathology of head and neck injuries in young children. Presented at the AAFS 52nd Annual Meeting. February 21, 2000. Reno NV.

8. Kelley JS, Purtscher's retinopathy related to chest compression by safety belts. *Am J Ophthalmol* 1972; 74:278-283.

9. Price EA, et al., Cardiopulmonary resuscitation — related injuries and homicidal blunt abdominal trauma in children. *Amer J. Forensic Med. Path 2000*; 21(4):307-310.

10. Bush CM, et al., Pediatric injuries from cardiopulmonary resuscitation. *Ann Emerg Med* 1996; 28:40-44.

11. Moritz AR and Henriques FC, Studies of thermal injury: 11. The relative importance of time and surface temperature in the causation of cutaneous burns. *Amer J Pathol* 1947; 23:695-720.

12. Rosen CL, et al., Two siblings and recurrent cardiorespiratory arrest: Munchausen syndrome by proxy or child abuse? *Pediatrics* 1983; 71:715-720.

13. Southall DP, et al., Apneic episodes induced by smothering: Two cases identified by covert video surveillance. *Br Med J* 1987; 294:1637-1641.

14. Zitelli BI, Seltman MF, and Shannon RM, Munchausen's syndrome by proxy and its professional participants. *Am J Dis Children* 1987; 141:1099-1102.

15. DiMaio VIM and Bernstein CG, A case of infanticide. *J Forensic Sci* 1974; 19:744-754.

16. Berger D, Child abuse simulating "near-miss" sudden infant death syndrome. *J Pediatr* 1979;95:554-556.

17. Minford AMB, Child abuse presenting as apparent "near-miss" sudden infant death syndrome. *Br Med J* 1981;282:521.

18. Steinschneider A, Prolonged apnea and the sudden infant death syndrome: Clinical and laboratory observations. *Pediatrics* 1972;50:646-653.

19. Firstman R and Talan J, *The Death of Innocents*. New York-Bantam Books, 1997.

20. Merten DF, Radkowski MA, and Leonidas JC, The abused child: A radiological reappraisal. *Radiology* 1983; 146:37-381.

21. Leonidas JC, Skeletal trauma in the child abuse syndrome. *Pediatr Ann* 1983; 12:875-881.

22. Kleinman PK, Marks SC, and Blackbourne B, The metaphyseal lesion in abused infants: A radiologic-histopathologic study. *Am J Radiol* 1986; 146:895-905.

23. Brogdon BG, *Forensic Radiology*. 1998 CRC Press. Boca Raton, FL.

24. Billmire ME and Myers PA, Serious head injury in infants: Accident or abuse.*Pediatrics* 1985; 75:340-342.

25. Helfer RE, Slovis TL, and Black M, Injuries resulting when small children fall out of bed. *Pediatrics* 1977; 60:533-535.

26. Feldman KW and Brewer DK, Child abuse, cardiopulmonary resuscitation and rib fractures. *Pediatrics* 1980; 73:339-342.

27. Betz P and Liebhardt, Rib fractures in children — resuscitation or child abuse? *Int J Leg Med* 1994. 106:215-218.

28. Caffey J, On the theory and practice of shaking infants. *Am Dis Children* 1972; 124:161-169.

29. Duhaime A, et al., The Shaken Baby Syndrome: A clinical, pathological and biomechanical study. *J. Neurosurg.* 1987; 66:409-415, 1987.

30. Bruce DA and Zimmerman RA, Shaken impact syndrome. *Ped. Ann.* 18:482-94, 1989.

31. Thibault LE and Gennarelli TA, Biomechanics of diffuse brain injury in: *Proc. 4th Exper Safety Vehicle Conf*, New York: American Association of Automotive Engineers. 1985.

32. Duhaime A-C, et al., Nonaccidental head injury in infants — The "Shaken-Baby Syndrome," *NEJM* 1998 338(25): 1822-1829.

33. Knight B, *Forensic Pathology.* 2nd ed. 1996 Hodder Headline Group, London, Oxford University Press. New York. 1996.

34. Harris LS and Adelson L, Spinal injury and sudden infant death. *J. Clin Path.* 1969; 52:289-295.

35. Plunkett J, Sudden death in an infant caused by rupture of a basilar artery aneurysm. *Am J Forens Med Path* 1999; 20(2):211-214.

36. Rutty GN, Smith CM, and Malia RG, Late-form hemorrhagic disease of the newborn: A fatal case report with illustration of investigations that may assist in avoiding the mistaken diagnosis of child abuse. *Am J Forens Med Path* 1999; 20(1):48-51.

Fire Deaths

13

There are approximately 4000 fire deaths a year in the U.S.[1] Approximately 90% occur in the home and are caused by smoking, defective electrical wiring, defective or misused heaters, children playing with matches, or clothing catching on fire. This last phenomenon occurs more commonly in the elderly and, to a lesser degree, in young children.

Burns can be divided into five categories:

1. Flame
2. Contact
3. Radiant heat
4. Scalding
5. Chemical
6. Microwave

Burns

In **flame burns**, there is actual contact of body and flame, with scorching of the skin progressing to charring. **Flash burns** are a variant of flame burns. They are caused by the initial ignition (or "flash") from flash fires that result from the sudden ignition or explosion of gases, petrochemicals or fine particulate material. Typically, the initial flash is of short duration, a few seconds at most. All exposed surfaces are burned uniformly. If the victim's clothing is ignited, a combination of flash and traditional flame burn occurs. Flash burns usually result in partial-thickness burns and singed hair (Figure 13.1). If the heat pulse is very short, because the thermal conductivity of the skin is low, the burn is superficial.

Contact burns involve physical contact between the body and a hot object. At surface temperatures of 70°C and higher, trans-epidermal necrosis occurs in less than a second.[2] **Radiant heat burns** are caused by heat waves,

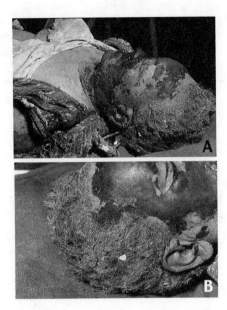

Figure 13.1 (A) and (B) Flash burns from methane explosion. Hair singed.

a type of electromagnetic wave. There is no contact between body and flame, or contact with a hot surface. Initially, the skin appears erythematous and blistered, with areas of skin slippage. With prolonged exposure to low heat, the skin will become light brown and leathery such as one sees in a well-done turkey (Figure 13.2). With most radiant heat burns, the hair is intact, at least initially. If the radiant heat continues long enough, there will be charring of the body. Three factors determine whether radiant heat burns occur, their extent and their severity. These are:

1. Temperature of the heat wave contacting the skin
2. Time of exposure
3. Whether the skin is covered with clothing

Extremely high radiant heat temperatures can cause burns in seconds. Thus, Ripple et al. concluded that air temperatures above 1500°C will cause second-degree burns on bare skin in less than 10 milliseconds.[3]

Scalding burns are caused by contact with hot liquids, most commonly water. Scalding burns generally occur on exposed skin, since even one layer of clothing can be sufficient to protect the body. The last two forms of burns are **chemical burns** and **microwave burns.**

Severity of Burn Injuries

The severity of thermal injury in an individual depends on:

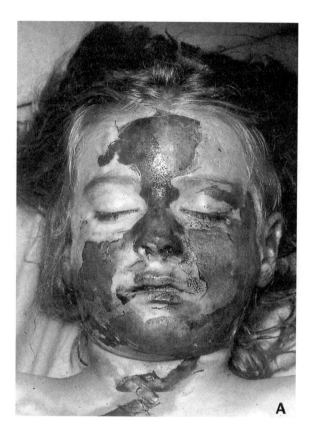

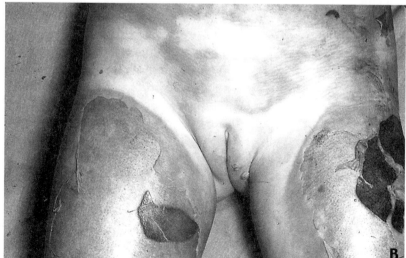

Figure 13.2 (A and B) Radiant heat burns with erythema, blistering of skin and skin slippage *(continued)*.

Figure 13.2 *(continued)* (C) "Cooked" skin caused by prolonged exposure to low heat.

- The extent of the burned area
- The severity of the burn
- The victim's age
- The presence of inhalation injuries

In living individuals, the extent of the burn is indicated as the percentage of total body surface area involved by the thermal injury. This is determined by the "rule of nines." If one considers the total body surface as 100%, then the head is 9%, the upper extremities are each 9%, the front of the torso is 18%, the back is 18%, each lower extremity is 18%, and the perineum is 1%.

Burns can be described as being first-, second-, third-, or fourth-degree; superficial, partial-thickness, or full-thickness burns; or a combination of both systems of nomenclature. In **first-degree (superficial) burns**, the skin is erythematous without blisters. Microscopically, there are dilated congested vessels in the dermis. The epidermis is intact, but there is some injury of the cells. There is subsequent desquamation of necrotic epidermal cells, e.g., peeling in sunburns. First-degree burns can be caused by prolonged exposure to low-intensity heat or light (e.g., sunburn), or a short-duration exposure to high-intensity heat or light.

Second-degree (partial-thickness) burns are subdivided into superficial and deep. Classically, in second-degree burns, the external appearance is a moist, red, blistered lesion. In superficial second-degree (partial-thickness) burns, there is destruction of the striatum granulosum and corneum, with the basal layer not totally destroyed and edema at the dermal–epidermal junction. This injury heals without scarring. In deep second-degree (partial-thickness) burns, there is complete disruption of the epidermis and destruction of most of the basal layer. There might be blistering. The dermal appendages (the hair and sweat glands) are spared and act as the source of regenerating epidermis. Second-degree burns heal without scarring.

In **third-degree (full-thickness) burns**, there is coagulation necrosis of the epidermis and dermis with destruction of the dermal appendages. Externally, the lesions usually have a dry white leathery appearance. There are no blisters. The lesions might also be brown or black, caused by charring and eschar formation. This wound heals as a scar. In **fourth-degree burns**, there are incinerating injuries extending deeper than the skin.

It should be understood that the surface appearance of a burn does not necessarily indicate the depth of injury. The extent of necrosis or degree of burn can be diagnosed only in retrospect if the victim survives. Thus, a person who has been in contact with a hot surface might have a pale lesion with a white leathery appearance that seems to be a third-degree or full-thickness burn. It will subsequently be found, however, to be only a deep, second-degree (partial-thickness) burn.

The thickness of the skin in the area in which the injury is inflicted can have an effect on the appearance of the wound. Thus, in thick skin, such as the palm, what appears to be a third-degree burn may be only a second-degree (partial-thickness) burn, while, in a thin area of skin, what appears to be a second-degree burn could turn out to be a third-degree (full-thickness) burn.

Clothing

Accidental ignition of an individual's clothing causes approximately 150 to 200 deaths a year.[1] The victims tend to be the very young and the old. Flame burns in women not uncommonly occur during cooking when they reach across a stove while wearing a long-sleeved nightgown, robe, or dress and the clothing is ignited by the flame of a gas burner.

Clothing can offer some protection from burns, especially flash and radiant heat, by reflecting and absorbing heat. Burns may be diminished in extent and depth. If the clothing ignites, however, flame burns are produced. The protective quality of clothing depends on the type of heat exposure (e.g., flame, flash, etc.), the physical properties of the fabric and the tightness of the fit. The severity of a burn may be decreased when the clothing is light colored or loose fitting, such that it provides an air space between the material and the skin; dry and multi-layered. Burn severity is increased by dark clothing that is wet with perspiration and stretched tightly over the skin.

Deaths Caused by Fire

Deaths caused by fire might be either immediate or delayed. **Immediate deaths** are caused by either direct thermal injury to the body, that is, burns, or, more commonly, to a phenomenon called "smoke inhalation." **Delayed deaths** within the first two or three days are caused by shock, fluid loss, or acute respiratory failure caused by inhalation of gases with injury to the respiratory tree. Deaths after this period are generally caused by sepsis or chronic respiratory insufficiency.

The Burned Body

On gross examination, it is usually impossible to distinguish acute antemortem from postmortem burns. Microscopic examination of the burns is not helpful unless the victim has survived long enough to develop an inflammatory response. Lack of such a response, however, does not necessarily indicate that the burn was postmortem. One of the authors (VJMD) had occasion to examine microscopic slides of third-degree burns incurred in Vietnam, with the patients subsequently evacuated to Japan where they died 2 or 3 days later. In some of these burns, there was no inflammatory reaction, presumably caused by heat thrombosis of dermal vessels such that inflammatory cells could not reach the area of burn and produce a reaction.

If a body is severely burned, the skin might split or be completely burned away, exposing muscle (Figure 13.3). This muscle often shows rupture caused by heat. Any unburned skin will usually have a seared leathery consistency. If the victim was lying on a flat surface, while the body as a whole might be severely charred, the skin resting on the surface may be perfectly preserved. In severely burned bodies, portions of the chest and abdominal walls might be burned away, exposing the viscera. The internal organs may appear seared or charred.

Burned bone has a gray-white color, often showing a fine superficial network of heat fractures on its cortical surface (Figure 13.4). It may crumble on handling. It is quite common for the soft tissue of the face to be burned away, revealing the skull (Figure 13.5). The outer table of the exposed cranial vault may show a network of fine crisscrossing heat fractures. In some cases, the outer table can fragment and be absent. Bodies will often be brought in without hands and feet, which have been burned so badly that they are either unrecognizable at the scene or have fragmented.

Burned bodies may present with a **pugilistic** attitude. Coagulation of the muscle caused by heat causes contraction of muscle fibers with resultant flexion of the limbs. Thus, the upper extremities assume the position of a boxer holding his hands up in front of him. Assumption of the pugilistic

Figure 13.3 Charred body with skin burned away; muscle exposed and ruptured.

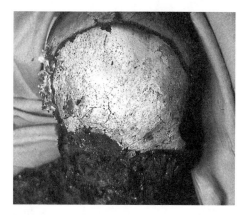

Figure 13.4 Scalp burned away exposing cranial vault. Linear heat fractures of grey, white, crumbling (calcined) bone.

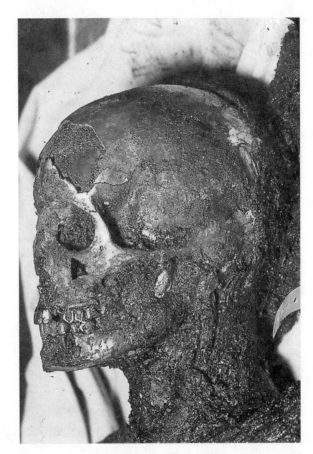

Figure 13.5 Partial skeletonization of face caused by soft tissue burned away. Portions of outer table of skull have fallen away in left frontal region.

attitude is unrelated to whether the individual was alive or dead prior to the fire.

A common artifact in severely burned bodies with charring of the head is the presence of a **postmortem epidural hematoma** (Figure 13.6). There should be no difficulty in distinguishing these from antemortem epidural hematomas. Postmortem fire epidurals are a chocolate brown color and have a crumbly or honeycomb appearance. They are large, fairly thick (up to 1.5 cm), and typically overlie the frontal, parietal, and temporal areas, in some cases with extension to the occipital area.

Smoke Inhalation

Not all bodies in a fire end up charred and disfigured. Some show no evidence of injury at all, while others demonstrate only searing burns. In the latter instance, the skin is a light brown color with a stiff leathery consistency

Figure 13.6 (A) and (B) Postmortem epidural thermal hematoma

(Figure 13.2). Blisters may also be present. Blisters do not necessarily indicate that the deceased was alive at the time the burns were incurred, since they can be produced postmortem. A mistaken impression exists that an erythematous rim surrounding blisters or burns indicates that the individual was alive at the time they were incurred (Figure 13.7). This is incorrect. Blisters with a red rim have been produced on dead bodies. Heat applied to the skin causes contraction of dermal capillaries forcing liquid blood to the periphery of the blister or burn, simulating an antemortem hyperemic inflammatory response.

For the victim of a fire whose body shows no or minimum evidence of thermal injuries, the cause of death is often attributed to "smoke inhalation."

Figure 13.7 Postmortem burn with erythematous rim.

Figure 13.8 Soot in larynx and trachea.

This is often used synonymously with carbon monoxide poisoning (intoxication). Examination of individuals overcome by smoke inhalation will usually reveal soot in the nostrils and mouth as well as coating the larynx, trachea, and bronchi (Figure 13.8). Absence of soot, however, does not necessarily mean that the individual was dead prior to the start of the fire. The authors have seen numerous cases in which there was no soot in the larynx or trachea, yet analysis of blood for carbon monoxide revealed lethal levels.

At autopsy, it is usually relatively easy to determine whether the individual died of carbon monoxide intoxication. The livor mortis, the muscles, and internal organs, as well as the blood, will have a cherry-red coloration. In spite of this coloration, a carbon monoxide determination on the blood is mandatory. The cherry-red coloration can be produced by other factors (e.g., cyanide). A cherry-red coloration to livor mortis is very common in bodies exposed to cold for long periods of time. In addition, an individual could have a fatal carbon monoxide level, yet a prominent cherry-red color be absent.

Attributing the cause of death in smoke inhalation cases to carbon monoxide intoxication is a simplification of a complicated process. The actual mechanism of death in individuals dying of smoke inhalation is not always clear. In individuals who die during fires, actual carbon monoxide levels, while toxic, are often insufficiently high to have caused death. These levels are characteristically 20% lower than in deaths caused by inhalation of carbon monoxide exhaust fumes. Thus, in the authors' experience, in individuals whose deaths are caused by inhalation of automobile exhaust, the average carbon monoxide level is 79%, with 82% of cases having levels of 70% or greater. In fires, the average carbon monoxide concentration is 57%, with carbon monoxide levels of 30 or 40% common, and with some levels in the 20% range. In some instances, this is aided by underlying disease. Thus, an individual with severe coronary atherosclerosis could die at lower carbon monoxide levels than a healthy individual. In other cases, drugs or alcohol can act as contributory factors.

A number of factors other than carbon monoxide have been suggested as causing death in smoke inhalation cases. These are oxygen deprivation, cyanide, free radicals, and nonspecified toxic substances. Oxygen deprivation caused by the fire's consumption of oxygen is not realistic as a causation of death in house fires. If there were insufficient oxygen to maintain life, the fire would go out.

Cyanide is produced in the burning of many common synthetic substances. It may, in a few rare instances, be a contributory cause of death, but to ascribe most or even many deaths to cyanide poisoning is a mistake. Cyanide as a cause of death in fires is a favorite theory of attorneys in cases of civil litigation. They picture the deceased as having been rapidly overcome and succumbing to a cloud of cyanide produced by burning synthetics. In fact, the amount of cyanide produced in fires is relatively small, with actual concentrations in real-life situations very low. Even in closed rooms with the introduction of pure gaseous cyanide in high concentrations, as occurred in the Nazi death chambers, incapacitation is not necessarily immediate and death may not occur for a number of minutes.

The detection and quantitation of cyanide in the blood is beset with difficulty. Cyanide can be produced postmortem in blood in both the body or a test tube, through the process of decomposition. In addition, if the method of analysis is not absolutely specific, other substances in the blood (sulfides) can react like cyanide, giving falsely elevated levels of cyanide.[4] One extensively quoted study ascribing numerous deaths to cyanide is suspect because of its methodology.[5] Free radicals have been proposed as one possibility in causing death, because they can inactivate surfactants, thus preventing oxygen from crossing the alveoli into the blood.[6]

Inhalation Injuries

Inhalation injuries are often ascribed to the inhalation of hot gases with "burning" of the air passages. As early as 1945, Moritz et al. found that inhalation of hot dry air sufficient to cause instantaneous burning of the skin had little or no effect on the lungs.[7] In their experiments, animals were made to inhale dry room air heated to 350 and 500ºC. This dry air lost most of its heat before reaching the lungs such that there was no injury to either the lungs or lower trachea. Injury to the upper trachea was described as mild. If the air was hot and moist, however, there were burns of the airways.

Thermal burns of the tracheobronchial tree are rare, most often caused by steam, which contains 4000 times more heat than air.[7,8] Hot air, whether dry or moist, can produce a rapidly fatal obstructive edema of the larynx. This, however, is very uncommon. The inhalation injuries of the lungs are chemical injuries caused by the byproducts of incomplete combustion.[8] These produce pulmonary edema due to injury at the endothelial–epithelial interface, alveolar collapse due to decreased production of surfactant, and bronchocilliary injury. The concept of laryngospasm caused by inhalation of extremely hot gases has been suggested. The laryngospasm is supposed to prevent inhalation of gases produced by the fire (e.g., carbon monoxide). This concept, however, is just conjecture.

Identification of the Deceased

In many fire deaths, thermal injuries to the body are insignificant. Death is said to be caused by smoke inhalation. There are no distinct disfiguring burns and establishment of identity is readily performed by personal identification, photographs, or fingerprints. If a body is charred to such a degree that facial structures are mutilated and no fingerprints can be obtained, other methods of identification must be used. Most commonly, this is dental identification. In all severely burned bodies where fingerprints are unobtainable, dental charts should be prepared and X-rays of the jaws obtained. These can be used to compare with the dental X-rays and charts of the individual who is believed to be the deceased. While dental charts and X-rays can be made with the teeth *in situ*, it is simpler to remove the jaws, especially for adequate X-raying. The jaws then can be split down the middle and more accurate lateral X-ray films taken.[9] These procedures should cause no problem with the next of kin, as the body cannot be viewed because it has been disfigured by the fire. In some cases, it is a wise practice to keep the jaws for further reference. It should be realized that dental identification utilizing X-rays does not require the presence of fillings but can be made on the bony structure of the jaws and the orientation, structure, and appearance of the teeth alone. In fact, positive dental identification can be made using only one tooth. Properly used and interpreted, dental identification is just as reliable as fingerprinting.

Another method of identification that can be just as reliable as dental identification, but is less commonly utilized, is the comparison of postmortem X-rays to the antemortem X-rays of the individual the deceased is suspected of being. If one has a tentative identification on a body, one should inquire whether the individual ever had any trauma or even a routine chest

X-ray. These X-rays can then be obtained to use for comparison with those of the unidentified body. X-rays of virtually any area of the body can be suitable for comparison. Identification can be based not only on peculiarities of the bones but on soft tissue calcification; enteric accretions (e.g., gallstones, kidney stones, etc.) and opaque stints, filters, clips, surgical screws, etc. Positive identification might be made on either a cluster of relatively common changes or a single unique finding.

If identification cannot be made by fingerprints, dental records or X-ray, then positive identification can be made by DNA techniques. If none of the aforementioned methods of identification is possible, then only a tentative identification based on circumstances; personal possessions; or nonspecific characteristics such as tattoos, scars, or absence of organs, can be made.

Cremation

The most thorough study of the changes a body undergoes as it is burned is by Bohnert et al., who observed the cremation of 15 bodies.[10] The 15 bodies, in either oak or fir coffins, were cremated at temperatures between 670 and 810°C. It took between 2 and 3 h to reduce the bodies to ash and pieces of calcined bone. Cremation of a body in a crematorium occurs under controlled conditions where the body is continuously exposed to a uniform heat source. This is not true in accidental fires, where exposure to the fire might be intermittent and the temperature of the fire might fluctuate, never reaching that of a crematorium. Thus, in the article by Bohnert et al., the time taken to go from one stage of cremation to another is not so important, but rather the sequence of the changes that occur as a body burns.

Bohnert et al. found that, 10 min into the cremation, the scalp had burned away, exposing the cranial vault, which was not calcined. The soft tissue of the face was charred. After 20 minutes, the external table showed fissures or the coronal and saggital sutures burst. By 30 min, there were large gaping fractures in the cranial vault with the external table beginning to fragment. The facial bones were calcined with only sparse soft tissue, if any. By 40 min, the calvarium had burned away, exposing a shrunken and blackened brain. The facial bones were free of soft tissue, calcined and disintegrating. The soft tissue of the neck was absent in half the cases and charred in the rest. By 50 min, the base of the skull was visible and the facial bones disintegrating. By 60 min, only the core of the facial bones and the base of the skull were left.

As to the trunk, after 20 min, the skin of the anterior chest was burned away, exposing charred muscle. In slightly more than half the cases, the anterior aspect of the ribs was visible, with the sternum and costal cartilage burned away in three of these cases. By 30 min, the thoracic and abdominal cavities were exposed, with the internal organs blackened and shrunken except for the intestines, which, though blackened anteriorly, were moist posteriorly. The anterior aspect of the ribs was calcined. After 40 min, the ribs were exposed and calcined up to the posterior axillary lines. The thoracic and abdominal organs, which were shrunken with a sponge-like surface, were, with the exception of the liver, unrecognizable by 50 min and reduced to ash by 60 min.

In regard to the extremities, after 20 min, the skin of the arms and legs was burned away, with the exposed muscle charred and the radius and ulna partially visible. The bones of the hands were visible, calcined and connected by charred soft tissue, except in cases where they were completely destroyed. The forearms were generally reduced to their proximal portions by 30 min and absent by 40 min. The upper arms were largely devoid of soft tissue by 40 min, with the head of the humerus visible and the humeri calcined with extensive longitudinal fractures. As to the legs, by 30 min the distal femurs and the tibiae were mostly free of soft tissue, with the exposed bones calcined with longitudinal fractures with rolled-up edges. By 50 min, the arms were gone and the femurs reduced to calcined stumps.

Causes of Fires

Smoking is a common cause of house fires. In some situations, one might not know whether the individual was a smoker and, if so, whether this was a possible cause of the fire. One can always analyze urine for the presence of nicotine, which would suggest that the deceased was a smoker.

Children are often the initiators as well as the victims of fires. This is often associated with lack of supervision — either none for an extended time or inadequate quality of supervision. Often, children start the fires that kill them. When a fire does start, children tend to panic and hide in closets, under beds, or in bathrooms. In urban areas, where there is extensive substandard housing, fires with the death of large numbers of children are not uncommon. The reaction of authorities is to arrest the parent for criminal negligent homicide and endangering the welfare of the dead children. This usually eases the conscience of the officials, who are often responsible for the social conditions that led to the situation that resulted in the fire and deaths.

Homicide by Fire

Deaths in fires are, for the most part, accidental. If, however, the fire is deliberately set, these deaths are properly classified as homicides. In cases where there is suspicion of arson, a ruling as to the manner of death should be delayed until a complete investigation by the fire department is carried out.

Fires are purposely set for a number of reasons. The most common is for profit, i.e., insurance fraud. Fires might also be set for revenge, because of mental instability (pyromania), or to conceal a crime such as burglary or homicide. Arson in an attempt to burn a body or conceal the cause of death, while infrequent, occurs. Such attempts are usually in vain, as the first thing the medical examiner establishes is that the individual was dead prior to the fire. It is, in fact, extremely difficult to burn a body, because of its high water content. Thus, a body that on the outside shows extensive charring, with heat fractures and partial loss of the extremities, will often show perfect preservation of the internal viscera. Fires seldom generate a high enough temperature, over a long enough time, to cremate a body. The temperatures to which the body is exposed fluctuate widely, depending on the materials burning; how rapidly they are consumed; what new materials, if any, replace the burned materials and how rapidly firefighters intervene. Outside a crematorium, fires lack the intensity and the time to completely incinerate a human body. The only way to properly cremate a body outside a crematorium is to elevate it on a grill-like structure, so that as it burns, the melting fat will feed the fire and contribute to the consumption of the body.

Self Immolation

Self immolation is rare. Individuals usually douse themselves with a flammable liquid, generally gasoline, and set themselves on fire. The container and matches (cigarette lighter) are usually present at the scene. These should be examined for fingerprints. Generally, individuals incur second- or third-degree burns over most of their bodies, with the burns more concentrated on the front. Death may not be immediate; rather, the individuals die of complications of their burns. In a study of 32 cases by Shkum and Johnston, 56.25% of individuals were dead at the scene.[11] This corresponds almost exactly with the study of Leth and Hart-Madsen, who found that 56% of the deaths in their series of 43 cases occurred at the scene.[12]

The forensic pathologist should retain portions of clothing for the analysis of volatile substances. This clothing should be placed in a glass container with a screw-top cap. It should not be placed in a plastic bag, as the volatile material may escape through the plastic. Another way to preserve clothing for examination for volatile substances is to place it in a clean paint can and close the can. One might also want to pick up soil from beneath where the individuals initially ignited themselves to analyze for the presence of volatile substances.

In deaths caused by self immolation, comment is often made that blood carbon monoxide concentrations may not be elevated but be in the normal range since these are "flash" fires. What is often not appreciated is that, in most deaths caused by self-immolation and in most deaths caused by flash fire, carbon monoxide is elevated. It is when the self immolation occurs outdoors or in a large enclosure (a large room) that one tends to get a low or negative carbon monoxide. Even here, carbon monoxide may be elevated. Shkum and Johnston reviewed 32 cases of self immolation, 18 of which involved individuals dead at the scene.[11] Eleven of the 18 died in motor vehicles. The accelerants used in these 11 cases were gasoline in 9 cases, kerosene in one and propane in one. All 11 individuals had elevated carbon monoxide ranging from 28% to 80% with an average of 58%.

Five individuals killed themselves in houses. Carbon monoxide levels were 9, 11, 14, 33 and 38%. The average was 21%. Two individuals died outdoors. Their carbon monoxide levels were 17 and 25%. In the review by Leth and Hart-Madsen, six of seven individuals testing negative for carbon monoxide committed suicide in the open air, with the seventh in a large room.[12] Only two of their cases occurred in a motor vehicle and both of those had a carbon monoxide of greater than 50%. Thus, it appears that, in small enclosures such as a motor vehicle, self immolation can result in high carbon monoxide levels. In larger enclosures or the outdoors, carbon monoxide may range from "normal," to slightly elevated to moderately elevated.

This section would not be complete without mention of spontaneous human combustion. This phenomenon or concept is absurd and warrants no further discussion.

Scalding Burns

Scalding burns are of three types: immersion burns following accidental or deliberate immersion in a hot liquid, usually water; splash or spill burns — usually accidental — and steam burns caused by exposure to superheated steam. Hot water accounts for most of the immersion, spill, and splash burns (Figure 13.9). These may be homicidal or accidental. Scalding of children is a common form of child abuse (see Chapter 12). While most splash burns are accidents, the authors have seen cases where individuals have boiled water, then intentionally thrown it on a victim. These are usually domestic homicides, with the victim the husband. The severe nature of burns from boiling water is appreciated when one realizes that water heated to 158°F can cause a full-thickness burn in adult skin in 1 s of contact.[2] Splash burns in accidents tend to be multiple and of varying depths.

Accidental spill burns typically involve children in kitchens who pull a pot, or cup of hot tea, coffee or water down onto themselves. The burns are on the face, neck, upper chest, and arms. Clothing protects the skin from these burns. The hot fluid cools as it falls onto the skin and flows down the body, producing superficial scald burns with a red, moist surface. As the fluid moves down the body, the burns become progressively less severe.

An individual exposed to superheated steam sustains severe scald-like burns of the body. With inhalation, there are laryngeal, tracheal, and respiratory burns. The latter may progress to adult respiratory distress syn-

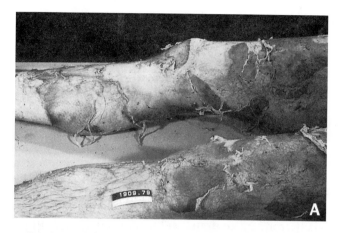

Figure 13.9 (A) and (B) Scalding burns. Deceased fell into vat of hot fluid (160°F). Hair did not burn.

drome. In some instances, there is massive edema of the larynx, with an asphyxial death.

Chemical Burns

In chemical burns, the amount of tissue damaged depends on the agent, its strength and concentration, the quantity of the chemical, the duration of contact, and the extent of penetration of the body by the chemical. Chemicals continue to act on tissue until they are either neutralized by another agent or inactivated by the tissue reaction.[13]

Chemicals coagulate protein by reduction, oxidation, salt formation, corrosion, protoplasmic poisoning, metabolic competition or inhibition, desiccation, or as a result of the ischemic complication of vesicants. More simply, chemical burns are classified as caused by acids, alkali, and vesicants (blister-producing substances).

Strong acids generally have a pH of less than 2. Alkaline agents usually need a pH of 11.5 or greater to injure tissue. The percentage of chemical in a solution will usually determine the degree of tissue damage. Alkalies produce more severe injury than acids because they tend to dissolve protein and saponify fat. They produce a liquefaction necrosis, permitting deeper invasion of tissue by chemicals, with deep burns and marked edema. In contrast, acids precipitate protein, producing a coagulation necrosis with a resultant hard eschar, or scab. The burns produced by acid tend to be clearly demarcated, dry, and hard. Edema is mild. The burns are often second-degree-deep partial-thickness. If there is prolonged contact, there can be third-degree burns, especially from concentrated sulfuric or nitric acid. In this case, the scab tends to be dark, leather-like, and dry. Hydrofluoric acid gives much deeper burns than most acids. The color of the eschar depends to a degree on the acid. Nitric acid produces a yellow scab; sulfuric, black or brown; hydrochloric, white or gray; and phenol, light gray or light brown.

Some agents, such as phenol, yellow phosphorus, and ammonium sulfide, cause not only chemical burns but systemic poisoning. Thus, phenol is associated with acute tubular necrosis; phosphorus with liver and kidney necrosis.

Some very common compounds can produce chemical burns. Prolonged contact with gasoline or cement can result in chemical burns. Cement has a pH of 12.5 to 14 and thus is a very strong alkaline compound. Prolonged contact with hydrocarbons, such as gasoline, can cause chemical burns through their irritant effect and their high lipid solubility (Figure 13.10). The latter permits dissolution of fatty tissue. Gasoline chemical burns are partial-thickness burns.

Microwave Burns

Microwaves create heat through molecular agitation. The greater the water content of a particular tissue, the greater the heat produced. Thus, muscle, which has more water than fat, tends to be heated more than fat. While conventional ovens employing radiant heat cook from the outside in, microwaves directly heat the internal tissue. With radiant heat, the maximum injury occurs to the outside of the body, while with microwave ovens, the opposite may occur.

Burns caused by microwave ovens, as reported in the literature, tend to be indirect. These are usually cases where a microwave heats a liquid to a very high temperature and the person ingests the liquid without realizing how hot it is. Direct microwave injures are rare. Those having forensic relations are even rarer. Alexander et al. reported two children who incurred full- and partial-thickness burns caused by being placed in microwave ovens.[14] The burns were well demarcated without charring. Biopsies of the burns in

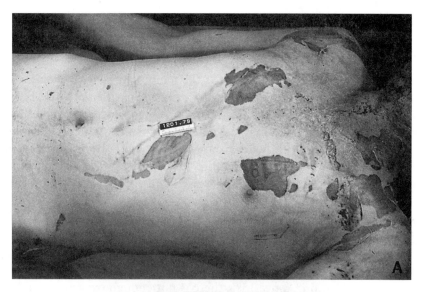

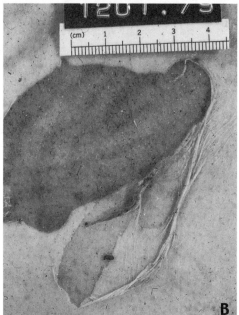

Figure 13.10 (A) and (B) Postmortem chemical burns caused by gasoline.

one case showed sparing of different tissues, with a sandwich-type appearance to the burns. Thus, there were burns of the skin, sparing of the subcutaneous fat, and burns of the muscle. The burns were based on the distribution of water in these tissues.

Miscellaneous

Flash Fires: Fires Involving Flammable Hydrocarbon Liquids

The flash point of hydrocarbons is the temperature at which sufficient fuel has evaporated to sustain a brief flash of fire. The flame, however, will not continue to burn until the hydrocarbon reaches a slightly higher temperature, the flame or fire point. Here, the flame will continue to burn until the fuel is consumed. With hydrocarbon fuels, it is the vapors from evaporation that burn, not the fuel. When the vapor ignites, it raises the temperature of the hydrocarbon, causing increased and rapid evaporation of fuel and thus sustaining the fire.

Hydrocarbon fuels have a characteristic range of concentrations over which they vaporize and will burn. This is their flammability range. For example, for natural gas (which is principally methane), it is between 4 and 15%. At vapor concentrations below 4%, there is not enough vaporized fuel to sustain combustion. Above 15%, there is not enough oxygen available to sustain combustion. Thus, natural gas will only burn when the vapor concentration is between 4 and 15%. The flame in a flash fire moves out in all directions from the point of ignition. After the initial flash, the ensuing fire causes evaporation of fuel that then sustains the fire.[15] The temperature in flash fires from hydrocarbon fuels is around 500 to 975°C.

In flash fires in rooms, within 45 s of ignition, the oxygen falls markedly and the CO_2 rises proportionately. CO production follows 15 to 30 s after the maximum temperature, occurring as oxygen is depleted. Oxygen can fall to 8.5% in 1.5 to 3 min, while CO_2 can increase up to 12 to 16% in less than 1.5 min. In the initial portion of the fires, the CO might reach a concentration of 9500 parts per million in a matter of 1.5 to 2 min. If the flash fire is confined to a limited space such as one room and there is no significant introduction of new air the fire will go out through lack of sufficient oxygen.

Flashover

Fires in confined spaces such as a room can produce a phenomenon called a **flashover**. Once a fire starts, even if it is initially small, it produces radiant heat, hot gases and smoke. The gases and smoke rise, forming a layer immediately below the ceiling. As the smoke and hot gases accumulate, this layer thickens, extending downward toward the floor. Initially, the hot gases heat the ceiling and adjacent upper walls. Radiant heat from the fire and hot gases begin to heat objects in the lower portion of the room. The combustible materials in the room begin to give off flammable gases (this process is called pyrolysis). If the original fire burns out, or if sufficient oxygen cannot get into the room, the fire dies out. If, however, the fire continues to burn, at some point the combustible objects in the room reach their ignition temper- atures. If this occurs more or less simultaneously, flame sweeps over the room involving most combustible objects. This is called flashover. The pre-flash- over period lasts 5–20 min in most circumstances. Time to flashover cannot be predicted with certainty, as it depends on many factors (e.g., fuel, oxygen supply). The temperature in a room at time of flashover is between 500–600°C or 932–1112°F.

References

1. National Safety Council, Accident Facts (1998) Itasca. IL.

2. Moritz AR and Henriques FC, Studies of thermal injury: II. The relative importance of time and surface temperature in the causation of cutaneous burns. *Am J Pathol* 1947; 23:695-720.

3. Ripple GR, Torrington KG, and Phillips YY, Predictive criteria for burns from brief thermal exposures. *J Occ Med.* 32(3):215-9, 1990.

4. McAnnalley BH, et al., Determination of inorganic sulfide and cyanide in blood using specific ion electrodes: Application to the investigation of hydro- gen sulfide and cyanide poisoning. *J Anal Toxicol* 1979; 3:111-114.

5. Silverman SH, et al., Cyanide toxicity in burned patients. *J Trauma* 1988; 28:171-176.

6. Lowry WT, et al., Free radical production from controlled low energy fires: Toxicity consideration. *J Forens Sci* 1985; 30:73-85.

7. Moritz AR, Henriques FC, and McLean R. The effects of inhaled heat on the air passages and lungs. *Am J Pathol* 1945; 21:311-331.

8. Zajtchuk R, (Ed.), *Textbook of Military Medicine*, Part I, Volume 5, Conven- tional Warfare: Ballistics, Blast and Burn Injuries. U.S. Government Printing Office, Washington, D.C. 1991.

9. Norton LE, The Norton technique for dental identification. *Forens Sci Gaz* 1978; 9(4):1-2.

10. Bohnert M, Rost T, and Pollak S, The degree of destruction of human bodies in relation to the duration of the fire. *Forens Sci. Intern*, 1998 95:11-21.

11. Shkum MJ and Johnston KA, Fire and suicide: a three year study of self- immolation deaths. *J. Forens Science.* 1992 37(1):208-221.

12. Leth P and Hart-Madsen M, Suicide by self-incineration. *Am J Forens Med Path*, 1997 18(2):113-118.

13. Jelenko C, Chemicals that "burn." *J Trauma* 1974; 14:65-72..

14. Alexander RC, Surrell JA, and Cohle SD, Microwave oven burns to children: An unusual manifestation of child abuse. *Pediatrics* 1987; 79:255-260.

15. Deltaan JD, The Dynamics of Flash Fires Involving Flammable Hydrocarbon liquids *Am J Forens Med Path*, 17 (1): 24-31, 1996.

Carbon Monoxide Poisoning

14

Carbon monoxide (CO) is a colorless, odorless, tasteless, non-irritating gas whose relative density is a little less than that of air. The most common sources of carbon monoxide in deaths are fires, automobile exhaust, defective heaters, and incomplete combustion of burning products, such as charcoal briquets. Carbon monoxide is produced whenever organic materials are burned with an inadequate supply of oxygen necessary to produce complete combustion. Excluding deaths during fires, there are approximately 2700 deaths caused by carbon monoxide annually in the U.S. Approximately 2000 of these are suicides and 700 are accidents.[1] Virtually all the suicides involve inhalation of automobile exhaust.

Mechanism of Action

Carbon monoxide produces tissue hypoxia by competing with oxygen for binding sites on the oxygen-carrying hemeproteins (hemoglobin, myoglobin, cytochrome c oxidase, cytochrome P-450).[2] The affinity of carbon monoxide for hemeproteins varies from 30 to 500 times as much as oxygen, depending on the hemeproteins.[2,3] For hemoglobin, it is from 250 to 300 times greater than that for oxygen. In addition to the greater affinity of hemoglobin for carbon monoxide, the presence of carboxyhemoglobin alters the oxygen affinity of the hemoglobin by shifting the oxyhemoglobin dissociation curve to the left, decreasing the release of oxygen to tissue. This results in a hypoxia of the tissue greater than what would be produced by an equivalent degree of anemia. It is believed that carbon monoxide has a direct toxic effect at the cellular level by impairing mitochondrial respiration, caused by carbon monoxide's binding to the cytochrome oxidase complex.[4] Unlike hemoglobin, the affinity of cytochrome oxidase is much greater for oxygen. However, during cellular anoxia, carbon monoxide might bind. When the oxygen atmosphere is returned, the displacement of carbon monoxide is slow.

The percent saturation of carbon monoxide is defined as the percentage of hemoglobin combined with carbon monoxide in the form of carboxyhemoglobin. Because of the greater affinity of hemoglobin for carbon monoxide, extremely low concentrations in the atmosphere can produce very high blood saturation with this gas. A concentration of 0.5 to 1% (5–10,000 parts per million) in the atmosphere can produce carboxyhemoglobin saturation levels of 75% in 2 to 15 min (Table 14.1). Humidity, high environmental temperature, high altitude and physical activity increase the respiratory rate and, thus, the absorption of carbon monoxide. The Occupational Safety and Health Administration (OSHA) recommended maximum allowable exposure limit is 35 ppm over 8 h.[5] For safety purposes, workers exposed to carbon monoxide should never have a blood carboxyhemoglobin level above 5%. In practice, this is not always possible. While non-smokers have blood carboxyhemoglobin levels of 1–3%, smokers often have "normal" levels of carboxyhemoglobin of 5–6%, commonly reach 10% and may even exceed 15%.[6] Blood carboxyhemoglobin levels of 10–14% have been observed in firefighters after a blaze.[7] Elevated levels of carboxyhemoglobin (up to 13%) can also be found in police officers working in tunnels or workers in garages where motor vehicles are running, if the individuals are also smokers.

Deaths from Motor Vehicle Exhaust

After fires, the second most common source of carbon monoxide in fatalities is inhalation of the exhaust fumes of automobiles. Most such deaths are suicide, but accidental deaths do occur. These are due almost exclusively to a faulty vehicle, though deaths have happened when cars have been trapped in snow. Some deaths have occurred while the vehicle was in motion, and some with partly open (2- to 4-in)windows.[8]

Rarely, accidental deaths occur when a car is started and left running in a garage to warm up while the driver goes back to the house. Carbon mon-

Table 14.1   Time Required for Various Concentrations of Carbon Monoxide to Produce 80% Equilibrium Value of Blood Saturation

Concentration of CO in air (%)	Blood Saturation (%)	Time
0.02-0.03	23-30	5-6 h
0.04-0.06	36-44	4-5 h
0.07-0.10	47-53	3-4 h
0.11-0.15	55-60	1.5-3 h
0.16-0.20	61-64	1-1.5 h
0.20-0.30	64-68	30-45 min
0.30-0.50	68-73	20-30 min
0.50-1.00	73-76	2-15 min

Reproduced from Von Oettingen WF, *Carbon Monoxide: Its Hazards and the Mechanism of Its Action,* U.S. Public Health Service, Bulletin 290. Washington, D.C., U.S. Government Printing Office.

oxide from the exhaust then leaks into the house, killing the residents. Occasionally, someone commits suicide in a garage by leaving the car running, and, at the same time, inadvertently kills the occupants of the house as well.

The quantity of CO produced by a gasoline engine depends on a number of factors, including idling speed, air–fuel ratio, compression ratio, and the presence of a catalytic converter. Prior to the introduction of catalytic converters, an idling engine could produce 7% CO, while the same engine in a vehicle traveling at 60 mph, with the carburetor adjusted for efficient operation, produced less than 0.5% CO.[9] Diesel engines have traditionally produced smaller quantities of carbon monoxide than gasoline engines.

By 1975, most new cars were equipped with catalytic converters designed to convert CO to CO_2. The 1980s saw the introduction of even more sophisticated converters, oxygen sensors and computers to increase the efficiency of the converters. Catalytic converters, if properly adjusted, eliminate most of the carbon monoxide, meaning that idling engines can produce exhaust with less than 0.1% CO.[10] Because of this, forensic pathologists have begun to see occasional deaths caused by inhalation of exhaust fumes in which the CO level is in the normal range.[11] Such deaths are thought to be caused by displacement of oxygen by CO_2, the toxic effects of CO_2, and possibly the actions of other compounds in the exhaust.

Catalytic converters have limitations. They do not become fully operational until they and the engine reach a certain temperature. Thus, there is an initial rise in CO exhaust to a high level with a subsequent decline to a constant lower level. The warmer the engine, and, thus, the converter, prior to starting, the lower the maximum CO level.[10] If the catalytic converter becomes overheated, it becomes less efficient.

Survival Time

Survival time in an atmosphere heavily saturated with carbon monoxide is short. Flanagan et al. reported a case in which the individual committing suicide left a tape recorder on, recording his dying sounds.[12] On the basis of this, a determination could be made on how long the person survived. The deceased was a 36-year-old male found sitting in a car, with the engine running and a rubber hose running from the exhaust through the rear window of the car. Blood carboxyhemoglobin was 70% saturation. The tape recorder was on the front passenger seat. On the tape, the deceased was heard to start the car engine. For 20 min a variety of sounds were heard, after which they ceased, although the tape continued to run. Reconstruction of the scene allowed continuous monitoring of the buildup of carbon monoxide in the car. After the engine had been running 1 min, the percent carbon monoxide saturation in the atmosphere was 0.2%. At 5 min, it was 1.5%; at 6 min, 1.7%; at 7 min, 2.2%; at 9 min, 2.5%; at 13 min, 3.7%; and by 17 min it was over 4%.

The tape showed occasional coughing at 2 min, with vigorous coughing and retching at 3 min. By 5 min, there was severe coughing and expiratory wheezing with marked inspiratory stridor. By 6 min, the coughing had gradually lessened in intensity, with respiration becoming shallow, but increasing in rate. At 7 min, there was shallow respiration, with the rate slowing and intermittent periods of apnea. At 9 min, the respiratory rate was 6 per min. At 13 min, there was a definite change in the pattern, felt to be that of a comatose or stuporous type. There was a prolonged expiratory phase. At 17 min, the respiratory frequency was 3 per minute. The last sound heard was at approximately 20 min. The authors concluded that, while it was difficult to decide at what stage the situation became irretrievable, certainly by 6–7 minutes, there was evidence of rapid downhill progress.

Elevated Temperatures in Passenger Compartment Caused by Exhaust

Carbon monoxide diverted into the passenger compartment of an automobile can significantly raise the temperature in this space. Thus, a 26-year-old female was found dead in a small van with a hose running from the exhaust to the left side door window.[9] Blood carboxyhemoglobin was 41.5%. The engine was tested and found to produce 3.3% CO in the exhaust gases while idling. The CO concentration of the cabin rose sharply, peaking at 0.7–0.8% in 25–35 min, plateauing at this level for 10–15 min, and gradually decreasing to 0.3% at 90 min. The exhaust gases caused a gradual rise in cabin temperature from 21.6 to 40.50°C in the front of the cabin and to 34.9°C at the rear. This elevation in cabin temperature is consistent with the observation that many individuals found dead of carbon monoxide poisoning in automobiles show postmortem slippage of the skin, though they have been dead only a short time.

Outdoor Deaths Caused by Carbon Monoxide

DiMaio and Dana reported three deaths as a result of inhalation of carbon monoxide from automobile exhaust fumes while outdoors.[13] Blood carboxyhemoglobin concentrations ranged from 58% (in a decomposing body) to 81%. All individuals were found lying adjacent to the exhaust pipe of an automobile. Two deaths were suicides. These cases illustrate the fact that, even in the outdoors, deaths from carbon monoxide inhalation can occur if the individual is in proximity to a rich source of carbon monoxide for a prolonged time.

Carbon Monoxide Deaths from Sources Other than Exhaust

Charcoal briquets are made to smolder, not burn with a flame. The incomplete burning that takes place produces carbon monoxide. Thus, if these grills are used in an unventilated environment such as a residence, garage, trailer, tent, or even a porch, death can be caused by the large amount of carbon monoxide produced. Occasionally, individuals camping out will use charcoal briquets to keep warm. This has resulted in a number of fatal CO poisonings. Carbon monoxide poisoning has also occurred with natural and butane gas heaters following buildup of carbon deposits, with resultant incomplete combustion of gas.

Carbon monoxide can get into the air tanks of scuba divers. Here, carbon monoxide emitted by gasoline-driven compressors might be accidentally sucked up and mixed with the air being pumped into the scuba air tanks.

Decomposition and Carbon Monoxide

Carbon monoxide levels in blood and body cavity fluids of decomposed bodies are dependent on the carbon monoxide level of the blood prior to the death. They are not produced by postmortem carbon monoxide formation through the decomposition of hemoglobin, myoglobin, and other substances. Dominguez et al. found that carboxyhemoglobin saturation in blood was not markedly altered during postmortem decomposition, with values of not more than 6% determined in dogs submerged in seawater for 4 d.[14] They also found that carboxyhemoglobin saturation in blood was not significantly different from that in the fluids of the thoracic cavities.

Signs and Symptoms of Carbon Monoxide Poisoning

The studies by Haldane and Killick probably give the best description of the effects of exposure to carbon monoxide (CO).[15,16] The symptoms, when they appear, are progressive, roughly paralleling the blood levels of CO. Initially, the signs and symptoms are often subtle. At levels of 0–10% carboxyhemoglobin saturation, there are generally no symptoms. In individuals at rest, CO levels from 10 to 20% are often symptomless, except for a headache. If tested, however, these individuals will show impairment in the execution of complex tasks. Haldane experienced no ill effects at levels up to 18–23%. Killick's symptoms were negligible below 30%, though, between 30 and 35%, she had a headache with throbbing and fullness of the head.[16] Between 30–40% CO, there was a throbbing headache, nausea, vomiting, faintness and drowsiness even at rest. As levels approach 40%, the slightest exertion caused faintness. Pulse and respiration are rapid. Blood pressure falls. Between 40–60% CO, there is mental confusion, weakness and loss of coordination. Haldane at 56% was unable to walk unaided.[15] At 60% CO and beyond, individuals lose consciousness, develop Cheyne-Stokes respiration, have intermittent convulsions, depressed heart action and respiratory failure, and die. An elevated body temperature may be present.

Fatal Levels of Carbon Monoxide

The carboxyhemoglobin levels of individuals who die of CO poisoning can vary greatly, depending on the source of the CO, the circumstances surrounding the death, and the health of the individual. In elderly individuals, and those suffering severe diseases, such as coronary artery disease or chronic obstructive pulmonary disease, saturations as low as 20–30% can be fatal. Carboxyhemoglobin levels in house fires average 57%, with carbon monoxide levels of 30 or 40% common. In contrast, in individuals dying from the inhalation of exhaust fumes, levels are mostly over 70%, averaging 79%. Low levels in individuals dying of inhalation of exhaust fumes might be found if the car stops running after the victims are in an irreversible coma but continue breathing, gradually decreasing their carboxyhemoglobin concentration in spite of irreversible hypoxic injury to the brain. The half-life of carbon monoxide, breathing room air at sea level, is approximately 4–6 h. Oxygen therapy reduces the half-life elimination, depending on the concentration of oxygen. Half-life elimination with oxygen therapy is shortened to 40–80 min breathing 100% oxygen at 1 atm, and 15–30 min breathing hyperbaric oxygen.[6] If an individual reaches an emergency room alive, a pulse oximeter cannot be relied on to accurately determine oxygenation levels. It cannot distinguish carboxyhemoglobin from oxyhemoglobin at the usual wavelengths employed.[17,18]

Suicide or Accident

In suicides from CO, the diagnosis is often immediately apparent at the scene. A victim will usually be found either in a garage or a car with the ignition on. The car may be running, but more commonly is not. Pipes or hoses connected to the exhaust might lead into the compartment of the vehicle.

Accidental deaths caused by carbon monoxide can be subtle in their presentation. A person might be found dead in a parked car with the ignition on and the motor either running or stalled. Death is caused by carbon monoxide entering a defect in the vehicle. An investigator, however, could mistakenly ascribe the cause of death to heart disease. When more than one individual is found dead in a car whose ignition is on, almost inevitably, death is caused by CO. If more than one person is found dead in a residence, or one individual dead and others comatose, without any evidence of trauma, the first agent one should suspect is carbon monoxide poisoning caused by a defective heating unit.

Sometimes, people will try to make a suicide look like an accident. They will be found in a garage, with the door closed, the ignition of the car on, the hood open, and tools on the fender. The expected conclusion is that such individuals were overcome by exhaust fumes while repairing the vehicle. Such cases, however, are invariably suicide. This is because, if one were to run a car in a closed garage, within 2–3 min the atmosphere would be so noxious, so irritating to the respiratory system, that one could not effect any repair at all. It would be necessary to turn the car off and open the garage door to let the fumes escape.

Autopsy Findings

Autopsy findings in CO deaths are fairly characteristic. In Caucasians, the first impression one gets on viewing the body is that the person looks very healthy. The pink complexion is caused by coloration of the tissue by carboxyhemoglobin, which has a characteristic cherry-red or bright-pink appearance that can be seen in the tissue. Cherry-red livor mortis suggests the diagnosis even before autopsying the individual. It must be realized, however, that this color can be simulated by prolonged exposure of the body to a cold environment (either at the scene of death or in a morgue "cooler") or cyanide poisoning. With blacks, the discoloration is prominent in the conjunctivae, nailbeds, and mucosa of the lips.

Internally, the musculature and the internal viscera will have a bright cherry-red coloration. This coloration of the viscera will persist even if tissue is removed and placed in formaldehyde. Nor will embalming change the color of the viscera. Blood withdrawn from the vessels will also have this characteristic color. This is not invariable, however. One of the authors autopsied an individual with a carboxyhemoglobin level of 45% in whom the characteristic coloration was not present. He at first ascribed the cause of death to heart disease. The individual had such a "healthy complexion." However, the author's suspicions were aroused enough to order a carbon monoxide determination. Death had been caused by CO, produced by a defective heating unit in the residence.

While elevated CO levels are virtually the rule in house fires, there might be no elevation of CO in a death from a flash fire that occurs in an open environment. Individuals who die in motor vehicle accidents in which a gas tank explodes, theoretically might not show an elevated carbon monoxide. This latter occurrence is very rare, usually involving unusual circumstances.

In some individuals, death from carboxyhemoglobin poisoning is not immediate. In such cases, if production of the carbon monoxide ceases after the onset of irreversible coma, the individual will gradually eliminate the carbon monoxide from the body, even though irreversible injury has occurred. Thus, the authors have seen individuals who died from carboxyhemoglobin poisoning register low or even negative carboxyhemoglobin levels at autopsy. Such a diagnosis is made on the basis of scene investigation. For example, a man is found dead in a parked car. The ignition is on and the gas tank is empty. An autopsy and complete toxicological analysis fail to reveal a cause of death. Examination of the car, however, reveals defects in the exhaust system such that high concentrations of CO built up in the car while it was running.

Carbon monoxide can pass from the maternal to the fetal blood. The carboxyhemoglobin (COHB) concentration of the fetus is dependent on the percent saturation of the mother's hemoglobin with CO. Saturation of fetal hemoglobin with CO lags behind saturation of the maternal hemoglobin because of the slow dissociation of maternal carboxyhemoglobin. After a time, however, equilibrium will be reached. The final COHB is 10% higher than maternal COHB.[19] Carbon monoxide can produce intrauterine death of the infant even though the mother may survive.

The brain is the organ most sensitive to the actions of carbon monoxide. Brain damage is characteristically localized to certain selective areas. If death does not occur immediately, the injury to these areas may increase over hours and days. Carbon monoxide produces selective injury to the cerebral gray matter. Bilateral necrosis of the globus pallidus is the most characteristic lesion, though other affected areas include the cerebral cortex, hippocampus, cerebellum, and substantia nigra. The lesions in the globus pallidus, however, are nonspecific and can be seen in drug overdoses as well.

Neurological *sequelae* caused by CO poisoning can develop during the acute phase of poisoning or post exposure after a period ranging from days to weeks without overt symptoms.[20–23] In this situation, after an asymptomatic interval, the patient can develop severe headache, fever, nuchal rigidity, and neuropsychiatric symptoms. Transitory cortical blindness and memory defects are common. In addition, there can be aphasia, apathy, disorientation, hallucinations, incontinence, slow movements, and muscular rigidity. The permanent *sequelae* of CO intoxication include dementia, amnestic syndromes, psychosis, paralysis, chorea, cortical blindness, peripheral neuropathy, and incontinence. In a study by Choi, 11.8% of individuals requiring hospitalization for carbon monoxide poisoning exhibited delayed neurological deterioration.[22] Virtually all demonstrated mental deterioration, with the majority having incontinence and gait disturbances. The median age of the individuals showing delayed deterioration was older than that of the hospitalized group as a whole. A lucid interval of 2–4 weeks commonly preceded the onset of the neurological *sequelae*. Three-quarters of the patients recovered within a year, though some showed persistent mild neurological injury. There were no clinical signs at the time of admission that would permit the physician to deduce which patients would incur the delayed neurological injury.

It has been demonstrated that some cells, for example, CAI pyramidal cells in the hippocampus, may resume their functioning after exposure to the carbon monoxide only to die days later.[23] It has been hypothesized that this delayed injury is caused by post ischemic re-perfusion injury and the effects of CO on vascular endothelium and oxygen radical mediated brain oxygen re-oxygenation.

The delayed neurological syndrome in carbon monoxide intoxication is associated with lesions of the cerebral white matter.[21] These lesions are non-specific, however, and are found in other conditions associated with hypoxia and hypotension. It appears that a combination of hypotension and hypoxia is necessary to produce these lesions.

References

1. *National Safety Council: Accident Facts* (1998 edition). Itasca IL.

2. Caughey WS, Carbon monoxide bonding in hemeproteins. *Ann NY Acad Sci* 1970; 174:148-153.

3. Wald G and Allen DW, The equilibrium between cytochrome oxidase and carbon monoxide. *J Gen Physiol* 1957; 40:593-608.

4. Dolan MC, Carbon monoxide poisoning. *Can Med Assoc* 11985; 133:392399.

5. Occupational Safety and Health Administration. Occupational Safety and Health Guideline for Carbon Monoxide, http:/www.osha-slc.gov/SLTC/healthguidelines/carbonmonoxide/recognition.html.

6. Ernst A and Zibrak JD, Carbon monoxide poisoning (Current concepts). *NEJM* 1998; 339(22):1603-1608.

7. Radford EP and Levine MS, Occupational exposure to carbon monoxide in Baltimore firefighters. *J Occup Med* 1976; 18:628-632.

8. Baker SP, et al., Fatal unintentional carbon monoxide poisoning in motor vehicles. *Am J Public Health* 1972; 62:1463-1467.

9. Tsunenari S, et al., Suicidal carbon monoxide inhalation of exhaust fumes. *Am J Forens Med Pathol* 1985;6:233-239.

10. Morgen C, et al., Automobile exhaust as a means of suicide: an experimental study with a proposed model. *J Forens Sci*, 1998; 43(4):827-836.

11. Atkinson P, et al., Suicide, carbon dioxide and suffocation. *Lancet.* 1994; 344:192-3.

12. Flanagan NG, et al., An unusual case of carbon monoxide poisoning. *Med Sci Law* 1978; 18:117-119.

13. DiMaio VJM and Dana SE, Deaths caused by carbon monoxide poisoning in an open environment (outdoors). *J Forens Sci* 1987; 32:1794-1795.

14. Dominguez A, Halstead JR, and Domanski TJ, The effect of postmortem changes on carboxyhemoglobin results. *J Forens Sci* 1964; 9:330-341.

15. Haldane J, Carbon monoxide poisoning *Brit Med J* 1930; ii 16-18.

16. Killick EM, The acclimatization of the human subject to atmospheres containing low concentration of carbon monoxide. *J Physiol* 1936; 87:41-55.

17. Buckley RG, et al., The pulse oximetry gap in carbon monoxide intoxication. *Ann Emerg Med* 1994; 24:252-255.

18. Vegfors M and Lennmarken C, Carboxyhemoglobinaemia and pulse oximetry. *Br J Anesth* 1991; 66:625-6.

19. Farrow JR, et al., Fetal death caused by nonlethal maternal carbon monoxide poisoning. *J Forens Sci*, 1990; 35(6):1448-1452.

20. Werner B, et al., Two cases of acute carbon monoxide poisoning with delayed neurological *sequelae* after a "free interval." *J Toxicol-Clin Toxicol* 1985; 23(4-6):249-265.

21. Ginsberg MD, Carbon monoxide intoxication: Clinical features, neuropathology and mechanisms of injury. *J Toxicol-Clin Toxicol* 1985; 23(46):281-288.

22. Choi HS, Delayed neurologic *sequelae* in carbon monoxide intoxication. *Arch Neurol* 1983;4:433-435.

23. Seisjo BK, Oxygen deficiency and brain damage: Localization, evaluation in time and mechanisms of damage, *J Toxicol-Clin Toxicol* 1985;23(46):267-280.

Death by Drowning

15

Drowning can be defined as death caused by submersion in a liquid. It can occur in an ocean or, in the case of alcoholic stupor, epileptics, or infants, in water as shallow as 6 in. The mechanism of death in acute drowning is irreversible cerebral anoxia. The original concept of drowning deaths was that they were asphyxial in nature, with water occluding the airways. Experiments in the late 1940s and early 1950s suggested that death was caused by electrolyte disturbances or cardiac arrhythmias produced by large volumes of water entering the circulation through the lungs.[1,2] Present thought, however, is that the original concept was correct and that the most important physiological consequence of drowning is asphyxia.[3]

In drowning, the volume of water inhaled can range from relatively small to very large. In freshwater drowning especially, large volumes of water can pass through the alveolar–capillary interface and enter the circulation. Even when large volumes of water are absorbed, there is no evidence that the increase in blood volume causes significant electrolyte irregularities or hemolysis, or that it is beyond the capacity of the heart or kidneys to compensate for the fluid overload.[3,4]

Some individuals who drown are considered to be victims of "dry drowning." Here, the lungs do not have the heavy, boggy and edematous appearance typical of drowning lungs. Rather, the fatal cerebral hypoxia is alleged to be caused by laryngeal spasm. Dry drowning is said to occur in 10–15% of all drownings. What is theorized to occur is that when a small amount of water enters the larynx or trachea, there is a sudden laryngeal spasm mediated as a vagal reflex. Thick mucous, foam, and froth may develop, producing an actual physical plug at this point. Thus, water never enters the lungs. The authors have never seen the "physical plug" said to occur in the larynx and the "laryngospasm" cannot be demonstrated at autopsy, as death causes relaxation of the musculature. While the aforementioned explanation for dry drowning is interesting, it is a hypothesis and not proven. Thus, the authors do not endorse use of this term or concept. It is probable that dry drowning is just one end of a spectrum of changes seen in the lung produced by occlusion of the airways by water, with the other end the heavy, boggy lung containing a massive amount of edema fluid.

Physiology of Drowning

When people sink beneath the surface of water, their initial reaction is to hold their breath. This continues until a breaking point is reached, at which time the individuals have to take a breath. The breaking point is determined by a combination of high carbon dioxide levels and low oxygen concentrations. According to Pearn, the breaking point occurs at PCO_2 levels below 55 mm Hg when there is associated hypoxia, and at PAO_2 levels below 100 mm Hg when the PCO_2 is high.[3]

Upon reaching the breaking point, the individual involuntarily inhales, taking in large volumes of water. Some water is also swallowed and will be found in the stomach. During this interval of submersed breathing, the patient may also vomit and aspirate some gastric contents. The involuntary gasping for air under water will continue for several minutes, until respiration ceases. The developing cerebral hypoxia will continue until it is irreversible and death occurs.

The point at which cerebral anoxia becomes irreversible is dependent on both the age of the individual and the temperature of the water. With warm water, this time is somewhere between 3 and 10 min.[3] Submersion of children in extremely cold or icy water has resulted in successful resuscitation with intact neurological outcome for as long as 66 min following drowning.[5] No matter what the time interval involved, consciousness is usually lost within 3 min of submersion.[3]

The sequence of events is:

Breath holding
Involuntary inspiration and gasping for air at the breaking point
Loss of consciousness
Death

The sequence can be altered if the individual hyperventilates prior to sinking under water. Hyperventilation can cause significant decrease in the CO_2 levels. Thus, cerebral hypoxia due to low blood PO_2, with development of unconsciousness, might occur before the breaking point is reached. In this case, the sequence would be:

Voluntary holding of breath
Unconsciousness
Aspiration of water

The type of water that is inhaled, fresh versus salt, probably has very little influence on whether the individual will survive. In fresh water, as previously noted, large volumes of water can pass through the alveolar capillary membranes. Fresh water alters or denatures pulmonary surfactant, while seawater dilutes or washes it away. [3,6] The presence of either chlorine or soap in fresh water apparently has no effect on this property.[3] The denaturization of surfactant can continue even after a person has been apparently successfully resuscitated. Loss or inactivation of pulmonary surfactant and alveolar collapse decrease lung compliance, resulting in profound ventilation perfusion mismatch with up to 75% of the blood perfusing non-ventilated areas.[7] When water is inhaled, vagal reflexes cause increased peripheral airway resistance, with pulmonary vasoconstriction, development of pulmonary hypertension, decreased lung compliance, and fall of ventilation perfusion ratios.[7] Even in individuals who are successfully resuscitated and appear healthy, redistribution of blood perfusion takes several days to return fully to its normal status.

The term "near drowning" is occasionally encountered. This refers to a submersion victim who arrives at an emergency facility and survives for 24 h.[8] This definition does not take into account whether these individuals subsequently survive or, if they survive, whether they have any neurological impairment. It is in the near drowning cases that physicians have been able to observe electrolyte changes. They have found that the electrolyte disturbances and hemoglobinemia are mild, if present at all, and rarely have any clinical significance.[3,4]

As previously mentioned, survival following prolonged underwater submersion in ice cold water may be for as long as 66 min in the case of children and infants.[5] The traditional explanations for this have been that immature brains are more resistant to anoxia and that the "diving reflex" is still present in children. The diving reflex refers to vasoconstriction in the vascular beds (except for the heart and brain), shunting of blood to the brain and heart and bradycardia, all triggered by immersion of the face in cold water. There is, however, some question as to whether the diving reflex exists in humans exactly as it does in animals.[8] Bradycardia does occur, but there has been no proof of the vasoconstriction in the vascular beds with shunting of blood to the heart and brain. Many people feel that these children survive because of the rapid development of hypothermia.[5–8] Because of the relatively large surface area and lack of adequate insulation in children, the body cools very rapidly. This is especially true in conjunction with the swallowing and aspiration of large quantities of cold fluid. There is rapid cooling of the body caused by immersion in cold water and aspiration of cold water with absorption of this water into the circulation. Thus, while in warm water, a submersion time of 3–10 min is thought to represent the maximum time prior to irreversible neurological injury, in ice water, submersion times as long as 66 min have been reported with neurological recovery.[5]

Autopsy Findings

At autopsy, there are no pathognomonic findings to indicate the diagnosis of drowning. The diagnosis is based on the circumstances of the death, plus a variety of nonspecific anatomical findings. Chemical tests put forth to make the diagnosis are nonspecific and essentially unreliable. A diagnosis of drowning cannot be made without a complete autopsy, especially a complete toxicological screen, because this is a diagnosis of exclusion. If individuals are found in water and all other causes of death have been excluded, they are presumed to have drowned. It must be remembered, however, that people have fatal heart attacks and fall into water, and that victims of a fatal drug overdose are occasionally "dumped" into a body of water. Attachments of heavy weights to a body to keep it under water is consistent with both homicidal and suicidal drownings, as is disposal of the body of an individual who has died from some other cause than drowning.

When a person drowns, the body sinks, assuming a position of head down, buttocks up, and extremities dangling downward. Unless there are strong currents, the body will not move very far from its initial position. In relatively shallow water, the extremities or face may bump or drag against the bottom of the body of water, often causing postmortem injuries to the face, back of the hands, knees, and toes. The crown of the head and the buttocks can be seen at water level. In deeper water, the body stays below the surface until decomposition begins and gas forms; the body then gradually rises to the surface. In very cold water, the body might stay submerged for months before decomposition creates enough gas to bring it to the surface. Depending on how long a body has been in the water, there might be evidence of animal activity, for example, fish, turtles, crabs, or shrimp. The authors have seen bodies that appear relatively intact but, when opened up, reveal complete absence of the thoracic and abdominal viscera. Examination of the exterior of the body will reveal a defect(s) in the trunk that communicates with the chest or abdominal cavity, through which water denizens have eaten their way inside, where they consume the internal viscera.

The hands and soles typically have a "washerwoman" appearance if the deceased has been in the water for more than 1–2 h (Figure 15.1). Experiments have shown that if you place the hands of a corpse in water whose temperature ranges between 10 and 18°C, initial formation of washerwoman's skin appears at the fingertips in 20–30 min (maximum of 100 min), with the whole finger involved at 50–60 min (maximum of 150 min).[9] This appearance of the hands and feet does not indicate that the deceased drowned, as it will develop whether they were alive or dead when they entered the water. The same is true for "goose flesh" (cutis anserina). This is a spasm of the erector pilae muscles caused by rigor mortis and, again, does not indicate whether the person was alive or dead when entering the water.

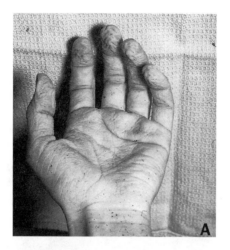

Figure 15. 1 (A and B) "Washerwoman" palms caused by prolonged immersion in water.

In the classic wet drowning, white or hemorrhagic edema fluid is present in the nostrils, mouth, and airways. Compression of the chest can cause it to flow out. Pulmonary edema is, however, nonspecific. An individual dying of a drug overdose and disposed of in water can also have pulmonary edema. The lungs of the typical wet drowning victim are large and bulky, completely occupying their respective pleural cavities. On cut section, they usually have a brick-red appearance, with large quantities of edema fluid flowing from the cut surfaces (Figure 15.2). A white or hemorrhagic foam is commonly found in the trachea and bronchi. Water may be found in the lumen of the

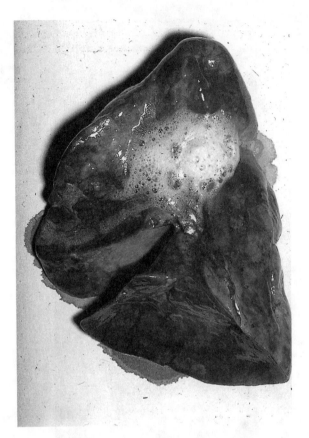

Figure 15.2 Hemorrhagic pulmonary edema.

stomach. There could be dilatation of the right ventricle. When the brain is examined, it is swollen with flattening of the gyri caused by nonspecific brain swelling.

Hemorrhage may appear in the petrous or mastoid bones. This, again, is nonspecific and, if sought, can be found in individuals dying of heart disease, drug overdose, or other causes of death. Thus, the drug overdose victim dumped in water and the heart attack victim collapsing into water can have the washerwoman appearance of the palms and soles, goose flesh, pulmonary edema, and hemorrhage into the petrous and mastoid bones. The presence of vegetation and stones such as would be found at the bottom of the body of water found clutched in the hands indicates that the cause of death was, in fact, drowning, because they imply that the deceased was alive when entering the water.

When initially recovered from the water, the body might be in full rigor mortis, even though only a short time has passed from the time of the drowning. This is caused by violent struggling at the time of drowning, with a decrease in ATP and rapid development of rigor mortis. Bodies cool much more rapidly in water than air. Thus, decomposition of bodies in water takes longer.

Immersion of a body in water for several hours may cause leaching out of the blood from antemortern wounds. Thus, an individual might be found with a number of what appear to be bloodless postmortem wounds that are, in actual fact, antemortem and the cause of death. This can cause problems when a body is pulled out of the water exhibiting propellor cuts. There may be no bleeding around these injuries, initially leading to the conclusion that these were postmortem injuries when, in fact, they were antemortem, the blood having been leached out by the action of the water. The authors have seen leaching out of blood as early as 3–4 h following immersion.

Tests for Drowning

A number of tests have been developed over the years to determine whether a person has drowned. The most famous is the Gettler chloride test,[10] in which blood was analyzed from the right and left sides of the heart. If the chloride level was less on the right than on the left, the person was assumed to have drowned in saltwater. If it was elevated on the right side of the heart over the left, then one was thought to be dealing with a freshwater drowning. Tests have also been done for other elements in the blood, as well as comparing the specific gravity of blood in the right versus the left atria. All of the aforementioned tests are unreliable and of no help in diagnosing drowning.

A more exotic, though controversial, test involves the identification of diatoms in the tissue of drowning victims. Diatoms are microscopic unicellular algae varying in size from 5 to more than 500 μm. These organisms have a silica skeleton in the shape of two valves. They are found everywhere in all types of water (fresh, brackish, and saltwater), on moist soil, and in the atmosphere. Some authors contend that the identification of diatoms in human organs is clear proof of drowning, while others say that it is not possible to come to this conclusion because of the widespread distribution of these organisms throughout the environment.[11,12] The whole question revolves around whether diatoms are normally present in human organs, their density if present, and what types are present. Lung, liver, kidney, and bone marrow have been analyzed for diatoms and conclusions have been reached based on the presence or absence of these organisms. Some medical professionals have found diatoms in the organs of non-drownings, while others have not.

If diatoms are present in a body, there are three possible ways they could have gotten there. First is by inhalation of airborne diatoms, second is by ingestion of material containing diatoms, and third is by aspiration of water containing diatoms, with subsequent circulation of these throughout the body. Complicating all this is the fact that diatoms are so ubiquitous that some of the analyses may have been contaminated by the glassware and reagents used.

Today, people who use diatom analysis tend to deal with closed organ systems, such as femoral bone marrow or an encapsulated kidney from a non-decomposed body. Contact of the sample with water is limited to triple distilled water. The instruments are specially cleaned to prevent contamination with diatoms. The material, such as bone marrow, is digested in concentrated acid. The deposit is examined with a standard microscope for the presence of the diatoms. The water in which the individual has allegedly drowned is sampled to see what type of diatoms are present and a comparison is made between those in the water and those found in the body. While a positive comparison is helpful, a negative result does not rule out drowning.

Drownings in Bathtubs

Drownings in bathtubs are relatively uncommon, usually involving young children left unattended by a parent. Some undoubtedly are homicides. Adults in the throes of a seizure can drown in a bathtub (Figure 3.8). Less clear are instances where an individual found in a tub has toxic or lethal drug levels. Did they pass out and drown, die of the drugs and eventually slide under water, or were they placed in the tub following an overdose in a futile attempt to revive them? Similar questions arise in regard to the individual with severe heart disease found in a bathtub under water. Did they die of a heart attack and then slip under the water or did they have an incapacitating heart attack, slip under the water and drown? The presence of pulmonary edema is of no help, as it might be present in drug overdoses, heart failure or drowning.

Rarely, a case involving an adult will be homicide. If, while taking a bath, one's feet are grasped and one is pulled underwater by them, there can be an involuntary inhalation of water as the water rushes into the nasopharynx. This, exacerbated by panic and being in a smooth-walled, wet, slippery container, could result in an inability to save oneself, with rapid loss of consciousness and death. Possibly no injuries will be seen at autopsy. Rarely, the authors have seen well-documented cases where an individual slipped in the bathtub, struck his head, and drowned.

Scuba Divers

Deaths occurring with use of scuba equipment can be caused by:
Natural disease
As a consequence of being underwater at increased pressure
An environmental hazard
As a result of defective equipment

Too rapid an ascent to the surface can cause air embolism, pneumothorax, or interstitial emphysema. Divers occasionally get trapped by underwater debris or in caves. Equipment can be the cause of death if it is defective or if there is contamination of the contained air by a substance such as carbon monoxide. Severe rusting of the interior of the tank could result in a tank atmosphere depleted of oxygen due to formation of iron oxide. In any scuba death, the authors suggest examination of the equipment by a person knowledgeable in this field, analysis of the residual atmosphere in the tank, and consultation with someone in your area experienced in scuba diving.

References

1. Swann HG and Spafford NR, Body salt and water changes during fresh and sea water drowning. *Texas Rep Biol Med* 1951; 9:356-382.

2. Swann HG, et al., Fresh- and sea-water drowning: A study of the terminal cardiac and biochemical events. *Texas Rep Biol Med* 1947; 5:423-437.

3. Pearn J, Pathophysiology of drowning. *Med J Australia* 1985; 142:586-588.

4. Modell JH and Davis JH, Electrolyte changes in human drowning victims. *Anesthesiology* 1969; 30:414-420.

5. Bolte RG, et al., The use of extracorporeal rewarming in a child submerged for 66 minutes. *JAMA* 1988; 260:377-379.

6. Giammona ST and Modell JH, Drowning by total immersion: Effects on pulmonary surfactant of distilled water, isotonic saline and sea water. *Am J Dis Children* 1967; 114:612-616.

7. Ornato JP, The resuscitation of near-drowning victims. *JAMA* 1986; 256: 75-77.

8. Conn AW and Barker CA: Fresh water drowning and near-drowning — An update. *Can Anaesth Soc*, 1984; 31: S38-S44.

9. Reh H, On the early postmortem course of "washerwoman's skin at the fingertips." *Z Rechtsmed* 1984; 92(31:183-188. (In German).

10. Gonzales TA, Vance M, Helpern M, *Legal Medicine and Toxicology*. New York, Appleton-Century Co, 1937.

11. Peabody AJ, Diatoms and drowning – A review, *Med Sci Law* 1980; 20(4): 254-261.

12. Foged N, Diatoms and drowning — Once more. *Forens Sci Int* 1983; 21: 153-159.

Electrocution

16

Deaths caused by electrocution are infrequent. Virtually all are accidents, with suicides rare and homicides even rarer. These deaths involve both low-voltage (<600 V) and high-voltage (>600–750 V) currents. They virtually always involve alternating currents, because direct current is used less. In addition, humans are four to six times as sensitive to alternating currents as to direct. Alternating currents between 39 and 150 cycles per s have the greatest lethality. In the U.S., alternating current is generated at a 60-Hz frequency; in Europe at 50-Hz.

Amperage, or the amount of current flow, is the most important factor in electrocution. It is directly related to the voltage and inversely related to the resistance. Voltage is a measure of the electromotive force and ohms are the resistance to the conduction of electricity. This is expressed in the formula:

$$A = V/R$$

Residential voltage in the U.S. is approximately 110–120 V from line to ground. High-voltage lines in suburban and urban areas are approximately 7500–8000 V line to ground with transcontinental high-tension lines 100,000 V or greater. For electrocution from low-voltage (110–120 V) household current, there must be direct contact with the electrical circuit, with death primarily caused by ventricular fibrillation. In high-voltage accidents, direct contact with the wire is not necessary. As the body approaches the high-voltage line, an electric current (arc) may jump from the line to the body. Death from high-voltage electrocution is usually caused by either the electro-thermal injury produced by the current, or respiratory arrest. The temperature generated by an arc current can be as high as 40,000°C.

In urban areas, the usual high-voltage line carries 7000–8000 V, line to ground. Electrocution from these lines occurs when they break, fall to the ground and are touched, or when an intact or "live" line is touched by a tall metal object such as a ladder, pole, or crane with which a person is in contact.

Resistance to electrocution in humans involves the skin. With 120 V, dry skin may have a resistance of 100,000 ohms; dry and calloused skin up to a million ohms; moist skin 1,000 ohms or less, and moist, thin skin as low as

Table 16.1   The Distance An Electric Arc Can Jump*

Voltage	Distance Current Can Arc
1,000	few mm
5,000	1 cm
20,000	6 cm
40,000	13 cm
100,000	35 cm

* as given by Somogyi and Tedeschi[1]

100 ohms.[2] With high-voltage currents, skin condition plays no significant role in resistance to electrocution.

Mechanism of Death

Amperage is the most important factor in electrocution. Since voltage is usually constant, the main factor in determining the amount of amperage that enters the body is the resistance, as expressed in ohms. The minimal amount of amperage perceptible to a human as a tingle is 1 mA (0.001 A). A current of 5 mA will produce tremors of the musculature while 15–17 mA will cause contracture of the muscles, which prevents release of the electrical source. This latter current is the "no-let-go" threshold. At 50 mA, there is contracture of all muscles, respiratory paralysis and death if the current is sustained. Ventricular fibrillation occurs at currents between 75 and 100 mA. Extremely high currents, ~1 A and higher, do not cause ventricular fibrillation, but rather ventricular arrest. If the current is then turned off, and there is no significant electrothermal injury to the heart, the heart should begin to beat normally.

When electrical current enters the body, it runs from the point of contact to the point of grounding, following the shortest path. Most commonly, the path is from hand to foot or hand to hand. The time necessary for a current to cause death depends on the amperage. Thus, in very low-amperage electrocutions, where death is caused by paralysis of the muscles with secondary asphyxia, prolonged contact, (i.e., several minutes) with the electrical current would be necessary. With household current, in which the mechanism of death is ventricular fibrillation, the duration of contact necessary to produce fibrillation may be measured in seconds or tenths of seconds, depending on the amperage. This is, of course, determined by the resistance. Thus, with 120-V current and 1000 ohms of skin resistance, 120 mA reach the body. In such a case, contact for 5 s would be necessary to produce ventricular fibrillation.[3] If the point of contact is thin moist skin, resistance may be as low as 100 ohms. In such cases, the current entering the body would be approximately 1200 mA (1.2 A) and ventricular fibrillation could occur in 0.1s. With high-voltage electrocution, cardiac arrest is essentially instantaneous.

In low-voltage electrocution with ventricular fibrillation, consciousness may not be lost immediately. In fact, it is very common for the individual receiving a fatal electric shock to not lose consciousness, but to yell out or state that he just "burned" himself prior to collapse. This is because the brain has approximately 10–15 s of oxygen reserve, irrespective of the heart. Thus, an individual can remain conscious for 10–15 s after cessation of the heart as a pumping organ. In cases of low-voltage electrocution, resuscitation and defibrillation may prevent death. It should be kept in mind that ventricular fibrillation is occasionally self-reversible in that the heart will revert to spontaneous rhythm following a short time of fibrillation.

In high-voltage electrocution, there may be irreversible electrothermal injury. While the heart may start again spontaneously following cardiac arrest, respiration might not resume because of paralysis of the respiratory center. This is probably caused by damage to the respiratory center of the brain stem by the hyperthermic effects of the current.

The hyperthermic effects of high-voltage currents can be seen in judicial execution, where third-degree burns develop at the site of contact between the electrodes and skin, as well as in the observation by Werner that, following execution, the brain temperature was as high as 63°C.[4]

Fractures Caused by Electrocution

When an individual contacts an electrified source having a current of 50 mA or greater, there is generalized muscular contraction. Whether the current is low- or high-volatage, these contractions can fracture bones. Tarquinio et al. reported bilateral scapular fractures from a 440-V, 60-Hz current; Dumas and Walker from exposure to a 220-V, 50 Hz current.[5,6] Stueland et al. described a case of bilateral humeral fractures from contact with 110 V; Shaheen and Sabet bilateral fractures of the femoral necks secondary to contact with a 220-V current.[7,8] Fractures of T12 and L1 vertebrae have been reported.[9] Tarquinio et al. mention that fractures were frequently seen as complications of electroconvulsive or "shock" therapy prior to the use of muscle relaxants in this therapy.[5]

Involuntary Movements Caused by Electricity-Induced Contraction of Muscle

Contact with current, especially high-voltage current, may produce violent muscle contractions. As previously noted, these can cause fractures. Wright et al. describe the following reactions that can result from electrically induced contraction of muscle:[10]

The back and neck arch backward.

The arms rotate inward the elbows flex and the hands form fists.

The hips and knees lock straight and the feet extend

If the individuals are grasping something, they will continue to do so.

Wright et al. feel that these muscular contractions, if violent enough, can propel an individual forward or backward, depending on the original position.

Autopsy Findings

In all cases of high-voltage electrocution but in only about half (50%) the cases of low-voltage electrocution, electrical burns will appear on the body. In low-voltage electrocution, these may occur at the point of entry or the point of exit, at both, or at neither. If the current enters over a broad surface area that offers minimal resistance, there may be no electrical burn. The best example of this is an individual electrocuted in a bathtub. Absence of burns in low-voltage electrocutions, however, can occur with only a small area of contact. Electrocution can produce accelerated onset of rigor mortis caused by the muscle contractions and depletion of ATP. If this does occur, it may be eccentric, reflecting the passage of the current through the body.

Electrical burns tend to be on the palms of the hands and tips of the fingers (entry sites) and soles of the feet (exit sites) (Figure 16.1). In low-voltage electrocutions, they may appear as either an erythematous area of blistering or as an irregular chalky white lesion, often with raised borders and a central crater. There may be some yellowish or black discoloration of the burn sites caused by heat. Generally, the burns are small in size, from a few millimeters up to 1–1.5 cm. Microscopically, the epidermis shows a Swiss cheese appearance. If there is only brief contact with a live wire, there may be no burns. The person may collapse from ventricular fibrillation and fall away from the wire. When there is prolonged contact, there will be severe burns caused by the heat generated by the electrical current. One cannot differentiate antemortem from postmortem electrical burns. The burns indicate only that current has passed through the skin. Minute particles of metal from the conducting surface may be deposited in the burns, especially in high-voltage electrocutions. These can be located and identified by scanning electron microscopy.

In contrast to low-voltage burns, high-voltage burns may be extremely severe, with charring of the body. If the burns occur from contact or proximity to a high-voltage line, numerous individual and confluent areas of third-degree burns will present (Figure 16.2). The multiple small burns are caused by arcing of the current. If the contact with the high-voltage current is not direct, but through current running through an intermediary object such as a ladder or pole, the burns are large and irregular, chalky white in

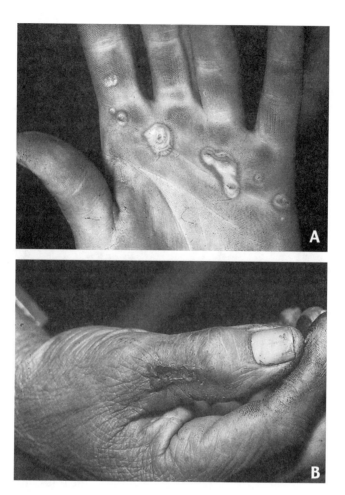

Figure 16.1 (A and B) Electrical burns of hands representing points of entry. *(continued)*.

color, often with raised borders and a central crater with yellowish or black discoloration of the burn sites caused by heat. If the individual is wearing shoes, and the exit site is a foot, there may be arcing exit burns. With very high voltage, there can be massive destruction of tissue with loss of extremities and rupture of organs.

In all cases of suspected electrocution, there should be an examination of the alleged source of the electrical current including electrical devices the individual was handling at the time of death. In low-voltage electrocutions, examination of the device rather than examination of the body will often provide the cause of death, because burns may not be present. Thus, one can make a diagnosis of electrocution without an electrical burn, based on the circumstances of the death, negative autopsy findings and the examination

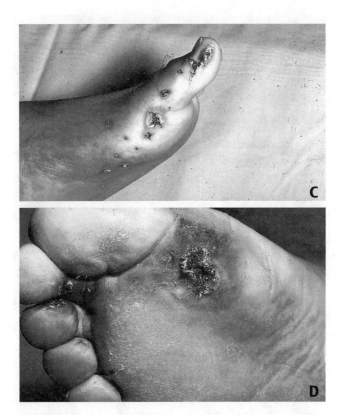

Figure 16.1 *(continued)* (C and D) Electrical burns of feet representing exit sites

of the electrical device in use. In high-voltage electrocution, tissue from the victim may be adherent at the point of contact with the source of the current (e.g., a metal ladder).

Manner of Death

Most deaths caused by electrocution are accidental in manner. Not infrequently, these can be blamed on defective tools or electrical appliances. Electrocutions caused by high-voltage wires occur secondary to inadvertent contact with a high-voltage line when operating or in contact with a device such as a "cherry picker." Other causes of electrocution are touching a downed electrical line or inadvertently making contact with a line via a radio antenna or kite. The authors have also seen cases of a sexual nature where electrodes have been found in the anus or attached to the penis.

Suicides are rare, although occasionally, individuals will build elaborate devices to electrocute themselves. Homicides are even rarer. The most common method of homicide with electrical current is to drop a plugged-in

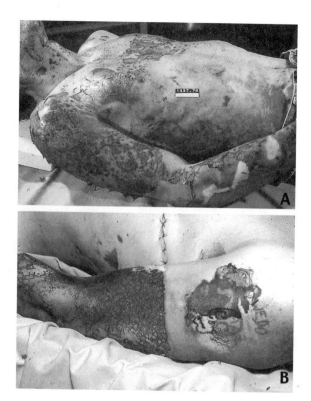

Figure 16.2 (A and B) High-voltage electrical burns with multiple individual and confluent burn areas *(continued).*

electrical device into a bathtub while an individual is taking a bath. There are usually no electrical burns in such a case and, if the electrical device is removed, the cause of death will be missed.

Bathtub electrocutions, both homicidal and accidental, are becoming less common, because of the fairly widespread use of low-voltage Ground-Fault Current Interrupters (GFCI). These are required in kitchens, bathrooms and outside outlets. This device monitors the current flow. If there is a greater than 5-mA difference, the circuit is broken, thus preventing electrocution. A normal circuit breaker does not function until a 15-A difference is detected. Thus, in most cases of electrocution, the house fuse is unaffected by the electrocution. Electrocution in water could also be caused by defective lights in a swimming pool. GFCIs prevent this type of accident.

Lightning

A lightning bolt is produced when the charged undersurface of a thunder-cloud sends its electrical charge to the ground. Since the undersurface is usually negatively charged, virtually all discharges are also negative. Approx-

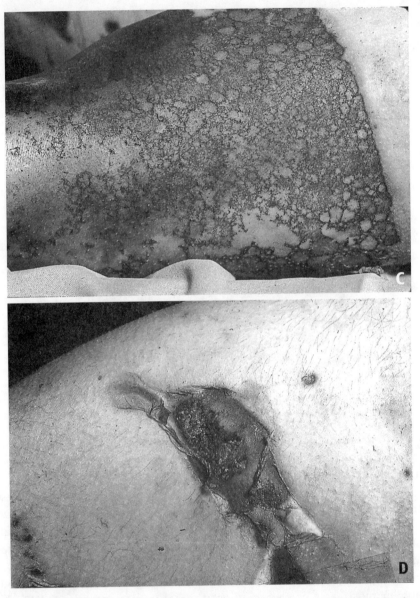

Figure 16.2 *(continued)* (C) High-voltage electrical burns with multiple individual and confluent burn areas (D) Burn from high-voltage current conducted into body by a metal plate.

imately 5% of lightning flashes, however, are positive discharges. These are most frequent in mountainous regions.

A lightning bolt may injure or kill an individual by a direct strike, a side flash, or conduction through another object. An example of the last instance would be a lightning bolt's hitting a crane, with the electricity's flowing down the metal structure and striking a grounded worker who is touching the crane. The injuries produced would be the same as if the crane had hit a high-power electrical line, that is, burns at the entrance and exit sites, often multiple and severe.

In a side-flash strike, the bolt of lightning hits an object, such as a tree, and then ricochets, striking the individual. In a direct strike or a side-flash strike where the individual is relatively close to the object from which the bolt jumps, the current can either spread over the surface of the body or enter it, or it can follow both routes. In most cases seen by the forensic pathologist, the current has both flowed over the surface of the body and entered. In such cases, it is quite common to find the clothing torn, shoes burst, hair seared, burns on the skin caused by zippers and other metal objects heated by the lightning, and burns caused by the entrance and exit of current. Cutaneous burns are not severe but always present.[11] On histological examination, the epidermis is separated from the papillary dermis. Rupture of the tympanic membrane is present in approximately 81% of cases.[11] Objects constructed of ferrous metal on the body may be magnetized. Other metal objects, such as coins, may show burns. The torn clothing and burst shoes sometimes have led to misinterpretation of the nature of the injuries. People struck by lightning and found next to a road have been thought to be hit-and-run victims. If one is inside a metal vehicle, such as a car or train, when it is struck by lightning, the probability of injury is extremely small. On rare occasions, death or injury has been reported when an individual was using a telephone and the line was hit by lightning.[12]

Deaths from lightning are caused by high-voltage direct current. Death is caused by cardiopulmonary arrest or electrothermal injuries. With a direct hit by lightning, death is probably inevitable, because of burns and injury to the respiratory center of the brain. Amperage in this case would be in the kiloampere range. If the electrocution is secondary to a close point of impaction, survival may be possible. In fact, most individuals injured by lightning do survive. One of the lesions considered pathognomonic for lightning injury is the "arborescent" or fern-like injury of the skin called Lichtenberg figures (Figure 16.3). This lesion is a patterned area of transient erythema that appears within 1 h of the accident and then gradually fades within 24 h. The erythematous marks are not burns. Ten Duis et al. believe that this lesion is caused by positive discharges over the skin.[13] They hypothesize that the lesion occurs when an individual struck by a negative lightning bolt is then hit by a secondary positive flashover from a nearby grounded object. Another possibility is that it represents an entrance point in an individual struck by a positively charged lightning bolt. Both explanations, neither of which are exclusive of the other, would explain the relative rarity of the arborescent lesion in individuals struck by lightning.

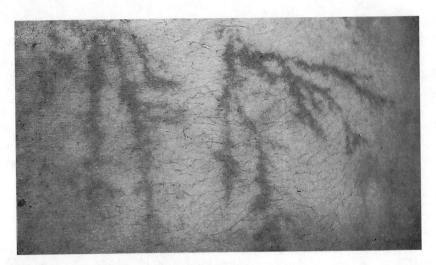

Figure 16.3 "Arborescent" burn of lightning.

References

1. Sornogyi E and Tedeschi CG, Injury by electrical force, in Tedeschi CG, Eckert WG, Tedeschi LG (Eds): *Forensic Medicine*. Philadelphia, WB Saunders Co, 1977, pp 645-676.

2. Bruner JMR, Hazards of electrical apparatus. *Anesthesiology* 1967; 28: 396-425.

3. Ferris LP, et al., Effect of electroshock and health. *AIEE Trans* 1936; 55:498.

4. Werner AH, Death by electricity, *NY Med J* 1923; 118:498-500.

5. Tarquinio T, Weinstein, ME and Virgilio, RW, Bilateral scapular fractures from accidental electric shock. *J. Trauma.* 1979; 19(2): 132-133.

6. Dumas JL and Walker N, Bilateral scapular fractures secondary to electrical shock. *Arch. Orthopaed & Trauma Surg*, 1992; 111(5):287-8.

7. Stueland DT, et al., Bilateral humeral fractures from electrically induced muscular spasm. *J. of Emerg. Med.* 1989; 7(5):457-9.

8. Shaheen MA and Sabet NA, Bilateral simultaneous fracture of the femoral neck following electrical shock. *Injury.* 1984; 16(1): 13-14.

9. Rajam KH, et al., Fracture of vertebral bodies caused by accidental electric shock. *J. Indian Med Assoc.* 1976; 66:35.

10. Wright RK, Broisz HG, and Shuman M, The investigation of electrical injuries and deaths. Presented at the meeting of the American Academy of Forensic Science, Reno, NV, February 2000.

11. Wetli CV, Keraunopathology: An analysis of 45 fatalities, *Am J Forens Med Path* 1996; 17 (2): 89-98.

12. Johnstone BR, Harding DL, and Hocking B: Telephone-related lightning injury. *Med J Aust* 1986; 144:706-709.

13. ten Duis HJ, Klasen H1, Nijsten MWN, et al., Superficial lightning injuries — Their "fractal" shape and origin. *Burns* 1987; 13:141-146.

Hyperthermia and Hypothermia: the Effects of Heat and Cold

17

Normal body temperature is generally considered to be 98.6°F (37°C) orally and approximately 1°F (0.6°C) higher rectally. Body temperature, however, can vary from individual to individual, by age, time of day, physical exertion, etc. Thus, newborns and the elderly have temperatures averaging 1°C higher. Cyclic changes in body temperature occur with decreases of 0.5°C early in the morning (approximately 1:00 to 2:00 a.m.) and slight elevations later in the morning and afternoon. Hard exercise can raise the rectal temperature up to 104°F.[1] Rectal temperatures of 39–40°C are common in marathoners after a race.[2]

To further complicate this matter, the normal oral temperature is based on 19th-century data. More-recent work by Mackowiak et al. indicates that 98.2°F (36.8°C) is the mean normal oral temperature, with 99.9°F (37.7°C) the upper limit.[3] Maximum temperatures varied with time of day with a low in the early morning. They thought that 98.9°F (37.2°C) in the morning and 99.9° F (37.7°C) overall should be regarded as the upper limits of oral temperature in adults. Thus, we see that there is no exact "normal" temperature, but rather a range.

Maintenance of normal body temperature is a delicate balance between heat load and heat loss. Heat load is the sum of heat generated by oxidation of metabolic products and heat acquired from the environment. Heat is lost by three mechanisms: **conduction**, **radiation**, and **evaporation**.[1]

Loss of heat by conduction is either by direct conduction from the surface of the body to another object or by conduction to air. Loss of heat by direct conduction to objects is relatively minor. For example, if an individual sits in a chair, heat conducted from the body will raise the temperature of the chair to that of the body. When this has occurred, heat loss will stop.

In contrast to limited heat loss by direct conduction, sizable quantities of heat can be lost by conduction to air. The molecules composing the skin transfer heat to contiguous air molecules, producing a thin zone of heated air adjacent to the skin. This zone usually remains relatively stationary. Once this layer of air absorbs heat until it is equal to the temperature of the body, heat loss ceases. If, however, this layer of heated air is continually removed and new air introduced (by a fan or wind), the loss of heat by conduction will continue. This movement of air around the body, with resultant continued loss of heat, is known as **convection**. Winds will blow away the layer of air immediately adjacent to the skin, thus accounting for the feeling of cold and increased heat loss when the wind blows. There is, however, a limitation on this process. Once the wind has cooled the skin to a certain temperature, the rate at which heat flows from the core of the body to the skin is the limiting factor in heat loss, rather than the rate of conduction and convection.

The second method of heat loss is by **radiation**. Here, there is loss of heat in the form of infrared rays. These radiate from the body in all directions. Heat rays, however, radiate from all masses. Thus, walls, floors, the ground, etc. all radiate infrared heat rays. If the environment becomes hotter than the body, radiant heat given up by the surroundings will exceed the loss of heat from the body by radiation.

The third method of heat loss is by **evaporation**. This is the primary method of cooling the overheated body. As water evaporates from the body, 0.58 calories of heat are lost for each gram of water that evaporates.[1] The two mechanisms of heat loss by evaporation are **insensible** heat loss and **sweating**. Insensible heat loss is loss of moisture from the non-sweating individual. This is water that evaporates from the skin and lungs. It occurs at a rate of about 600 mL per day, that is, a continual heat loss of 12-16 cal/h.[1] Insensible heat loss is caused by continued diffusion of water molecules through the skin and respiratory surfaces regardless of the body temperature.

The more important of the two methods of evaporation that produce cooling of the body is sweating. In cold weather, the rate of sweat production is essentially zero. In hot weather, the maximum rate of sweat production varies from 700 mL/h in the unacclimatized person to 1.5 to 2 L/h in a person maximally acclimatized to heat.[1] In individuals sweating heavily, dehydration can rapidly develop. Dehydration, in turn, predisposes an individual to the development of hyperthermia and heat stroke. To prevent this, individuals exposed to high temperatures are urged to increase their fluid intake. This is especially necessary in those engaging in strenuous activities such as manual labor or jogging. Some people ingest too much fluid and develop hyponatremia.[4] The symptoms of this are nonspecific — nausea, vomiting, headache, muscle weakness, confusion, and seizures. Symptoms occur when serum sodium levels decrease to <130 mmol/L, becoming severe at levels <125 mmol/L. When serum sodium drops below 120 mmol/L, more than 50% of individuals have seizures.

When people are exposed to hot weather for several weeks, they begin to progressively sweat more and more. First, they sweat 700 mL/h. This doubles within 10 days, increasing up to three times as much within 6 weeks. This is caused by increased sweat capability of the sweat glands. Sweat contains sodium chloride or salt. When the rate of sweat secretion is very low, the sodium chloride concentration of the sweat is also very low because sodium and chloride are reabsorbed before they reach the surface of the body. As the rate of secretion becomes progressively greater, the rate of sodium chloride re-absorption does not increase equally, so that the concentration of sodium in the sweat can rise almost to the level of the plasma. Extreme sweating can deplete the extracellular fluids of electrolytes, particularly sodium and chloride. Thus, extra sodium and chloride must usually be added to the diet in tropical climates. Persons who sweat profusely can lose as much as 15–30 g of sodium chloride each day until they become acclimatized.[1] After 4 to 6 weeks, the loss of sodium decreases and may be as little as 3–5 g per day. A person who has lived in the tropics since childhood actually has more active sweat glands in the body than an individual from a cold climate. People are born with an excess of sweat glands. When they live in a temperate zone, many of these become permanently inactive during childhood. If, however, they remain in the tropics, they remain functional throughout life.

The skin, subcutaneous tissues, and fat act as heat insulators in the body. Fat is especially important because it conducts heat only one third as readily as other tissues. When no blood is flowing from internal organs to the skin, the insulating properties of the male body are approximately equal to three fourths the insulating properties of the usual suit of clothes. In women, because of greater body fat, this insulation is still better.

Increased loss of heat from the body can be caused by increased flow of blood to the skin. Immediately beneath the skin is a venous plexus that is supplied by an inflow of blood. Full dilatation of these vessels can increase the rate of heat transfer to the skin eightfold. Such a high rate of blood flow causes heat to be conducted from the internal portions of the body to the skin with great efficiency. Reduction in the rate of blood flow decreases the efficiency in heat conduction, Thus, the skin is used as a radiator system, with the flow of blood to the skin the mechanism of heat transfer from the body core to the skin. As long as the body temperature is greater than that of the surroundings, heat is lost principally by radiation and conduction. Thus, a nude person sitting in a room at normal room temperature would lose approximately 3% of heat by conduction to objects, 15% by conduction to air, 60% by radiation, and 22% by evaporation (insensible heat loss).[1]

When the temperature of the surroundings is greater than that of the skin, instead of losing heat, the body gains heat by radiation and conduction from the surroundings. In this situation, the only means by which the body can rid itself of heat is by evaporation. Any factor preventing adequate evaporation under such circumstances causes the body temperature to rise. If this continues long enough, the individual will develop heat stroke and die.

High humidity interferes with heat loss by sweating. With high humidity, the air holds almost as much moisture as possible. As a result, the rate of evaporation is greatly reduced or totally prevented so that the secreted sweat remains in a fluid state. Consequently, the body temperature approaches the temperature of the surroundings or rises above this temperature, even though sweat continues to pour forth.

It has already been mentioned that a thin zone of air adjacent to the skin usually remains relatively stationary and is not exchanged for new air at a rapid rate unless convection air currents are present. Such lack of air movement prevents effective evaporation in the same way that it prevents effective cooling by conduction of heat to the air. The local air becomes saturated with water vapors and further evaporation cannot occur. When convection currents occur, the saturated air is swept away from the skin and unsaturated air replaces it. Convection is of even more importance with heat loss from the body by evaporation than by conduction to air. This explains why fans are so helpful in keeping the body temperature down.

Clothing has the opposite effect. It traps the air around the body, decreasing the flow of convection air currents. Thus, the rate of heat loss from the body by convection and conduction is greatly decreased. Ordinarily, clothes decrease the rate of heat loss from the body to about half that from a nude body.[5] Arctic clothing can decrease heat loss to as little as one sixth of the nude state. When clothing becomes wet, the rate of heat transmission increases as much as 20-fold because of the high conductivity of heat by water. This is why wet clothing is so deadly in arctic regions.

In an individual who is clothed, the effectiveness of heat loss by evaporation is dependent upon the material. Fabric that is pervious to moisture, such as cotton, allows almost normal heat loss by the body by evaporation. This is because, when sweating occurs, the sweat dampens the clothing and evaporation then occurs on the surface of the clothing. This cools the clothing, which, in turn, cools the skin. Thus, in tropical regions, light clothing that is pervious to sweat but impervious to radiant heat from the sun prevents the body from gaining radiant heat, while at the same time allowing it to lose heat by evaporation, almost as if one were not wearing clothing.

Heat Stroke

When individuals' ability to cool the body can no longer compensate for the heat load, they develop heat stroke. This is a life-threatening condition classically manifested by hyperthermia (a rectal temperature of 105–106°F or higher), hot, dry skin, altered sensorium, tachycardia, hypotension, and hyperventilation. The very old and very young are more susceptible to heat stroke. Predisposing health conditions and individual susceptibility include alcoholism, dehydration, obesity, preexisting disease (cardiac and neurological), and the use of diuretics and major tranquilizers such as phenothiazines, tricyclic antidepressants, and monoamine oxidase inhibitors. Relative humidity also plays a role. As humidity increases, the apparent temperature may be significantly higher than the actual recorded temperature (Table 17.2).

Obese individuals show a greater susceptibility to heat stroke. This is due to a number of factors: (1) Increased adipose tissue creates an greater demand on the heart; (2) the fat provides extra insulation for the body, preventing loss of heat; (3) since metabolic heat is produced in proportion to the bulk of the tissue and is lost in proportion to the surface area, the larger bulk-to-area ratio in the obese reduces efficient heat loss.

While the classic definition of heat stroke requires a minimum rectal temperature of between 105 and 106°F, there is some variability in this, just as there is with the hot, dry skin. In individuals who develop heat stroke following extreme exertion (e.g., military recruits), there may initially be some sweating, though a hot, flushed, dry skin is more common. The skin may also appear blanched and relatively cool because of intense catecholamine release.[6] Individuals who develop heatstroke secondary to extreme exertion have a greater tendency to develop rhabdomyolysis and disseminated intravascular coagulopathy than those individuals whose heat stroke is unrelated to exertion.

Heat stroke is generally seen in two settings. First is that involving relatively young individuals exposed to high temperatures while undergoing extreme exertion — military recruits and football players in training are examples. The other setting is a prolonged heat wave. In this latter circumstance, affected individuals are generally over the age of 60. Deaths

Table 17.2 Heat Index Chart:
Air Temperature and Relative Humidity versus Apparent Temperature

Temp.	Relative Humidity (%)										
F	50	55	60	65	70	75	80	85	90	95	100
110	**150**										
105	**135**	**142**	**149**								
100	*120*	*126*	**132**	**138**	**144**						
95	*107*	*110*	*114*	*119*	*124*	**130**	**136**				
90	96	98	100	102	*106*	*109*	*113*	*117*	*122*		
85	88	89	90	91	93	95	97	99	102	*105*	*108*
80	81	81	82	83	85	86	86	87	88	89	91
75	75	75	76	76	77	77	78	78	79	79	80
70	69	69	70	70	70	70	71	71	71	71	72

Note: Danger = *Italic*; Extreme danger = **Bold**

caused by heat stroke during heat waves usually do not present the first day or two of the heat wave, but appear toward the end of the first week, as the victims' heat-adaptive systems give out. Many also have preexisting cardiovascular disease.

Deaths from heat stroke also occur in children left unattended in automobiles for long periods of time in the summer. In a study by Zumwalt et al., thermometers with a temperature range of 100–320° F were placed out of direct sunlight on the back seats and in the trunks of two passenger cars, one white and the other light blue.[7] The cars were then left in direct sunlight. Readings were taken on 39 separate days at 12 noon, 3 p.m., and 5 p.m., with the outside ambient temperatures also recorded. Table 17.2 summarizes the results of the tests. Outside temperatures ranged from 82 to 97°F; corresponding passenger compartment temperatures ranged from 82 to 136°F. There were no significant differences between the temperatures in the passenger compartments of the white and blue cars. The trunk temperature of the blue car was essentially identical to that in the passenger compartment, while the trunk temperatures in the white car were consistently lower than the compartment temperatures. It is speculated that, in the passenger compartments, radiant heat readily enters through the glass, with car color playing no role, while, in the trunks, the reflective qualities of the white car were responsible for the lower temperatures.

In a second study by Surpure, two cars, one large and one small, were parked in direct sunlight and shade.[8] In direct sunlight, the maximum temperatures in the small and large cars were 70 and 65°C, respectively. The smaller car heated up more rapidly than the larger car. Leaving the windows partially open was not particularly helpful. Thus, in the small car, with the front windows open 2 in., the maximum temperature was 70°C. If, however, the front windows were left fully open, the maximum temperature in the sun reached 50°C. When the small car was parked in the shade, there was a significant difference, with a maximum temperature of only 44°C.

Symptoms of heat stroke may come on suddenly or be preceded by prodromic symptoms — nausea, vomiting, vertigo, muscle cramps, dyspnea, a feeling of warmth. Experiments have been carried out to determine the

Table 17.2 Temperature Range in Two Test Cars (°F)

Location	Noon.		3:00 p.m.		5:00 p.m	
	Outside	Inside	Outside	Inside	Outside	Inside
Passenger compartment						
Blue car	82-92	104-128	87-96	115-132	89-97	117-136
White car	82-92	102-126	87-96	109-128	89-97	114-132
Trunk						
Blue car	89-92	102-126	87-96	112-131	89-97	112-128
White car	86-92	100-108	87-96	100-118	89-97	101-112

subjective impressions of individuals exposed to heat stress.[9] Initially, there is a loss of ability to concentrate and a vague feeling of impending physiologic deterioration. Awareness of body heat and profuse perspiration is replaced by the realization that sweating has diminished and then suddenly ceased. The face feels dry and hot, while, at the same time, the individual notes the feeling of a film of dried salt on the cheeks, forehead, and corners of the mouth. Then comes the realization that the slightest movement of the body produces an increase in heart rate and a premonition of a fainting spell. Paresthesias develop in the hands, feet, and ankles. The face, which until now was pinkish red, abruptly turns ashen gray, suggesting impending cardiocirculatory collapse. Exposure in volunteers ended at this point, to prevent their becoming stuporous and lapsing into the coma of heat stroke.

As the circulating blood temperature rises to a level higher than 42.4°C, there is generalized vasodilation, with resultant effective reduction in blood volume. Diminished peripheral resistance leads to increased and rapid venous return and increased cardiac output. The left side of the heart cannot keep pace with the right. The increase in venous return results in elevation of venous pressure that triggers high-output cardiac failure and circulatory collapse.[9,10] The resulting tissue anoxia may explain the paresthesias. The same increase in venous pressure is ultimately thought to be responsible for the cessation of sweating seen at the peak of the heat stroke syndrome. Thus, it has been noted that if venous pressure increases, sweating begins to decrease; as venous pressure decreases, sweating is restored.

Diagnosis of heat stroke antemortem is relatively easy because of the characteristic symptoms and signs, as well as the elevated body temperature. The autopsy findings of heat stroke, however, are not specific. Individuals surviving more than 24 h may show lobular pneumonia, acute tubular necrosis of the kidneys, adrenal hemorrhage, or necrosis of the liver. Also noted is subendocardial hemorrhage, degeneration of myocardial fibers, and disseminated intravascular coagulopathy. If the diagnosis of heat stroke has not been made prior to death, the diagnosis, if it can be made, is often circumstantial, based on history, exclusion of other causes of death and perhaps a rectal or core temperature. If an individual's time of death is known and if a rectal temperature taken shortly thereafter shows hyperthermia, a diagnosis of heat stroke can be made if, at autopsy, there is no other explanation for the hyperthermia, such as central nervous system bleeding or salicylate overdose. If the time of death is unknown, a rectal temperature may be of help in making the diagnosis of heat stroke. If an individual is found at 8 a.m., when the environmental temperature is 78°F and he has a rectal temperature of 103°F, and no medical explanation for the increased temperature is found at autopsy, the individual can be diagnosed as having had heat stroke. The same individual found dead at 3 p.m. with an environmental temperature of 105°F and a rectal temperature of 105°F cannot be diagnosed as dying of heat stroke, because the elevated body temperature may be caused by radiant heat and conduction from adjacent heated surfaces. Unfortunately, there are no diagnostic anatomical criteria at autopsy for heat stroke.

Malignant Hyperthermia

Malignant hyperthermia is an inherited disorder of the muscle-cell membrane predominantly associated with the administration of halogenated anesthetic agents and succinylcholine.[2,11] In this disorder, the triggering agent raises myoplasmic Ca (2+) levels, with resultant rise in body temperature and muscle rigidity. Three clinical myopathies that predispose to malignant hyperthermia are known. The most common is Evans myopathy, which is inherited as a mendelian dominant. Manifestation of this condition may be insidious or fulminant and may not occur every time anesthesia is administered. In its most dramatic presentation, following administration of succinylcholine or halogenated volatile anesthetics, there is a rapid sustained rise in temperature. There can be generalized muscle rigidity, tachycardia, cardiac arrhythmia or arrest. Complications include:

- Rhabdomyolysis (with elevated CPK peaking the second or third day)
- Renal failure secondary to rhabdomyolysis
- Acidosis
- Electrolyte disturbances (especially hyperkalemia and hypocalcemia)
- Disseminated intravascular coagulopathy

While malignant hyperthermia typically occurs immediately after administration of the anesthetic agents, it can be delayed up to 11 hrs.[11]

In individuals with the genetic susceptibility to malignant hyperthermia, attacks can occur unassociated with anesthesia. Thus, vigorous exercise in a hot environment can precipitate an attack. Neuroleptic agents can trigger an attack by raising myoplasmic levels of Ca 2+ (the neuroleptic malignant syndrome). This syndrome occurs in approximately 0.2% of patients receiving neuroleptic agents, usually within the first 30 d following institution of therapy.[2]

Miscellaneous Causes of Hyperthermia

Hyperthermia can be due to various other causes. Though body temperature may be normal or only slightly elevated in thyrotoxicosis, in thyrotoxic crisis, rectal temperatures of 40°C can occur. Severe dehydration with volume depletion can lead to cutaneous vasoconstriction with decreased sweating, impaired heat loss and hyperthermia. Cocaine, methamphetamine and aspirin intoxication can all cause hyperthermia through excess heat production. In severe salicylate intoxication, there is excess heat production as salictylates uncouple the bonds formed by oxidative phosphorylation in skeletal-muscle mitochondria.[2]

Saunas

In a sauna, there is exposure to an extremely hot and relatively dry environment with air temperatures ranging from 170–250° F (60–120°C).[12] The "bather" is usually able to remain in this environment 10–30 min. Core temperature begins to rise in 1–3 min with a constant rate of increase after 3 min. Rectal temperatures, which are an approximate reflection of core temperature, rise from 37.6 to 40.0°C. Once outside the sauna and back at normal room temperature, the body's core temperature returns to normal in approximately 30 min. In hot dry environments such as a sauna, sweating is the only means of cooling. Perspiration rates may increase to 0.8 to 2.0 kg/hr. Individuals with severe heart disease are at risk in a sauna because of the strain on the cardiovascular system from the body's attempt to adapt to the high environmental temperatures and the potential risk of hyperthermia.

Exercise, Body Temperature, Humidity and Exhaustion

Individuals in a sauna are exposed to extremely high temperatures in a very dry environment. During this time, they do not engage in any significant physical activity. Thus, increase in body temperature is due solely to exposure to a hot environment. This is an artificial situation. In ordinary life, individuals are usually exposed to a hot environment, and possibly a high humidity, while undertaking physical activity.

Experiments have been conducted in which trained athletes have engaged in continuous and strenuous activity (on bicycle ergometers) to the point of complete exhaustion in a hot environment.[13,14] The humidity varied from dry (10% relative humidity) to humid (87%). The body temperature increased due to both the heat of the environment and the heat generated by the metabolism of work. The tests were continued over 8–13 consecutive days to evaluate heat acclimation.

In a **hot dry environment** (40°C, 10% relative humidity), endurance increased from an initial 48 ± 1.9 min to 80 ± 3.3 min.[13] Mean core (esophageal) temperatures were 39.8 ± 0.13° C the first day; 39.7 ± 0.15°C the last day.

In hot humid air (35°C; 87% relative humidity), exhaustion was reached in 44.6 ± 2.8 min.[14] After acclimation, the subjects reached exhaustion at 52.0 ± 1.9 minutes. The mean core temperature at exhaustion was 39.9 ± 0.1°C both before and after acclimation. Sweating increased with acclimatization with both tests.

In view of these studies, it appears that a high core temperature is the critical factor for exhaustion during exercise in a hot environment. With exposure to a hot environment, whether it be dry or humid, exhaustion sets in and physical exertion ceases with a core temperature of approximately 40°C. Even if there is no physical activity, when core temperature approaches 40°C, the body senses danger. Thus, the individuals in the sauna, exposed to a hot dry environment without physical activity, leave the sauna when their core temperature is approximately 40ºC.

Hypothermia

The term hypothermia is used when an individual's body temperature is below 95°F (35°C). This will occur when the loss of body heat exceeds heat production. The most common cause of hypothermia is exposure to low temperatures. Accidental hypothermia occurs in alcoholics going to sleep or passing out in a cold environment, individuals lost while hiking or skiing, and those who have been immersed in ice-cold water. This last condition, immersion hypothermia, is extremely dangerous because of the more rapid loss of heat in water than in air. Body heat is lost three times faster in water than in dry, cold air of the same temperature, as water conducts heat 20 to 25 times faster than dry air.[15]

The elderly may die of hypothermia in their homes because of inadequate heating coupled with debilitating diseases or inadequate nutrition. The latter conditions impair the ability of the body to maintain normal temperature. Infants are much more susceptible to hypothermia than adults. This is because their surface area in relation to body mass is considerably greater than that of adults. In newborn infants, vasomotor reflexes are underdeveloped and the heat-regulating center is insufficient for at least several hours after birth. Thus, hypothermia is more frequent in the first few weeks of life and is associated with a very high mortality.

The body's defense against cold is vasoconstriction of blood vessels in the skin and muscles so as to conserve heat, combined with an increase in generation of heat. Heat production is increased in two ways: First, there is shivering. During maximum shivering, heat production can rise as high as five times normal. Second, there is chemical thermogenesis, i.e., an immediate increase in the rate of cellular metabolism. The degree of thermogenesis that occurs is directly proportional to the amount of brown fat. In adults, who have almost no brown fat, it is rare that chemical thermogenesis increases the rate of heat production more than 10–15%. In infants, who have a large amount of brown fat, the increased heat production is as much as 100%. The thickness of an individual's subcutaneous fat also affects whether hypothermia will develop and how soon. Fat individuals tolerate cold better than skinny individuals. Because of the thicker layer of subcutaneous fat, women endure cold better than men.

Compensatory increases of heat production by the body, such as that caused by shivering, can maintain body temperature to about 90°F (32°C), where impairment of cerebral functioning, manifested by analgesia, clouding of consciousness, hallucinations, and slowing of reflexes, begins. Shivering ceases between 90 and 85°F. Respiration becomes less frequent and more shallow and there is a decrease in the pulse rate. Below 85°F, the ability of the hypothalamus to regulate temperature is completely lost. Cold narcosis appears at 85°F and reflexes are abolished at 81°F. As hypothermia develops, electrocardiographs show prolongation of the PQRS waves with inverted T waves. At about 86°F, atrial fibrillation often appears. Between 82 and 77°F, death may occur from ventricular fibrillation.

Hypothermia can cause a hemoconcentration by two mechanisms. The first is cold diuresis.[16] Exposure to an environmental temperature of 59°F (15°C) is sufficient to trigger diuresis in an individual. The second mechanism is the leaking of plasma into the extracellular spaces. This is known as "cold edema." Hyperglycemia occurs in the early phases of hypothermia.[17] It is caused by the action of glucocorticoids and epinephrine on the liver, with resultant depletion of glycogen. With prolonged hypothermia, hypoglycemia may develop.[16,18–19] This is more common in alcoholics. The hypoglycemia may be accompanied by elevated levels of insulin.[19]

Many cases of hypothermia seen by the forensic pathologist involve individuals who die of exposure while under the influence of alcohol. Alcohol is said to contribute to the fatal outcome by causing cutaneous dilatation of peripheral vessels and thus loss of heat. This is the warm flush that an individual experiences when drinking alcohol. However, a number of individuals have been reported as surviving deep hypothermia because of alcohol intake. This survival is attributed to protection against cardiac fibrillation by the alcohol. This protective effect has been reproduced in dogs as well as individuals during surgery with body temperatures reduced to 25–26°C.[20] In these individuals, alcohol was administered to maintain a blood concentration of approximately 400 mg%. Increase in circulation and reduction of oxygen consumption in the brain might explain some of the protective effects of alcohol.

Hypothermia in Water

A fair amount of data concerning survival time in cold water is known from experiences in World War II, as well as from experiments carried out in concentration camps.[15,17,21] In concentration camps, it was found that it takes 70–90 min for a man to die when immersed in water at 4–9°C.[17] Data on shipwreck victims showed that survival time of these individuals, who were better nourished than the concentration camp victims, was 2 h.[15]

In immersion in cold water, the thickness of an individual's subcutaneous fat is the most important internal factor affecting the rate at which the body cools. In water at 15° C, obese individuals cool at a rate that may be hardly discernable, while a thin individual's body temperature can fall by 2.5°C in the first half hour.[22] In children, the ratio of skin surface area to body mass is greater than in adults, thus, the rate of body cooling is faster. Boys under 10 years of age, in water at 20.4°C, often showed falls in body temperature below 35° after as little as 30 minutes.[23] Clothing retards body cooling in water, though not as effectively as in air. In very cold water, exercise accelerates the rate at which the body temperature falls, because increased flow of blood to exercising muscles carries away more heat than is produced by the exercise.[24]

Deaths have been reported within a half hour following immersion in water at 32°F (0°C). The individuals who die under these circumstances probably do not die primarily of hypothermia. Death is probably caused by cardiovascular etiology due to the effects on the heart of the sudden cooling of the skin, i.e., constriction of blood vessels, and reflex stimulation of the heart, with increased blood pressure and cardiac output, with resultant sudden increase in the work of the left ventricle. Both ventricular and atrial ectopic beats are common during the first few minutes of cold immersion.[25] They usually cease after a few minutes, as the temperature receptors in the skin adapt to the low temperature. Rarely, the arrhythmias progress to ventricular fibrillation, followed by sudden death. Ventricular fibrillation caused by these mechanisms probably accounts for the occasional case of a swimmer's diving into cold water only to float up or sink to the bottom, dead. Older individuals may be especially susceptible to a cardiovascular mechanism of death in cold water immersion.

Reflex disturbances of breathing could also account for some of the rapid deaths following immersion in cold water. Sudden cooling of the skin following immersion in water with a temperature approaching 0°C causes marked reflex stimulation of breathing for a few minutes such that breathing can often not be controlled voluntarily.[26] In instances where the water is choppy, waves breaking over the head of an individual can result in inhalation of water and drowning before hypothermia causes death.

Post-immersion deaths can occur following the rescue from cold water of individuals who appear to be in no danger of dying. The individual may be conscious when taken out of the water, only to lose consciousness when taken into the warmth of the facility. This appears to be related to the "afterdrop phenomenon."[27] Following removal from cold water, an individual's body temperature continues to fall for a period of time before it starts to rise. This occurs even if the subject is rapidly rewarmed. The first graphic records of the after-drop were in experiments at Dachau. These observations were subsequently reproduced in experiments, though the body cooling was restricted to safe limits. The exact mechanism causing death is not understood, but appears to be manifested by cardiac arrest.

The critical temperature to maintain thermo-equilibrium in water was determined to be 35°C (95°F) by Burton and Bazett.[28]

Hypothermia on Land

Determination of survival time in dry cold on land is more complicated than in cold water because of the multiple factors that play a role in determining to what temperature the body is actually exposed. On land, the principal factors that determine whether an individual becomes hypothermic are the environmental temperature, wind speed, and clothing. Wind, by dispersing the warm air surrounding the body, causes a chilling effect by magnifying the effects of the environmental temperature. This observation has led to the construction of the wind-chill index. This index computes the combined effects of air temperature and wind speed. Thus at 10°F, if the wind blows at 2 mph, an individual will feel cold; at 5 mph very cold; at 10 bitterly cold and at 15 mph exposed flesh will freeze. If the clothing an individual wears is soaked through with water, the air temperature used in the wind-chill index should be adjusted down 6°C (11° F) from the measured temperature before using the index.[29]

The critical temperature to maintain thermo-equilibrium in dry air was determined to be 25°C (77°F) by Wilkerson, Raven and Horvath.[30]

Individuals suffering from hypothermia on land may show either red patches on the skin or pale areas of subcutaneous edema. Mental disorientation is common. They are often unconscious with a low or unrecordable blood pressure, a slow, irregular pulse, and slow, shallow respiration. They may appear dead. Heart sounds may not be detected with a stethoscope at 86°F (30°C). The pupil reflex can vanish at 77°F (25°C).[31] If such individuals are found dead, at autopsy the livor mortis will have a cherry-red color. This is due to increased amounts of oxyhemoglobin caused by antemortem binding of oxygen to the hemoglobin. In some cases, however, bodies have been reported as being totally white. Areas of bluish discoloration might also be seen on the hands, elbows, knees, and feet, probably representing minor frostbite areas. Histologically, these lesions are characterized by edema and hyperemia of the dermis with occasional foci of inflammatory cell infiltrates.

In individuals who do not immediately die from hypothermia, but survive a while, there may be development of hemorrhagic pancreatitis; erosions and hemorrhages of the gastric mucosa, ileum and colon; bronchopneumonia; acute tubular necrosis, and cardiac muscle degeneration. In individuals who die of uncomplicated hypothermia, that is, are found "frozen," there are no specific lesions that can be attributable to the hypothermia. Victims of hypothermia are often found undressed (paradoxical undressing). This is explained by terminal hallucinations and feelings of warmth that are caused by paralysis of the thermal regulatory mechanism.[32]

In addition to hypothermic deaths, cold weather is often associated with sudden death in individuals with coronary artery disease. The lower the temperature, the greater the risk of a coronary attack. Individuals with angina pectoris almost invariably experience pain on exposure to air temperature of less than 15°F (-10°C).[33] This pain is caused by coronary spasm or increased stroke volume induced by breathing cold air.

References

1. Guyton AC and Hall JE, *Textbook of Medical Physiology*. 10th ed, Philadelphia, WB Saunders, 2000.

2. Simon HB, Hyperthermia: Review article *NEJM* 1993; 329(7): 483-487.

3. Mackowiak PA, Wasserman SS, and Levine MM, A critical appraisal of 98.6°F, the upper limit of the normal body temperature, and other legacies of Carl Reinhold August Wunderlich. *JAMA* 1992; 268:1578-1580.

4. Backer HD, Shopes E, Collins, and Barkan H, Exertional heat illness and hyponatremia in hikers. *Am J Emerg Med* 1999; 17:532-539.

5. Pugh LGC, Clothing insulation and accidental hypothermia in youth. *Nature* 1966; 209:1281-1286.

6. Knochel JP, Heat Illness, in Callahan ML (Ed): *Current Therapy in Emergency Medicine*. Philadelphia, BC Decker Inc, 1987.

7. Zumwalt RE, Petty CS, and Holman W, Temperature in closed automobiles in hot weather. *Forens Sci Gazette* 1976; 7:7-8.

8. Surpure JS, Heat-related illness and the automobile. *Ann Emerg Med* 1982; 11:263-265.

9. Gold J, Development of heat pyrexia. *JAMA* 1960; 173:1175-1182.

10. Daily WM and Harrison TR, Study of mechanism and treatment of heat pyrexia. *Am J Med Sci* 1948; 215:42-55.

11. Denborough M, Malignant hyperthermia: Seminar, *Lancet* 1998; 352: 1131-1136.

12. Hasan J, Karvonen MJ, and Piironen P, Special Review. Part 1:Physiological Effects of Extreme Heat , as studied in the Finnish "sauna" bath. *Am J. Physical Med,* 1966; 45: 296-314.

13. Nielsen B, et al., Human circulatory and thermoregulatory adaptations with heat acclimation and exercise in a hot, dry environment, *J Physiol*, 1993; 460:467-485.

14. Nielsen B, et al., Acute and adaptive responses in humans to exercise in a warm, humid environment, *Eur J Physiol* 1997; 434:49-56.

15. Molnar GW, Survival of hypothermia by men immersed in the ocean. *JAMA* 1946; 131:1045-1050.

16. Paton BC, Accidental hypothermia. *Pharmacol Ther* 1983; 22:331-377.

17. Simpson K, Exposure to cold-starvation and neglect, in Simpson K (Ed): *Modern Trends in Forensic Medicine.* St Louis, MO, Mosby Co, 1953.

18. Fitzgerald FT, Hypoglycemia and accidental hypothermia in an alcoholic population. *West J Med* 1980; 133:105-107.

19. Stoner HB et al., Metabolic aspects of hypothermia in the elderly. *Clin Sci* 1980; 59:19-27.

20. MacGregor DC et al., The effects of ether, ethanol, propanol and butanol on tolerance to deep hypothermia. *Dis Chest* 1966; 50:523-529.

21. Cooper KE, Hunter AR, and Keatinge WR, Accidental hypothermia. *Int Anesthesia Clin* 1964; 2:999-1013.

22. Keatinge WR. The effects of subcutaneous fat and of previous exposure to cold on the body temperature, peripheral blood flow and metabolic rate of men in cold water. *J Physiol* 1960; 153:166-178.

23. Sloan REG and Keatinge WR, Cooling rates of young people swimming in cold water. *J Appl Physiol* 1973; 35:371-375.

24. Keatinge WR, Role of cold and immersion accidents. In Adam JM (Ed) *Hypothermia – Ashore and Afloat.* 1981, Chapter 4, Aberdeen Univ. Press, GB.

25. Keatinge WR and Evans M, The respiratory and cardiovascular responses to immersion in cold and warm water. *QJ Exp Physiol* 1961; 46:83-94.

26. Keatinge WR and Nadel JA, Immediate respiratory response to sudden cooling of the skin. *J Appl Physiol* 1965; 20:65-69.

27. Golden F. St C. and Hurvey GR, The "After Drop" and death after rescue from immersion in cold water. In Adam JM (Ed). *Hypothermia – Ashore and Afloat*, Chapter 5, Aberdeen Univ. Press, GB 1981.

28. Burton AC and Bazett HC, Study of average temperature of tissue, of exchange of heat and vasomotor responses in man by means of bath coloremeter. *Am J Physiol* 1936; 117:36-54.

29. Adam JM, Cold Weather: Its characteristics, dangers and assessment, In Adam JM (Ed). *Hypothermia – Ashore and Afloat* Chapter 1, Aberdeen Univ. Press, GB1981.

30. Wilkerson, Raven and Horvath (1972). Cited in Adam JM (Ed). *Hypothermia – Ashore and Afloat*, Aberdeen Univ. Press 1981.

31. Stewart TM, Mountain rescue and the exposure syndrome, some case reports and observations. In Adam JM (Ed). *Hypothermia – Ashore and Afloat*, Chapter 3, Aberdeen Univ. Press, GB 1981.

32. Bedin B, Vangaard L, and Hirvonen J, Paradoxical undressing in fatal hypo-
    thermia. *J Forens Sci*, 1979; 24:543-553.

33. Kavanagh T, A cold-weather "jogging mask" for angina patients. *Can Med
    Assoc J* 1970; 103:1290-1291.

Rape

18

Three elements are necessary for rape of a female: carnal knowledge, force, and commission without consent. Carnal knowledge is the slightest penetration of the labia minora by the penis. Hymenal penetration or ejaculation is not necessary. Force may involve the use of violence, threat of violence or coercion. The actual number of rapes that occur annually is unknown, because of a significant number of unreported cases.

The Living Rape Victim

Rape presents a unique problem to physician clinicians in that they often inherit the burden of not only treatment, but proper collection of evidence. For the correct handling of rape cases, both medically and legally, there must be coordination between the physicians examining the victims and the police agency with jurisdiction. It is preferable that victims of rape be examined at one central hospital by experienced physicians trained in the handling and treatment of such patients and in the proper collection of evidence. In a number of areas, rape examination is being conducted by specially trained forensic nurses. If victims are treated at multiple hospitals, by different physicians, documentation of the rape and collection of the evidence will suffer. At the time of examination, the examiner should have a rape examination kit that contains the necessary materials for collection and packaging of the collected evidence. Such kits also contain forms with pertinent questions to be asked and diagrams that can be used to illustrate injuries.

When the victim of a rape is brought into the hospital, she should be triaged ahead of the non-emergency patients. Written, witnessed consent should be obtained before the examination, collection of specimens, release of information to authorities, and taking of photographs. A female chaperone should always be present. The name of the victim is recorded, along with the date and time of the alleged assault, the date and time of the examination, and, if the police have been notified, the attending law officer's name and badge. The law officer is not present at the examination. The only people present should be the examiner and a nurse, one of whom is usually the female chaperone.

Treatment of life-threatening injuries is, of course, given precedence over the collection of evidence. After collection, the chain of evidence must be maintained. The examining physician should either hand the evidence directly over to a police officer or a representative of the crime laboratory, or place it in a secure storage area for subsequent transmittal.

If examination of victims is by physicians, they should preferably be senior staff obstetrician /gynecologists and not residents. Senior staff members are more experienced and their testimony will carry greater weight in court. In addition, a resident might have moved out of the area by the time the case comes to court. In court, the physician or forensic nurse is never expected to state whether the crime of rape has occurred. Rape is not a diagnosis, it is a matter of jurisprudence. All that the examiner can do is document any evidence of trauma, determine, if possible, whether there has been recent sexual intercourse, and collect trace evidence.

The first step is to obtain a history from the patient. This includes a medical history and a brief account of the alleged assault. Three important questions should be asked:

Did the assailant's penis penetrate the vulva?
Did the assailant experience orgasm?
Did the assailant wear a condom?

Similar questions regarding anal and oral intercourse should also be asked. The victim is asked whether she douched, bathed, showered, defecated, or urinated prior to the examination. All the aforementioned factors can influence whether the physical evidence needed to document sexual intercourse is present. Vertical drainage from the vagina is the worst enemy to the collection of evidence. Because of this, it is recommended that the examiner retain the panty the victim was wearing. Thus, any drainage of semen into the panty can be documented.

After taking a history, the patient is examined. The physician or forensic nurse will conduct the examination in such a manner that objectively acquired evidence can be used to prosecute an assailant in an actual case of rape, or to disprove a false charge of sexual assault. The patient's general appearance and emotional state are noted, as well as whether she is under the influence of alcohol or drugs. The patient's emotional state does not necessarily reflect on the validity of her charges. Some rape victims will appear cold and detached, while others will be hysterical.

All clothing should be examined for stains, tears, missing buttons, dirt, gravel, grease, leaves, etc. The patient herself is then examined. The examiner will look for bruises, bites, and lacerations. He will examine the hands to see if the fingernails are broken. Is the pubic hair matted? Are there any foreign

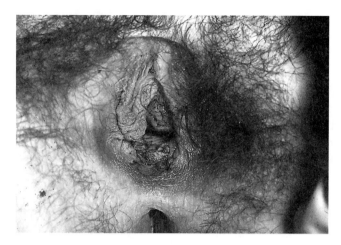

Figure 18.1 Rape-homicide with laceration of vagina at 6 o'clock position.

hairs mixed with the patient's pubic hair? The external genitalia are examined for abrasions, lacerations, and hematomas (Figure 18.1). The vagina and cervix are then examined internally by the use of an unlubricated speculum. All injuries are described.

If there is a bite mark on the patient or if the patient gives a history of the perpetrator's licking a portion of her body (e.g., the nipples), these areas should be swabbed in an attempt to recover saliva. These swabs can then be analyzed for DNA. Positive DNA identification has been made in a number of cases from saliva on the body of the victim. After the swabbing of the bite mark, photographs should be taken. A metric ruler should be included in the photographs. Ideally, one should have a forensic odontologist on call so that they can examine and document the bite mark. They might take casts of the bite mark in addition to photographing it.

During the physical examination, evidence will be collected to document the rape. The only significant differences in the collecting of evidence between the living rape victim and the dead individual are that, in the living individual, a culture will be made from the cervix to detect the presence of venereal disease, and swabs of the mouth and rectum may not be taken if there was no penetration of these orifices.

Absence of trauma to a rape victim does not negate the validity of her claim of rape. Thus, in an analysis of 451 rape victims examined at Parkland Hospital in Dallas by staff gynecologists, Stone found that only 34% showed any evidence of trauma (abrasions, contusions, or lacerations) (I. Stone, personal communication). Of the total number of victims, only 18% had any trauma to the genitalia (reddening, abrasions, contusions, or lacerations). Examination of fluid from the vaginal pool revealed the presence of motile spermatozoa in 19.3% of patients, with motile and non-motile spermatozoa observed in 47% of all patients. Subsequent examination of vaginal smears in the crime laboratory showed spermatozoa present in 62% of all smears.

Following the examination, the patient is treated for her injuries, as well as being given drugs for prevention of pregnancy, and medication for prevention of venereal disease. The patient should be seen 2 weeks after the assault in a follow-up examination. Repeated testing for A.I.D.S. should be performed over the next months.

Rape-Homicides

Rape-homicides are relatively uncommon. When they do occur, they are usually more vicious than routine homicides and generate more publicity and public outcry. They are often extremely difficult to solve because they frequently represent the purest form of stranger-to-stranger crime — that is, the victim and assailant are unknown to each other. There is usually only one assailant, so there is no one to "squeal" to the police. In addition, it is not the type of crime that most people brag about in bars.

In rape-homicides, the cause of death is usually strangulation, stabbing, or blunt force injuries. Rape victims are rarely shot. Excessive force and unnecessary savagery are common in rape-homicides. Occasionally, there is mutilation of the body (Figure 18.2).

In cases of rape-homicide, the medical examiner, in addition to determining the cause of death, has to document evidence of sexual assault and collect trace evidence that can be used subsequently at a trial to convict the perpetrator. In rape-homicides, as in all homicides, the medical examiners' involvement with the body should begin at the scene. This does not mean that they have to be present personally, but at least an investigator from their office should be present. At the scene, the body should be manipulated and touched as little as possible. The scene is not the place for examination of the body, either by a physician or an investigator. Manipulation of a body at the scene could result in destruction of trace evidence.

Transport of the Body

Prior to transporting the body from the scene, paper bags should be placed on the hands to preserve any trace evidence that might be clutched in them or beneath the fingernails. Paper bags should be used instead of plastic, because there will be condensation of moisture inside plastic bags as the body is shifted from cold to warm environments. In addition to covering the hands, the body should be wrapped in a clean white sheet or placed in a clean body bag. This serves two purposes: to prevent loss of trace evidence from the body in transporting it to the morgue, and to prevent the body from picking up debris from the vehicle transporting the body that might subsequently be confused with legitimate trace evidence.

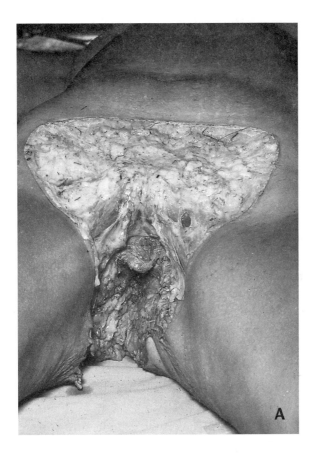

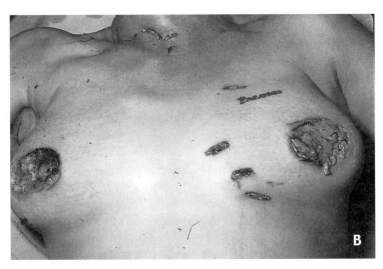

Figure 18.2 (A &B) A 39-yr-old prostitute stabbed and beaten. Nipples cut off and "skinned" in pubic and perineal region.

Examination of the Body

On arriving at the morgue, the body should never be undressed or finger-printed prior to examination by the medical examiner. A number of authorities are now attempting to lift fingerprints from the skin of a body in which there has been close contact between the assailant and victim. Rape-homicides are ideally suited for such attempts because of the physical contact necessary in such an assault. Such procedures, however, are virtually always non-productive. If attempts to recover fingerprints from the body are to be made, the skin should not be touched with the bare hand. If possible, there should be no handling of the thighs, breasts, or upper arms. Unfortunately, the procedures used in an attempt to recover fingerprints might involve fuming of the skin with various chemicals. This can obscure injuries. Because of this, the forensic pathologist should examine the areas to be fumed prior to attempts to lift fingerprints.

Prior to the autopsy, the medical examiner should be thoroughly knowledgeable as to the circumstances surrounding the death, as well as any special tests the police may deem necessary. An autopsy should never be conducted until the medical examiner fully understands the circumstances surrounding the death.

Trace Evidence Recovery from the Hands

The first part of the autopsy consists of examining the hands for foreign material clutched in the hands or present under the fingernails. The body should never be fingerprinted prior to examination of the hands by the medical examiner. Any material removed from the hands, as well as nail clippings, should be put in labeled containers. It is not uncommon to find hair clutched in the hands of rape-homicide victims who have been strangled or beaten about the head. In most instances, however, this turns out to be their own head hair. Thus, it is necessary at the time of the examination to obtain head hair from the victim for a control.

After examining the hands for trace evidence, the fingernails are clipped and placed in marked containers. Clipping and retention of the fingernails is recommended over just scraping and retaining material under the nails. The fingernail clippings can subsequently be examined by the Crime Laboratory for foreign material that might have come from the assailant. The most important of the materials sought is tissue that might have been deposited under the nails if the deceased scratched her assailant. This tissue can be typed for DNA. A number of identifications of assailants have been made through DNA typing of tissue recovered from under the fingernails. A clean pair of scissors or nail clippers should be used to prevent contamination of the cuttings by DNA material from a non-associated source.

Examination of the Clothing

After examining the hands, one should examine the clothing while it is still on the body. The medical examiner should carefully search for fibers, hair, glass, paint, or any foreign material that might have been transferred to the deceased's body from the assailant, his weapon, or a vehicle he used to transport the body of the victim. The medical examiner should note whether any defects in the clothing correspond to the wounds in the deceased to determine whether the individual was attacked with the clothing still on or whether the body was subsequently dressed. Any material removed from the clothing should be put into an envelope and labeled with the deceased's name, case number, date, what is present in the envelope, where it came from, and who recovered it.

The Body

The body now can be undressed. The clothing is reexamined after removal for additional trace evidence. The medical examiner can now begin the examination of the body, documenting any evidence of trauma by written notes, diagrams, x-rays, or photography. At the same time, the medical examiner will begin to collect trace evidence from the body. Samples of head hair should be obtained and retained. These can be compared with hair found clutched in the hands; in a vehicle used to transport a body; on a suspected assailant or, if there was blunt trauma to the head, hair recovered from a suspected murder weapon. The pubic hair is combed to recover any foreign hair deposited there from the pubic hair of the assailant. The combings and the comb are placed in a labeled envelope. In the case of a deceased victim, 15–20 pubic hairs are pulled with forceps and placed in a separate envelope to serve as controls when examining the loose hair. In a living victim, an equal number of pubic hairs are cut, not pulled.

Hair

Prior to current developments in DNA technology, analysis of hair was, for the most part, limited to microscopic examination. One could determine hair color, the race of the individual, its source on the body and its general characteristics. One could never make a positive identification of a hair as coming from a specific individual. All that one could say was that, in all measurable characteristics, two hairs were identical. It is now possible to perform DNA analyses on hair. If one has an intact hair, tandem repeat analysis on the root can be performed. If no root is present, mitochondrial DNA typing can be performed on the shaft. Microscopic examination of hair is only performed as a screening method to determine if DNA analysis is warranted and what type of DNA testing to perform.

Experiments have been conducted to determine the frequency of pubic hair transfer during sexual intercourse. Exline et al. determined that, under optimum conditions, there was transfer of pubic hair to males in 23.6% of cases and to females in 10.9%.[1]

Evidence of Sexual Intercourse

The next step is to obtain samples from the vaginal pool. If death was fairly recent, a hanging drop preparation for motile sperm can be made. Vaginal smears on glass slides are prepared and air dried. Two cotton-tip swabs soaked with material from the vaginal pool should be air dried and placed in cardboard boxes (not test tubes). Any apparent seminal stains on the skin of the victim should be recovered with saline-moistened pieces of cloth. Oral and rectal smears and swabs should also be obtained and retained in all autopsy cases.

The slides should be placed either in clean plastic slide holders or in new cardboard holders. The latter should not be reused to prevent carryover of vaginal or seminal material to a subsequent slide placed in the cardboard container. Vaginal, rectal and oral slides should be stained in an attempt to identify any spermatozoa. If sperm are present, DNA analysis of the swabs is performed. When no sperm are observed, part of each of the swabs from the vagina, rectum, and mouth can be used for presumptive tests for acid phosphatase. If, however, sexual intercourse is still strongly suspected, or if the acid phosphatase test was weakly positive or questionable, an assay for semen-specific protein P30 should be performed. Occasionally, P30 is positive in the face of a negative acid phosphatase. If the acid phosphatase or P30 tests are positive, even if no spermatozoa are seen, DNA analysis should be performed.[2]

In living individuals, motile sperm are usually seen only up to 6 h, occasionally 12 h, and, very rarely, up to 24 h. In the latter case, it is probable that the sperm was obtained from cervical mucus. Thus, it is important when searching for motile sperm in an individual alleged to have been raped only a few hours before to obtain this material from the vaginal pool and not from the cervix.

Non-motile sperm with tails in the living individual are usually seen up to 26 h, with occasional reports of 2 to 3 days. In the latter cases, these are probably sperm trapped in cervical mucus. The identification of only a single sperm on one or two slides should make the examiner wary that he may have one of those cases in which there is unusual prolonged survival of the sperm, that is, sperm from cervical mucus. In most rape cases, numerous sperm will be seen on each smear. The presence of several sperm on a slide, with a history of the last voluntary intercourse 2 or 3 days before, would be inconsistent with the sperm's originating at that time, but would be consistent with a recent rape.

The survival time of spermatozoa in the vagina of living individuals as reported in the medical literature is quite variable. This can be explained by two factors: where the sample was collected, and what criteria are used to identify sperm. Swabs should be taken from the vaginal pool and not the cervix, because sperm can survive in cervical mucus much longer than in the vagina. Thus, sperm seen on a cervical swab may not be caused by the rape but by sexual intercourse 2 to 3 days before. More important is what criteria are used to identify sperm. Some clinicians identify sperm only when they see a complete spermatozoa — one with a head and tail. Other individuals require only the head to be present. This difference in criteria of identification explains some of the differences in reports of the persistence of sperm.

The best study of the persistence of sperm in the vagina of living individuals is by Willott and Allard.[3] They examined 1332 vaginal swabs taken in alleged rape cases and found 57% positive for sperm. The longest time for identification of sperm with tails was 26 h. Sperm heads were identified up to 120 h. A cervical swab was positive for sperm at 179 h (7 days).

Willott and Allard also examined 225 anal and 212 rectal swabs.[3] Sperm were identified in 37% of the former and in 32% of the latter. They found that it was rare to find sperm with tails, especially after more than 6 h. Sperm heads were identified on an anal swab 45 h after intercourse and on a rectal swab 65 h after intercourse. They also examined 74 oral swabs, of which 12% were positive. Sperm with tails were identified up to 3 h and sperm heads up to 6 h.

A number of points should be remembered about the identification of sperm in vaginal, rectal, and oral swabs. Failure to demonstrate sperm does not preclude intercourse. In addition, the times previously quoted for persistence of sperm are for living individuals. Sperm have been identified in the vagina of dead individuals 1 to 2 weeks after death. In dead individuals, the sperm are destroyed by decomposition, not drainage or the action of the vaginal secretions or cells. Sperm that is deposited on material like cotton, cloth, or paper and air dried can be identified years after the event.

In some cases of undoubted rape, no sperm have been identified. This could be caused by use of a condom, failure to ejaculate, drainage of semen or aspermia secondary to disease or a vasectomy. Because of this problem, substances were looked for in semen besides sperm that could be identified by biochemical means to indicate recent intercourse. The substance most widely analyzed for has been acid phosphatase. Acid phosphatase is found in high concentrations in semen.[4] It is usually present in the vagina for up to 18–24 h after sexual intercourse and occasionally up to 72 h. The highest levels are within the first 12 h, with gradual disappearance by 48–72 h. Because it usually disappears in the first 24 h after intercourse, it is most useful as an indicator of recent intercourse, compared with non-motile sperm, which can be identified up to 2–3 days after intercourse.

In 1978, a semen-specific glycoprotein (P30) of prostatic origin was discovered.[2] This substance is present in semen only and cannot be detected in any body fluids from females. P30 is present in both normal and aspermic semen. In a report by Graves et al., P30 was found to be detectable in vaginal fluid for a mean period of 27 h after intercourse (a range of 13–47 h), as compared with 14 h for acid phosphatase (8–24 h).[2] All specimens collected more than 48 h from intercourse were negative for P30. Graves et al. also found that, in some instances, the test for P30 was positive when the acid phosphatase was negative. Thus, of 27 females allegedly raped in which acid phosphatase was negative, 26% were positive for P30, thus indicating sexual intercourse had taken place.

Bite Marks

One form of evidence previously alluded to is bite marks (Figure 18.3). Bite marks can be as individual as fingerprints. A number of individuals have been positively identified and convicted on the basis of bite marks. Thus, in any case in which a bite mark is present on an individual, whether living or dead, the mark should first be swabbed for recovery of saliva for DNA testing. The bite mark should then be documented photographically, with a scale present in the picture. If a forensic odontologist is on call, he should be summoned at the time of the examination to perform the aforementioned steps as well as taking a cast. If a suspect is arrested, a court order can be obtained to get an impression of his teeth to be compared with the injuries on the victim.

Homosexual Rape

For completeness, we should mention the victims of homosexual rape. The victims are usually children or persons incarcerated in jail or prison. Essentially the same procedures as those performed on the female rape victim should be performed on the male.

Of interest are homosexual-related homicides. These tend to be more violent than their heterosexual counterparts. There is "overkill." The victim is often nude and the number and extent of injuries on the body tend to be greater.[5] The cause of death is usually stabbing, strangulation, blunt force, or a combination of them all. The case might be extremely bizarre, with evidence of torture (Figure 18.4).

DNA Analysis

Until the late 1980s, serological testing in cases of rape involved traditional enzyme studies. DNA typing has virtually eliminated such testing. DNA "fingerprinting," i.e., DNA typing for forensic purposes, was developed by

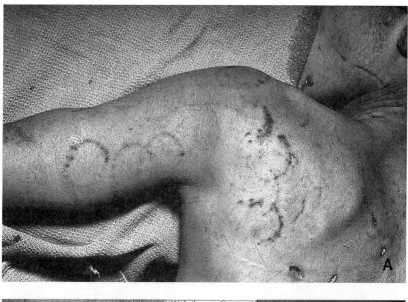

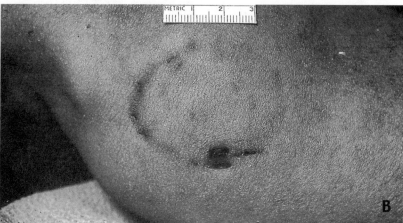

Figure 18.3 (A and B) Bite marks.

Dr. Alec Jeffreys in 1985.[6–8] He determined that, in each strand of DNA, there are thousands of identical DNA sequences. The length, constitution, and number of the repetitive sequences are different for each person. The identification and demonstration of the sequences of nucleotides possessed by an individual cell is the basis for DNA identification.

The importance of DNA fingerprinting is that any tissue containing nucleated cells can potentially be linked to an individual, usually to the statistical exclusion of all other individuals. DNA can be obtained from sperm, nucleated blood cells, cells from soft tissue, teeth, bone, fingernails, saliva, urine and hair — essentially, any tissue in which there are

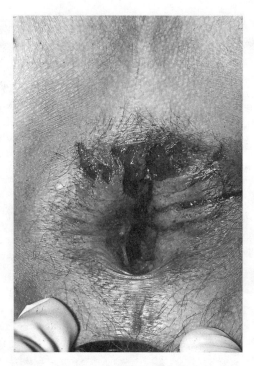

Figure 18.4 Lacerations of the anus. The deceased was beaten and stabbed. A toilet bowl brush was rammed up the rectum and the body set on fire.

nucleated cells. DNA can be extracted from these specimens, chemically divided into fragments, and formed into a pattern that will serve as an identification profile. This pattern can then be compared with a DNA pattern obtained from a suspect's blood specimen. If these match, and the test is done with sufficient probes, there is virtually no doubt that the suspect is the source of the tissue to the exclusion of all other individuals, except for an identical twin. If the patterns do not match, then the suspect is not the perpetrator.

In addition to the absolute nature of DNA identification, there are other advantages. DNA is much more stable than the enzymes and proteins formerly used in blood identification. There are no false positives caused by degradation. If the DNA is altered, it will fail to form a pattern. DNA is fairly resistant to degradation and analysis has been made on human remains thousands of years old.

In addition to its application in criminal matters, DNA identification can be used in paternity suits. A child inherits half its DNA from each parent. If the half of the child's DNA pattern that is different from the mother's pattern matches that of the alleged father, then there is no doubt that he is the biological father.

Two basic concepts must be understood in dealing with DNA analyses:

1. If the DNA profile of the evidence DNA is different from that of the suspect in any aspect, then the suspect is absolutely excluded.
2. If the evidence DNA and the suspect DNA match then there are three possibilities:
   a. The evidence DNA came from the suspect.
   b. The evidence DNA came from another individual who has the same DNA profile. This is possible if the second individual is a monozygotic twin, or because an insufficient number of tests were performed to differentiate the suspect from the other individual.
   c. An error was made in either the collection or analysis of the specimen DNA.

Many individuals do not know what is meant by a DNA match. Except for monozygotic twins, the DNA pattern is unique for each individual. DNA profiling, however, does not compare the whole DNA pattern of an individual and that of the evidence DNA, only a minute portion. A match is made by the statistical exclusion of all other individuals. To determine this, the frequency of occurrence of selected alleles in the major population groups is determined, and testing is performed to determine the presence of these selected alleles. If the evidence DNA and the suspect's DNA are tested for an allele that occurs in one in ten individuals, and they match, then 9 out of 10 people in the population are excluded as sources of the DNA. If the second allele tested for also occurs and this matches, then 99 out of 100 people are excluded. If sufficient alleles are tested for, the probabilities for exclusion go into the millions or even billions. Thus, a match is made on statistics.

All nucleated cells in the body contain 23 pairs of chromosomes except for sperm and ova, which contain 23 chromosomes rather than 23 pairs. Each chromosome consists of a double spiral of deoxyribonucleic acid (DNA) in the shape of a twisted ladder, the double helix. The sides of the ladder consist of alternating sugar (deoxyribose) and phosphate molecules; the rungs of the ladder consist of nitrogen bases. The weakest part of the helix or ladder is the rungs, where the nitrogen bases are weakly linked by hydrogen bonds. DNA is composed of units called nucleotides, which consist of a sugar, a phosphate group, and a base. Millions of these nucleotides form a single strand. Despite the millions of nucleotides, only four different bases are used. Two of these are purines (adenine and guanine) and two are pyrimidines (thymine and cytosine). In forming the rungs of the ladder, guanine always binds to cytosine and adenine always binds to thymine. These are the only two possible combinations and these are called complementary base pairs. Because of the millions of nucleotides forming a single strand and the fact that there are 23 pairs of chromosomes in each cell, there is an almost infinite variety in the arrangement of the nucleotides. The order or sequence of the bases in a DNA molecule forms a code of the genetic information of the cells.

A gene is a series of these bases that occupies a specific location (locus) on a chromosome, producing a specific product. There is usually more than one form of a gene for each locus. These are called alleles. Most of the chromosome, however, serves no known function. These areas consist of multiple copies of identical base sequences, 50–60 base pairs in length, arranged one behind the other, that is, in tandem. The repeated sequences are known as tandem repeats, with the areas made up of tandem repeats known as VNTR (variable number of tandem repeats). Just like a gene, a loci of VNTR can have multiple alleles. The VNTR loci were the first areas used in DNA typing because of the multiple alleles.

The original method of DNA analysis was RFLP (restriction fragment length polymorphism). This was a prolonged, complicated method that took a minimum of 6–8 weeks to conduct. DNA was chemically extracted from the submitted biological specimen and purified. It was then cut into fragments by a restriction enzyme. These substances cut the DNA molecule at specific base sequences. The number of DNA fragments and their length as produced by a particular restriction enzyme depend on how often the enzyme's base sequence occurs in the DNA specimen. Because every individual's DNA sequence is different, the fragments in the DNA specimen from one individual to another are different in number and length from those in a DNA specimen from another individual.

The DNA fragments were then separated into bands by electrophoresis. DNA carries a negative charge and thus travels toward the positive pole in electrophoresis. The distance that each fragment travels depends on its length. The longer the fragment, the slower its rate of migration. This creates a number of DNA bands in the gel. These are transferred to a nylon membrane by a technique known as Southern blotting. The membrane is then exposed to a DNA probe having a radioactive tag. The probe looks for a complementary sequence of bases. Thus, adenine looks for thymine, and guanine looks for cytosine. The probe then binds to the DNA pattern. X-ray film is placed next to the membrane to detect the radioactive patterns that appear as a series of bands similar to the bar code on items in grocery stores. Each dark stripe or band represents a point where the DNA probe is bound to its complementary base sequences. The pattern of bands is unique for each individual (excepting identical twins), just as a fingerprint is. While two individuals may have identical patterns for one or two probes, if a sufficient number of probes are used, at some point, the probes will begin to not match and the individual is ruled out. If the DNA being tested came from the individual it is being tested against, and a sufficient number of probes are run, then statistically, the probability that the individual was the source of the DNA approaches 100%. With the use of sufficient DNA probes, the probability that an identification is positive can be as great as 30 billion to one.[8]

Short Tandem Repeats

RFLP has been replaced by a new technique that uses analysis of short tandem repeats. STR are loci on chromosomes normally 2 to 6 bases long. While shorter than VNTR, they are more numerous. There are approximately 8 to 10 alleles per STR loci. Using the 13 STR loci recommended by the FBI, the average match probability is less than one in a trillion.

Problems can arise if an insufficient number of loci are tested for or if the DNA sample being tested is degraded so that only a limited number of loci can be typed. If close relatives are typed, they can be expected to be genetically similar, with numerous identical loci. Thus, it would not be unexpected for siblings to match at 4–5 STR loci. A match has even been reported at 10 loci.[9] Because of this, if only a limited number of loci are or can be tested, there is the potential for misidentification.

STR typing of urine is based on recovery of nucleated cells present in the urine. These are epithelial cells of the genito-urinary tract and white blood cells. Typically, women have more nucleated cells in their urine than men. Because of this, STR typing of urine and urine stains is more successful on urine from women than from men. In view of this, mitochondrial typing is a better analytical technique for analysis of urine of male origin.

In STR analysis, the DNA is extracted from the submitted specimen, quantitated and then replicated by the polymerase chain reaction (PCR). Identification of STR loci can then be performed by gel-based electrophoresis methods utilizing fluorescent dyes, or by capillary electrophoresis using laser-induced fluorescence detection. The advantages of the STR method of DNA analysis are:

- Because of the unlimited ability to reproduce the STR segments by PCR, testing can be performed on very small quantities of DNA, e.g., wipings from apparently clean full metal-jacketed bullets that have perforated the body.
- The analytical techniques are simple to perform.
- It is more rapid to perform (2–3 days).
- It can be automated.

The main disadvantage is that, because the method is exquisitely sensitive, it is susceptible to contamination.

Mention should be made of examination of the suspect in a case of alleged rape. If the individual is apprehended shortly after the incident, his pubic hair should be combed for pubic hair from the victim. Any foreign hair recovered should be submitted for DNA analysis. In addition to collection of foreign pubic hair, swabs of the penis should also be made. In a number of cases, DNA from the victim has been recovered from these swabs using STR. Cina et al. conducted an experimental study on the ability to identify female DNA on postcoital penile swabs.[10] They were able to identify female DNA on swabs taken as long as 24 h after intercourse if the individual did not bathe or shower. Analysis identified the X chromosome and 8 STR loci.

Combined DNA Index System

Combined DNA Index System (CODIS) is a nationwide electronic database of DNA profiles. Cities, counties and states throughout the U.S. are in the process of collecting DNA samples from individuals convicted of various crimes in their jurisdictions, performing DNA profiles (at present 13 specified STR loci), and submitting the results to CODIS. When a crime occurs in which biological material is recovered, the DNA profile of this material can be submitted to CODIS for possible identification of the individual who is the source of the DNA.

Mitochondrial DNA Analysis

Mitochondrial DNA (mtDNA) analysis[11,12] is used when the biological evidence recovered is either small in quantity or degraded. MtDNA typing can be done on a single hair shaft. It is of value in typing old bones and decomposed tissue, where nuclear DNA typing is not possible. MtDNA differs from nuclear DNA in its location in the cell, its quantity and its mode of inheritance. While the cell nucleus contains only two sets of 23 chromosomes, the cell contains hundreds, even thousands, of mitochondria. Thus, more mtDNA is available for analysis than nuclear DNA.

While nuclear DNA is inherited from both parents, mtDNA is inherited solely from the mother. Because of this, the mtDNA sequences of a mother and her children exactly match. This means that mtDNA analysis is limited in that it cannot differentiate between individuals of the same maternal line. This attribute, however, makes it valuable in identifying unknown bodies. MtDNA has a higher mutation rate than nuclear DNA. In spite of this, the transmission of mtDNA is consistent over many generations.

As a rule, mtDNA does not undergo recombination. Individuals, however, can have more than one type of mtDNA (heteroplasmy). This can occur in either a single tissue or different tissues. Variation between the types is usually only one base, though greater variation may occur. Heteroplasmy does not invalidate the use of mtDNA for forensic analysis.

MtDNA analysis is tedious and labor intensive. The DNA is extracted, amplified by the polymerase chain reaction, purifed and quantitated, and finally sequenced. In sequencing, the DNA is fluorescently labeled and separated using gel electrophoresis. An automated fluorescence detector records the wavelength of the fluorescent dyes on each base as they migrate through the gel past the detection area of the instrument, generating a chromatogram. The mtDNA sequences are then compared with a standard mtDNA reference, the Anderson sequence. The resultant report is made up of the number of the positions different from the Anderson sequence and the different bases at these positions. Because of its exquisite sensitivity, there is always danger of contamination at the scene, in collection and in analysis.

References

1. Exline DL, Smith FP, and Drexler SG, Frequency of pubic hair transfer during sexual intercourse. *J Forens Sci*, 1998; 43(3):505-508.

2. Graves HCB, Sensabaugh GF, and Blake ET, Postcoital detection of a male-specific semen protein. *NEJM*, 1985; 312:338-343.

3. Willott GM and Allard JE, Spermatozoa — their persistence after sexual intercourse. *Forens Sci Int* 1982; 19:135-154.

4. Ricci LR and Hoffman SA, Prostatic acid phosphatase and sperm in the postcoital vagina. *Ann Emerg Med*, 1982; 11: 530-534.

5. Bell MD and Vila RI, Homicide and Homosexual Victims: A Study of 67 cases from Broward County Florida Medical Examiner's Office (1982–1992), with Special Emphasis on "Overkill," *Am J Forens Med Path* 1996; 17 (1): 65-69.

6. Jeffreys AJ, Wilson V, and Thein SL, Individual-specific fingerprints of human DNA. *Nature* 1985; 316:76-79.

7. Gill P, Jeffreys AJ, and Werret DJ, Forensic application of DNA fingerprints. *Nature* 1985; 318:577-579.

8. Merz B, DNA fingerprints come to court. *JAMA* 1988; 259:2193-2194.

9. Bourke MT et al., Sib pair identity at multiple STR loci: Implications for interpretations of forensic DNA casework. Presented at the annual meeting of the American Academy of Forensic Sciences, February 2000, Reno.

10. Cina SJ, et al., Isolation and identification of female DNA on postcoital penile swabs. *Am J Forens Med Path*, 2000; 21(2):97-100.

11. Isenberg AR and Moore JM, Mitochondrial DNA Analysis at the FBI laboratory. *Forens Sci Comm*, 1999; 1(2).

12. Bar W, et al., DNA Commission of the International Society for Forensic Genetics: Guidelines for mitochondrial DNA typing. 2000; *Int J Legal Med* 113:193-196.

Emboli

19

Gas Embolism

Gas emboli may involve either or both the venous and arterial systems. In most instances, the gas is air, though, in some diagnostic situations, it could be carbon dioxide, nitrous oxide or nitrogen.[1] In the venous system, death from air embolism depends on the size of the bolus and the rate of delivery. In arterial embolism, these factors are not as important, because only a small number of air bubbles occluding a coronary artery or a cerebral vessel can result in death. In venous air embolism, between 75 and 250 cm^3 of air delivered rapidly is necessary to cause death.

Venous air embolism may occur during therapeutic or diagnostic procedures secondary to trauma, during childbirth or abortion, and during oral-genital sex in a pregnant woman when her partner blows air into the vagina. Arterial air embolism occurs secondary to cardiopulmonary bypass, arterial catherization, surgical procedures involving arteries, or injury to the pulmonary veins after chest trauma. One might also incur a paradoxical air embolism, that is, air crossing from the venous to the arterial circulation.

Air entering the venous system is carried to the heart and pulmonary arteries, with resultant mechanical occlusion of the pulmonary arterial vasculature by air bubbles. This is followed by a transient vasoconstriction. Obstruction of the pulmonary blood flow results in churning of the blood and air, producing the frothy appearance of the blood seen at autopsy. This churning can result in the development of complexes of air bubbles, fibrin, platelet aggregates, erythrocytes, and fat globules, thus further occluding the vasculature.[2] Death is caused by obstruction of the pulmonary blood flow secondary to obstruction of the pulmonary arterial system by the air bubbles, the pulmonary vasoconstriction, and the cellular aggregates. With a very large bolus of air, the obstruction occurs not only in the pulmonary vasculature but also in the right ventricle.

Paradoxical air emboli occur when air or gas that has entered the venous system crosses over to the arterial system. Typically, these have been described in association with septal defects of the heart. These permit air to go from the right side of the heart to the left without passing through the pulmonary vasculature. If a large air embolism is carried to the heart, the sudden rise in the right-sided heart pressure may result in a right-to-left shunt through a probe patent, but physiologically closed, foramen ovale. Increased right-sided heart pressure also causes air to be forced into the epicardial veins on the surface of the heart. Paradoxical emboli can also occur secondary to arteriovenous anastomoses in the lung. In addition, with sufficiently high pressures and delivery of large quantities of air, the ability of the lungs to filter out air can be exceeded and bubbles of gas may traverse the pulmonary circulation and enter the left atrium. This has been demonstrated by Butler and Hills in experiments on dogs.[3] Air entering the arterial circulation causes death by occluding the cerebral or coronary arteries. Only a very small quantity of air is necessary.

Forensic pathologists will encounter air emboli most commonly in knife wounds of the neck, and secondary to surgical procedures. Air enters an open vein whenever there is a negative pressure gradient between the vein and the right atrium. This is facilitated by the negative intrathoracic pressure generated during inspiration. The higher the open vein is above the right atrium, the greater the pressure gradient and the more likely air is to enter the vessel. This is why wounds to the neck can result in air emboli. Thus, in individuals incurring stab or incised wounds of the neck with injury to the veins, the prosector may want to explore the possibilities of air embolism at the time of autopsy.

The true incidence of venous air embolism during surgical and diagnostic procedures is unknown, with one exception — craniotomy in the sitting position. Here, air emboli occur in 21 to 29% of all craniotomies and 40% of all occipital craniotomies.[4,5] Air emboli have also been reported in a host of other therapeutic and diagnostic procedures. Any surgical procedure that causes a negative pressure gradient between the right side of the heart and a vein is a potential risk for venous air embolism. Individuals have been seated or prone, supine, in the lithotomy position, and in the lateral knee-chest position at the time they incurred air emboli.[6]

Air emboli were more common when blood and other fluids were delivered in glass bottles rather than the present collapsible plastic bags. Even with plastic bags, there is the possibility, though rare, of an air embolus.[7] Air emboli have also occurred following cesarean section, placenta previa, and subclavian venipuncture.[8–10] With a large-bore channel to a vein, a fatal amount of air can pass quickly into a vessel. Theoretically, 100 cm^3 of air per second can enter through a 14-gauge needle with a 5-cm water pressure drop across it.[10] Fortunately for people with subclavian lines, this is more theoretical than actual.

Homicides secondary to injection of air into the venous system using a syringe are rare because of the large quantity of air one has to introduce in a bolus (100–250 cm3), the expertise necessary to administer the injection intravenously, and the necessary passivity of the patient. Individuals with established intravenous lines, such as hospital patients, will, of course, be easier to kill in this way.

When abortions were, for the most part, illegal, occasional deaths caused by air emboli were encountered. This occurred following dilatation of the cervical os, with resultant tears of the margins of the placenta or the cervical veins. In some cases, there was a delay in the air embolus. Thus, in one case, after having an illegal abortion, the woman left the premises, only to collapse and die 2 h later. At autopsy, air could be seen in the inferior vena cava, right atrium, and right ventricle.

Death caused by air embolism in association with pregnancy may also occur secondary to cesarean section and placenta previa.[8–10] Just as in an abortion, there can be a time delay prior to the onset of the fatal air embolus. In deaths of pregnant females during sexual intercourse, one should always suspect air emboli. This occurs during oral–genital intercourse, with the partner blowing air into the vagina during cunnilingus.

Suicide from an air embolus is rare. The authors have seen it in individuals who have slit their throats, severing their jugular veins, as well as in patients hooked up to dialysis machines who disconnected their tubing, with resultant massive air embolus.

The broad spectrum of deaths caused by air embolism is illustrated by the following cases: The first involved a 22-year-old woman, 34 weeks pregnant, who was having intercourse with her husband. Her husband blew into her vagina and she suddenly "passed out." She was dead on arrival at the emergency room. At autopsy, there was air in the right atrium and ventricle. The epicardial veins had a beaded appearance caused by air bubbles. Bubbles of air were also present in the pelvic veins. The blood of the heart had a frothy appearance.

The second case involved an obese 40-year-old man who was prone in the semi knee-chest position for a lumbar laminectomy. Five hours into the procedure, he developed bradycardia and an agonal rhythm. The autopsy revealed air in the right ventricle, with beading of the epicardial veins by air bubbles.

The third case was a 39-year-old woman who went into premature labor. She presented with vaginal bleeding. On admission to the hospital, she had a complete central placenta previa and a breech presentation. The child was delivered by cesarean section at 8:51 in the evening. The operation was over at 9:30 p.m. She then was returned to the recovery room. At midnight, she was taken to her room. As she was being placed into bed, she had a grandmal seizure and went into cardiopulmonary arrest. Attempts at resuscitation were unsuccessful. At autopsy, there was air in the right atrium and ventricle with beading of the epicardial veins by massive numbers of air bubbles.

In a living patient, the diagnosis of venous air embolism to the heart can be made by auscultation of the mill-wheel murmur or by detection of intracardiac air using dopler ultrasonography or transesophageal echocardiography. In the deceased individual, to make the diagnosis of air embolism, one must consider the diagnosis prior to the autopsy. The first step may be a chest X-ray to look for air in the heart (Figure 19.1). A Y-shaped incision can then be made into the skin and musculature of the chest and the skin and muscle retracted. Instead of then removing the chest plate in the ordinary way, a "window" should be cut in the sternum and ribs overlying the heart. The bony plate should then be retracted very carefully, so as not to introduce air into the venous system. The pericardial sac can then be cut open and the heart visualized. The epicardial veins should be examined for the presence of air. One or two bubbles in an epicardial vein do not make a diagnosis of air embolism.

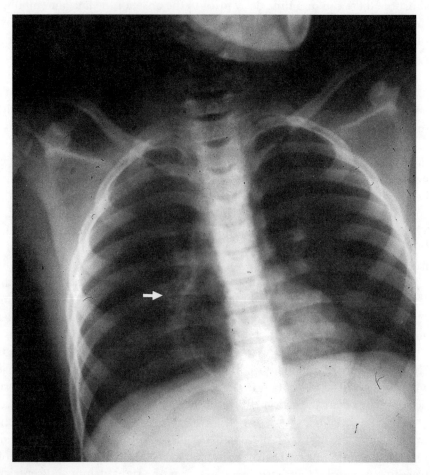

Figure 19.1 Massive air embolus with air in the right atrium and ventricle. Note outline of right ventricular wall.

With air embolism, the epicardial veins usually have a beaded appearance, with numerous air bubbles the length of these vessels (Figure 19.2). The pericardial sac should then be flooded, the plunger removed from a 50-cc syringe, a large-bore needle attached, and the syringe filled with water. The tip of the needle can then be pushed into the right ventricle. If there is air in this chamber, it will be seen to bubble up through the water in the syringe. The water should then be removed and the right side of the heart opened. The blood typically has a frothy appearance. Following this, the incision can be extended through the anterior abdominal wall to the pubic area. If the air entered in the pelvic region, the inferior vena cava is examined for air bubbles. One should be careful about interpreting one or two bubbles in this vessel as evidence of air embolism. If the deceased has been vigorously resuscitated with a thoracotomy and internal cardiac massage, it is usually impossible to make the diagnosis of air embolus based on the autopsy, because the air observed in vessels could be caused by resuscitation. Air in the coronary arteries cannot be identified at autopsy because air bubbles cannot be seen through the wall of these vessels. In the brain, the process of removing the skull cap, cutting through the dura, and putting traction on the brain to see the cerebral circulation might introduce air bubbles into the circulation. Thus, the presence of a few air bubbles in the cerebral circulation

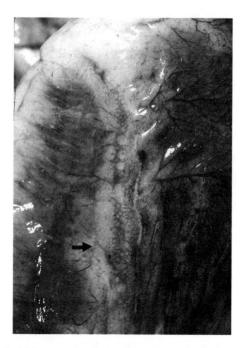

Figure 19.2 Air bubbles in epicardial veins of heart in death caused by air embolism.

does not necessarily indicate an embolus. If individuals survive the initial insult of air in the coronary and cerebral circulation, they might develop myocardial or cerebral infarcts.

The technique described to demonstrate air in the heart using a 50-cc syringe is very basic and very crude. A much better and more sophisticated method is to use an aspirometer. This device not only demonstrates the presence of air but measures the amount and stores it for subsequent analysis by gas chromatography.[11] Embolized air differs from atmospheric air in that CO_2 is less than 15%; N_2 is higher than 70% and O_2 is reduced, usually measuring between 8 and 15%.[10] Detection of CH_4 and H_2 indicates that decomposition has begun. Most individuals feel that decomposition, with its formation of gases of putrefaction, precludes the diagnosis of air emboli. Bajanowski et al. disagree.[12] They analyzed gas recovered from the ventricles of 15 individuals, exhumed after 10–45 weeks burial, who were believed to have been killed by injection of air. They found that analysis in 8 of the 15 cases gave results typical of air embolism, with only small amounts of the gases of putrefaction present.

Fat Embolism Syndrome

Fat embolism is characterized by the presence of globules of fat in the lung and peripheral circulation. Fat embolization occurs in 90–100% of individuals with long-bone or pelvic fractures. Following trauma, fat droplets enter the circulation. The larger droplets are strained out by the lungs, where they lodge in the vasculature. The smaller fat globules travel through the pulmonary capillaries, enter the arterial circulation, and are carried to the brain and other organs. In only a small percentage of individuals with fat emboli, however, does this condition become symptomatic. When this occurs, the individual is said to have the **fat embolism syndrome**.[13–15] This syndrome is characterized by progressive pulmonary insufficiency, mental deterioration, and a petechial rash. Typically, symptoms do not appear for 24 to 72 h following injury. There is, however, a severe fulminating form of fat emboli in which both pulmonary and cerebral deterioration begins within the first 12 h. Fat embolism syndrome is rare in children.

The incidence of fat emboli syndrome increases with the multiplicity of the long-bone fractures. Ten Duis noted that the syndrome developed in 3% of patients with a single fracture of the femur and 33% of patients with two fractured femora.[13]

While the fat embolism syndrome is usually associated with long-bone or pelvic fractures, it can also be seen in association with acute pancreatitis, extensive burns, liposuction, decompression sickness, and parenteral infusion of lipids.[14] It can also be precipitated by reaming and nailing procedures for long-bone fractures.

The major clinical signs of fat embolism are respiratory insufficiency, mental deterioration, and a petechial rash. The petechiae are typically seen in the conjunctivae, as well as on the chest and the axillae. These major signs may be accompanied by fever; tachycardia; thrombocytopenia; fat globules in the urine, sputum and retina; as well as renal failure. Most individuals who die from fat embolism do so as a result of pulmonary failure. There are two theories as to the cause of pulmonary injury. The first holds that the injury is caused by the mechanical obstruction of the pulmonary vasculature by large globules of fat. The second theory is that free fatty acids, released from either the marrow directly or from fat lodged in the lungs, cause direct toxic injury to the pneumocytes and endothelium, with resultant abnormalities in gas exchange. Microscopically, there are fat emboli in the pulmonary vasculature, with edema, transudate, and exudate in the alveoli. Visualization of fat emboli within the pulmonary vasculature requires the use of frozen sections and fat stains. If the individual survives a few days, the brain will show small perivascular hemorrhages in the white matter around vessels containing fat emboli (Figure 19.3). In the early stages, the brain may appear grossly normal.

Amniotic Fluid Emboli

This is an uncommon but highly lethal complication of pregnancy, first described by Steiner and Lushbough.[16] While early studies reported an 86% mortality, more recent work indicates that the mortality has decreased to

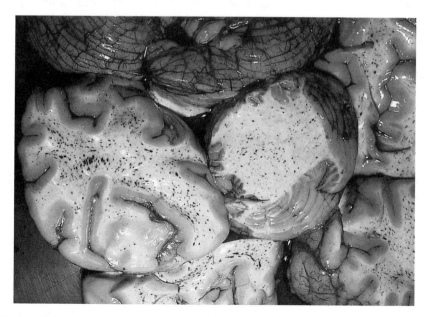

Figure 19.3 Petechial hemorrhages of brain caused by fat embolism in 21-year-old female with fracture of right femur.

61%.[16,17] Unfortunately, the increased survival was accompanied by a 24% incidence of permanent neurological injury. Thus, only 15% of patients survived neurologically intact. There are no demographic factors predisposing to amniotic fluid embolism as well as no relationship to route of delivery, prolonged hard labor, or use of oxytocin.

Most cases of amniotic emboli occur during active labor, though cases have occurred as late as 90 min postpartum.[16–18] Clark et al. reviewed 46 cases of amniotic fluid emboli.[17] Thirty women had amniotic fluid emboli during labor but before delivery, and 13 after delivery. Of these 13 cases, five had emboli following vaginal delivery, and eight during cesarean section but after delivery. Three of the patients who had cesarean sections were in labor prior to the section. Of the 13 individuals developing symptoms of amniotic fluid emboli after delivery, nine (69%) did so within 5 min of delivery.

Three of the cases reported by Clark et al. involved individuals undergoing second-trimester abortions. Ammotic fluid emboli have been reported in first- and second-trimester abortions as well as following abdominal trauma and amniocentesis.[19–21]

Clinical Presentation

The clinical presentation of amniotic fluid emboli is sudden dyspnea, hypotension, and seizures, followed by cardiovascular arrest.[18,22,23] Of the 40 individuals studied by Clark et al. who had cardiac arrest, all but two arrested within the first hour.[17] If death does not occur immediately, consumptive coagulopathy usually develops. Clark et al. reported that 38 of the 46 patients they studied had clinical or laboratory evidence of a coagulopathy; eight individuals died before their clotting status could be evaluated, either clinically or by laboratory testing. Typically, laboratory studies show decreased fibrinogen, elevated levels of fibrin split products, prolonged partial thromboplastin and prothrombin times, and thrombocytopenia.

Etiology

The syndrome of amniotic fluid embolism has been attributed to the acute embolization of amniotic fluid and debris of fetal origin into the maternal venous circulation, with resultant pulmonary microvascular obstruction. On reaching the lung, this material is presumed to produce severe transient vasospasm of the pulmonary vasculature, pulmonary hypertension, right heart failure, and hypoxia. Clark et al. disagree with this hypothesis.[17] They feel that, in some individuals, no matter how small the amount of amniotic fluid involved, simple exposure of the maternal circulation to amniotic fluid triggers a pathophysiologic cascade similar to anaphylactic or septic shock generating the physiological derangements characterizing these syndromes. This would explain the observation that fetal debris is not seen at autopsy in all cases where there is no doubt, clinically, that the patient had "amniotic fluid emboli." Thus, in the 22 cases coming to autopsy in the study by Clark et al., in six of the individuals (27%) no fetal elements (squamous cells, hair, fat droplets, mucin or trophoblasts) were identified in the lungs.[17]

Autopsy Findings

Traditionally, the diagnosis of amniotic fluid embolism was made at autopsy by a combination of clinical signs and symptoms and the finding of mucin derived from meconium, fetal squamous cells, lanugo hair, or vernix fat globules in the pulmonary vasculature. These materials can usually be seen on hematoxylin and eosin slides, though special stains might better demonstrate individual elements. Mucin is virtually always present, with cellular elements seen less frequently.[23] As pointed out by Clark et al., in a substantial number of cases where there is no doubt clinically that the patient has had amniotic fluid emboli, no fetal elements are identified.[17] This is especially true in deaths during early pregnancy caused by the less abundant nature of these elements in amniotic fluid at this stage.[20]

The presence of squamous cells in the pulmonary arterial circulation at autopsy has traditionally been regarded as one of the pathognomonic elements of amniotic fluid emboli. A study by Clark et al. to see whether squamous cells are routinely present in the maternal pulmonary circulation of all pregnant women, showed squamous cells in the blood of 16 pregnant women undergoing pulmonary arterial catherization for a variety of medical indications.[24] Even more interesting was the fact that squamous cells were also identified in the blood of 17 non-pregnant patients, though the difference in cell count between the pregnant and non-pregnant patients was significant. The squamous cells in the non-pregnant patients apparently came from epidermal contamination secondary to venipuncture. Thus, the detection of squamous cells alone in the pulmonary arterial blood would not be sufficient for the diagnosis of amniotic fluid embolism. Just as the presence of squamous cells is not pathegnomonic of amniotic fluid embolus, neither is the presence of trophoblastic cells. Trophoblastic cells can be found in the blood and lungs of women who do not have amniotic fluid emboli.

Deaths During Abortion

While amniotic fluid embolism is typically a complication of term pregnancy, it can also be a cause of death in abortion-related deaths. From 1972 to 1978, 12% of all deaths (15 cases) from legal abortion were caused by amniotic fluid embolism.[20] Twelve were caused by installation of hypertonic saline solution, one to intra-amniotic installation of prostaglandin, one to installation of hypertonic urea, and one following a hysterotomy. No deaths were associated with curettage abortions in this study, though some have occurred.

Three of the individuals became symptomatic 3, 9, and 12 h after delivery of the fetus. Death was rapid, with five women dying before expelling the fetus, nine within 4 h, and one 24 h after. Disseminated intravascular coagulopathy was present in 60% of the women and in 75% of those who survived more than an hour. No deaths occurred at 12 weeks of gestation or less. At 21 weeks of gestation or more, the risk of death was 24 times that from 13 to 15 weeks. These observations make sense if one realizes that the mean volume of amniotic fluid is approximately 50 ml at 12 weeks gestation and 400 ml by mid pregnancy.

References

1. Muth CM and Shank ES, Gas embolism. *NEJM* 200; 342(7): 476-482.

2. O'Quin RJ and Lakshminarayn S, Venous air embolism. *Arch Intern Med* 1982; 142:2173-2176.

3. Butler BD and Hills B, Transpulmonary passage of venous air emboli. *J Appl Physiol* 1985; 59:543-547.

4. Hybels C, Venous air embolism in head and neck surgery. *Laryngoscope* 1980; 90:946-954.

5. Tateishi T, Prospective study of air embolism. *Br J Anaesth* 1972; 44:1306-1310.

6. Albin MS, Venous air embolism and lumbar disk surgery. *JAMA* 1978; 240:1713. (Letter).

7. Yeakel A, Lethal air embolism from plastic blood-storage container. *JAMA* 1968; 204:267-268.

8. Davies DE, Digwood KI, and Hilton IN, Air embolism during cesarean section, *Med J Australia* 1980; 1:644-646.

9. Nelson PK, Pulmonary gas embolism in pregnancy and the puerperium. *Obstet Gynecol Survey* 1960; 15:449-4819.

10. Flannagan et al., Air embolism: A lethal complication of subclavian venipuncture, *NEJM* 1969; 281:488489.

11. Bajanowski T, West A, and Brinkmann B, Proof of fatal air embolism. *Int J Legal Med*, 1998; 111:208-211.

12. Bajanowski T et al., Proof of air embolism after exhumation, *Int J Legal Med* 1998; 112:2-7.

13. ten Duis HJ, The fat embolism syndrome: Review, *Injury* 1997; 28(2):77-85

14. Fabian TC, Unraveling the fat embolus syndrome (Editorial). *NEJM*; 1993. 329(13): 961-963.

15. Bulger EM et al., Fat embolism syndrome: A 10-year review. *Arch Surg*. 1997; 132(4):435-9.

16. Steiner PE and Lushbough CG, Maternal pulmonary embolism by amniotic fluid as a cause of obstetric shock and unexpected deaths in obstetrics. *JAMA* 1941; 117:1245-1254, 1340-1345.

17. Clark SL et al., Amniotic fluid embolism: Analysis of the national registry. *Am J Obstet Gynecol*, 1995; 172(4):1158-1169.

18. Liban E and Raz S, A clinicopathologic study of fourteen cases of amniotic fluid embolism. *Am J Clin Pathol* 1969; 51:477-486.

19. Cromley MG, Taylor PJ, and Cummings DO, Probable amniotic fluid embolism after first trimester pregnancy termination. *J Reprod Med* 1983; 28:209.

20. Guidotti RJ, Grimes DA, and Cates W, Fatal amniotic fluid embolism during legally induced abortion, United States, 1972 to 1978. *Am J Obstet Gynecol* 1981; 141:257-261.

21. Olcott CO, et al., Amniotic fluid embolism and disseminated intravascular coagulopathy after blunt maternal trauma. *J Trauma* 1973; 13:737-740.

22. Clark SL, Amniotic fluid embolism. *Clinics Perinatol* 1986; 13:801-811.

23. Sperry K, Amniotic fluid embolism, *JAMA* 1986; 255:2183-2186.

24. Clark SL et al., Squamous cells in the maternal pulmonary circulation. *Am J Obstet Gynecol* 1986; 154:104-106.

Topics in Forensic Pathology

20

Primary Cardiac Arrest during Exercise

Myocardial ischemia, arrhythmias, and sudden death can occur during or immediately after exercise.[1] Cardiovascular function is under the regulatory control of the sympathetic nervous system, with sympathetic stimulation causing an increase in heart rate, force of myocardial contraction, and blood pressure. During exercise, there is a progressive rise in systolic pressure, though usually very little, if any, change in diastolic pressure. Diastolic pressure may fall slightly in younger individuals and rise in middle-aged and older individuals.[2] Heart rate increases progressively with exercise before reaching a plateau. The average maximum heart rate is approximately 180–200 beats per minute. Systolic blood pressure increases to between 162 and 216 mm. Hg.[2] The increase in systolic blood pressure and heart rate is accompanied by a decrease in peripheral resistance. With isometric exercise such as weight lifting, there is almost no increase in heart rate, an increase in both systolic and diastolic blood pressure, and an increase in peripheral resistance.

Sudden death is seen not only during exercise, but often immediately after cessation. The term "post-exercise peril" has been used to refer to the risk of cardiac arrhythmias during the first few minutes after cessation of strenuous exercise.[3] Dimsdale found that the highest levels of catecholamines occurred during the first 3 min after cessation of exercise.[3] During the same period, plasma potassium concentration falls rapidly.[4,5] During exercise, the levels of both norepinephrine and epinephrine increase, with norepinephrine increasing more sharply. Immediately following cessation of exercise, the levels of both these catecholamines, instead of plateauing or decreasing, continue to rise, with norepinephrine levels increasing seven- to tenfold over baseline values and epinephrine 3 to 8 times.[3,4] Even 10 min after cessation of activity, serum levels of the catecholamines were approximately twice the resting values.[5] During exercise, serum potassium levels increase. Following cessation of exercise, the levels fall rapidly, reaching hypokalemic levels within

1–2 min post exercise.[4,5] The combination of falling potassium and rising catecholamines during the first few minutes post exercise may make the individuals susceptible to post exercise arrhythmias.

Episodes of sudden death occurring after exercise are probably caused by this phenomenon, with ischemia sensitizing the heart to the arrhythmogenic properties of the catecholamines and hypokalemia.

Sudden cardiac death has also been described in association with psychological stress.[6] It has been documented that psychological stress can induce either fatal or potentially fatal cardiac arrhythmias with and without underlying heart disease. This is apparently caused by stress-induced sympathetic stimulation.

Starvation

Deaths caused by starvation are relatively rare in America. For the most part, they occur either as a result of child abuse or fasting (Figure 20.1). The average 70-kg man, lying in bed, not exerting himself, requires approximately 1650 cal of energy per day. Asleep, he utilizes 65 cal per h and, while awake, uses 77 cal per h.[7] If he walks slowly, he utilizes 200 cal per h, running 570 cal per h, and walking up stairs 1100 cal per h. A manual laborer can require up to 6000–7000 cal per day.

Food can be grouped into three general categories: carbohydrates, fat, and protein. Tissues prefer to use carbohydrates for energy. The amount of carbohydrate stored in the body (glycogen in liver and muscle; glucose in blood) has a combined caloric value of approximately 1200 cal, insufficient to supply a 70-kg man with 1 d worth of calories. Therefore, if one stops eating, the body has to utilize fat and protein after the first 24 h of starvation. As fasting continues, there will be a progressive depletion of fat and protein, with fat depletion progressing at a faster rate than protein because fat provides more calories per weight of tissue. As fat is utilized for calories, ketones are produced and appear in the blood. Thus, after 12 h of fasting, blood acetone concentrations of approximately 1.0 mg/100 mL develop, with concentrations of 10–50 mg% in 36 h (J.C. Garriott, personal communication).

As starvation continues, protein is gradually depleted in three different phases. First is a rapid mobilization of protein stores that are converted by the liver to glucose, with the glucose used principally to supply energy to the brain. This is followed by a reduction in the utilization of protein. As total depletion of the fat stores approaches, protein is again rapidly utilized as a source of calories. Death usually occurs shortly after. If one assumes that fat

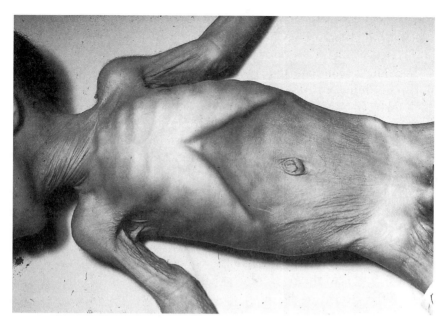

Figure 20.1 Starvation.

constitutes 20–25% of the body weight in males and 25–30% in females and then assumes 2000 cal are needed per day, for the average individual there would be sufficient energy supply for 60–70 days. This correlates very well with actual fasting conditions.

Frommel et al. describe four individuals who went on a voluntary fast for political reasons.[8] With sedentary activities, no problem was encountered up to 18% of original body loss (28–35 days of fasting). When weight loss exceeded 18%, they developed muscle weakness, syncopal episodes, and decreased mental alertness. Fasting was stopped at 40 days following development of Wernicke's syndrome by one of the four.

There appears to be no definite level of weight loss that can be considered lethal.[9] When loss of original body weight for adults reaches 40%, deaths begin to occur. With semi-starvation over a long period of time, the level is somewhat higher. For children, the level at which death begins is significantly lower.

Leiter and Marlis reported on the fasting to death of 10 young healthy males in Northern Ireland.[10] Information on these cases was obtained from the media, which gave reports of their ages, weights, and duration of fasts. Individuals consumed no calories or vitamins, only water. Their average age was 25.6 ± 0.7 years. One died after 45 d of fasting. The other nine survived from 57 to 73 d. The mean survival time for all 10 was 61.6 ± 2.5 d. These authors concluded that the maximum limit of total fasting in healthy, nonobese individuals in their mid to late 20s is approximately 60 d. Death in these individuals occurred when approximately 70–94% of the body fat and approximately 19–21% of body protein were lost.

Individuals who have undergone starvation report an initial feeling of hunger and hunger pains, with craving for food wearing off very rapidly. This is followed by both mental and physical lethargy, fatigue, and progressive loss of weight.[9,11,12] As the starvation continues, the lethargy becomes extreme, with mental impairment and loss of interest in everything.

At autopsy, there is essentially complete lack of fat in the subcutaneous and deep fat depots. The skin is pale and cadaverous in 82.5% of the cases and dark brown in 17.5% of the cases.[12] Edema is present in one third of the cases and may mask the amount of weight loss. Peritoneal effusions may occur. Edema is rare in individuals with brown-colored skin. There is severe atrophy of skeletal muscles, the heart, liver, spleen, and kidneys, but not the brain.[9,12] The small intestinal wall appears swollen, with reddish discolored mucosa in 27.2% of the cases. Almost half the cases in one study had ulcerations of the mucosa of the colon, described as "pseudo-dysentery.[12]

Anaphylactic Deaths

Most anaphylactic deaths seen by a medical examiner are caused by insect bites, drugs, or foods. The symptoms of anaphylactic attack are faintness, itching of the skin, urticaria, tightness in the chest, wheezing, respiratory difficulty, and collapse. In anaphylactic deaths, the onset of symptoms is usually immediate or within the first 15 to 20 min. Beyond that time, one would need a well-documented medical history of gradually developing symptoms to implicate an anaphylactic reaction, e.g., the development of itching or wheals and flares. Death usually occurs within 1 to 2 h. In some insects, e.g., fire ants, the venom is directly toxic and death can occur without anaphylactic reaction if there were a large number of bites.[13] In such cases, death typically occurs after 24 h.

A fatal anaphylactic reaction results in acute respiratory distress or circulatory collapse. Obstruction of the upper airway can be caused by pharygeal or laryngeal edema; of the lower airway, by bronchospasm with contraction of the smooth muscle of the lungs, vasodilation, and increased capillary permeability.[14] Cardiac arrest may be caused by respiratory arrest; the direct effects of the chemical mediators of anaphylaxsis on the heart or shock caused by a combination of intravascular fluid loss from edema and vasodilatation. Pumphrey and Roberts studied 56 anaphylactic deaths coming to autopsy.[15] They found that, in all 16 deaths that were caused by food allergy, there was difficulty in breathing, with death in 13 of the cases caused by respiratory arrest. In contrast, shock without any difficulty in breathing occurred in eight of 19 cases caused by insect venom and 12 of 21 caused by iatrogenic reactions.

At autopsy, the findings are often nonspecific. There is often laryngeal edema, but rarely complete obstruction of the airway. Pumphrey and Roberts reported larygeal or pharygeal edema in 8% and 49%, respectively, of individuals who died immediately.[15] Emphysema caused by the bronchoconstriction might be present. Visceral and pulmonary congestion, edema, and pulmonary hemorrhage are present, but are nonspecific. In Pumphrey and Roberts' study, 23 of 56 anaphylactic deaths had no macroscopic findings at autopsy.

To make a diagnosis of an anaphylactic reaction, one needs either a history of an allergy or a witnessed collapse and death following an insect bite, ingestion of food, or administration of a drug. Most deaths attributed to therapeutic agents involve the administration of either penicillin or an iodine-containing contrast agent used for diagnostic purposes. Death, however, has been associated with a multitude of other therapeutic agents. The introduction of low-osmolar contrast agents in radiology should reduce the number of adverse and fatal reactions to iodinated contrast agents.

In death caused by an anaphylactic reaction to an insect bite, it is possible to detect elevated levels of venom-specific IgE antibodies in postmortem blood.[13,15,16] Elevated levels of a specific IgE antibody do not necessarily indicate that an anaphylactic reaction took place, only that the individual is sensitive to the venom. The presence of such an antibody would be confirmatory evidence of an anaphylactic reaction caused by a sting from an insect. One percent of normal blood donors have been found to have elevated venom-specific IgE antibodies in their serum. Not all individuals dying of an anaphylactic reaction demonstrate antibodies to the specific insect that stung them. In such cases, a cross-reaction to antigens of another insect to which the deceased is allergic is suspected.

When IgE interacts with specific antigens, mast cells are activated, releasing a number of potent chemical mediators, including beta tryptase and histamine, from secretory granules in the cells. The level of tryptase rises rapidly, becoming detectible within 30 min, with peak concentrations reached in the first 2–3 h. Half-life of tryptase is 2 h. Resting mast cells secrete alpha tryptase. In mastocytosis, blood levels are raised. Anaphylaxis-like reactions in individuals with mastocytosis might not require IgE antibodies. Both IgE and tryptase can be measured in postmortem blood.

Injury of the Eye Caused by Acids and Alkalis

The degree of injury to the eye from either an acid or an alkaline compound depends on the pH of the compound, its concentration, and the period of contact with the eye. The corneal epithelium is a barrier to injury from acid, because acid produces a coagulative necrosis that limits penetration through tissue. Alkali, on the other hand, produces a liquefaction necrosis enabling greater penetration of tissue. Animal experiments have revealed that damage to eyes is not always related to pH. The concept that acid solutions with a pH below 2.5 produce severe damage to the cornea is not always correct. Thus, hydrochloric acid with a pH of 1.28 produced no corneal opacity. Phenol with a pH of 7.7 and acetic acid with a pH of 2.7 produced opacities.[17]

Just as a pH below 2.5 was believed to always cause corneal damage to eyes, it is generally felt that alkali, with a pH value of 11.45 or greater, will produce severe ocular damage. This also is not absolutely correct. Sodium hydroxide solutions with pH values of 12.8 and 12.3 did not produce corneal opacities. If, however, the pH was elevated to 13.1, then opacities occurred. One must, therefore, conclude that the degree of eye damage cannot be based on pH alone and that pH values of 2.5 and 11. 5 can be used only as general guidelines for the prediction of ocular injury. The concentration of the chemical and period of contact with the eye prior to washing must be taken into account.

Death in the Dental Chair

Deaths associated with dentistry are extremely uncommon. Some deaths are coincidental, caused by the stress, fear, and pain of dental procedures precipitating a fatal heart attack. "Few men are heroes … at the moment of visiting their dentist."[18] In any death during a dental procedure, the forensic pathologist must separate the natural coincidental deaths from those that are non-natural. Most non-natural deaths are associated with general anesthesia.

One of the best study of deaths associated with dentistry appears to be that of Coplans and Curson in England.[19] They examined 120 deaths over a 10-year period. One hundred were associated with general anesthesia, 10 with local anesthesia, 6 with neither of these, and, in 4 cases, there was insufficient or inadequate information for classification. Coplans and Curson used the term "general anesthesia" to include not only conventional general anesthesia, but any sedation with analgesia where there was loss of consciousness at some time during the procedure. Of the 100 deaths associated with general anesthesia, in 54 of the cases the general anesthesia was directly responsible for the death of a healthy individual; in 29 cases there was some underlying disease that made a significant contribution to the death, but, nonetheless, the general anesthesia provoked the fatal outcome, and, in 17 cases, the general anesthesia was incidental to the outcome.

Some deaths in the dental chair are attributed to allergic reactions to the drugs given, principally local anesthetics. There is controversy as to the validity of this etiology, however. True allergic reactions to a local anesthetic or a substance used as a preservative or stabilizer in the local anesthetic are probably extremely rare.[20,21] Most so-called allergic reactions are probably overdoses of the local anesthetic caused by an intravascular injection of the drug, due to failure to aspirate after placement of the needle; injection of large doses of a local anesthetic into a highly vascular area or unusually rapid absorption.[20,22] This last cause is aided by the fact that local anesthetics by themselves are vasodilators that enhance absorption in vascular areas.

Naguib et al. produced an extensive review of adverse effects and drug interactions associated with the use of local anesthetics.[20] They concluded, as previously noted, that the adverse effects of local anaesthetics were usually caused by excessive dosage, unusually rapid absorption, or inadvertent intravascular injection, with the last cause the most common. Severe adverse reactions were caused by either central nervous system or cardiovascular toxicity. The amount ol local anesthetic necessary to produce cardiovascular toxicity is 3.5 to 6.7 times higher than that needed to produce CNS toxicity. High levels of local anesthetics produce direct depression of the myocardium, with impairment of myocardial contractility, and decreased conduction velocity. There is peripheral vasodilatation with hypotension and bradycardia. This can progress to arrythmias and cardiac arrest. Bupivacaine and etidocaine are apparently more cardiotoxic than other commonly used local anesthetics, with bupivacaine arrhythmias more refractory to treatment. CNS toxicity is first manifested by excitement (stimulation), followed by depression, drowsiness, respiratory failure and coma.

Addition of epinephrine will reduce the systemic absorption of the anesthetic injected in such areas and tends to reduce the probability of an overdose. Unfortunately, epinephrine has the potential of being dangerous in itself. If too much epinephrine is used in conjunction with the anesthetic, the epinephrine might be absorbed and, in conjunction with the local anesthetic, cause cardiac arrhythmias. This danger is more theoretical than actual.[23]

One of the most common causes of death during general anesthesia in a dental office is an overdose of drugs. This could be caused by an error in dosage, ignorance of proper dosage, or carelessness. More common, however, is the tendency to give multiple medications during induction and maintenance of general anesthesia or deep sedation, with resultant synergestic action of these drugs. The dentist often gives a barbiturate, a tranquilizer, and an opiate (all central nervous system depressants) and then perhaps uses nitrous oxide. The three central nervous system depressant drugs produce a synergistic action, so that the combined effect of three different drugs is greater than any one of their individual actions. Another common mistake is failure to take a good medical history or, if it is taken, to appreciate its significance. For example, one must realize that epileptics under general anesthesia may have seizures. In addition, they may already be and, in fact, should be, on central nervous system depressant drugs such as barbiturates and phenytoin. General anesthetics can also produce asthma-like attacks that are not as apparent in an unconscious patient. Other problems involving anesthesia in the dental office include failure to monitor the patient's vital functions and failure to have the proper drugs and equipment to resuscitate an individual who is having difficulty.

Over one 5-year period, one of the authors saw four deaths involving dentistry that were not coincidental — one in the operating room and three in a private office.[24,25] The operating room fatality was a 36-year-old male admitted to the hospital to have his teeth capped. It was decided to cap 21 teeth all at the same time. The patient received premedication of meperidine, promethazine, and scopolamine 1 h prior to surgery. General anesthesia was induced with an ultra-short-acting barbiturate, with general anesthesia maintained by halothane and nitrous oxide. At 2 h and 45 min after induction of the anesthesia, 10 min after the placement of a gingival retraction cord around 21 teeth, the patient became cyanotic, with labored breathing. Ventricular fibrillation was noted and cardiopulmonary resuscitation was unsuccessful. The patient died of a cardiac arrhythmia caused by the combined action of halothane and epinephrine.[24] The epinephrine was in the gingival retraction cord. This cord, impregnated with 8% racemic epinephrine, is used to provide hemostasis. The cord can contain as much as 1 mg of epinephrine per inch. Absorption of epinephrine from the gingiva can produce significant arrhythmias, especially in the presence of a halogenated hydrocarbon anesthestic such as halothane. The epithelial lining of the gingival sulcus is semipermeable, as well as being highly vascular. Thus, anywhere from 24 to 92% of epinephrine applied to the gingival sulcus is absorbed into the systemic circulation. The potential problem with using a gingival retraction cord is recognized.[23]

Within a 14-month period, the author also saw three other victims of death in a dentist's office.[25] The patients involved were a 7-year-old boy, a 38-year-old woman, and a 25-year-old woman. All three were given diazepam, pentazocine, and methohexital intravenously. All died after the administration of the presurgical anesthetic medication, during or immediately after the procedure. Toxicological analysis for the drugs involved and a review of the medical records confirmed that the three individuals had all received potentially lethal doses of pentazocine, a narcotic analgesic, along with unusually high and potentially lethal doses of diazepam. All had also received anesthetic doses of methohexital, an ultra-short-acting barbiturate. Doxapram, a respiratory stimulant, was given in all cases, without beneficial effect; caffeine was administered in the first case. Narcotic antagonists were not administered in any of the cases. All three deaths involved the same oral surgeon.

Maternal Mortality: Criminal Abortion

The most common causes of maternal death in the U.S. are hemorrhage, embolism, hypertensive disease of pregnancy, and infection, approximately in that order. In 1998, there were 281 reported deaths caused by complications of pregnancy, childbirth, and the puerperium.[26] This number is lower than the actual number of deaths, as it includes only those reported on the death certificate and assigned to the cause of death. Death complicating an abortion is uncommon.[27] In 1998, there were six deaths following legally induced abortions, none from illegal abortion and two from spontaneous abortions.[26] All deaths following an abortion should be reported to a medicolegal office. Under most circumstances, such cases should be autopsied, as there is a good probability of civil litigation.

One of the authors had extensive experience with illegal abortions in the time prior to the Supreme Court's decision making abortion legal. At that time, abortion was produced by one of three methods: abortifacient drugs, local abortifacients, and instrumentation.

Abortifacient Drugs

These were taken in an attempt to produce an abortion. In small doses, these drugs were generally ineffective. In large doses, the toxic effects of the drugs, and not their alleged abortifacient effect, could cause the woman to abort. On occasion, the toxic effects of the drug caused death with or without causing abortion. The first category of drugs was **essential oils** (oil of pennyroyal, oil of rue, cantharides, and purgatives). These drugs really have no direct stimulating action on the uterine muscle, rather they act indirectly by causing marked pelvic congestion and irritation of the colon, which allegedly cause excitation and contraction of the adjacent uterus, followed by expulsion of the fetus.

The second category of drugs is **ecbolics**, which had a direct stimulating action on the uterine muscle. Examples would be ergot, quinine, and oxytocin. Quinine in healthy women rarely produced abortion. Oxytocin was generally used by physicians. In the case of ergots, while they may cause abortion, more frequently they cause ergot poisoning, with a possible fatal outcome. While these abortifacient drugs might cause contraction of the uterine muscle, they do not relax or dilate the cervical canal and external cervical os, which is a necessary preliminary step to expel the fetus. Thus, usually, these drugs did not cause abortion.

Local Abortifacient

The second method of inducing abortion was by the use of local abortifacients. This involves the introduction of a certain chemical intravaginally or

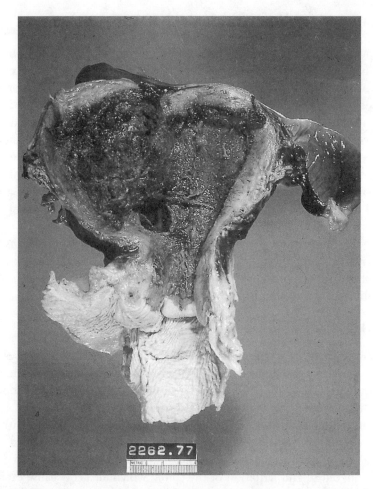

Figure 20.2 A 23-year-old female who died 7 hours after a therapeutic abortion. Death was caused by perforation of the uterus. Two liters of blood were found in the retroperitoneal space.

in the cervix. Potassium permanganate was commonly used. The tablet was inserted in the cervix, causing ulceration of the cervix or vaginal fornix with bleeding. This method of abortion was not very effective.

Instrumentation

The third and most effective method of illegal abortion was the use of instrumentation. The exact instrumental procedure that was employed depended on whether the abortionists were physicians, midwifes, nurses, or lay persons and their training, experience, and skill. Criminal abortion by instrumental means generally was of three types: douching, syringing, and direct instrumentation.

In induction by **douching**, a stream of water, hot or cold, with or without an irritant soap or antiseptic solution (Lysol®), was injected forcefully into the vagina at the external cervical os. More-experienced abortionists placed the nozzle of the tubing directly into the cervical canal. The successful abortion depended on the injected fluid's separating the fetal membrane and placenta from the uterine wall attachments. While the mechanical action could be produced just by the injection of ordinary water, most often a soapy solution composed of tap water and household soap was used. Lysol was also frequently used. The water was usually delivered by a household enema can or bag with attached rubber tubing and a long, slender, hard nozzle.

Because of the small cervical opening, failures using douching fluids were unusually high in the primigravida. The injected fluid would enter the vagina, but not the cervical canal. Abortion by douching was often self-induced, and was more common among multiparous women.

Abortion by **syringing** essentially used the same principle as that of douching. A large-capacity syringe or douche syringe was used, with the nozzle inserted into the cervix. Again, this was a favorite self-induced method of abortion.

Deaths due to abortion by douching or syringing were caused by:

- Cardiac arrhythmia
- Sepsis
- Air embolism
- Perforation of the uterus or vagina (rare)

Insertion of the douching or syringe nozzle into the cervix, combined with the rapid forceful injection of fluids or the rapid separation of the placenta from the uterine wall apparently produces a vagal reaction, with a cardiac arrhythmia and death. A number of these deaths were witnessed by relatives of the deceased. The patient died immediately upon insertion of the syringe or tubing into the cervical os and injecting of the fluid.

Sepsis was secondary to the nonsterile nature of the method of induced abortion. A corrosive endometritis caused by the fluid was common. On occasion, the soapy solution or solution containing Lysol would enter the uterine veins, initiating a hemolytic anemia, hemoglobinemia, and hemoglobinuric nephrosis, with uremia and death.

Air embolism could occur two ways. First is when air became trapped in the rubber tubing and was forcefully injected into the uterine cavity and into torn veins. Second, in the process of separating the fetal membranes from the uterine wall, veins were torn through which air from the atmosphere could be sucked in. While most deaths caused by air embolism occur within a few minutes of the procedure, in some cases, there have been delays of hours. One hypothesis for this delay is that the injected irritating fluid that caused separation and tearing also caused severe contraction of the uterus. Subsequently, as the uterus relaxed, the air then was able to enter the circulation.

The third method of inducing criminal abortion by instrumental means is **induction by instruments**. This was usually not self-induced, though in some instances women, especially multiparous women, were able to do so using knitting needles and coat hangers. Essentially, this method is a variation on dilatation and uterine curettage. Catheters, soft or hard, and other instruments were used to dilate the cervical os or at least to pass through the cervical os into the uterine cavity. The experienced non-physicians would typically insert a soft or hard catheter into the cervix and uterus. A cervical packing or tampon was then placed immediately adjacent to the cervix to hold the catheter in place and absorb any blood that might flow from the cervix or uterus during the woman's journey home. The woman was then instructed to go home and expect painful forceful uterine contractions and vaginal bleeding within 24 h, but not later than 48 h. This would indicate expulsion of the fetus and placenta. If the inserted catheter had perforated or ruptured the fetal membrane, causing loss of amniotic fluid and immediate contraction, the fetus and placenta would be expelled within hours. The woman was often instructed that, if she bled profusely, she was to dispose of the catheter and vaginal packing, go to the nearest doctor or hospital and tell them that she had severe vaginal bleeding. She would then attempt to pass this off as a spontaneous abortion. (Anyone working the emergency room of a large county hospital in urban areas noticed that there was an unusually large number of "spontaneous abortions" on Thursday and Friday nights, This was because hospitalization in such cases was only for three days. Thus, a woman having a "spontaneous abortion" on a Thursday night lost only one day of work, Friday, while the woman having one on Friday night lost only Monday.)

Deaths from instrumentation were caused by:

- Primary cardiac arrest caused by a vagal reaction produced by forceful dilation of the cervix and/or insertion of a catheter or sound into the uterus
- Complications of anesthesia
- Hemorrhage (Figure 20.2)
- Sepsis caused by perforation of the uterus, cervix, or vagina
- Air embolus
- Thrombotic embolus

Sepsis was the most common cause of death by instrumental abortion (Figure 20.3).

Figure 20.3 Self-induced septic abortion with perforation of the uterus.

One of the authors (DD) had the opportunity to autopsy or supervise the autopsies of 105 cases of criminal abortion in Brooklyn, New York, from 1960 to 1973. The causes of death in these 105 cases were:

- Deaths caused by abortifacients: 4
  a. Deaths caused by douching: 22
  b. Sudden cardiac deaths: 10
  c. Air embolism: 3
- Sepsis: 9
- Deaths caused by instrumentation: 9
  a. Postabortal sepsis following insertion of catheter into uterus: 8
  b. Postabortal sepsis following insertion of wire coat hanger into uterus: 1
- Deaths caused by postabortal sepsis — method of abortion unknown: 60
- Deaths caused by postabortal hemorrhage — method of abortion unknown: 10

Of the four deaths caused by abortifacients, one was caused by potassium permanganate, two by quinine, and in one, the substance was unknown. The woman who took the potassium permanganate inserted the pills into the cervix and subsequently aborted. She developed methemoglobinemia, hemolytic anemia, methemoglobinuric nephrosis, and uremia. Those who took the quinine died from quinine overdoses. In the fourth case, an unknown number of pills were taken to induce abortion. The victim subsequently developed postabortal sepsis, subacute bacterial endocarditis and sepsis, and died. The 70 cases in which the method of abortion was unknown were, in virtually all instances, thought to be caused by instrumentation.

Stillborn Infants

Delivery of a severely macerated infant indicates to even the most inexperienced observer that the child was dead intrauterine for a prolonged time. Presentation to an emergency room, EMS crew, or police agency, of a full-term child born without a physician present and showing very early or minimal signs of maceration has resulted in misinterpretation of maceration as evidence of trauma during or immediately after delivery. This is illustrated by the following case.

A full-term child delivered at home by a midwife did not immediately cry and was placed in warm water for "stimulation," and scrubbed to remove the vernix caseosa. The child did not respond and "died." The midwife contended that the child had taken a few breaths prior to being placed in the water, though no one else had witnessed this. The child was brought to an emergency room to be pronounced dead. The emergency room physician saw the child and called the police, stating that there were scalding burns of almost the complete body. On examination of the body by one of the authors (VJMD), there was slippage of the skin of the trunk, extremities, and lower half of the face, with sparing only of the palms and soles of the feet (Figure 20.4). Internal examination showed early decomposition, with non-aerated, totally atelectatic lungs that sank on placement in water. Blood-tinged fluid was in the pleural and peritoneal cavities. The child was obviously a stillborn showing early signs of maceration.

Delivery of a macerated infant is absolute evidence of an intrauterine death. When a fetus dies *in utero*, it is suspended in sterile fluid within an intact amniotic sac. There, it undergoes aseptic autolytic changes, i.e., maceration, due to the infant's tissue and cellular enzymes aided by the favorable body temperature. The earliest sign of maceration in a stillborn is skin slippage (separation of the epidermis from the dermis). This may be present as early as 6 h after death *in utero* and is expected after more than 12 h.[28,29] As intrauterine decomposition proceeds, bullae may form under the skin. On rupture, the exposed skin, initially raw, dries out, becoming reddish brown. The tissue will develop a reddish coloration caused by hemolysis. Serosanguinous fluid will accumulate in the thoracic and abdominal cavities. The internal organs will undergo decomposition, becoming diffluent. If the child is retained several days intrauterine, the skull will collapse and the brain will become semi-liquefied.

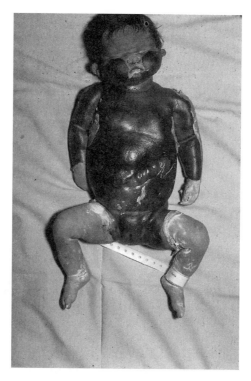

Figure 20.4 A stillborn showing evidence of intrauterine decomposition. Incorrectly diagnosed as scalding injuries following a live birth.

Traumatic Lesions of Birth

Birth is traumatic to both the mother and child. Depending on the ease of delivery, the amount of trauma that the child may incur can vary from minor to fatal. A small amount of hemorrhage into the scalp is normal. It is not rare for children to present with caput succedaneum, a hemorrhagic edema of the scalp, and superficial fascia caused by the trauma of delivery. Subperiosteal and epidural hemorrhage are rare. Epidural hemorrhage is usually associated with a skull fracture, tends to be small in extent, and is usually not a cause of death.

The cranial vault of an infant is formed of poorly mineralized plates of bone with membranous sutures. This results in the child's being able to withstand considerable cranial distortion without fracture of the bone. Fractures, when they occur, usually involve the parietal bone and are linear, extending along the lines of cleavage.[30] Such fractures in themselves are probably not life threatening, but indicate that significant force has been exerted on the head. They are seen in difficult extractions where forceps are used. A more significant form of cranial injury is separation of the squamous and lateral parts of the occipital bone. These do not fuse until the second year of life. In difficult deliveries, the squamous and lateral portion of the occipital bone may be displaced forward, tearing the dura and occipital sinuses, with resultant subdural hemorrhage in the posterior fossa and laceration of the cerebellum. This injury is seen most commonly in occipital posterior presentations and is commonly missed at autopsy.

Subdural hemorrhage can also occur from tearing of the bridging veins and, rarely, of the dural folds. Tears of the dural folds require significant deformation of the head. Thus, death could be associated with such tears even without a subdural hematoma, because the brain itself would be injured by the deformation.

In unwitnessed births outside the hospital in which the infant is brought in with fractures of the skull, the mother may state that the injury was caused by precipitous delivery in the erect position with the infant's head striking the ground. Such an occurrence would, in theory, be more common in a multiparous woman with a large birth canal, a small child, and vigorous labor. Klein, however, felt such fractures to be rare.[31] He reported 183 cases of precipitous delivery in women kneeling, sitting, or standing with the infant falling to the ground. Only one child died and there were no instances in which a skull fracture could be detected externally. It must be remembered that when the child is delivered, the umbilical cord is still attached. The cord (average length, 20 in.) will tend to pull the child short, thus preventing the head from hitting the ground with full force.

Water Intoxication

Deaths resulting from water intoxication are rare. Most of those seen by a forensic pathologist involve psychotic patients who, for some reason, drink large quantities of water.[32] Deaths also have been seen in individuals in jail involved in water-drinking contests. In hospitalized individuals, the administration of large quantities of intravenous fluids devoid of electrolytes can also produce water intoxication. This is seen predominantly in infants and young children. Whatever the etiology of the water intoxication, death is caused by a cardiac arrhythmia produced by electrolyte imbalance.

Diagnosis postmortem is based on history plus abnormal electrolyte levels in the vitreous fluid. One cannot use electrolyte values on blood obtained postmortem to make a diagnosis of electrolyte imbalance due to the artifacts produced by postmortem breakdown of cells. Vitreous levels of sodium and chloride are valid in making the diagnosis as long as postmortem decomposition has not set in. In water intoxication, one would expect low levels of sodium and chloride in the vitreous. Normal vitreous sodium levels range from 135 to 151 meq/L and chloride levels range from 105 to 132 meq/L.[33] In water intoxication, levels well below these concentrations are seen. Theoretically, one should also see low levels of potassium. This is not seen, however, because potassium is rapidly released from the cells of the body after death, even in the vitreous. Thus, typically, one sees high or normal levels of potassium in the vitreous, even if the individual was hypokalemic. If the vitreous potassium is 15 meq/L or higher, this indicates decomposition. At this point, there is artifactual depression of sodium and chloride levels, making interpretation of these values suspect.

Vitreous

Next to blood, the most important tissue for toxicological purposes is vitreous. In some ways, vitreous has an advantage over blood in that, caused by its acellular nature and relative isolation, it is less susceptible to biochemical changes and contamination. Because of this, valid electrolyte studies can be done on the vitreous that cannot be performed on blood. In the case of certain drugs, such as alcohol, vitreous can provide a picture of the blood concentration 1–2 h prior to death. Unlike spinal fluid, vitreous is also easy to obtain.

Analysis of postmortem blood for concentrations of sodium, potassium, and chloride give erroneous results. Sodium and chloride decrease in the blood after death, while potassium increases, due to breakdown of cells. Thus, one cannot use postmortem blood to accurately determine an individual's electrolyte status immediately prior to death. Fortunately, electrolyte abnormalities in living individuals are often reflected in the vitreous. Because vitreous levels of sodium and chloride are valid, this makes diagnosis of antemortem electrolyte imbalances possible. Unfortunately, this does not hold true for vitreous potassium.

The normal levels of sodium and chloride in vitreous are 135 to 151 meq/L and 105–132 meq/L, respectively, if significant cellular and tissue breakdown (decomposition) has not set in.[33] Decomposition of a body is reflected in the vitreous by a potassium level of 15 meq/L or above. When potassium is 15 meq/L or greater, the sodium and chloride values fall, making electrolyte evaluation of questionable value.[34]

If potassium values are less than 15 meq/L, then sodium values below 135 meq/L and chloride values below 105 meq/L indicate that one is dealing with low salt syndrome. This is seen most commonly in association with severe fatty metamorphosis of the liver or micronodular cirrhosis. Coe described six cases of profound salt depletion. In one case, sodium was106 meq/L; chloride 87 meq/L, and potassium 6.2 meq/L due to prolonged use of diuretic therapy.[35] The same picture of a low salt syndrome can be caused by overhydration, or water intoxication. In a fatal case of water intoxication seen by one of the authors, vitreous sodium was 115 meq/L, chloride 105 meq/L, and potassium 7.6 meq/L.[32] In individuals with dehydration, sodium is greater than 155 meq/L, chloride greater than 135 meq/L, and urea greater than 40 mg/dL. In uremia, sodium and chloride are usually within normal limits, with vitreous urea usually greater than 150 mg/dL.[35]

Vitreous potassium levels are of no help in determining what the potassium status of an individual was immediately prior to death, because potassium is released almost immediately postmortem, even in the vitreous. Elevated levels of potassium, therefore, have no diagnostic value in the vitreous. Low levels of potassium in the vitreous, indicative of hypokalemia, are valid, but the authors have virtually never seen this, even in cases where the individual is known to be hypokalemic. Attempts have been made to determine the time of death by vitreous potassium levels. Such attempts have been unsatisfactory.

Normal levels of glucose in the vitreous range anywhere from 0 to 180 mg%. Vitreous glucose levels are of significance if elevated, but are of no significance if low. An elevated vitreous glucose is an accurate reflection of an elevated antemortem blood glucose. Glucose levels significantly above 200 mg/dL in the vitreous are considered diagnostic of diabetes mellitus.[36]

Agonal hyperglycemia is extremely common, especially if there has been attempted resuscitation. It plays no part in contributing to the death, however. Agonal hyperglycemia is not reflected in the vitreous. Thus, Coe reported that, in all of 102 nondiabetics in whom postmortem peripheral blood glucose concentration exceeded 500 mg/dL from a terminal rise in blood sugar, the vitreous glucose was below 100 mg/dL.[37] Even if intravenous glucose infusions are administered prior to death, the vitreous glucose levels in normal subjects are generally less than 200 mg/dL.

In individuals with elevated levels of glucose in the vitreous due to hyperglycemia, there is a gradual fall in vitreous levels postmortem. The fall is gradual enough to allow diagnosis of hyperglycemia for a considerable time after death. Unfortunately, because normal individuals start at significantly lower levels of vitreous glucose, the decline is sufficiently rapid that low levels of glucose are the rule. Because of this, one cannot differentiate a low vitreous glucose level caused by hypogycemia from that of normal postmortem decline in an indiviual who had a normal glucose level at the time of death. Thus, perfectly normal individuals who die of trauma might be found to have a vitreous glucose level of 0 or 5 mg/dL, which is obviously an artifactual phenomenon.

Vitreous bilirubin is of no value diagnostically, with normal values in jaundiced individuals who have antemortem serum levels of greater than 30 mg/dL.[33] Values for alkaline phosphatase, SGOT, and calcium are also of no value. Vitreous urea, however, is valuable for diagnostic purposes. Its normal range is within the same normal range as blood urea nitrogen. It is the most stable component of vitreous. Blood urea nitrogen levels postmortem are also valid over prolonged time. Creatinine determinations are valid in both vitreous and blood.

Because of the work of Dr. John Coe, the importance of vitreous as an agent in postmortem chemistry has been realized.[33-35,37] What still is not fully appreciated is that vitreous can also be of great value in drug identification and interpretation. Vitreous alcohol concentrations are often of value in making the diagnosis of death from acute alcohol intoxication occurring in both the absorptive and the nonabsorptive phases. A young boy may present with a fatal blood alcohol level of 0.450 g/dL and a vitreous alcohol of 0.12 g/dL. This indicates that he was ingesting large quantities of alcohol over a short time and died before there could be any equilibration between blood and vitreous. Other individuals take in a large amount of alcohol over a longer period of time, lapse into an irreversible coma due to the central nervous depressant action of the alcohol, and suffer irreversible brain injury, yet still "live" for a significant time after ingestion. In such cases, one may find a vitreous alcohol of 0.400% and a blood alcohol of 0.250%.

In addition to analysis for alcohol, one of the authors (VJMD) has had extensive experience with the use of vitreous for other drug determinations. Thus, cocaine, morphine, propoxyphene, and the tricyclic antidepressants and their metabolites have all been identified in vitreous. The levels of the drugs and metabolites in the vitreous can be used in conjunction with blood levels to make determinations as to the manner of death, because, just like those of alcohol, these levels are a reflection of what the blood levels were an hour or two prior to death. Thus, one can better evaluate the status of how an individual took a drug, whether as an acute overdose, an acute overdose with prolonged survival, or was a chronic abuser of the drug.

Electrolyte Disorders

Deaths due primarily to electrolyte imbalance that are seen by the forensic pathologist generally involve gastrointestinal infections in infants, overdoses of diuretics or potassium chloride pills, water intoxication, and repeatedly induced vomiting. Obviously, electrolyte imbalances are present in many other medical examiner cases, but they are usually a secondary factor in the deaths, while, in the aforementioned cases, they are the primary mechanism of death.

Postmortem diagnosis of death caused by an electrolyte imbalance depends on analysis of the vitreous for sodium, chloride, and urea nitrogen. Assuming normal renal function, one would expect elevated levels of sodium, chloride, urea nitrogen and creatinine in the vitreous with any entity producing dehydration. With ingestion or administration of abnormally large

quantities of fluid, markedly depressed levels of sodium and chloride could
be expected. The authors have seen a number of deaths caused by water
intoxication and a few caused by repeatedly induced vomiting. In both
groups, the individuals were, for the most part, psychotic. In young children,
gastrointestinal infections can produce severe vomiting or diarrhea with
development of electrolyte imbalances. In infants, vomiting and diarrhea can
cause dehydration, electrolyte imbalance, and death in a matter of several
hours.

Rarely, deaths are caused by an overdose of potassium chloride or diuretics. The overdose in these instances might be either suicidal or accidental
through abuse of these drugs by an individual who has a history of taking
more than the prescribed medication. Obviously, ingestion of large quantities
of potassium chloride pills can produce hyperkalemia, while, taking a diuretic
in abnormal amounts can produce hypokalemia. In both instances, the
abnormal levels of blood potassium can produce cardiac arrhythmias and
death. At autopsy, there are no specific findings. Unfortunately, the diagnosis
of death caused by hyper- or hypokalemia, in most instances, can be made
only on the basis of history. Blood potassium levels postmortem are invalid
for interpretation caused by postmortem release of potassium. Vitreous
potassium levels are valid only if indicative of hypokalemia. Unfortuantely,
the authors have almost never seen abnormally low concentrations of potassium in the vitreous, even in the case of individuals who took large amounts
of diuretics. This is because, almost immediately after death, cells begin to
break down and release potassium. This causes elevated levels of potassium
in both the blood and vitreous. Thus, with a low potassium concentration
in the vitreous prior to death, unless the vitreous was collected immediately
after death, the release of potassium would return the hypokalemic individual
to a "normal" or elevated potassium level.

Blast Injuries

Blast injuries can occur from either a single exposure to a high-energy pressure wave or repeated exposure to lower impulse levels. Injury is primarily
to the middle ears, the lungs, and gastrointestinal tract. Death is commonly
caused by air emboli. The lungs are hemorrhagic and edematous. Pnemotho-
rax or hemothorax are often present.

Intra-Operative Deaths

Deaths during diagnostic or therapeutic procedures can be divided into a
number of categories based on etiology. First are the deaths unrelated to the

procedures, but caused by the underlying disease for which the procedure is being performed. An example of this involving a diagnostic procedure would be cardiac catheterization following an individual's arrival at the hospital with chest pain. During cardiac angiography, the patient develops a fatal arrhythmia and dies. Surgically, the cases seen most commonly by the authors are deaths during cardiac bypass surgery. The individual is put on a cardiac bypass pump and the surgery is successfully performed, but the patient's heartbeat does not come back when the pump is removed.

A second category includes those related to the anesthesia, whether local or general. Most anesthetic-related deaths are caused by human error, with the most common problems related to ventilation. An intra-operative death could be caused by as simple a mistake as inserting the intubation tube into the esophagus. There may be unrecognized extubation, disconnection from the ventilator, or inadequate ventilation. There may be allergic reaction to the anesthetic agent (rare) or contamination of the gas being administered. In some instances, due to mix-ups in bottled gases, the wrong gas is administered. The patient may develop malignant hyperthermia.[38] This is usually associated with the use of halogenated anesthetics and succinycholine. The individual usually has a genetic predisposition, but this condition may not occur every time anesthesia is administered. The onset of signs can be insidious or fulminant, with a rapid rise in body temperature, tachycardia, arrhythmias and skeletal muscle rigidity. The patient might then develop disseminated intravascular coagulopathy, electrolyte abnormalities — especially hyperkalemia — and rhabdomyolysis. Deaths from local anesthetics have been discussed in another section.

Death can be caused by administration of the wrong medication or the right medication in the wrong dose. This is virtually always missed unless toxicology is performed. There could be an allergic reaction to a dye that is administered. Even with all the precautions taken nowadays, sometimes the wrong blood type is administered, with resultant transfusion reaction.

Death may be caused by inadvertent mechanical disruption of a vital organ. There might be perforation of the coronary artery during angioplasty or angiography, or unrecognized perforation of the uterus during curretage. In individuals with extensive pericardial adhesions, procedures involving splitting the sternum down the middle have occasionally resulted in perforation of the heart. A significant number of deaths have occurred during catheterization of vessels.[39] Catheters have perforated the vena cava, right atrium and ventricle, and the pulmonary arteries. The authors have seen cases of intravenous alimentation where the tubing was inserted into the pleural cavity.

Mechanical disruption of vessels during surgery can result in the introduction of air into the vascular system. This occurs most commonly during laminectomy and central nervous system procedures.[40,41]

References

1. Mittleman MA and Siscovic KDS, Physical exertion as a trigger of myocardial infarction and sudden cardiac death. *Cardiology Clinics* 1996; 14(2): 263-70.

2. Wolthus RA et al., The response of healthy men to treadmill exercise. *Circulation* 1977; 55:153.

3. Dimsdale JE, et al., Post exercise peril: Plasma catecholamine and exercise. *JAMA* 1984; 252:630-632.

4. Young DB, et al., Potassium and catecholamine concentrations in the immediate post exercise period. *Am J Med Sci,* 1992; 304(3): 150-153.

5. Lindinger M, Potassium regulation during exercise and recovery in humans: Implications for skeletal and cardiac muscle. *J Mol Cell Cardiol* 1995; 27:1011-1022.

6. Brodsky MA, et al., Ventricular tachyarrhythmia associated with psychological stress: Role of the sympathetic nervous system. *JAMA* 1987; 257:2064-2067.

7. Guyton AC and Hall JE, *Textbook of Medical Physiology.* 10th ed. WB Saunders Co. Philadelphia, 2000.

8. Frommel D, et al., Voluntary total fasting: a challenge for the medical community, *Lancet,* 1984; 1:1451-29.

9. Keys A, et al., *The Biology of Human Starvation.* University of Minnesota Press, 1950.

10. Leiter LA and Marlis EB, Survival during fasting may depend on fat as well as protein stores. *JAMA* 1982; 248:2306-2307.

11. Simpson K, Exposure to cold/starvation and neglect, in Simpson K (Ed): *Modern Trends in Forensic Medicine.* St Louis, Mo, CV Mosby Co, 1953.

12. Winick M (Ed), *Hunger Disease: Studies by the Jewish Physicians in the Warsaw Ghetto.* New York, John Wiley & Sons, 1979.

13. Prahlow JA and Barnard JJ, Fatal anaphylaxis caused by fire ant stings. *Am J Forens Med & Path* 1998; 19(2):137-142.

14. Delage C and Irey NS, Anaphylactic deaths: A clinicopathologic study of 43 cases. *J Forens Sci* 1972; 17:525-540.

15. Pumphrey RSH and Roberts IS, Postmortem findings after fatal anaphylactic reactions. *J. Clin Path* 2000; 53(4):273-276.

16. Schwartz HJ, et al., Studies in stinging insect hypersensitivity: Postmortem demonstration of antivenom IgE antibody and possible sting-related sudden death. *Am J Clin Pathol* 1986; 85:607–610.

17. Murphy JC et al., Ocular irritancy responses to various pHs of acid and bases with/without irrigation, *Toxicology* 1982; 23:281-291.

18. Christie A, *An Overdose of Death,* 1940.

19. Coplans MP and Curson I, Deaths associated with dentistry. *Br Dental J* 1982; 153:357-362.

20. Naguib M, et al., Adverse effects and drug interactions associated with local and regional anaesthesia. *Drug Safety* 1998; 18(4):221-250.

21. Chen AH, Toxicity and allergy to local anesthesia. *CDA Journal* 1998; 26(9):683-692.

22. Lalli AF and Amaranath L, A critique on mortality associated with local anesthetics. *Anesthes Rev* 1982; 9(6):29-36.

23. Pallasch TJ, Vasoconstrictors and the heart, *CDA J* 26(9):668-676.

24. Hilley MD, et al., Fatality associated with the combined use of halothane and gingival retraction cord. *Anesthesiology* 1984; 60:587-588.

25. Garriott JC and DiMaio VJM, Death in the dental chair: Three drug fatalities in dental patients. *J Toxicol-Clin Toxicol* 1982-3; 19:987-995

26. Centers for Disease Control and Prevention. National Vital Statistics Report. Deaths: Final Data for 1998. 48(11):95

27. Lawson HW, et al., Abortion mortality, United States, 1972 through 1987. *Am J Obstet Gyn* 1994; 171(5):1365-1372.

28. Wigglesworth JS, The macerated stillborn fetus, in *Perinatal Pathology*. 2nd ed, Philadelphia, WB Saunders Co, 1996, pp 78-86.

29. Strachan GI, The pathology of fetal maceration. *Br Med J* 1922; 2:80-82.

30. Wigglesworth JS, Intrapartum and early neonatal death: the interaction of asphyxia and trauma, in *Perinatal Pathology*. 2nd ed Philadelphia, WB Saunders Co, 1996, pp 87-103.

31. Klein, cited by Taylor AS., *Medical Jurisprudence*, 7th ed, London, 1961.

32. DiMaio VJM and DiMaio SJ, Fatal water intoxication in a case of psychogenic polydipsia. *J Forens Sci* 1980; 25:332-335

33. Coe JI, Postmortem chemistries on human vitreous humor. *Am J Clin Pathol* 1969; 51:741-750.

34. Coe JI, Some further thoughts and observations on postmortem chemistries. *Forens Sci Gazette* 1973; 4(5):2-5.

35. Coe JI, Case # 7, Forensic Pathology Dinner Seminar (# 410), American Society of Clinical Pathology.

36. DiMaio VJM, Sturner WQ, and Coe JJ, Sudden and unexpected deaths after the acute onset of diabetes mellitus. *J Forens Sci* 1977; 22:147-151.

37. Coe JI, Peripheral blood glucose and cardiopulmonary resuscitation. *Forens Sci Gazette* 1975; 6(4):1-239.

38. Hopkins PM, Malignant hyperthermia: advance in clinical management and daignosis. *Br J. Anaesth* 2000; 85(1):118-28.

39. Robinson JF, et al., Perforation of the great vessels during central venous line placement. *Arch Intern. Med* 1995; 155(11):1225-1228.

40. Palmon SC, et al., Venous air embolism: a review. *J Clin Anesth*, 1997; 9(3):251-257.

41. Albin M et al.,Venous air embolism during lumbar laminectomy in the prone position: report of three cases. *Anesth. Analg.* 1991 73:346-349.

Nursing Home Deaths

21

Approximately 17, 000 nursing homes exist in the U.S., housing 1.5 million patients over the age of 65 years. Deaths in Nursing Homes (NH) are, for the most part, natural and usually do not fall under the medical examiner's jurisdiction. There are exceptions, such as:

Drug Overdoses

Such deaths may be either inadvertent or intentional. The authors have investigated a number of cases where a patient was given either too much medication or the wrong medication. This situation is probably fairly common, but, in most instances, does not cause death. When death does occur, the nursing home is probably often unaware of the mix-up and assumes the death to be natural. In virtually all the cases where death was caused by an inadvertent overdose and the death was investigated, the circumstances of the case came to light only when an employee surreptitiously notified the medical examiner or the family. Insulin seems to be quite commonly involved in these situations.

In rare instances, the drug overdose is intentional. A number cases of health care workers who believed it their calling to end "suffering" by killing a patient have been reported. The only cases such as this seen by the authors involved potassium chloride. In one case, it was a concentrated oral medication administered via a PEG tube.

Accidents Not Involving Medications

These include asphyxial deaths caused by bedrails and restraint vests, drinking of cleaning fluids by senile patients, burns caused by immersion in hot bath water, falls etc. It is not uncommon for the NH staff to attempt to conceal a fatal accident.

Homicides

The perpetrators of the homicides may be NH personnel, visiting family members, or fellow patients. In two recent cases, patients were beaten to death by fellow patients who suffered from Alzheimer's disease. Weapons used were a metal crutch and part of a wheelchair.

Suicides

These are very uncommon. More common are the spouses of patients with chronic or fatal disease who come in, kill the patient, and then kill themselves.

Gross Neglect of Patients

Nursing homes or personnel have been charged with homicide for improper and inadequate care of patients.[1-2] In one case involving a death resulting from infected decubitus ulcers (pressure sores), the care-home provider was convicted of manslaughter.[2] In another case, an attending nurse pled guilty to the felony offense of injury to an elderly individual, second degree, because she did not promptly notify a physician or summon EMS personnel when a patient was obviously suffering a heart attack.[3] In all probability, the numbers of cases in which individuals and perhaps institutions will be charged with homicide in the death of patients will increase.

Signs of Neglect

Signs of neglect are:
- Contractures
- Malnutrition
- Dehydration
- Decubitus ulcers

Of course, these complications overlap and one can contribute to the development of another.

The biggest problem in many, if not most, Nursing Homes in this country is staffing. Unskilled individuals are hired at very low salaries to minister to sick, debilitated and often confused patients. Employees may not be adequately screened and it is not uncommon for individuals with criminal records to be hired. Training is minimal. To make matters even worse, staff numbers are generally inadequate. Thus, in many nursing homes a CNA (certfied nursing assistant) is required to feed seven to nine residents during the day and 12 to 15 at the evening meal; the ideal caseload is one CNA for two to three residents.[4] It may take 1–2 min to feed a spoonful of food to an impaired patient —30 to 40 minutes for a meal. If you are required to feed six patients in an hour, it is not possible. Food is rammed into the mouth, only to be spit out. The record shows, however, that the patient "consumed" 100% of the meal. Thus, records will show that all food is eaten, but severe weight loss and malnutrition ensue.

Records of the administration of care should always be approached with caution. Records will show that patients are turned every 2 h, but decubitus ulcers develop, that they eat all their meals but lose weight. Medications are always given, even when it turns out that they were not available. In some instances, care is documented as being given even after the patient has died.

Contractures

A **contracture** is an abnormal, often permanent, condition characterized by flexion and fixation of a limb at a joint. Contractures leave the joint in a non-functional position, resistant to bending. They are caused by atrophy and abnormal shortening of muscle fibers. Their primary cause is disuse. Prolonged bed rest, even in "normal" individuals, results in loss of lean muscle mass through lack of use. The muscles become weak, atrophic, change shape, and shorten with disuse. The muscle decreases in diameter and in the number of muscle cells. Eventually, there may be replacement with fibrous connective tissue, progressing to fibrosis and development of contractures.

Contractures are seen in NH patients with impaired sensorium who are confined to bed. In such patients, a nurse should administer a passive range-of-motion exercises on a daily basis to prevent development of contractures. Often, this is not done and contractures develop. Development of contractures indicates poor nursing care i.e., that the individual is not receiving appropriate joint exercises. Approximately 20% of nursing home residents nationwide have contractures.[4]

Malnutrition

Malnutrition is manifested by a deficit, excess, or imbalance in essential components of a balanced diet. The type of malnutrition seen in nursing homes is usually protein-caloric malnutrition. Thirty-five to 80 percent of patients in nursing homes are malnourished, with 30–40% of patients sub-standard in weight.[4] A weight loss of 5% or greater in 30 d, 7.5% in 3 months and 10% in 6 months, indicates a patient's nutrition should be evaluated.

The amount of nutrition required by a person to live depends on body size, age, health, the environment, and degree of activity. The **basal metabolic rate** (BMR) is the amount of energy required of an individual who is awake but at rest, to maintain cellular function at the lowest rate. For a 25-year-old male weighing 154 lbs, it is 1744 cal; for a 132-lb, 25-year-old woman, 1281 cal. The number of calories required by a person increases with activity and health problems. Since we are discussing bedridden patients for the most part, we can ignore activity. In such patients, however, health problems are frequent. Stress caused by infections or decubitus ulcers can increase the caloric requirement by a factor of 1.2 to 1.6. For the 25-year-old male, the calories needed would increase to 2100–2800 cal. The BMR increases 5% for every 1°F rise in body temperature, which necessitates an increase in caloric intake. As to protein intake, in a normal individual, 0.8 to 1.0 g/kg/day of protein is needed. With infection or decubitus ulcers, this can increase up to 1.2 to 1.5 g/kg/day.

Malnutrition in nursing home patients can be caused by:

- Chronic disease conditions that make eating difficult, e.g., paralysis caused by a stroke
- Increased caloric or protein requirements due to infection or the healing of wounds
- Medications that impair the desire to eat, e.g., psychotropic drugs
- Failure of the nursing home to feed the patients

Obviously, the first three causes have to do with why the patient is in the nursing home. It is the duty of the nursing home to overcome these problems and see that the patient is offered and consumes adequate amounts of food.

Malnutrition predisposes an individual to the development of decubitus ulcers and infection. These, in turn, lead to increased caloric and protein requirements, thus making the malnutrition worse, which, again, predisposes to decubitus ulcers and infection.

While loss of weight often is an indicator of malnutrition, this is not always the case. The easiest way of determining malnutrition is by measuring serum albumin. The level of albumin in the blood is a reflection of the nutritional status of the patient. (Table 21.1) Low levels are associated with protein deprivation (inadequate intake of protein). They are also seen in chronic disease, infection, surgical stress, and trauma, all of which result in demand for more protein. Individuals in nursing homes suffering from these conditions should be given additional food (calories and protein).

Low levels of albumin reflect longstanding malnutrition. The half-life of albumin is 12 to 20 d, but is shortened in the presence of infection.[5] Thus, low levels of albumin generally reflect what happened to the patient 1–2 months in the past. In contrast, acute starvation reduces the concentrations of proteins that have a short half-life: transferrin (half-life 5 d) and pre-albumin (half-life 2 d).[5]

Table 21.1 Blood Albumin*	
Normal	3.5 - 4.5 g/dl
Mild protein depletion	3.0 - 3.4 g/d
Moderate depletion	2.5 - 2.9 g/dl
Severe depletion	< 2.5 g/dl

* There is some variation in normal ranges among laboratories.

Dehydration

Dehydration is very common in NH patients. It is caused by illness (diarrhea, fever, infection), the effects of medications (e.g., diuretics), and decreased fluid intake. When personnel do not monitor the intake of fluid and provide extra fluids when required, dehydration develops.

Decubitus Ulcers

Decubitus ulcers (pressure sores) are entirely preventable. They need not and should never occur. Factors predisposing to pressure sores are:

- Depressed sensory or motor function
- Altered consciousness
- Pressure over bony prominences
- Malnutrition
- Shearing forces
- Moisture (fecal and urinary incontinence)

The most common cause of decubitus ulcers is **pressure**, usually over bony prominences, in an individual with altered consciousness or impaired motor activity. When the pressure on soft tissue is greater than 32 mm of mercury, it closes capillary blood flow. This results in deprivation of oxygen to the tissue in this area and accumulation of metabolic end products. If these continue to accumulate for more than 2 h, there is irreversible tissue damage. The inability to shift one's body because of depressed sensory or motor function or unconsciousness leads to abnormal pressure and, thus, development of decubitus ulcers. The most common sites are the sacrum, the coccygeal areas, and the greater trochantars from lying in bed, as well as the ischial tuberosities if the patient is able to sit.

The second major cause of decubitus ulcers is **malnutrition**. This results in muscle atrophy and decrease in subcutaneous tissue, reducing the padding over the muscles, making the pressure more significant and producing ulcers. **Obesity** also contributes to pressure ulcers. A normal amount of fat protects the skin by acting as a cushion. Large quantities of fat, however, lead to ulceration because the adipose tissue is poorly vascularized and the underlying tissue then becomes more susceptible to ischemia.

Another major factor causing ulcers is **shearing forces**. Here, there is sliding of one tissue layer over another with stretching and angulation of blood vessels, which results in injury and thrombosis. This commonly occurs when the head of the bed is raised too high and the individual's body tends to slide downward. Friction and perspiration cause fixation of the skin and the superficial fascia to the sheets, while the deeper fascia slides down. Shearing forces in the elderly are aggravated by the loose skin common in the elderly because of loss of subcutaneous tissue and dehydration.

Moisture, usually caused by urinary and fecal incontinence, is also a major factor predisposing to development of pressure sores. Moisture reduces skin resistance to the other factors and increases the possibility of decubitus ulcers fivefold.

Decubitus ulcers (pressure sores) are divided into four (4) stages based on their clinical appearance and extent.

Stage 1 — The initial lesion seen following compression of skin and tissue is **reactive hyperemia** (reddening of the skin). The redness is caused by sudden increase in blood flow to the area compressed, after relief from the pressure of compression. If there is no injury to the tissue, the redness will disappear in less than 1 h. If the compression is long enough to produce ischemia but not irreversible injury, then you have an abnormal reactive hyperemia, which can last several hours. If the pressure is maintained long enough, one then has a stage 1 pressure sore manifested by erythema that lasts longer than 24 h, does not blanch on pressure, and shows induration of the tissue caused by edema. These sores can occur in a matter of a few hours. In our opinion, while stage 1 pressure sores are an indication of a potential problem, they do not in themselves indicate neglect. They are readily treatable and should not progress.

Stage 2 — These range in severity from a blister to ulceration of the skin. They may involve the full thickness of the skin but do not penetrate into the subcutaneous fat. These lesions are in a grey zone as indicators of neglect. They shouldn't occur, but do. They are readily treatable.

Stage 3 — These are full-thickness ulcers extending through the skin and subcutaneous fat up to the fascia. There is usually undermining of the skin. The base of the ulcer is usually necrotic, foul-smelling and infected.

Stage 4 — Here the ulcer extends down through the fascia into muscle, often to the bone. Osteomyelitis may develop (Figure 21.1).

Stage 3 and Stage 4 ulcers, in our opinion, indicate poor or lack of nursing treatment and thus neglect. Preventive measures involve basic nursing techniques. In bed, the patient should be turned or repositioned at least every 2 h; in wheelchairs, every hour. Adequate nutrition and hydration should be given; the skin must be kept dry by preventing patients from lying in their urine and feces; the head of the bed should not be raised to such a degree that the patient will slide down and, if necessary, extra padding over bony prominences should be provided. If a sore develops, the physician should be notified immediately.

The incidence of pressure sores in individuals in nursing homes varies from study to study. A conservative approximation is 7–8%. Tsokos et al. conducted a prospective study of 10,222 bodies coming to cremation in Hamburg,

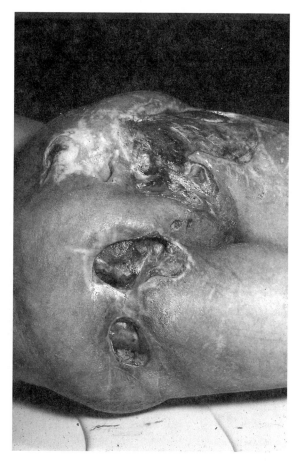

Figure 21.1 Stage IV decubitus ulcers

Germany, from various sources including nursing homes, hospitals and private residences. [6] Pressure sores were observed in 11.2% of the individuals. The distribution of the sores by grades was Stage 1–6.1%; Stage 2–3%; Stage 3–1.1% and stage 4–0.9%. Stage 3 and 4 sores were found principally on the sacrum (69.6%). Seventy-three percent of all Stage 4 sores were in individuals 80 years of age and older. For Stage 4 sores, the place of death was:

- 36.2%: senior citizen or nursing home
- 23.4%: private home
- 17%: hospital
- 23.4%: unknown

The site where the individuals developed the sores was not necessarily the same as where they died.

Both the presence of pressure sores and deaths caused by them are under-reported. The authors have reviewed hospital admission records of patients with pressure sores where the sores are not mentioned at all in the physical examinations by the physicians or in the diagnoses. Pressure sores are dismissed as inevitable by many physicians. In fact, there is no doubt that pressure sores can be successfully prevented by determining the patients at risk for development of sores, consistently monitoring them for development of sores and instituting prophylactic procedures to prevent their development. If sores develop, they can be effectively treated by conservative or surgical means.

Decubitus ulcers, Stages 2–4, lose both fluids and proteins. The more severe the lesion, the greater the loss. These open sores are invariably colonized by bacteria. The resultant infection can cause septicemia. The exact incidence of this complication is unknown, because many physicians fail to attempt to conclusively determine the source of a fatal septicemia in these patients.

Homicide by Decubitus Ulcers

How can one defend a ruling of homicide in a death from decubitus ulcers? In these cases, what one attempts to show is that the patient died of the decubitus ulcers and that the ulcers developed secondary to gross neglect, or failure to provide the most basic nursing services. Quite commonly in such cases, a pattern of falsified records is found, delay in notifying attending physicians of the presence or severity of the ulcer, and failure to promptly institute therapy ordered by the physician.

Physicians, both clinicians and forensic pathologists, have a tendency to write off the deaths of nursing home patients as inevitable. Some individuals and institutions argue that, because of the patients' condition (i.e., they are bedridden, do not have control of their bowels, and cannot feed themselves), then it is expected that they will become malnourished and develop contractures and bed sores. There are two problems with this argument. First, if these same individuals were moved into institutions where they were provided good nursing care the decubitus ulcers would heal; the patients would gain weight and overall health would improve. Second, infants are bedridden, have no control over their bowels and can't feed themselves. If a caretaker starved a child, leaving it in its urine and feces so that it developed sores and infections, that caretaker would be arrested; charged with child abuse, and put in prison. A death in such circumstances would be ruled homicide.

Deaths Caused by Hospital Bed Side-Rails

Bed side-rails are intended to prevent patients from injuring themselves. They are not suitable for and will not restrain individuals who are active or ambulatory, no matter the mental status. Bed rails cause injury indirectly in that most falls from beds in elderly individuals occur when they attempt to climb over the rails. On occasion, bed rails may cause death directly by entrapment.[7,8] The majority of such cases involve nursing homes, where the patients are elderly and tend to have cognitive and physical disabilities.

Parker and Miles reviewed 74 deaths attributed solely to bed rails. In 52 (70%) of the cases, there was entrapment between the mattress and bed rail, with the face pressed against the mattress.[8] Thirteen (18%) of the deaths were caused by entrapment of the neck within the rails (eight had inserted their heads between the vertical bars; the bed-rail latch failed and the rail dropped on their necks; five patients died because their heads and necks were draped over the top of the rails). Nine (12%) of the 74 patients died when they slid partially off the bed. This resulted in their being suspended by either their heads or pelvises with, in the latter circumstance, the necks hyperflexed or hyperextended by contact with the floor.

In a number of deaths involving bed rails seen by the authors, attempts to conceal the cause of death were made. This involved placing the individual back in bed and notifying the attending physician that the patient had died naturally. Such cases were uncovered only when NH personnel reported the deaths to the medical examiner or a member of the family.

Deaths Caused by Medical Restraints

Restraints are mechanical devices, materials, or equipment that restrict individuals' freedom of movement or normal access to their bodies. If individuals attempt to escape from such devices, they run the danger of ligature strangulation or traumatic/positional asphyxia.[9,10] Miles and Irvine reviewed 122 deaths caused by vest and strap restraints, in which 85% occurred in nursing homes.[10] The victims were elderly, with a median age of 81. They were found suspended from chairs in 58% of the cases and from beds in 42%. Typically, there was a history of sliding down in or escaping restraints. Victims are placed in a vest or strap restraint and left alone. They then slide off the bed or chair, with the restraint catching them across the chest or, less commonly, under the chin. Unfortunately, they do not slide down far enough to reach a weight-bearing surface. If the restraint catches them under the neck, they strangle. If the restraint stops at the chest, their weight on the restraint reduces chest movement, causing traumatic asphyxia.

References

1. Long S, *Death Without Dignity*, Texas Monthly Press, Austin TX 1987.
2. *State of Hawaii v. Bermissa*, 2000.

3. *State of Texas vs. Jo Ann Maddox,* 1999.

4. Burger SG, Kayser-Jones J and Bell JP, Malnutrition and dehydration in nursing homes: Key issues in prevention and treatment. June 2000. Research supported by the Commonwealth Fund. http://www.cmwf.org/programs/elders/burger_mal_386.asp.

5. Neale G, Diet and disease. In Tomlinson S, Heagerty AM and Weetman AP (Eds). *Mechanisms of Disease.* Cambridge University Press Cambridge, UK 1997.

6. Tsokos M, Heinemann A, and Puschel K, Pressure sores: epidemiology, medicolegal implications and forensic argumentation concerning causality. *Int J Legal Med,* 2000 113:283-287.

7. Todd JF, Ruhl CE and Gross TP, Injury and death associated with hospital bed side-rails: Reports to the U.S. Food and Drug Administration from 1985 to 1995. *Am J Pub Hlth,* 1997; 87(10):1675-1677.

8. Parker K and Miles SH, Deaths caused by bed rails. *J Am Geriatrics Soc.* 1997; 45(7):797-802.

9. Di Maio VJ, Dana SE, and Bux RC, Deaths caused by restraint vests. *JAMA* 1986; 255:905.

10. Miles SH and Irvine P, Deaths cause by physical restraints. *Gerontologist.* 1992; 32:762-766.

Sudden Death During or Immediately after a Violent Struggle

22

Periodically, a forensic pathologist is presented with a case of sudden death during or immediately after a violent struggle in which a complete autopsy fails to reveal an anatomical cause of death. Such deaths usually involve police or medical personnel who have attempted to restrain a violent, irrational individual. When the forensic pathologist reports that there was insufficient trauma to explain the death, they are often accused of a cover-up or incompetence because it is "quite evident" the individual was "killed" by the police or medical personnel. When it is finally accepted that there was insufficient physical evidence of trauma to the body to explain the death, allegations that the individual died from a "choke hold" or "positional asphyxia" are frequently made.

In cases in which individuals die during a struggle with either police or medical personnel, the following procedures should be followed:

- A complete investigation of the circumstances leading up to and surrounding the death should be conducted. The medical examiner should obtain as much information and as many different accounts of the incident. Any medical records of the deceased should be obtained and reviewed.
- A complete autopsy should be performed. This should be accompanied by a microscopic survey of all organs, especially the heart.
- A complete toxicological screen should be performed.

Because of the controversial nature of such deaths, especially when they involve the police, it is recommended that the autopsy be performed by or under the direct supervision of an experienced forensic pathologist, and photographs of the body taken, even if there are no visible injuries. No ruling as to the cause of death should be made until all testing is complete.

Excited Delirium

The usual presentation in such deaths is that of individuals in **excited delirium.** They are confused, irrational, hyperactive, and usually violent. In an attempt to restrain them from injuring themselves or others, a violent struggle ensues. Immediately after the struggle ends, the individual abruptly becomes unresponsive, develops cardiopulmonary arrest, and does not respond to cardiopulmonary resuscitation. In cases involving the police, individuals usually become unresponsive after being handcuffed and placed or wrestled to the ground. In some instances, this occurs as they are being transported to jail or a hospital. At autopsy, there is no anatomical cause for the death, though minor injuries, e.g., abrasions, may be present. In the cases involving the police, toxicologic testing will usually reveal drugs such as cocaine or methamphetamine. It is the cocaine or another stimulant that is presumably causing the excited delirium. The authors would like to reiterate that the lapse into unresponsiveness and development of cardiopulmonary arrest almost invariably occurs after the struggle has ended.

Catecholamine Release

In cases such as the aforementioned, most deaths are caused by the combined effect of the physiological consequences of violent physical activity and the effects of the drugs. During high intensity exercise, e.g., a struggle, there is release of catecholamines (norepinephrine and epinephrine) from the adrenals into the circulation. The effects of these substances are to increase the rate and force of contraction of the heart, the conduction velocity and the blood pressure. This results in an increase in demand for oxygen by the heart. The highest levels of catecholamines occur not during physical activity (a struggle in this case) but approximately 3 min after cessation of the activity.[1,2]

Potassium

During the struggle, not only do the levels of the catecholamines increase in the blood but so do blood potassium concentrations.[2-4] The increase may be as much as 5 mEq/l or more in some individuals.[4] Following cessation of exercise, there is an immediate, rapid drop in blood potassium to concentrations that approach 2 mEq/l.[3-5] Five minutes after cessation of the exercise, potassium levels may be lower than when they were at rest. There may be a pronged hypokalemia lasting 90 min or more.[3,5] These extremes in potassium concentrations can have cardiac arrhythmogenic effects. The arrhythmogenic effects of the hyperkalemia, however, are neutralized by the cardioprotective effect of the elevated levels of catecholamines.[6] Thus, the danger time for arrhythmias is immediately following cessation of physical activity, when blood catecholamine concentrations continue to rise while potassium levels drop dramatically to hypokalemic levels. This period has been referred to by Dimsdale et al. as the time of **post-exercise peril**, in that there is a risk of cardiac arrhythmias during this period.[1]

Effects of Catecholamines on the Heart

Upon commencement of high-intensity physical activity (a struggle in these cases), the adrenal glands secrete epinephrine and norepinephrine into the blood. Most of the alpha adrenergic receptors on effector organs (cardiac muscle, smooth muscle) are alpha-1 receptors. Stimulation results in smooth muscle contraction of blood vessels, with resultant vasospasm. The beta-1 receptors are primarily in the heart; the beta-2 receptors in the heart and peripherally. Stimulation of the beta-1 receptors causes an increase in heart rate, contractility and conduction velocity. Beta-2 stimulation results in smooth muscle relaxation. Epinephrine reacts with alpha and beta receptors both peripherally and in the cardiovascular system. Norepinephrine has its predominant effect on the cardiovascular system, reacting with the alpha-1 and beta-1 receptors in the effector cells of the heart. Thus, both epinephrine and norepinephrine react with beta-1 receptors with resultant increase in heart rate, contractility and conduction velocity. Coronary arteries have in their walls both beta-2 and alpha-1 receptors, with the beta-2 more plentiful. Norepinephrine interacting only with the alpha-1 receptors causes vasoconstriction, thus decreasing the amount of oxygenated blood being supplied to the myocardium by the coronary arteries. Therefore, any drug that causes increased exposure of receptor sites to norepinephrine predisposes to coronary artery constriction at the time the heart needs more — not less — oxygen. At the same time that changes in catecholamine concentrations are occurring, the aforementioned changes in blood potassium levels also occur.

Actions of Drugs

Following cessation of a violent struggle, the levels of catecholamine continue to increase for approximately three minutes, while the level of potassium drops dramatically.[1-5] These two factors predispose to the development of an arrhythmia. This is the time of "**post exercise peril**" described by Dimsdale.[1] Stimulants such as cocaine and methamphetamine can cause excited delirium. If the individual has taken amphetamine, cocaine or another stimulant, the physiologic effects of the struggle can be magnified by the drugs and a fatal arrhythmia more readily ensue. Cocaine has a double effect. It causes increased release of catecholamines from the adrenals and inhibits norepinephrine reuptake. The latter action causes norepinephrine to accumulate at the neuroeffector junction, intensifying its effect. Thus, by these actions, cocaine works on the beta-1 receptors to increase heart rate, force of contraction and conduction velocity, while, at the same time, acting on the alpha receptors in the coronary arteries to cause contraction, reducing myocardial perfusion. Thus, as the myocardium needs increasing amounts of oxygen, due to the stimulation of the beta-1 receptors, the amount of blood perfusing the myocardium is reduced by constriction of the coronary arteries. Amphetamine has the same effect as cocaine, but, instead of blocking the reuptake of norepinephrine, it causes release of norepinephrine from the sympathetic fibers.

Alcohol

Sudden death of an individual with a history of alcohol abuse and in whom only alcohol may be present also occurs during a struggle. Alcohol is a recognized cause of a variety of atrial and ventricular arrhythmias.[7–9] In addition, chronic alcoholics have been found to have a prolonged QT interval, an affliction associated with sudden death, as well as increased levels of norepinephrine.[10–12] All these predispositions to arrhythmias can be aggravated by catecholamines released during a violent struggle. Thus, if the heart is predisposed to fatal arrhythmias by the action of alcohol, then, under conditions such as a violent struggle, the released catecholamines can produce a fatal arrhythmia.

Endogenous Mental Disease: Acute Psychotic Episodes

Excited delirium may also occur in the absence of stimulant drugs such as cocaine, methamphetamine or alcohol in individuals with endogenous mental disease. Clinically, these are usually referred to as acute psychotic episodes, and tend to occur in individuals with schizophrenia, schizoaffective disorders or delusional disorders. Acute psychotic episodes happen both in and out of mental facilities. They may occur because of the patient's discontinuance of medications or development of tolerance to the medications. If the episode occurs outside a mental health facility, the police are usually called on to deal with the individual; if inside the facility, it is nursing or support personnel. Sudden death can be caused by either the physiological effects of catecholamine and hypokalemia following the struggle or a combination of these effects and the effects of the medications the patient is or was on. Many patients, nowadays, are on medications, some of which have a cardiotoxic potential. The tricyclic antidepressants, just like cocaine, block reuptake of norepinepnrine. The action of these drugs can predispose an individual to a cardiac arrhythmia.

Natural Disease without Anatomical Manifestations

In some instances, sudden death during or following a struggle can be caused by natural disease that is not diagnosable anatomically. In such instances, a medical history is absolutely necessary to make the diagnosis. Some examples are Wolfe-Parkinson-White syndrome, the prolonged Q-T syndrome, etc. In one case, an interview with the family revealed a history of "fluttering" or "pounding" heartbeats, a "funny pulse," suggestive that the individual had an underlying physiological lesion of the conduction system of the heart predisposing him to develop an arrhythmia.

Most medical professionals, including forensic pathologists, have no experience with individuals who are in the throes of excited delirium. They do not comprehend the violence or the intensity of the struggle. Thus, to restrain a 12-yr-old child during an acute psychotic episode may take four large adults, one to each extremity, while a fifth administers a tranquilizing injection. Nursing articles recommend that, when attempting to physically restrain a violent individual experiencing an acute psychotic episode, at least six individuals be used.[13]

When someone dies during a struggle, the natural question is why. An explanation involving catecholamines, alpha and beta receptors, and potassium levels, is difficult for most people to understand. Choke holds and positional asphyxia can be demonstrated and are simple to understand, therefore, it is normal to gravitate to this simpler explanation for a death. Even if there is absolutely no evidence of use of a choke hold or positional asphyxia, and the law enforcement or medical personnel deny using either, the denials are sometimes dismissed as a cover-up. The concept of death caused by a choke hold is very popular because, when no evidence of trauma to the neck is found, this would seem to "prove" that the choke hold was "expertly" applied. Of course, use of a choke hold is just a form of manual strangulation. It always amazes me when a 200-lb adult male is allegedly killed with a choke hold without a mark on the throat and no petechiae in the eyes, while a 100-lb woman, manually strangled by an individual twice her weight, is able to put up sufficient struggle so as to have bruises on the neck and petechiae of the conjunctivae and sclerae. Since use of a choke hold is manual strangulation, the individual applying the choke hold must maintain it for close to 2 min to cause cessation of respiration.

Deaths Ascribed to Positional Asphyxia

For respiration, one has to have an open airway; lungs capable of gas exchange and the ability to ventilate the lungs. In deaths ascribed to positional asphyxia, it is alleged that there is interference with ventilation of the lungs. Ventilation involves movement of the chest wall, diaphragm and abdominal wall. Positional asphyxia occurs when an individual is placed in or somehow gets into a position where there is interference with his ventilatory efforts (Figure 8.12). A number of deaths occurring after episodes of manic delirium have been ascribed to positional asphyxia.

Law enforcement personnel routinely employ physical restraints to control prisoners. The most common of these are handcuffs. When the prisoner is violent, there may be escalation to ankle shackles, restraint chairs, etc. Until the mid-1990s, use of "hogtie" restraints was common. In the hogtie position, the prisoner is placed face down on the ground, his wrists and ankles bound behind his back and then tied together by a rope or cord. This type of restraint began to fall in disuse when it was alleged that sudden death could be produced utilizing this position and type of restraint. Numerous civil suits were filed in regard to prisoners dying while hogtied. It was alleged that securing an individual in this position caused hypoventilatory respiratory failure, i.e., positional asphyxia. Studies by Chan et al. refuted these contentions.[14] In experiments involving high-intensity physical activity followed by hogtie restraint, Chan et al. demonstrated that, while there was impairment in respiratory activity, it "did not result in clinically relevant changes in oxygenation or ventilation." Eisele et al. continued this line of research, with the addition of placing 25- and 50-lb weights between the shoulder blades while the subjects were prone and hogtied, to simulate an individual pressing down on the back of someone hogtied. The tests showed no significant effect on oxygen saturation of the blood. [15]

While virtually all deaths in manic delirium are probably caused by the physiological reactions to a violent struggle (with or without interaction with drugs), in occasional cases, positional asphyxia may play a role in a death. Thus, if individuals are placed in hogtie restraint and put in the back of a vehicle so that their abdomens lie over the transmission hump, a reasonable argument for positional asphyxia can be made. There is also the problem with massively obese individuals. There is a potential for positional asphyxia if a hogtie is applied and they are left face down. In both situations, pressure on the abdomen would impair the abdominal component of respiration as well as forcing the diaphragm up, reducing its capacity for excursion.

Certification of Death

In the aforementioned cases, the authors suggest two ways of certifying the cause of death. First is to sign out the cause of death as "excited delirium" and then list "struggle," "cocaine intoxication," etc., as contributory causes. The other way is to sign out the cause of death in a descriptive manner, e.g. "Cardiopulmonary arrest during violent struggle in individual under influence of cocaine, alcohol, etc." In individuals with psychoses, this is listed either as a contributory cause or incorporated in the descriptive diagnosis.

The greater difficulty is designating a manner of death. Because of the effects of the violent struggle, one cannot classify such a case as a natural death. The choice then is either homicide or accident. Since a violent struggle has occurred with interaction between two or more individuals, the best classification of the manner of death is probably homicide. A good argument for an accident can be made, however. If the case is called a homicide, it is necessary to explain that the designation does not indicate that there was necessarily any criminal activity involved. The difference between homicide and murder should be carefully explained.

Pepper Spray

Oleoresin Capsaicin (Pepper Spray, OC) is an extract of hot peppers consisting of capsaicin and four derivatives.[16] When sprayed in an individual's face it acts within seconds on the membranes of the eyes to cause stinging, tearing and blepharospasm with involuntary closure of the eyes. Capsaicin also affects the respiratory membranes, causing coughing, broncho-constriction, mucous secretion, and shortness of breath, as well as some brief laryngeal paralysis with resultant inability to speak. The effects disappear in 20–30 minutes. The substances in Pepper Spray produce depletion of neurotransmitter substances of the sensory nerves with resultant activation of mast cells and release of histamine. This causes the broncho-constriction and mucous formation.

OC spray canisters consist of a carrier for the capsaicin, a propellant, and an aerosol valve nozzle. The carrier is either water or alcohol. The concentration of the capsaicin varies from 1% in canisters sold to the public, to 5 to 10% for police.

Pepper spray is widely used throughout the U.S. and also worldwide. A number of deaths have occurred in individuals after being sprayed. Investigation of these deaths has failed to reveal any evidence that the pepper spray played any role in the deaths. Virtually all of the individuals were in the throes of excited delirium at the time of spraying. Toxicologic analysis virtually always revealed the presence of cocaine or methamphetamine. Other individuals gave a history of a psychotic disease. The authors have had a number of cases in which individuals in excited delirium have been sprayed repeatedly with absolutely no effect. This included individuals whose excited delirium was caused by cocaine, as well as other individuals experiencing an acute psychotic episode.

References

1. Dimsdale JE, et al., Post exercise peril: Plasma catecholamine and exercise. *JAMA* 1984; 252:630-632.

2. Young DB, et al., Potassium and catecholamine concentrations in the immediate post exercise period. *Am J Med Sci,* 1992; 304(3):150-153.

3. Lindinger MI, Potassium regulation during exercise and recovery in humans: Implications for skeletal and cardiac muscle. *J Mol Cell Card* 1995; 27:1011-1022.

4. Medbo JI and Sejersted OM, Plasma potassium changes with high intensity exercise. 1990 *J Physiol*; 421:105-122.

5. Lindinger MI, et al, Blood ion regulation during repeated maximal exercise and recovery in humans. *Am J Physiol,* 1992; 262:R126-136.

6. Paterson DJ, et al., Effect of catecholamines on the ventricular myocyte action potential in raised extracellular potassium. *Acta Physiol Scand* 1993; 148:177-186.

7. Singer K and Lundberg WB, Ventricular arrhythmias associated with the ingestion of alcohol. *Ann Intern Med* 1972; 77:247-248.

8. Gould L et al., Cardiac effects of two cocktails in normal man. *Chest* 1974; 63:943-947.

9. Ettinger PO et al., Arrhythmias and the "holiday heart": Alcohol-associated cardiac rhythm disorders. *Am Heart* 1 1978; 95:555-562.

10. Day CP et al., QT prolongation and sudden cardiac death in patients with alcoholic liver disease. *Lancet* 1993 342:1425-1428

11. Bernardi M et al., Q-T interval prolongation in cirrhosis: Prevalence, relationship with severity, and etiology of the disease and possible pathogenetic factors. *Hepatology* 1998; 27(1): 28-34

12. Newsome HH, Ethanol modulation of plasma norepinephrine response to trauma and hemorrhage. *J Trauma* 1988; 28:1-9.

13. Farrell SP, Harmon RB and Hastings S. Nursing management of acute psychotic episodes. Nursing Clinics of North America 1998; 33(1):187-200.

14. Chan TC et al., Restraint position and positional asphyxia. *Ann Emerg Med* 1997 30(5):578-586.

15. Eisele JW, et al., Comparison of respiratory function in the prone maximal restraint position with and without additional weight force on the back. Presented at the annual meeting of the American Academy of Forensic Science, Reno NV, Feb.21-26, 2000.

16. Busker RW and van Helden HPM, Toxicologic examination of pepper spray as a possible weapon for the Dutch police. *Am J Forens Med Path* 1998; 19(4): 309-316.

Interpretive Toxicology: Drug Abuse and Drug Deaths

23

The three curses of mankind: alcohol, morphine and cocaine

Forensic toxicology is the study and practice of the application of toxicology to the purposes of the law. It involves, not just the identification and quantifying of a drug, poison or substance in human tissue, but also the ability to interpret the results of those findings. Every year in the U.S., tens of thousands of people die directly or indirectly because of drugs. Because of this, the toxicology laboratory is as important to the medical examiner as the investigative section. It is absolutely necessary for a medicolegal system to have access to a well-equipped, adequately staffed toxicology laboratory. Without this, rulings as to cause and manner of death may be erroneous.

In medical examiner's offices, the results of toxicologic testing are correlated with the medical history of the deceased, the autopsy findings, and the circumstances leading up to or surrounding the death, so as to determine whether a drug was a cause of death, a contributing factor, or played no role. In many instances, drug levels alone cannot be interpreted. All physicians and toxicologists have had cases where an individual was found to have a fatal level of drug in the blood but was functioning with this level; the drug had nothing to do with the death. This is seen typically in drug abusers who acquire a tolerance to drug levels that would kill an ordinary person, but are normal functioning levels to them. This same situation is seen by clinical physicians — the patient admitted to the emergency room conscious and coherent, with drug levels that would be associated with unconsciousness or death in most individuals.

No matter how good one's toxicology laboratory, it cannot function if there is failure to collect the proper specimens, in adequate quantity, and in the proper containers.

Collection of Tissue for Analysis

In all autopsy cases, at a minimum, blood, urine, bile, and vitreous should be collected if available.

Collection of Specimens

- All specimens should be collected with a clean needle and a new syringe.
- The specimens of blood, urine, bile, and vitreous should be placed in glass containers, not plastic, because these fluids can leach out plastic polymers from the wall of a plastic container. If the blood is subsequently analyzed by gas chromatography, the polymers will give peaks that could mask certain compounds and interfere with analysis. In some cases, substances such as volatiles can be lost, due to absorption by the plastic.
- Collect the blood from the femoral vessels. If this is not possible, the other sites for collection, in descending order of preference, are:
  - The subclavian vessels
  - The root of the aorta
  - The pulmonary artery
  - The superior vena cava
  - The heart
- Collect a minimum of 50 mL of blood.
  - 20 ml in a 20-mL red-top glass test tube
  - 20 ml in two 10 mL gray-top glass test tubes (preservative potassium oxalate and sodium fluoride)
  - 10 ml in a purple top glass test tube (preservative EDTA) for DNA analysis
  - Collect all the vitreous
  - Collect 20 ml of urine
  - Collect up to 20 ml of bile
  - Label the specimens with name of deceased; case number; date of examination; name of the pathologist and, in the case of the blood, the source of the blood, e.g., the femorals.

If the blood is to be analyzed for volatiles, some should be kept in a test tube with a Teflon-lined screw top rather than a rubber stopper through which volatile compounds can diffuse.

The practice of opening the pericardial sac, positioning a tube or jar under the heart, then cutting the heart and letting blood drain into the receptacle should be condemned, because it is very easy to contaminate the contents of the jar with pericardial fluid and other material that might be present in the chest cavities. This may dilute the blood (with resultant fallacious low levels) or, if there has been diffusion of a drug from the stomach into pericardial or chest fluid, may actually contaminate it with the drug such that inaccurately high levels are detected in the "heart blood."

Blood is preferentially collected from the femoral and subclavian vessels to prevent the possibility or contention of postmortem release (redistribution) artifacts. In the case of certain drugs, postmortem levels in heart blood have been challenged on the basis of postmortem drug redistribution. The best examples are the tricyclic antidepressants. In cases involving these drugs, quantitation of the liver has been suggested as being superior to blood levels in determining whether one is dealing with an acute overdose or levels caused by chronic medication.[1] Pounder et al., however, have called this into question by demonstrating postmortem diffusion of drugs from the stomach into the liver, principally the left lobe.[2] Also demonstrated was diffusion into the left lung base, the spleen and the pericardial fluid. To a lesser degree, there was diffusion into the cardiac blood, aortic blood and inferior vena cava. All work was done on cadavers with postmortem instilling of the drugs.

Diffusion of alcohol into the cardiac chambers, the superior vena cava and the aorta is more controversial. The general feeling is that, while this can occur, it is uncommon. Diffusion appears to be associated with very high concentrations of alcohol in the stomach; failure to refrigerate the body for more that 24 hours, and an increasing time from death to collection of the blood.[3] Pounder found that diffusion is markedly inhibited by refrigeration. Because of the phenomenon of postmortem diffusion, Pound et al. recommended that, for toxicological purposes, peripheral blood (e.g., that from the femoral vessels), should be used for toxicologic analyses. If tissue is desired, then deep tissue from the right lobe of the liver; the apex of the lung, or muscle from an extremity should be used.

In individuals who have died after several hours or days of hospitalization, one would expect that any drugs in the blood at the time of admission would be metabolized. This is usually, but not always, the case. In these instances, not only should blood be obtained at autopsy, but the hospital in which the individual was a patient should be contacted to see if any blood obtained at or shortly after hospitalization is still in existence. This should then be obtained for toxicologic analysis. In trauma cases, blood is usually drawn immediately on admission to the emergency room and sent to the blood bank for typing and cross-match; it should then be retained in the blood bank for at least 2 weeks.

In deaths caused by a drug overdose or suspected drug overdose, the pathologist may wish to retain portions of liver, kidney and muscle for subsequent toxicological analysis. Collect at least 50 g of each of the aforementioned tissues. With the present-day state of the art in toxicology, this is generally not necessary. Unless there has been unusually prolonged survival, the drug that causes death will be present in the blood. Even with prolonged survival, the drug can usually be detected in the vitreous, bile, or urine. Drugs tend to be found in higher concentrations in the liver than the blood, as drug metabolism occurs there. In cases of a suspected oral overdose of drugs, the entire stomach contents should be retained.

On occasion, in instances of massive trauma to a body, no blood can be collected from the vasculature, though there is free blood in the body cavities. If this blood is collected, tested for alcohol and drugs and found to be negative then one is safe in assuming the individual was not under the affects of alcohol or drugs at the time of death. A positive test, on the other hand, must take into account the possibility of contamination. In such a case, another material such as vitreous or muscle must be analyzed to evaluate the accuracy of the test results on the blood.

If it is elected not to do an autopsy, but rather just an external examination of the body, then blood, urine and vitreous should be collected. Urine can be collected by inserting the needle from a clean syringe through the lower abdominal wall, just above the pubic symphysis. Blood is collected from either the femoral or subclavian vessels. Blood should never be collected by way of a blind stab through the anterior chest wall into the heart. This is to preclude inadvertent contamination of the blood with fluid contents from the esophagus, pericardial sac, stomach or pleural cavity.

Tissue Analyses

The tissue of most importance for analysis is blood. This is logical, when one realizes that it is the blood level of the drug that has the effect on the individual. A drug detected in the urine or bile had an effect on the individual but one cannot say that it is having an effect at the time the patient died. Thus, toxicologic analysis should be oriented to analysis of blood. With rare exception, virtually all drugs and their major metabolites can now be detected in blood in any modern toxicology lab. Heroin is an exception. But even in this case one can usually prove conclusively that it was taken. Thus, heroin (di-acetylmorphine) is almost immediately metabolized to mono-acetylmorphine and then to morphine in the blood after injection. In drug deaths, the detection of morphine in the blood was assumed to indicate that the individual died of an overdose of heroin. In some deaths in an emergency room, it was contended that the individual was inadvertently given morphine, thus causing death, i.e., the deceased was not a drug addict. With the recent ability to easily detect mono-acetylmorphine, it is now possible to positively prove the individual died of an overdose of heroin. Mono-acetylmorphine can often be detected in the vitreous after it has disappeared from the blood. In cases of head trauma, where there is a subdural collection of blood and the individual survives a number of days, subdural blood can be analyzed for alcohol. The results will be a crude approximation of the alcohol level of the deceased at the time the head trauma was incurred.

After blood, vitreous humor is next in value. Allowing for appropriate distribution ratios, vitreous reflects the drugs and their levels in the blood 1–2 h prior to death. Virtually any drug detectable in the blood is detectable in the vitreous if one uses analytical techniques and equipment of sufficient sensitivity. The significance of the level present is another matter. Vitreous is analyzed for alcohol when a positive blood alcohol is obtained, as this reflects the blood alcohol level 1–2 hours prior to death. In some cases, a routine electrolyte screen for sodium, chloride, urea nitrogen and creatinine is run on the vitreous. If analysis of the vitreous fluid for electrolytes is to be performed, the vitreous should be spun down and the supernatant analyzed, otherwise proteinaceous material in the vitreous may jam the analyzer.

Most drugs are excreted in the urine. Analysis of urine for drugs is easy because there is no protein binding to hinder extraction and many drugs are concentrated in the urine. It should be realized, however, that the level of a drug in the urine is usually of no significance in the interpretation of the cause of death. It is the level in the blood that determines whether an individual lives or dies.

Bile was useful when toxicological procedures were relatively crude because it concentrated drugs as they were excreted, thus making analysis for these drugs relatively easy. Nowadays, it is very rarely of any use other than to detect prior drug use and abuse. An example would be the case of an individual who died of hypoxic encephalopathy believed caused by a heroin overdose. In such a case, an analysis for morphine in the bile is conducted to see if an opiate had been used in the past several days. Liver and kidney are rarely used nowadays because there is no direct correlation between levels in these organs and blood levels. Hair and fingernails can be retained for analysis if one suspects arsenic poisoning.

One tissue whose potential for toxicological analysis is not appreciated is muscle. Muscle is of great value in decomposed bodies. Here, one cannot usually collect blood, urine, or vitreous. Instead, one tends to rely on the solid organs, such as the liver and kidney. These, however, decompose fairly rapidly. The muscle, especially that of the thigh, is often well preserved, in spite of advanced decomposition. In one case involving cocaine, even after embalming and disinterment of the body months after burial, cocaine and two of its metabolites, in lethal levels, were identified and quantitated in the muscle. Levels of drugs in the muscle more accurately reflect blood levels than the liver or kidney.

The authors believe the residual specimens should be kept for 2 years at a minimum, and preferably 5 years, after the specimens are analyzed.

Analysis of insects, e.g., maggots, feeding on a severely decomposed body have demonstrated the presence of drugs such as barbiturates, benzodiazepines, opiates and cocaine. In some cases, this has been used to make a diagnosis as to the cause of death. Thus, in a case reported by Levine et al., secobarbital was found in maggots recovered from a decomposed and skeletonized body.[4] Adjacent to the body was a bottle of secobarbital.

In summary, we would make the following suggestions concerning toxicological analysis. In bodies in which only an external examination is performed, we would suggest collecting blood, vitreous, and urine; in routine autopsies, blood, vitreous, urine, and bile; in suspected oral overdoses of a drug, blood, vitreous, urine, bile, and stomach contents, with liver, muscle and kidney optional; in drug overdoses not caused by oral ingestion, blood, vitreous, urine, and bile, with liver, muscle and kidney optional; in decomposed bodies, blood, urine, vitreous, and bile if present (usually they are not) as well as muscle, liver, and kidney. Body fluids and tissue should be retained even after analysis for 2–5 years, depending on storage capability.

Analysis

Analysis of biological tissues for toxicological purposes involves three fundamental steps applicable to any specimen:

1. Separation of the drug from the biological tissue
2. Purification of the drug
3. Analytical detection and quantitation

With some drugs, specimens and methodologies, Steps 1 and 2 can be eliminated and direct analytical analysis performed. Thus, analysis for drugs of abuse in urine using immunoassay techniques do not require Steps 1 and 2.

Separation of a drug from the biological specimen, e.g., blood, is usually accomplished using a solvent. Purification is carried out by additional extraction procedures using alkaline and acid solutions. Analysis is then conducted by gas chromatography (GC), gas chromatography-mass spectrometry (GC-MS), high performance liquid chromatography, immunoassay or UV spectrophotometry. It must be realized that, except for GC-MS, none of the methods is totally specific. All that the other analytical methods provide is presumptive evidence of the presence of the drug. While the presumptive evidence may be very strong — in the high 90% range with some drugs and analytical tests — another test must be performed for positive identification. The confirmatory test must involve a totally different method of analysis from the one originally used. If a method of analysis other than GC-MS is used for initial identification, it is often easier to make positive identification and even quantitation using the GC-MS. If initial analysis is made with the GC-MS, there is no necessity to redo the identification, because this method is specific.

Thin-layer chromatography should be mentioned as it is widely used in hospital toxicology. As a method of analysis in the forensic toxicology lab, it is, and has been for a considerable time, obsolete. It is neither sensitive nor specific enough for present-day use. The role that it used to play in a forensic laboratory, as a screening device, has been replaced by more sensitive and more rapid methods of screening involving immunoassay.

One of the more recently developed tools of the forensic toxicologist is the immunoassays. There are four types: radioimmunoassay, enzyme immunoassay, fluorescent immunoassay and kinetic interaction of microparticles. The major advantage to these systems is that large numbers of tests can be performed in a small amount of time using an extremely small volume of specimen, with semi-automated and automated systems to speed the rate of analysis. While radio-immuoassays can be used on blood, the other types of immunoassay should be confined to analysis of urine. These systems were never intended for the analysis of blood. Some laboratories have developed extraction techniques for blood that they allege makes analysis possible. If these methods are used on blood, drugs that are present will be missed.

There are two disadvantages to immunoassay techniques. First, the analysis is usually very narrow in scope; i.e., one analyzes for either a specific drug or a specific family of drugs, rather than for the several hundred drugs that can be analyzed for in one test with a GC or GC-MS. In addition, this method of analysis is not absolutely specific, although, with some of the newer kits, the specificity is extremely good. A positive test result must be confirmed by another analytical method, usually GC-MS. In a high-volume forensic lab, immunoassay methods can be used to screen for opiates, cocaine, amphetamines and methamphetamines, barbiturates, and cannabinoids in the urine. Negative results indicate that the compounds are not present; positive results indicate that the compound may be present. *A positive identification with any of the immunoassay tests should never be reported unless it has been confirmed by another method of analysis.* A positive immunoassay test cannot be confirmed with another immunoassay test — even using different assay techniques.

The minimum equipment necessary for an adequately equipped toxicology laboratory is a GC-MS, a GC, a UV spectrophotometer, and an immunoassay system. Minimum equipment for a population of one million would be three gas chromatographs (one dedicated to alcohol analysis), two GC-MSs (to confirm and quantitate material picked up by GC screens), an immunoassay system, one UV spectrometer, a CO oximeter, and an inductive coupled plasma spectrometer (ICP).

Toxicology Screens

Generally, toxicological screens can be divided into four general groups. First is the screen for lower alcohols. This involves analysis by gas chromatography and will identify acetone, isopropyl alcohol, n-propyl alcohol, ethyl alcohol, and methyl alcohol. Blood for this test should be collected in a tube containing sodium fluoride and potassium oxalate to prevent postmortem alcohol formation or loss.

The second screen is the acidic and neutral screen. This is performed on urine by immunoassay. It detects primarily barbiturates, salicylates, ethchlorvynol, and carbarnates. Confirmation and quantitation is usually by GC-MS.

The third screen is the basic screen. It detects tranquilizers, synthetic narcotics, local anesthetics, antihistamines, antidepressants, alkaloids, and other agents extractable from alkaline aqueous solution. Hundreds of drugs and metabolites can be detected by this procedure, depending on how it is structured. The equipment necessary for these screens is either a GC or GC-MS. General screening can be done with a GC, with confirmation and quantitation by GC-MS.

The fourth screen is the narcotics screen. It can be readily accomplished nowadays with immunoassay on urine. This test screens for the opiates, cocaine, and methadone. A positive test by the immunoassay requires positive identification and quantitation by a GC-MS on blood. It must be realized that, in very acute heroin overdoses, the urine may test negative for morphine or monoacetyl-morphine. Therefore, in cases where it is felt that the death is caused by heroin, even with a negative urine screen, analysis of the blood by GC-MS should be conducted.

Less used is the screen for higher volatiles, a gas chromatographic method used to detect toluene, the most commonly abused inhalant; benzene; trichlorethane; and trichlorethylene. Another screen now being performed routinely is for cannabis components. Blood from the test tube containing sodium fluoride and potassium oxalate should be used, because some of the active components of cannabis will otherwise deteriorate with time. We generally use an immunoassay screen on the urine for metabolites of delta-9-tetrahydrocannabinol. If positive, then we analyze the blood by GC-MS. Rarely, we use a heavy-metal screen. Depending on the metal, one can use either ICP or a specific chemical test.

Drugs not detected in the aforementioned screen include some whose blood therapeutic or abuse levels are extremely low. These can be picked up by GC-MS. Examples are phencyclidine, fentanyl derivatives, etc. If these drugs are suspected or common in one's population, an immunoassay screen can be performed on urine. Cyanide can be analyzed for by using a specific ion electrode or other chemical techniques. Alkaloid poisons, such as strychnine and nicotine, are detected in the basic screen.

It is the authors' opinion that the more thorough the toxicologic approach, the better. Therefore, we make the following recommendations as to types of tests to be performed, depending on the type of case.

In all homicides, accidents, and suicides, the authors recommend the lower alcohol screen; the acidic and neutral screen; and the basic screen. In stranger-to-stranger homicides and those in which the use of narcotics is suspected, the narcotic screen is also recommended. In natural deaths, the authors recommend the alcohol, the acidic and neutral screen, and the basic screen. Some medical professionals think that this is unnecessary, especially in the elderly. The authors, however, have detected a number of suicidal and accidental overdoses in individuals in their sixties and seventies, and homicides in alleged SIDS cases by this routine screening. Where the cause of death is undetermined at autopsy, the authors recommend the alcohol, acidic and neutral screen, basic screen, and narcotics screen. A cannabis screen is strongly recommended in all drivers of motor vehicles and work-related deaths.

Deaths

Deaths caused by ingestion, injection, snorting, or inhalation of drugs fall into four categories by manner: homicide, suicide, accident, and undetermined. The last category is used when a decision as to manner of death cannot be made. For the most part, the accidental category is made up of deaths caused by drug abuse. In the nineteenth century, the "three curses of mankind" were said to be alcohol, morphine, and cocaine. Little has changed since then, except that a more potent opiate, heroin, has replaced morphine.

The most commonly abused drug in the U.S. is alcohol. It is responsible for tens of thousands of deaths each year both directly and indirectly. While deaths caused by an acute overdose of alcohol are uncommon, deaths caused by the chronic effects of alcohol are seen every day. Thus, between 25,000 and 30,000 people a year die of chronic liver disease caused by alcohol. Alcohol is the major cause of motor vehicle accidents. Approximately half of all motor vehicle accidents are related to use of alcohol. Alcohol has also been linked to congenital anomalies and the development of malignant tumors. Acute alcohol intoxication is a factor in suicides and homicides.

After alcohol and marijuana, the most commonly abused drugs are probably heroin and cocaine. There are numerous other drugs of abuse: the synthetic narcotics, phencyclidine, amphetamine and methamphetamine, propoxyphene, inhalants, and so on. These drugs, however, come and go on the drug scene, but the "three curses" always remain. In the next section, we will discuss the three main drugs of abuse, a number of other drugs of abuse, and some drugs that cause deaths because their lethal potential is not appreciated or because they fall into the hands of a child.

Ethyl Alcohol

Ethyl alcohol is the most abused drug in American society and probably the world. Any drink containing from 0.5 to 95% alcohol is considered an alcoholic beverage.[5] The term "proof" is used to describe the strength of an alcoholic beverage. Proof is defined as twice the percentage of the alcohol content of the drink. Thus, an 80-proof beverage is 40% alcohol. The alcohol content of beer ranges between 3.2 and 4%, table wines 7.1 to 14%, whiskey 40–75%, vodka 40–50%, gin 40–85%, and rum 40–95%.[5]

Alcohol is rapidly absorbed from all the mucosal surfaces of the gastrointestinal tract. In fasting individuals, 20–25% of a dose of alcohol is absorbed from the stomach and 75–80% from the small intestine.[6] Food delays the absorption of alcohol. Following ingestion of alcohol on an empty stomach, peak blood alcohol concentration occurs within one half to 2 h (average 0.75–1.35 h), whereas with food in the stomach, peak levels are reached within 1–6 h (average 1.06–2.12 h). The delay in reaching peak blood alcohol is directly proportional to the size of the meal and inversely proportional to the amount of time between food and alcohol consumption. The makeup of the meal appears to have very little influence at all on the rate of absorption.

Because alcohol is soluble in water, it is present in the body tissue in direct relation to the amount of water content of the tissue or fluid. Specimens with high water content, such as blood or vitreous, will have high concentrations of alcohol compared with tissues such as the liver or brain. Forensic pathologists tend to deal in whole blood when performing alcohol determinations, while clinicians often use serum or plasma. The plasma or serum to whole blood alcohol concentration ratio averages 1.18 (a range of 1.10 to 1.35). It is often not realized that there may be a significant difference in the alcohol concentration of arterial blood and venous blood in the absorptive phase, with arterial blood up to 40% higher in alcohol concentration than venous blood.[7] There is little difference, however, in the concentration of alcohol in the venous and arterial blood in the postabsorptive phase. At autopsy, one should obtain the blood from either the femoral or subclavian vessels, with the former preferred.

Aside from blood, the best material to analyze for alcohol is vitreous. Alcohol disperses throughout the body in proportion to the water content of the tissue. Vitreous, with a high water content, has proportionally more alcohol than blood when at equilibrium. Thus, at equilibrium, for every unit of alcohol in blood, there are 1.2 units of alcohol in vitreous. A vitreous level of 0.120 g/dL is equivalent to a level of 0.100 g/dL of ethyl alcohol in blood. Because of its isolated location, the equilibration of vitreous alcohol with blood alcohol lags by 1–2 h. Thus, the vitreous alcohol levels provide a method for looking back in time. They will tell what the blood alcohol level was 1–2 h prior to death after one compensates for the greater amount of water in the vitreous. In the absorptive phase of alcohol, vitreous alcohol levels are lower than in the blood. If the individuals stop drinking, their blood alcohol will continue to rise for a short time as absorption continues, plateaus, and then begins to go down. Vitreous alcohol, which lags behind blood alcohol, will continue to rise as the blood alcohol plateaus. The vitreous alcohol then plateaus and begins to decline. At the point of equilibration of blood and vitreous, the vitreous alcohol will be higher numerically because of the greater amount of water in the vitreous. This constant ratio of 1.2 to1 will continue as the vitreous alcohol declines following the decline in the blood alcohol. Thus, only in the absorptive phase will vitreous alcohol be lower than blood alcohol.

After vitreous, the next-best tissue to analylze for alcohol is muscle. We prefer muscle from the thigh since it is isolated from other organs, unlike psoas muscle, and appears to be fairly resistant to decomposition. Garriott found a blood to muscle ratio of 0.94 ± 0.086 when blood alcohol concentration was greater than 0.10 g/dL; 1.48 ± 0.13 with blood alcohols less than 0.10 g/dL.[8]

If the body is not discovered immediately and decomposition sets in, there may be production of ethyl alcohol by the microbes. The amount of alcohol produced endogenously is to a degree related to the length of decomposition. It should be noted that not in all decomposed bodies will there be endogenous production of alcohol. When it does occur, the alcohol rarely reaches high levels in postmortem blood. In the study by Zumwalt et al., 80% of mildly decomposing bodies and 55% of mild to moderately decomposed bodies contained no alcohol.[9] Endogenously produced alcohol was present in 27% of the mild to moderately decomposed bodies. In moderately decomposed bodies, no alcohol was found in 29%; exogenous alcohol in 33%; endogenous alcohol in 19%, and no determination was reached in 17%. In severely decomposed bodies, no alcohol was found in 13%, exogenous alcohol in 30%, endogenous alcohol in 13%, and no determination was reached in 43%. Thus, in the study of 130 cases of decomposing bodies, in only 23 cases was there presumed production of alcohol postmortem in the blood. Of these, 19 had levels of 0.07 g/dL or less, with four having levels of between 0.110 and 0. 220 g/ dL.

In embalming a body, the blood is, for the most part, removed and replaced by embalming fluid. Alcohol determination, however, can still be performed on either the vitreous or muscle. If vitreous is present, it is the preferred specimen. A small amount of embalming fluid will enter the vitreous fluid and produce minor dilution. Embalming fluid contains methanol but not ethyl alcohol. Thus, any ethyl alcohol present in the vitreous fluid should be presumed to have been ingested.

Almost immediately on entering the body, alcohol begins to undergo metabolism. It is metabolized to acetaldehyde, acetaldehyde to acetic acid, and acetic acid to carbon dioxide and water. The vast majority of the metabolism (95%) occurs in the liver. Blood alcohol in males is metabolized at an average rate of 15 mg/dL per hour (a range of 11–22 mg), and in females at 18 mg/ dL per hour (a range of 11–22 mg).[10] Alcoholics are able to metabolize alcohol at a faster rate than non-alcoholics, apparently because of an increase in liver enzymes. Thus, Clothier et al. reported an average rate of blood alcohol decline of 27 mg/dL per hour (a range of 16–43 mg/dL per hour).[11]

Alcohol is excreted to a small degree unchanged in the urine. The urine alcohol concentration is in equilibrium with blood at the time it is formed. The urine in the bladder generally lags behind blood concentration until the blood concentration reaches its peak. The urine concentration then remains higher than the blood values during the declining blood alcohol concentrations. Urine and blood alcohol ratios have been reported as ranging anywhere from 0.32 to 2.44, in spite of the fact that the usually accepted average urine to blood concentration ratio is 1.3.[6] All that the urine concentration reflects is an average over the period of time the urine was produced, and the average is related to a number of factors, including alcohol concentration in the blood. By virtue of this, urine alcohol concentrations are not useful for predicting blood alcohol.[12]

Alcohol, being a drug, has measurable effect on many of the physiological activities of the body. Alcohol impairs visual acuity, adaption to both light and darkness, discrimination of colors, persistence or speed of response to visual stimulation, focusing, etc.[13] Decrease in driving skills is measurable with blood alcohol concentrations as low as 30 mg/dL, though risk of involvement in an accident is not increased. Risk of an accident begins to increase markedly around 0.08 mg/dL. By 0.10 mg/dL, risk of involvement in a fatal accident increases 12-fold compared with non-drinkers. Alcohol impairs reaction time at blood concentrations in excess of 50 mg/dL. It has been known since 1919 that the effects of acute alcohol intoxication are more pronounced when the blood level is rising than falling (the Mellanby effect).[13] The individual psychological reaction to acute alcohol intoxication is variable. In all individuals, however, there is impairment of judgment by 0.10 mg/dL. In regard to alcohol's effect on the personality, some people become sleepy, placid, and friendly, whereas others become antagonistic, hostile, and violent. There is no way to say how individuals will react by blood alcohol level alone. The best indication of reaction would be an account of how they have reacted at prior times when intoxicated.

Of all the organ systems in the body, the most affected by alcohol is the central nervous system. Table 23.1 gives the stages of acute alcohol intoxication, that is, symptomatology versus the actual blood alcohol concentration.

Table 23.1 Acute Alcohol Intoxication

Blood Alcohol (g/100 mL)	Signs/Symptoms
0.01-0.05	Slight physiological impairment detectable on careful testing by 0.05 g/100 mL.
0.05-0.07	Euphoria; increased self-confidence. Consistent impairment of reaction responses and attention by 0.07 g/100 mL.
0.07-0.10	Increasing impairment of reaction responses, attention, visual acuity, sensory-motor coordination, and judgment. Individual may still appear sober.
0.10-0.20	Increasing impairment of sensory-motor activities, reaction times, attention, visual acuity, and judgment. Progressive increase in drowsiness, disorientation, and emotional lability. By 0.20 g/100 mL loss of coordination, staggering gait, slurred speech.
0.20-0.30	Staggering, grossly impaired, drunk; may be lethargic and sleepy or hostile and aggressive. By 0.30 g/100 mL, many individuals fall asleep or pass out.
0.30-0.40	Impaired consciousness, stupor, unconsciousness.
0.40+	Unconsciousness, coma. Possible death.

Chronic alcoholics are often able to mask many of the signs of acute alcohol intoxication, though there is still physiological impairment. Thus, a chronic alcoholic with a blood level of 150 mg% may superficially appear sober, though there is still impairment in the reflexes, visual acuity, memory, concentration, and judgment. Young individuals, inexperienced with alcohol, are more susceptible to the physiological actions of acute alcohol intoxication and to lethal CNS depression.

Most deaths caused by acute alcohol intoxication occur with blood alcohol levels of 400 mg% or greater. Inexperienced drinkers are more susceptible than chronic alcoholics. Chronic alcoholics have been apprehended operating motor vehicles with blood alcohols of 450–500 mg% and have actually survived alcohol levels as high as 600–700 mg%. The actual blood alcohol concentration at time of autopsy may be lower than the normally accepted lethal levels, if the individual suffered irreversible hypoxic brain injury caused by the CNS depressant action of the alcohol, yet managed to survive a while and metabolize alcohol. In such a case, one may see blood alcohol levels in the 300 mg% or high 200 mg% range. The vitreous, however, will show significantly higher alcohol levels, indicating that the individual is in the metabolizing phase.

Methyl Alcohol

Poisoning caused by methyl alcohol is relatively uncommon. Methanol is oxidized by the liver to formaldehyde, which in turn is oxidized to formic acid. Formic acid is six times more toxic than methanol. Symptoms of acute methanol poisoning are weakness, nausea, vomiting, headache, epigastric pain, dyspnea, and cyanosis. Inebriation is not a prominent symptom. The symptoms may occur within half an hour after ingestion or may not appear for 24 h. If a fatal amount of methyl alcohol has been ingested, the afore-mentioned symptoms will be followed by stupor, coma, convulsions, hypo-thermia, and death. Death is nearly always preceded by blindness. If the individual does survive, he may be permanently blind, due apparently to a specific toxicity for the retinal cells. Death in methyl alcohol poisoning is caused by the acidosis from production of organic acids and the CNS depres-sant action of the alcohol.[14,15]

Acidosis is the primary toxic factor in methyl alcohol poisoning, with the central nervous system depression a relatively minor factor. Formic acid is the primary agent responsible for the severe metabolic acidosis and ocular toxicity of methanol. Ingestion of 70–100 mL of methyl alcohol is usually fatal, though death may occur with ingestion of as little as 30–60 mL. As little as 10 mL of methanol can cause permanent blindness. Of 725 cases of meth-anol poisoning caused by ingestion reported by Keeney and Mellinkoff, 54% of the individuals died, 12% were blinded, and 12% had visual impairment.[15] Methyl alcohol can usually be detected up to 48 h after ingestion because of the slow rate of oxidation. The minimum lethal blood level in methyl alcohol poisoning is approximately 80 mg%. The autopsy findings are nonspecific.

Isopropanol

Isopropanol is available to the public as rubbing alcohol in a 70% aqueous solution. It has twice the CNS depressant potential of ethanol. Unlike meth-anol, it is not in itself toxic. It is metabolized in the liver to acetone. A lethal dose of isopropanol is estimated at 250 mL for an adult. It should be noted that the appearance of small amounts of isopropanol in the blood is not necessarily indicative of ingestion of this alcohol. In diabetics with ketoaci-dosis, and in cases of starvation with high levels of acetone, acetone may be converted to isopropyl alcohol. In such cases, there will be a high level of acetone and a low level of isopropyl alcohol.[14,16]

Ethylene Glycol

Ethylene glycol is the principal component of most automotive antifreeze solutions. In humans, it is metabolized to a number of compounds, the most important of which is oxalic acid. Upon ingestion, individuals develop central nervous system depression with severe metabolic acidosis. If they survive these, they develop acute renal failure. Microscopic sections of the kidneys viewed under polarized light show deposition of oxalate crystals in the renal tubules and brain.[14,17]

Ethylene glycol itself is not toxic; it is the metabolites (principally oxalic acid) that are. Minimum lethal dose is estimated at 100 mL for an adult, though individuals have survived significantly higher amounts. The clinical manifestations of acute ethylene glycol intoxication can be divided into neurological, cardiorespiratory, and renal. Neurological symptoms usually develop within a half hour to 12 h after ingestion. The individual develops nausea, vomiting, convulsions, and coma. Cardiorespiratory manifestations usually appear 12–24 h after ingestion. Tachycardia, tachypnea, and congestive heart failure are present. If individuals still survive, they then develop acute tubular necrosis. This usually is seen 24–72 h after ingestion.

Phencyclidine (PCP)

PCP is a hallucinogenic agent that predisposes an individual to violent behavior. Originally developed as an intravenous anesthetic, it is no longer legally manufactured. PCP may be injected, smoked, snorted or ingested. When smoked, peak levels are reached in 15–20 minutes; when taken orally in 2.5 h. PCP blocks dopamine re-uptake and causes release of catecholamines. It is both a respiratory and cardiac depressant. PCP is detectable in urine for 5–6 days after use. Just like cocaine, there is no correlation between blood levels and death.[18]

Heroin

Heroin was introduced to medicine and the public in the early part of the 20th century as a replacement for morphine and codeine. When introduced, one of the claims made for it was that it was non-addictive. While it does have certain therapeutic advantages over morphine and codeine, heroin is much more addictive. Because of this, it is not used therapeutically. Until the widespread introduction of cocaine to the American population, heroin was probably the most popular of the "hard" drugs. Depending on geographical area, it is sold in small plastic envelopes, capsules, or balloons. It has typically been cut with a sugar such as lactose. On the East Coast, quinine is often added, giving it a bitter taste. The typical "bag" of heroin traditionally contained a 1–2% concentration of the drug. With the introduction of the cheaper black tar form of heroin from Mexico, the quality of heroin being sold increased dramatically. Bags of heroin showing 20–30% purity, with some up to 50%, are now routine in some parts of the country (personal communication Samantha A. Di Maio). For many years, people hypothesized that deaths due to heroin were caused by an allergic reaction to some component used as a cutting agent. It is now realized that these are just overdose deaths from a very strong CNS depressant — heroin. In virtually all cases, individuals who die of an overdose of heroin are either under the influence of alcohol or intoxicated at the time of death. More recently, we have seen a number of deaths caused by "speedballs," a combination of heroin and cocaine.[14,18]

In the Far East, where heroin is cheap and plentiful, it has been smoked. In the U.S., it is injected intravenously. The addict places the powder in either a bottle cap or spoon, adds water, and then heats the mixture over a flame (Figure 23.1). A piece of cotton may be added to the mixture to "strain out" the impurities. The solution is then taken up into a syringe and injected intravenously. With repeated injection into veins, the addicts will develop "needle tracks" (Figure 23.2). These are raised hyperpigmented scars produced by the repeated intravenous injection of the solutions, usually with a dull contaminated needle. Needle tracks are seen in hard-core addicts, especially on the East Coast. Needle tracks are often more prominent in geographical areas where the addict has a difficult time acquiring syringes and needles. In a state like Texas, where no prescription is necessary to buy a

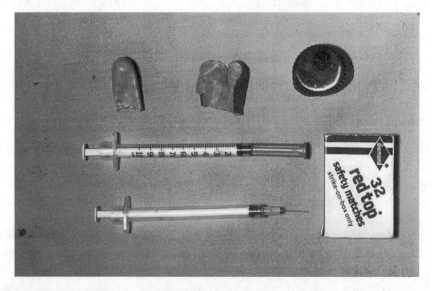

Figure 23.1 Intravenous heroin paraphernalia: syringes, two balloon tips (one opened) that contained heroin, and a bottle cap that functioned as a cooker.

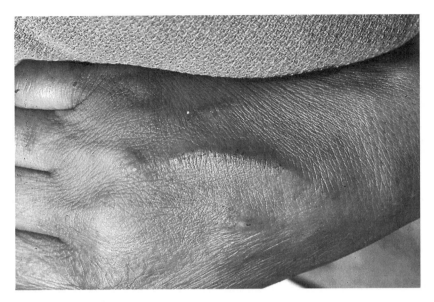

Figure 23.2   Needle track.

syringe and needle, the addicts tend to buy tuberculin or insulin syringes that have very fine needles. Thus, in this population, needle tracks are not as prominent as on the East Coast. In fact, in many deaths, the injection site is often not discovered.

At autopsy of an individual who has died of an overdose of heroin, the lungs are heavy and show congestion, though the classic pulmonary edema mentioned in some of the older textbooks is not always present. Microscopic examination of the lungs commonly reveals foreign-body granulomas with talc crystals and cotton fibers. The cotton originates from the "strainer." The talc probably has been used as a cutting agent. There is usually enlargement of the periportal lymph nodes. Microscopic examination of the liver will reveal a chronic triaditis with a mononuclear cell infiltrate.

Following injection, heroin (diacetylmorphine) is almost immediately metabolized to monoacetylmorphine (half-life 9 min). Monoacetylmorphine is then hydrolyzed to morphine (half-life 38 min). Because of this, if one performs a toxicologic analysis on an individual who died from an overdose of heroin, one does not detect heroin in the blood, but rather morphine and monoacetyl morphine. If both monoacetylmorphine and morphine are detected in the blood, then the individual took heroin. Both monoacetylmorphine and morphine can also be detected in the vitreous in heroin overdoses if death is not immediate.

Small amounts of codeine may be detected in the blood or urine. Morphine is not metabolized to codeine, rather the codeine detected represents impurities in the compound used. Thus, in heroin overdoses, on toxicological analysis one may detect morphine, monoacetylmorphine, and extremely low levels of codeine. The morphine and codeine are excreted into the bile, where the former drug may be detected for several days. Following injection, morphine and monoacetylmorphine enter the urine almost immediately. In some very acute deaths from heroin overdose, the urine is negative but the blood positive. Death is not directly related to blood concentration, due to the high tolerance individuals can build up. Thus, a level that makes one individual "high" will kill another.

Propoxyphene

Propoxyphene falls into the opiate category. It is derived from methadone but, unlike methadone, is a mild narcotic. Most deaths are accidents that result from an individual's taking too much medication over too short a time. Propoxyphene has a narrow margin of safety, as not only does it cause respiratory depression as opiates usually do, but also acts as a local anesthetic with resultant cardiac toxicity. The minimum lethal dose of propoxyphene in adults is approximately 650 to 780 mg. Following ingestion, peak levels are reached in 1 to 2 h. Propoxyphene is rapidly metabolized to norpropoxyphene. In chronic users of propoxyphene, norpropoxyphene levels are always higher than propoxyphene, often by a factor of 2 or 3 times. In individuals who die of an acute overdose, the concentration of propoxyphene is higher than norpropoxyphene, with the propoxypnene concentration 1 mg/L and higher. In some propxyphene related deaths, the individual presents with a lethal concentration of propoxyphene accompanied by a higher level of norpropoxyphene, though not 2–3 times higher. This is the picture of either an individual who died of an acute overdose but survived long enough to metabolize a significant amount of the propoxyphene ingested to norpropoxyphene, or of a chronic user of propoxyphene who took an acute overdose.

Fentanyl

Fentanyl is 50–100 times more potent than morphine. It is the preferred drug of abuse of anesthesiologists. It is available both in hospitals and clandestinely. It can be taken intravenously, orally, smoked, snorted or by way of skin patches, with the intravenous route the most common. Therapeutic levels are in the low ng/mL levels (1–3 ng/mL). Fatalities are seen at levels begining at 3 ng/mL.

Cocaine

Cocaine has replaced heroin in some areas as the most commonly abused of the hard drugs.[14,18] It is one of the most potent of the CNS stimulants. Introduced to medicine and the public in the late 19th century, it soon became the "third scourge of mankind." Cocaine can be sniffed, shot intravenously, or smoked as "crack." While originally said to be nonaddictive (just like heroin), it is now realized that it is a very potent addictive compound, especially the crack (free base) form. When smoked as crack, it is immediately absorbed by the lungs and reaches the brain within seconds. It takes slightly longer for its action to affect the brain when injected intravenously. Cocaine is a relatively short-acting drug such that to maintain a high, one has to take it every 15 min to an hour. Since it is a potent vasoconstrictor, snorting the drug can occasionally cause ulceration and perforation of the nasal septum with long-term use. Cocaine has also been linked to myocardial infarctions, cerebral hemorrhages and dissecting aortic aneurysms.[18-21]

Sudden death caused by an overdose of cocaine is linked to all three routes of abuse. It is more common, however, following intravenous injection and smoking of crack than snorting. Cocaine-related deaths are generally not dose related. Cocaine causes sudden death by two mechanisms: (1) cardiac arrhythmia caused by the direct action of the cocaine on the myocardium, and (2) cardiopulmonary arrest induced by the CNS action of the drug. Cocaine, being a potent stimulant of the CNS, in overdoses can overstimulate the CNS with subsequent cardiopulmonary arrest.

Cocaine acts on the heart to increase heart rate and force of contraction by blocking the reuptake of norepinephrine at the neuroeffector junctions. It also causes increased release of catecholamines, which also stimulate the heart. Cocaine works on the alpha receptors in the coronary arteries to cause contraction, reducing myocardial perfusion. Thus, as the myocardium needs increasing amounts of oxygen, due to the stimulation of the beta-1 receptors, the amount of blood perfusing the myocardium is reduced by vasoconstriction of the coronary arteries.

Cocaine is rapidly hydrolyzed to benzoylecgonine and other derivatives by blood cholinesterases. Continued breakdown of cocaine will continue in the test tube unless it is inhibited by the addition of fluoride. After being taken, cocaine appears almost immediately in the urine. If the urine screen is negative for cocaine metabolites, the blood will also be negative.

Habitual, prolonged, heavy use of cocaine can make an individual aggressive, violent, and paranoid. A chemical paranoid psychosis may be induced by the prolonged and heavy use of cocaine. Such individuals may become extremely violent and assaultive. They are often immune to the effects of pepper spray. They may die suddenly and unexpectedly during or immediately after a struggle.

Methamphetamine and Amphetamine

Methamphetamine is a potent CNS stimulant that is readily produced illicitly.[14,18] In the brain, it acts by both increasing release of dopamine and blocking its re-absorption, causing hyperstimulation of receptor neurons. Methamphetamine is also a cardiovascular stimulant. It blocks re-uptake of norepinephrine and causes an increase in catecholamine release. The euphoric effect is similar to cocaine but may last as long as ten times that of cocaine. Methamphetamine is metabolized to amphetamine, its major active metabolite. Amphetamine itself is rarely encountered. In overdoses, methamphetamine causes restlessness, confusion, hallucinations, coma, convulsions, and cardiac arrhythmias. With chronic abuse, just like cocaine, it can produce a chemical paranoid psychosis. Methamphetamine may be sold as cocaine. It is usually taken orally or intravenously though it may be snorted or smoked. Methamphetamine may be transformed into amphetamine hydrochloride ("ice") which is smoked like crack cocaine. Methamphetamine has a half-life of 11–12 hours, with 45% excreted in urine unchanged over a number of days. Long-term use may be associated with myocardial fibrosis.[22,23] Chronic use of methamphetamine may cause psychoses[24] that can persist for months. Just like cocaine, methamphetamine-related deaths are generally not dose related. There is substantial overlap in blood methamphetamine concentrations in individuals dying of a methamphetamine overdose and those in whom it is an incidental finding.[23,25] The highest concentrations were, however, seen in the drug overdose deaths. Just like cocaine, individuals may die suddenly during or immediately after a manic episode.

Miscellaneous Narcotics

Other drugs that should be mentioned briefly are morphine, meperidine, codeine, and methadone. Deaths from **morphine** and **meperidine** are uncommon and usually involve a hospital setting where an inadvertent overdose is administered. In an overdose from morphine, monoacetylmorphine will not be detected. **Codeine** is a relatively safe drug. Overdose deaths by codeine alone are uncommon. Usually an individual dying from an overdose of codeine is also intoxicated from the use of alcohol. In individuals with high concentrations of codeine in the blood very low levels of morphine will be detected; that is, the codeine is metabolized to a very slight degree to morphine (J. Garriott, personal communication). Codeine is excreted in the bile as both codeine and morphine. If an individual lives for a few days, analysis of the bile may reveal relatively high levels of morphine and no or trace amounts of codeine. This is because the morphine is bound to glucuronide and stored in the bile, while codeine is unbound and excreted faster. Thus, detection of morphine in the bile does not necessarily indicate that an individual took either heroin or morphine, since it can also be formed from codeine.[14,18]

Dilaudid (hydromorphone) deaths are occasionally encountered. It is prescribed for use in chronic pain. Deaths are usually accidents caused by a patient's taking too much medication. It is 7–10 times as potent as morphine. **Oxycodone** (percodan) and **meperidine** (demerol) deaths are uncommon.

Methadone is a long-acting synthetic narcotic with a half-life of approximately 15 h. It is not preferred by addicts, but they will use it if it is the only drug available. Methadone is used in therapy programs for heroin addicts. Many times, the addicts will sell the methadone on the street for money to buy heroin. Deaths from methadone usually occur in communities that have methadone programs. Occasionally, young children access a parent's methadone and die of an overdose. The lethal quality of methadone is its long duration of action.

Inhalants

Toluene is a constituent of paints, paint thinners, and glues. It, along with **gasoline** and **chlorinated hydrocarbons**, is inhaled to get a "high." Occasional deaths caused by cardiac arrhythmias occur from the chlorinated hydrocarbons as a result of their direct cardiotoxic action on the myocardium. Exertion may trigger an arrhythmia in an individual high on these drugs. Toluene, in contrast to the chlorinated hydrocarbons, rarely, if ever causes sudden death (J. Garriott, personal communication).

Lead

Lead is the major cause of heavy-metal toxicity in present-day society. Lead is found in storage batteries and was used as a constituent of paint and gasoline for many years. The most common causes of lead poisoning in the U.S. are ingestion of lead-based paint and industrial or environmental exposure. The symptoms of chronic lead poisoning are abdominal cramps, vomiting, constipation, lethargy, anemia, weight loss, muscle paralysis, nephropathy, and convulsions. Death is uncommon. When it does occur, it most often involves children in tenement areas who have a history of pica. These children, ages 18 months to 3 years, eat the lead-containing paint peelings that fall off the walls of their homes. Lead deposited in the bone produces a dense band at the ends of the long bones that can be seen on X-ray. Deaths of these children peak during the summer. At autopsy, the most striking finding is the brain, which is massively swollen, with flattening of the gyri, and is extremely pale, almost white. Blood smears show basophilic stippling of erythrocytes. Characteristic eosinophilic intranuclear inclusions may be seen in hepatocytes and cells of the proximal tubules of the kidneys (Figure 23.3). PAS-positive, pink-staining homogeneous material may be seen in the perivascular spaces in the brain.

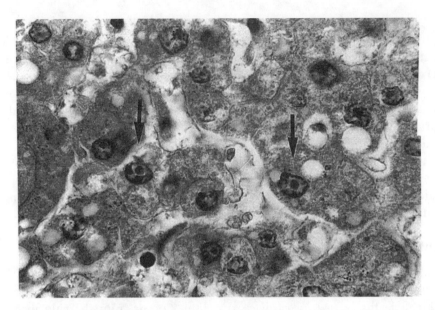

Figure 23.3 Eosinophilic inclusions in nuclei of liver cells in individual with chronic lead poisoning.

In adults, 0.20 mg/L in venous blood is now considered the normal upper limit for blood lead. The upper limit of normal for lead in venous blood for children is 0.10 mg/L. Children with lead levels between 0.10 and 0.20 mg/L usually require observation with follow-up venous testing every 2 to 3 months, because levels can continue to rise. Children whose blood lead levels are >= 0.20 mg/L need clinical management, including a detailed environmental, nutritional, and medical history. Generally, levels >= 0.45 mg/L are treated with chelation, the removal of lead from the blood. Some physicians, however, order chelation with levels as low as 0.3 mg/L.[14]

Iron

Death caused by iron poisoning usually involves children who accidentally ingest a large number of iron sulfate tablets. Rarely, these tablets have been used by adults for suicidal purposes. Following ingestion, there is severe pain in the abdomen, vomiting, and diarrhea. The vomitus is often bloody. At autopsy, the gastric mucosal folds are thickened, corroded, and dark brown to black.

Lye (NaOH)

Every year large numbers of children accidentally ingest lye.[26] Most make a full recovery, a few die, and many more suffer severe injury requiring surgical intervention and *sequelae* that may accompany them the rest of their lives.

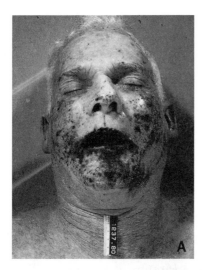
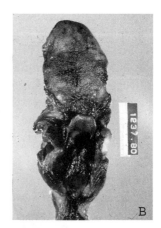

Figure 23.4 Elderly man who ingested lye with lye burns of (A) skin, (B) tongue, trachea, and (C) esophagus and stomach.

Occasionally, adults attempt and sometimes succeed in committing suicide by ingestion of lye (Figure 23.4).

The severity of injuries depends in part on the form of the lye ingested. Originally, it was available only in a crystalline form. Accidental ingestion was difficult, because only a few crystals caused severe pain, prompting a rapid cessation of such intake. Individuals attempting suicide commonly diluted the crystals with water to produce a solution of relatively low alkaline concentrations. Thus, the injuries produced were generally limited to the esophagus and were relatively superficial. Injury to the stomach was uncommon. Esophageal stricture was the most common complication, with occasional perforation. Lye is now available in a liquid form that is colorless and odorless. It can produce transmural necrosis of the esophagus after only 1 s of contact. Liquid lye commonly reaches the stomach, producing gastric necrosis. Occasionally, perforation of the small intestine can occur. In a case seen by one of the authors, a 41-year-old woman exsanguinated 4 weeks after ingesting liquid lye, when she developed an esophagoaortic fistula.

Arsenic

Homicide by poisoning is relatively rare today. The traditional poisons used in homicide were arsenic, cyanide, and strychnine. The poison with the longest history is arsenic, which has been used since the time of the Roman Empire.[14,27] It is found throughout the environment, being naturally present in soil in amounts as high as 20 parts per million. It is present in all living organisms, including humans. The average daily human intake of arsenic is between 0.5 and 1 mg contained in food and water. Traditionally, arsenic has been used in herbicides, pesticides, and wood preservatives. It is also used as a glass clarifier in the electronics industry. For the most part, arsenic has been replaced by other compounds. The only exceptions are its use as a wood preservative and in the electronics industry, in both of which it is still extensively used.

Arsenic is a popular poison because it is tasteless, odorless, and fairly easy to obtain. However, it is not too effective, because death is usually slow and painful rather than instantaneous. The most common form of arsenic used for poisoning is arsenic trioxide. Arsenic in this and other forms is cytotoxic, apparently due to the inhibition of sulfhydryl-containing enzymes. Arsenic is almost completely absorbed from the gastrointestinal tract, with excretion primarily through the urine in the form of methylated arsenic. On absorption, it is bound to the protein portion of hemoglobin. Within 24 h of ingestion, large concentrations of it are present in the liver, kidney, spleen, lungs, and gastrointestinal tract. It is also deposited in hair, nails, and skin.

A fatal dose of arsenic trioxide is somewhere between 200 and 300 mg. Following ingestion, symptoms may begin within 30 min. They tend to be centered about the gastrointestinal tract with nausea, vomiting, colicky abdominal pain, and diarrhea with rice-water stools. The patient may have a dry mouth with a metallic taste, a slight garlicky odor to the breath, and difficulty swallowing. Damage to the capillary endothelium by the arsenic leads to transudation of plasma. In the bowel, this causes accumulation of fluid in the bowel lumen. Arsenic in the gastrointestinal tract causes sloughing of the mucosa and vesicle formation, not caused by any corrosive action of arsenic, but rather the consequence of its vascular actions. With large doses of arsenic, death can occur in a few hours, caused by shock as a result of the vascular actions. If individuals survive this initial insult, they may develop hepatic and renal failure. Electrocardiographic changes may occur with prolonged QT intervals and nonspecific ST segment changes. At autopsy, in acute deaths, the gastric mucosa is congested and shows some oozing of blood. If the individual lives a day or two, the whole small intestine may have this appearance, with formation of a pseudomembrane in some instances. Within a matter of a few days, there are fatty deposits in the heart, liver, and kidneys as well as acute tubular necrosis.

Some poisonings are not accomplished with one large dose, but with multiple smaller doses. Here, the action of the arsenic on the skin causes an initial erythematous flush with subsequent development of melanosis, hyperkeratosis, and desquamation. Months after an acute ingestion of arsenic, transverse white bands (Mees's lines) can be seen on the nails. Arsenic can also cause anemia, leukopenia, thrombocytopenia, and basophilic stippling.

Individuals may develop a peripheral neuropathy of both the sensory and motor nerves. There is paralysis of the muscles of the hands and feet, with sensory loss. This neuropathy can be seen following both acute and chronic arsenic poisoning. In chronic poisoning, other symptoms may be minor and the person may present just with the neuropathy. In some individuals who take very large doses of arsenic, death may be so rapid that there is no chance to develop gastrointestinal symptoms. Rather, the individual becomes comatose, develops convulsions, and dies within several hours. This presentation, however, is unusual. Normal levels of arsenic in the blood range between 0.002 and 0.062 mg/L. Fatal blood levels are from 0.62 to 9.3 mg/L. High levels of arsenic may be present in the urine after consumption of seafood.

Cyanide

The second drug that comes to mind when one talks about homicidal poisoning is cyanide. Cyanide has been discussed in detail in another section of the book and this discussion will not be repeated.

Strychnine

Strychnine is a powerful alkaloid found in the seeds of Strychnos nux-vomica. Strychnine poisoning is rarely encountered. Strychnine was used in the early part of the 20th century medicinally, but, at present, is mostly used as an animal poison. A lethal dose is between 50 and 100 mg. It is rapidly absorbed from the stomach, with symptoms occurring within a few minutes. On ingestion, there is often a bitter taste. Because of this, the use of strychnine as a homicidal agent is difficult and it is better suited for suicide. The principal action of strychnine is on the CNS. Symptoms begin, on the average, 10–15 min following ingestion of the poison. There are violent convulsions with opisthotonos, whereby the body rests only on the heels and head. Convulsions can last from half a minute to several minutes. During violent convulsions, respiration is impossible. The convulsions come in consecutive waves. In between, the individual appears relaxed and can breathe. Death can occur in as short as 2 min but usually takes 1 or 2 h. If the individual survives, the convulsions will generally disappear within 12–24 h. During attacks, individuals are alert and oriented. Because they die in convulsions, there is rapid onset of rigor mortis. Lethal levels of strychnine in adults who die within 1 h of ingestion have ranged from 5 to 90 mg/L. Average blood level is 26 mg/L.[14,28]

Digoxin, Succinylcholine, and Insulin

Before ending this section, three more drugs should be mentioned: digoxin, succinylcholine, and insulin. Two of the three are medications and one is a muscle relaxant. In the older forensic literature, these were three drugs that could be used to commit murder, with a fair certainty that they could not be detected. This is no longer the case. **Digoxin** is a cardiac glycoside used in the treatment of congestive heart failure and other cardiac disorders. It is the most common form of digitalis prescribed. On an empty stomach, the maximum serum concentration is reached approximately 1 h after oral ingestion. Serum concentrations of over 2 ug/L are generally considered toxic. Following death, there is postmortem release of digoxin into the blood. This can cause artifactually high levels. Because of this, the authors recommend that any analysis of digoxin be done on the vitreous. In the cases the authors have seen in which death was caused by an overdose of digoxin, levels in the vitreous have generally been 10 ug/L and above. Victims of homicidal poisoning have generally been the elderly or young children. Analysis for digoxin is now extremely simple, and is performed on a routine basis in virtually all hospitals by immunoassay.

Succinylcholine is a neuromuscular blocking agent first synthesized in 1906, though its properties as a blocking agent were not recognized until 1949. Unlike D-tubocurarine, which combines with the cholinergic receptor sites blocking competitively the transmitter action of acetylcholine, succinylcholine is a depolarizing agent. It depolarizes the membrane the same as acetylcholine. This depolarization is longer lasting, however, and results in repetitive excitation, which may be seen as transient muscular fasciculation. This, in turn, is followed by a phase of blocking of transmission with neuromuscular paralysis. Following intravenous injection of succinylcholine, there is a brief period of muscular fasciculation, followed by complete paralysis that disappears usually within 5 min. During this time, though there is complete paralysis of the musculature, the individual is completely conscious. If the individual is not maintained on a respirator, he will die of anoxia due to an inability to breathe. Succinylcholine is rapidly hydrolyzed by plasma cholinesterase and liver esterases to succinylmonocholine and then succinic acid and choline.

Prior to the early 1980s, there was no valid method of analysis for succinylcholine in tissues. Analysis is now possible using GC-MS. The authors have seen a number of cases of suicide from succinylcholine, usually involving medical personnel, and one case of documented homicide. The latter case involved a 15-month-old girl injected in the thigh with succinylcholine by a nurse. The child developed apnea and died. She was subsequently autopsied by a hospital physician and death was ascribed to SIDS. The internal viscera were returned to the body cavity and the body was embalmed and buried. The child was disinterred approximately 8 months later. The body was in an excellent state of preservation. Muscle from both thighs, the kidneys, and a portion of liver were retained for toxicological purposes. On analysis, succinylcholine was demonstrated in the musculature of both thighs, as well as in the liver and kidneys. The nurse was subsequently tried and convicted of homicide.

Until the introduction of radioimmunoassay, death caused by **insulin** was extremely difficult to prove. Most deaths from insulin are accidental. Suicides are infrequent and homicides rare. Insulin, of course, is used for the treatment of diabetes. An overdose of insulin will cause hypoglycemia with irreversible injury to the brain. In one 6-month period, one of the authors (VJMD) saw five deaths caused by insulin: a homicide, a suicide, and three accidents. The homicide involved a 43-year-old nondiabetic male who was found dead in bed by his wife. She summoned the police and told them he had been hospitalized for bleeding caused by liver disease, but refused to stay in the hospital. She also told them he had been drinking heavily since he had returned home. A physician at one of the hospitals he had been seen at was contacted and agreed to sign the death certificate. Subsequently, it turned out that this was not the deceased's treating physician. The body was transported to a funeral home and arterially embalmed. Relatives of the deceased contacted the medical examiner's office and stated that he had been separated from his wife and had just gone to visit her. They also claimed that she used to beat him. The body was transported to the medical examiner's office, where a complete autopsy was performed. No evidence of any significant disease was found at autopsy. In spite of the arterial embalming, a large quantity of blood mixed with embalming fluid was still present in the heart and aorta. A complete drug screen was performed on this fluid and was negative. Vitreous showed an alcohol level of 20 mg%.

The deceased's medical records were obtained and reviewed. They showed an interesting pattern of multiple hospital and emergency room admissions over a 1-year period for severe hypoglycernia. Blood insulin levels taken on one admission showed a level of 170 /IU/mL. Analysis for porcine and bovine insulin antibodies was positive. At the time of all of these incidents, the deceased had apparently been drinking and had been "found" unconscious or seizing by his wife. Because of this history, insulin levels were performed on the blood obtained at autopsy in spite of the fact that it had been contaminated with embalming fluid. The "blood" insulin level was 934 IU/ml. Subsequent investigation disclosed that the patient's wife was diabetic and on insulin. The cause and manner of this death were certified as acute insulin overdose, homicide. No one was ever charged with this death.

Insulin is produced in the beta cells of the islets of Langerhans by the enzymatic cleavage of the precursor polypeptide proinsulin. For every molecule of insulin formed, a corresponding molecule of C-peptide is formed. Classically, diabetes has been treated by the administration of insulin obtained either from cattle or swine. Synthetic human insulin has virtually replaced them. The administration of insulin from either cattle or swine may result in the production of antibodies to these forms of insulin. Such antibodies, however, are not as common as one would expect, due to newer methods of purification of insulin. Thus, individuals who have been taking insulin of animal origin for many years may not have antibodies.

It was the introduction of radioimmunoassay (RIA) that made the measurement of insulin in the body practical. Analysis for insulin is now performed in most large hospital laboratories. The method most used is chemiluminescent immunoassay. In the case seen by the author, the measurement of blood insulin was possible even when embalming fluid had contaminated the blood. This was confirmed by a second death in which a nurse accidentally administered an overdose of insulin and the body was also embalmed before the case was reported to the medical examiner's office. Again, an elevated level of insulin was found in the blood. In a limited series of experiments, blood was spiked with both embalming fluid and insulin. The only result of adding the embalming fluid was the expected dilutional effect. Insulin was detected and quantitated in all samples.

Blood glucose levels postmortem are of no help in the diagnosis of hypoglycemia, because there is release of glucose postmortem. Thus, one might get normal or elevated levels of glucose in postmortem blood in an overdose from insulin. The vitreous is of no help either, because abnormally low values of glucose in the vitreous have no significance. Only elevated levels of glucose are of any significance. If the increase in concentration of insulin in the blood is caused by endogenous production either by the pancreas or a tumor, then the concentration of C-peptide should theoretically be elevated. Thus, if one finds high insulin and high C-peptide, one assumes that the insulin is endogenous. If, however, one sees high concentrations of insulin and normal or depressed concentrations of C-peptide, then one would conclude that the insulin is of exogenous origin, that is, it was administered. Unfortunately, the expected response of C-peptide is not absolute. In addition, C-peptide is very unstable and analysis for it in postmortem blood is not satisfactory and, in fact, in our experience, is of no use. In the cases that have just been described, insulin levels were also done on urine and bile. Both showed elevated levels. The significance of this was unknown by the author, so he had routine tests for insulin levels performed on urine and bile of individuals who died of trauma, that is, homicide and accident victims. The levels of insulin in the urine or bile in these cases showed tremendous variation.

Antidepressants

Drug overdose is the second most common method of suicide in the U.S. after shooting. For many years, the drug of choice was one of the barbiturates. This has changed dramatically in the past 20 years such that deaths caused by barbiturates are now relatively uncommon. The most common family of drugs used in suicides now are the antidepressants, specifically, the tricyclics. There are now three generations of **tricyclic antidepressants**. The first included amitriptyline, nortriptyline, imipramine, desipramine, and doxepin; the second, amoxapine, trazodone, bupropion and maprotiline and the third venlafaxine, nefazodone and mirtazapine. The mechanism of death from an overdose of a tricyclic antidepressant is cardiac. Overdoses of tricyclic antidepressants produce intraventricular conduction abnormalities, tachycardia, a widening of the QRS complex, and arrhythmias that range from premature ventricular contractions to ventricular fibrillation. The CNS effects of the tricyclics are confusion, hallucinations, lethargy, and agitation that progress to seizures or coma. There is allegedly an increased incidence of seizures in epileptics taking the tricyclics. They can also cause hyperpyrexia. The therapeutic, toxic, and overdose concentrations of the first two generations of these drugs are listed in Table 23.2.

A number of individuals have contended that there is significant postmortem redistribution of the tricyclic antidepressants and that concentrations of these drugs in postmortem blood do not accurately reflect their perimortem concentration. Apple and Bandt contend that only liver levels of the tricyclic antidepressants should be used for diagnosis of overdoses.[1] The authors of this book agree that the tricyclic antidepressants are highly tissue bound and that there is postmortem tissue release that may give rise to elevated blood levels. However, we believe that, in only rare instances, would there be sufficient release of the drug postmortem so as to even suggest that a case was a fatal overdose when it was not, if one uses the levels in Table 23.2. Even in the paper by Apple and Bandt, in the nine cases of fatal overdoses of tricyclics, the concentration of the tricyclic and its major metabolite in the

Table 23.2 Therapeutic, Toxic, and Fatal Blood Concentrations of Various Drugs and Chemicals

Drug name	Dose in milligrams	Therapeutic or Normal level mg/L*	Toxic mg/L	Fatal mg/L	Half-life in hours
Acetaminophen	324	2.4-6.4 (6)	30-300	160-387	1-3
	1000	9.0 (1-3)			
	1800	26 (1)			
Acetone	normal	<10	2500	?	3-6
	controlled diabetes	<30			
	fasting/keto-acidosis	100-700			
Alprazolam	1.0	0.019 (1.3)		0.122-2.1	6-27
(*Xanax*)	1.5-6/day	0.025-0.055			
Aminophylline	170 IV	4.5 (1)	>20	63-250	6-9
	500 oral	1.4-7.7 (1-4)			(<6-month-old)
					4.1 (child)
					3-11 (adult)
Amitriptyline	50 oral	0.016-0.035 (2-4) A	0.5-3.4	>2.0 A	8-51
(A)		0.014 N	(A + N)		
Nortriptyline	150/day	0.038-.162 A			
(N)		0.022-.242 N			
(*Elavil, Endep*)					
Amobarbital	120 oral	1.8 (2)	8-21	13-96	15-40 dose
	600 oral	6.4-12.3 (0.5)			dependent
Amoxapine	50	0.03 (1.5)	>0.3	0.9-20	8
(*Asendin*)	300/day	0.017-0.093			
Amphetamine	5-15 oral	0.035 (2)		0.5-41	7-34
	30 oral	0.111 (2.5)			
	160 IV	0.59 (abuse)(1)			
Arsenic	0.025-0.033 mg/kg/day (average dietary intake)	0.002-0.062	?	0.6-9.3	7
Brom-pheniramine	8	0.015 (3)	>0.05	0.2	15-22
		0.005 (24)			
Bupropion	32-55	0.06-0.125 (3)	?	?	4-24
	100	0.140 (3)			
Butabarbital	600	7.6-16.9 (.5)	>10	30-88	>30
Butalbital	100	2.1 (2)	?	13-26	35-88
		1.5 (24)			
Caffeine	120	2-4 (1)	>40	79-344	2.3-12
	300	6-9 (1)			
	500	14 (0.5)			
Carbamazepine	420	6.5 (3.2)		35-70	18-65
(*Tegretol*)		4-8 (optimal)			

Table 23.2 Therapeutic, Toxic, and Fatal Blood Concentrations of Various Drugs and Chemicals (continued)

Drug name	Dose in milligrams	Therapeutic or Normal level mg/L*	Toxic mg/L	Fatal mg/L	Half-life in hours
Carbon monoxide	urban non-smoker smoker	1-2% CoHb 5-6% CoHb	15-25%	>50%	4-5 (without O_2 therapy)
Carisoprodol (*Soma*)	350 700	2.1 (1) 3.5 (0.8)	>30	39-110	0.9-2.4
Chloral hydrate (*Noctec*)	1000 oral	2-12 (1) 6.5-8 (2) 3-6.3 (6)	50?	100-640	4 min chloral hydrate; 6-10 h tri- chloroethanol
Chlordiazepoxide (*Librium*)	30 55/d	1.6 (4) 2.3	9-60	>20	6-27
Chloroform	500 oral anesthesia	1-5 (1) 20-232		10-194	1.5
Chloroquine	50/day 300/d	0.022 0.176	>0.6	3-16	3-14 days
Chlor- pheniramine	4 IV 12 oral	0.01 0.017 (2) 0.010 (12) 0.004 (24)	>0.5	>1.0	12-43
Chlorpromazine (*Thorazine*)	25 oral 150 oral 600 mg/d 2400 mg/d	0.001 (2.8) 0.018 (3) 0.02-0.08 1.1	>0.5	3-35	18-30
Chlorpropamide (*Diabinese*)	250 500-1000/d	28.5 (3) 102-363	300-750	?	25-42
Clonazepam	2 6/d	0.017 (1-4) 0.029-0.075	>0.1	?	19-60
Clorazepate (*Tranxene*)	15 50/d	0.16 (2) 1.21-2.64	?	?	2
Cocaine	17-48 oral 2mg/Kg intranasal 2 mg/Kg oral 32 IV 50 smoked	0.011-0.149(.4-2) 0.161 (1) 0.210 (1) 0.308 (5 min) 0.203 (5 min)	?	0.9-21	0.7-1.5
Codeine	15 60	0.03 (2) 0.134 (1)	0.5	1-8.8	1.9-3.9
Cyanide	non-smoker smoker fire victim	0.004 0.006 0.17-2.2	0.01-4.36	1.1-53 (ingestion) 1-15 (inhalation)	0.7-2.1
Desipramine	82mg/70Kg/d	0.021-0.064	1.0	3-15	12-54

Table 23.2 Therapeutic, Toxic, and Fatal Blood Concentrations of Various Drugs and Chemicals (continued)

Drug name	Dose in milligrams	Therapeutic or Normal level mg/L*	Toxic mg/L	Fatal mg/L	Half- life in hours
Diazepam	10	0.148 (1)	>5	5-19	21-37
	30/d	1.03			
Dicumarol	150	17 (10)	22-192	?	21 (average)
Digoxin	0.25 oral	0.001 (1)	2.1-9	15 ng/ml	30-45
	0.5 oral	0.0014 (2)	ng/ml		
	0.75 IV	0.013 (10 min)			
Digitoxin	0.05-0.3/d	3-39 ng/ml	?	>320 ng/ml	
Di-	50	0.083 (3)	>1	8-31	3-14
phenhydramine	100	0.112 (2)			
		0.014 (24)			
Doxepin	75	0.024 (2)	>0.14	0.7-29	8-25
(*Sinequan,*	113/d	0.005-0.115			
Adapin)					
Doxylamine	25 mg	0.07-0.14 (4)	?	0.7-12	10
Ephedrine	19.4	0.081 (3.9)	?	3.5-21	5-7.5
	24	0.10 (1)			
Ethchlorvynol	200	1.2 (1)	>50	14-400	19-32
(*Placidyl*)	500	6.5 (1)			
Ether	workers	18	>90	600-3750	?
	sub-anesthesia	100-500			
	anesthesia	500-1500			
Ethylene glycol		?	any amount	300-4300	3-5
Fentanyl	2μg/Kg IV	0.011	0.02	0.003-0.03	3-12
		0.001 (1)			
Fluoride	normal	0.01	?	2.6-56	2-9
	1.5-10	0.06-0.4 (0.5)			
Fluoxetine	40	0.015-0.055(6-8)		1.3-6.8	1-3 days
(*Prozac*)	20-60/d	0.025-0.473			(7-14 days for metabolites)
Flurazepam	15	<0.002 (0.5)	?	0.5-4	1-3
	30	0.0021 (1)			
Fluvoxamine	50	0.008-0.028 (4.8)	>0.115	3.4-11	8-28
(*Luvox*)	100	0.021-0.06 (4.5)			
Haloperidol	20-200/d	0.006-0.245	0.01	1-1.9	14-41
Halothane	surgical anesthesia	80-260	?	33-650	43 (from fat)
Hydrocodone	5	0.011 (1.5)	?	0.13-7	3.4-8.8
	10	0.024 (1.5)			
Hydrogen sulfide	normal	<0.05	any amount	0.9-3.8	?
Hydromorphone	4	0.018-0.027(.8-1.5)	0.02	0.02-1.2	1.5-3.8

Table 23.2 Therapeutic, Toxic, and Fatal Blood Concentrations of Various Drugs and Chemicals (continued)

Drug name	Dose in milligrams	Therapeutic or Normal level mg/L*	Toxic mg/L	Fatal mg/L	Half- life in hours
Hydroxyzine	100	0.078 (4)	?	4.2-39	13-27
Ibuprofen	200	26 (1.5)			0.9-2.5
(*Motrin, Advil*)	400	17-36 (1-1.3)		>80	
	800	49 (1)			
Imipramine (I)	75	0.037 I (4)			6-20
Desipramine(D)	150/d	0.008-0.105 I 0.15-.24 I&D (optimal)	>0.5	2.8-7 (I)	
Insulin	normal fasting	11 µU/ml (range 6-24)	?	>700 (free)	3.5-4.3
	normal, non-fasting	27 µU/ml (range 7-37)			
	insulin treated	10-440 µU/ml (free insulin) 67-17,020 (total insulin)			
Iron	normal serum	0.27-2.93	2.76-25.5	18.8-50	?
	normal whole blood	380-560			
Isoniazid	5/kg oral	1.2-4.8 (1)	>20	43-168	0.6-6.7
	450	0.2-2.7 (4)			
Isopropanol			0.04 g/dL	0.1-0.33 g/dL	2.5-3
Ketamine	2.5/kg	1.0 (12 min) 0.5 (0.5)	?	7-27	3-4
Lead	normal industrial society	0.07-0.22	0.20 (children)	1.11-3.5	Up to 7 years
	normal taxi drivers	0.16-0.49			
Lidocaine	500 oral	0.6-1.1 (1-2)	>8	6-33	0.7-1.8
	1/Kg IV	0.96 (.25) 0.4 (1)			
Lithium (as carbonate)	1500	1.66 mmol/L (1) 0.5-1.3 mmol/L optimum	>2 mmol/L	0.3-4.6 mmol/L	17-58
Lorazepam	2	0.018 (2) 0.009 (12)	0.3	?	9-16
	10/d	0.140-0.24			
Maprotiline	150	0.091 (8)	0.237-0.317 (seizures)	1.3-13	36-105
	150/d	0.168-0.718			

continued

Table 23.2 Therapeutic, Toxic, and Fatal Blood Concentrations of Various Drugs and Chemicals (continued)

Drug name	Dose in milligrams	Therapeutic or Normal level mg/L*	Toxic mg/L	Fatal mg/L	Half- life in hours
Meperidine	100 IM	0.17 (1.3)	?	8-20	2-5
	50 IV	0.31 (1)		oral	
		0.52 (12 min)		1-8 IV	
Meprobamate	400	7.7(2)	>60	35-300	6-17
	800	12-19 (2)			
	1600	8.6-27 (2)			
Mercury	fish eaters "acceptable"	0.006-0.2 0.02	0.2	0.8-22	24 days (inorganic mercury)
Methadone	15	0.075 (4)	0.1	0.4-1.8	15-55
	100-200/d	0.83 (4)			
		0.46 (24)			
d-Metha- mphetamine	0.125/kg	0.02 (3.6)	>0.1	2.0	12-34
	10	0.03 (1)			
	12.5	0.02 (2.5)			
		0.01 (24)			
Methanol	normal chronic bourbon consumption	<1.5 27	?	>400	2-24
Methaqualone	250	1-4 (2)	2-12	5-42	20-60
		1.1 (5)			
	600	7.0 (1)			
Metoclopromide	10	0.054 (0.9)	>2.0	?	3-6
Mexiletine	300	0.4 (4)	>2.0	21-45	8-17
	400	0.9-1.6 (2-4)			
	750/day	0.9-1.4			
		0.75-2 (optimal therapeutic level)			
Mirtazapine (*Remeron*)	20 20/day	0.032 (1.7) 0.007-0.046	>0.2	?	20-40
Morphine	0.125/kg IV	0.44 (0.5 min)	0.2	0.2-2.3	1.3-6.7
		0.02 (2)			
	0.125/kg IM	0.07 (10 min)			
Nefazodone (*Serzone*)	200 400/day	0.39 (1.3) 2.0	?	?	1-4
Nicotine	non-smokers smokers	0-0.006 0.012-0.054	?	11-63	24-84 min
Nitrous oxide	surgical anesthesia	170-220 ml/L	?	46-180 ml/L	? (min)
Nortriptyline (*Pamelor*)	75/d 150-250/d	0.01-0.275 0.171-0.375	1.0	1-26	15-90

Table 23.2 Therapeutic, Toxic, and Fatal Blood Concentrations of Various Drugs and Chemicals (continued)

Drug name	Dose in milligrams	Therapeutic or Normal level mg/L*	Toxic mg/L	Fatal mg/L	Half- life in hours
Oxycodone	4.88	0.009-.037 (1)	?	4.3-14	4-6
		0.016 (2)			
		0.009 (4)			
		0.005 (8)			
Paraldehyde	10 ml IM	77 (1.2)	?	115-480	3-10
		62 (2.3)			
Paroxetine	20	0.011	>0.2	1.4-4	7-37
	30	0.062 (5.2)			
Pentobarbital	100	1.2-3.1 (.5-2)	8	10-51	20-30
Phenacetin	250	0.09-0.22 (1-2)	?	>100	0.6-1.3
Phencyclidine		0.007-0.24	0.09-0.22	0.3-25	7-46
Phenmetrazine	75	0.13 (2)	>0.5	0.1-4.9	8
		0.06 (12)			
Phenobarbital	30	0.7	40	55-114	2-6 days
	30/d	8.1			
	600	18 (4.5)			
		10-30 optimal			
Phenol	normal	0.10	?	46-90	0.5
Phentermine	0.375/kg	0.09 (4)		1.5-7.6	19-24
Phenylbutazone	200	16 (3)	>100	400	29-175
	400	60 (max conc)			
Phenytoin	100	1.6-2.8 (2.4)	>30	45	8-60
(*Dilantin*)	300-400/d	7.8-17.5			
		(10-20 optimal)			
Primidone	250	4.9 (4)	>50	?	6-22
	500	6.7			
	1000	11-15			
Procainamide	1000	4.5 (1)			2-5
	1000 IM	5.9 (.5)	>16	80-260	
	1000 IV	16 (10 min)			
Promethazine	30	0.011 (2)	?	?	9-16
		0.005 (12)			
	50	0.008-0.023 (3)			
		0.003-0.004 (12)			
Propoxyphene	130 (as H Cl)	0.23 (2)	>1	1-17	8-24
	800-1600/d for narcotic withdrawal	0.13-1.07			
Propranolol	80	0.097 (1.5-2)	?	4-29	2-4
	160/d	0.46			
Propylhexedrine		0.01	?	0.3-2.7	?
					continued

Table 23.2 Therapeutic, Toxic, and Fatal Blood Concentrations of Various Drugs and Chemicals (continued)

Drug name	Dose in milligrams	Therapeutic or Normal level mg/L*	Toxic mg/L	Fatal mg/L	Half- life in hours
Quinidine	600	3.2 (2.25) 2-5 (optimal)	>8	45	5-12
Quinine	650	2.8 (2) 1.9 (8)	>10	6-24	3-15
Salicylamide	1000	3-32 (1) 0-22 (3) 0-15 (5)	?	27 (?)	26-35 min
Salicylate (acetylsalicylic acid)	3000-5000/d for arthritis 1000 3000/d	31-114 (2) 44-330	>500	61-7320	13-20 min 3-20 hours for salicylic acid
Secobarbital	3.3/kg 600	2.0 (3) 1.3 (20) 3.4-5.3 (0.5) 2.7 (18)	5-12	5-52	22-29
Sertraline	50 100	0.0095 (6-8) 0.016 (6-8)		0.6-3	24-26
Strychnine			?	0.5-61	10-11
Δ⁹-Tetrahydro-cannabinol	10 mg = 1 cigarette 8.8	0.005 (2) 0.046-0.188	?	None	20-57 hours, infrequent user; 3-13 days, frequent user
Thallium	normal	0-0.08	1-8	0.5-11	2-4 days
Theophylline	500 470 (syrup)	1.4 (1) 4.5 (2) 7.7 (4) 9 (1.5) 5-15 optimal range	>20	63-250	3-11
Thioridazine	100 400/d	0.24 (1.7) 0.64	>2.4	0.3-18	26-36
Toluene	workers	0.4-1.2	0.3-30 (sniffers)	10-79	72
Trazodone (Desyrel)	100 150	1.1 (2) 2.1 (2-4)	?	15-23	4-7
Triazolam (Halcion)	0.25	0.003 (1)		0.01-0.22	1.8-3.9
Trichloroethane	Exposure to 955 ppm	7-10 (1)		1.5-720	53
Trichloro-ethylene	Exposure to 100 ppm	1.0 (6)	?	3-110 (average 27)	30-38

Table 23.2 Therapeutic, Toxic, and Fatal Blood Concentrations of Various Drugs and Chemicals (continued)

Drug name	Dose in milligrams	Therapeutic or Normal level mg/L*	Toxic mg/L	Fatal mg/L	Half- life in hours
Valproic acid	400 1400-2520/d	32-42 (1.5-3) 81-106 50-100 optimal range	?	720-1969	8-12
Venlafaxine	50 150/day	0.071 (2.2) 0.194	6	6.6-89	3-7

*Numbers in parentheses are hours post dose

blood ranged from 2.4 to 11.1 mg/L. In contrast, in the deaths from other causes in individuals taking therapeutic doses of tricyclic antidepressants, the range was 0.16 to 0.30 mg/L. Most of the aforementioned discussion is academic, because the authors recommend that blood for toxicologic analyses be obtained from either the femoral or subclavian vessels.

The newest group of antidepressants are the **selective serotonin reuptake inhibitors (SSRI)**.[29] These include fluoxetine, paroxetine, fluvoxamine and sertraline. Fluoxetine (Prozac) is the best known of the group. Fluoxetine is metabolized to norfluoxetine, which is an active metabolite. The SSRI are significantly less toxic than the tricyclics in that they do not have the cardiotoxic component. They still can cause death, however. Most deaths encountered seem to involve an SSRI and one or more other drugs. Deaths from these drugs alone are uncommon.

Mixed Drug Overdose

After the tricyclic antidepressants, the "drug" most responsible for suicidal deaths in our experience (though it has been the first in other series) is not a drug, but a combination of drugs, or mixed drug overdose. The two most common drugs involved in mixed drug overdoses are alcohol and the tricyclic antidepressants, followed by the benzodiazepines, most commonly diazepam. The benzodiazepines, used principally as anti-anxiety and muscle relaxant agents, are probably one of the most benign groups of drugs on the market if taken alone. Mixed with alcohol or other drugs, however, they can contribute to a fatal outcome.

Barbiturates

Until the early 1970s, the most popular family of drugs for overdose purposes was the barbiturates. Barbiturates are mostly of historical interest. Except for phenobarbital used in the treatment of epilepsy, these drugs are rarely encountered by the forensic pathologist. Barbiturates are, of course, CNS depressants. Therapeutic, toxic, and lethal levels can be found in Table 23.2. In discussing barbiturate overdoses, one has to mention the concept of "drug automatism."[30,31] This concept is indelibly linked to the barbiturates. If one accepts this theory, some deaths caused by overdose that are classified as suicide should be classified as accident in that the drugs were taken without intention, after the first dose produced confusion. There is, however, no evidence that this entity exists. It is essentially an unproven hypothesis and should be considered just another one of the theories put forth by people in an effort to change a suicide ruling to accident.

References

1. Apple FS and Bandt CM, Liver and blood postmortem tricyclic antidepressant concentrations, *Am J Clin Pathol* 1988; 89:794-795.

2. Pounder DJ, et al., Postmortem diffusion of drugs from gastric residue: An experimental study, *Am J Forens Med & Path;* 1996 17(1):1-7.

3. Pounder DJ and Smith DRW, Postmortem diffusion of alcohol from the stomach, *Am J Forens Med & Path;* 16 (2): 89-96, 1995.

4. Levine B, Golle M, and Smialek JE, An unusual drug death involving maggots. *Am J Forens Med & Path* 2000; 21(1):59-61

5. McAnalley BH, Chemistry of alcoholic beverages, in Garriott JC (Ed): *Medicolegal Aspects of Alcohol* 3rd ed. Lawyers and Judges Pub. Co., Tucson AZ. 1996.

6. Baselt RC, Danhof IE, Disposition of alcohol in man, in Garriott JC (Ed): *Medicolegal Aspects of Alcohol* 3rd ed. Lawyers and Judges Pub. Co., Tucson AZ. 1996.

7. Garriott J, Analysis for alcohol in postmortem specimens, in Garriott JC (Ed): *Medicolegal Aspects of Alcohol* 3rd ed. Lawyers and Judges Pub. Co., Tucson AZ. 1996.

8. Garriott JC, Skeletal muscle as an alternative specimen for alcohol and drug analysis. *J Forensic Sci* 1991; 36:60-69.

9. Zumwalt RE, Bost RO, and Sunshine I, Evaluation of ethanol concentrations in decomposed bodies. *J Forens Sci* 1982; 27:549-554.

10. Dubowski KM, Human pharmacokinetics of alcohol. *Alcohol Technol Rep* 1976; 5:55-63.

11. Clothier J, et al, Varying rates of alcohol metabolism in relation to detoxication medication. *Alcohol* 1985; 2:443-445.

12. Kuroda N, Williams K, and Pounder DJ, Estimating blood alcohol from urinary alcohol at autopsies *Am J Forens Med & Path*, 1995; 16 (3) 219-222.

13. Manno JE and Manno BR, Experimental basis of alcohol-induced psychomotor performance impairment (PMPI) in Garriott JC. (Ed) *Medicolegal Aspects of Alcohol* 3rd ed. Lawyers and Judges Pub. Co., Tucson AZ. 1996.

14. Baselt RC, *Disposition of Toxic Drugs and Chemicals in Man*, 5th ed. Chemical Toxicology Institute, Foster City CA, 2000.

15. Keeney AH and Mellinkoff SM, Methyl alcohol poisoning. *Ann Int Med* 1951; 34:331-338.

16. Alexander CB, McBay AJ, and Hudson RP, Isopropanol and isopropanol deaths-Ten years' experience. *J Forens Sci* 1982; 27:541-548.

17. Linnanvuo-Laitinen M and Huttunen K, Ethylene glycol intoxication. *Clin Toxicol* 1986; 24:167-174.

18. Karch SB, *The Pathology of Drug Abuse* 2nd ed. CRC Press, Boca Raton, FL 1996.

19. Karch SB and Billingham ME, The pathology and etiology of cocaine-induced heart disease. *Arch Pathol Lab Med* 1988; 112:225-230.

20. Rashid J, Eisenberg MJ, and Topol EJ. Cocaine-induced aortic dissection. *Am Heart J*, 1996; 132(6):1301-1304.

21. Rowbotham MC, Neurological aspects of cocaine abuse (medical staff conference). *West J Med* 1988; 149:442-448.

22. Hong R, Matsuyama E, and Nur K, Cardiomyopthy associated with the smoking of crystal methamphetamine. *JAMA* 1991; 265:1152-1154.

23. Karch SB, Stephens BG, and Ho C-H. Methamphetamine-related deaths in San Francisco: Dermographic, pathologic and toxicologic profiles. *J Forens Sci* 1999; 44(2):359-368.

24. Iwanami A et al, Patients with methamphetamine psychosis admitted to a psychiatric hospital in Japan. *Acta Psychiatry Scand.* 1994; 89:428-432.

25. Logan BK. Fligner CL, and Haddix T, Cause and manner of death in fatalities involving methamphetamine, *J Forens Sci*, 1998; 43(1):28-34.

26. Ray J, Myers WO, and Sautter RD, Lye ingestion. *JAMA* 1974; 229(7):765. (letter).

27. Gorby MS, Arsenic poisoning. (clinical conference). *West J Med* 1988; 149:308-315.

28. Smith BA, Strychnine poisoning. *J Emerg Med* 1990; 8(3):321-5.

29. Levine B. (Ed). *Principles of Forensic Toxicology. Am Assoc Clinical Chem.* USA 1999.

30. Imajo T: Drug automatism. *Am J Forens Med Pathol* 1984; 5:7-10.

31. Drug automatism: A myth (Editorial). *JAMA* 1974; 230:265.

Appendix

The Forensic Autopsy

The forensic autopsy differs from the hospital autopsy in its objectives and relevance. Besides determining the cause of death, the forensic pathologist must establish the manner of death (natural, accidental, suicidal, or homicidal), the identity of the deceased if unknown, and the time of death or injury. The forensic autopsy may also involve collection of evidence from the body, which can subsequently be used to either prove or disprove an individual's guilt, and confirm or deny his account of how the death occurred.

Because of the possible medicolegal implications of forensic cases, not only must the aforementioned determinations be made, but the findings or lack of them must be documented. In many cases, the cause and manner of death may be obvious. It is the documentation of the injuries or lack of them, as well as the interpretation of how they occurred and the determination or exclusion of other contributory or causative factors that are important.

The forensic autopsy involves not only the actual examination of the body at the autopsy table, but the consideration of other aspects that the general pathologist does not believe to be part of the autopsy—the scene, clothing and toxicology. The forensic autopsy begins at the scene. Pathologists should not perform a forensic autopsy unless they know the circumstances leading up to and surrounding the death. This is a very basic principle that is often violated. What would one think of a physician who examined a patient without asking what the patient's symptoms or complaints were? As in all examinations of patients, one must have a medical history. In the case of the forensic pathologist, the "patient" is unable to render this history. Therefore, the history must be obtained by either the medical examiner or police investigators. This history should be known before the autopsy begins.

The scene should be documented either with diagrams or photographs, preferably both. People should be interviewed and a written report should be given to the pathologist prior to the autopsy. It makes good television dramatics to poke and prod a body at the scene, but it does not make sense scientifically. At the scene, there is often pressure to move the body, people milling around, inadequate lighting, no instruments, and no running water. A body cannot be examined adequately at a scene. What can be done, however, is destroy evidence or introduce fallacious evidence. Powder can be dislodged from the clothing, primer residue can be wiped away from the hands, the body can be contaminated with the examiner's hair or with the hair of the police officer who helps turn, poke, and prod the body, and so on.

The body should be touched and moved as little as possible at the scene. In cases of violent death, paper bags should be secured about the victim's hands so that no trace evidence will be lost. If plastic bags are used and the body then placed in a cooler, there will be condensation of water vapor on the hands (with possible loss of trace evidence) when it is moved back into a warm environment. Prior to transportation, the body should be either wrapped in a clean white sheet or placed in a clean body bag. It should never be placed directly onto a cart in the back of an ambulance. Who knows what or who was lying on the cart prior to the body transport? Trace evidence from a prior body could be deposited on this body, or trace evidence from this body can be lost and subsequently transferred to another body.

At the morgue, the body should never be undressed prior to the medical examiner's seeing it. This includes removing shoes and socks to place toe tags. Examination of the clothing is as much a part of the autopsy as examination of the wounds. The clothing must be examined for blood stains and trace evidence as well as to see if the wounds in the body correlate with the defects in the clothing. How does one know that the individual was not shot and then dressed?

The body should never be embalmed prior to the autopsy. Embalming ruins toxicologic analysis, changes the appearance of the wounds, and can induce artifacts. The body should never be fingerprinted prior to examination of the hands. In fingerprinting, the hands are pried open to ink the fingers. In the process, trace evidence can be lost or false evidence deposited. Tests for firearms residue can be rendered invalid by prying apart fingers and fingerprinting a body.

In all gunshot deaths and severely burnt bodies, X-rays should be taken. X-rays are especially important in gunshot wound cases in which the bullet appears to have exited. This is because the entire bullet may not have exited but rather only a piece of the bullet or a piece of bone. With the semijacketed ammunition now in widespread use, it is common for the lead core to exit the body and the jacket to remain. The core is of no interest ballistically. It is the jacket that is important. The jacket might be retained beneath the skin adjacent to the exit site. It is very easy to miss the jacket material at autopsy, unless one knows, by X-ray, that it is there.

The Autopsy Report

The first part of the forensic autopsy is the **External Description**.

The external description should include the age, sex, race, physique, height, weight, and nourishment of the deceased. Congenital malformations, if present, should be noted. Following this, a description of the clothing should be given. This description, initially, does not need to be very detailed. Essentially, a simple listing of the articles found or accompanying the body should be given, for example, a short-sleeved white shirt, or a long-sleeved white shirt unbuttoned down the front, or a bloodstained white T-shirt. If the case is a traumatic death with significant alterations of the garments due to trauma, the clothing will be described in further detail in another section of the autopsy.

After the description of the clothing, at least the following should be described:

- Degree and distribution of rigor and livor mortis.
- Hair and eye color.
- The appearance of the eyes.
- Any unusual appearance to the ears, nose, or face, for example, congenital malformations, scarring, or severe acne. (Excluded should be evidence of trauma, which will have its separate section.)
- The presence of teeth or dental plates.
- The presence of vomitus in the nostrils or mouth.
- Significant scars, tattoos, moles.
- External evidence of disease.
- Old injuries.
- Evidence of recent medical and/or surgical intervention (*Note:* You may want to put this in a separate section entitled "Evidence of Medical and/or Surgical Intervention").

At this time, if fingerprints have not been taken, they should be. In addition, it is strongly recommended that identification photos, with the number of the case, be taken.

If there is injury to the body, it should now be described in the next section, entitled "Evidence of Injury." All recent injuries, whether minor or major, external or internal, should be described in this section. There is no need to repeat the description of these injuries in the subsequent "Internal Examination" section or to describe them in the "External Description." The age of the lesions should be described, if possible, at least in a general way.

There are many ways to handle the "Evidence of Injury" section. Excluding gunshot and stab wounds, it is easiest to divide it into two broad areas:

external evidence and internal evidence. Some examiners intermingle these two. They describe the external evidence of injury to the head and then say "Subsequent autopsy reveals ..." and go on to describe the internal injuries of the head. They will then describe the external injuries of the trunk, followed by the internal injuries of the trunk.

Gunshot wounds and, to a degree, stab wounds are a different situation. In gunshot wound cases, if at all possible, each individual wound should be described in its entirety before going on to a second wound. Each wound should be located on the body (in inches or centimeters) in relation to the top of the head or the sole of the foot and to the right or left of the midline. It should then be described (in inches or centimeters) in relation to a local landmark, such as the nipple or the umbilicus. The features of the wound that make it an entrance and that determine at what range the bullet was fired should be described — for example, abrasion ring, soot, or tattooing. Pertinent negatives should be noted. Then, the course of the bullet through the body should be described. All organs perforated or penetrated by the missile should be noted.

It is useful to give an overall description of the missile path through the body in relation to the planes of the body. Thus, one will say, "The bullet traveled from back to front, left to right, and sharply downward." If the bullet exits, the exit wound should be described in relation to the entrance.

If the bullet is found, one should state where it was found, whether it is intact, deformed, or fragmented, whether it is lead or jacketed, and the approximate caliber. A letter or number should be inscribed on the bullet, which should then be placed in an envelope with the name of the victim, the date, case number, and location from which the bullet was recovered, the letter or number assigned it, and the name of the prosector.

If at all possible, the same general procedures should be used to describe stab wounds. One should indicate, if possible, whether the weapon was single- or double-edged, which edge of the wound was produced by the cutting edge of the knife, the exact dimensions of the stab wound, and an estimation of the depth of the wound track. In instances where there are dozens of knife wounds, it may not be possible to handle each wound separately and it might be necessary to handle them in groups.

The last part of the "Evidence of Injury" section should concern the clothing. The location of defects, whether they correspond to the injuries, and the presence of trace evidence, such as powder, soot, or car paint, should be described.

Next is the "Internal Examination" section. Here, the major organ systems as well as the organ cavities are described. The usual subdivisions of this section are:

- Head
- Body cavities
- Neck
- Respiratory tract
- Cardiovascular system
- Gastrointestinal tract
- Biliary tract
- Pancreas
- Spleen
- Adrenals
- Urinary tract
- Reproductive tract
- Musculoskeletal system

In these sections, one would give organ weights (not necessary for adrenal and pancreas) as well as a brief description of the organs with pertinent negatives. With the pancreas, adrenals, and spleen, if there are no positive findings, using the term "unremarkable" as the sole description is acceptable. Do not use the term "normal" as organs are rarely normal – whatever that is.

The next section is the "Microscopic Examination." Microscopic slides should be made when indicated. Samples of tissue from all major organs should be saved, but are often not needed in forensic cases, especially in trauma cases.

Next is the "Toxicology Section" where the results of the toxicological analyses are listed.

The next section is "Findings." This, and the last section, "Opinion," should be on a separate page. List the major findings in order of importance. It is not necessary to list every minute, often extraneous finding, as is done in some hospital autopsies. This autopsy will most likely be seen by nonphysicians, and having spent a half hour trying to explain acute passive congestion of the liver to a jury in a gunshot death, we feel the inconsequential observations should not be listed in "Findings."

The last section is "Opinion." This should briefly describe the cause of death in language as simple as possible, as well as stating the manner of death. This section is intended for the public, not for physicians Thus, for example, one can say, "… died of a heart attack due to coronary atherosclerosis ('hardening' of the blood vessels that supply blood and oxygen to the heart muscle)." Or "…died of massive internal bleeding due to a gunshot wound of the aorta (the major blood vessel of the body)."

Speculation as to circumstances surrounding the death should be absent or kept to a minimum.

Index